A MODERN SOUTHERN READER

*Major Stories, Drama,
Poetry, Essays, Interviews
and Reminiscences from the
Twentieth-Century South*

Edited by Ben Forkner and Patrick Samway, S.J.

Peachtree Publishers, Ltd.

Published by
PEACHTREE PUBLISHERS, LTD.
494 Armour Circle, N.E.
Atlanta, Georgia 30324

Manufactured in the United States of America

1st printing

Design by Paulette L. Lambert

Library of Congress Cataloging-in-Publication Data

A Modern southern reader.

    1. American literature--Southern States.   2. American
literature--20th century.   3. Southern States--Literary
collections.   4. Authors, American--Southern States--
Biography.   5. Authors, American--Southern States--
Interviews.   6. Southern States in literature.
I. Forkner, Ben.   II. Samway, Patrick H.
PS551.M64   1986   810'.8'0975   86-21218
ISBN 0-934601-01-1
ISBN 0-934601-08-9 (pbk.)

• CONTENTS •

A MODERN
SOUTHERN
READER

• INTRODUCTION •

AS THE LAST DECADE of the century approaches, and as we look back at what should remain alive in the next, there seems a good chance that Southern literature of the twentieth century will be remembered and read as one of the permanent gifts of modern times. A list of the best of Southern writers — William Faulkner, Katherine Anne Porter, Flannery O'Connor, Eudora Welty, Peter Taylor, Ernest Gaines, Reynolds Price, Robert Penn Warren, Walker Percy, and all the rest — would be recognized anywhere in the world where modern writing counts, just as the best of Southern music — blues, jazz, bluegrass, and the modern country song — has given us the most original, vital, and far-reaching regional music of the century.

Looking back, it is difficult to realize that as late as 1917 H.L. Mencken condemned the South as a cultural desert, the Sahara of the Bozart. To be fair to Mencken, the great age of Southern letters — the age represented in this collection — was to begin several years after his thundering dismissal. But to be fair to the South, Mencken was in many ways blind and deaf to the deep springs of vigorous traditional arts — homemade music and compulsive storytelling — that had been there all the time when the modern spirit of the South began to awaken.

This anthology is intended as one way of setting forward the best of modern Southern writing in a single volume, a representative choice from a remarkably fertile time and place. Of course the century is not finished, and there are still good Southern writers at work, many of them included here, but the natural chronological brackets of a nearly complete century is only one of the good reasons for making the collection now. For one thing, the South, even in its most traditional and stubborn enclaves, has become more and more indistinguishable from the rest of the United States, especially in the last twenty years. Differences do remain, and sometimes seem to hold on crazily despite all odds. You can stand in the center of Columbus, Mississippi, or Hillsboro, North Carolina, or in the larger towns of Natchez or Savannah, and still feel part of a permanent Southern community, at least as far as the vegetation and the architecture are concerned. But in the middle of each house and on the outskirts of each town the South has given way to the common national norm. Television and the suburban shopping mall have pushed it further into the backcountry, and the small town rural world of the early decades of the century is now most fully alive in the fiction it helped create.

Good writing will continue to come out of the South, but it will have to be a good deal different from the stories of Faulkner and Welty and Gaines to reflect the Sun Belt South of tomorrow. Even the contemporary Southern writers most alert to the absurdities and contrasts of today's transformed South — Walker Percy and Barry Hannah come immediately to mind — rely on a well-defined Southern community to make their satires of doubt and alienation work. The community might be based on memory rather than immediate experience, but the notion of a complete community underlies almost all modern Southern writing. Flannery O'Connor once answered an attack that Southern writing — of the 1940's and 1950's — often dealt with grotesques by observing that the Southern writer writes about grotesques because he is still able to recognize one. O'Connor's fanatic eccentrics and Percy's rudderless castaways are perhaps in no other way comparable, but they both are clearly defined against a community that exerts powerful forces even when doomed.

To a large degree, it has been precisely the Southern writer's keen awareness of a community *different* from the rest of the United States that has stamped his stories and poems and reminiscences. Many of these differences come readily to mind: the history of a rural, agrarian society dominated by the plantation and slave labor; the powerful impact of nineteenth-century sectionalism that led to the Southern secession and the War; the haunting and helpless memory of reckless courage and resounding defeat that lasted through the Reconstruction and on into the twentieth century; the myth of an antebellum golden age which, like all myths, tended to draw the curtains in front of the grim realities it could never fully face, and the most pervasive difference of all, the often cruel, always humiliating oppression of blacks by whites — a forced segregation between two races who nevertheless lived so close to each other that individual reconciliations were more common than not. Historians, social theorists, and economists — all could add to this list. The modern South has had its share of compelling dissections. And the modern Southern writer, growing up at the beginning of the century, has had his share of ripe obsessions and dramatic oppositions to deliver into literature.

There is another important difference, an obvious one to a reader opening a book of stories and poems: the distinctive character of Southern speech. Perhaps the fact that it is so obvious helps account for the relatively little attention it has been given in discussions of what sets the South apart. Yet the language of the South has always been bound up with its special identity. When Mark Twain revisited the Mississippi River in 1882 to write his impressions of the changes that had occurred since the War, there was at least one element of Southern life that had not changed at all, the characteristic sound of its speech: "I found the half-forgotten Southern intonations and elisions as pleasing to my ear as they had formerly been. A Southerner talks music. At least it is music to me, but then I was born in the South. The educated Southerner has no use for an r, except at the beginning of a word. He says 'honah,' and 'dinnah,' and 'Gove'nuh,' and 'befo' the waw,' and so on. The words may lack charm to the eye, in print, but they have it to the ear."

That these same examples could be taken from Southern speech today without too much hunting around argues in several directions. It proves that language is a powerful force of community identity, time-resistant, and, as Mark Twain himself suggests, space-resistant as well. He was born in Florida, Missouri, north of St. Louis. But he speaks of himself as being born in the South. What he means is that the small frontier town of Florida, and later, of Hannibal, were at the very least outposts of the South, where the majority of the inhabitants spoke and acted and ate the way they had in Tennessee, Kentucky, or Virginia before they moved West. If anything, the displacement made them more attached to what they had brought from home. Mark Twain was born "in the South," but he was also born a Southern exile, an origin that may help explain the sense of loss and of looking back all through his work. At the end of his life, in Connecticut, he is capable of complaining that corn bread, hot biscuits, and fried chicken have "never been properly cooked in the North."

Twain's examples of Southern speech suggest something else for the reader of modern Southern literature, that the South affirms its identity as much in the ways of expression than in what is expressed. The objection could be made that in the examples given, Twain limits himself to mere sounds, a characteristic accent or pronunciation. But just two years after he published *Life on the Mississippi* and his observations on Southern "intonations," he finished what Allen Tate has called the first modern Southern novel, *Huckleberry Finn*, a book that exploits the resources of vocabulary, idiomatic invention, and poetic power of an uneducated Southern boy in a revolutionary way. *Huckleberry Finn* had no immediate successors, but as the one great example of a wholly Southern narrative capable of giving astonishing voice to a wide range of Southern realities, it prepared the way for the literary revival of the twentieth-century South. So many modern Southern writers — Faulkner, Warren, Welty, Percy — have mentioned it as an important literary influence in their careers that it will be worthwhile coming back to it later on as one of the best introductions to their writing.

Eighty years after Twain's observations, Flannery O'Connor also turned to language in a definition of Southern qualities. Like Twain, she did not write under any regional spells, and she was not given to sentimental praise of Southern myths; but for her, too, one of the great fortunes of a Southern writer was his native English: "There are two qualities that make fiction. One is the sense of mystery and the other is the sense of manners. You get the manners from the texture of existence that surrounds you. The great advantage of being a Southern writer is that we don't have to go anywhere to look for manners; bad or good, we've got them in abundance. We in the South live in a society that is rich in contradictions, rich in irony, rich in contrast, and particularly rich in its speech."

Perhaps one reason Flannery O'Connor felt called on to praise the wealth of behavior and speech she saw and heard every day around her in the present, was that at the time she was writing, in the 1950's, the most common distinction of the South was its struggle with the predominantly negative legacies of its past: the burden of its special history.

This last phrase is of course the title of the well-known book by Southern historian C. Vann Woodward. *The Burden of Southern History* was published in 1960, but the essays it contains were written during the 1950's, and they represent the most forceful statement of what had become the dominant version of Southern difference. Woodward was greatly influenced by the new Southern writing of the first half of the century; he readily acknowledged — even insisted on the fact — that his reading of Faulkner, Katherine Anne Porter, Thomas Wolfe, Robert Penn Warren — to whom *The Burden* is dedicated — helped sharpen his vision of Southern history. The Southern writer who influenced him most powerfully was Allen Tate: poet, novelist, critic, and Southern theorist. Even though he is best known as a poet, Tate's Southern essays exceed everything else he wrote as rich fuel for all sorts of recent speculations about the South.

In an essay published in 1935, "The Profession of Letters in the South," Tate had pointed out the "peculiarly historical consciousness" of the Southern writer. And in a later essay, "The New Provincialism," he made the claim that the historical compulsion of the modern Southern writer was the driving force behind the brilliant burst of literary achievement after World War I: "With the war of 1914-1918, the South reentered the world — but gave a backward glance as it slipped over the border: that backward glance gave us the Southern renascence, a literature conscious of the past in the present." As Tate suggested, and as Woodward developed the idea in his essays, Southern history was considerably different from the common experience of the rest of the United States. Instead of the usual American story of success, industrial progress, social mobility, accessible wealth, equal rights, and confidence in the future, the Southern historical legacy was one of defeat, dispossession, poverty, racial oppression, rural inertia, and, for many, a corrosive guilt. For Tate, and for Woodward, the first half of the century was marked in the South by a necessary struggle with this legacy, a continual wrestling with the past in order to better confront the tormenting realities of the present.

The struggle took many forms and expressed as many attitudes as there were writers. What all the writers did share, however, were a spirit of critical inquiry and a willingness to apply the lessons of modern literary realism. Faulkner, Porter, Caroline Gordon, Andrew Lytle, Warren, all make use of the Southern problem of the past, but always dramatically. They were well-read in the Southern literature of the nineteenth century, and realized that its weaknesses were largely attributable to the way political simplifications often shoved aside social realities and obscured the contradictions of individual character.

The single intellectual movement in modern Southern letters, the Fugitive-Agrarian group at Vanderbilt University in the 1920's, did tend to look back to certain community values of the Southern past as preferable to the urban uniformity and mass culture of modern times, but their attachment was never blind; they were in fact first to admit that earlier Southern literature was "hag-ridden" by politics and political rhetoric. The poets of this group are best considered individually, since Ransom, Tate, and especially Warren, were to have long careers as independent moderns. But their collection of essays published as an Agrarian "manifesto" in 1930, *I'll Take My Stand*, did mark an important step in their lives and in the intellectual history of the South, even though, as most polemical tracts, it seems today more valuable as an historical document than as a seedbed for Southern theory. Certainly the idea behind most of the essays, that society is most fully human when based on the simple fact of "the family on the land," has remained a powerful countercurrent to the enormous changes the traditional rural South has undergone.

As a collection of twelve essays, *I'll Take My Stand* served as a document that mirrored the thinking about Southern society, culture, religion, industry, and the arts up to 1930, much as in a more sustained way Matthew Arnold, Thomas Carlyle, and others of their generation did in Victorian England; it also served as lamp to light up the way for the rest of the twentieth century and give direction, as the essayists fervently hoped, to future decision makers in the South. American society has changed in ways that these writers could never have imagined in 1930; one has only to think of the differences made by jet planes, lasers, the civil rights, gay and feminist movements, the growth of universities, computers, industrial robots, moon landings, World War II and the war in Vietnam, television, Moog synthesizers, Dacron, and wonder drugs. Today, in hindsight, some of the views of these agrarians, as stated in the introduction to the book, seem not to have weathered well the test of time: "Art depends, in general, like religion, on a right attitude to nature; and in particular on a free and disinterested observation of nature that occurs only in leisure. Neither the creation nor the understanding of works of art is possible in an industrial age except by some local and unlikely suspension of the industrial drive." And yet, contrary to the expectations of these agrarians, American (and Southern) art and belles lettres prosper and have continued to thrive during the last fifty years.

In spite of their reluctance to a changing American society, these twelve Southern thinkers are not arguing for a nostalgic return to the Old South; rather, they are concerned with articulating a workable philosophy rooted in a love of land and the concomitant values that emerge from such stewardship, among which are a strong family unit, a commitment to the incarnational theology of the Bible, the development of a legal system that respects the differences that exist in various parts of the United States, and an expressive use of language that reveals the foundation of a rich literary tradition. None of these essayists gives a more sympathetic overview of Southern society than does Andrew Lytle in "The Hind Tit." Lytle believed that one must understand, in particular, the rapid alterations that the Cotton Kingdom underwent after the Civil War in order to appreciate the transformation that took place in the South and the subsequent demands his agrarian-minded confreres were making. The rise of the poor white sharecropper who supplanted the black slave, the use of fertilizers that insured a faster growing cotton and thus a greater reliance on a cash economy, and the expansion of the railroads that brought an end to regional isolationism — all created a fabric, he believed, that could be torn apart by an unchallenged proclamation of thoughtless notions about manifest destiny. In his portrayal of the South, Lytle never loses a sense of the demands, rewards, and specificity of daily life; yet his lyric raptures lead to an untenable conclusion: Until the small Southern farmers and the conservative communities across the United States unite politically, Southerners must not buy any products that the industrialists offer for sale. Unfortunately, his position prevents genuine growth or advancement.

In his essay "Reconstructed But Unregenerate," John Crowe Ransom, provides a glimmer of hope in suggesting a solution to industrialism's grip on the Southern economy; in his view, the South has the potential to provide moral leadership for the rest of the country: "I wish that the whole force of my own generation in the South would get behind his principles and make them an idea which the nation at large would have to reckon with." In general, Ransom saw the South as the place where European principles of culture can continue to flourish and exert an influence over the rest of the country. Unlike life in England, however, where people have successfully adapted to the environment, he wrote, the American way of life is progressive, urbanized, and in a constant state of flux. Although Ransom and his colleagues could well be accused of setting up a too neat dichotomy between the progress of industrialism (and its counterpart, service) and undisturbed nature, they apodictically believed, and with good common sense to support them, that progress "never defines its ultimate objective, but thrusts its victims at once into an infinite series." Not too subtly, they imply that progress will have deleterious effects on society and that, more importantly, intelligent men and women cannot provide the answers needed to solve the ongoing congeries of complex problems that steadily confront them.

What eventually happened in the years since *I'll Take My Stand* was published is that Southerners have, rightly or wrongly, been conscious of the principles that Ransom alluded to. Ransom wisely had no concrete plan for development in the South; he knew that a philosophical approach would win the day since it would set guidelines that would have to be accommodated at each stage of industrial development. One way to adapt would be for "the South to reenter the American political field with a determination and an address quite beyond anything she has exhibited during her half-hearted national life of the last half a century." By joining the mainstream of American life and not remaining apart from it, Southerners, ever conscious of the sources of their talents and genius, have constantly nourished American society without depleting their own creative wellsprings. The problem, of course, was and will always remain how to prevent a partial or even complete dissolution of the Southern way of life in spite of the tremendous ebb and flow in American society. At least two of the contributors, Allen Tate and Robert Penn Warren, continued to revise and develop their interpretations on religion and race relations respectively in later essays. But given the far greater worth of the poetry of these two writers, it is probably best to remember *I'll Take My Stand* as an exceptional — and limited — expression of the modern writer's conviction that in the South, as Faulkner's Gavin Stevens argues, "the past is not dead. It is not even past."

There can be no question that the pressures and problems of Southern history — as Allen Tate and C. Vann Woodward have claimed — dominated the beginnings of modern Southern fiction. Even the characteristic form of many of the novels and stories was, appropriately enough, the retrospective monologue. Remembering and, to use an old Southernism, disremembering, became the most vital acts of central characters in a Faulkner novel or a Katherine Anne Porter story. But the burden of Southern history is only a partial explanation of the force and vividness found in these writers. Southern language and Southern attitudes toward language are equally important. We need a term such as a renewed "verbal consciousness" to match the new "historical consciousness" Allen Tate singled out. This brings us back to Flannery O'Connor's reference to the rich vein of Southern speech which seemed to her in the 1950's one of the abiding gifts of Southern life.

There is a way, of course, in which the Southern writer's special use of his native English coincides with his historical preoccupations. Stories out of the past are always on the threshold of legend and myth, and the reverential or automatic repetition of these stories are closely bound up with the conscious or unconscious attitude towards the language that embodies them. The power of language to trap, betray, and distort is as great as its power to reveal or give meaning, and for a Faulkner character, for example, the sacred myths and the sacred words are never far from the mechanical rite that has been emptied of all value. The modern Southerner, because of his history, is perhaps more keenly aware than others of the universal fact that an individual can only express his nature in a language he has inherited. He should constantly be sounding his words out, thumping them for what is rotten or ripe. Eudora Welty begins one of her essays by remarking that "we start from scratch, and words don't; which is the thing that matters — matters over and over again."

Another dimension of this new "verbal consciousness" — more closely related to Flannery O'Connor's praise of the Southern idiom — was the fresh appreciation of Mark Twain's discovery that poetry, wit, expressive power, and range reside as much in the vernacular as they do in the literary tradition. Mark Twain, of course, was not the only Southern writer to exploit the resources of the spoken word, but he was the first to free it from conventional stereotypes. When the modern Southern writer looked back at the Southern literature of the nineteenth century, he could not help but be struck by the ease with which most books could be classified in terms of literary schools.

There was the plantation novel, launched by John Pendleton Kennedy's *Swallow Barn* in 1832 and culminating in Thomas Nelson Page's *In Ole Virginia* in 1887. Most of the plantation novels and stories follow the same pattern of nostalgia and regret, looking back to a better age of social and racial harmonies. With their genteel descriptions of the fine-mannered master and the faithful slave, both full of good humor and mutual sympathy, they helped fix the myth of the antebellum plantation in the Southern and, for that matter, the Northern imagination. There were the historical romances of the colonial South by William Gilmore Sims and dozens more now forgotten names. There were also the Southwestern humorists — the Southwest referring to what is now known principally as the Deep South: Georgia, Alabama, Tennessee, Mississippi, and Louisiana in the decades just before the Civil War — who brought to the civilized East the exotic stories of the wild and unlettered frontier. Finally, there were the local color writers of the post-Civil War South: Irwin Russell, Joel Chandler Harris, George Washington Cable, and others, who turned to profit an accurate description of regional Southern dialects and folkways, attractive and archaic to Northern readers whose own language was becoming standardized, and whose cities promoted the modern and the brand-new at all costs.

The main problem with much of this writing — and the reason it is so easy to classify — stems from its reliance on social and racial types, and on a rigid division of language into two kinds: educated and not. This same division plays an important role in fictional narration. Dialect, both black and white, even when accurately rendered, was reserved almost exclusively for comic effect, and the eccentricities of native Southern speech were made even more so by surrounding them by the overblown, excessively "literary" style of the author. Many of these writers were professional lawyers, and all too often the thesaurus oratory and the Latin tags are as suffocating as a summer courtroom. Given the conventions of the genteel literary tradition that most nineteenth-century Southern writers adhered to, we are often left with the impression of two extremely opposed versions of experience, each in its own way limited and isolated.

Characterization was almost wholly determined by social position demanding well-defined, and too often one-dimensional roles. The capacity of a human being to slip in and out of several roles, sometimes at cross-purposes with each other, and despite this, remaining himself, is rarely acknowledged in early Southern fiction.

The attitude that made it so rare was not confined to the Southern writer. In *The Cotton Kingdom* by Frederick Law Olmsted, one of the most perceptive and informative accounts we have of the South just before the Civil War, the Northerner Olmsted is gratified whenever he meets the expected Southern "type" in the flesh. He can thus give his reader faithful snapshots of a pipe-smoking female "cracker," a rich absentee planter, or a gesticulating black preacher. He does so with a great deal of sympathy, but there is always the question of what is hidden by the artificial light of the photographic flash. To Olmsted's credit, he is not always satisfied with his categories, and can confess his confusion when he discovers someone inhabited by more than a single form of social behavior. For Olmsted, it is interesting to note, this strange self-contradiction was more Southern than Northern: "I found that, more than any people I had ever seen, they were unrateable by dress, taste, forms, and expenditures. I was perplexed by finding, apparently united in the same individual, the self-possession, confidence, and the use of expressions of deference, of the well-equipped gentleman, and the coarseness and low tastes of the uncivilized boor — frankness and reserve, recklessness and self-restraint, extravagance and penuriousness." The problem with much of early Southern fiction is that it too finds it difficult to do justice to the complex ironies and unpredictable shifts of an actual human being, and this is exactly one of the strengths of the modern Southern writer, from William Faulkner to Walker Percy.

As has been implied up to now, twentieth-century Southern literature has been marked especially by the works of one writer: William Faulkner. For those who were his contemporaries and followed after him, they had, in the marvelous image of Flannery O'Connor, to get off the tracks quickly when the Dixie Limited came roaring down. Born in 1897 in northern Mississippi, Faulkner came from a family that was known both in that area and beyond. His great-grandfather, for example, Col. William Clark Falkner (without the "u"), wrote the best seller *The White Rose of Memphis* (1881) and other works; he was also noted as someone who had killed two men before being murdered himself by one of his business partners. Young William grew up in the post-Civil War years and though he incorporated situations from this war into a number of works, including *The Unvanquished* (1938), his genius was rooted more in his desire to explore his native region, his own "little postage stamp of native soil," and to expand continually the frontiers of fiction.

His first important novel, *Sartoris* (1929), relying to some degree on his own family genealogy, portrayed the clash of values that the South experienced in the late 1920's, particularly in the emotional shock a young Southerner feels when returning to Mississippi at the end of World War I. Though Faulkner had never seen battle in Europe (he had joined the Royal Air Force and trained in Toronto, Canada), he was acutely conscious of the changes taking place in the South during his lifetime. In this novel and in subsequent ones, he dealt both with the South's ability or inability to find strength to overcome the obstacles time inevitably brings. In *The Sound and the Fury* (1929), for example, a title taken from the last act of *Macbeth*, Faulkner tells the story of the decline and fall of the Compson family and the efforts of the black servant, Dilsey Gibson, to hold the family together. The story is presented by four narrators, three of whom are brothers: Benjy Compson, a retarded man who is preoccupied by the disappearance of his sister, Caddy; Quentin, a suicidal freshman at Harvard, who likewise cannot cope with what has happened to Caddy; Jason, the more pragmatic brother, who lets life slip through his hands as he chases after power and money, and finally, Dilsey, who becomes a surrogate mother for Benjy and for Caddy's daughter. Dilsey's tremendous faith in God and her willingness to carry on with life's difficulties make her an admirable character, so much so that in the appendix to the novel, Faulkner designated her a symbol of all black women by stating simply, "They endured."

Not only did Faulkner attempt to push this novel to its limits by having the first section told from the first-person point of view by someone who has no comprehension of self or time, but the same story, essentially about Caddy, is told from multiple perspectives, a literary device reminiscent of Wallace Stevens's poem, "Thirteen Ways of Looking at a Blackbird," which deals with the idea that in literature one version of story does not suffice; only multiple viewpoints can adequately deal with the truth of a situation.

In a subsequent novel, *As I Lay Dying* (1930), the literary perspective is even further fragmented, as fifteen characters (members of the Bundren family, and their neighbors, for the most part) deal with the events surrounding the death and burial of Addie Bundren. As with *The Sound and the Fury*, Faulkner is dealing with the theme of the loss of a woman; yet in both novels it should be noted that he does not allow his Eurydice to fall back completely into the nether world. His novel, like the music of Orpheus, keeps both women alive; in the first case, Caddy is last seen in a photograph with a German staff general and, in the second, Addie comes back from the dead in one chapter of the novel and explains directly her views concerning her husband and children, love, experience, sin, and salvation. In these two novels and subsequent ones, Faulkner created his own 2,400 square-mile Yoknapatawpha County and populated it with 6,298 whites and 9,313 blacks. By fusing the local with the mythic, he made his fiction not only accessible but universal, and thus has escaped the tag of being called a "regional writer" by those readers who have never seen kudzu, okra, or white cotton in a field.

Unlike Flannery O'Connor, whose stories tend to be apologetically formulaic in nature, and thus have a fairly consistent tone and density to them, Faulkner never stopped experimenting with narrative technique. *Light in August* (1932), perhaps Faulkner's most lyrical novel, juxtaposes the wonderfully humane Lena Grove, a young woman who gives birth to a child during the course of the novel while all the time looking for the father of her child, with Joe Christmas, an outcast from society who is unable to decide his racial identity. These two protagonists, so opposite in many ways, are in physical proximity throughout most of the novel though they never meet. To a great extent, this novel has a more optimistic tone to it than previous ones since the last scene presents a vignette of Lena, her child, and Bryon Bunch (who could well become her future husband) as they move slowly towards Tennessee and perhaps a future together. Lena and her child have not been dragged down into the abyss of Christmas's death.

Faulkner's masterpiece, *Absalom, Absalom!* (1936), rates as one of the most important novels of the twentieth century. Though this novel was written after the publication of *The Sound and the Fury*, it is chronologically anterior for the most part to the story of the Compson family. Two narrators, Quentin Compson and Shreve McCannon, share with one another the history of Thomas Sutpen and the events leading up to the murder of Charles Bon (most likely Sutpen's son) by Henry Sutpen (most likely his half-brother). Though Quentin has a good deal of information that his father and grandfather have passed down, he does not have all the "facts" of Sutpen's history; ironically, Shreve, who has never visited the South and clearly has not talked with any of those who know the Sutpen history firsthand, makes logical sense out of the reasons why Bon was killed. Not only is Faulkner dealing with the problem of the tellers in the tale, but he relates a story that says essentially that the history of the South cannot be known in every detail. As Mr. Compson says, "We have a few old mouth-to-mouth tales; we exhume from old trunks and boxes and drawers letters without salutation or signature, in which men and women who once lived and breathed are now merely initials or nicknames out of some incomprehensible affection which sound to us like Sanskrit or Chocktaw; we see dimly people, the people in whose living blood and seed we ourselves lay dormant and waiting, in this shadowy attenuation of time possessing now heroic proportions, performing their acts of simple passion and simple violence, impervious to time and inexplicable. . . ." *Absalom, Absalom!* provides a thorough study of history, narrative technique, and epistemology, and embodies in one volume Faulkner's most penetrating and sustained view of Southern life and theory of literature.

As scholars know, the fertility of Faulkner's imagination as revealed in these and his other great works [*The Wild Palms* (1939), the Snopses trilogy — *The Hamlet* (1940), *The Town* (1957), and *The Mansion* (1959), *Go Down, Moses* (1942), *A Fable* (1954), *The Reivers* (1962), *The Collected Stories* (1950), *The Uncollected Stories* (1979)] has not by any means been plumbed sufficiently. Textual and intertextual analyses, cultural history, and problems associated with literary creativity need to be further addressed. Contemporaries of Faulkner, other noted Southern fiction writers, particularly William Styron, Reynolds Price, Walker Percy, Cormac McCarthy, and, of course, Flannery O'Connor, have acknowledged their enormous debt to Faulkner and struggled long and hard to find their own authentic voices. Each one had to listen carefully to the voice within and allow the fullness of that voice to emerge and be structured in written words.

Not surprisingly, one of the forces that changed the Southern writer's conception of characterization came not from literature, but from life, from a rich oral tradition capable of expressing much more than the coarse and the comic. The change was similar to the impulse behind the Irish Literary Revival, which began when the various forms of native Irish English were suddenly discovered to be not only the most legitimate, but the richest and most complete expression of Irish life. In fact, the example of the remarkable Irish writers at the beginning of the century probably helped turn the modern Southern writer toward his own special mysteries and manners, to use the Flannery O'Connor conjunction. But an earlier example, *Huckleberry Finn,* was much closer to home, and provided the greatest influence of all, especially in its use of Southern speech.

There are several ways the language of *Huckleberry Finn* can be directly linked to the literature of the modern South. First of all, Twain was by nature and by experience open to all sorts of language, as long as it meant something. Like the Southwestern humorists, he had a keen ear for the rough wit and bold metaphor of the Southern countryman. And like the local colorists, especially Joel Chandler Harris, he fully appreciated the emphatic humor and subtle indirections of the Southern black. His famous preface to *Huckleberry Finn* shows just how conscious he was of the sheer variety of Southern speech. He distinguishes seven different dialects, and makes the claim that these verbal "shadings have not been done in a hap-hazard fashion, or by guess-work; but painstakingly, and with the trustworthy guidance and support of personal familiarity with these several forms of speech."

This same attention to the details of actual speech can be found all through the writings of the modern South. When Katherine Anne Porter remarked of Eudora Welty that she has an ear "sharp, shrewd, and true as a tuning fork," she could have said the same thing about herself, or William Faulkner, or Flannery O'Connor, or a dozen other Southern contemporaries. It becomes one of the few generalizations possible about every writer in this collection. Like the modern Irish writer, the modern Southerner has recognized that the sound of the speaking voice is the genuine source of modern realism, and he will not give it to us muddied up or diluted.

Huckleberry Finn is full of the sounds of different Southern voices, but it also proves that a single Southern voice is capable of enough range and depth to carry a full-scale narrative along by itself. Huck gives the reader wonderful descriptions of river life, the best in literature according to T.S. Eliot, but he also gives us — perhaps more unwittingly than the descriptions — an honest and direct look at some of the native wrongs of Southern society. And he allows himself to listen to a black voice equally capable of a full range of expression, including justifiable indignation. It takes Huck almost a third of the novel before he is able to do so, but when Jim reproaches him for one of his tricks, and he is moved enough to ask Jim's pardon, we are witnessing one of the central experiences of Southern life. Only in the twentieth century did the Southern black fully enter into American literature — in the remarkable portraits of Faulkner, Welty, Hurston, Taylor, Gaines, and Wright — and he did so largely because the white Southern writer realized finally that a full vision of the South needed the eyes of both races.

The realization went far beyond the mere recognition by each race of the other. For one thing, the mutual influence of black and white in the South had been at work for so long that the character of both races had been permanently affected. In *The Mind of the South,* W.J. Cash identifies this relationship as one of the features that set Southern society apart: "Negro entered the white man as profoundly as white man entered into Negro — subtly influencing every gesture, every emotion and idea, every attitude." But at the same time, Southern history saw to it that each race would remain itself, within well-marked bounds; so much so that the segregation imposed by white supremacy often presented the strange spectacle of a single society united by two alien worlds.

As opposed to the white, the black had to struggle against strong odds to maintain an identity he could value. Most of his creative energies had to be invested in music and storytelling, and along the way he intensified an already powerful oral tradition. In so doing, he presented a stubborn, original, and imaginative cultural presence that continually inspired modern Southern fiction. It made the white Southerner more conscious of his own oral traditions, and it enlarged the scope of Southern realism — in the writings of both black and white — by asserting that legend, collective memory, and dream are essential to the full reality of the human mind.

Generally speaking then, the peculiar situation in the modern South made it impossible for either race to define itself in complete isolation from the other. The odd irony of close living and mutual influence, combined with, for each, black and white, the daily contact of a half-foreign presence, became the inescapable condition of the modern South. And it is one of the triumphs of modern Southern fiction that it faces up to this condition — including its share of tragic consequences — with completeness and understanding.

A final remark on *Huckleberry Finn* as a forerunner of modern Southern fiction brings us back to Allen Tate, and the essay included here: "A Southern Mode of the Imagination." Tate takes as his argument the well-known epigram of W.B. Yeats: "Out of the quarrel with others we make rhetoric; out of the quarrel with ourselves, poetry." For Tate, the nineteenth-century Southern writers were primarily rhetoricians, addressing an audience. The main mode of discourse, in formal speech and formal writing, was political oratory. And since political oratory depends so much on exaggerated contrasts and certainties, it was wholly inadequate in dealing with fine gradations and lack of certainty in the modern South. The crucial shift — and for Tate this was an enormous shift in quality — from earlier Southern fiction to the modern writers of Tate's generation was a shift away from the easy judgments of rhetoric, and toward a more faithful account of the often uneasy movements of self-consciousness. *Huckleberry Finn* looks forward to the twentieth century because in it the "action is generated inside the characters: there is internal dialogue, a conflict within the self."

Tate does not attempt to transform Huck's fresh look at life into the tortured conscience of Faulkner's Quentin Compson, but in pointing out that Huck is capable of revising his view of the world, of Jim, and especially of himself, Tate convincingly directs us to another feature of Southern literature. We have already mentioned that the Southern writer is fully conscious of the special powers of language, and fully alert to the whole range of living Southern voices. What Tate suggests is that one of the consequences of this heightened consciousness is a special divided attitude toward language. The Southern writer frequently writes about language, and not merely by means of it.

Faulkner's fascination with the deceptive inadequacies of a single voice to tell all the story; Flannery O'Connor's shrewd pursuit of the dogmatic formula, no matter where it leads; Eudora Welty's power of making the simplest figure of folk speech reveal an ancient myth still at work; Robert Penn Warren's restless use of any word or phrase at hand as long as they move the poem forward; Walker Percy's ironic speculations on the role of language in our daily alienations, are all part of the same concern. In every case, the deep delight in the actual presence of an individual voice is matched by an equally deep wariness about taking any human utterance at face value. In a century where language has been so often used to evade, distort, and destroy, not just in the South but in the world at large, this mixture of fascination and skepticism is one reason the appeal of modern Southern literature has moved far beyond Southern boundaries.

Of course, as this collection should demonstrate, there is more than one good reason these writers are read and admired. Not the least of these is the fundamental enjoyment of witnessing the real world of a remarkable region achieve vivid dramatic life again and again. The modern Southern writer has somehow been able to strengthen the impression of a collective Southern character, and at the same time do justice to wide differences in individual and racial experiences of Southern society. He has been able to marry the best of a vigorous traditional Southern culture — its delight in storytelling and the spoken word — with all the exigencies of modern realism. If at the beginning of the century a Southern writer almost invariably had to look for his literary models outside the South, the Southern writer at the end of the century has quite a different problem: Faced with the prodigious display of literary achievement, he might well wonder if there is anything left to say.

• SHORT STORIES •

MODERN SOUTHERN LITERATURE, everyone agrees, had its beginnings in the 1920's with the past-haunted but wide-awake poetry of the Fugitives, and the searching new realism found in the novels of Ellen Glasgow, Thomas Wolfe, and, above all, William Faulkner. But in looking back over the decades of writing that followed, it is no surprise that for many readers, the major achievement of Southern writing has been the wealth of powerful short stories produced almost yearly since World War II. A simple list of the monuments alone makes the case: William Faulkner's *Collected Stories* in 1950, Katherine Anne Porter's *Collected Stories* in 1965, Peter Taylor's *Collected Stories* in 1971 followed recently by the two remarkable collections *In the Miro District* and *The Old Forest*, Flannery O'Connor's posthumous *Complete Stories* in 1971, Eudora Welty's *Collected Stories* and Caroline Gordon's *Collected Stories* in 1980, Elizabeth Spencer's *Collected Stories* in 1981. The list could continue with the names of many other individual collections springing readily to mind: those of Carson McCullers, Reynolds Price, Doris Betts, Ernest Gaines, Fred Chappell, and Barry Hannah. Though all of these writers have written novels, and though there are a few Southern writers who have written only a very few stories (Anne Tyler, for example) or none at all (Walker Percy), the short story is generally recognized as the predominant Southern genre. It is also the most characteristic, and in fact the one helps to explain the other.

However much the modern Southern short story shares with the original impulses of the Southern novel or poem, it has come to dominate the center of the stage simply because it is the most congenial form to the Southern literary mind. Certainly it is the one genre most capable of fusing modern literary concerns and techniques with a native Southern idiom and oral storytelling tradition. Fusion, however, is perhaps not in every case the best description. In many modern Southern stories, there are more painful tensions between the narrator and the South than there are effortless reconciliations. The central narrative voice is almost always an individual at odds with himself or with the outside world, and almost invariably — sometimes comically, sometimes not — a local community voice enters into the story to complicate and deepen its final meaning. Often the voice emanates from the watchful presence of the Southern black, at times hidden and unpredictable, but always a vital organic element in the connective community tissue.

It has often been suggested that the modern South is full of fragments and scattered reminders of a once whole and coherent culture, and that these isolated remains are more suited to the short story than to the novel — thus the great success of the Southern short story. But it may be that something close to an opposite explanation makes more sense. The novel is capable of creating a full sense of a complete society, with all its variations of class and manners. But a short story can only suggest the fullness of society; it depends on the extra-textual world of the story being known and recognized by the reader. And whatever social and sectional unity there was, it is quite possible that the South as a region broken up into isolated enclaves is a more faithful account of antebellum realities than it is of the South just after the turn of the century. The South became much more coherent after the War, when the great Southern myth of a separate fate took hold and refused to let go. Certainly the most distinctive cultural manifestations of the Southern world — its music and its literature — did not develop until that world could be taken for granted. Even today, despite all the uprootings and convulsive changes, the South still gives the impression of a community that can be defined. Everyone knows what the South is, or thinks he does, and the modern Southern writer can thus depend on — or play against — the representative gesture or word and the individual tendancy to represent anything but what the community wants him to.

It would be editorial blindness, or pigheadedness, to insist too freely on shared themes or on any single common basis for the stories we have chosen. In each of them the individual mind of the writer rings out with clear, unmistakable signals right from the opening sentences. No reader could confuse the long, tireless, uncoiling, but finally taut and conclusive Faulknerian line of "Barn Burning" — in which the "old fierce pull of the blood" sharply dismisses the boy's overburdened hunger — with the exuberant irony of Flannery O'Connor's theatrically set porch scene in "The Life You Save May Be Your Own;" nor could he confuse either of them with any of the other stories. They succeed first of all as individual creations: definite, odd, singular, and complete. But at the same time, the reader will recognize — though one should be careful about this — that behind the frank individual differences of tone and treatment, there are powerful, but sometimes obscure, family resemblances. They are there even though the Southern story has been able to accommodate an astonishing range of character and locale, stretching from the well-housed, white upper-class Tennesseans of Peter Taylor's stories to the weatherbound black sharecroppers of Ernest Gaines's Louisiana. And strangely enough, the family resemblances are probably as fundamental and as mysterious as all the clearly isolated individual differences. They go beyond the familiar recognitions of Southern idiom, racial themes, and small-town, rural manners. To speak of them we must go back to the earlier statement that claimed that the short story is the literary form most congenial to the modern Southern mind.

This is a rather bewildering proposition, but it might help to look again at two standard features of modern Southern writing: its preoccupation with the past, with Southern history, and its rediscovery of the hidden resources of Southern language. There is a third resemblance that comes to mind, the general tendency of the Southern writer to speculate on the form and purpose of the short story. All these resemblances reflect the peculiar situation of the modern Southern writer steadily contemplating a home he has known all his life, with a full new understanding of its meaning, standing inside the front door, with his hand on the doorknob, but looking in instead of out. The attention the Southern writer has given to history and language has, of course, been felt in every form of Southern literature: poetry, drama, and the essay. But in a deeper, more organic way than in the other genres, a special Southern attitude toward history in terms of a personal past and toward language as human speech informs almost every major Southern story.

In Peter Taylor's "In the Miro District," in Katherine Anne Porter's "The Jilting of Granny Weatherall," in Caroline Gordon's "Old Red," just to mention three obvious examples among the stories presented here, the preoccupation with the past, the compulsive probing of the "backward glance," establishes not only the dramatic subject of the story but the shape of the narrative itself.

In a similar way, a new Southern attitude toward language, especially its unusual combination of fascination and wariness when addressing the power of what has been called "the speaking voice," helps explain both the choice of the short story as the favorite form and the particular type of story the modern Southerner writes. Even though it is rarely a straightforward "told" tale — Thomas Wolfe's "Chickamauga" would be the outstanding exception, and probably the most convincing piece of fiction he every wrote — it owes far more than other modern stories to the conditions of traditional storytelling, and to the permanent needs that storytelling satisfies. None of the major Southern stories permits any sort of merely stylistic artifice to divert the flow of narration. Even the dense Faulknerian sentence with its emphatic discordances and studied choice of vocabulary is always driven by the desire to express meaning, never to artfully conceal it or diplomatically let it slip by. The modern Southern narrative voice can be complicated, fully conscious and deliberate; it may digress freely — in fact delights in the relevent digression and improvisation — and often shifts perspective. This expansiveness is usually justified, however, and in any case the spirit behind the narration is much more fearful of incompleteness than redundancy. Like the teller who speaks to a listener, it can not contrive, or bluff, or fabricate at will. If it does, the hold is broken. And it certainly can not suddenly stop short. When Eudora Welty was asked in an interview about what made the Southern story distinctive, she responded: "I think the Southerner is a talker by nature, but not only a talker — we are used to an audience. We are used to a listener and that does something to our narrative style. We like to entertain and please, and we also rejoice in response." What Eudora Welty suggests is that the modern writer must be both teller and listener at the same time, and as such demands that a story declare its purpose and fulfill it. The instinct of mystification is always subordinate to the more powerful instincts of communicability and completeness. There are no open-ended stories in the modern Southern tradition, and that may be one good reason the stories of Faulkner, Porter, Welty, O'Connor, and Taylor so quickly established themselves as permanent classics.

A wary faith in language and a wary faith in the past to disclose significant patterns; both can be traced to the brutal acceleration of change the entire South has undergone during the last fifty years. Language, especially the stubborn repetitions of spoken language, thrusts us into the past every day, whether we like it or not. Memory, too, especially in the modern South where memories seem riper and more persistent than anywhere else in the United States, makes daily claims, at times against our will. In the three stories grouped together earlier — "The Jilting of Granny Weatherall," "Old Red," and "In the Miro District" — the act of memory that irrepressibly seeks out meaning in the past is stressed almost as much as the remembered event; and this extra stress of a remembering mind unable to stay still is a telling symptom of the modern South.

Katherine Anne Porter's portrait of Granny Weatherall is the earliest of the three stories, written in the 1920's, the first decade of the Southern revival. And it is appropriate that, more so than in the later stories of Gordon and Taylor, the memory of Granny Weatherall is almost wholly bound by the past. She is on her deathbed, nearing eighty years old, and images out of her long life insist on crowding out the present. They succeed each other in what seems at first an arbitrary sequence, shifting among her dead husband, her children, and her worries about the farm. Her South is not the modern South at all. It has consisted of hard rural work — after the death of her husband she once dug post holes to fence a hundred acres of land — and the spectacle of nature as a daily and nightly presence. The spectacle has not been without its rewards: "Lighting the lamps had been beautiful. The children huddled up to her and breathed like little calves waiting at the bars in the twilight. Their eyes followed the match and watched the flame rise and settle in a blue curve, then they moved away from her. The lamp was lit, they didn't have to be scared and hang on to mother any more." She can look back approvingly on her success as a hard-working widow who has kept a good house and has provided well for her children. But as the story continues, the mass of shifting family images is suddenly cast into shadow by the single flash of the day she had been jilted as a young bride. The mixture of grief and guilt this memory awakens dominates everything else. She is a Catholic, like Katherine Anne Porter herself, but she is also a native Southerner and thus much more preyed on by the terrors of guilt than, say, a European Catholic. At the end of the story, dying, she is unable to rid herself of the loss and unrelieved grief her bridal day represents — she will not forgive — and the final impression is one of a life wholly burdened by the past. Her memory has overcome her.

Caroline Gordon's story, "Old Red," was published in 1933, and revolves around the memories of Aleck Maury, a sixty-year old teacher with a sound classical education whose consuming passion is fishing. His mind also reaches back deeply into the past, but he has accommodated himself to the new Southern world he has to live in. He has retired to Florida, and is pleased to use the rapid modes of transportation to get away by himself. In many ways, though, like Granny Weatherall, his present life is constantly solicited by his past. He has trouble remembering the name of his son-in-law, but none at all in picturing in exact detail the long-ago accidental fall of Uncle James from his horse, or the progress of the fox hunt which winds its way in his mind during the last half of the story. What strikes the reader about Mr. Maury's memories is the way he uses them to help him survive his declining strength and particularly the constraints he feels pressing around him in the household of his wife's family. His attitude toward Southern traditions is a divided one. He fully appreciates the pleasures of batter bread and home-smoked ham, but for him the family rituals of the South can be dangerous traps as well. On this May visit to the family home, Merry Point, two sets of memory prevail. On one hand, there are the images of loss and death: He remembers the death of his first child, and the way his wife — she has been dead for some years — turned fatalistically to religion which so consumed her that their marriage was never the same afterwards. When he learns that he is expected to cancel a fishing trip because of the funeral of a nearby relative, it seems a natural development of what he has tried to forget. But side by side with these oppressive associations of decline and death moves another stream of images, of hunting trips and the hunter's fascinating lore. These images are dominated by "Old Red," the hunted fox who always escaped, and who comes to be for Mr. Maury a kindred spirit. Maury himself is in many ways selfish and irresponsible, but he knows where his salvation lies, and when the story ends he is no longer lost in reverie, or chafing against the present, but thinking ahead, preparing to escape the funeral duty the family has imposed with one more triumphant ruse of a knowing independent will.

Peter Taylor's "In the Miro District" is a recent story, written almost forty years after "Old Red." But once more, the ambivalent force of memory is the central theme. The narrator, in late middle age, looks back on a series of painful confrontations with his grandfather, a Civil War veteran who lives alone in the country, but who on his visits to his son's house in Nashville is paired off uncomfortably with his grandson. The meetings are painful because both the boy and his grandfather have little to say to each other. For the boy, especially as he begins to assert himself as an independent adolescent, the stories his grandfather tells threaten to smother his own fragile identity. The grandfather's exploits are genuinely heroic, above all the revenge he took on some murderous nightriders well after the War when he was close to sixty years old. The grandfather does not use his stories to boast about his earlier life, but they are so full of will and strong character that the grandson dreads them as a reminder of his own tentative maturity. This is the negative reversal of the Southern storytelling tradition. It comes to afflict the boy's life like a disease. At one point, he undergoes a sort of ritualistic purgation of his grandfather's — and the South's — overwhelming history: "I hear myself going on and on that Sunday night. As I babbled away, it was not just that night but every night that I had ever been alone in the house with him. I had the sensation of retching or of actually vomiting, not the whiskey I had in my stomach but all the words I had not ever wanted to hear. My confusion was such that some of the time I did not know at all what I was saying. I knew only that this was the beginning of my freedom from him." He does eventually break away, or seems to. The end of the story concentrates more on his grandfather than on himself, and we are given a rather tragic portrait of a solitary man who has resigned himself to living in the city and entertaining the guests in his son's house. Of course, what finally emerges from the story is the power of the narrator to use his own memory to understand what had escaped him before in his grandfather's. It has taken him all the intervening years to realize, but he learns what neither he nor his grandfather ever would have admitted when forced together as dutiful but alien companions, that in an important sense they have more in common with each other than either of them has with the grandson's parents who had disappeared into the active life of the adult present.

As each of these three stories demonstrates, the retrospective monologue has become a characteristically Southern form of the modern short story. It is remarkable just how many Southern stories assume — in part or in whole — a comparable form. In this collection, there are Andrew Lytle's "Jericho, Jericho, Jericho" — whose dramatic situation is almost identical to that of Granny Weatherall, but whose tone and characterization are radically different — and Reynolds Price's autobiographical "Uncle Grant." Elsewhere, Faulkner's "The Bear," Katherine Anne Porter's "Holiday," James Agee's "1928 Story," Robert Penn Warren's "Blackberry Winter," are all stories in which a single narrator looks back on the past — either his own or his family's — in order to mine out a part of his own purpose or fate that had been up to then hidden to him.

And in all these stories of retrospection, the language and narrative compulsion of the remembering character ring out convincingly with the sound of the spoken word and the finality of the told story. No matter how involved or detailed the actual writing, the presence of human speech hovers above them like a higher authority. It is tempting to argue that such a constant presence is an inheritance from one of the traditional convictions that has resisted the longest in the modern South: Individual character is revealed most fully and most faithfully through individual speech. In this respect the South seems closer in spirit to a country such as Ireland than to any other region of the United States. Like the traditional Irishman, the Southerner still tends to judge a man by his words — rather than by acts alone — and still has a certain faith in the power of speech to express not only information, but also value, belief, entertainment, and dream.

In the contemporary South, there are still exceptional storytellers in the oral tradition. Probably the best example of the existence and the importance of the told tale today is the series of recordings Theodore Rosengarten made in the early 1970's with a black sharecropper, Ned Cobb. Published in 1974, *All God's Dangers* testifies to the continuing power of the tradition. Ned Cobb's imaginative manipulation of language, his large and searching memory, and his natural impulse to make meaning out of each of his problems or successes by giving it dramatic form align him closely with the literary art of the modern Southern authors mentioned above. He is one of the master storytellers of his time.

Of the short story writers of the modern South, Ernest Gaines is the one whose stories derive most directly from the oral traditions. He has been especially influenced by the power of Southern black speech to maintain a cohesive spirit in a victimized race threatened on all sides by disruption and discontinuity. All of the stories in his collection *Bloodline* are told by individual blacks who participate in or are deeply affected by the stories they tell. The tellers range in age from the six-year-old boy of "A Long Day in November" to a seventy-year-old man in the title story. The final story, "Just Like a Tree," organized around the structural principle of Faulkner's *As I Lay Dying*, is told by a group of relatives and friends, each in his turn, as they attend the leavetaking ceremonies surrounding Aunt Fe, an old black woman who has been invited North to escape white reprisals against the civil rights movement. More than any other story in the collection, "Just Like a Tree" affirms the force of the community. The only outsider, a black from the North, is clearly alien to the shared assumptions and beliefs of the others. He speaks a different "language;" he sets himself apart by his loud manners, his condescension, and his lack of feeling. The other people gathered in the house, even the white lady who has walked to the house to say good-bye, form a whole, united by shared speech and shared feelings. Gaines has a keen, sure ear for the vocabulary, idioms, accents, and rhythms of native black speech, but more than that, he recognizes the power in what for a long time was a predominantly oral culture to assert, affirm, and keep hold of personal and collective values. His stories deliberately call attention to the special virtues of the spoken word as a rich storehouse capable of keeping alive an otherwise impoverished community.

A strong oral tradition — both black and white — certainly helps account for some of the special qualities of the Southern story, but it must be remembered that the modern story is always a deliberately crafted work of art, and that the Southern writer this century is fully conscious of belonging to the modern *literary* tradition as well as to a specific society and region. The South is a large country, and apart from the small group of intellectuals and poets who formed the Fugitive-Agrarian membership in Nashville, there was never a well-defined literary movement such as in William Butler Yeats's Ireland, where diverse individuals were drawn into constant contact in a single city. What the modern South lacked in the way of a definite literary center, it compensated for by means of a different kind of literary community, one made of universities, textbooks, university-based journals, and private correspondence.

What was true of the first generation of modern Southern writers was even more true of the following generations. Not only did they benefit from the universities, but they also had the careers of William Faulkner, Thomas Wolfe, John Crowe Ransom, and Allen Tate as encouraging examples; and they had the advantage of being close to some of the best literary criticism being written in the English-speaking world. Journals such as *The Southern Review*, founded in 1935 by Cleanth Brooks and Robert Penn Warren, were particularly important to the great creative burst of Southern short stories in the 1940's and 1950's. These journals provided a place where Southern writers could publish their stories, and perhaps more important, in the long run, they provided a continuing forum where literary criticism, analysis, and speculation were made readily available. Southern text-book-anthologies were a direct result of this new critical activity, and the popular *Understanding Fiction* (1943) by Cleanth Brooks and Robert Penn Warren and *The House of Fiction* (1950) by Allen Tate and Caroline Gordon were influential through their judicious choice of stories and their high standards of critical commentary. Flannery O'Connor's letters mention both these books as having helped shape her own literary aims and judgment. Her letters also demonstrate, at least in her case, the importance of advice and encouragement from other writers. She developed many of her theories of the short story by corresponding with friends who asked her to read and criticize their stories; the letters she herself received from Caroline Gordon are models of clarity, precise detail, insight, and practical advice on the stories and novels O'Connor sent her.

One of the important results of this lively interest in critical theory behind the short-story textbooks, the professional journals, and the examples of personal correspondence we have is the fact that almost every major Southern writer has written criticism on the short-story form. In a field that is notoriously meager — in France today, for example, there is not a single anthology of modern French stories, nor a single critical study of the modern short story — Southern writers have been particularly original and productive. Once more, the only comparable situation to the Southern one is modern Ireland, out of which two of the rare full-length studies of the short story have emerged: Frank O'Connor's *The Lonely Voice* and Sean O'Faolain's *The Short Story*. Caroline Gordon, Katherine Anne Porter, Robert Penn Warren, Flannery O'Connor, and Eudora Welty have all been willing to discuss they own stories in as much instructive detail as they discuss those of others. Flannery O'Connor's various speeches and articles were collected posthumously in the volume *Mystery and Manners* (1969), her letters in *The Habit of Being* (1979). Eudora Welty has published her wry, original essays in *The Eye of the Story* (1978). More of her short story commentary can be found in her recent mini-autobiography, *One Writer's Beginnings* (1984), and in a collection of her interviews, *Conversations with Eudora Welty* (1984), one of an invaluable series of interviews published by the University Press of Mississippi.

Another telling sign that the short story seems to have natural roots in the Southern mind is the curious fact that almost every writer in the South has an original theory about the form; there is something so general and so compulsive about speculating on the role of story in the South that one is tempted again to consider the genre a Southern mode of perception. We can consider very briefly the following passages from three contemporary Southern writers: Reynolds Price, Harry Crews, and Robert Penn Warren.

The first is taken from the introductory essay in Reynolds Price's *A Palpable God* (1978), a selection of stories he translated from the Bible. The essay is entitled "A Single Meaning: Notes on the Origins and Life of Narrative." In the midst of discussing the source and narrative form of some of the earliest Biblical stories, Price makes the following statement:

> The oldest prose stories were set in virtually their present verbal form in about 950 B.C. by one of the greatest of epic writers, anonymous, known to us only as the Yahwist. There is considerable evidence of various sorts however — including the personal experience of anyone reared in a powerful oral-narrative tradition (contemporary American Southerners, for instance, or conservative Jews) — that the stories developed their present narrative armature and perhaps the greater part of their verbal form long before the Yahwist's editing.

The second passage is taken from Harry Crew's moving autobiographical portrait of his Bacon County, south Georgia home, *A Childhood: The Biography of a Place* (1978):

> It was always the women who scared me. The stories that women told and that men told were full of violence, sickness, and death. But it was the women whose stories were unrelieved by humor and filled with apocalyptic vision. No matter how awful the stories were that the men told they were always funny. The men's stories were stories of character, rather than of circumstances, and they always knew the people the stories were about. But the women would repeat stories about folks they did not know and had never seen, and consequently, without character counting for anything, the stories were as stark and cold as legend or myth.

The third passage, taken from a recent review-article by Robert Penn Warren on Eudora Welty, offers an interesting contrast to the distinctions Crews makes above:

There is another fact, a special kind of conversational flow among Southern women — or at least a remarkable plenty of them — that has provided another contribution to Southern literature. This was not ordinary gossip (although gossip no doubt thrived) but gossip providing the tale for its own sake, sad or humorous: the character sketch, the narrative, grotesque, comic or poetic description; gusts of feelings, delicate ironies and small, astute observations, bright as a needle point — all the things that characterize a "woman's talk," which is somehow so different from a man's tale, even when it is, itself, a tale.

These passages are placed together not to call attention to their differences — however provocative they are — but to demonstrate how vital the oral storytelling tradition remains in the mind even of the contemporary Southern writer. Reynolds Price's parenthetical aside is part of a long, carefully argued thesis on biblical narration; Harry Crews's distinction appears undeveloped, almost offhandedly, in an autobiography that talks about much more than storytelling traditions, and Robert Penn Warren's remarks on gossip are just that, brief remarks in a short newspaper review. What is striking in these three passages is the natural use of a common experience of story to support each writer's different theory, and this seems unique in the history of modern letters. Writers from Russia, England, France, Ireland, especially Ireland, and most recently several countries in South America have all contributed modern classics in the short story. In none of these countries, however, is the convergence of native traditions and individual speculation on the art of the story — Frank O'Connor and Sean O'Faolain in Ireland, Jorge Luis Borges in Argentina, V.S. Pritchett in England, are the exception, not the rule — as widespread as in the American South. Perhaps this is one reason the modern Southern story continues to thrive and to breed new forms, and continues to reflect, more than any other region or country, the successful union of the communal, popular mind with an individual, original voice.

TRUMAN CAPOTE

Children on Their Birthdays

(This story is for Andrew Lyndon)

YESTERDAY AFTERNOON THE six-o'clock bus ran over Miss Bobbit. I'm not sure what there is to be said about it; after all, she was only ten years old, still I know no one of us in this town will forget her. For one thing, nothing she ever did was ordinary, not from the first time that we saw her, and that was a year ago. Miss Bobbit and her mother, they arrived on that same six-o'clock bus, the one that comes through from Mobile. It happened to be my cousin Billy Bob's birthday, and so most of the children in town were here at our house. We were sprawled on the front porch having tutti-frutti and devil cake when the bus stormed around Deadman's Curve. It was the summer that never rained; rusted dryness coated everything; sometimes when a car passed on the road, raised dust would hang in the still air an hour or more. Aunt El said if they didn't pave the highway soon she was going to move down to the seacoast; but she'd said that for such a long time. Anyway, we were sitting on the porch, tutti-frutti melting on our plates, when suddenly, just as we were wishing that something would happen, something did; for out of the red road dust appeared Miss Bobbit. A wiry little girl in a starched, lemon-colored party dress, she sassed along with a grown-up mince, one hand on her hip, the other supporting a spinsterish umbrella. Her mother, lugging two cardboard valises and a wind-up victrola, trailed in the background. She was a gaunt shaggy woman with silent eyes and a hungry smile.

All the children on the porch had grown so still that when a cone of wasps started humming the girls did not set up their usual holler. Their attention was too fixed upon the approach of Miss Bobbit and her mother, who had by now reached the gate. "Begging your pardon," called Miss Bobbit in a voice that was at once silky and childlike, like a pretty piece of ribbon, and immaculately exact, like a movie-star or a schoolmarm, "but might we speak with the grown-up persons of the house?" This, of course, meant Aunt El; and, at least to some degree, myself. But Billy Bob and all the other boys, no one of whom was over thirteen, followed down to the gate after us. From their faces you would have thought they'd never seen a girl before. Certainly not like Miss Bobbit. As Aunt El said, whoever heard tell of a child wearing makeup? Tangee gave her lips an orange glow, her hair, rather like a costume wig, was a mass of rosy curls, and her eyes had a knowing, penciled tilt; even so, she had a skinny dignity, she was a lady, and, what is more, she looked you in the eye with manlike directness. "I'm Miss Lily Jane Bobbit, Miss Bobbit from Memphis, Tennessee," she said solemnly. The boys looked down at their toes, and, on the porch, Cora McCall, who Billy Bob was courting at the time, led the girls into a fanfare of giggles. "*Country* children," said Miss Bobbit with an understanding smile, and gave her parasol a saucy whirl. "My mother," and this homely woman allowed an abrupt nod to acknowledge herself, "my mother and I have taken rooms here. Would you be so kind as to point out the house? It belongs to a Mrs. Sawyer." Why, sure, said Aunt El, that's Mrs. Sawyer's, right there across the street. The only boarding house around here, it is an old tall dark place with about two dozen lightning rods scattered on the roof: Mrs. Sawyer is scared to death in a thunderstorm.

Coloring like an apple, Billy Bob said, please ma'am, it being such a hot day and all, wouldn't they rest a spell and have some tutti-frutti? and Aunt El said yes, by all means, but Miss Bobbit shook her head. "Very fattening, tutti-frutti; but *merci* you kindly," and they started across the road, the mother half-dragging her parcels in the dust. Then, and with an earnest expression, Miss Bobbit turned back; the sunflower yellow of her eyes darkened, and she rolled them slightly sideways, as if trying to remember a poem. "My mother has a disorder of the tongue, so it is necessary that I speak for her," she announced rapidly and heaved a sigh. "My mother is a very fine seamstress; she has made dresses for the society of many cities and towns, including Memphis and Tallahassee. No doubt you have noticed and admired the dress I am wearing. Every stitch of it was handsewn by my mother. My mother can copy any pattern, and just recently she won a twenty-five-dollar prize from the *Ladies' Home Journal*. My mother can also crochet, knit and embroider. If you want any kind of sewing done, please come to my mother. Please advise your friends and family. Thank you." And then, with a rustle and a swish, she was gone.

Cora McCall and the girls pulled their hair-ribbons nervously, suspiciously, and looked very put out and prune-faced. I'm *Miss* Bobbit, said Cora, twisting her face into an evil imitation, and I'm Princess Elizabeth, that's who I am, ha, ha, ha. Furthermore, said Cora, that dress was just as tacky as could be; personally, Cora said, all my clothes come from Atlanta; plus a pair of shoes from New York, which is not even to mention my silver turquoise ring all the way from Mexico City, Mexico. Aunt El said they ought not to behave that way about a fellow child, a stranger in the town, but the girls went on like a huddle of witches, and certain boys, the sillier ones that liked to be with the girls, joined in and said things that made Aunt El go red and declare she was going to send them all home and tell their daddies, to boot. But before she could carry forward this threat Miss Bobbit herself intervened by traipsing across the Sawyer porch, costumed in a new and startling manner.

The older boys, like Billy Bob and Preacher Star, who had sat quiet while the girls razzed Miss Bobbit, and who had watched the house into which she'd disappeared with misty, ambitious faces, they now straightened up and ambled down to the gate. Cora McCall sniffed and poked out her lower lip, but the rest of us went and sat on the steps. Miss Bobbit paid us no mind whatever. The Sawyer yard is dark with mulberry trees and it is planted with grass and sweet shrub. Sometimes after a rain you can smell the sweet shrub all the way into our house; and in the center of this yard there is a sundial which Mrs. Sawyer installed in 1912 as a memorial to her Boston bull, Sunny, who died after having lapped up a bucket of paint. Miss Bobbit pranced into the yard toting the victrola, which she put on the sundial; she wound it up, and started a record playing, and it played the Court of Luxemborg. By now it was almost nightfall, a firefly hour, blue as milkglass; and birds like arrows swooped together and swept into the folds of trees. Before storms, leaves and flowers appear to burn with a private light, color, and Miss Bobbit, got up in a little white skirt like a powderpuff and with strips of gold-glittering tinsel ribboning her hair, seemed, set against the darkening all around, to contain this illuminated quality. She held her arms arched over her head, her hands lily-limp, and stood straight up on the tips of her toes. She stood that way for a good long while, and Aunt El said it was right smart of her. Then she began to waltz around and around, and around and around she went until Aunt El said, why, she was plain dizzy from the sight. She stopped only when it was time to rewind the victrola; and when the moon came rolling down the ridge, and the last supper bell had sounded, and all the children had gone home, and the night iris was beginning to bloom, Miss Bobbit was still there in the dark turning like a top.

We did not see her again for some time. Preacher Star came every morning to our house and stayed straight through to supper. Preacher is a rail-thin boy with a butchy shock of red hair; he has eleven brothers and sisters, and even they are afraid of him, for he has a terrible temper, and is famous in these parts for his green-eyed meanness: last fourth of July he whipped Ollie Overton so bad that Ollie's family had to send him to the hospital in Pensacola; and there was another time he bit off half a mule's ear, chewed it and spit it on the ground. Before Billy Bob got his growth, Preacher played the devil with him, too. He used to drop cockleburrs down his collar, and rub pepper in his eyes, and tear up his homework. But now they are the biggest friends in town: talk alike, walk alike, and occasionally they disappear together for whole days, Lord knows where to. But during these days when Miss Bobbit did not appear they stayed close to the house.

They would stand around in the yard trying to slingshot sparrows off telephone poles; or sometimes Billy Bob would play his ukulele, and they would sing so loud Uncle Billy Bob, who is Judge for this county, claimed he could hear them all the way to the courthouse: *send me a letter, send it by mail, send it in care of the Birming-ham jail.* Miss Bobbit did not hear them; at least she never poked her head out the door. Then one day Mrs. Sawyer, coming over to borrow a cup of sugar, rattled on a good deal about her new boarders. You know, she said, squinting her chicken-bright eyes, the husband was a crook, uh huh, the child told me herself. Hasn't an ounce of shame, not a mite. Said her daddy was the dearest daddy and the sweetest singing man in the whole of Tennessee. . . . And I said, honey, where is he? and just as off-hand as you please she says, Oh, he's in the penitentiary and we don't hear from him no more. Say, now, does that make your blood run cold? Uh huh, and I been thinking, her mama, I been thinking she's some kinda foreigner: never says a word, and sometimes it looks like she don't understand what nobody says to her. And you know, they eat everything *raw*. *Raw* eggs, *raw* turnips, carrots — no meat whatsoever. For reasons of health, the child says, but ho! she's been straight out on the bed running a fever since last Tuesday.

That same afternoon Aunt El went out to water her roses, only to discover them gone. These were special roses, ones she'd planned to send to the flower show in Mobile, and so naturally she got a little hysterical. She rang up the Sheriff, and said, listen here, Sheriff, you come over here right fast. I mean somebody's got off with all my Lady Anne's that I've devoted myself to heart and soul since early spring. When the Sheriff's car pulled up outside our house, all the neighbors along the street came out on their porches, and Mrs. Sawyer, layers of cold cream whitening her face, trotted across the road. Oh shoot, she said, very disappointed to find no one had been murdered, oh shoot, she said, nobody's stole them roses. Your Billy Bob brought them roses over and left them for little Bobbit. Aunt El did not say one word. She just marched over to the peach tree, and cut herself a switch. Ohhh, Billy Bob, she stalked along the street calling his name, and then she found him down at Speedy's garage where he and Preacher were watching Speedy take a motor apart. She simply lifted him by the hair and, switching blueblazes, towed him home. But she couldn't make him say he was sorry and she couldn't make him cry. And when she was finished with him he ran into the backyard and climbed high into the tower of a pecan tree and swore he wasn't ever going to come down. Then his daddy stood at the window and called to him: Son, we aren't mad with you, so come down and eat your supper. But Billy Bob wouldn't budge. Aunt El went and leaned against the tree. She spoke in a voice soft as the gathering light. I'm sorry, son, she said, I didn't mean whipping you so hard like that. I've fixed a nice supper, son, potato salad and boiled ham and deviled eggs. Go away, said Billy Bob, I don't want no supper, and I hate you like all-fire. His daddy said he ought not to talk like that to his mother, and she began to cry. She stood there under the tree and cried, raising the hem of her skirt to dab at her eyes. I don't hate you, son. . . . If I didn't love you I wouldn't whip you. The pecan leaves began to rattle; Billy Bob slid slowly to the ground, and Aunt El, rushing her fingers through his hair, pulled him against her. Aw, Ma, he said, Aw, Ma.

After supper Billy Bob came and flung himself on the foot of my bed. He smelled all sour and sweet, the way boys do, and I felt very sorry for him, especially because he looked so worried. His eyes were almost shut with worry. You're s'posed to send sick folks flowers, he said righteously. About this time we heard the victrola, a lilting faraway sound, and a night moth flew through the window, drifting in the air delicate as the music. But it was dark now, and we couldn't tell if Miss Bobbit was dancing. Billy Bob, as though he were in pain, doubled up on the bed like a jackknife; but his face was suddenly clear, his grubby boy-eyes twitching like candles. She's so cute, he whispered, she's the cutest dickens I ever saw, gee, to hell with it, I don't care, I'd pick all the roses in China.

Preacher would have picked all the roses in China, too. He was as crazy about her as Billy Bob. But Miss Bobbit did not notice them. The sole communication we had with her was a note to Aunt El thanking her for the flowers. Day after day she sat on her porch, always dressed to beat the band, and doing a piece of embroidery, or combing curls in her hair, or reading a Webster's dictionary — formal, but friendly enough; if you said good-day to her she said good-day to you. Even so, the boys never could seem to get up the nerve to go over and talk with her, and most of the time she simply looked through them, even when they tomcatted up and down the street trying to get her eye. They wrestled, played Tarzan, did foolheaded bicycle tricks. It was a sorry business. A great many girls in town strolled by the Sawyer house two and three times within an hour just on the chance of getting a look. Some of the girls who did this were: Cora McCall, Mary Murphy Jones, Janice Ackerman. Miss Bobbit did not show any interest in them either. Cora would not speak to Billy Bob any more. The same was true with Janice and Preacher. As a matter of fact, Janice wrote Preacher a letter in red ink on lace-trimmed paper in which she told him he was vile beyond all human beings and words, that she considered their engagement broken, that he could have back the stuffed squirrel he'd given her. Preacher, saying he wanted to act nice, stopped her the next time she passed our house, and said, well, hell, she could keep that old squirrel if she wanted to. Afterwards, he couldn't understand why Janice ran away bawling the way she did.

Then one day the boys were being crazier than usual; Billy Bob was sagging around in his daddy's World War khakis, and Preacher, stripped to the waist, had a naked woman drawn on his chest with one of Aunt El's old lipsticks. They looked like perfect fools, but Miss Bobbit, reclining in a swing, merely yawned. It was noon, and there was no one passing in the street, except a colored girl, baby-fat and sugar-plum shaped, who hummed along carrying a pail of blackberries. But the boys, teasing at her like gnats, joined hands and wouldn't let her go by, not until she paid a tariff. I ain't studyin' no tariff, she said, what kinda tariff you talkin' about, mister? A party in the barn, said Preacher, between clenched teeth, mighty nice party in the barn. And she, with a sulky shrug, said, huh, she intended studyin' no barn parties. Whereupon Billy Bob capsized her berry pail, and when she, with despairing, piglike shrieks, bent down in futile gestures of rescue, Preacher, who can be mean as the devil, gave her behind a kick which sent her sprawling jellylike among the blackberries and the dust. Miss Bobbit came tearing across the road, her finger wagging like a metronome; like a schoolteacher she clapped her hands, stamped her foot, said: "It is a well-known fact that gentlemen are put on the face of this earth for the protection of ladies. Do you suppose boys behave this way in towns like Memphis, New York, London, Hollywood or Paris?" The boys hung back, and shoved their hands in their pockets. Miss Bobbit helped the colored girl to her feet; she dusted her off, dried her eyes, held out a handkerchief and told her to blow. "A pretty pass," she said, "a fine situation when a lady can't walk safely in the public daylight."

Then the two of them went back and sat on Mrs. Sawyer's porch; and for the next year they were never far apart, Miss Bobbit and this baby elephant, whose name was Rosalba Cat. At first, Mrs. Sawyer raised a fuss about Rosalba being so much at her house. She told Aunt El that it went against the grain to have a nigger lolling smack there in plain sight on her front porch. But Miss Bobbit had a certain magic, whatever she did she did it with completeness, and so directly, so solemnly, that there was nothing to do but accept it. For instance, the tradespeople in town used to snicker when they called her *Miss* Bobbit; but by and by she was Miss Bobbit, and they gave her stiff little bows as she whirled by spinning her parasol. Miss Bobbit told everyone that Rosalba was her sister, which caused a good many jokes; but like most of her ideas, it gradually seemed natural, and when we would overhear them calling each other Sister Rosalba and Sister Bobbit none of us cracked a smile. But Sister Rosalba and Sister Bobbit did some queer things. There was the business about the dogs. Now there are a great many dogs in this town, rat terriers, bird dogs, bloodhounds; they trail along the forlorn noon-hot streets in sleepy herds of six to a dozen, all waiting only for dark and the moon, when straight through the lonesome hours you can hear them howling: someone is dying, someone is dead. Miss Bobbit complained to the Sheriff; she said that certain of the dogs always planted themselves under her window, and that she was a light sleeper to begin with; what is more, and as Sister Rosalba said, she did not believe they were dogs at all, but some kind of devil. Naturally the Sheriff did nothing; and so she took the matter into her own hands. One morning, after an especially loud night, she was seen stalking through the town with Rosalba at her side, Rosalba carrying a flower basket filled with rocks; whenever they saw a dog they paused while Miss Bobbit scrutinized him. Sometimes she would shake her head, but more often she said, "Yes, that's one of them, Sister Rosalba," and

Sister Rosalba, with ferocious aim, would take a rock from her basket and crack the dog between the eyes.

Another thing that happened concerns Mr. Henderson. Mr. Henderson has a back room in the Sawyer house; a tough runt of a man who formerly was a wildcat oil prospector in Oklahoma, he is about seventy years old and, like a lot of old men, obsessed by functions of the body. Also, he is a terrible drunk. One time he had been drunk for two weeks; whenever he heard Miss Bobbit and Sister Rosalba moving around the house, he would charge to the top of the stairs and bellow down to Mrs. Sawyer that there were midgets in the walls trying to get at his supply of toilet paper. They've already stolen fifteen cents' worth, he said. One evening, when the two girls were sitting under a tree in the yard, Mr. Henderson, sporting nothing more than a nightshirt, stamped out after them. Steal all my toilet paper, will you? he hollered, I'll show you midgets. . . . Somebody come help me, else these midget bitches are liable to make off with every sheet in town. It was Billy Bob and Preacher who caught Mr. Henderson and held him until some grown men arrived and began to tie him up. Miss Bobbit, who had behaved with admirable calm, told the men they did not know how to tie a proper knot, and undertook to do so herself. She did such a good job that all the circulation stopped in Mr. Henderson's hands and feet and it was a month before he could walk again.

It was shortly afterwards that Miss Bobbit paid us a call. She came on Sunday and I was there alone, the family having gone to church. "The odors of a church are so offensive," she said, leaning forward and with her hands folded primly before her. "I don't want you to think I'm a heathen, Mr. C.; I've had enough experience to know that there is a God and that there is a Devil. But the way to tame the Devil is not to go down there to church and listen to what a sinful mean fool he is. No, love the Devil like you love Jesus: because he is a powerful man, and will do you a good turn if he knows you trust him. He has frequently done me good turns, like at dancing school in Memphis. . . . I always called in the Devil to help me get the biggest part in our annual show. That is common sense; you see, I knew Jesus wouldn't have any truck with dancing. Now, as a matter of fact, I have called in the Devil just recently. He is the only one who can help me get out of this town. Not that I live here, not exactly. I think always about somewhere else, somewhere else where everything is dancing, like people dancing in the streets, and everything is pretty, like children on their birthdays. My precious papa said I live in the sky, but if he'd lived more in the sky he'd be rich like he wanted to be. The trouble with my papa was he did not love the Devil, he let the Devil love him. But I am very smart in that respect; I know the next best thing is very often the best. It was the next best thing for us to move to this town; and since I can't pursue my career here, the next best thing for me is to start a little business on the side. Which is what I have done. I am sole subscription agent in this county for an impressive list of magazines, including *Reader's Digest*, *Popular Mechanics*, *Dime Detective* and *Child's Life*. To be sure, Mr. C., I'm not here to sell you anything. But I have a thought in mind. I was thinking those two boys that are always hanging around here, it occurred to me that they are men, after all. Do you suppose they would make a pair of likely assistants?"

Billy Bob and Preacher worked hard for Miss Bobbit, and for Sister Rosalba, too. Sister Rosalba carried a line of cosmetics called Dewdrop, and it was part of the boys' job to deliver purchases to her customers. Billy Bob used to be so tired in the evening he could hardly chew his supper. Aunt El said it was a shame and a pity, and finally one day when Billy Bob came down with a touch of sunstroke she said, all right, that settled it, Billy Bob would just have to quit Miss Bobbit. But Billy Bob cussed her out until his daddy had to lock him in his room; whereupon he said he was going to kill himself. Some cook we'd had told him once that if you ate a mess of collards all slopped over with molasses it would kill you sure as shooting; and so that is what he did. I'm dying, he said, rolling back and forth on his bed, I'm dying and nobody cares.

Miss Bobbit came over and told him to hush up. "There's nothing wrong with you, boy," she said. "All you've got is a stomach ache." Then she did something that shocked Aunt El very much: she stripped the covers off Billy Bob and rubbed him down with alcohol from head to toe. When Aunt El told her she did not think that was a nice thing for a little girl to do, Miss Bobbit replied: "I don't know whether it's nice or not, but it's certainly very refreshing." After which Aunt El did all she could to keep Billy Bob from going back to work for her, but his daddy said to leave him alone, they would have to let the boy lead his own life.

Miss Bobbit was very honest about money. She paid Billy Bob and Preacher their exact commission, and she would never let them treat her, as they often tried to do, at the drugstore or to the picture show. "You'd better save your money," she told them. "That is, if you want to go to college. Because neither one of you has got the brains to win a scholarship, not even a football scholarship." But it was over money that Billy Bob and Preacher had a big falling out; that was not the real reason, of course: the real reason was that they had grown cross-eyed jealous over Miss Bobbit. So one day, and he had the gall to do this right in front of Billy Bob, Preacher said to Miss Bobbit that she'd better check her accounts carefully because he had more than a suspicion that Billy Bob wasn't turning over to her *all* the money he collected. That's a damned lie, said Billy Bob, and with a clean left hook he knocked Preacher off the Sawyer porch and jumped after him into a bed of nasturtiums. But once Preacher got a hold on him, Billy Bob didn't stand a chance. Preacher even rubbed dirt in his eyes. During all this, Mrs. Sawyer, leaning out an upper-story window, screamed like an eagle, and Sister Rosalba, fatly cheerful, ambiguously shouted, Kill him! Kill him! Kill him! Only Miss Bobbit seemed to know what she was doing. She plugged in the lawn hose, and gave the boys a close-up, blinding bath. Gasping, Preacher staggered to his feet. Oh, honey, he said, shaking himself like a wet dog, honey, you've got to decide. "Decide *what*?" said Miss Bobbit, right away in a huff. Oh, honey, wheezed

Preacher, you don't want us boys killing each other. You got to decide who is your real true sweetheart. "Sweetheart, my eye," said Miss Bobbit. "I should've known better than to get myself involved with a lot of country children. What sort of businessman are you going to make? Now, you listen here, Preacher Star: I don't want a sweetheart, and if I did, it wouldn't be you. As a matter of fact, you don't even get up when a lady enters the room."

Preacher spit on the ground and swaggered over to Billy Bob. Come on, he said, just as though nothing had happened, she's a hard one, she is, she don't want nothing but to make trouble between two good friends. For a moment it looked as if Billy Bob was going to join him in a peaceful togetherness; but suddenly, coming to his senses, he drew back and made a gesture. The boys regarded each other a full minute, all the closeness between them turning an ugly color: you can't hate so much unless you love, too. And Preacher's face showed all of this. But there was nothing for him to do except go away. Oh, yes, Preacher, you looked so lost that day that for the first time I really liked you, so skinny and mean and lost going down the road all by yourself.

They did not make it up, Preacher and Billy Bob; and it was not because they didn't want to, it was only that there did not seem to be any straight way for their friendship to happen again. But they couldn't get rid of this friendship: each was always aware of what the other was up to; and when Preacher found himself a new buddy, Billy Bob moped around for days, picking things up, dropping them again, or doing sudden wild things, like purposely poking his finger in the electric fan. Sometimes in the evenings Preacher would pause by the gate and talk with Aunt El. It was only to torment Billy Bob, I suppose, but he stayed friendly with all of us, and at Christmas time he gave us a huge box of shelled peanuts. He left a present for Billy Bob, too. It turned out to be a book of Sherlock Holmes; and on the flyleaf there was scribbled, "Friends Like Ivy On the Wall Must Fall." That's the corniest thing I ever saw, Billy Bob said. Jesus, what a dope he is! But then, and though it was a cold winter day, he went in the backyard and climbed up into the pecan tree, crouching there all afternoon in the blue December branches.

But most of the time he was happy, because Miss Bobbit was there, and she was always sweet to him now. She and Sister Rosalba treated him like a man; that is to say, they allowed him to do everything for them. On the other hand, they let him win at three-handed bridge, they never questioned his lies, nor discouraged his ambitions. It was a happy while. However, trouble started again when school began. Miss Bobbit refused to go. "It's ridiculous," she said, when one day the principal, Mr. Copland, came around to investigate, "really ridiculous; I can read and write and there are *some* people in this town who have every reason to know that I can count money. No, Mr. Copland, consider for a moment and you will see neither of us has the time nor energy. After all, it would only be a matter of whose spirit broke first, yours or mine. And besides, what is there for you to teach me? Now, if you knew anything about dancing, that would be another matter; but under the circumstances, yes, Mr. Copland, under the circumstances, I suggest we forget the whole thing." Mr. Copland was perfectly willing to. But the rest of the town thought she ought to be whipped. Horace Deasley wrote a piece in the paper which was titled "A Tragic Situation." It was, in his opinion, a tragic situation when a small girl could defy what he, for some reason, termed the Constitution of the United States. The article ended with a question: *Can she get away with it?* She did; and so did Sister Rosalba. Only she was colored, so no one cared. Billy Bob was not as lucky. It was school for him, all right; but he might as well have stayed home for the good it did him. On his first report card he got three F's, a record of some sort. But he is a smart boy. I guess he just couldn't live through those hours without Miss Bobbit; away from her he always seemed half-asleep. He was always in a fight, too; either his eye was black, or his lip was split, or his walk had a limp. He never talked about these fights, but Miss Bobbit was shrewd enough to guess the reason why. "You are a dear, I know, I know. And I appreciate you, Billy Bob. Only don't fight with people because of me. Of course they say mean things about me. But do you know why that is, Billy Bob? It's a compliment, kind of. Because deep down they think I'm absolutely wonderful."

And she was right: if you are not admired no one will take the trouble to disapprove. But actually we had no idea of how wonderful she was until there appeared the man known as Manny Fox. This happened late in February. The first news we had of Manny Fox was a series of jovial placards posted up in the stores around town: Manny Fox Presents the Fan Dancer Without the Fan; then, in smaller print: Also, Sensational Amateur Program Featuring Your Own Neighbors — First Prize, A Genuine Hollywood Screen Test. All this was to take place the following Thursday. The tickets were priced at one dollar each, which around here is a lot of money; but it is not often that we get any kind of flesh entertainment, so everybody shelled out their money and made a great todo over the whole thing. The drugstore cowboys talked dirty all week, mostly about the fan dancer without the fan, who turned out to be Mrs. Manny Fox. They stayed down the highway at the Chucklewood Tourist Camp; but they were in town all day, driving around in an old Packard which had Manny Fox's full name stenciled on all four doors. His wife was a deadpan pimento-tongued redhead with wet lips and moist eyelids; she was quite large actually, but compared to Manny Fox she seemed rather frail, for he was a fat cigar of a man.

They made the pool hall their headquarters, and every afternoon you could find them there, drinking beer and joking with the town loafs. As it developed, Manny Fox's business affairs were not restricted to theatrics. He also ran a kind of employment bureau: slowly he let it be known that for a fee of $150 he could get for any adventurous boys in the county high-class jobs working on fruit ships sailing from New Orleans to South America. The chance of a lifetime, he called it. There are not two boys around here who readily lay their hands on so much as five dollars; nevertheless, a good dozen managed to raise the money. Ada

Willingham took all she'd saved to buy an angel tombstone for her husband and gave it to her son, and Acey Trump's papa sold an option on his cotton crop.

But the night of the show! That was a night when all was forgotten: mortgages, and the dishes in the kitchen sink. Aunt El said you'd think we were going to the opera, everybody so dressed up, so pink and sweetsmelling. The Odeon had not been so full since the night they gave away the matched set of sterling silver. Practically everybody had a relative in the show, so there was a lot of nervousness to contend with. Miss Bobbit was the only contestant we knew real well. Billy Bob couldn't sit still; he kept telling us over and over that we mustn't applaud for anybody but Miss Bobbit; Aunt El said that would be very rude, which sent Billy Bob off into a state again; and when his father bought us all bags of popcorn he wouldn't touch his because it would make his hands greasy, and please, another thing, we mustn't be noisy and eat ours while Miss Bobbit was performing. That she was to be a contestant had come as a last-minute surprise. It was logical enough, and there were signs that should've told us; the fact, for instance, that she had not set foot outside the Sawyer house in how many days? And the victrola going half the night, her shadow whirling on the window shade, and the secret, stuffed look on Sister Rosalba's face whenever asked after Sister Bobbit's health. So there was her name on the program, listed second, in fact, though she did not appear for a long while. First came Manny Fox, greased and leering, who told a lot of peculiar jokes, clapping his hands, ha, ha. Aunt El said if he told another joke like that she was going to walk straight out: he did, and she didn't. Before Miss Bobbit came on there were eleven contestants, including Eustacia Bernstein, who imitated movie stars so that they all sounded like Eustacia, and there was an extraordinary Mr. Buster Riley, a jug-eared old wool-hat from way in the back country who played "Waltzing Matilda" on a saw. Up to that point, he was the hit of the show; not that there was any marked difference in the various receptions, for everybody applauded generously, everybody, that is, except Preacher Star. He was sitting two rows ahead of us, greeting each act with a donkey-loud boo. Aunt El said she was never going to speak to him again. The only person he ever applauded was Miss Bobbit. No doubt the Devil was on her side, but she deserved it. Out she came, tossing her hips, her curls, rolling her eyes. You could tell right away it wasn't going to be one of her classical numbers. She tapped across the stage, daintily holding up the sides of a cloud-blue skirt. That's the cutest thing I ever saw, said Billy Bob, smacking his thigh, and Aunt El had to agree that Miss Bobbit looked real sweet. When she started to twirl the whole audience broke into spontaneous applause; so she did it all over again, hissing, "Faster, faster," at poor Miss Adelaide, who was at the piano doing her Sunday-school best. "I was born in China, and raised in Jay-pan . . ." We had never heard her sing before, and she had a rowdy sandpaper voice. ". . . if you don't like my peaches, stay away from my can, o-ho o-ho!" Aunt El gasped; she gasped again when Miss Bobbit, with a bump, up-ended her skirt to display blue-lace underwear, thereby collecting most of the whistles the boys had been saving for the fan dancer without the fan, which was just as well, as it later turned out, for that lady, to the tune of "An Apple for the Teacher" and cries of gyp gyp, did her routine attired in a bathing suit. But showing off her bottom was not Miss Bobbit's final triumph. Miss Adelaide commenced an ominous thundering in the darker keys, at which point Sister Rosalba, carrying a lighted Roman candle, rushed onstage and handed it to Miss Bobbit, who was in the midst of a full split; she made it, too, and just as she did the Roman candle burst into fiery balls of red, white and blue, and we all had to stand up because she was singing "The Star Spangled Banner" at the top of her lungs. Aunt El said afterwards that it was one of the most gorgeous things she'd ever seen on the American stage.

Well, she surely did deserve a Hollywood screen test and, inasmuch as she won the contest, it looked as though she were going to get it. Manny Fox said she was: honey, he said, you're real star stuff. Only he skipped town the next day, leaving nothing but hearty promises. Watch the mails, my friends, you'll all be hearing from me. That is what he said to the boys whose money he'd taken, and that is what he said to Miss Bobbit. There are three deliveries daily, and this sizable group gathered at the post office for all of them, a jolly crowd growing gradually joyless. How their hands trembled when a letter slid into their mailbox. A terrible hush came over them as the days passed. They all knew what the other was thinking, but no one could bring himself to say it, not even Miss Bobbit. Postmistress Patterson said it plainly, however: the man's a crook, she said, I knew he was a crook to begin with, and if I have to look at your faces one more day I'll shoot myself.

Finally, at the end of two weeks, it was Miss Bobbit who broke the spell. Her eyes had grown more vacant than anyone had ever supposed they might, but one day, after the last mail was up, all her old sizzle came back. "O.K., boys, it's lynch law now," she said, and proceeded to herd the whole troupe home with her. This was the first meeting of the Manny Fox Hangman's Club, an organization which, in a more social form, endures to this day, though Manny Fox has long since been caught and, so to say, hung. Credit for this went quite properly to Miss Bobbit. Within a week she'd written over three hundred descriptions of Manny Fox and dispatched them to Sheriffs throughout the South; she also wrote letters to papers in the larger cities, and these attracted wide attention. As a result, four of the robbed boys were offered good-paying jobs by the United Fruit Company, and late this spring, when Manny Fox was arrested in Uphigh, Arkansas, where he was pulling the same old dodge, Miss Bobbit was presented with a Good Deed Merit award from the Sunbeam Girls of America. For some reason, she made a point of letting the world know that this did not exactly thrill her. "I do not approve of the organization," she said. "All that rowdy bugle blowing. It's neither good-hearted nor truly feminine. And anyway, what is a good deed? Don't let anybody fool you, a good deed is something you do because you want something in return." It would be reassuring to report she was wrong, and that her just reward, when at last it came, was given out of kindness and love. However, this is not the case. About a week ago the boys involved in the swindle all received from Manny Fox checks covering their losses, and Miss Bobbit, with clodhopping determination, stalked into a meeting of the Hangman's Club, which is now an excuse for drinking beer and playing poker every Thursday night. "Look, boys," she said, laying it on the line, "none of you ever thought to see that money again, but now that you have, you ought to invest it in something practical — like me." The proposition was that they should pool their money and finance her trip to Hollywood; in return, they would get ten percent of her life's earnings which, after she was a star, and that would not be very long, would make them all rich men. "At least," as she said, "in this part of the country." Not one of the boys wanted to do it: but when Miss Bobbit looked at you, what was there to say?

Since Monday, it has been raining buoyant summer rain shot through with sun, but dark at night and full of sound, full of dripping leaves, watery chimings, sleepless scuttlings. Billy Bob is wide-awake, dry-eyed, though everything he does is a little frozen and his tongue is as stiff as a bell tongue. It has not been easy for him, Miss Bobbit's going. Because she'd meant more than that. Than what? Than being thirteen years old and crazy in love. She was the queer things in him, like the pecan tree and liking books and caring enough about people to let them hurt him. She was the things he was afraid to show anyone else. And in the dark the music trickled through the rain: won't there be nights when we will hear it just as though it were really there? And afternoons when the shadows will be all at once confused, and she will pass before us, unfurling across the lawn like a pretty piece of ribbon? She laughed to Billy Bob; she held his hand, she even kissed him. "I'm not going to die," she said. "You'll come out there, and we'll climb a mountain, and we'll all live there together, you and me and Sister Rosalba." But Billy Bob knew it would never happen that way, and so when the music came through the dark he would stuff the pillow over his head.

Only there was a strange smile about yesterday, and that was the day she was leaving. Around noon the sun came out, bringing with it into the air all the sweetness of wisteria. Aunt El's yellow Lady Anne's were blooming again, and she did something wonderful, she told Billy Bob he could pick them and give them to Miss Bobbit for good-bye. All afternoon Miss Bobbit sat on the porch surrounded by people who stopped by to wish her well. She looked as though she were going to Communion, dressed in white and with a white parasol. Sister Rosalba had given her a handkerchief, but she had to borrow it back because she couldn't stop blubbering. Another little girl brought a baked chicken, presumably to be eaten on the bus; the only trouble was she'd forgotten to take out the insides before cooking it. Miss Bobbit's mother said that was all right by her, chicken was chicken; which is memorable because it is the single opinion she ever voiced. There was only one sour note. For hours Preacher Star had been hanging around down at the corner, sometimes standing at the curb tossing a coin, and sometimes hiding behind a tree, as if he didn't want anyone to see him. It made everybody nervous. About twenty minutes before bus time he sauntered up and leaned against our gate. Billy Bob was still in the garden picking roses; by now he had enough for a bonfire, and their smell was as heavy as wind. Preacher stared at him until he lifted his head. As they looked at each other the rain began again, falling fine as sea spray and colored by a rainbow. Without a word, Preacher went over and started helping Billy Bob separate the roses into two giant bouquets: together they carried them to the curb. Across the street there were bumblebees of talk, but when Miss Bobbit saw them, two boys whose flower-masked faces were like yellow moons, she rushed down the steps, her arms outstretched. You could see what was going to happen; and we called out, our voices like lightning in the rain, but Miss Bobbit, running toward those moons of roses, did not seem to hear. That is when the six-o'clock bus ran over her.

WILLIAM FAULKNER

Barn Burning

THE STORE IN WHICH the Justice of the Peace's court was sitting smelled of cheese. The boy, crouched on his nail keg at the back of the crowded room, knew he smelled cheese, and more: from where he sat he could see the ranked shelves close-packed with the solid, squat, dynamic shapes of tin cans whose labels his stomach read, not from the lettering which meant nothing to his mind but from the scarlet devils and the silver curve of fish — this, the cheese which he knew he smelled and the hermetic meat which his intestines believed he smelled coming in intermittent gusts momentary and brief between the other constant one, the smell and sense just a little of fear because mostly of despair and grief, the old fierce pull of blood. He could not see the table where the Justice sat and before which his father and his father's enemy (*our enemy* he thought in that despair; *ourn! mine and hisn both! He's my father!*) stood, but he could hear them, the two of them that is, because his father had said no word yet:

"But what proof have you, Mr. Harris?"

"I told you. The hog got into my corn. I caught it up and sent it back to him. He had no fence that would hold it. I told him so, warned him. The next time I put the hog in my pen. When he came to get it I gave him enough wire to patch up his pen. The next time I put the hog up and kept it. I rode down to his house and saw the wire I gave him still rolled on to the spool in his yard. I told him he could have the hog when he paid me a dollar pound fee. That evening a nigger came with the dollar and got the hog. He was a strange nigger. He said, 'He say to tell you wood and hay kin burn.' I said, 'What?' 'That whut he say to tell you,' the nigger said. "Wood and hay kin burn." That night my barn burned. I got the stock out but I lost the barn."

"Where is the nigger? Have you got him?"

"He was a strange nigger, I tell you. I don't know what became of him."

"But that's not proof. Don't you see that's not proof?"

"Get that boy up here. He knows." For a moment the boy thought too that the man meant his older brother until Harris said, "Not him. The little one. The boy," and, crouching, small for his age, small and wiry like his father, in patched and faded jeans even too small for him, with straight, uncombed, brown hair and eyes gray and wild as storm scud, he saw the men between himself and the table part and become a lane of grim faces, at the end of which he saw the Justice, a shabby, collarless, graying man in spectacles, beckoning him. He felt no floor under his bare feet; he seemed to walk beneath the palpable weight of the grim turning faces. His father, stiff in his black Sunday coat donned not for the trial but for the moving, did not even look at him. *He aims for me to lie,* he thought, again with that frantic grief and despair. *And I will have to do hit.*

"What's your name, boy?" the Justice said.

"Colonel Sartoris Snopes," the boy whispered.

"Hey?" the Justice said. "Talk louder. Colonel Sartoris? I reckon anybody named for Colonel Sartoris in this country can't help but tell the truth, can they?" The boy said nothing. *Enemy! Enemy!* he thought; for a moment he could not even see, could not see that the Justice's face was kindly nor discern that his voice was troubled when he spoke to the man named Harris: "Do you want me to question this boy?" But he could hear, and during those subsequent long seconds while there was absolutely no sound in the crowded little room save that of quiet and intent breathing it was as if he had swung outward at the end of a grape vine, over a ravine, and at the top of the swing had been caught in a prolonged instant of mesmerized gravity, weightless in time.

"No!" Harris said violently, explosively. "Damnation! Send him out of here!" Now time, the fluid world, rushed beneath him again, the voices coming to him again through the smell of cheese and sealed meat, the fear and despair and the old grief of blood:

"This case is closed. I can't find against you, Snopes, but I can give you advice. Leave this country and don't come back to it."

His father spoke for the first time, his voice cold and harsh, level, without emphasis: "I aim to. I don't figure to stay in a country among people who . . ." he said something unprintable and vile, addressed to no one.

"That'll do," the Justice said. "Take your wagon and get out of this country before dark. Case dismissed."

His father turned, and he followed the stiff black coat, the wiry figure walking a little stiffly from where a Confederate provost's man's musket ball had taken him in the heel on a stolen horse thirty years ago, followed the two backs now, since his older brother had appeared from somewhere in the crowd, no taller than the father but thicker, chewing tobacco steadily, between the two lines of grim-faced men and out of the store and across the worn gallery and down the sagging steps and among the dogs and half-grown boys in the mild May dust, where as he passed a voice hissed:

"Barn burner!"

Again he could not see, whirling; there was a face in a red haze, moonlike, bigger than the full moon, the owner of it half again his size, he leaping in the red haze toward the face, feeling no blow, feeling no shock when his head struck the earth, scrabbling up and leaping again, feeling no blow this time either and tasting no blood, scrabbling up to see the other boy in full flight and himself already leaping into pursuit as his father's hand jerked him back, the harsh, cold voice speaking above him: "Go get in the wagon."

It stood in a grove of locusts and mulberries across the road. His two hulking sisters in their Sunday dresses and his mother and her sister in calico and sunbonnets were already in it, sitting on and among the sorry residue of the dozen and more movings which even the boy could remember — the battered stove, the broken beds and chairs, the clock inlaid with mother-of-pearl, which would not run, stopped at some fourteen minutes past two o'clock of a dead and forgotten day and time, which had been his mother's dowry. She was crying, though when she saw him she drew her sleeve across her face and began to descend from the wagon. "Get back," the father said.

"He's hurt, I got to get some water and wash his . . ."

"Get back in the wagon," his father said. He got in too, over the tail-gate. His father mounted to the seat where the older brother already sat and struck the gaunt mules two savage blows with the peeled willow, but without heat. It was not even sadistic; it was exactly that same quality which in later years would cause his descendants to over-run the engine before putting a motor car into motion, striking and reining back in the same movement. The wagon went on, the store with its quiet crowd of grimly watching men dropped behind; a curve in the road hid it. *Forever* he thought. *Maybe he's done satisfied now, now that he has* . . . stopping himself, not to say it aloud even to himself. His mother's hand touched his shoulder.

"Does hit hurt?" she said.

"Naw," he said. "Hit don't hurt. Lemme be."

"Can't you wipe some of the blood off before hit dries?"

"I'll wash to-night," he said. "Lemme be, I tell you."

The wagon went on. He did not know where they were going. None of them ever did or ever asked, because it was always somewhere, always a house of sorts waiting for them a day or two days or even three days away. Likely his father had already arranged to make a crop on another farm before he . . . Again he had to stop himself. He (the father) always did. There was something about his wolflike independence and even courage when the advantage was at least neutral which impressed strangers, as if they got from his latent ravening ferocity not so much a sense of dependability as a feeling that his ferocious conviction in the rightness of his own actions would be of advantage to all whose interest lay with his.

That night they camped, in a grove of oaks and beeches where a spring ran. The nights were still cool and they had a fire against it, of a rail lifted from a nearby fence and cut into lengths — a small fire, neat, niggard almost, a shrewd fire; such fires were his father's habit and custom always, even in freezing weather. Older, the boy might have remarked this and wondered why not a big one; why should not a man who had not only seen the waste and extravagance of war, but who had in his blood an inherent voracious prodigality with material not his own, have burned everything in sight? Then he might have gone a step farther and thought that that was the reason: that niggard blaze was the living fruit of nights passed during those four years in the woods hiding from all men, blue or gray, with his strings of horses (captured horses, he called them). And older still, he might have divined the true reason: that the element of fire spoke to some deep mainspring of his father's being, as the element of steel or of powder spoke to other men, as the one weapon for the preservation of integrity, else breath were not worth the breathing, and hence to be regarded with respect and used with discretion.

But he did not think this now and he had seen those same niggard blazes all his life. He merely ate his supper beside it and was already half asleep over his iron plate when his father called him, and once more he followed the stiff back, the stiff and ruthless limp, up the slope and on to the starlit road where, turning, he could see his father against the stars but without face or depth — a shape black, flat, and bloodless as though cut from tin in the iron folds of the frockcoat which had not been made for him, the voice harsh like tin and without heat like tin:

"You were fixing to tell them. You would have told him." He didn't answer. His father struck him with the flat of his hand on the side of the head, hard but without heat, exactly as he had struck the two mules at the store, exactly as he would strike either of them with any stick in order to kill a horse fly, his voice still without heat or anger: "You're getting to be a man. You got to learn. You got to learn to stick to your own blood or you ain't going to have any blood to stick to you. Do you think either of them, any man there this morning, would? Don't you know all they wanted was a chance to get at me because they knew I had them beat? Eh?" Later, twenty years later, he was to tell himself, "If I had said they wanted only truth, justice, he would have hit me again." But now he said nothing. He was not crying. He just stood there. "Answer me," his father said.

"Yes," he whispered. His father turned.

"Get on to bed. We'll be there tomorrow."

To-morrow they were there. In the early afternoon the wagon stopped before a paintless two-room house identical almost with the dozen others it had stopped before even in the boy's ten years, and again, as on the other dozen occasions, his mother and aunt got down and began to unload the wagon, although his two sisters and his father and brother had not moved.

"Likely hit ain't fitten for hawgs," one of the sisters said.

"Nevertheless, fit it will and you'll hog it and like it," his father said. "Get out of them chairs and help your Ma unload."

The two sisters got down, big, bovine, in a flutter of cheap ribbons; one of them drew from the jumbled wagon bed a battered lantern, the other a worn broom. His father handed the reins to the older son and began to climb stiffly over the wheel. "When they get unloaded, take the team to the barn and feed them." Then he said, and at first the boy thought he was still speaking to his brother: "Come with me."

"Me?" he said.

"Yes," his father said. "You."

"Abner," his mother said. His father paused and looked back — the harsh level stare beneath the shaggy, graying, irascible brows.

"I reckon I'll have a word with the man that aims to begin to-morrow owning me body and soul for the next eight months."

They went back up the road. A week ago — or before last night, that is — he would have asked where they were going, but not now. His father had struck him before last night but never before had he paused afterward to explain why; it was as if the blow and the following calm, outrageous voice still rang, repercussed, divulging nothing to him save the terrible handicap of being young, the light weight of his few years, just heavy enough to prevent his soaring free of the world as it seemed to be ordered but not heavy enough to keep him footed solid in it, to resist it and try to change the course of its events.

Presently he could see the grove of oaks and cedars and the other flowering trees and shrubs where the house would be, though not the house yet. They walked beside a fence massed with honeysuckle and Cherokee roses and came to a gate swinging open between two brick pillars, and now, beyond a sweep of drive, he saw the house for the first time and at that instant he forgot his father and the terror and despair both, and even when he remembered his father again (who had not stopped) the terror and despair did not return. Because, for all the twelve movings, they had sojourned until now in a poor country, a land of small farms and fields and houses, and he had never seen a house like this before. *Hit's big as a courthouse* he thought quietly, with a surge of peace and joy whose reason he could not have thought into words, being too young for that: *They are safe from him. People whose lives are a part of this peace and dignity are beyond his touch, he no more to them than a buzzing wasp: capable of stinging for a little moment but that's all; the spell of this peace and dignity rendering even the barns and stable and cribs which belong to it impervious to the puny flames he might contrive . . .* this, the peace and joy, ebbing for an instant as he looked again at the stiff black back, the stiff and implacable limp of the figure which was not dwarfed by the house, for the reason that it had never looked big anywhere and which now, against the serene columned backdrop, had more than ever that impervious quality of something cut ruthlessly from tin, depthless, as though, sidewise to the sun, it would cast no shadow. Watching him, the boy remarked the absolutely undeviating course which his father held and saw the stiff foot come squarely down in a pile of fresh droppings where a horse had stood in the drive and which his father could have avoided by a simple change of stride. But it ebbed only for a moment, though he could not have thought this into words either, walking on in the spell of the house, which he could even want but without envy, without sorrow, certainly never with that ravening and jealous rage which unknown to him walked in the ironlike black coat before him: *Maybe he will feel like it too. Maybe it will even change him now from what maybe he couldn't help but be.*

They crossed the portico. Now he could hear his father's stiff foot as it came down on the boards with clocklike finality, a sound out of all proportion to the displacement of the body it bore and which was not dwarfed either by the white door before it, as though it had attained to a sort of vicious and ravening minimum not to be dwarfed by anything — the flat, wide, black hat, the formal coat of broadcloth which had once been black but which had now that friction-glazed greenish cast of the bodies of old house flies, the lifted sleeve which was too large, the lifted hand like a curled claw. The door opened so promptly that the boy knew the Negro must have been watching them all the time, an old man with neat grizzled hair, in a linen jacket, who stood barring the door with his body, saying, "Wipe yo foots, white man, fo you come in here. Major ain't home nohow."

"Get out of my way, nigger," his father said, without heat too, flinging the door back and the Negro also and entering, his hat still on his head. And now the boy saw the prints of the stiff foot on the doorjamb and saw them appear on the pale rug behind the machinelike deliberation of the foot which seemed to bear (or transmit) twice the weight which the body compassed. The Negro was shouting "Miss Lula! Miss Lula!" somewhere behind them, then the boy, deluged as though by a warm wave by a suave turn of carpeted stair and a pendant glitter of chandeliers and a mute gleam of gold frames, heard the swift feet and saw her too, a lady — perhaps he had never seen her like before either — in a gray, smooth gown with lace at the throat and an apron tied at the waist and the sleeves turned back, wiping cake or biscuit dough from her hands with a towel as she came up the hall, looking not at his father at all but at the tracks on the blond rug with an expression of incredulous amazement.

"I tried," the Negro cried. "I tole him to . . ."

"Will you please go away?" she said in a shaking voice. "Major de Spain is not at home. Will you please go away?"

His father had not spoken again. He did not speak again. He did not even look at her. He just stood stiff in the center of the rug, in his hat, the shaggy iron-gray brows twitching slightly above the pebble-colored eyes as he appeared to examine the house with brief deliberation. Then with the same deliberation he turned; the boy watched him pivot on the good leg and saw the stiff foot drag round the arc of the turning, leaving a final long and fading smear. His father never looked at it, he never once looked down at the rug. The Negro held the door. It closed behind them, upon the hysteric and indistinguishable woman-wail. His father stopped at the top of the steps and scraped his boot clean on the edge of it. At the gate he stopped again. He stood for a moment, planted stiffly on the stiff foot, looking back at the house. "Pretty and white, ain't it?" he said. "That's sweat. Nigger sweat. Maybe it ain't white enough yet to suit him. Maybe he wants to mix some white sweat with it."

Two hours later the boy was chopping wood behind the house within which his mother and aunt and the two sisters (the mother and aunt, not the two girls, he knew that; even at this distance and muffled by walls the flat loud voices of the two girls emanated an incorrigible idle inertia) were setting up the stove to prepare a meal, when he heard the hooves and saw the linen-clad man on a fine sorrel mare, whom he recognized even before he saw the rolled rug in front of the Negro youth following on a fat bay carriage horse — a suffused, angry face vanishing, still at full gallop, beyond the corner of the house where his father and brother were sitting in the two tilted chairs; and a moment later, almost before he could have put the axe down, he heard the hooves again and watched the sorrel mare go back out of the yard, already galloping again. Then his father began to shout one of the sisters' names, who presently emerged backward from the kitchen door dragging the rolled rug along the ground by one end while the other sister walked behind it.

"If you ain't going to tote, go on and set up the wash pot," the first said.

"You, Sarty!" the second shouted. "Set up the wash pot!" His father appeared at the door, framed against that shabbiness, as he had been against that other bland perfection, impervious to either, the mother's anxious face at his shoulder.

"Go on," the father said. "Pick it up." The two sisters stooped, broad, lethargic; stooping, they presented an incredible expanse of pale cloth and a flutter of tawdry ribbons.

"If I thought enough of a rug to have to git hit all the way from France I wouldn't keep hit where folks coming in would have to tromp on hit," the first said. They raised the rug.

"Abner," the mother said. "Let me do it."

"You go back and git dinner," his father said. "I'll tend to this."

From the woodpile through the rest of the afternoon the boy watched them, the rug spread flat in the dust beside the bubbling wash-pot, the two sisters stooping over it with that profound and lethargic reluctance, while the father stood over them in turn, implacable and grim, driving them though never raising his voice again. He could smell the harsh homemade lye they were using; he saw his mother come to the door once and look toward them with an expression not anxious now but very like despair; he saw his father turn, and he fell to with the axe and saw from the corner of his eye his father raise from the ground a flattish fragment of field stone and examine it and return to the pot, and this time his mother actually spoke: "Abner. Abner. Please don't. Please, Abner."

Then he was done too. It was dusk; the whippoorwills had already begun. He could smell coffee from the room where they would presently eat the cold food remaining from the mid-afternoon meal, though when he entered the house he realized they were having coffee again probably because there was a fire on the hearth, before which the rug now lay spread over the backs of the two chairs. The tracks of his father's foot were gone. Where they had been were now long, water-cloudy scoriations resembling the sporadic course of a lilliputian mowing machine.

It still hung there while they ate the cold food and then went to bed, scattered without order or claim up and down the two rooms, his mother in one bed, where his father would later lie, the older brother in the other, himself, the aunt, and the two sisters on pallets on the floor. But his father was not in bed yet. The last thing the boy remembered was the depthless, harsh silhouette of the hat and coat bending over the rug and it seemed to him that he had not even closed his eyes when the silhouette was standing over him, the fire almost dead behind it, the stiff foot prodding him awake. "Catch up the mule," his father said.

When he returned with the mule his father was standing in the black door, the rolled rug over his shoulder. "Ain't you going to ride?" he said.

"No. Give me your foot."

He bent his knee into his father's hand, the wiry, surprising power flowed smoothly, rising, he rising with it, on to the mule's bare back (they had owned a saddle once; the boy could remember it though not when or where) and with the same effortlessness his father swung the rug up in front of him. Now in the starlight they retraced the afternoon's path, up the dusty road rife with honeysuckle, through the gate and up the black tunnel of the drive to the lightless house, where he sat on the mule and felt the rough warp of the rug drag across his thighs and vanish.

"Don't you want me to help?" he whispered. His father did not answer and now he heard again that stiff foot striking the hollow portico with that wooden and clocklike deliberation, that outrageous overstatement of the weight it carried. The rug, hunched, not flung (the boy could tell that even in the darkness) from his father's shoulder struck the angle of wall and floor with a sound unbelievably loud, thunderous, then the foot again, unhurried and enormous; a light came on in the house and the boy sat, tense, breathing steadily and quietly and just a little fast, though the foot itself did not increase its beat at all, descending the steps now; now the boy could see him.

"Don't you want to ride now?" he whispered. "We kin both ride now," the light within the house altering now, flaring up and sinking. *He's coming down the stairs now,* he thought. He had already ridden the mule up beside the horse block; presently his father was up behind him and he doubled the reins over and slashed the mule across the neck, but before the animal could begin to trot the hard, thin arm came round him, the hard knotted hand jerking the mule back to a walk.

In the first red rays of the sun they were in the lot, putting plow gear on the mules. This time the sorrel mare was in the lot before he heard it at all, the rider collarless and even bareheaded, trembling, speaking in a shaking voice as the woman in the house had done, his father merely looking up once before stooping again to the hame he was buckling, so that the man on the mare spoke to his stooping back:

"You must realize you have ruined that rug. Wasn't there anybody here, any of your women . . ." he ceased, shaking, the boy watching him, the older brother leaning now in the stable door, chewing, blinking slowly and steadily at nothing apparently. "It cost a hundred dollars. But you never had a hundred dollars. You never will. So I'm going to charge you twenty bushels of corn against your crop. I'll add it in your contract and when you come to the commissary you can sign it. That won't keep Mrs. de Spain quiet but maybe it will teach you to wipe your feet off before you enter her house again."

Then he was gone. The boy looked at his father, who still had not spoken or even looked up again, who was now adjusting the logger-head in the hame.

"Pap," he said. His father looked at him — the inscrutable face, the shaggy brows beneath which the gray eyes glinted coldly. Suddenly the boy went toward him, fast, stopping as suddenly. "You done the best you could!" he cried. "If he wanted hit done different why didn't he wait and tell you how? He won't git no twenty bushels! He won't git none! We'll gether hit and hide hit! I kin watch . . ."

"Did you put the cutter back in that straight stock like I told you?"

"No, sir," he said.

"Then go do it."

That was Wednesday. During the rest of that week he worked steadily, at what was within his scope and some which was beyond it, with an industry that did not need to be driven nor even commanded twice; he had this from his mother, with the difference that some at least of what he did he liked to do, such as splitting wood with the half-size axe which his mother and aunt had earned, or saved money somehow, to present him with at Christmas. In company with the two older women (and on one afternoon, even one of the sisters), he built pens for the shoat and the cow which were a part of his father's contract with the landlord, and one afternoon, his father being absent, gone somewhere on one of the mules, he went to the field.

They were running a middle buster now, his brother holding the plow straight while he handled the reins, and walking beside the straining mule, the rich black soil shearing cool and damp against his bare ankles, he thought *Maybe this is the end of it. Maybe even that twenty bushels that seems hard to have to pay for just a rug will be a cheap price for him to stop forever and always from being what he used to be;* thinking, dreaming now, so that his brother had to speak sharply to him to mind the mule: *Maybe he even won't collect the twenty bushels. Maybe it will all add up and balance and vanish — corn, rug, fire; the terror and grief, the being pulled two ways like between two teams of horses — gone, done with for ever and ever.*

Then it was Saturday; he looked up from beneath the mule he was harnessing and saw his father in the black coat and hat. "Not that," his father said. "The wagon gear." And then, two hours later, sitting in the wagon bed behind his father and brother on the seat, the wagon accomplished a final curve, and he saw the weathered paintless store with its tattered tobacco- and patent-medicine posters and the tethered wagons and saddle animals below the gallery. He mounted the gnawed steps behind his father and brother, and there again was the lane of quiet, watching faces for the three of them to walk through. He saw the man in spectacles sitting at the plank table and he did not need to be told this was a Justice of the Peace; he sent one glare of fierce, exultant, partisan defiance at the man in collar and cravat now, whom he had seen but twice before in his life, and that on a galloping horse, who now wore on his face an expression not of rage but of amazed unbelief which the boy could not have known was at the incredible circumstance of being sued by one of his own tenants, and came and stood against his father and cried at the Justice: "He ain't done it! He ain't burnt . . ."

"Go back to the wagon," his father said.

"Burnt?" the Justice said. "Do I understand this rug was burned too?"

"Does anybody here claim it was?" his father said. "Go back to the wagon." But he did not, he merely retreated to the rear of the room, crowded as that other had been, but not to sit down this time, instead, to stand pressing among the motionless bodies, listening to the voices:

"And you claim twenty bushels of corn is too high for the damage you did to the rug?"

"He brought the rug to me and said he wanted the tracks washed out of it. I washed the tracks out and took the rug back to him."

"But you didn't carry the rug back to him in the same condition it was in before you made the tracks on it."

His father did not answer, and now for perhaps half a minute there was no sound at all save that of breathing, the faint, steady suspiration of complete and intent listening.

"You decline to answer that, Mr. Snopes?" Again his father did not answer. "I'm going to find against you, Mr. Snopes. I'm going to find that you were responsible for the injury to Major de Spain's rug and hold you liable for it. But twenty bushels of corn seems a little high for a man in your circumstances to have to pay. Major de Spain claims it cost a hundred dollars. October corn will be worth about fifty cents. I figure that if Major de Spain can stand a ninety-five dollar loss on something he paid cash for, you can stand a five-dollar loss you haven't earned yet. I hold you in damages to Major de Spain to the amount of ten bushels of corn over and above your contract with him, to be paid to him out of your crop at gathering time. Court adjourned."

It had taken no time hardly, the morning was but half begun. He thought they would return home and perhaps back to the field, since they were late, far behind all other farmers. But instead his father passed on behind the wagon, merely indicating with his hand for the older brother to follow with it, and crossed the road toward the blacksmith shop opposite, pressing on after his father, overtaking him, speaking, whispering up at the harsh, calm face beneath the weathered hat: "He won't git no ten bushels neither. He won't git one. We'll . . ." until his father glanced for an instant down at him, the face absolutely calm, the grizzled eyebrows tangled above the cold eyes, the voice almost pleasant, almost gentle: "You think so? Well, we'll wait till October anyway."

The matter of the wagon — the setting of a spoke or two and the tightening of the tires — did not take long either, the business of the tires accomplished by driving the wagon into the spring branch behind the shop and letting it stand there, the mules nuzzling into the water from time to time, and the boy on the seat with the idle reins, looking up the slope and through the sooty tunnel of the shed where the slow hammer rang and where his father sat on an upended cypress bolt, easily, either talking or listening, still sitting there when the boy brought the dripping wagon up out of the branch and halted it before the door.

"Take them on to the shade and hitch," his father said. He did so and returned. His father and the smith and a third man squatting on his heels inside the door were talking, about crops and animals; the boy, squatting too in the ammoniac dust and hoof-parings and scales of rust, heard his father tell a long and unhurried story out of the time before the birth of the older brother even when he had been a professional horsetrader. And then his father came up beside him where he stood before a tattered last year's circus poster on the other side of the store, gazing rapt and quiet at the scarlet horses, the incredible poisings and convolutions of tulle and tights and the painted leers of comedians, and said, "It's time to eat."

But not at home. Squatting beside his brother against the front wall, he watched his father emerge from the store and produce from a paper sack a segment of cheese and divide it carefully and deliberately into three with his pocket knife and produce crackers from the same sack. They all three squatted on the gallery and ate, slowly, without talking; then in the store again, they drank from a tin dipper tepid water smelling of the cedar bucket and of living beech trees. And still they did not go home. It was a horse lot this time, a tall rail fence upon and along which men stood and sat and out of which one by one horses were led, to be walked and trotted and then cantered back and forth along the road while the slow swapping and buying went on and the sun began to slant westward, they — the three of them — watching and listening, the older brother with his muddy eyes and his steady, inevitable tobacco, the father commenting now and then on certain of the animals, to no one in particular.

It was after sundown when they reached home. They ate supper by lamplight, then, sitting on the doorstep, the boy watched the night fully accomplish, listening to the whippoorwills and the frogs, when he heard his mother's voice: "Abner! No! No! Oh, God. Oh, God. Abner!" and he rose, whirled, and saw the altered light through the door where a candle stub now burned in a bottle neck on the table and his father, still in the hat and coat, at once formal and burlesque as though dressed carefully for some shabby and ceremonial violence, emptying the reservoir of the lamp back into the five-gallon kerosene can from which it had been filled, while the mother tugged at his arm until he shifted the lamp to the other hand and flung her back, not savagely or viciously, just hard, into the wall, her hands flung out against the wall for balance, her mouth open and in her face the same quality of hopeless despair as had been in her voice. Then his father saw him standing in the door.

"Go to the barn and get that can of oil we were oiling the wagon with," he said. The boy did not move. Then he could speak.

"What . . ." he cried. "What are you . . ."

"Go get that oil," his father said. "Go."

Then he was moving, running, outside the house, toward the stable: this the old habit, the old blood which he had not been permitted to choose for himself, which had been bequeathed him willy nilly and which had run for so long (and who knew where, battening on what of outrage and savagery and lust) before it came to him. *I could keep on,* he thought. *I could run on and on and never look back, never need to see his face again. Only I can't. I can't,* the rusted can in his hand now, the liquid sploshing in it as he ran back to the house and into it, into the sound of his mother's weeping in the next room, and handed the can to his father.

"Ain't you going to even send a nigger?" he cried. "At least you sent a nigger before!"

This time his father didn't strike him. The hand came even faster than the blow had, the same hand which had set the can on the table with almost excruciating care flashing from the can toward him too quick for him to follow it, gripping him by the back of his shirt and on to tiptoe before he had seen it quit the can, the face stooping at him in breathless and frozen ferocity, the cold, dead voice speaking over him to the older brother who leaned against the table, chewing with that steady, curious, sidewise motion of cows:

"Empty the can into the big one and go on. I'll catch up with you."

"Better tie him up to the bedpost," the brother said.

"Do like I told you," the father said. Then the boy was moving, his bunched shirt and the hard, bony hand between his shoulder-blades, his toes just touching the floor, across the room and into the other one, past the sisters sitting with spread heavy thighs in the two chairs over the cold hearth, and to where his mother and aunt sat side by side on the bed, the aunt's arms about his mother's shoulders.

"Hold him," the father said. The aunt made a startled movement. "Not you," the father said. "Lennie. Take hold of him. I want to see you do it." His mother took him by the wrist. "You'll hold him better than that. If he gets loose don't you know what he is going to do? He will go up yonder." He jerked his head toward the road. "Maybe I'd better tie him."

"I'll hold him," his mother whispered.

"See you do then." Then his father was gone, the stiff foot heavy and measured upon the boards, ceasing at last.

Then he began to struggle. His mother caught him in both arms, he jerking and wrenching at them. He would be stronger in the end, he knew that. But he had no time to wait for it. "Lemme go!" he cried. "I don't want to have to hit you!"

"Let him go!" the aunt said. "If he don't go, before God, I am going up there myself!"

"Don't you see I can't?" his mother cried. "Sarty! Sarty! No! No! Help me, Lizzie!"

Then he was free. His aunt grasped at him but it was too late. He whirled, running, his mother stumbled forward on to her knees behind him, crying to the nearer sister: "Catch him, Net! Catch him!" But that was too late too, the sister (the sisters were twins, born at the same time, yet either of them now gave the impression of being, encompassing as much living meat and volume and weight as any other two of the family) not yet having begun to rise from the chair, her head, face, alone merely turned, presenting to him in the flying instant an astonishing expanse of young female features untroubled by any surprise even, wearing only an expression of bovine interest. Then he was out of the room, out of the house, in the mild dust of the starlit road and the heavy rifeness of honeysuckle, the pale ribbon unspooling with terrific slowness under his running feet, reaching the gate at last and turning in, running, his heart and lungs drumming, on up the drive toward the lighted house, the lighted door. He did not knock, he burst in, sobbing for breath, incapable for the moment of speech; he saw the astonished face of the Negro in the linen jacket without knowing when the Negro had appeared.

"De Spain!" he cried, panted. "Where's . . ." then he saw the white man too emerging from a white door down the hall. "Barn!" he cried. "Barn!"

"What?" the white man said. "Barn?"

"Yes!" the boy cried. "Barn!"

"Catch him!" the white man shouted.

But it was too late this time too. The Negro grasped his shirt, but the entire sleeve, rotten with washing, carried away, and he was out that door too and in the drive again, and had actually never ceased to run even while he was screaming into the white man's face.

Behind him the white man was shouting, "My horse! Fetch my horse!" and he thought for an instant of cutting across the park and climbing the fence into the road, but he did not know the park nor how high the vine-massed fence might be and he dared not risk it. So he ran on down the drive, blood and breath roaring; presently he was in the road again though he could not see it. He could not hear either: the galloping mare was almost upon him before he heard her, and even then he held his course, as if the very urgency of his wild grief and need must in a moment more find him wings, waiting until the ultimate instant to hurl himself aside and into the weed-choked roadside ditch as the horse thundered past and on, for an instant in furious silhouette against the stars, the tranquil early summer night sky which, even before the shape of the horse and rider vanished, stained abruptly and violently upward: a long, swirling roar incredible and soundless, blotting the stars, and he springing up and into the road again, running again, knowing it was too late yet still running even after he heard the shot and, an instant later, two shots, pausing now without knowing he had ceased to run, crying "Pap! Pap!", running again before he knew he had begun to run, stumbling, tripping over something and scrabbling up again without ceasing to run, looking backward over his shoulder at the glare as he got up, running on among the invisible trees, panting, sobbing, "Father! Father!"

At midnight he was sitting on the crest of a hill. He did not know it was midnight and he did not know how far he had come. But there was no glare behind him now and he sat now, his back toward what he had called home for four days anyhow, his face toward the dark woods which he would enter when breath was strong again, small, shaking steadily in the chill darkness, hugging himself into the remainder of his thin, rotten shirt, the grief and despair now no longer terror and fear but just grief and despair. *Father. My father,* he thought. "He was brave!" he cried suddenly, aloud but not loud, no more than a whisper: "He was! He was in the war! He was in Colonel Sartoris' cav'ry!" not knowing that his father had gone to that war a private in the fine old European sense, wearing no uniform, admitting the authority of and giving fidelity to no man or army or flag, going to war as Malbrouck himself did: for booty — it meant nothing and less than nothing to him if it were enemy booty or his own.

The slow constellations wheeled on. It would be dawn and then sun-up after a while and he would be hungry. But that would be to-morrow and now he was only cold, and walking would cure that. His breathing was easier now and he decided to get up and go on, and then he found that he had been asleep because he knew it was almost dawn, the night almost over. He could tell that from the whippoor-wills. They were everywhere now among the dark trees below him, constant and inflectioned and ceaseless, so that, as the instant for giving over to the day birds drew nearer and nearer, there was no interval at all between them. He got up. He was a little stiff, but walking would cure that too as it would the cold, and soon there would be the sun. He went on down the hill, toward the dark woods within which the liquid silver voices of the birds called unceasing — the rapid and urgent beating of the urgent and quiring heart of the late spring night. He did not look back.

ERNEST J. GAINES

Just Like a Tree

I shall not;
   I shall not be moved.
I shall not;
   I shall not be moved.
Just like a tree that's
planted 'side the water.
   Oh, I shall not be moved.

I made my home in glory;
   I shall not be moved.
Made my home in glory;
   I shall not be moved.
Just like a tree that's
planted 'side the water.
   Oh, I shall not be moved.

(from an old Negro spiritual)

Chuckkie

PA HIT HIM ON the back and he jeck in them chains like he pulling, but ever'body in the wagon know he ain't, and Pa hit him on the back again. He jeck again like he pulling, but even Big Red know he ain't doing a thing.

"That's why I'm go'n get a horse," Pa say. "He'll kill that other mule. Get up there, Mr. Bascom."

"Oh, let him alone," Gran'mon say. "How would you like it if you was pulling a wagon in all that mud?"

Pa don't answer Gran'mon; he just hit Mr. Bascom on the back again.

"That's right, kill him," Gran'mon say. "See where you get mo' money to buy another one."

"Get up there, Mr. Bascom," Pa say.

"You hear me talking to you, Emile?" Gran'mon say. "You want me hit you with something?"

"Ma, he ain't pulling," Pa say.

"Leave him alone," Gran'mon say.

Pa shake the lines little bit, but Mr. Bascom don't even feel it, and you can see he letting Big Red do all the pulling again. Pa say something kind o' low to hisself, and I can't make out what it is.

I low' my head little bit, 'cause that wind and fine rain was hitting me in the face, and I can feel Mama pressing close to me to keep me warm. She sitting on one side o' me and Pa sitting on the other side o' me, and Gran'mon in the back o' me in her setting chair. Pa didn't want bring the setting chair, telling Gran'mon there was two boards in that wagon already and she could sit on one of 'em all by herself if she wanted to, but Gran'mon say she was taking her setting chair with her if Pa liked it or not. She say she didn't ride in no wagon on nobody board, and if Pa liked it or not, that setting chair was going.

"Let her take her setting chair," Mama say. "What's wrong with taking her setting chair."

"Ehhh, Lord," Pa say, and picked up the setting chair and took it out to the wagon. "I guess I'll have to bring it back in the house, too, when we come back from there."

Gran'mon went and clambed in the wagon and moved her setting chair back little bit and sat down and folded her arms, waiting for us to get in, too. I got in and knelt down 'side her, but Mama told me to come up there and sit on the board 'side her and Pa so I could stay warm. Soon 's I sat down, Pa hit Mr. Bascom on the back, saying what a trifling thing Mr. Bascom was, and soon 's he got some mo' money he was getting rid o' Mr. Bascom and getting him a horse.

I raise my head to look see how far we is.

"That's it, yonder," I say.

"Stop pointing," Mama say, "and keep your hand in your pocket."

"Where?" Gran'mon say, back there in her setting chair.

" 'Cross the ditch, yonder," I say.

"Can't see a thing for this rain," Gran'mon say.

"Can't hardly see it," I say. "But you can see the light little bit. That chinaball tree standing in the way."

"Poor soul," Gran'mon say. "Poor soul."

I know Gran'mon was go'n say "poor soul, poor soul," 'cause she had been saying "poor soul, poor soul," ever since she heard Aunt Fe was go'n leave from back there.

Emile

Darn cane crop to finish getting in and only a mule and a half to do it. If I had my way I'd take that shotgun and a load o' buckshots and — but what's the use.

"Get up, Mr. Bascom — please," I say to that little dried-up, long-eared, tobacco-color thing. "Please, come up. Do your share for God sake — if you don't mind. I know it's hard pulling in all that mud, but if you don't do your share, then Big Red'll have to do his and yours, too. So, please, if it ain't asking you too much to —"

"Oh, Emile, shut up," Leola say.

"I can't hit him," I say, "or Mama back there'll hit me. So I have to talk to him. Please, Mr. Bascom, if you don't mind it. For my sake. No, not for mine; for God sake. No, not even for His'n; for Big Red sake. A fellow mule just like yourself is. Please, come up."

"Now, you hear that boy blaspheming God right in front o' me there," Mama say. "Ehhh, Lord — just keep it up. All this bad weather there like this whole world coming apart — a clap o' thunder come there and knock the fool out you. Just keep it up."

Maybe she right, and I stop. I look at Mr. Bascom there doing nothing, and I just give up. That mule know long's Mama's alive he go'n do just what he want to do. He know when Papa was dying he told Mama to look after him, and he know no matter what he do, no matter what he don't do, Mama ain't go'n never let me do him anything. Sometimes I even feel Mama care mo' for Mr. Bascom 'an she care for me her own son.

We come up to the gate and I pull back on the lines.

"Whoa up, Big Red," I say. "You don't have to stop, Mr. Bascom. You never started."

I can feel Mama looking at me back there in that setting chair, but she don't say nothing.

"Here," I say to Chuckkie.

He take the lines and I jump down on the ground to open the old beat-up gate. I see Etienne's horse in the yard, and I see Chris new red tractor 'side the house, shining in the rain. When Mama die, I say to myself, Mr. Bascom, you going. Ever'body getting tractors and horses and I'm still stuck with you. You going, brother.

"Can you make it through?" I ask Chuckkie. "That gate ain't too wide."

"I can do it," he say.

"Be sure to make Mr. Bascom pull," I say.

"Emile, you better get back up here and drive 'em through," Leola say. "Chuckkie might break up that wagon."

"No, let him stay down there and give orders," Mama say, back there in that setting chair.

"He can do it," I say. "Come on, Chuckkie boy."

"Come up, here, mule," Chuckkie say.

And soon 's he say that, Big Red make a lunge for the yard, and Mr. Bascom don't even move, and 'fore I can bat my eyes I hear *pow-wow; sagg-sagg; pow-wow*. But above all that noise, Leola up there screaming her head off. And Mama — not a word; just sitting in that chair, looking at me with her arms still folded.

"Pull Big Red," I say. "Pull Big Red, Chuckkie."

Poor little Chuckkie up there pulling so hard till one of his little arms straight out in back; and Big Red throwing his shoulders and ever'thing else in it, and Mr. Bascom just walking there just 's loose and free, like he's suppose to be there just for his good looks. I move out the way just in time to let the wagon go by me, pulling half o' the fence in the yard behind it. I glance up again, and there's Leola still hollering and trying to jump out, but Mama not saying a word — just sitting there in that setting chair with her arms still folded.

"Whoa," I hear little Chuckkie saying. "Whoa up, now."

Somebody open the door and a bunch o' people come out on the gallery.

"What the world—?" Etienne say. "Thought the whole place was coming to pieces there."

"Chuckkie had a little trouble coming in the yard," I say.

"Goodness," Etienne say. "Anybody hurt?"

Mama just sit there about ten seconds, then she say something to herself and start clambing out the wagon.

"Let me help you there, Aunt Lou," Etienne say, coming down the steps.

"I can make it," Mama say. When she get on the ground she look up at Chuckkie. "Hand me my chair there, boy."

Poor little Chuckkie, up there with the lines in one hand, get the chair and hold it to the side, and Etienne catch it just 'fore it hit the ground. Mama start looking at me again, and it look like for at least a' hour she stand there looking at nobody but me. Then she say, "Ehhh, Lord," like that again, and go inside with Leola and the rest o' the people.

I look back at half o' the fence laying there in the yard, and I jump back on the wagon and guide the mules to the side o' the house. After unhitching 'em and tying 'em to the wheels, I look at Chris pretty red tractor again, and me and Chuckkie go inside: I make sure he kick all that mud off his shoes 'fore he go in the house.

Leola

Sitting over there by that fireplace, trying to look joyful when ever'body there know she ain't. But she trying, you know; smiling and bowing when people say something to her. How can she be joyful, I ask you; how can she be? Poor thing, she been here all her life — or the most of it, let's say. 'Fore they moved in this house, they lived in one back in the woods 'bout a mile from here. But for the past twenty-five or thirty years, she been right in this one house. I know ever since I been big enough to know people I been seeing her right here.

Aunt Fe, Aunt Fe, Aunt Fe, Aunt Fe; the name's been 'mongst us just like us own family name. Just like the name o' God. Like the name of town — the city. Aunt Fe, Aunt Fe, Aunt Fe, Aunt Fe.

Poor old thing; how many times I done come here and washed clothes for her when she couldn't do it herself. How many times I done hoed in that garden, ironed her clothes, wrung a chicken neck for her. You count the days in the year and you'll be pretty close. And I didn't mind it a bit. No, I didn't mind it a bit. She there trying to pay me. Proud — Lord, talking 'bout pride. "Here." "No, Aunt Fe; no." "Here, here; you got a child there, you can use it." "No, Aunt Fe. No. No. What would Mama think if she knowed I took money from you? Aunt Fe, Mama would never forgive me. No. I love doing these thing for you. I just wish I could do more."

And there, now, trying to make 'tend she don't mind leaving. Ehhh, Lord.

I hear a bunch o' rattling round in the kitchen and I go back there. I see Louise stirring this big pot o' eggnog.

"Louise," I say.

"Leola," she say.

We look at each other and she stir the eggnog again. She know what I'm go'n say next, and she can't even look in my face.

"Louise, I wish there was some other way."

"There's no other way," she say.

"Louise, moving her from here's like moving a tree you been used to in your front yard all your life."

"What else can I do?"

"Oh, Louise, Louise."

"Nothing else but that."

"Louise, what people go'n do without her here?"

She stir the eggnog and don't answer.

"Louise, us'll take her in with us."

"You all no kin to Auntie. She go with me."

"And us'll never see her again."

She stir the eggnog. Her husband come back in the kitchen and kiss her on the back o' the neck and then look at me and grin. Right from the start I can see I ain't go'n like that nigger.

"Almost ready, honey?" he say.

"Almost."

He go to the safe and get one o' them bottles of whiskey he got in there and come back to the stove.

"No," Louise say. "Everybody don't like whiskey in it. Add the whiskey after you've poured it up."

"Okay, hon."

He kiss her on the back o' the neck again. Still don't like that nigger. Something 'bout him ain't right.

"You one o' the family?" he say.

"Same as one," I say. "And you?"

He don't like the way I say it, and I don't care if he like it or not. He look at me there a second, and then he kiss her on the ear.

"Un-unnn," she say, stirring the pot.

"I love your ear, baby," he say.

"Go in the front room and talk with the people," she say.

He kiss her on the other ear. A nigger do all that front o' public got something to hide. He leave the kitchen. I look at Louise.

"Ain't nothing else I can do," she say.

"You sure, Louise? You positive?"

"I'm positive," she say.

The front door open and Emile and Chuckkie come in. A minute later Washington and Adrieu come in, too. Adrieu come back in the kitchen, and I can see she been crying. Aunt Fe is her godmother, you know.

"How you feel, Adrieu?"

"That weather out there," she say.

"Y'all walked?"

"Yes."

"Us here in the wagon. Y'all can go back with us."

"Y'all the one tore the fence down?" she ask.

"Yes, I guess so. That brother-in-law o' yours in there letting Chuckkie drive that wagon."

"Well, I don't guess it'll matter too much. Nobody go'n be here, anyhow."

And she start crying again. I take her in my arms and pat her on the shoulder, and I look at Louise stirring the eggnog.

"What I'm go'n do and my nan-nane gone? I love her so much."

"Ever'body love her."

"Since my mama died, she been like my mama."

"Shhh," I say. "Don't let her hear you. Make her grieve. You don't want her grieving, now, do you?"

She sniffs there 'gainst my dress few times.

"Oh, Lord," she say. "Lord, have mercy."

"Shhh," I say. "Shhh. That's what life's 'bout."

"That ain't what life's 'bout," she say. "It ain't fair. This been her home all her life. These the people she know. She don't know them people she going to. It ain't fair."

"Shhh, Adrieu," I say. "Now, you saying things ain't your business."

She cry there some mo'.

"Oh, Lord, Lord," she say.

Louise turn from the stove.

"About ready now," she say, going to the middle door. "James, tell everybody to come back and get some."

James

Let me go on back here and show these country niggers how to have a good time. All they know is talk, talk, talk. Talk so much they make me buggy round here. Damn this weather — wind, rain. Must be a million cracks in this old house.

I go to that old beat-up safe in that corner and get that fifth of Mr. Harper (in the South now; got to say Mister), give the seal one swipe, the stopper one jerk, and head back to that old wood stove. (Man, like, these cats are primitive — goodness. You know what I mean? I mean like wood stoves. Don't mention TV, man, these cats here never heard of that.) I start to dump Mr. Harper in the pot and Baby catches my hand again and say not all of them like it. You ever heard of anything like that? I mean a stud's going to drink eggnog, and he's not going to put whiskey in it. I mean he's going to drink it straight. I mean, you ever heard anything like that? Well, I wasn't pressing none of them on Mr. Harper. I mean, me and Mr. Harper get along too well together for me to go around there pressing.

I hold my cup there and let Baby put a few drops of this egg stuff in it; then I jerk my cup back and let Mr. Harper run a while. Couple of these cats come over (some of them aren't so lame) and set their cups, and I let Mr. Harper run for them. Then this cat says he's got 'nough. I let Mr. Harper run for this other stud, and pretty soon he says, "Hold it. Good." Country cat, you know. "Hold it. Good." Real country cat. So I raise the cup to see what Mr. Harper's doing. He's just right. I raise the cup again. Just right, Mr. Harper; just right.

I go to the door with Mr. Harper under my arm and the cup in my hand and I look into the front room where they all are. I mean, there's about ninety-nine of them in there. Old ones, young ones, little ones, big ones, yellow ones, black ones, brown ones — you name them, brother, and they were there. And what for? Brother, I'll tell you what for. Just because me and Baby are taking this old chick out of these sticks. Well, I'll tell you where I'd be at this moment if I was one of them. With that weather out there like it is, I'd be under about five blankets with some little warm belly pressing against mine. Brother, you can bet your hat I wouldn't be here. Man, listen to that thing out there. You can hear that rain beating on that old house like grains of rice; and that wind coming through them cracks like it does in those old Charlie Chaplin movies. Man, like you know — like *whooo-ee; whooo-ee*. Man, you talking about some weird cats.

I can feel Mr. Harper starting to massage my wig and I bat my eyes twice and look at the old girl over there. She's still sitting in that funny-looking little old rocking chair, and not saying a word to anybody. Just sitting there looking into the fireplace at them two pieces of wood that aren't giving out enough heat to warm a baby, let alone ninety-nine grown people. I mean, you know, like that sleet's falling out there like all get-up-and-go, and them two pieces of wood are lying there just as dead as the rest of these way-out cats.

One of the old cats — I don't know which one he is — Mose, Sam, or something like that — leans over and pokes in the fire a minute; then a little blaze shoots up, and he raises up, too, looking as satisfied as if he'd just sent a rocket into orbit. I mean, these cats are like that. They do these little bitty things, and they feel like they've really done something. Well, back in these sticks, I guess there just isn't nothing big to do.

I feel Mr. Harper touching my skull now — and I notice this little chick passing by me with these two cups of eggnog. She goes over to the fireplace and gives one to each of these old chicks. The one sitting in that setting chair she brought with her from God knows where, and the other cup to the old chick that Baby and I are going to haul from here sometime tomorrow morning. Wait, man, I mean like, you ever heard of anybody going to somebody else's house with a chair? I mean, wouldn't you call that an insult at the basest point? I mean, now, like tell me what you think of that? I mean — dig — here I am at my pad, and in you come with your own stool. I mean, now, like man, you know. I mean that's an insult at the basest point. I mean, you know . . . you know, like way out. . . .

Mr. Harper, what you trying to do boy? — I mean, sir. (Got to watch myself, I'm in the South. Got to keep watching myself.)

This stud touches me on the shoulder and raise his cup and say, "How 'bout a taste?" I know what the stud's talking about, so I let Mr. Harper run for him. But soon 's I let a drop get in, the stud say, " 'Nough." I mean I let about two drops get in, and already the stud's got enough. Man, I mean, like you know. I mean these studs are 'way out. I mean like 'way back there.

This stud takes a swig of his eggnog and say, "Ahhh." I mean this real down-home way of saying "Ahhhh." I mean, man, like these studs — I notice this little chick passing by me again, and this time she's crying. I mean weeping, you know. And just because this old ninety-nine-year-old chick's packing up and leaving. I mean, you ever heard of anything like that? I mean, here she is pretty as the day is long and crying because Baby and I are hauling this old chick away. Well, I'd like to make her cry. And I can assure you, brother, it wouldn't be from leaving her.

I turn and look at Baby over there by the stove, pouring eggnog in all these cups. I mean, there're about twenty of these cats lined up there. And I bet you not half of them will take Mr. Harper along. Some way-out cats, man. Some way-out cats.

I go up to Baby and kiss her on the back of the neck and give her a little pat where she likes for me to pat her when we're in the bed. She say, "Uh-uh," but I know she likes it anyhow.

Ben O

I back under the bed and touch the slop jar, and I pull back my leg and back somewhere else, and then I get me a good sight on it. I spin my aggie couple times and sight again and then I shoot. I hit it right square in the middle and it go flying over the fireplace. I crawl over there to get it and I see 'em all over there drinking they eggnog and they didn't even offer me and Chuckkie none. I find my marble on the bricks, and I go back and tell Chuckkie they over there drinking eggnog.

"You want some?" I say.

"I want shoot marble," Chuckkie say. "Yo' shot. Shoot up."

"I want some eggnog," I say.

"Shoot up, Ben O," he say. "I'm getting cold staying in one place so long. You feel that draft?"

"Coming from that crack under that bed," I say.

"Where?" Chuckkie say, looking for the crack.

"Over by that bedpost over there," I say.

"This sure's a beat-up old house," Chuckkie say.

"I want me some eggnog," I say.

"Well, you ain't getting none," Gran'mon say, from the fireplace. "It ain't good for you."

"I can drink eggnog," I say. "How come it ain't good for me? It ain't nothing but eggs and milk. I eat chicken, don't I? I eat beef, don't I?"

Gran'mon don't say nothing.

"I want me some eggnog," I say.

Gran'mon still don't say no more. Nobody else don't say nothing, neither.

"I want me some eggnog," I say.

"You go'n get a eggnog," Gran'mon say. "Just keep that noise up."

"I want me some eggnog," I say; "and I 'tend to get me some eggnog tonight."

Next thing I know, Gran'mon done picked up a chip out o' that corner and done sailed it back there where me and Chuckkie is. I duck just in time, and the chip catch old Chuckkie side the head.

"Hey, who that hitting me?" Chuckkie say.

"Move, and you won't get hit," Gran'mon say.

I laugh at old Chuckkie over there holding his head, and next thing I know here's Chuckkie done haul back there and hit me in my side. I jump up from there and give him two just to show him how it feel, and he jump up and hit me again. Then we grab each other and start tussling on the floor.

"You, Ben O," I hear Gran'mon saying. "You, Ben O, cut that out. Ya'll cut that out."

But we don't stop, 'cause neither one o' us want be first. Then I feel somebody pulling us apart.

"What I ought to do is whip both o' you," Mrs. Leola say. "Is that what y'all want?"

"No'm," I say.

"Then shake hand."

Me and Chuckkie shake hand.

"Kiss," Mrs. Leola say.

"No, ma'am," I say. "I ain't kissing no boy. I ain't that crazy."

"Kiss him, Chuckkie," she say.

Old Chuckkie kiss me on the jaw.

"Now, kiss him, Ben O."

"I ain't kissing no Chuckkie," I say. "No'm. Uh-uh. You kiss girls."

And the next thing I know, Mama done tipped up back o' me and done whop me on the leg with Daddy belt.

"Kiss Chuckkie," she say.

Chuckkie turn his jaw to me and I kiss him. I almost wipe my mouth. I even feel like spitting.

"Now, come back here and get you some eggnog," Mama say.

"That's right, spoil 'em," Gran'mon say. "Next thing you know, they be drinking from bottles."

"Little eggnog won't hurt 'em, Mama," Mama say.

"That's right, never listen," Gran'mon say. "It's you go'n suffer for it. I be dead and gone, me."

Aunt Clo

Be just like wrapping a chain round a tree and jecking and jecking, and then shifting the chain little bit and jecking and jecking some in that direction, and then shifting it some mo' and jecking and jecking in that direction. Jecking and jecking till you get it loose, and then pulling with all your might. Still it might not be loose enough and you have to back the tractor up some and fix the chain round the tree again and start jecking all over. Jeck, jeck, jeck. Then you hear the roots crying, and then you keep on jecking, and then it give, and you jeck some mo', and then it falls. And not till then that you see what you done done. Not till then you see the big hole in the ground and piece of the taproot still way down in it — a piece you won't never get out no matter if you dig till doomsday. Yes, you got the tree — least got it down on the ground, but did you get the taproot? No. No, sir, you didn't get the taproot. You stand there and look down in this hole at it and you grab yo' axe and jump down in it and start chopping at the taproot, but do you get the taproot? No. You don't get the taproot, sir. You never get the taproot. But, sir, I tell you what you do get. You get a big hole in the ground, sir; and you get another big hole in the air where the lovely branches been all these years. Yes, sir, that's what you get. The holes, sir, the holes. Two holes, sir, you can't never fill no matter how hard you try.

So you wrap yo' chain round yo' tree again, sir, and you start dragging it. But the dragging ain't so easy, sir, 'cause she's a heavy old tree — been there a long time, you know — heavy. And you make yo' tractor strain, sir, and the elements work 'gainst you, too, sir, 'cause the elements, they on her side, too, 'cause she part o' the elements, and the elements, they part o' her. So the elements, they do they little share to discourage you — yes, sir, they does. But you will not let the elements stop you. No, sir, you show the elements that they just elements, and man is stronger than elements, and you jeck and jeck on the chain, and soon she start to moving with you, sir, but if you look over yo' shoulder one second you see her leaving a trail — a trail, sir, that can be seen from miles and miles away. You see her trying to hook her little fine branches in different little cracks, in between pickets, round hills o' grass, round anything they might brush 'gainst. But you is a determined man, sir, and you jeck and you jeck, and she keep on grabbing and trying to hold, but you stronger, sir — course you the strongest — and you finally get her out on the pave road. But what you don't notice, sir, is just 'fore she get on the pave road she leave couple her little branches to remind the people that it ain't her that want leave, but you, sir, that think she ought to. So you just drag her and drag her, sir, and the folks that live in the houses 'side the pave road, they come out on they gallery and look at her go by, and then they go back in they house and sit by the fire and forget her. So you just go on, sir, and you just go and you go — and for how many days? I don't know. I don't have the least idea. The North to me, sir, is like the elements. It mystify me. But never mind, you finally get there, and then you try to find a place to set her. You look in this corner and you look in that corner, but no corner is good. She kind o' stand in the way no matter where you set her. So finally, sir, you say, "I just stand her up here a little while and see, and if it don't work out, if she keep getting in the way, I guess we'll just have to take her to the dump."

Chris

Just like him, though, standing up there telling them lies when everybody else feeling sad. I don't know what you do without people like him. And, yet, you see him there, he sad just like the rest. But he just got to be funny. Crying on the inside, but still got to be funny.

He didn't steal it, though; didn't still it a bit. His grandpa was just like him. Mat? Mat Jefferson? Just like that. Mat could make you die laughing. 'Member once at a wake. Who was dead? Yes — Robert Lewis. Robert Lewis laying up in his coffin dead as a door nail. Everybody sad and droopy. Mat look at that and start his lying. Soon, half o' the place laughing. Funniest wake I ever went to, and yet —

Just like now. Look at 'em. Look at 'em laughing. Ten minutes ago you would 'a' thought you was at a funeral. But look at 'em now. Look at her there in that little old chair. How long she had it? Fifty years — a hundred? It ain't a chair no mo', it's little bit o' her. Just like her arm, just like her leg.

You know, I couldn't believe it. I couldn't. Emile passed the house there the other day, right after the bombing, and I was in my yard digging a water drain to let the water run out in the ditch. Emile, he stopped the wagon there 'fore the door. Little Chuckkie, he in there with him with that little rain cap buckled up over his head. I go out to the gate and I say, "Emile, it's the truth?"

"The truth," he say. And just like that he say it. "The truth."

I look at him there, and he looking up the road to keep from looking back at me. You know, they been pretty close to Aunt Fe ever since they was children coming up. His own mom, Aunt Lou, and Aunt Fe, they been like sisters, there, together.

Me and him, we talk there little while 'bout the cane cutting, then he say he got to get on to the back. He shake the lines and drive on.

Inside me, my heart feel like it done swole up ten times the size it ought to be. Water come in my eyes, and I got to 'mit I cried right there. Yes sir, I cried right there by that front gate.

Louise come in the room and whisper something to Leola, and they go back in the kitchen. I can hear 'em moving things round back there, still getting things together they go'n be taking along. If they offer me anything, I'd like that big iron pot out there in the back yard. Good for boiling water when you killing hog, you know.

You can feel the sadness in the room again. Louise brought it in when she come in and whispered to Leola. Only, she didn't take it out when her and Leola left. Every pan they move, every pot they unhook keep telling you she leaving, she leaving.

Etienne turn over one o' them logs to make the fire pick up some, and I see that boy, Lionel, spreading out his hands over the fire. Watch out, I think to myself, here come another lie. People, he just getting started.

Anne-Marie Duvall

"You're not going?"

"I'm not going," he says, turning over the log with the poker. "And if you were in your right mind, you wouldn't go either."

"You just don't understand, do you?"

"Oh, I understand. She cooked for your daddy. She nursed you when your mama died."

"And I'm trying to pay her back with a seventy-nine-cents scarf. Is that too much?"

He is silent, leaning against the mantel, looking down at the fire. The fire throws strange shadows across the big, old room. Father looks down at me from against the wall. His eyes do not say go nor stay. But I know what he would do.

"Please go with me, Edward."

"You're wasting your breath."

I look at him for a long time, then I get the small package from the coffee table.

"You're still going?"

"I am going."

"Don't call for me if you get bogged down anywhere back there."

I look at him and go out to the garage. The sky is black. The clouds are moving fast and low. A fine drizzle is falling and the wind coming from the swamps blows in my face. I cannot recall a worse night in all my life.

I hurry into the car and drive out of the yard. The house stands big and black in back of me. Am I angry with Edward? No, I'm not angry with Edward. He's right. I should not go out into this kind of weather. But what he does not understand is I must. Father definitely would have gone if he were alive. Grandfather definitely would have gone, also. And, therefore, I must. Why? I cannot answer why. Only, I must go.

As soon as I turn down that old muddy road, I begin to pray. Don't let me go into that ditch, I pray. Don't let me go into that ditch. Please, don't let me go into that ditch.

The lights play on the big old trees along the road. Here and there the lights hit a sagging picket fence. But I know I haven't even started yet. She lives far back into the fields. Why? God, why does she have to live so far back? Why couldn't she have lived closer to the front? But the answer to that is as hard for me as is the answer to everything else. It was ordained before I — before father — was born — that she should live back there. So why should I try to understand it now?

The car slides toward the ditch, and I stop it dead and turn the wheel, and then come back into the road again. Thanks, father. I know you're with me. Because it was you who said that I must look after her, didn't you? No, you did not say it directly, father. You said it only with a glance. As grandfather must have said it to you, and as his father must have said it to him.

But now that she's gone, father, now what? I know. I know. Aunt Lou, Aunt Clo, and the rest.

The lights shine on the dead, wet grass along the road. There's an old pecan tree, looking dead and all alone. I wish I was a little nigger gal so I could pick pecans and eat them under the big old dead tree.

The car hits a rut, but bounces right out of it. I am frightened for a moment, but then I feel better. The windshield wipers are working well, slapping the water away as fast as it hits the glass. If I make the next half mile all right, the rest of the way will be good. It's not much over a mile now.

That was too bad about that bombing — killing that woman and her two children. That poor woman; poor children. What is the answer? What will happen? What do they want? Do they know what they want? Do they really know what they want? Are they positively sure? Have they any idea? Money to buy a car, is that it? If that is all, I pity them. Oh, how I pity them.

Not much farther. Just around that bend and — there's a water hole. Now what?

I stop the car and just stare out at the water a minute; then I get out to see how deep it is. The cold wind shoots through my body like needles. Lightning comes from towards the swamps and lights up the place. For a split second the night is as bright as day. The next second it is blacker than it has ever been.

I look at the water, and I can see that it's too deep for the car to pass through. I must turn back or I must walk the rest of the way. I stand there a while wondering what to do. Is it worth it all? Can't I simply send the gift by someone tomorrow morning? But will there be someone tomorrow morning? Suppose she leaves without getting it, then what? What then? Father would never forgive me. Neither would grandfather or great-grandfather, either. No, they wouldn't.

The lightning flashes again and I look across the field, and I can see the tree in the yard a quarter of a mile away. I have but one choice: I must walk. I get the package out of the car and stuff it in my coat and start out.

I don't make any progress at first, but then I become a little warmer and I find I like walking. The lightning flashes just in time to show up a puddle of water, and I go around it. But there's no light to show up the second puddle, and I fall flat on my face. For a moment I'm completely blind, then I get slowly to my feet and check the package. It's dry, not harmed. I wash the mud off my raincoat, wash my hands, and I start out again.

The house appears in front of me, and as I come into the yard, I can hear the people laughing and talking. Sometimes I think niggers can laugh and joke even if they see somebody beaten to death. I go up on the porch and knock and an old one opens the door for me. I swear, when he sees me he looks as if he's seen a ghost. His mouth drops open, his eyes bulge — I swear.

I go into the old crowded and smelly room, and every one of them looks at me the same way the first one did. All the joking and laughing has ceased. You would think I was the devil in person.

"Done, Lord," I hear her saying over by the fireplace. They move to the side and I can see her sitting in that little rocking chair I bet you she's had since the beginning of time. "Done, Master," she says. "Child, what you doing in weather like this? Y'all move; let her get to that fire. Y'all move. Move, now. Let her warm herself."

They started scattering everywhere.

"I'm not cold, Aunt Fe," I say. "I just brought you something — something small — because you're leaving us. I'm going right back."

"Done, Master," she says. Fussing over me just like she's done all her life. "Done, Master. Child, you ain't got no business in a place like this. Get close to this fire. Get here. Done, Master."

I move closer, and the fire does feel warm and good.

"Done, Lord," she says.

I take out the package and pass it to her. The other niggers gather around with all kinds of smiles on their faces. Just think of it — a white lady coming through all of this for one old darky. It is all right for them to come from all over the plantation, from all over the area, in all kinds of weather: this is to be expected of them. But a white lady, a white lady. They must think we white people don't have their kind of feelings.

She unwraps the package, her bony little fingers working slowly and deliberately. When she sees the scarf — the seventy-nine cents scarf — she brings it to her mouth and kisses it.

"Y'all look," she says. "Y'all look. Ain't it the prettiest little scarf y'all ever did see? Y'all look."

They move around her and look at the scarf. Some of them touch it.

"I go'n put it on right now," she says. I go'n put it on right now, my lady."

She unfolds it and ties it round her head and looks up at everybody and smiles.

"Thank you, my lady," she says. "Thank you, ma'am, from the bottom of my heart."

"Oh, Aunt Fe." I say, kneeling down beside her. "Oh, Aunt Fe."

But I think about the other niggers there looking down at me, and I get up. But I look into that wrinkled old face again, and I must go back down again. And I lay my head in that bony old lap, and I cry and I cry — I don't know how long. And I feel those old fingers, like death itself, passing over my hair and my neck. I don't know how long I kneel there crying, and when I stop, I get out of there as fast as I can.

Etienne

The boy come in, and soon, right off, they get quiet, blaming the boy. If people could look little farther than the tip of they nose — No, they blame the boy. Not that they ain't behind the boy, what he doing, but they blame him for what she must do. What they don't know is that the boy didn't start it, and the people that bombed the house didn't start it, neither. It started a million years ago. It started when one man envied another man for having a penny mo' 'an he had, and then the man married a woman to help him work the field so he could get much 's the other man, but when the other man saw the man had married a woman to get much 's him, he, himself, he married a woman, too, so he could still have mo'. Then they start having children — not from love; but so the children could help 'em work so they could have mo'. But even with the children one man still had a penny mo' 'an the other, so the other man went and bought him a ox, and the other man did the same — to keep ahead of the other man. And soon the other man had bought him a slave to work the ox so he could get ahead of the other man. But the other man went out and bought him two slaves so he could stay ahead of the other man, and the other man went out and bought him three slaves. And soon they had a thousand slaves apiece, but they still wasn't satisfied. And one day the slaves all rose and kill the masters, but the masters (knowing slaves was men just like they was, and kind o' expected they might do this) organized theyself a good police force, and the police force, they come out and killed the two thousand slaves.

So it's not this boy you see standing here 'fore you, 'cause it happened a million years ago. And this boy here's just doing something the slaves done a million years ago. Just that this boy here ain't doing it they way. 'Stead of raising arms 'gainst the masters, he bow his head.

No, I say; don't blame the boy 'cause she must go. 'Cause when she's dead, and that won't be long after they get her up there, this boy's work will still be going on. She's not the only one that's go'n die from this boy's work. Many mo' of 'em go'n die 'fore it's over with. The whole place — everything. A big wind is rising, and when a big wind rise, the sea stirs, and the drop o' water you see laying on top the sea this day won't be there tomorrow. 'Cause that's what wind do, and that's what life is. She ain't nothing but one little drop o' water laying on top the sea, and what this boy's doing is called the wind . . . and she must be moved. No, don't blame the boy. Go out and blame the wind. No, don't blame him, 'cause tomorrow, what he's doing today, somebody go'n say he ain't done a thing. 'Cause tomorrow will be his time to be turned over just like it's hers today. And after that, be somebody else time to turn over. And it keep going like that till it ain't nothing left to turn — and nobody left to turn it.

"Sure, they bombed the house," he say; "because they want us to stop. But if we stopped today, then what good would we have done? What good? Those who have already died for the cause would have just died in vain."

"Maybe if they had bombed your house you wouldn't be so set on keeping this up."

"If they had killed my mother and my brothers and sisters, I'd press just that much harder. I can see you all point. I can see it very well. But I can't agree with you. You blame me for their being bombed. You blame me for Aunt Fe's leaving. They died for you and for your children. And I love Aunt Fe as much as anybody in here does. Nobody in here loves her more than I do. Not one of you." He looks at her. "Don't you believe me, Aunt Fe?"

She nods — that little white scarf still tied round her head.

"How many times have I eaten in your kitchen, Aunt Fe? A thousand times? How many times have I eaten tea cakes and drank milk on the back steps, Aunt

Fe? A thousand times? How many times have I sat at this same fireplace with you, just the two of us, Aunt Fe? Another thousand times — two thousand times? How many times have I chopped wood for you, chopped grass for you, ran to the store for you? Five thousand times? How many times have we walked to church together, Aunt Fe? Gone fishing at the river together — how many times? I've spent as much time in this house as I've spent in my own. I know every crack in the wall. I know every corner. With my eyes shut, I can go anywhere in here without bumping into anything. How many of you can do that? Not many of you." He looks at her. "Aunt Fe?"

She looks at him.

"Do you think I love you, Aunt Fe?"

She nods.

"I love you, Aunt Fe, much as I do my own parents. I'm going to miss you much as I'd miss my own mother if she were to leave me now. I'm going to miss you, Aunt Fe, but I'm not going to stop what I've started. You told me a story once, Aunt Fe, about my great-grandpa. Remember? Remember how he died?"

She looks in the fire and nods.

"Remember how they lynched him — chopped him into pieces?"

She nods.

"Just the two of us were sitting here beside the fire when you told me that. I was so angry I felt like killing. But it was you who told me get killing out of my mind. It was you who told me I would only bring harm to myself and sadness to the others if I killed. Do you remember, Aunt Fe?"

She nods, still looking in the fire.

"You were right. We cannot raise our arms. Because it would mean death for ourselves, as well as for the others. But we will do something else — and that's what we will do." He looks at the people standing round him. "And if they were to bomb my own mother's house tomorrow, I would still go on."

"I'm not saying for you not to go on," Louise says. "That's up to you. I'm just taking Auntie from here before hers is the next house they bomb."

The boy look at Louise, and then at Aunt Fe. He go up to the chair where she sitting.

"Good-bye, Aunt Fe," he say, picking up her hand. The hand done shriveled up to almost nothing. Look like nothing but loose skin's covering the bones. "I'll miss you," he say.

"Good-bye, Emmanuel," she say. She look at him a long time. "God be with you."

He stand there holding the hand a while longer, then he nods his head, and leaves the house. The people stir round little bit, but nobody say anything.

Aunt Lou

They tell her good-bye, and half of 'em leave the house crying, or want cry, but she just sit there 'side the fireplace like she don't mind going at all. When Leola ask me if I'm ready to go, I tell her I'm staying right there till Fe leave that house. I tell her I ain't moving one step till she go out that door. I been knowing her for the past fifty some years now, and I ain't 'bout to leave her on her last night here.

That boy, Chuckkie, want stay with me, but I make him go. He follow his mon and paw out the house and soon I hear that wagon turning round. I hear Emile saying something to Mr. Bascom even 'fore that wagon get out the yard. I tell myself, well, Mr. Bascom, you sure go'n catch it, and me not there to take up for you — and I get up from my chair and go to the door.

"Emile?" I call.

"Whoa," he say.

"You leave that mule 'lone, you hear me?"

"I ain't done Mr. Bascom a thing, Mama," He say.

"Well, you just mind you don't," I say. "I'll sure find out."

"Yes'm," he say. "Come up here, Mr. Bascom."

"Now, you hear that boy. Emile?" I say.

"I'm sorry, Mama," he say. "I didn't mean no harm."

They go out in the road, and I go back to the fireplace and sit down again. Louise stir round in the kitchen a few minutes, then she come in the front where we at. Everybody else gone. That husband o' hers, there, got drunk long 'fore midnight, and Emile and them had to put him to bed in the other room.

She come there and stand by the fire.

"I'm dead on my feet," she say.

"Why don't you go to bed," I say. "I'm go'n be here."

"You all won't need anything?"

"They got wood in that corner?"

"Plenty."

"Then we won't need a thing."

She stand there and warm, and then she say good night and go round the other side.

"Well, Fe?" I say.

"I ain't leaving here tomorrow, Lou," she say.

" 'Course you is," I say. "Up there ain't that bad."

She shake her head. "No, I ain't going nowhere."

I look at her over in her chair, but I don't say nothing. The fire pops in the fireplace, and I look at the fire again. It's a good little fire — not too big, not too little. Just 'nough there to keep the place warm.

"You want sing, Lou?" she say, after a while. "I feel like singing my 'termination song."

"Sure," I say.

She start singing in that little light voice she got there, and I join with her. We sing two choruses, and then she stop.

"My 'termination for Heaven," she say. "Now — now —"

"What's the matter, Fe?" I say.

"Nothing," she say. "I want get in my bed. My gown hanging over there."

I get the gown for her and bring it back to the firehalf. She get out of her dress slowly, like she don't even have 'nough strength to do it. I help her on with her gown, and she kneel down there 'side the bed and say her prayers. I sit in my chair and look at the fire again.

She pray there a long time — half out loud, half to herself. I look at her kneeling down there, little like a little old girl. I see her making some kind o' jecking motion there, but I feel she crying 'cause this her last night here, and 'cause she got to go and leave ever'thing behind. I look at the fire.

She pray there ever so long, and then she start to get up. But she can't make it by herself. I go to help her, and when I put my hand on her shoulder, she say, "Lou? Lou?"

I say, "What's the matter, Fe?"

"Lou?" she say. "Lou?"

I feel her shaking in my hand with all her might. Shaking, shaking, shaking — like a person with the chill. Then I hear her take a long breath, longest I ever heard anybody take before. Then she ease back on the bed — calm, calm, calm.

"Sleep on, Fe," I tell her. "When you get up there, tell 'em all I ain't far behind."

CAROLINE GORDON

Old Red

I

WHEN THE DOOR HAD closed behind his daughter, Mr. Maury went to the window and stood a few moments looking out. The roses that had grown in a riot all along that side of the fence had died or been cleared away, but the sun lay across the garden in the same level lances of light that he remembered. He turned back into the room. The shadows had gathered until it was nearly all in gloom. The top of his minnow bucket just emerging from his duffel bag glinted in the last rays of the sun. He stood looking down at his traps all gathered neatly in a heap at the foot of the bed. He would leave them like that. Even if they came in here sweeping and cleaning up — it was only in hotels that a man was master of his own room — even if they came in here cleaning up he would tell them to leave all his things exactly as they were. It was reassuring to see them all there together, ready to be taken up in the hand, to be carried down and put into a car, to be driven off to some railroad station at a moment's notice.

As he moved toward the door he spoke aloud, a habit that was growing on him:

"Anyhow I won't stay but a week. . . . I ain't going to stay but a week, no matter what they say. . . ."

Downstairs in the dining room they were already gathered at the supper table: his white-haired, shrunken mother-in-law; his tall sister-in-law who had the proud carriage of the head, the aquiline nose, but not the spirit of his dead wife; his lean, blond, new son-in-law; his black eyed daughter who, but that she was thin, looked so much like him, all of them gathered there waiting for him, Alexander Maury. It occurred to him that this was the first time he had sat down in the bosom of the family for some years. They were always writing saying that he must make a visit this summer or certainly next summer — ". . . all had a happy Christmas together, but missed you. . . ." They had even made the pretext that he ought to come up to inspect his new son-in-law. As if he hadn't always known exactly the kind of young man Sarah would marry! What was the boy's name? Stephen, yes, Stephen. He must be sure and remember that.

He sat down and, shaking out his napkin, spread it over his capacious paunch and tucked it well up under his chin in the way his wife had never allowed him to do. He let his eyes rove over the table and released a long sigh.

"Hot batter bread," he said, "and ham. Merry Point ham. I sure am glad to taste them one more time before I die."

The old lady was sending the little Negro girl scurrying back to the kitchen for a hot plate of batter bread. He pushed aside the cold plate and waited. She had bridled when he spoke of the batter bread and a faint flush had dawned on her withered cheeks. Vain she had always been as a peacock, of her housekeeping, her children, anything that belonged to her. She went on now, even at her advanced age, making her batter bread, smoking her hams according to that old recipe she was so proud of, but who came here now to this old house to eat or to praise?

He helped himself to a generous slice of batter bread, buttered it, took the first mouthful and chewed it slowly. He shook his head.

"There ain't anything like it," he said. "There ain't anything else like it in the world."

His dark eye roving over the table fell on his son-in-law. "You like batter bread?" he inquired.

Stephen nodded, smiling. Mr. Maury, still masticating slowly, regarded his face, measured the space between the eyes — his favorite test for man, horse, or dog. Yes, there was room enough for sense between the eyes. How young the boy looked! And infected already with the fatal germ, the *cacoëthes scribendi*. Well, their children — if he and Sarah ever had any children — would probably escape. It was like certain diseases of the eye, skipped every other generation. His own father had had it badly all his life. He could see him now sitting at the head of the table spouting his own poetry — or Shakespeare's — while the children watched the preserve dish to see if it was going around. He, Aleck Maury, had been lucky to be born in the generation he had. He had escaped that at least. A few translations from Heine in his courting days, a few fragments from the Greek; but no, he had kept clear of that on the whole. . . .

His sister-in-law's eyes were fixed on him. She was smiling faintly. "You don't look much like dying, Aleck. Florida must agree with you."

The old lady spoke from the head of the table. "I can't see what you do with yourself all winter long. Doesn't time hang heavy on your hands?"

Time, he thought, *time!* They were always mouthing the word, and what did they know about it? Nothing in God's world! He saw time suddenly, a dull, leaden-colored fabric depending from the old lady's hands, from the hands of all of them, a blanket that they pulled about between them, now here, now there, trying to cover up their nakedness. Or they would cast it on the ground and creep in among the folds, finding one day a little more tightly rolled than another, but all of it everywhere the same dull gray substance. But time was a banner that whipped before him always in the wind! He stood on tiptoe to catch at the bright folds, to strain them to his bosom. They were bright and glittering. But they whipped by so fast and were whipping always ever faster. The tears came into his eyes. Where, for instance, had this year gone? He could swear he had not wasted a minute of it, for no man living, he thought, knew better how to make each day a pleasure to him. Not a minute wasted and yet here it was already May. If he lived to the biblical threescore-and-ten, which was all he ever allowed himself in his calculations, he had before him only nine more Mays. Only nine more Mays out of all eternity and they wanted him to waste one of them sitting on the front porch at Merry Point!

The butter plate which had seemed to swim before him in a glittering mist was coming solidly to rest upon the white tablecloth. He winked his eyes rapidly and, laying down his knife and fork, squared himself about in his chair to address his mother-in-law:

"Well, ma'am, you know I'm a man that always likes to be learning something. Now this year I learned how to smell out fish." He glanced around the table, holding his head high and allowing his well-cut nostrils to flutter slightly with his indrawn breaths. "Yes, sir," he said, "I'm probably the only white man in this country knows how to smell out feesh."

There was a discreet smile on the faces of the others. Sarah was laughing outright. "Did you have to learn how or did it just come to you?"

"I learned it from an old nigger woman," her father said. He shook his head reminiscently. "It's wonderful how much you can learn from niggers. But you have to know how to handle them. I was half the winter wooing that old Fanny. . . ."

He waited until their laughter had died down. "We used to start off every morning from the same little cove and we'd drift in there together at night. I noticed how she always brought in a good string, so I says to her: 'Fanny, you just lemme go 'long with you.' But she wouldn't have nothing to do with me. I saw she was going to be a hard nut to crack, but I kept right on. Finally I began giving her presents. . . ."

Laura was regarding him fixedly, a queer glint in her eyes. Seeing outrageous pictures in her mind's eye, doubtless. Poor Laura. Fifty years old if she was a day. More than half her lifetime gone and all of it spent drying up here in the old lady's shadow. She was speaking with a gasping little titter:

"What sort of presents did you give her, Aleck?"

He made his tone hearty in answer. "I give her a fine string of fish one day and I give her fifty cents. And finally I made her a present of a Barlow knife. That was when she broke down. She took me with her that morning. . . ."

"Could she really *smell* fish?" the old lady asked curiously.

"You ought to a seen her," Mr. Maury said. "She'd sail over that lake like a hound on the scent. She'd row right along and then all of a sudden she'd stop rowing." He bent over and peered into the depths of imaginary water. " 'Thar they are, White Folks, thar they are. Cain't you smell 'em?' "

Stephen was leaning forward, eyeing his father-in-law intently. "Could you?" he asked.

"I got so I could smell feesh," Mr. Maury told him. "I could smell out the feesh but I couldn't tell which kind they were. Now Fanny could row over a bed and tell just by the smell whether it was bass or bream. But she'd been at it all her life." He paused, sighing. "You can't just pick these things up. . . . Who was it said, 'Genius is an infinite capacity for taking pains'?"

Sarah was rising briskly. Her eyes sought her husband's across the table. She was laughing. "Sir Izaak Walton," she said. "We'd better go in the other room. Mandy wants to clear the table."

The two older ladies remained in the dining room. Mr. Maury walked across the hall to the sitting room, accompanied by Steve and Sarah. He lowered himself cautiously into the most solid-looking of the rocking chairs that were drawn up around the fire. Steve stood on the hearthrug, his back to the fire.

Mr. Maury glanced up at him curiously. "What you thinking about, feller?" he asked.

Steve looked down. He smiled but his gaze was still contemplative. "I was thinking about the sonnet," he said, "in the form in which it first came to England."

Mr. Maury shook his head. "Wyatt and Surrey," he said. "Hey, nonny, nonny. . . . You'll have hardening of the liver long before you're my age." He looked past Steve's shoulder at the picture that hung over the mantelshelf: Cupid and Psyche holding between them a fluttering veil and running along a rocky path toward the beholder. It had been hanging there ever since he could remember; would hang there, he thought, till the house fell down or burned down, as it was more likely to do with the old lady wandering around at night carrying lighted lamps the way she did. "Old Merry Point," he said. "It don't change much, does it?"

He settled himself more solidly in his chair. His mind veered from the old house to his own wanderings in brighter places. He regarded his daughter and son-in-law affably.

"Yes, sir," he said, "this winter in Florida was valuable to me just for the acquaintances I made. Take my friend Jim Yost. Just to live in the same hotel with that man is an education." He paused, smiling reminiscently into the fire. "I'll never forget the first time I saw him. He came up to me there in the lobby of the hotel. 'Professor Maury,' he says, 'you been hearin' about me for twenty years and I been hearin' about you for twenty years. And now we've done met.' "

Sarah had sat down in the little rocking chair by the fire. She leaned toward him now, laughing. "They ought to have put down a cloth of gold for the meeting," she said.

Mr. Maury regarded her critically. It occurred to him that she was, after all, not so much like himself as the sister whom, as a child, he had particularly disliked. A smart girl, Sarah, but too quick always on the uptake. For his own part he preferred a softer-natured woman.

He shook his head. "Nature does that in Florida," he said. "I knew right off the reel it was him. There were half a dozen men standing around. I made 'em witness. 'Jim Yost,' I says, 'Jim Yost of Maysville or I'll eat my hat.'"

"Why is he so famous?" Sarah asked.

Mr. Maury took out his knife and cut off a plug of tobacco. When he had offered a plug to his son-in-law and it had been refused, he put the tobacco back into his pocket. "He's a man of imagination," he said slowly. "There ain't many in this world."

He took a small tin box out of his pocket and set it on the little table that held the lamp. Removing the top, he tilted the box so that they could see its contents: an artificial lure, a bug with a dark body and a red, bulbous head, a hook protruding from what might be considered its vitals.

"Look at her," he said. "Ain't she a killer?"

Sarah leaned forward to look and Steve, still standing on the hearthrug, bent above them. The three heads ringed the light. Mr. Maury disregarded Sarah and addressed himself to Steve. "She takes nine strips of pork rind," he said, "nine strips cut just thick enough." He marked off the width of the strips with his two fingers on the table, then, picking up the lure and cupping it in his palm, he moved it back and forth quickly so that the painted eyes caught the light.

"Look at her," he said, "look at the wicked way she sets forward."

Sarah was poking at the lure with the tip of her finger. "Wanton," she said, "simply wanton. What does he call her?"

"This is his Devil Bug," Mr. Maury said. "He's the only man in this country makes it. I myself had the idea thirty years ago and let it slip by me the way I do with so many of my ideas." He sighed, then, elevating his tremendous bulk slightly above the table level and continuing to hold Steve with his gaze, he produced from his coat pocket the oilskin book that held his flies. He spread it open on the table and began to turn the pages. His eyes sought his son-in-law's as his hand paused before a gray, rather draggled-looking lure.

"Old Speck," he said. "I've had that fly for twenty years. I reckon she's taken five hundred pounds of fish in her day. . . . ."

The fire burned lower. A fiery coal rolled from the grate and fell onto the hearthrug. Sarah scooped it up with a shovel and threw it among the ashes. In the circle of the lamplight the two men still bent over the table looking at the flies. Steve was absorbed in them, but he spoke seldom. It was her father's voice that, rising and falling, filled the room. He talked a great deal but he had a beautiful speaking voice. He was telling Steve now about Little West Fork, the first stream ever he put a fly in. "My first love," he kept calling it. It sounded rather pretty, she thought, in his mellow voice. "My first love. . . ."

II

When Mr. Maury came downstairs the next morning the dining room was empty except for his daughter, Sarah, who sat dawdling over a cup of coffee and a cigarette. Mr. Maury sat down opposite her. To the little Negro girl who presented herself at his elbow he outlined his wants briefly: "A cup of coffee and some hot batter bread, just like we had last night." He turned to his daughter. "Where's Steve?"

"He's working," she said. "He was up at eight and he's been working ever since."

Mr. Maury accepted the cup of coffee from the little girl, poured half of it into his saucer, set it aside to cool. "Ain't it wonderful," he said, "the way a man can sit down and work day after day? When I think of all the work I've done in my time . . . Can he work *every* morning?"

"He sits down at his desk every morning," she said, "but of course he gets more done some mornings than others."

Mr. Maury picked up his saucer, found the coffee cool enough for his taste. He sipped it slowly, looking out of the window. His mind was already busy with his day's program. No water — no running water — nearer than West Fork, three miles away. He couldn't drive a car and Steve was going to be busy writing all morning. There was nothing for it but a pond. The Willow Sink. It was not much, but it was better than nothing. He pushed his chair back and rose.

"Well," he said, "I'd better be starting."

When he came downstairs with his rod a few minutes later the hall was still full of the sound of measured typing. Sarah sat in the dining room in the same position in which he had left her, smoking. Mr. Maury paused in the doorway while he slung his canvas bag over his shoulders. "How you ever going to get anything done if you don't take advantage of the morning hours?" he asked. He glanced at the door opposite as if it had been the entrance to a sick chamber. "What's he writing about?" he inquired in a whisper.

"It's an essay on John Skelton."

Mr. Maury looked out at the new green leaves framed in the doorway. "John Skelton," he said, "God Almighty!"

He went through the hall and stepped down off the porch onto the ground that was still moist with spring rains. As he crossed the lower yard he looked up into the branches of the maples. Yes, the leaves were full-grown already even on the late trees. The year, how swiftly, how steadily it advanced! He had come to the far corner of the yard. Grown up it was in pokeberry shoots and honeysuckle, but there was a place to get through. The top strand of wire had been pulled down and fastened to the others with a ragged piece of rope. He rested his weight on his good leg and swung himself over onto the game one. It gave him a good, sharp twinge when he came down on it. It was getting worse all the time, that leg, but on the other hand he was learning better all the time how to handle it. His mind flew back to a dark, startled moment, that day when the cramp first came on him. He had been sitting still in the boat all day long and that evening when he stood up to get out his leg had failed him utterly. He had pitched forward among the reeds, had lain there a second, face downward, before it came to him what had happened. With the realization came a sharp picture out of his faraway youth. Uncle James, lowering himself ponderously out of the saddle after a hard day's hunting, had fallen forward in exactly the same way, into a knot of yowling little Negroes. He had got up and cursed them all out of the lot. It had scared the old boy to death, coming down like that. The black dog he had had on his shoulder all that fall. But he himself had never lost one day's fishing on account of his leg. He had known from the start how to handle it. It meant simply that he was slowed down that much. It hadn't really made much difference in fishing. He didn't do as much wading but he got around just about as well on the whole. Hunting, of course, had had to go. You couldn't walk all day shooting birds, dragging a game leg. He had just given it up right off the reel, though it was a shame when a man was as good a shot as he was. That day he was out with Tom Kensington, last November, the only day he got out during the bird season. Nine shots he'd had and he'd bagged nine birds. Yes, it was a shame. But a man couldn't do everything. He had to limit himself. . . .

He was up over the little rise now. The field slanted straight down before him to where the pond lay, silver in the morning sun. A Negro cabin was perched halfway up the opposite slope. A woman was hanging out washing on a line stretched between two trees. From the open door little Negroes spilled down the path toward the pond. Mr. Maury surveyed the scene, spoke aloud:

"Ain't it funny now? Niggers always live in the good places."

He stopped under a wild cherry tree to light his pipe. It had been hot crossing the field, but the sunlight here was agreeably tempered by the branches. And that pond down there was fringed with willows. His eyes sought the bright disc of the water, then rose to where the smoke from the cabin chimney lay in a soft plume along the crest of the hill.

When he stooped to pick up his rod again it was with a feeling of sudden keen elation. An image had risen in his memory, an image that was familiar but came to him infrequently of late and that only in moments of elation: the wide field in front of his uncle's house in Albemarle, on one side the dark line of undergrowth that marked the Rivanna River, on the other the blue of Peters' Mountain. They would be waiting there in that broad plain when they had the first sight of the fox. On that little rise by the river, loping steadily, not yet alarmed. The sun would glint on his bright coat, on his quick turning head as he dove into the dark of the woods. There would be hullabaloo after that and shouting and riding. Sometimes there was the tailing of the fox — that time Old Whiskey was brought home on a mattress! All of that to come afterwards, but none of it ever like that first sight of the fox there on the broad plain between the river and the mountain.

There was one fox, they grew to know him in time, to call him affectionately by name. Old Red it was who showed himself always like that there on the crest of the hill. "There he goes, the damn, impudent scoundrel. . . ." Uncle James would shout and slap his thigh and yell himself hoarse at Whiskey and Mag and the pups, but they would already have settled to their work. They knew his course, every turn of it, by heart. Through the woods and then down again to the river. Their hope was always to cut him off before he could circle back to the mountain. If he got in there among those old field pines it was all up. But he always made it. Lost 'em every time and dodged through to his hole in Pinnacle Rock. A smart fox, Old Red. . . .

He descended the slope and paused in the shade of a clump of willows. The little Negroes who squatted, dabbling in the water, watched him out of round eyes as he unslung his canvas bag and laid it on a stump. He looked down at them gravely.

"D'you ever see a white man that could conjure?" he asked.

The oldest boy laid the brick he was fashioning out of mud down on a plank. He ran the tip of his tongue over his lower lip to moisten it before he spoke. "Naw, suh."

"I'm the man," Mr. Maury told him. "You chillun better quit that playin' and dig me some worms."

He drew his rod out of the case, jointed it up, and laid it down on a stump. Taking out his book of flies, he turned the pages, considering. "Silver Spinner," he said aloud. "They ought to take that . . . in May. Naw, I'll just give Old Speck a chance. It's a long time now since we had her out."

The little Negroes had risen and were stepping quietly off along the path toward the cabin, the two little boys hand in hand, the little girl following, the baby astride her hip. They were pausing now before a dilapidated building that might long ago have been a hen house. Mr. Maury shouted at them: "Look under them old boards. That's the place for worms." The biggest boy was turning around. His treble "Yassuh" quavered over the water. Then their voices died away. There was no sound except the light turning of the willow boughs in the wind.

Mr. Maury walked along the bank, rod in hand, humming: "Bangum's gone to the wild boar's den. . . . *Bangum's* gone to the wild boar's den. . . ." He stopped where a white, peeled log protruded six or seven feet into the water. The pond made a little turn here. He stepped out squarely upon the log, still humming. The line rose smoothly, soared against the blue, and curved sweetly back upon the still water. His quick ear caught the little whish that the fly made when it clove the surface, his eye followed the tiny ripples made by its flight. He cast again, leaning a little backwards as he did sometimes when the mood was on him. Again and again his line soared out over the water. His eye rested now and then on his wrist. He noted with detachment the expert play of the muscles, admired each time the accuracy of his aim. It occurred to him that it was four days now since he had wet a line. Four days. One whole day packing up, parts of two days on the train, and yesterday wasted sitting there on that front porch with the family. But the abstinence had done him good. He had never cast better than he was casting this morning.

There was a rustling along the bank, a glimpse of blue through the trees. Mr. Maury leaned forward and peered around the clump of willows. A hundred yards away Steve, hatless, in an old blue shirt and khaki pants, stood jointing up a rod.

Mr. Maury backed off his log and advanced along the path. He called out cheerfully: "Well, feller, do any good?"

Steve looked up. His face had lightened for a moment but the abstracted expression stole over it again when he spoke. "Oh, I fiddled with it all morning," he said, "but I didn't do much good."

Mr. Maury nooded sympathetically. *"Minerva invita erat,"* he said. "You can do nothing unless Minerva perches on the roof tree. Why, I been castin' here all morning and not a strike. But there's a boat tied up over on the other side. What say we get in it and just drift around?" He paused, looked at the rod Steve had finished jointing up. "I brought another rod along," he said. "You want to use it?"

Steve shook his head. "I'm used to this one," he said.

An expression of relief came over Mr. Maury's face. "That's right," he said, "a man always does better with his own rod."

The boat was only a quarter full of water. They heaved her over and dumped it out, then dragged her down to the bank. The little Negroes had come up, bringing a can of worms. Mr. Maury threw them each a nickel and set the can in the bottom of the boat. "I always like to have a few worms handy," he told Steve, "ever since I was a boy." He lowered himself ponderously into the bow and Steve pushed off and dropped down behind him.

The little Negroes still stood on the bank staring. When the boat was a little distance out on the water the boldest of them spoke:

"You reckon 'at ole jawnboat going to hold you up, Cap'm?"

Mr. Maury turned his head to call over his shoulder. "Go 'way, boy. Ain't I done tole you I's a conjure?"

The boat dipped ominously. Steve changed his position a little and she settled to the water. Sitting well forward, Mr. Maury made graceful casts, now to this side, now to that. Steve, in the stern, made occasional casts but he laid his rod down every now and then to paddle though there was really no use in it. The boat drifted well enough with the wind. At the end of half an hour seven sizable bass lay on the bottom of the boat. Mr. Maury had caught five of them. He reflected that perhaps he really ought to change places with Steve. The man in the bow certainly had the best chance at the fish. "But no," he thought, "it don't make no difference. He don't hardly know where he is now."

He stole a glance over his shoulder at the young man's serious, abstracted face. It was like that of a person submerged. Steve seemed to float up to the surface every now and then, his expression would lighten, he would make some observation that showed he knew where he was, then he would sink again. If you asked him a question he answered punctiliously, two minutes later. Poor boy, dead to the world and would probably be that way the rest of his life. A pang of pity shot through Mr. Maury and on the heels of it a gust of that black fear that occasionally shook him. It was he, not Steve, that was the queer one. The world was full of people like this boy, all of them going around with their heads so full of this and that they hardly knew what they were doing. They were all like that. There was hardly anybody — there was *nobody* really in the whole world like him. . . .

Steve, coming out of his abstraction, spoke politely. He had heard that Mr. Maury was a fine shot. Did he like to fish better than hunt?

Mr. Maury reflected. "Well," he said, "they's something about a covey of birds rising up in front you . . . they's something . . . and a good dog. Now they ain't anything in this world that I like better than a good bird dog." he stopped and sighed. "A man has got to come to himself early in life it he's going to amount to anything. Now I was smart, even as a boy. I could look around me and see all the men of my family, Uncle Jeems, Uncle Quent, my father, every one of 'em weighed two hundred by the time he was fifty. You get as heavy on your feet as all that and you can't do any good shooting. But a man can fish as long as he lives. . . . Why, one place I stayed last summer there was an old man ninety years old had himself carried down to the river every morning. Yes, sir, a man can fish as long as he can get down to the water's edge. . . ."

There was a little plop to the right. He turned just in time to see the fish flash out of the water. He watched Steve take it off the hook and drop it on top of the pile in the bottom of the boat. Seven bass that made and one bream. The old lady would be pleased. "Aleck always catches me fish," she'd say.

The boat glided over the still water. There was no wind at all now. The willows that fringed the bank might have been cut out of paper. The plume of smoke hung perfectly horizontal over the roof of the Negro cabin. Mr. Maury watched it stream out in little eddies and disappear into the bright blue.

He spoke softly: "Ain't it wonderful . . . ain't it wonderful now that a man of my gifts can content himself a whole morning on this here little old pond?"

III

Mr. Maury woke with a start. He realized that he had been sleeping on his left side again. A bad idea. It always gave him palpitations of the heart. It must be that that had waked him up. He had gone to sleep almost immediately after his head hit the pillow. He rolled over, cautiously, as he always did since that bed in Leesburg had given down with him and, lying flat on his back, stared at the opposite wall.

The moon rose late. It must be at its height now. That patch of light was so brilliant he could almost discern the pattern of the wallpaper. It hung there, wavering, bitten by the shadows into a semblance of a human figure, a man striding with bent head and swinging arms. All the shadows in the room seemed to be moving toward him. The protruding corner of the washstand was an arrow aimed at his heart, the clumsy old-fashioned dresser was a giant towering above him.

They had put him to sleep in this same room the night after his wife died. In the summer it had been, too, in June; and there must have been a full moon, for the same giant shadows had struggled there with the same towering monsters. It would be like that here on this wall every full moon, for the pieces of furniture would never change their position, had never been changed, probably, since the house was built.

He turned back on his side. The wall before him was dark but he knew every flower in the pattern of the wallpaper, interlacing pink roses with, thrusting up between every third cluster, the enormous, spreading fronds of ferns. The wallpaper in the room across the hall was like it too. The old lady slept there, and in the room next to his own, Laura, his sister-in-law, and in the east bedroom downstairs, the young couple. He and Mary had slept there when they were first married, when they were the young couple in the house.

He tried to remember Mary as she must have looked that day he first saw her, the day he arrived from Virginia to open his school in the old office that used to stand there in the corner of the yard. He could see Mr. Allard plainly, sitting there under the sugar tree with his chair tilted back, could discern the old lady — young she had been then! — hospitably poised in the doorway, hand extended, could hear her voice: "Well, here are two of your pupils to start with. . . ." He remembered Laura, a shy child of nine hiding her face in her mother's skirts, but Mary that day was only a shadow in the dark hall. He could not even remember how her voice had sounded. "Professor Maury," she would have said, and her mother would have corrected her with "Cousin Aleck. . . ."

That day she got off her horse at the stile blocks she had turned as she walked across the lawn to look back at him. Her white sunbonnet had fallen on her shoulders. Her eyes, meeting his, had been dark and startled. He had gone on and had hitched both the horses before he leaped over the stile to join her. But he had known in that moment that she was the woman he was going to have. He could not remember all the rest of it, only that moment stood out. He had won her, she had become his wife, but the woman he had won was not the woman he had sought. It was as if he had had her only in that moment there on the lawn. As if she had paused there only for that one moment and was ever after retreating before him down a devious, a dark way that he would never have chosen.

The death of the first baby had been the start of it, of course. It had been a relief when she took so definitely to religion. Before that there had been those sudden, unaccountable forays out of some dark lurking place that she had. Guerilla warfare and trying to the nerves, but that had been only at first. For many years they had been two enemies contending in the open. . . . Toward the last she had taken mightily to prayer. He would wake often to find her kneeling by the side of the bed in the dark. It had gone on for years. She had never given up hope. . . .

Ah, a stouthearted one, Mary! She had never given up hope of changing him, of making him over into the man she thought he ought to be. Time and again she almost had him. And there were long periods, of course, during which he had been worn down by the conflict, one spring when he himself said, when she had told all the neighbors, that he was too old now to go fishing anymore. . . . But he had made a comeback. She had had to resort to stratagem. His lips curved in a smile, remembering the trick.

It had come over him suddenly, a general lassitude, an odd faintness in the mornings, the time when his spirits ordinarily were at their highest. He had sat there by the window, almost wishing to have some ache or pain, something definite to account for his condition. But he did not feel sick in his body. It was rather a dulling of all his senses. There were no longer the reactions to the visible world that made his days a series of adventures. He had looked out of the window at the woods glistening with spring rain; he had not even taken down his gun to shoot a squirrel.

Remembering Uncle Quent's last days he had been alarmed, had decided finally that he must tell her so that they might begin preparations for the future — he had shuddered at the thought of eventual confinement, perhaps in some institution. She had looked up from her sewing, unable to repress a smile.

"You think it's your mind, Aleck. . . . It's coffee. . . . I've been giving you a coffee substitute every morning. . . ."

They had laughed together over her cleverness. He had not gone back to coffee but the lassitude had worn off. She had gone back to the attack with redoubled vigor. In the afternoons she would stand on the porch calling after him as he slipped down to the creek. "Now, don't stay long enough to get that cramp. You remember how you suffered last time. . . ." He would have forgotten all about the cramp until that moment but it would hang over him then through the whole afternoon's sport and it would descend upon him inevitably when he left the river and started for the house.

Yes, he thought with pride. She was wearing him down — he did not believe there was a man living who could withstand her a lifetime — she was wearing him down and would have had him in another few months, another year certainly. But she had been struck down just as victory was in her grasp. The paralysis had come on her in the night. It was as if a curtain had descended, dividing their life sharply into two parts. In the bewildered year and a half that followed he had found himself forlornly trying to reconstruct the Mary he had known. The pressure she had so constantly exerted upon him had become for him a part of her personality. This new, calm Mary was not the woman he had lived with all these years. She had lain there — heroically they all said — waiting for death. And lying there, waiting, all her faculties engaged now in defensive warfare, she had raised, as it were, her lifelong siege; she had lost interest in his comings and goings, had once even encouraged him to go for an afternoon's sport! He felt a rush of warm pity. Poor Mary! She must have realized toward the last that she had wasted herself in conflict. She had spent her arms and her strength against an inglorious foe when all the time the real, the invincible adversary waited. . . .

He turned over on his back again. The moonlight was waning, the contending shadows paler now and retreating toward the door. From across the hall came the sound of long, sibilant breaths, ending each one on a little upward groan. The old lady. . . . She would maintain till her dying day that she did not snore. He fancied now that he could hear from the next room Laura's light, regular breathing and downstairs were the young couple asleep in each other's arms. . . .

All of them quiet and relaxed now, but they had been lively enough at dinner-time. It had started with the talk about Aunt Sally Crenfew's funeral tomorrow. Living now, as he had for some years, away from women of his family, he had forgotten the need to be cautious. He had spoken up before he thought:

"But that's the day Steve and I were going to Barker's Mill. . . ."

Sarah had cried out at the idea. "Barker's Mill!" she had said. "Right on the Crenfew land . . . well, if not on the very farm, in the very next field. It would be a scandal if he, Professor Maury, known by everybody to be in the neighborhood, could not spare one afternoon, one insignificant summer afternoon, from his fishing long enough to attend the funeral of his cousin, the cousin of all of them, the oldest lady in the whole family connection. . . ."

Looking around the table he had caught the same look in every eye; he had felt a gust of that same fright that had shaken him there on the pond. That look! Sooner or later you met it in every human eye. The thing was to be up and ready, ready to run for your life at a moment's notice. Yes, it had always been like that. It always would be. His fear of them was shot through suddenly with contempt. It was as if Mary were there laughing with him. *She* knew that there was not one of them who could have survived as he had survived, could have paid the price for freedom that he had paid. . . .

Sarah had come to a stop. He had to say something. He shook his head.

"You think we just go fishing to have a good time. The boy and I hold high converse on that pond. I'm starved for intellectual companionship, I tell you. . . . In Florida I never see anybody but niggers. . . ."

They had all laughed out at that. "As if you didn't *prefer* the society of niggers!" Sarah said scornfully.

The old lady had been moved to anecdote:

"I remember when Aleck first came out here from Virginia, Cousin Sophy said: 'Professor Maury is so well educated. Now Cousin Cave Maynor is dead who is there in the neighborhood for him to associate with?' 'Well,' I said, 'I don't know about that. He seems perfectly satisfied with Ben Hooser. They're off to the creek together every evening soon as school is out.'"

Ben Hooser. . . . He could see now the wrinkled face, overlaid with that ashy pallor of the aged Negro, smiling eyes, the pendulous lower lip that, drooping away, showed always some of the rotten teeth. A fine nigger, Ben, and on to a lot of tricks, the only man really that he'd ever cared to take fishing with him.

But the first real friend of his bosom had been old Uncle Teague, the factotum at Hawkwood. Once a week or more likely every ten days he fed the hounds on the carcass of a calf that had had time to get pretty high. They would drive the spring wagon out into the lot; he, a boy of ten, beside Uncle Teague on the driver's seat. The hounds would come in a great rush and rear their slobbering jowls against the wagon wheels. Uncle Teague would wield his whip, chuckling while he threw the first hunk of meat to Old Mag, his favorite.

"Dey goin' run on dis," he'd say. "Dey goin' run like a shadow. . . ."

He shifted his position again, cautiously. People, he thought . . . people . . . so bone ignorant, all of them. Not one person in a thousand realized that a foxhound remains at heart a wild beast and must kill and gorge and then, when he is ravenous, kill and gorge again. . . . Or that the channel cat is a night feeder. . . . Or . . . His daughter had told him once that he ought to set all his knowledge down in a book. "Why?" he had asked. "So everybody else can know as much as I do?"

If he allowed his mind to get active, really active, he would never get any sleep. He was fighting an inclination now to get up and find a cigarette. He relaxed again upon his pillows, deliberately summoned pictures before his mind's eye. Land-scapes — and streams. He observed their outlines, watched one flow into another. The Black River into West Fork, that in turn into Spring Creek and Spring Creek into the Withlicoochee. Then they were all flowing together, merging into one broad plain. He watched it take form slowly: the wide field in front of Hawkwood, the Rivanna River on one side, on the other Peters' Mountain. They would be waiting there till the fox showed himself on that little rise by the river. The young men would hold back till Uncle James had wheeled Old Filly, then they would all be off pell-mell across the plain. He himself would be mounted on Jonesboro. Almost blind, but she would take anything you put her at. That first thicket on the edge of the woods. They would break there, one half of them going around, the other half streaking it through the woods. He was always of those going around to try to cut the fox off on the other side. No, he was down off his horse. He was coursing with the fox through the trees. He could hear the sharp, pointed feet padding on the dead leaves, see the quick head turned now and then over the shoulder. The trees kept flashing by, one black trunk after another. And now it was a ragged mountain field and the sage grass running before them in waves to where a narrow stream curved in between the ridges. The fox's feet were light in the water. He moved forward steadily, head down. The hounds' baying grew louder. Old Mag knew the trick. She had stopped to give tongue by that big rock and now they had all leaped the gulch and were scrambling up through the pines. But the fox's feet were already hard on the mountain path. He ran slowly, past the big boulder, past the blasted pine to where the shadow of the Pinnacle Rock was black across the path. He ran on and the shadow swayed and rose to meet him. Its cool touch was on his hot tongue, his heaving flanks. He had slipped in under it. He was sinking down, panting, in black dark, on moist earth while the hounds' baying filled the valley and reverberated from the mountainside.

Mr. Maury got up and lit a cigarette. He smoked it quietly, lying back upon his pillows. When he had finished smoking he rolled over on his side and closed his eyes. It was still a good while till morning, but perhaps he could get some sleep. His mind played quietly over the scene that would be enacted in the morning. He would be sitting on the porch after breakfast, smoking, when Sarah came out. She would ask him how he felt, how he had slept.

He would heave a groan, not looking at her for fear of catching that smile on her face — the girl had little sense of decency. He would heave a groan, not too loud or overdone. "My kidney trouble," he would say, shaking his head. "It's come back on me, daughter, in the night."

She would express sympathy and go on to talk of something else. She never took any stock in his kidney trouble. He would ask her finally if she reckoned Steve had time to drive him to the train that morning. He'd been thinking about how much good the chalybeate water of Estill Springs had done him last year. He might heave another groan here to drown her protests. "No. . . . I better be getting on to the Springs. . . . I need the water. . . ."

She would talk on a lot after that. He would not need to listen. He would be sitting there thinking about Elk River, where it runs through the village of Estill Springs. He could see that place by the bridge now: a wide, deep pool with plenty of lay-bys under the willows.

The train would get in around one o'clock. That nigger, Ed, would hustle his bags up to the boardinghouse for him. He would tell Mrs. Rogers he must have the same room. He would have his bags packed so he could get at everything quick. He would be into his black shirt and fishing pants before you could say Jack Robinson. . . . Thirty minutes after he got off the train he would have a fly in that water.

BARRY HANNAH

All the Old Harkening Faces at the Rail

A FEW OF THE old liars were cranking it up around the pier when Oliver brought his one-man boat out. He was holding the boat in one hand and the motor in the other. Oliver probably went about fifty-seven or eight. He had stringy hair that used to be romantic-looking in the old days. But he still had his muscles, for a short guy.

"What you got there?" said Smokey.

"Are you blind, you muttering old dog? It's a one-man boat," said Oliver. Oliver didn't want to be troubled.

"I seen one of them in the Sears book, didn't I? How much that put you back?"

"I don't recall ever studying your checkbook," said Oliver.

"This man's feisty this afternoon, ain't he?" said a relative newcomer named Ulrich. He was sitting on the rail next to the steps where Oliver wanted to get his boat down them and to the water. For a moment this Ulrich didn't move out of Oliver's way. "You buy it on credit?"

Oliver never answered. He stared at Ulrich until the old man moved, then went down the steps with his little boat to the water and eased the thing in. It was fiberglass of a factory hue that is no real color. Then Oliver went back up the steps where he'd left the motor. It was brand new. He pondered for a moment. Then he pulled the back of the boat up and screwed on the boat clamps of the motor. It was nifty. You had something ready to go in five minutes.

All the old liars were peering over the edge at his operation.

"Don't you need fuel and a battery?" said Smokey, lifting up his sunglasses. One of his eyes was taped over from cataract surgery.

"A man that buys on credit is whipped from the start," said Ulrich.

When Oliver looked up the pier on all the old harkening faces at the rail, he felt young in an ancient way. He had talked with this crew many an evening into the night. There was a month there when he thought he was one of them, with his

hernia and his sciatica, his lies, and his workman's compensation, out here with
his cheap roachy lake house on the reservoir that formed out of the big Yazoo.
Here Oliver was with his hopeful poverty, his low-rent resort, his wife who never
had a bad habit in her life having died of an unfair kidney condition. All it's unfair,
he'd often thought. But he never took it to heart until Warneeta passed over to the
other side.

There was a gallery of pecking old faces scrutinizing him from the rail. Some of
them were widowers too, and some were leaking away toward the great surrender
very fast. Their common denominator was that none of them was honest.

They perhaps had become liars by way of joining the evening pier crowd. One
old man spoke of the last manly war, America against Spain. Another gummed
away about his thirty pints and fifteen women one night in Mexico. Oliver had
lied too. He had told them that he loved his wife and that he had a number of
prosperous children.

Well, he had respected his wife, and when the respect wore off, he had twenty
years of habit with her. One thing was he was never unfaithful.

And he had one son who was the drum major of the band for Lamar Tech in
Beaumont, and who had graduated last year utterly astonished that his beautiful
hair and outgoing teeth wouldn't get him employment.

But now I'm in love, thought Oliver. God help me, it's unfair to Warneeta in the
cold ground, but I'm in love. I'm so warm in love I don't even care what these old
birds got to say.

"Have you ever drove one of them power boats before, son?" This was asked by
Sergeant Fish, who had had some education and was a caring sort of fellow with
emphysema.

Oliver walked through them and back across the planks of the pier to his car that
was parked in the lot at the end. He opened the trunk of his car and lifted out the
battery and the gas can. He managed to hold the marine oil under his armpit. He
said something into the car, and then all the men at the end of the pier saw the
woman get out of Oliver's Dodge and walk to him and pull the marine oil can
from under his arm to relieve the load. She was about thirty-five, lean, and looked
like one of those kind of women over at the Rolling Fork Country Club who might
play tennis, drink Cokes and sit around spraddle-legged with their nooks humped
out aimless.

Jaws were dropped on the end of the pier.

Smokey couldn't see that far and was agitated by the groans around him.

Sergeant Fish said: "My Gawd. It's Pearl Harbor, summer of forty-one!"

When she and Oliver got near enough the liars, they saw her face and it was
cute — pinkish big mouth, a jot pinched, but cute, though maybe a little scarred
by acne.

Oliver rigged up the gas line and mixed the oil into the tank. He attached the
battery cables. The woman sat two steps above him while he did this alone in the

back of the boat. There was one seat in the boat, about a yard wide. Oliver floated off a good bit while he was readying the boat. The woman had a scarf on her hair. She sat there and watched him float off thirty feet away as he was getting everything set. Then he pulled the crank on the motor. It took right up and Oliver was thrown back because the motor was in gear. The boat went out very fast about two hundred yards in the water. Then he got control and circled around and puttered back in.

The woman got in the boat. She sat in Oliver's lap. He turned the handle, and they scooted away so fast they were almost out of sight by the time one of the liars got his tongue going.

"It was Pearl Habor, summer of forty-one, until you saw her complexion," said Sergeant Fish.

"I'll bet they was some women in Hawawyer back then," said the tall proud man with freckles. He waved his cane.

"Rainbow days," lied Fish. "The women were so pretty they slept right in the bed with me and the wife. She forgave me everything. It was just like stroking puppies, all of them the color of a goldfish."

"Can that boat *hold* the two of 'em?" said Smokey.

"As long as it keeps goin' it can," said Ulrich, who featured himself a scientist.

"Oliver got him a babe," said another liar.

"I guess we're all old enough to see fools run their course," said old Dan. Dan was a liar who bored even the pier crowd. He lied about having met great men and what they said. He claimed he had met Winston Churchill. He claimed he was on friendly terms with George Wallace.

"You'd give your right one to have a chance with Oliver's woman, indifferent of face as she is," said Sergeant Fish.

"When the motor ever gives out, the whole thing will sink," said Ulrich.

They watched awhile. Then they all went home and slept.

ZORA NEALE HURSTON

The Gilded Six-Bits

IT WAS A NEGRO yard around a Negro house in a Negro settlement that looked to the payroll of the G. and G. Fertilizer works for its support.

But there was something happy about the place. The front yard was parted in the middle by a sidewalk from gate to doorstep, a sidewalk edged on either side by quart bottles driven neck down into the ground on a slant. A mess of homey flowers planted without a plan but blooming cheerily from their helter-skelter places. The fence and house were whitewashed. The porch and steps scrubbed white.

The front door stood open to the sunshine so that the floor of the front room could finish drying after its weekly scouring. It was Saturday. Everything clean from the front gate to the privy house. Yard raked so that the strokes of the rake would make a pattern. Fresh newspaper cut in fancy edge on the kitchen shelves.

Missie May was bathing herself in the galvanized washtub in the bedroom. Her dark-brown skin glistened under the soapsuds that skittered down from her wash-rag. Her stiff young breasts thrust forward aggressively, like broad-based cones with the tips lacquered in black.

She heard men's voices in the distance and glanced at the dollar clock on the dresser.

"Humph! Ah'm way behind time t'day! Joe gointer be heah 'fore Ah git mah clothes on if Ah don't make haste."

She grabbed the clean meal sack at hand and dried herself hurriedly and began to dress. But before she could tie her slippers, there came the ring of singing metal on wood. Nine times.

Missie May grinned with delight. She had not seen the big tall man come stealing in the gate and creep up the walk grinning happily at the joyful mischief he was about to commit. But she knew that it was her husband throwing silver dollars in the door for her to pick up and pile beside her plate at dinner. It was this way every Saturday afternoon. The nine dollars hurled into the open door, he scurried to a hiding place behind the Cape jasmine bush and waited.

Missie May promptly appeared at the door in mock alarm.

"Who dat chunkin' money in mah do'way?" she demanded. No answer from the yard. She leaped off the porch and began to search the shrubbery. She peeped under the porch and hung over the gate to look up and down the road. While she did this, the man behind the jasmine darted to the chinaberry tree. She spied him and gave chase.

"Nobody ain't gointer be chunkin' money at me and Ah not do 'em nothin'," she shouted in mock anger. He ran around the house with Missie May at his heels. She overtook him at the kitchen door. He ran inside but could not close it after him before she crowded in and locked with him in a rough-and-tumble. For several minutes the two were a furious mass of male and female energy. Shouting, laughing, twisting, turning, tussling, tickling each other in the ribs; Missie May clutching onto Joe and Joe trying, but not too hard, to get away.

"Missie May, take yo' hand out mah pocket!" Joe shouted out between laughs.

"Ah ain't, Joe, not lessen you gwine gimme whateve' it is good you got in yo' pocket. Turn it go, Joe, do Ah'll tear yo' clothes."

"Go on tear 'em. You de one dat pushes de needles round heah. Move yo' hand, Missie May."

"Lemme git dat paper sack out yo' pocket. Ah bet it's candy kisses."

"Tain't. Move yo' hand. Woman ain't got no business in a man's clothes nohow. Go way."

Missie May gouged way down and gave an upward jerk and triumphed.

"Unhhunh! Ah got it! It 'tis so candy kisses. Ah knowed you had somethin' for me in yo' clothes. Now Ah got to see whut's in every pocket you got."

Joe smiled indulgently and let his wife go through all of his pockets and take out the things that he had hidden there for her to find. She bore off the chewing gum, the cake of sweet soap, the pocket handkerchief as if she had wrested them from him, as if they had not been bought for the sake of this friendly battle.

"Whew! dat play-fight done got me all warmed up!" Joe exclaimed. "Got me some water in de kittle?"

"Yo' water is on de fire and yo' clean things is cross de bed. Hurry up and wash yo'self and git changed so we kin eat. Ah'm hongry." As Missie said this, she bore the steaming kettle into the bedroom.

"You ain't hongry, sugar," Joe contradicted her. "Youse jes' a little empty. Ah'm de one whut's hongry. Ah could eat up camp meetin', back off 'ssociation, and drink Jurdan dry. Have it on de table when Ah git out de tub."

"Don't you mess wid mah business, man. You git in yo' clothes. Ah'm a real wife, not no dress and breath. Ah might not look lak one, but if you burn me, you won't git a thing but wife ashes."

Joe splashed in the bedroom and Missie May fanned around in the kitchen. A fresh red-and-white checked cloth on the table. Big pitcher of buttermilk beaded with pale drops of butter from the churn. Hot fried mullet, crackling bread, ham hock atop a mound of string beans and new potatoes, and perched on the windowsill a pone of spicy potato pudding.

Very little talk during the meal but that little consisted of banter that pretended to deny affection but in reality flaunted it. Like when Missie May reached for a second helping of the tater pone. Joe snatched it out of her reach.

After Missie May had made two or three unsuccessful grabs at the pan, she begged, "Aw, Joe, gimme some mo' dat tater pone."

"Nope, sweetenin' is for us menfolks. Y'all pritty lil frail eels don't need nothin' lak dis. You too sweet already."

"Please, Joe."

"Naw, naw. Ah don't want you to git no sweeter than whut you is already. We goin' down de road a lil piece t'night so you go put on yo' Sunday-go-to-meetin' things."

Missie May looked at her husband to see if he was playing some prank. "Sho nuff, Joe?"

"Yeah. We goin' to de ice cream parlor."

"Where de ice cream parlor at, Joe?"

"A new man done come heah from Chicago and he done got a place and took and opened it up for a ice cream parlor, and bein' as it's real swell, Ah wants you to be one de first ladies to walk in dere and have some set down."

"Do Jesus, Ah ain't knowed nothin' 'bout it. Who de man done it?"

"Mister Otis D. Slemmons, of spots and places — Memphis, Chicago, Jacksonville, Philadelphia and so on."

"Dat heavyset man wid his mouth full of gold teeths?"

"Yeah. Where did you see 'im at?"

"Ah went down to de sto' tuh git a box of lye and Ah seen 'im standin' on de corner talkin' to some of de mens, and Ah come on back and went to scrubbin' de floor, and he passed and tipped his hat whilst Ah was scourin' de steps. Ah thought Ah never seen *him* befo'."

Joe smiled pleasantly. "Yeah, he's up-to-date. He got de finest clothes Ah ever seen on a colored man's back."

"Aw, he don't look no better in his clothes than you do in yourn. He got a puzzlegut on 'im and he so chuckleheaded he got a pone behind his neck."

Joe looked down at his own abdomen and said wistfully: "Wisht Ah had a build on me lak he got. He ain't puzzlegutted, honey. He jes' got a corperation. Dat make 'm look lak a rich white man. All rich mens is got some belly on 'em."

"Ah seen de pitchers of Henry Ford and he's a spare-built man and Rockefeller look lak he ain't got but one gut. But Ford and Rockefeller and dis Slemmons and all de rest kin be as many-gutted as dey please, Ah's satisfied wid you jes' lak you is, baby. God took pattern after a pine tree and built you noble. Youse a pritty man, and if Ah knowed any way to make you mo' pritty still Ah'd take and do it."

Joe reached over gently and toyed with Missie May's ear. "You jes' say dat cause you love me, but Ah know Ah can't hold no light to Otis D. Slemmons. Ah ain't never been nowhere and Ah ain't got nothin' but you."

Missie May got on his lap and kissed him and he kissed back in kind. Then he went on. "All de womens is crazy 'bout 'im everywhere he go."

"How you know dat, Joe?"

"He tole us so hisself."

"Dat don't make it so. His mouf is cut crossways, ain't it? Well, he kin lie jes' lak anybody else."

"Good Lawd, Missie! You womens sho is hard to sense into things. He's got a five-dollar gold piece for a stickpin and he got a ten-dollar gold piece on his watch chain and his mouf is jes' crammed full of gold teeths. Sho wisht it wuz mine. And whut make it so cool, he got money 'cumulated. And womens give it all to 'im."

"Ah don't see whut de womens see on 'im. Ah wouldn't give 'im a wink if de sheriff wuz after 'im."

"Well, he tole us how de white womens in Chicago give 'im all dat gold money. So he don't 'low nobody to touch it at all. Not even put dey finger on it. Dey tole 'im not to. You kin make 'miration at it, but don't tetch it."

"Whyn't he stay up dere where dey so crazy 'bout 'im?"

"Ah reckon dey done made 'im vast-rich and he wants to travel some. He says dey wouldn't leave 'im hit a lick of work. He got mo' lady people crazy 'bout him than he kin shake a stick at."

"Joe, Ah hates to see you so dumb. Dat stray nigger jes' tell y'all anything and y'all b'lieve it."

"Go 'head on now, honey, and put on yo' clothes. He talkin' 'bout his pritty womens — Ah want 'im to see *mine*."

Missie May went off to dress and Joe spent the time trying to make his stomach punch out like Slemmons's middle. He tried the rolling swagger of the stranger, but found that his tall bone-and-muscle stride fitted ill with it. He just had time to drop back into his seat before Missie May came in dressed to go.

On the way home that night Joe was exultant. "Didn't Ah say ole Otis was swell? Can't he talk Chicago talk? Wuzn't dat funny whut he said when great big fat ole Ida Armstrong come in? He asted me, 'Who is dat broad wid de forte shake?' Dat's a new word. Us always thought forty was a set of figgers but he showed us where it means a whole heap of things. Sometimes he don't say forty, he 'jes say thirty-eight and two and dat mean de same thing. Know whut he tole me when Ah wuz payin' for our ice cream? He say, 'Ah have to hand it to you, Joe. Dat wife of yours is 'jes thirty-eight and two. Yessuh, she's forte!' Ain't he killin'?"

"He'll do in case of a rush. But he sho is got uh heap uh gold on 'im. Dat's de first time Ah ever seed gold money. It lookted good on him sho nuff, but it'd look a whole heap better on you."

"Who, me? Missie May, youse crazy! Where would a po' man lak me git gold money from?"

Missie May was silent for a minute, then she said, "Us might find some goin' long de road some time. Us could."

"Who would be losin' gold money round heah? We ain't even seen none dese white folks wearin' no gold money on dey watch chain. You must be figgerin' Mister Packard or Mister Cadillac goin' pass through heah."

"You don't know whut been lost 'round heah. Maybe somebody way back in memorial times lost they gold money and went on off and it ain't never been found. And then if we wuz to find it, you could wear some 'thout havin' no gang of womens lak dat Slemmons say he got."

Joe laughed and hugged her. "Don't be so wishful 'bout me. Ah'm satisfied de way Ah is. So long as Ah be yo' husband, Ah don't keer 'bout nothin' else. Ah'd ruther all de other womens in de world to be dead than for you to have de toothache. Less we go to bed and git our night rest."

It was Saturday night once more before Joe could parade his wife in Slemmons's ice cream parlor again. He worked the night shift and Saturday was his only night off. Every other evening around six o'clock he left home, and dying dawn saw him hustling home around the lake, where the challenging sun flung a flaming sword from east to west across the trembling water.

That was the best part of life — going home to Missie May. Their whitewashed house, the mock battle on Saturday, the dinner and ice cream parlor afterwards, church on Sunday nights when Missie outdressed any woman in town — all, everything, was right.

One night around eleven the acid ran out at the G. and G. The foreman knocked off the crew and let the steam die down. As Joe rounded the lake on his way home, a lean moon rode the lake in a silver boat. If anybody had asked Joe about the moon on the lake, he would have said he hadn't paid it any attention. But he saw it with his feelings. It made him yearn painfully for Missie. Creation obsessed him. He thought about children. They had been married more than a year now. They had money put away. They ought to be making little feet for shoes. A little boy child would be about right.

He saw a dim light in the bedroom and decided to come in through the kitchen door. He could wash the fertilizer dust off himself before presenting himself to Missie May. It would be nice for her not to know that he was there until he slipped into his place in bed and hugged her back. She always liked that.

He eased the kitchen door open slowly and silently, but when he went to set his dinner bucket on the table he bumped it into a pile of dishes, and something crashed to the floor. He heard his wife gasp in fright and hurried to reassure her.

"Iss me, honey. Don't git skeered."

There was a quick, large movement in the bedroom. A rustle, a thud, and a stealthy silence. The light went out.

What? Robbers? Murderers? Some varmint attacking his helpless wife, perhaps. He struck a match, threw himself on guard and stepped over the doorsill into the bedroom.

The great belt on the wheel of Time slipped and eternity stood still. By the match light he could see the man's legs fighting with his breeches in his frantic desire to get them on. He had both chance and time to kill the intruder in his helpless condition — half in and half out of his pants — but he was too weak to take action. The shapeless enemies of humanity that live in the hours of Time had waylaid Joe. He was assaulted in his weakness. Like Samson awakening after his haircut. So he just opened his mouth and laughed.

The match went out and he struck another and lit the lamp. A howling wind raced across his heart, but underneath its fury he heard his wife sobbing and Slemmons pleading for his life. Offering to buy it with all that he had. "Please, suh, don't kill me. Sixty-two dollars at de sto'. Gold money."

Joe just stood. Slemmons looked at the window, but it was screened. Joe stood out like a rough-backed mountain between him and the door. Barring him from escape, from sunrise, from life.

He considered a surprise attack upon the big clown that stood there laughing like a chessy cat. But before his fist could travel an inch, Joe's own rushed out to crush him like a battering ram. Then Joe stood over him.

"Git into yo' damn rags, Slemmons, and dat quick."

Slemmons scrambled to his feet and into his vest and coat. As he grabbed his hat, Joe's fury overrode his intentions and he grabbed at Slemmons with his left hand and struck at him with his right. The right landed. The left grazed the front of his vest. Slemmons was knocked a somersault into the kitchen and fled through the open door. Joe found himself alone with Missie May, with the golden watch charm clutched in his left fist. A short bit of broken chain dangled between his fingers.

Missie May was sobbing. Wails of weeping without words. Joe stood, and after a while he found out that he had something in his hand. And then he stood and felt without thinking and without seeing with his natural eyes. Missie May kept on crying and Joe kept on feeling so much, and not knowing what to do with all his feelings, he put Slemmons's watch charm in his pants pocket and took a good laugh and went to bed.

"Missie May, whut you cryin' for?"

"Cause Ah love you so hard and Ah know you don't love *me* no mo'."

Joe sank his face into the pillow for a spell, then he said huskily, "You don't know de feelings of dat yet, Missie May."

"Oh Joe, honey, he said he wuz gointer give me dat gold money and he jes' kept on after me —"

Joe was very still and silent for a long time. Then he said, "Well, don't cry no mo', Missie May. Ah got yo' gold piece for you."

The hours went past on their rusty ankles. Joe still and quiet on one bed rail and Missie May wrung dry of sobs on the other. Finally the sun's tide crept upon the shore of night and drowned all its hours. Missie May with her face stiff and streaked towards the window saw the dawn come into her yard. It was day. Nothing more. Joe wouldn't be coming home as usual. No need to fling open the front door and sweep off the porch, making it nice for Joe. Never no more breakfast to cook; no more washing and starching of Joe's jumper-jackets and pants. No more nothing. So why get up?

With this strange man in her bed, she felt embarrassed to get up and dress. She decided to wait till he had dressed and gone. Then she would get up, dress quickly and be gone forever beyond reach of Joe's looks and laughs. But he never moved. Red light turned to yellow, then white.

From beyond the no-man's land between them came a voice. A strange voice that yesterday had been Joe's.

"Missie May, ain't you gonna fix me no breakfus'?"

She sprang out of bed. "Yeah, Joe. Ah didn't reckon you wuz hongry."

No need to die today. Joe needed her for a few more minutes anyhow.

Soon there was a roaring fire in the cookstove. Water bucket full and two chickens killed. Joe loved fried chicken and rice. She didn't deserve a thing and good Joe was letting her cook him some breakfast. She rushed hot biscuits to the table as Joe took his seat.

He ate with his eyes in his plate. No laughter, no banter.

"Missie May, you ain't eatin' yo' breakfus'."

"Ah don't choose none, Ah thank yuh."

His coffee cup was empty. She sprang to refill it. When she turned from the stove and bent to set the cup beside Joe's plate, she saw the yellow coin on the table between them.

She slumped into her seat and wept into her arms.

Presently Joe said calmly, "Missie May, you cry too much. Don't look back lak Lot's wife and turn to salt."

The sun, the hero of every day, the impersonal old man that beams as brightly on death as on birth, came up every morning and raced across the blue dome and dipped into the sea of fire every morning. Water ran downhill and birds nested.

Missie knew why she didn't leave Joe. She couldn't. She loved him too much, but she could not understand why Joe didn't leave her. He was polite, even kind at times, but aloof.

There were no more Saturday romps. No ringing silver dollars to stack beside her plate. No pockets to rifle. In fact, the yellow coin in his trousers was like a monster hiding in the cave of his pockets to destroy her.

She often wondered if he still had it, but nothing could have induced her to ask nor yet to explore his pockets to see for herself. Its shadow was in the house whether or no.

One night Joe came home around midnight and complained of pains in the back. He asked Missie to rub him down with liniment. It had been three months since Missie had touched his body and it all seemed strange. But she rubbed him. Grateful for the chance. Before morning youth triumphed and Missie exulted. But the next day, as she joyfully made up their bed, beneath her pillow she found the piece of money with the bit of chain attached.

Alone to herself, she looked at the thing with loathing, but look she must. She took it into her hands with trembling and saw first thing that it was no gold piece. It was a gilded half dollar. Then she knew why Slemmons had forbidden anyone to touch his gold. He trusted village eyes at a distance not to recognize his stickpin as a gilded quarter, and his watch charm as a four-bit piece.

She was glad at first that Joe had left it there. Perhaps he was through with her punishment. They were man and wife again. Then another thought came clawing at her. He had come home to buy from her as if she were any woman in the longhouse. Fifty cents for her love. As if to say that he could pay as well as Slemmons. She slid the coin into his Sunday pants pocket and dressed herself and left his house.

Halfway between her house and the quarters she met her husband's mother, and after a short talk she turned and went back home. Never would she admit defeat to that woman who prayed for it nightly. If she had not the substance of marriage she had the outside show. Joe must leave *her*. She let him see she didn't want his old gold four-bits, too.

She saw no more of the coin for some time though she knew that Joe could not help finding it in his pocket. But his health kept poor, and he came home at least every ten days to be rubbed.

The sun swept around the horizon, trailing its robes of weeks and days. One morning as Joe came in from work, he found Missie May chopping wood. Without a word he took the ax and chopped a huge pile before he stopped.

"You ain't got no business choppin' wood, and you know it."

"How come? Ah been choppin' it for de last longest."

"Ah ain't blind. You makin' feet for shoes."

"Won't you be glad to have a lil baby chile, Joe?"

"You know dat 'thout astin' me."

"Iss gointer be a boy chile and de very spit of you."

"You reckon, Missie May?"

"Who else could it look lak?"

Joe said nothing, but he thrust his hand deep into his pocket and fingered something there.

It was almost six months later Missie May took to bed and Joe went and got his mother to come wait on the house.

Missie May was delivered of a fine boy. Her travail was over when Joe came in from work one morning. His mother and the old women were drinking great bowls of coffee around the fire in the kitchen.

The minute Joe came into the room his mother called him aside.

"How did Missie May make out?" he asked quickly.

"Who, dat gal? She strong as a ox. She gointer have plenty mo'. We done fixed her wid de sugar and lard to sweeten her for de nex' one."

Joe stood silent awhile.

"You ain't ask 'bout de baby, Joe. You oughter be mighty proud cause he sho is de spittin' image of yuh, son. Dat's yourn all right, if you never git another one, dat un is yourn. And you know Ah'm mighty proud too, son, cause Ah never thought well of you marryin' Missie May cause her ma used tuh fan her foot round right smart and Ah been mighty skeered dat Missie May wuz gointer git misput on her road."

Joe said nothing. He fooled around the house till late in the day, then, just before he went to work, he went and stood at the foot of the bed and asked his wife how she felt. He did this every day during the week.

On Saturday he went to Orlando to make his market. It had been a long time since he had done that.

Meat and lard, meal and flour, soap and starch. Cans of corn and tomatoes. All the staples. He fooled around town for a while and bought bananas and apples. Way after while he went around to the candy store.

"Hello, Joe," the clerk greeted him. "Ain't seen you in a long time."

"Nope, Ah ain't been heah. Been round in spots and places."

"Want some of them molasses kisses you always buy?"

"Yessuh." He threw the gilded half dollar on the counter. "Will dat spend?"

"Whut is it, Joe? Well, I'll be doggone! A gold-plated four-bit piece. Where'd you git it, Joe?"

"Offen a stray nigger dat come through Eatonville. He had it on his watch chain for a charm — goin' round making out iss gold money. Ha ha! He had a quarter on his tiepin and it wuz all golded up too. Tryin' to fool people. Makin' out he so rich and everything. Ha! Ha! Tryin' to tole off folkses wives from home."

"How did you git it, Joe? Did he fool you, too?"

"Who, me? Naw suh! He ain't fooled me none. Know whut Ah done? He come round me wid his smart talk. Ah hauled off and knocked 'im down and took his old four-bits away from 'im. Gointer buy my wife some good ole lasses kisses wid it. Gimme fifty cents worth of dem candy kisses."

"Fifty cents buys a mighty lot of candy kisses, Joe. Why don't you split it up and take some chocolate bars, too? They eat good, too."

"Yessuh, they do, but Ah wants all dat in kisses. Ah got a lil boy chile home now. Tain't a week old yet, but he kin suck a sugar tit and maybe eat one them kisses hisself."

Joe got his candy and left the store. The clerk turned to the next customer. "Wisht I could be like these darkies. Laughin' all the time. Nothin' worries 'em."

Back in Eatonville, Joe reached his own front door. There was the ring of singing metal on wood. Fifteen times. Missie May couldn't run to the door, but she crept there as quickly as she could.

"Joe Banks, Ah hear you chunkin' money in mah do'way. You wait till Ah got mah strength back and Ah'm gointer fix you for dat."

MADISON JONES

The Fugitives

WALT HEARD THE TRAIN again. He slowed his steps until the clap of his shoes on the pavement was dimmed to a flesh-like padding. It reached him from far off beyond the field where cotton rows merged at a distance and wove a lush unruffled fabric that fanned out wide under the moon to a dark wall of thicket. From so far away the sound was only a wail, almost painful, like the surge of a childhood memory into the heart. It came to him that way often when on summer nights through his open window he heard the trains heading south out of the city. Then he would half rouse from his pillow and follow in spirit over the rolling farm-checkered land, along the delta that bounded the broad untamed river. Then he would think again of Uncle Tad, an old man hunched in a chair gripping a stick between his knees with hands burly as haunches of meat but strangely tender with mottled old-man's flesh. Walt used to sit at his feet. By the hour he sat there and looked up at him while the old man talked, recounting over and over violent tales of the days when he had been a railroad engineer. Walt used to watch his hands gripping the stick like a lever in his engine, growing white about the knuckles when he told about the time his coaches cut loose; or again, when he ran the barricade, how he throttled up his engine as he came on and hit with a force that knocked him half senseless against the iron-studded panel and yet found strength to lean out of the window and wave goodbye to the mob with a big ruddy hand. Walt used to think what those hands had done. And once he brought him an egg to break, long-ways in one hand like Uncle Tad had said he could. But now he said, "No; no more," because the strength had gone from his grip. Walt wanted his hands to be like Uncle Tad's and he used to pull at his fingers thinking that would help them grow, and hold them out ahead of him in the sun trying to make them red. Now they were big, as long as Uncle Tad's, he guessed. But the brawn and the redness were not there. People didn't have hands like his any more. And sometimes at his drafting table he had mused upon it, looking at his hands and at

Walker's next to him that were thin and fragile and capable only of wielding a compass. And then he would think of what they had told him in biology about hands and evolution and he thought about men reverting because they did nothing to develop their hands. Or again, he would look out of the window over the blue tiresome sheet into the sunlight and think of a muscular hand gripping a hot steel lever, whitening at the knuckles, or perhaps twisting a compass about a single finger.

Walt shifted the bag to his other hand and moved on down the empty highway. There had been no car for half an hour. An occasional truck went by droning south to Vicksburg or New Orleans or north Memphis. They wouldn't hail at night. But he didn't care. The air was live and fresh and the pavement stretched away like an unbroken line of soft manila paper. Perhaps he would have to walk all night. It didn't matter. He had a week and some money and a few clothes in the handbag. Maybe he would make New Orleans. It was the going he liked, the feel and privacy of night, the chance he took of catching a ride or being marooned until dawn on the highway. And back home they had no notion of it. By now, his mother was thinking, he was in Nashville at Woody's house asleep. She had kept him at the door what seemed an intolerable time, holding his hand, fondling him with her eyes. When at last he broke away he felt as though he had done her some violence. It made him angry at her. He could feel her eyes as he passed along the hedge, but he did not look back. Perhaps he should have; it did no good to be unkind. They had given him everything; whatever they knew of to do they had done. Except they seemed never to have known, or else to have forgotten, that stifling sense of tedium, of meeting yourself coming back in a tiny circle which was your birthright. And he had inherited a Lilliputian world precisely rendered in minute sketches of bridges and buildings on a sheet of dull blue drawing paper. He could nearly encircle it by extending the arm of his little silver compass. And he had drawn, he knew, a million such circles. They were everywhere in the world, an infinity of circles, only waiting to be drawn. But if you did not draw them — then they were only in the mind; they did not exist. Yet his was drawn already, a little one in which the heart grew calluses from its incessant pounding against the narrow ribs of its cage. The way out was to lower your head and break through and claim your real birthright — the right to draw your own circle, or to draw none at all. And why shouldn't he do that? He was grown now and free and the road stretched out from his feet through a hundred cities where he had never been heard of and nothing was required of him but that he should mind his business. He looked down at his free hand, at the paleness of his outstretched fingers. It was only the wan light, he knew, but somehow the hand looked bigger, broader than before, and harder. He clenched it into a fist and the knuckles, whitening, showed like bulbs of ivory under the moon.

The road curved in a gentle arc and the moon was higher and the shadows not so long as before. Through the cotton to his right an embankment like a tiny levee ran and converged with the road which straightened ahead and paralleled it. On its crest twin rails glimmered away and in the distance came together with a single splash of brightness. Now he was tiring. He sat down, folding his legs up beneath him against the warm pavement. Mosquitoes whined around. One bit his cheek. He slapped it fiercely and got up and went on. There was nothing in sight but fields of cotton. He wondered if he would have to walk all night.

It was late when he saw a town. It lay back from the highway, straggling, still, like a little fortress of impregnable sleep. He stopped at the turn-off where trees cast a ragged shadow. A sign said "Rolling Fork." Up the lane scattered streetlights made vague semicircles on the dark macadam. There was no other sign of life. To try there for a place seemed almost irreverent, as though he would be treading on graves. And besides, it was too late. He stood pondering it, conscious how his legs ached. There was not even a barn nearby. Then his eyes caught something he had not seen before — boxcars, two of them, on the track only a little distance beyond the town.

Somewhere he missed the crossing and had to push through weeds. He felt his pants wet to the hips as he stepped up on the embankment. The boxcar door was sealed. He passed on to the other car. That one too was closed, but he saw that the seal was broken. With his free hand he pushed solidly at the door and it did not budge and he set the bag down and with both hands pulled. The door slid and the rasp of grating steel echoed in the hollow interior. Inside, a rectangle of light extended half across the floor, but beyond, the cargo of darkness seemed piled impenetrably upon itself. He heard no sound from within and about him only the chirping noises of night. He took up the bag and set it inside and tried again to peer through the blackness. His hands rested on the steel sill and he vaulted and stood upright. Here it was still with a silence that muted the pulsing of night beyond. Then he had the feeling of eyes fixed on him out of the dark. Cautiously he turned his head and tried to see into the regions where no light fell. Words formed in his mind. But a timidity restrained him, as though his voice would make a tumult of the silence. He reached for a match. It struck noisily against the cover, but moonlight drowned its glow and he held it far out ahead and inched his way into the darkness. It burned his finger. He dropped it and took another and held it up and struck it. In the first bright flare his eye leaped to a face that watched him from the corner. His pulses sprang; he recoiled and the match fell extinguished from his hand. Half in the light he stood his ground and felt the quick beating of blood in his chest and the scrutiny of eyes from out of the dark. He felt the need for some word or action to break the hold of silence. His own voice startled him.

"I couldn't see you back there. Gave me a start at first." The empty car gave an unfamiliar resonance to his words. He got no answer, but he felt a slack in the tension, as though his speech had thawed a subtle bodiless ice. He waited, listening for some response. Then he said, "Mosquitoes about took me. I thought it'd be better in here." And now he began to wonder. Perhaps it had been his imagination and no one was there at all. He jumped at the sudden voice.

"Air this a town?"

The voice was deep and without inflection, but something in the speech, some uncertain quality, gave him new assurance.

"Just a little village," he said. "This is the road to Vicksburg. We're out on the delta."

He felt a certain awkwardness in his stance and he reached for a cigarette and lit it deliberately and knew that his countenance showed clearly in the blaze of the match. He blew a long puff and watched the smoke vanish into blackness. Then came a sudden rustling and he started again at footsteps which resounded as from a cavern and approached him out of the dark. But he held his ground. He saw a figure, tall, coming into the light. The figure moved past him, an arm's length out, and stopped a little back from the door. Walt turned cautiously and watched him sidelong from his eye. He seemed not to notice Walt's presence. He gazed through the door and out across the delta with the look of a man who watches something far away. He was tall, exceedingly tall. And in the light that reached him he stood with a straightness that seemed unnatural. He appeared to be wrought there, like the far-gazing monuments of soldiers Walt had seen, Confederates mounted on their footings in quiet southern towns. His face looked gaunt, with pockets of shadow settled in hollows beneath the protruding bones. And now Walt was conscious of smoke from his cigarette rising toward the light and the whisper of crickets outside and now, it seemed, a change in that face, a softening. The lips moved barely and the face turned to him. Walt met his gaze and knew that he wasn't afraid any more.

"How far air we from Memphis?" The man's voice had a familiar twang, like the speech of mountaineers Walt had heard over at Lupton's Cove.

"Hundred and fifty miles, I guess. Where are you headed for?"

The man didn't answer for a time. Then,

"A ways on down yet," he murmured.

Walt heard the thin crying of a mosquito and he struck at it with his hand. "I never saw so many of the devils. You can't rest for them out there."

The man didn't reply. He stood there pensively and gazed at the landscape and finally said, "How far's this Vicksburg?"

"I'm not sure. A long way. Seventy miles, I reckon."

"You say that's a town yonder?"

"Yeah. But it's all closed up. It's just a little place."

Again Walt glanced at the face beside him and now he noticed its gauntness, and he wondered if the man was hungry. He had a sandwich in his bag. He hesitated though, waiting for something. Finally he said, "If you're hungry I've got a sandwich you can have. I don't want it."

Walt saw his lips part and an eagerness in his face that touched it with boyishness. He was younger, much younger than he had seemed, Walt's own age perhaps. Walt took the sandwich and put it into the outstretched hand. The man tore it from the paper and ate it savagely. After he had finished he turned his eyes to Walt again and in that instant they caught the moonlight. Walt returned their gaze and he half grinned at the earnest question. There was no mistaking it. He was still a boy. Walt shook his head. "That's all I've got."

The boy smiled a little. "I'm obliged to you." Now his face seemed less grave, as though quickened by something he watched out there. "Do you reckon there's any water here about?"

"I don't know," Walt said. "Unless it's back in that little town."

"Ain't there no creeks?"

"Yeah. But they're not fit to drink, down here in this low country. No telling what you'd catch."

"I've got to have some," he said and stepped to the door and put his hand on the sill and dropped nimbly to the ground. Then he stood motionless outside the car. Walt looked down on his ruffled hair and in the moonlight it seemed to have an auburn tint. It looked like Woody's hair. A truck was passing on the highway a hundred yards beyond and the noisy hum of its engine seemed the only sound in all that still country. The boy was following its progress with a gradual turn of his head. Walt saw that he was waiting.

"Those mosquitoes'll carry you off out there." He thought the boy shifted as though to start and Walt moved forward and came down beside him on the embankment. "Let's go," he said. They started, walking along the embankment. The slope declined from the ends of the crossties and made hard walking and they stepped up onto the track.

"It'd be better down on the road."

For a while the boy didn't speak. Then, "Let's stay up here."

Walt stepped rapidly to keep beside his long striding that covered two ties at a time. He glanced sidelong at him waiting for some apology. But there was none. Gravel crunched beneath their feet. Sometimes a steel track rang from rock they kicked against it. Walt's eyes followed the rails, how they sped away like silver wires into the distance. Now he was sure of it. This boy's was no pleasure jaunt like his own. Why else should he prefer this gravel and ties to the smooth pavement of a highway. And why all that time in a boxcar hungry and thirsty, like a fugitive there in the dark. Maybe that was it. What else would a hill boy be doing there? Walt glanced up suddenly, half expecting to see him anew. But the boy looked far out ahead as though nature steered his feet, and even in the dim light his face seemed full of a strange bright exuberance. Walt watched the ties passing beneath them. Maybe he was right; maybe not. Somehow it didn't matter. Yesterday and what had come before were things shut out by the level horizon that encircled them.

The cotton field to the right never varied and in spite of their rapid walking seemed to have no end. Walt was feeling the weariness he had forgotten. "Let's stop a minute," he said. "I've been walking all night." Walt sat on the track. It was cool and wet with the dew. The boy stood for a time, then seated himself on the opposite track. The mosquitoes were back again. Walt slapped and reached for his cigarettes and held them out and the boy took one and thanked him.

"Smoke's all that'll keep them away," Walt said. He watched the smoke rise thinly from his hand.

"They wasn't hardly this bad back home. 'Less you went down in a hollow." He spoke as though thinking aloud.

"Where do you live?" Walt said.

He hesitated; then, "Point Creek," and then, "It's in Tennessee."

Walt dragged again at his cigarette. "How far is that from Carthage?"

"A right far piece. Fifty mile, I reckon."

After a moment Walt said, "Good fishing up around Carthage. I was up there once."

The boy looked down. "I used to fish all the time in Wolf creek. Used to grab for them — I could catch them, too. Pa said it was 'cause I was so long and gangling I could get back up under them rocks where nobody else couldn't." He paused and a smile was on his lips. "Once I pulled out a snake. Pa said I jumped clean up on the hill." He laughed deep and mellow and Walt laughed too. They were quiet again except for an occasional chuckle from deep inside the boy. Walt blew smoke up into the air. Then the boy looked at him and the moon reflected in his eyes. "Where do you live at?"

"Memphis." The boy seemed to ponder it a moment. "That's a big place," he said. Then he threw down his cigarette. "I got to have some water."

"I could use some myself."

The rest had done Walt good. His legs felt lighter. He caught the swing of his companion's stride, a rhythm like the cadence of marching men. After a long time the boy said, "Don't look like there's no water about."

"Naw it don't. Looks like we'd run on a house or something."

In his mind Walt could picture a spring welling out from rock at the foot of a hill and them on their bellies sucking deep, wetting the ends of their noses. The thought of it made him thirstier. Perhaps the boy too was thinking of a spring where he had drunk back in some mountain hollow. Walt thought how it would look and how pleasant it would be to go with him there and drink from the spring, or grab for fish in the mountain branch. Suddenly the boy began to whistle soft and fine. It was square-dance music, Walt knew; it sounded like "Turkey in the Straw." But he did not know the tune. "What's the name of that?" Walt said.

The boy reflected a moment. Finally, "I've forgot. Pa used to fiddle it all the time."

The tune ran in Walt's head. After a little he was whistling it between his teeth.

"Naw," the boy said. "It goes like this." He whistled a few bars and Walt joined in and then the boy stopped and Walt saw him nodding and heard him say, "Now you got it."

They walked for a long time and once stopped to rest and smoke and the boy sang "Barbara Allen," all of it he could remember, and laughed when he got through. But now their gaiety had passed. The boy was suffering for water, Walt knew, because he kept talking to him about it and twice stopped and pulled blades of the wet grass and put them in his mouth and chewed them. Walt was thirsty too. It had grown upon him in the last hour, as though the boy's thirst had infected him. Then the boy said, "Look," and pointed and Walt saw a roof there at the thicket which bounded the cotton field. They hurried; then they saw that it was a shed without walls and empty.

"Shore we'll find some directly," the boy said. Walt felt his disappointment, its keenness, in the wan hope of his voice.

Still the highway and the open field were on their left, but to the right now a thicket rose and shut out the light but for patches where it broke through the heavy foliage.

"I hear a frog," the boy said. "Must be water." He was right, for now Walt too could hear it. That was the reason for a thicket — because the land was too wet for cotton. "It must be a swamp," Walt said. "We can't drink swamp water."

They went on, peering down into the thicket. Now they heard clearly the frogs, their quiet clamor that swelled and died in a strange grating rhythm, like the pulse of the swamp whose breath reached up and touched their nostrils with its dankness. Here the mosquitoes were worse. Even walking they had to flail at them with their hands. Then, at the thicket's edge where the moon broke through, they saw water, slick and shining under the light. The boy stopped. Quickly Walt said, "You can't drink that. It'll kill you."

"I got to have some water," he said.

"But that stuff's full of fever. It'd be just like drinking poison."

The boy still looked down at it.

"Come on," Walt said. "We're bound to run on a house."

The boy did not answer, only grunted when again Walt warned him against the water. Now they could see that the swamp was not large, that up ahead the thicket broke as abruptly as it had begun onto another field of cotton. Then they saw the stream that fed it, how its bright placid face abruptly vanished into the shadows that darkened the swamp. Ahead it passed under the tracks. Once more Walt set his pace with the boy's, which had quickened at sight of the water.

They stepped onto the bridge and Walt looked down through the ties at the stream. It looked deep. No ripple stirred and the gloss of its surface lay tranquil as ice. Walt tasted the humid air.

"This ain't in the swamp," the boy said.

"It's the same stuff though. Look how still it is."

The boy kept on looking at it.

"Let's go," Walt said. "It'll be day pretty soon. Then we can catch a ride." But his words made him remember.

"Naw," the boy answered. "I got to have some." He started across the bridge and when Walt came up beside him he said, "I got to. I ain't had none since yesterday noon."

Walt followed him down the bank through weeds and onto a clearing beside the stream where someone had watered stock. The boy dropped to his knees and put his hands in the water; mud clouded upward to meet his face. He straightened up again and crawled a little down the bank and leaned out beyond the stance of his spraddled hands. But he paused a moment there above his shadow. Then he began to drink. Walt watched the ripples around his head, how they shimmered the water's face, and he heard the suck of his drinking.

"Don't get too much," Walt said.

The boy did not stop or even seem to hear, as though there was no sound in the world but the noise of water coursing down his throat. Walt went to him and put his hand on his shoulder, the hard muscle that quivered with the strain.

"Don't drink any more."

The boy stopped. Walt looked at his kneeling body, the heaving of his chest, the still head that drooped a little downward toward his shadow with the look of a man in prayer. Now Walt could not hear his breathing any more; only mosquitoes and the witless chorus of frogs. The boy rocked back on his heels and struck at his arm. Walt looked at the water.

"How is it?"

"Better than nothing."

Walt looked at the water, aware that the boy stood up. The coating of light lay like varnish on its pond-quiet face. Looking at the water he heard the boy speak. He answered, "Yeah" and stepped to where the boy had been and knelt and lowered his face. His nose touched warm water; the scent of it rose up rancid and unclean into his nostrils. Beneath his eyes the water was black and lifeless as oil sopping his lips and tongue. He swallowed once, then again. As he came upright he felt the warm languid surge of it downward in his gullet. After a moment it had passed, but he shuddered. He got up and the boy was watching him. Light was in his eyes. They were gray eyes, or seemed to be, gray for looking distances. Walt held out his cigarettes and the boy took one without speaking and Walt lit it for him and then his own.

"Let's get up on the track," Walt said.

The boy sat on the rail beside him. They watched their smoke rising on the windless air. Walt said, "They don't like smoke."

"Naw," the boy answered.

But still Walt could hear mosquitoes about his head and he slapped at his cheek. The boy got up. Walt watched him as he searched about in the weeds and pulled some grass, sage, Walt thought, that looked drier than the rest. He came back with his hands full and arranged it quickly in a criss-cross pile near Walt's feet. He tried to light it, this stem and that, and at length a flame flickered tinily. They nursed it with their breath and bits of grass they dropped on it until a slow flame with gentle hissing consumed its way through the pile.

"That'll fetch them," the boy said.

Walt listened. But now he heard the boy's whistling again, the tune he had whistled before.

"Ain't you going back?" Walt asked.

"Naw. That's the first place they'd look."

"Where you going to?"

The boy threw the stub of his cigarette into the fire. "I don't know. It don't matter. I ain't going back to Nashville."

After a little Walt said, "How long did you have?"

The little blaze was flickering.

"Life."

Walt leaned forward and laid unburnt stems on the flame. They writhed for an instant in the heat, smoking, then caught.

The boy said, "I'd rather be dead than back there." He watched the fire, its fluctuations like bursts of a dying candle. "But I ain't sorry. I give him fair warning — I told him to stay away from there."

The last of the flames swelled to a moment's brightness and reeled and vanished into embers that pulsed still with an inner fire. The smoke still rose. Walt heard only the frogs. He looked down the silver tracks.

"You might go to New Orleans. They'd have a hard time finding you there."

The boy answered, "Yeah" and yawned and in the middle of it said, "Reckon I will," and reached his hands above his head and stretched. Walt yawned too. "Catching, ain't it?" he said.

The smoke, all but a wisp, was gone. Walt saw him start to move and they stood up together and Walt reached for his handbag and stepped off. But the boy was not at his side. Walt turned back and started at the look of him, the fixed body and half-raised hand and his face rigid. The boy turned his back to him.

"What is it?" Walt said.

"Listen."

That tenseness, the set of his body, stopped Walt's own slow breathing.

"Don't you hear it?" the boy whispered.

"No."

"Listen."

Now he heard it, a distance off up the tracks. Then it sounded again, clearer.

"I hear dogs."

The boy didn't say anything. They heard again the throaty yelps coming intermittently — but not a sound like barking. Walt felt the tension, the strain of gazing through light that was too unsure. He heard the hasty whisper that spoke the thought in his mind.

"They ain't no ordinary dogs."

Then Walt pointed, "Look"; he saw it glint an instant under the moon. The boy wheeled. Walt read panic in his face. He had no words, but he seized the boy's arm and the bright eyes fixed on him a wild mute appeal.

"The water," Walt said; "they can't track in the water."

Comprehending, he cut his eyes from Walt's face and bolted into the weeds toward the clearing. Walt started to call and did not. He saw the boy drawing away from him with long bounds of his shifting body; he felt sudden loneliness. The yelp of the dogs, clearer now, was advancing on him. Walt sprang into his wake. Striking the weeds he saw the boy reach the stream; he saw something else, a glimpse screened quickly by his descent, a car crawling lightless along the highway beyond. The boy was in water hip-deep wading on toward the road.

"The swamp," Walt hissed; "they're on the highway." The boy heard and wheeled and lurched back like a man dizzy with turning and sprawled in the water. Trying to run he made his way back to Walt and grasped his arm and "Quiet," Walt said, "they'll hear," and the boy's wide eyes crossed his face and Walt struggled on by his side. Under the bridge they crossed its shadow and came into light again. The water grew deeper. It rose up onto Walt's chest. The boy was gaining on him. Walt let go his handbag. The swamp was ahead with its sudden line of shadow and they began to swim a long silent breast stroke. The boy passed into the shadow first and the light was shorn from his hair. They heard the dogs, clear-voiced, nearer now. They slid on through black slick water that swirled in hollow sucks above their hands and the voice of a million frogs dinned in their ears like soft rhythmic thunder. They made for the bank. Mud like paste gave way under their hands, but a vine was there and they seized it, the boy first, and dragged themselves on wet bellies over the shallow bank. They came upright and the boy led blindly off.

"Keep close to the creek," Walt said. They plowed on half stumbling through sticky mud and vines that caught at their feet or slid wetly across their legs. A glooming light was all around, like a spell misguiding their steps. Walt struck another vine and fell to his knees and got up and went on. They were in water, splashing, tugging against the mud. Someone called. "Wait," Walt said and the boy stopped. Above the sounds of the swamp Walt heard the dogs and then on the bridge behind them the voices of men. They waited. The voices still sounded, but they could not distinguish the words. Suddenly mosquitoes were about them thick as from a hive, brushing against their faces, swarming so that Walt held his breath for fear they would enter his nostrils. He heard the boy say, "God," and start again. But now Walt could feel a difference, a sense of something gone, some unclear haze like departed sleep that left him aware of wretchedness, of sweat and his aching legs, and then, of wonder. It was only this morning — or yesterday — he stood on his own front walk — as though it were someone else, not him, who was fleeing here through the swamp; someone who had no memory of the names of books on his shelf, of Litton's voice, the look of his mother's face. He sank in mud to his shins. He tugged free and plunged on again. Then, "Look yonder," the boy cried. He was right. A rim of clear light was there, dissected by trunks that intervened, but deep like crystal water reaching into the distance. They hurried; then they both stopped together. The men were ahead of them; they knew every swamp and thicket, the lay of every field, the habits of men in flight. "They ain't to the creek yet," the boy hissed and started angling toward the stream. Walt fought the mucky space that grew between them, calling to him as loud as he dared. Then a voice sounded beyond the swamp dead on line of their course. The boy stopped. Another voice back behind them answered. Walt came up beside him. The boy did not look at him.

"They're all around," Walt said. He watched the line of the boy's profile, the swamp light on his face. And again he felt the mosquitoes. Abruptly the boy began to flail with heavy wasteful strokes of his hands.

Walt said, "We can't stay here. It's almost day."

He quit beating the air and stood gently fanning with his hands.

"I'm going to try it — in the cotton yonder."

"You can't," Walt said. "It's too light. And besides — those dogs. Even if they missed —"

"I'm going to try it." The words were a whisper, strained, exhausted. But they did not pass; they whispered themselves like faint echoes inside the cavern of Walt's skull. He could hear nothing, think nothing, but the sound of that whispering. The boy's movement startled him; his mind filled up again. He was following through water half to his knees, through mire that sucked at his shoes and strained hot cramps into the muscles of his thighs. He shielded his face with his arms and broke through the vines; his wrists burned like sores. He felt he was blind, compelled on his course by a kind of groping instinct. Once he came hard against a stump and fell to his hands. He felt cool water on his lips, the muck like a cushion under him. Then ahead he saw light. His eyes searched the rim of the thicket, under the roof of foliage, along black trunks that stood like portals opening onto the field. He saw the boy's head. It was framed black as the trees in a square of light. Walt got up and started. The head had vanished, but he found the boy on his hands and knees in the last edge of the shadows. The boy turned his face to him as he came up and kneeled down. But the boy did not speak. His eyes looked almost white. It was dusk over the field. The moon was in the west the feeble color of milk, hung in the interregnum between day and night. Off somewhere the throaty bark of a dog, then a voice. Nothing stirred. It seemed long.

"Hear the owl?"

Walt wasn't sure the boy had said it. His head was turned away, as stiffly fixed as though he were scenting something. Then Walt saw a man. He was standing hip-deep in cotton a distance down the edge of the thicket. He had a gun.

"The creek," the boy whispered.

"They'll be looking for that," Walt answered.

They began to crawl painfully along the shadow to where it touched on the cotton. They paused. The man had not moved. Even the frogs had stopped. On a line with his eyes the cotton spread out like a glistening turgid lake.

"It's dawning," the boy said. The words came on a faint expiration of breath, like something imagined. The boy was gazing at him. Walt strained to see his face, but only the feeble whiteness of his eyes showed through the blur. He could tell when the eyes closed, deliberately, and opened again and then turned away into the field.

They were crawling in the cotton down a narrow aisle of lumpy dirt and uprooted vegetation that rustled against their arms and legs. For long spaces he held his breath and watched his hands passing one another like pale fragile duck's feet against the dark earth. Sometimes he touched the muddy sole of a shoe and hesitated. Sometimes back behind them there were voices calling. A bird in the swamp shattered the dawn with its raucous cry. He knew that they must hurry. A space grew between him and the shoes. He moved faster. Then a sudden noise startled him to a halt; a white tuft of hair bobbed off through the cotton. The rattling of stalks beat for an agonized moment against the membranes of his ears. He could not move; he felt his heart swelled up tight like stuffing against his ribs. Suddenly behind them came another crashing. He knew that this was it, but he felt only confusion, and feebleness in his muscles. Then a voice, thunderous, challenging. He felt the boy come to his feet, the earth tremble at each quick thud of the ponderous shoes. The voice calling "Halt" and again "Halt" shocked Walt into motion. But a shot answered the upward lurch of his body; the noise like a concussion blew him staggering forward in the tracks of the racing figure. He strained at the yielding dirt. And some hard object, it seemed, probed against the small of his back. Then he could not stand it any more. He dove onto his belly and behind him the voice cracked and then the shot. He heard the boy's body strike the ground, as though the gun had discharged some enormous awkward load of pulp. He bolted forward. He half heard the warning shout and came to his knees by the long still body. The boy was lying face down. An arm was crooked clumsily under him. He had the look of having been dropped there from a great height. But now his body was shuddering. Walt felt sudden panic. He hovered over the boy, forming words with his tongue that did not come out. Then, as suddenly, he felt it was all a ridiculous act and he wanted to shout, "Stop it, stop it." But he could not stand to see him lying like that. With a calm that surprised him he was gently turning the boy onto his back, gently murmuring to him in the accents of a lover. The boy's lips were faintly writhing; there was blood on them and Walt's hand was covered with blood. But he hardly noticed it. With the tail of his shirt he wiped the lips and he wiped dirt from the nostrils and forehead. And all the time those pale lidless eyes stared at him. He tried to look deep into them, past that look of white amazement, down through the channels of his mind. But the whiteness blinded him. The boy's body began to strain; a noise like gargling issued from his throat.

"Turn his head 'fore he chokes," a voice said.

He obeyed, unshaken even by the sudden intrusion of that voice. The mouth was open. The teeth looked nearly scarlet, like dirty rubies. He laid his hand on the boy's dark jacket over the heart. It was wet, grimy; it cleaved like paste to his fingers. He took his hand away. There was a sound of rattling foliage and other voices were around him answering quietly to one another. Then he knew he was being spoken to, querulously. He was answering, not looking up, not even thinking, as though the words came by rote to his tongue. Now others were kneeling beside him. They did not speak for a long time. Then one of them stood up.

"Bring him on," the man said.

Two men seized the boy's long arms and hoisted him. His head flopped back and rolled wandering on his shoulders as he came upright. Walt sprang to him. He shouldered the man aside and took the limp wet arm and encircled his own neck with it. He heard the man curse and another coldly answer him. Then he began to think with a kind of pain at his own heart, "We cannot carry him this way, with a hole through his chest." But as they plodded off and the boy's feet dragged behind him and his head toppled aimlessly on the yielding column of his neck, Walt understood that he carried a corpse.

The east was flaming bright when they got up onto the track. The arm about his neck was sticky, suffocating; his wrist and fingers ached from the grip he held on that dead hand which slipped persistently from his own on a slime of sweat and blood. He felt that he could not get his breath. Some object like a round stone seemed lodged in his gullet, swelling up, pressing the air from his lungs. He tried to swallow it back, but it surged up hot and acid into his throat and drenched his tongue. He vomited, bent under the weight of the body. The heaves came violently, knotting his muscles, straining his entrails dry. He did not know so much of that black water was in him.

It seemed a long time he was on his knees retching. When it ceased he felt too tired to get up. It was as though he had waked up from a drugged uneasy sleep and looked out at a new-risen sun. But one of the men was speaking to him. He got to his feet. The body was stretched out, staring. There were no shadows on the face now. It looked older than it had before, the features not so clean of cut. And deep indentations, like scars, angled down from the flanges of the nose past the open mouth. But more than these, death had frozen the face in a look of dull and wanton brutality. He turned away. He could not help to carry the body any more.

They left him there with one silent man and took the corpse away. He did not look after them. The sun threw coppery spangles into a dusty sky. It promised heat. He felt shattered, as though he had run hard against a barrier of stone. And as he looked up the track which they had come down so lustily last night, he imagined he saw his own figure walking slowly north. At the end of his walk his own front door was standing open and they were watching him approach and the expression on their faces was something between placid satisfaction and mild surprise.

ANDREW LYTLE

Jericho, Jericho, Jericho

SHE OPENED HER EYES. She must have been asleep for hours or months. She could not reckon; she could only feel the steady silence of time. She had been Joshua and made it swing suspended in her room. Forever she had floated above the counterpane; between the tester and the counterpane she had floated until her hand, long and bony, its speckled-dried skin drawing away from the bulging blue veins, had reached and drawn her body under the covers. And now she was resting, clear-headed and quiet, her thoughts clicking like a new-greased mower. All creation could not make her lift her thumb or cross it over her finger. She looked at the bed, the bed her mother had died in, the bed her children had been born in, her marriage bed, the bed the General had drenched with his blood. Here it stood where it had stood for seventy years, square and firm on the floor, wide enough for three people to lie comfortable in, if they didn't sleep restless; but not wide enough for her nor long enough when her conscience scorched the cool wrinkles in the sheets. The two foot posts, octagonal-shaped and mounted by carved pieces that looked like absurd flowers, stood up to comfort her when the world began to crumble. Her eyes followed down the posts and along the basket-quilt. She had made it before her marriage to the General, only he wasn't a general then. He was a slight, tall young man with a rolling mustache and perfume in his hair. A many a time she had seen her young love's locks dripping with scented oil, down upon his collar. . . . She had cut the squares for the baskets in January, and for stuffing had used the letters of old lovers, fragments of passion cut to warm her of a winter's night. The General would have his fun. *Miss Kate, I didn't sleep well last night. I heard Sam Buchanan make love to you out of that farthest basket. If I hear him again, I mean to toss this piece of quilt in the fire.* Then he would chuckle in his round, soft voice; reach under the covers and pull her over to his side of the bed. On a cold and frosting night he would sleep with his nose against her neck. His nose was so quick to turn cold, he said, and her neck was so warm. Sometimes her hair, the loose, unruly strands at the nape, would tickle his nostrils and he would wake up with a sneeze. This had been so long ago, and there had been so many years of trouble and worry. Her eyes, as apart from her as the mirror on the bureau, rested upon the half-tester, upon the enormous button that caught the rose-colored canopy and shot its folds out like the rays of the morning sun. She could not see but she could feel the heavy cluster of mahogany grapes that tumbled from the center of the headboard — out of its vines curling down the sides it tumbled. How much longer would these never-picked grapes hang above her head? How much longer would she, rather, hang to the vine of this world, she who lay beneath as dry as any raisin. Then she remembered. She looked at the blinds. They were closed.

"You, Ants, where's my stick? I'm a great mind to break it over your trifling back."

"Awake? What a nice long nap you've had," said Doctor Ed.

"The boy? Where's my grandson? Has he come?"

"I'll say he's come. What do you mean taking to your bed like this? Do you realize, beautiful lady, that this is the first time I ever saw you in bed in my whole life? I believe you've taken to bed on purpose. I don't believe you want to see me."

"Go long, boy, with your foolishness."

That's all she could say, and she blushed as she said it — she blushing at the words of a snip of a boy, whom she had diapered a hundred times and had washed as he stood before the fire in the round tin tub, his little back swayed and his little belly sticking out in front, rosy from the scrubbing he had gotten. *Mammy, what for I've got a hole in my stummick; what for, Mammy?* Now he was sitting on the edge of the bed calling her beautiful lady, an old hag like her, beautiful lady. A good-looker the girls would call him, with his bold, careless face and his hands with their fine, long fingers. Soft, how soft they were, running over her rough, skinny bones. He looked a little like his grandpa, but somehow there was something missing . . .

"Well, boy, it took you a time to come home to see me die."

"Nonsense. Cousin Edwin, I wouldn't wait on a woman who had so little faith in my healing powers."

"There an't nothing strange about dying. But I an't in such an all-fired hurry. I've got a heap to tell you about before I go."

The boy leaned over and touched her gently. "Not even death would dispute you here, on Long Gourd, Mammy."

He was trying to put her at her ease in his carefree way. It was so obvious a pretending, but she loved him for it. There was something nice in its awkwardness, the charm of the young's blundering and of their efforts to get along in the world. Their pretty arrogance, their patronizing airs, their colossal unknowing of what was to come. It was a quenching drink to a sin-thirsty old woman.

Somehow his vitality had got crossed in her blood and made a dry heart leap, her blood that was almost water. Soon now she would be all water, water and dust, lying in the burying ground between the cedar — and fire. She could smell her soul burning and see it. What a fire it would make below, dripping with sin, like a rag soaked in kerosene. But she had known what she was doing. And here was Long Gourd, all its fields intact, ready to be handed on, in better shape than when she took it over. Yes, she had known what she was doing. How long, she wondered, would his spirit hold up under the trials of planting, of cultivating, and of the gathering time, year in and year out — how would he hold up before so many springs and so many autumns. The thought of him giving orders, riding over the place, or rocking on the piazza, and a great pain would pin her heart to her backbone. She wanted him by her to train — there was so much for him to know: how the south field was cold and must be planted late, and where the orchards would best hold their fruit, and where the frosts crept soonest — that now could never be. She turned her head — who was that woman, that strange woman standing by the bed as if she owned it, as if . . .

"This is Eva, Mammy."

"Eva?"

"We are going to be married."

"I wanted to come and see — to meet Dick's grandmother . . ."

I wanted to come and see her die. That's what she meant. Why didn't she finish and say it out. She had come to lick her chops and see what she would enjoy. That's what she had come for, the lying little slut. The riches acres in Long Gourd valley, so rich hit'd make yer feet greasy to walk over'm, Saul Oberly at the first tollgate had told the peddler once, and the peddler had told it to her, knowing it would please and make her trade. *Before you die.* Well, why didn't you finish it out? You might as well. You've given yourself away.

Her fierce thoughts dried up the water in her eyes, tired and resting far back in their sockets. They burned like a smothered fire stirred up by the wind as they traveled over the woman who would lie in her bed, eat with her silver, and caress her flesh and blood. The woman's body was soft enough to melt and pour about him. She could see that; and her firm, round breasts, too firm and round for any good to come from them. And her lips, full and red, her eyes bright and cunning. The heavy hair crawled about her head to tangle the poor, foolish boy in its ropes. She might have known he would do something foolish like this. He had a foolish mother. There warn't any way to avoid it. But look at her belly, small and no-count. There wasn't a muscle the size of a worm as she could see. And those hips —

And then she heard her voice: "What did you say her name was, Son? Eva? Eva Callahan, I'm glad to meet you, Eva. Where'd your folks come from, Eva? I knew some Callahans who lived in the Goosepad settlement. They couldn't be any of your kin, could they?"

"Oh, no, indeed. My people . . ."

"Right clever people they were. And good farmers, too. Worked hard. Honest — that is, most of 'em. As honest as that run of people go. We always gave them a good name."

"My father and mother live in Birmingham. Have always lived there."

"Birmingham," she heard herself say with contempt. They could have lived there all their lives and still come from somewhere. I've got a mule older'n Birmingham. "What's your pa's name?"

"Her father is Mister E. L. Callahan, Mammy."

"First name not Elijah by any chance? Lige they called him."

"No. Elmore, Mammy."

"Old Mason Callahan had a son they called Lige. Somebody told me he moved to Elyton. So you think you're going to live with the boy here."

"We're to be married . . . that is, if Eva doesn't change her mind."

And she saw his arm slip possessively about the woman's waist. "Well, take care of him, young woman, or I'll come back and han't you. I'll come back and claw your eyes out."

"I'll take very good care of him, Mrs. McCowan."

"I can see that." She could hear the threat in her voice, and Eva heard it.

"Young man," spoke up Doctor Edwin, "you should feel powerful set up, two such women pestering each other about you."

The boy kept an embarrassed silence.

"All of you get out now. I want to talk to him by myself. I've got a lot to say and precious little time to say it in. And he's mighty young and helpless and ignorant."

"Why, Mammy, you forget I'm a man now. Twenty-six. All teeth cut. Long trousers."

"It takes a heap more than pants to make a man. Throw open them blinds, Ants."

"Yes'm."

"You don't have to close the door so all-fired soft. Close it naturally. And you can tip about all you want to — later. I won't be hurried to the burying ground. And keep your head away from that door. What I've got to say to your new master is private."

"Listen at you, Mistiss."

"You listen to me. That's all. No, wait. I had something else on my mind — what is it? Yes. How many hens has Melissy set? You don't know. Find out. A few of the old hens ought to be setting. Tell her to be careful to turn the turkey eggs every day. No, you bring them and set them under my bed. I'll make sure. We got a mighty pore hatch last year. You may go now. I'm plumb worn out, boy, worn out thinking for these people. It's that that worries a body down. But you'll know all about it in good time. Stand out there and let me look at you good. You don't let me see enough of you, and I almost forget how you look. Not really, you understand. Just a little. It's your own fault. I've got so much to trouble me that you, when you're not here, naturally slip back in my mind. But that's all over now. You are here to stay, and I'm here to go. There will always be Long Gourd, and there must always be a McCowan on it. I had hoped to have you by me for several years, but you would have your fling in town. I thought it best to clear your blood of it, but as God is hard, I can't see what you find to do in town. And now you've gone and gotten you a woman. Well, they all have to do it. But do you reckon you've picked the right one — you must forgive the frankness of an old lady who can see the bottom of her grave — I had in mind one of the Carlisle girls. The Carlisle place lies so handy to Long Gourd and would give me a landing on the river. Have you seen Anna Belle since she's grown to be a woman? I'm told there's not a better housekeeper in the valley."

"I'm sure Anna Belle is a fine girl. But Mammy, I love Eva."

"She'll wrinkle up on you, Son; and the only wrinkles land gets can be smoothed out by the harrow. And she looks sort of puny to me, Son. She's powerful small in the waist and walks about like she had worms."

"Gee, Mammy, you're not jealous are you? That waist is in style."

"You want to look for the right kind of style in a woman. Old Mrs. Penter Matchem had two daughters with just such waists, but 'twarnt natural. She would tie their corset strings to the bed posts and whip'm out with a buggy whip. The poor girls never drew a hearty breath. Just to please that old woman's vanity. She got paid in kind. It did something to Eliza's bowels and she died before she was twenty. The other one never had any children. She used to whip'm out until they cried. I never liked that woman. She thought a whip could do anything."

"Well, anyway, Eva's small waist wasn't made by any corset strings. She doesn't wear any."

"How do you know, sir?"

"Well . . . I . . . What a question for a respectable woman to ask."

"I'm not a respectable woman. No woman can be respectable and run four thousand acres of land. Well, you'll have it your own way. I suppose the safest place for a man to take his folly is to bed."

"Mammy!"

"You must be lenient with your Cousin George. He wanders about night times talking about the War. I put him off in the west wing where he won't keep people awake, but sometimes he gets in the yard and gives orders to his troops. 'I will sweep that hill, General' — and many's the time he's done it when the battle was doubtful — 'I'll sweep it with my iron brooms'; then he shouts out his orders, and pretty soon the dogs commence to barking. But he's been a heap of company for me. You must see that your wife humors him. It won't be for long. He's mighty feeble."

"Eva's not my wife yet, Mammy."

"You won't be free much longer — the way she looks at you, like a hungry hound."

"I was just wondering," he said hurriedly. "I hate to talk about anything like this . . ."

"Everybody has a time to die, and I'll have no maudlin nonsense about mine."

"I was wondering about Cousin George . . . if I could get somebody to keep him. You see, it will be difficult in the winters. Eva will want to spend the winters in town. . . ."

He paused, startled, before the great bulk of his grandmother rising from her pillows, and in the silence that frightened the air, his unfinished words hung suspended about them.

After a moment he asked if he should call the doctor.

It was some time before she could find words to speak.

"Get out of the room."

"Forgive me, Mammy. You must be tired."

"I'll send for you," sounded the dead voice in the still room, "when I want to see you again. I'll send for you and — the woman."

She watched the door close quietly on his neat square back. Her head whirled and turned like a flying jennet. She lowered and steadied it on the pillows. Four thousand acres of the richest land in the valley he would sell and squander on that slut, and he didn't even know it and there was no way to warn him. This terrifying thought rushed through her mind, and she felt the bed shake with her pain, while before the footboard the spectre of an old sin rose up to mock her. How she had struggled to get this land and keep it together — through the War, the Reconstruction, and the pleasanter after days. For eighty-seven years she had suffered and slept and planned and rested and had pleasure in this valley, seventy of it, almost a turning century, on this place; and now that she must leave it . . .

The things she had done to keep it together. No. The one thing. . . . From the dusty stacks the musty odor drifted through the room, met the tobacco smoke over the long table piled high with records, reports. Iva Louise stood at one end, her hat clinging perilously to the heavy auburn hair, the hard blue eyes and the voice:

"You promised Pa to look after me" — she had waited for the voice to break and scream — "and you have stolen my land!"

"Now, Miss Iva Louise," the lawyer dropped his empty eyes along the floor, "you don't mean . . ."

"Yes, I do mean it."

Her own voice had restored calm to the room: "I promised your pa his land would not be squandered."

"My husband won't squander my property. You just want it for yourself."

She cut through the scream with the sharp edge of her scorn: "What about that weakling's farm in Madison? Who pays the taxes now?"

The girl had no answer to that. Desperate, she faced the lawyer: "Is there no way, sir, I can get my land from the clutches of this unnatural woman?"

The man coughed; the red rim of his eyes watered with embarrassment: "I'm afraid," he cleared his throat, "you say you can't raise the money. . . . I'm afraid —"

That trapped look as the girl turned away. It had come back to her, now trapped in her bed. As a swoon spreads, she felt the desperate terror of weakness, more desperate where there has been strength. Did the girl see right? Had she stolen the land because she wanted it?

Suddenly, like the popping of a thread in a loom, the struggles of the flesh stopped, and the years backed up and covered her thoughts like the spring freshet she had seen so many times creep over the dark soil. Not in order, but as if they were stragglers trying to catch up, the events of her life passed before her sight that had never been so clear. Sweeping over the mounds of her body rising beneath the quilts came the old familiar odors — the damp, strong, penetrating smell of new-turned ground; the rank, clinging, resistless odor of green-picked feathers stuffed in a pillow by Guinea Nell, thirty-odd years ago; tobacco on the mantel, clean and sharp like smelling salts; her father's sweat, sweet like stale oil; the powerful ammonia of manure turned over in a stall; curing hay in the wind; the polecat's stink on the night air, almost pleasant, a sort of commingled scent of all the animals, man and beast; the dry smell of dust under a rug; the over-strong scent of too-sweet fruit trees blooming; the inhospitable wet ashes of a dead fire in a poor white's cabin; black Rebeccah in the kitchen; a wet hound steaming before a fire. There were other odors she could not identify, overwhelming her, making her weak, taking her body and drawing out of it a choking longing to hover over all that she must leave, the animals, the fences, the crops growing in the fields, the houses, the people in them. . . .

It was early summer, and she was standing in the garden after dark — she had heard something after the small chickens. Mercy and Yellow Jane passed beyond the paling fence. Dark shadows — gay, full voices. *Where you gwine, gal? I dunno. Jest a-gwine. Where you? To the frolic, do I live. Well, stay off'n yoe back tonight.* Then out of the rich, gushing laughter: *All right, you stay off'n yourn. I done caught de stumbles.* More laughter.

The face of Uncle Ike, head man in slavery days, rose up. A tall Senegalese, he was standing in the crib of the barn unmoved before the bush-whackers. *Nigger, whar is that gold hid? You better tell us, nigger. Down in the well; in the far-place. By God, you black son of a bitch, we'll roast ye alive if you air too contrary to tell. Now, listen ole nigger, Miss McCowan ain't nothen to you no more. You been set free. We'll give ye some of it, a whole sack. Come on, now* — out of the dribbling, leering mouth — *whar air it?* Ike's tall form loomed towards the shadows. In the lamp flame his forehead shone like the point, the core of night. He stood there with no word for answer. As she saw the few white beads of sweat on his forehead, she spoke.

She heard her voice reach through the dark — *I know your kind. In better days you'd slip around and set people's barns afire. You shirked the War to live off the old and weak. You don't spare me because I'm a woman. You'd shoot a woman quicker because she has the name of being frail. Well I'm not frail, and my Navy Six ain't frail. Ike, take their guns.* Ike moved and one of them raised his pistol arm. He dropped it, and the acrid smoke stung her nostrils. *Now, Ike, get the rest of their weapons. Their knives, too. One of us might turn our backs.*

On top of the shot she heard the soft pat of her servants' feet. White eyeballs shining through the cracks in the barn. Then: *Caesar, Al, Zebedee, step in here and lend a hand to Ike.* By sun the people had gathered in the yard. Uneasy, silent, they watched her on the porch. She gave the word, and the whips cracked. The mules strained, trotted off, skittish and afraid, dragging the white naked bodies bouncing and cursing over the sod: *Turn us loose. We'll not bother ye no more, lady. You ain't no woman, you're a devil.* She turned and went into the house. It is strange how a woman gets hard when trouble comes a-gobbling after her people.

Worn from memory, she closed her eyes to stop the whirl, but closing her eyes did no good. She released the lids and did not resist. Brother Jack stood before her, handsome and shy, but ruined from his cradle by a cleft palate, until he came to live only in the fire of spirits. And she understood, so clear was life, down to the smallest things. She had often heard tell of this clarity that took a body whose time was spending on the earth. Poor Brother Jack, the gentlest of men, but because of his mark, made the butt and wit of the valley. She saw him leave for school, where he was sent to separate him from his drinking companions, to a church school where the boys buried their liquor in the ground and sipped it up through straws. His letters: *Dear Ma, quit offering so much advice and send me more money. You send barely enough to keep me from stealing.* His buggy wheels scraping the gravel, driving up as the first roosters crowed. *Katharine, Malcolm, I thought you might want to have a little conversation.* Conversation two hours before sun! And down she would come and let him in, and the General would get up, stir up the fire, and they would sit down and smoke. Jack would drink and sing, *If the Little Brown Jug was mine, I'd be drunk all the time and I'd never be sob-er a-gin* — or, *Hog drovers, hog drovers, hog drovers we air, a-courting your darter so sweet and so fair.* They would sit and smoke and drink until she got up to ring the bell.

He stayed as long as the whiskey held out, growing more violent towards the end. She watered his bottles; begged whiskey to make camphor — *Gre't God, Sis Kate, do you sell camphor? I gave you a pint this morning.* Poor Brother Jack, killed in Breckinridge's charge at Murfreesboro, cut in two by a chain shot from an enemy gun. All night long she had sat up after the message came. His body scattered about a splintered black gum tree. She had seen that night, as if she had been on the field, the parties moving over the dark field hunting the wounded and dead. Clyde Bascom had fallen near Jack with a bad hurt. They were messmates. He had to tell somebody; and somehow she was the one he must talk to. The spectral lanterns, swinging towards the dirge of pain and the monotonous cries of *Water,* caught by the river dew on the before-morning air and held suspended over the field in its acrid quilt. There death dripped to mildew the noisy throats . . . and all the white relief parties, moving, blots of night, sullenly moving in the viscous blackness.

Her eyes widened, and she looked across the foot posts into the room. There was some mistake, some cruel blunder; for there now, tipping about the carpet, hunting in her wardrobe, under the bed, blowing down the fire to its ashes until they glowed in their dryness, stalked the burial parties. They stepped out of the ashes in twos and threes, hunting, hunting and shaking their heads. Whom were they searching for? Jack had long been buried. They moved more rapidly; looked angry. They crowded the room until she gasped for breath. One, gaunt and haggard, jumped on the foot of her bed; rose to the ceiling; gesticulated; argued in animated silence. He leaned forward; pressed his hand upon her leg. She tried to tell him to take it off. Cold and crushing heavy, it pressed her down to the bowels of the earth. Her lips trembled, but no sound came forth. Now the hand moved up to her stomach; and the haggard eyes looked gravely at her, alert, as if they were waiting for something. Her head turned giddy. She called to Dick, to Ants, to Doctor Ed; but the words struck her teeth and fell back in her throat. She concentrated on lifting the words, and the burial parties sadly shook their heads. Always the cries struck her teeth and fell back down. She strained to hear the silence they made. At last from a great distance she thought she heard . . . *too late* . . . *too late*. How exquisite the sound, like a bell swinging without ringing. Suddenly it came to her. She was dying.

How slyly death slipped up on a body, like sleep moving over the vague boundary. How many times she had laid awake to trick the unconscious there. At last she would know . . . But she wasn't ready. She must first do something about Long Gourd. That slut must not eat it up. She would give it to the hands first. He must be brought to understand this. But the spectres shook their heads. Well let them shake. She'd be damned if she would go until she was ready to go. She'd be damned all right, and she smiled at the meaning the word took on now. She gathered together all the particles of her will; the spectres faded; and there about her were the anxious faces of kin and servants. Edwin had his hands under the cover feeling her legs. She made to raise her own hand to the boy. It did not go up. Her eyes wanted to roll upward and look behind her forehead, but she pinched them down and looked at her grandson.

"You want to say something, Mammy?" — she saw his lips move.

She had a plenty to say, but her tongue had somehow got glued to her lips. Truly it was now too late. Her will left her. Life withdrawing gathered like a frosty dew on her skin. The last breath blew gently past her nose. The dusty nostrils tingled. She felt a great sneeze coming. There was a roaring; the wind blew through her head once, and a great cotton field bent before it, growing and spreading, the bolls swelling as big as cotton sacks and bursting white as thunderheads. From a distance, out of the far end of the field, under a sky so blue that it was painful-bright, voices came singing, *Joshua fit the battle of Jericho, Jericho, Jericho — Joshua fit the battle of Jericho, and the walls come a-tumbling down.*

FLANNERY O'CONNOR

The Life You Save May Be Your Own

THE OLD WOMAN AND her daughter were sitting on their porch when Mr. Shiftlet came up their road for the first time. The old woman slid to the edge of her chair and leaned forward, shading her eyes from the piercing sunset with her hand. The daughter could not see far in front of her and continued to play with her fingers. Although the old woman lived in this desolate spot with only her daughter and she had never seen Mr. Shiftlet before, she could tell, even from a distance, that he was a tramp and no one to be afraid of. His left coat sleeve was folded up to show there was only half an arm in it and his gaunt figure listed slightly to the side as if the breeze were pushing him. He had on a black town suit and a brown felt hat that was turned up in the front and down in the back and he carried a tin tool box by a handle. He came on, at an amble, up her road, his face turned toward the sun which appeared to be balancing itself on the peak of a small mountain.

The old woman didn't change her position until he was almost into her yard; then she rose with one hand fisted on her hip. The daughter, a large girl in a short blue organdy dress, saw him all at once and jumped up and began to stamp and point and make excited speechless sounds.

Mr. Shiftlet stopped just inside the yard and set his box on the ground and tipped his hat at her as if she were not in the least afflicted; then he turned toward the old woman and swung the hat all the way off. He had long black slick hair that hung flat from a part in the middle to beyond the tips of his ears on either side. His face descended in forehead for more than half its length and ended suddenly with his features just balanced over a jutting steeltrap jaw. He seemed to be a young man but he had a look of composed dissastisfaction as if he understood life thoroughly.

"Good evening," the old woman said. She was about the size of a cedar fence post and she had a man's gray hat pulled down low over her head.

The tramp stood looking at her and didn't answer. He turned his back and faced the sunset. He swung both his whole and his short arm up slowly so that they indicated an expanse of sky and his figure formed a crooked cross. The old woman watched him with her arms folded across her chest as if she were the owner of the sun, and the daughter watched, her head thrust forward and her fat helpless hands hanging at the wrists. She had long pink-gold hair and eyes as blue as a peacock's neck.

He held the pose for almost fifty seconds and then he picked up his box and came on to the porch and dropped down on the bottom step. "Lady," he said in a firm nasal voice, "I'd give a fortune to live where I could see me a sun do that every evening."

"Does it every evening," the old woman said and sat back down. The daughter sat down too and watched him with a cautious sly look as if he were a bird that had come up very close. He leaned to one side, rooting in his pants pocket, and in a second he brought out a package of chewing gum and offered her a piece. She took it and unpeeled it and began to chew without taking her eyes off him. He offered the old woman a piece but she only raised her upper lip to indicate she had no teeth.

Mr. Shiftlet's pale sharp glance had already passed over everything in the yard — the pump near the corner of the house and the big fig tree that three or four chickens were preparing to roost in — and had moved to a shed where he saw the square rusted back of an automobile. "You ladies drive?" he asked.

"That car ain't run in fifteen year," the old woman said. "The day my husband died, it quit running."

"Nothing is like it used to be, lady," he said. "The world is almost rotten."

"That's right," the old woman said. "You from around here?"

"Name Tom T. Shiftlet," he murmured, looking at the tires.

"I'm pleased to meet you," the old woman said. "Name Lucynell Crater and daughter Lucynell Crater. What you doing around here, Mr. Shiftlet?"

He judged the car to be about a 1928 or '29 Ford. "Lady," he said, and turned and gave her his full attention, "lemme tell you something. There's one of these doctors in Atlanta that's taken a knife and cut the human heart — the human heart," he repeated, leaning forward, "out of a man's chest and held it in his hand," and he held his hand out, palm up, as if it were slightly weighted with the human heart, "and studied it like it was a day-old chicken, and lady," he said, allowing a long significant pause in which his head slid forward and his clay-colored eyes brightened, "he don't know no more about it than you or me."

"That's right," the old woman said.

"Why, if he was to take that knife and cut into every corner of it, he still wouldn't know no more than you or me. What you want to bet?"

"Nothing," the old woman said wisely. "Where you come from, Mr. Shiftlet?"

He didn't answer. He reached into his pocket and brought out a sack of tobacco and a package of cigarette papers and rolled himself a cigarette, expertly with one hand, and attached it in a hanging position to his upper lip. Then he took a box of wooden matches from his pocket and struck one on his shoe. He held the burning match as if he were studying the mystery of flame while it traveled dangerously toward his skin. The daughter began to make loud noises and to point to his hand and shake her finger at him, but when the flame was just before touching him, he leaned down with his hand cupped over it as if he were going to set fire to his nose and lit the cigarette.

He flipped away the dead match and blew a stream of gray into the evening. A sly look came over his face. "Lady," he said, "nowadays, people'll do anything anyways. I can tell you my name is Tom T. Shiftlet and I come from Tarwater, Tennessee, but you never have seen me before: how you know I ain't lying? How you know my name ain't Aaron Sparks, lady, and I come from Singleberry, Georgia, or how you know it's not George Speeds and I come from Lucy, Alabama, or how you know I ain't Thompson Bright from Toolafalls, Mississippi?"

"I don't know nothing about you," the old woman muttered, irked.

"Lady," he said, "people don't care how they lie. Maybe the best I can tell you is, I'm a man; but listen lady," he said and paused and made his tone more ominous still, "what is a man?"

The old woman began to gum a seed. "What you carry in that tin box, Mr. Shiftlet?" she asked.

"Tools," he said, put back. "I'm a carpenter."

"Well, if you come out here to work, I'll be able to feed you and give you a place to sleep but I can't pay. I'll tell you that before you begin," she said.

There was no answer at once and no particular expression on his face. He leaned back against the two-by-four that helped support the porch roof. "Lady," he said slowly, "there's some men that some things mean more to them than money." The old woman rocked without comment and the daughter watched the trigger that moved up and down in his neck. He told the old woman then that all most people were interested in was money, but he asked what a man was made for. He asked her if a man was made for money, or what. He asked her what she thought she was made for but she didn't answer, she only sat rocking and wondered if a one-armed man could put a new roof on her garden house. He asked a lot of questions that she didn't answer. He told her that he was twenty-eight years old and had lived a varied life. He had been a gospel singer, a foreman on the railroad, an assistant in an undertaking parlor, and he come over the radio for three months with Uncle Roy and his Red Creek Wranglers. He said he had fought and bled in the Arm Service of his country and visited every foreign land and that everywhere he had seen people that didn't care if they did a thing one way or another. He said he hadn't been raised thataway.

A fat yellow moon appeared in the branches of the fig tree as if it were going to roost there with the chickens. He said that a man had to escape to the country to see the world whole and that he wished he lived in a desolate place like this where he could see the sun go down every evening like God made it to do.

"Are you married or are you single?" the old woman asked.

There was a long silence. "Lady," he asked finally, "where would you find you an innocent woman today? I wouldn't have any of this trash I could just pick up."

The daughter was leaning very far down, hanging her head almost between her knees watching him through a triangular door she had made in her overturned hair; and she suddenly fell in a heap on the floor and began to whimper. Mr. Shiftlet straightened her out and helped her get back in the chair.

"Is she your baby girl?" he asked.

"My only," the old woman said "and she's the sweetest girl in the world. I would give her up for nothing on earth. She's smart too. She can sweep the floor, cook, wash, feed the chickens, and hoe. I wouldn't give her up for a casket of jewels."

"No," he said kindly, "don't ever let any man take her away from you."

"Any man come after her," the old woman said, " 'll have to stay around the place."

Mr. Shiftlet's eye in the darkness was focused on a part of the automobile bumper that glittered in the distance. "Lady," he said, jerking his short arm up as if he could point with it to her house and yard and pump, "there ain't a broken thing on this plantation that I couldn't fix for you, one-arm jackleg or not. I'm a man," he said with a sullen dignity, "even if I ain't a whole one. I got," he said, tapping his knuckles on the floor to emphasize the immensity of what he was going to say, "a moral intelligence!" and his face pierced out of the darkness into a shaft of doorlight and he stared at her as if he were astonished himself at this impossible truth.

The old woman was not impressed with the phrase. "I told you you could hang around and work for food," she said, "if you don't mind sleeping in that car yonder."

"Why listen, lady," he said with a grin of delight, "the monks of old slept in their coffins!"

"They wasn't as advanced as we are," the old woman said.

The next morning he began on the roof of the garden house while Lucynell, the daughter, sat on a rock and watched him work. He had not been around a week before the change he had made in the place was apparent. He had patched the front and back steps, built a new hog pen, restored a fence, and taught Lucynell, who was completely deaf and had never said a word in her life, to say the word "bird." The big rosy-faced girl followed him everywhere, saying "Burrttddt ddbirrrttdt," and clapping her hands. The old woman watched from a distance, secretly pleased. She was ravenous for a son-in-law.

Mr. Shiftlet slept on the hard narrow back seat of the car with his feet out the side window. He had his razor and a can of water on a crate that served him as a bedside table and he put up a piece of mirror against the back glass and kept his coat neatly on a hanger that he hung over one of the windows.

In the evenings he sat on the steps and talked while the old woman and Lucynell rocked violently in their chairs on either side of him. The old woman's three mountains were black against the dark blue sky and were visited off and on by various planets and by the moon after it had left the chickens. Mr. Shiftlet pointed out that the reason he had improved this plantation was because he had taken a personal interest in it. He said he was even going to make the automobile run.

He had raised the hood and studied the mechanism and he said he could tell that the car had been built in the days when cars were really built. You take now, he said, one man puts in one bolt and another man puts in another bolt and another man puts in another bolt so that it's a man for a bolt. That's why you have to pay so much for a car: you're paying all those men. Now if you didn't have to pay but one man, you could get you a cheaper car and one that had had a personal interest taken in it, and it would be a better car. The old woman agreed with him that this was so.

Mr. Shiftlet said that the trouble with the world was that nobody cared, or stopped and took any trouble. He said he never would have been able to teach Lucynell to say a word if he hadn't cared and stopped long enough.

"Teach her to say something else," the old woman said.

"What you want her to say next?" Mr. Shiftlet asked.

The old woman's smile was broad and toothless and suggestive. "Teach her to say 'sugarpie,'" she said.

Mr. Shiftlet already knew what was on her mind.

The next day he began to tinker with the automobile and that evening he told her that if she would buy a fan belt, he would be able to make the car run.

The old woman said she would give him the money. "You see that girl yonder?" she asked, pointing to Lucynell who was sitting on the floor a foot away, watching him, her eyes blue even in the dark. "If it was ever a man wanted to take her away, I would say, 'No man on earth is going to take that sweet girl of mine away from me!' but if he was to say, 'Lady, I don't want to take her away, I want her right here,' I would say, 'Mister, I don't blame you none. I wouldn't pass up a chance to live in a permanent place and get the sweetest girl in the world myself. You ain't no fool,' I would say."

"How old is she?" Mr. Shiftlet asked casually.

"Fifteen, sixteen," the old woman said. The girl was nearly thirty but because of her innocence it was impossible to guess.

"It would be a good idea to paint it too," Mr. Shiftlet remarked. "You don't want it to rust out."

"We'll see about that later," the old woman said.

The next day he walked into town and returned with the parts he needed and a can of gasoline. Late in the afternoon, terrible noises issued from the shed and the old woman rushed out of the house, thinking Lucynell was somewhere having a fit. Lucynell was sitting on a chicken crate, stamping her feet and screaming, "Burrddttt! bddurrddtttt!" but her fuss was drowned out by the car. With a volley of blasts it emerged from the shed, moving in a fierce and stately way. Mr. Shiftlet was in the driver's seat, sitting very erect. He had an expression of serious modesty on his face as if he had just raised the dead.

That night, rocking on the porch, the old woman began her business, at once. "You want you an innocent woman, don't you?" she asked sympathetically. "You don't want none of this trash."

"No'm, I don't," Mr. Shiftlet said.

"One that can't talk," she continued, "can't sass you back or use foul language. That's the kind for you to have. Right there," and she pointed to Lucynell sitting cross-legged in her chair, holding both feet in her hands.

"That's right," he admitted. "She wouldn't give me any trouble."

"Saturday," the old woman said, "you and her and me can drive into town and get married."

Mr. Shiftlet eased his position on the steps.

"I can't get married right now," he said. "Everything you want to do takes money and I ain't got any."

"What you need with money?" she asked.

"It takes money," he said. "Some people'll do anything anyhow these days, but the way I think, I wouldn't marry no woman that I couldn't take on a trip like she was somebody. I mean take her to a hotel and treat her. I wouldn't marry the Duchesser Windsor," he said firmly, "unless I could take her to a hotel and giver something good to eat.

"I was raised thataway and there ain't a thing I can do about it. My old mother taught me how to do."

"Lucynell don't even know what a hotel is," the old woman muttered. "Listen here, Mr. Shiftlet," she said, sliding forward in her chair, "you'd be getting a permanent house and a deep well and the most innocent girl in the world. You don't need no money. Lemme tell you something: there ain't any place in the world for a poor disabled friendless drifting man."

The ugly words settled in Mr. Shiftlet's head like a group of buzzards in the top of a tree. He didn't answer at once. He rolled himself a cigarette and lit it and then he said in an even voice, "Lady, a man is divided into two parts, body and spirit."

The old woman clamped her gums together.

"A body and a spirit," he repeated. "The body, lady, is like a house: it don't go anywhere; but the spirit, lady, is like a automobile: always on the move, always . . ."

"Listen, Mr. Shiftlet," she said, "my well never goes dry and my house is always warm in the winter and there's no mortgage on a thing about this place. You can go to the courthouse and see for yourself. And yonder under that shed is a fine automobile." She laid the bait carefully. "You can have it painted by Saturday. I'll pay for the paint."

In the darkness, Mr. Shiftlet's smile stretched like a weary snake waking up by a fire. After a second he recalled himself and said, "I'm only saying a man's spirit means more to him than anything else. I would have to take my wife off for the weekend without no regards at all for cost. I got to follow where my spirit says to go."

"I'll give you fifteen dollars for a weekend trip," the old woman said in a crabbed voice. "That's the best I can do."

"That wouldn't hardly pay for more than the gas and the hotel," he said. "It wouldn't feed her."

"Seventeen-fifty," the old woman said. "That's all I got so it isn't any use you trying to milk me. You can take a lunch."

Mr. Shiftlet was deeply hurt by the world "milk." He didn't doubt that she had more money sewed up in her mattress but he had already told her he was not interested in her money. "I'll make that do," he said and rose and walked off without treating with her further.

On Saturday the three of them drove into town in the car that the paint had barely dried on and Mr. Shiftlet and Lucynell were married in the Ordinary's office while the old woman witnessed. As they came out of the courthouse, Mr. Shiftlet began twisting his neck in his collar. He looked morose and bitter as if he had been insulted while someone held him. "That didn't satisfy me none," he said. "That was just something a woman in an office did, nothing but paper work and blood tests. What do they know about my blood? If they was to take my heart and cut it out," he said, "they wouldn't know a thing about me. It didn't satisfy me at all."

"It satisfied the law," the old woman said sharply.

"The law," Mr. Shiftlet said and spit. "It's the law that don't satisfy me."

He had painted the car dark green with a yellow band around it just under the windows. The three of them climbed in the front seat and the old woman said, "Don't Lucynell look pretty? Looks like a baby doll." Lucynell was dressed up in a white dress that her mother had uprooted from a trunk and there was a Panama hat on her head with a bunch of red wooden cherries on the brim. Every now and then her placid expression was changed by a sly isolated little thought like a shoot of green in the desert. "You got a prize!" the old woman said.

Mr. Shiftlet didn't even look at her.

They drove back to the house to let the old woman off and pick up the lunch. When they were ready to leave, she stood staring in the window of the car, with her fingers clenched around the glass. Tears began to seep sideways out of her eyes and run along the dirty creases in her face. "I ain't ever been parted with her for two days before," she said.

Mr. Shiftlet started the motor.

"And I wouldn't let no man have her but you because I seen you would do right. Good-by, Sugarbaby," she said, clutching at the sleeve of the white dress. Lucynell looked straight at her and didn't seem to see her there at all. Mr. Shiftlet eased the car forward so that she had to move her hands.

The early afternoon was clear and open and surrounded by pale blue sky. Although the car would go only thirty miles an hour, Mr. Shiftlet imagined a terrific climb and dip and swerve that went entirely to his head so that he forgot his morning bitterness. He had always wanted an automobile but he had never been able to afford one before. He drove very fast because he wanted to make Mobile by nightfall.

Occasionally he stopped his thoughts long enough to look at Lucynell in the seat beside him. She had eaten the lunch as soon as they were out of the yard and now she was pulling the cherries off the hat one by one and throwing them out the window. He became depressed in spite of the car. He had driven about a hundred miles when he decided that she must be hungry again and at the next small town they came to, he stopped in front of an aluminum-painted eating place called The Hot Spot and took her in and ordered her a plate of ham and grits. The ride had made her sleepy and as soon as she got up on the stool, she rested her head on the counter and shut her eyes. There was no one in The Hot Spot but Mr. Shiftlet and the boy behind the counter, a pale youth with a greasy rag hung over his shoulder. Before he could dish up the food, she was snoring gently.

"Give it to her when she wakes up," Mr. Shiftlet said. "I'll pay for it now."

The boy bent over her and stared at the long pink-gold hair and the half-shut sleeping eyes. Then he looked up and stared at Mr. Shiftlet. "She looks like an angel of Gawd," he murmured.

"Hitchhiker," Mr. Shiftlet explained. "I can't wait. I got to make Tuscaloosa."

The boy bent over again and very carefully touched his finger to a strand of the golden hair and Mr. Shiftlet left.

He was more depressed than ever as he drove on by himself. The late afternoon had grown hot and sultry and the country had flattened out. Deep in the sky a storm was preparing very slowly and without thunder as if it meant to drain every drop of air from the earth before it broke. There were times when Mr. Shiftlet preferred not to be alone. He felt too that a man with a car had a responsibility to others and he kept his eye out for a hitchhiker. Occasionally he saw a sign that warned: "Drive carefully. The life you save may be your own."

The narrow road dropped off on either side into dry fields and here and there a shack or a filling station stood in a clearing. The sun began to set directly in front of the automobile. It was a reddening ball that through his windshield was slightly flat on the bottom and top. He saw a boy in overalls and a gray hat standing on the edge of the road and he slowed the car down and stopped in front of him. The boy didn't have his hand raised to thumb the ride, he was only standing there, but he had a small cardboard suitcase and his hat was set on his head in a way to indicate that he had left somewhere for good. "Son," Mr. Shiftlet said, "I see you want a ride."

The boy didn't say he did or he didn't but he opened the door of the car and got in, and Mr. Shiftlet started driving again. The child held the suitcase on his lap and folded his arms on top of it. He turned his head and looked out the window away from Mr. Shiftlet. Mr. Shiftlet felt oppressed. "Son," he said after a minute, "I got the best old mother in the world so I reckon you only got the second best."

The boy gave him a quick dark glance and then turned his face back out the window.

"It's nothing so sweet," Mr. Shiftlet continued, "as a boy's mother. She taught him his first prayers at her knee, she give him love when no other would, she told him what was right and what wasn't, and she seen that he done the right thing. Son," he said, "I never rued a day in my life like the one I rued when I left that old mother of mine."

The boy shifted in his seat but he didn't look at Mr. Shiftlet. He unfolded his arms and put one hand on the door handle.

"My mother was a angel of Gawd," Mr. Shiftlet said in a very strained voice. "He took her from heaven and giver to me and I left her." His eyes were instantly clouded over with a mist of tears. The car was barely moving.

The boy turned angrily in the seat. "You go to the devil!" he cried. "My old woman is a flea bag and yours is a stinking pole cat!" and with that he flung the door open and jumped out with his suitcase into the ditch.

Mr. Shiftlet was so shocked that for about a hundred feet he drove along slowly with the door still open. A cloud, the exact color of the boy's hat and shaped like a turnip, had descended over the sun, and another, worse looking, crouched behind the car. Mr. Shiftlet felt that the rottenness of the world was about to engulf him. He raised his arm and let it fall again to his breast. "Oh Lord!" he prayed. "Break forth and wash the slime from this earth!"

The turnip continued slowly to descend. After a few minutes there was a guffawing peal of thunder from behind and fantastic raindrops, like tin-can tops, crashed over the rear of Mr. Shiftlet's car. Very quickly he stepped on the gas and with his stump sticking out the window he raced the galloping shower into Mobile.

KATHERINE ANNE PORTER

The Jilting of
Granny Weatherall

SHE FLICKED HER WRIST neatly out of Doctor Harry's pudgy careful fingers and pulled the sheet up to her chin. The brat ought to be in knee breeches. Doctoring around the country with spectacles on his nose! "Get along now, take your schoolbooks and go. There's nothing wrong with me."

Doctor Harry spread a warm paw like a cushion on her forehead where the forked green vein danced and made her eyelids twitch. "Now, now, be a good girl, and we'll have you up in no time."

"That's no way to speak to a woman nearly eighty years old just because she's down. I'd have you respect your elders, young man."

"Well, Missy, excuse me." Doctor Harry patted her cheek. "But I've got to warn you, haven't I? You're a marvel, but you must be careful or you're going to be good and sorry."

"Don't tell me what I'm going to be. I'm on my feet now, morally speaking. It's Cornelia. I had to go to bed to get rid of her."

Her bones felt loose, and floated around in her skin, and Doctor Harry floated like a balloon around the foot of the bed. He floated and pulled down his waistcoat and swung his glasses on a cord. "Well, stay where you are, it certainly can't hurt you."

"Get along and doctor your sick," said Granny Weatherall. "Leave a well woman alone. I'll call for you when I want you. . . . Where were you forty years ago when I pulled through milk-leg and double pneumonia? You weren't even born. Don't let Cornelia lead you on," she shouted, because Doctor Harry appeared to float up to the ceiling and out. "I pay my own bills, and I don't throw my money away on nonsense!"

She meant to wave good-by, but it was too much trouble. Her eyes closed of themselves, it was like a dark curtain drawn around the bed. The pillow rose and floated under her, pleasant as a hammock in a light wind. She listened to the leaves rustling outside the window. No, somebody was swishing newspapers: no, Cornelia and Doctor Harry were whispering together. She leaped broad awake, thinking they whispered in her ear.

"She was never like this, *never* like this!" "Well, what can we expect?" "Yes, eighty years old. . . ."

Well, and what if she was? She still had ears. It was like Cornelia to whisper around doors. She always kept things secret in such a public way. She was always being tactful and kind. Cornelia was dutiful; that was the trouble with her. Dutiful and good: "So good and dutiful," said Granny, "that I'd like to spank her." She saw herself spanking Cornelia and making a fine job of it.

"What'd you say, Mother?"

Granny felt her face tying up in hard knots.

"Can't a body think, I'd like to know?"

"I thought you might want something."

"I do. I want a lot of things. First off, go away and don't whisper."

She lay and drowsed, hoping in her sleep that the children would keep out and let her rest a minute. It had been a long day. Not that she was tired. It was always pleasant to snatch a minute now and then. There was always so much to be done, let me see: tomorrow.

Tomorrow was far away and there was nothing to trouble about. Things were finished somehow when the time came; thank God there was always a little margin over for peace: then a person could spread out the plan of life and tuck in the edges orderly. It was good to have everything clean and folded away, with the hair brushes and tonic bottles sitting straight on the white embroidered linen: the day started without fuss and the pantry shelves laid out with rows of jelly glasses and brown jugs and white stone-china jars with blue whirligigs and words painted on them: coffee, tea, sugar, ginger, cinnamon, allspice: and the bronze clock with the lion on top nicely dusted off. The dust that lion could collect in twenty-four hours! The box in the attic with all those letters tied up, well, she'd have to go through that tomorrow. All those letters — George's letters and John's letters and her letters to them both — lying around for the children to find afterwards made her uneasy. Yes, that would be tomorrow's business. No use to let them know how silly she had been once.

While she was rummaging around she found death in her mind and it felt clammy and unfamiliar. She had spent so much time preparing for death there was no need for bringing it up again. Let it take care of itself now. When she was sixty she had felt very old, finished, and went around making farewell trips to see her children and grandchildren, with a secret in her mind: This is the very last of your mother, children! Then she made her will and came down with a long fever. That was all just a notion like a lot of other things, but it was lucky too, for she had once for all got over the idea of dying for a long time. Now she couldn't be worried. She hoped she had better sense now. Her father had lived to be one hundred and two years old and had drunk a noggin of strong hot toddy on his last birthday. He told the reporters it was his daily habit, and he owed his long life to that. He had made quite a scandal and was very pleased about it. She believed she'd just plague Cornelia a little.

"Cornelia! Cornelia!" No footsteps, but a sudden hand on her cheek. "Bless you, where have you been?"

"Here, Mother."

"Well, Cornelia, I want a noggin of hot toddy."

"Are you cold, darling?"

"I'm chilly, Cornelia. Lying in bed stops the circulation. I must have told you that a thousand times."

Well, she could just hear Cornelia telling her husband that Mother was getting a little childish and they'd have to humor her. The thing that most annoyed her was that Cornelia thought she was deaf, dumb, and blind. Little hasty glances and tiny gestures tossed around her and over her head saying, "Don't cross her, let her have her way, she's eighty years old," and she sitting there as if she lived in a thin glass cage. Sometimes Granny almost made up her mind to pack up and move back to her own house where nobody could remind her every minute that she was old. Wait, wait, Cornelia, till your own children whisper behind your back!

In her day she had kept a better house and had got more work done. She wasn't too old yet for Lydia to be driving eighty miles for advice when one of the children jumped the track, and Jimmy still dropped in and talked things over: "Now, Mammy, you've a good business head, I want to know what you think of this? . . ." Old. Cornelia couldn't change the furniture around without asking. Little things, little things! They had been so sweet when they were little. Granny wished the old days were back again with the children young and everything to be done over. It had been a hard pull, but not too much for her. When she thought of all the food she had cooked, and all the clothes she had cut and sewed, and all the gardens she had made — well, the children showed it. There they were, made out of her, and they couldn't get away from that. Sometimes she wanted to see John again and point to them and say, Well, I didn't do so badly, did I? But that would have to wait. That was for tomorrow. She used to think of him as a man, but now all the children were older than their father, and he would be a child beside her if she saw him now. It seemed strange and there was something wrong in the idea. Why, he couldn't possibly recognize her. She had fenced in a hundred acres once, digging the post holes herself and clamping the wires with just a negro boy to help. That changed a woman. John would be looking for a young woman with the peaked Spanish comb in her hair and the painted fan. Digging post holes changed a woman. Riding country roads in the winter when women had their babies was another thing: sitting up nights with sick horses and sick negroes and sick children and hardly ever losing one. John, I hardly ever lost one of them! John would see that in a minute, that would be something he could understand, she would't have to explain anything!

It made her feel like rolling up her sleeves and putting the whole place to rights again. No matter if Cornelia was determined to be everywhere at once, there were a great many things left undone on this place. She would start tomorrow and do them. It was good to be strong enough for everything, even if all you made melted and changed and slipped under your hands, so that by the time you finished you almost forgot what you were working for. What was it I set out to do? she asked herself intently, but she could not remember. A fog rose over the valley, she saw it marching across the creek swallowing the trees and moving up the hill like an army of ghosts. Soon it would be at the near edge of the orchard, and then it was time to go in and light the lamps. Come in, children, don't stay out in the night air.

Lighting the lamps had been beautiful. The children huddled up to her and breathed like little calves waiting at the bars in the twilight. Their eyes followed the match and watched the flame rise and settle in a blue curve, then they moved away from her. The lamp was lit, they didn't have to be scared and hang on to mother any more. Never, never, never more. God, for all my life I thank Thee. Without Thee, my God, I could never have done it. Hail, Mary, full of grace.

I want you to pick all the fruit this year and see that nothing is wasted. There's always someone who can use it. Don't let good things rot for want of using. You waste life when you waste good food. Don't let things get lost. It's bitter to lose things. Now, don't let me get to thinking, not when I am tired and taking a little nap before supper. . . .

The pillow rose about her shoulders and pressed against her heart and the memory was being squeezed out of it: oh, push down the pillow, somebody: it would smother her if she tried to hold it. Such a fresh breeze blowing and such a green day with no threats in it. But he had not come, just the same. What does a woman do when she has put on the white veil and set out the white cake for a man and he doesn't come? She tried to remember. No, I swear he never harmed me but in that . . . and what if he did? There was the day, the day, but a whirl of dark smoke rose and covered it, crept up and over into the bright field where everything was planted so carefully in orderly rows. That was hell, she knew hell when she saw it. For sixty years she had prayed against remembering him and against losing her soul in the deep pit of hell, and now the two things were mingled in one and the thought of him was a smoky cloud from hell that moved and crept in her head when she had just got rid of Doctor Harry and was trying to rest a minute. Wounded vanity, Ellen, said a sharp voice in the top of her mind. Don't let your wounded vanity get the upper hand of you. Plenty of girls get jilted. You were jilted, weren't you? Then stand up to it. Her eyelids wavered and let in streamers of blue-gray light like tissue paper over her eyes. She must get up and pull the shades down or she'd never sleep. She was in bed again and the shades were not down. How could that happen? Better turn over, hide from the light, sleeping in the light gave you nightmares. "Mother, how do you feel now?" and a stinging wetness on her forehead. But I don't like having my face washed in cold water!

Hapsy? George? Lydia? Jimmy? No, Cornelia, and her features were swollen and full of little puddles. "They're coming, darling, they'll all be here soon." Go wash your face, child, you look funny.

Instead of obeying, Cornelia knelt down and put her head on the pillow. She seemed to be talking but there was no sound. "Well, are you tongue-tied? Whose birthday is it? Are you going to give a party?"

Cornelia's mouth moved urgently in strange shapes. "Don't do that, you bother me, daughter."

"Oh, no, Mother. Oh, no. . . ."

Nonsense. It was strange about children. They disputed your every word. "No what, Cornelia?"

"Here's Doctor Harry."

"I won't see that boy again. He just left five minutes ago."

"That was this morning, Mother. It's night now. Here's the nurse."

"This is Doctor Harry, Mrs. Weatherall. I never saw you look so young and happy!"

"Ah, I'll never be young again — but I'd be happy if they'd let me lie in peace and get rested."

She thought she spoke up loudly, but no one answered. A warm weight on her forehead, a warm bracelet on her wrist, and a breeze went on whispering, trying to tell her something. A shuffle of leaves in the everlasting hand of God, He blew on them and they danced and rattled. "Mother, don't mind, we're going to give you a little hypodermic." "Look here, daughter, how do ants get in this bed? I saw sugar ants yesterday." Did you send for Hapsy too?

It was Hapsy she really wanted. She had to go a long way back through a great many rooms to find Hapsy standing with a baby on her arm. She seemed to herself to be Hapsy also, and the baby on Hapsy's arm was Hapsy and himself and herself, all at once, and there was no surprise in the meeting. Then Hapsy melted from within and turned flimsy as gray gauze and the baby was a gauzy shadow, and Hapsy came up close and said, "I thought you'd never come," and looked at her very searchingly and said, "You haven't changed a bit!" They leaned forward to kiss, when Cornelia began whispering from a long way off, "Oh, is there anything you want to tell me? Is there anything I can do for you?"

Yes, she had changed her mind after sixty years and she would like to see George. I want you to find George. Find him and be sure to tell him I forgot him. I want him to know I had my husband just the same and my children and my house like any other woman. A good house too and a good husband that I loved and fine children out of him. Better than I hoped for even. Tell him I was given back everything he took away and more. Oh, no, oh, God, no, there was something else besides the house and the man and the children. Oh, surely they were not all? What was it? Something not given back. . . . Her breath crowded down under her ribs and grew into a monstrous frightening shape with cutting edges; it bored up into her head, and the agony was unbelievable: Yes, John, get the Doctor now, no more talk, my time has come.

When this one was born it should be the last. The last. It should have been born first, for it was the one she had truly wanted. Everything came in good time. Nothing left out, left over. She was strong, in three days she would be as well as ever. Better. A woman needed milk in her to have her full health.

"Mother, do you hear me?"

"I've been telling you —"

"Mother, Father Connolly's here."

"I went to Holy Communion only last week. Tell him I'm not so sinful as all that."

"Father just wants to speak to you."

He could speak as much a he pleased. It was like him to drop in and inquire about her soul as if it were a teething baby, and then stay on for a cup of tea and a round of cards and gossip. He always had a funny story of some sort, usually about an Irishman who made his little mistakes and confessed them, and the point lay in some absurd thing he would blurt out in the confessional showing his struggles between native piety and original sin. Granny felt easy about her soul. Cornelia, where are your manners? Give Father Connolly a chair. She had her secret comfortable understanding with a few favorite saints who cleared a straight road to God for her. All as surely signed and sealed as the papers for the new Forty Acres. Forever. . . heirs and assigns forever. Since the day the wedding cake was not cut, but thrown out and wasted. The whole bottom dropped out of the world, and there she was blind and sweating with nothing under her feet and the walls falling away. His hand had caught her under the breast, she had not fallen, there was the freshly polished floor with the green rug on it, just as before. He had cursed like a sailor's parrot and said, "I'll kill him for you." Don't lay a hand on him, for my sake leave something to God. "Now, Ellen, you must believe what I tell you. . . ."

So there was nothing, nothing to worry about any more, except sometimes in the night one of the children screamed in a nightmare, and they both hustled out shaking and hunting for the matches and calling, "There, wait a minute, here we are!" John, get the doctor now, Hapsy's time has come. But there was Hapsy standing by the bed in a white cap. "Cornelia, tell Hapsy to take off her cap. I can't see her plain."

Her eyes opened very wide and the room stood out like a picture she had seen somewhere. Dark colors with the shadows rising towards the ceiling in long angles. The tall black dresser gleamed with nothing on it but John's picture, enlarged from a little one, with John's eyes very black when they should have been blue. You never saw him, so how do you know how he looked? But the man insisted the copy was perfect, it was very rich and handsome. For a picture, yes, but it's not my husband. The table by the bed had a linen cover and a candle and a crucifix. The light was blue from Cornelia's silk lampshades. No sort of light at all, just frippery. You had to live forty years with kerosene lamps to appreciate honest electricity. She felt very strong and she saw Doctor Harry with a rosy nimbus around him.

"You look like a saint, Doctor Harry, and I vow that's as near as you'll ever come to it."

"She's saying something."

"I heard you, Cornelia. What's all this carrying-on?"

"Father Connolly's saying —"

Cornelia's voice staggered and bumped like a cart in a bad road. It rounded corners and turned back again and arrived nowhere. Granny stepped up in the cart very lightly and reached for the reins, but a man sat beside her and she knew him by his hands, driving the cart. She did not look in his face, for she knew without seeing, but looked instead down the road where the trees leaned over and bowed to each other and a thousand birds were singing a Mass. She felt like singing too, but she put her hand in the bosom of her dress and pulled out a rosary, and Father Connolly murmured Latin in a very solemn voice and tickled her feet. My God, will you stop that nonsense? I'm a married woman. What if he did run away and leave me to face the priest by myself? I found another a whole world better. I wouldn't have exchanged my husband for anybody except St. Michael himself, and you may tell him that for me with a thank you in the bargain.

Light flashed on her closed eyelids, and a deep roaring shook her. Cornelia, is that lightning? I hear thunder. There's going to be a storm. Close all the windows. Call the children in. . . . "Mother, here we are, all of us." "Is that you, Hapsy?" "Oh, no, I'm Lydia. We drove as fast as we could." Their faces drifted above her, drifted away. The rosary fell out of her hands and Lydia put it back. Jimmy tried to help, their hands fumbled together, and Granny closed two fingers around Jimmy's thumb. Beads wouldn't do, it must be something alive. She was so amazed her thoughts ran round and round. So, my dear Lord, this is my death and I wasn't even thinking about it. My children have come to see me die. But I can't, it's not time. Oh, I always hated surprises. I wanted to give Cornelia the amethyst set — Cornelia, you're to have the amethyst set, but Hapsy's to wear it when she wants, and, Doctor Harry, do shut up. Nobody sent for you. Oh, my dear Lord, do wait a minute. I meant to do something about the Forty Acres, Jimmy doesn't need it and Lydia will later on, with that worthless husband of hers. I meant to finish the altar cloth and send six bottles of wine to Sister Borgia for her dyspepsia. I want to send six bottles of wine to Sister Borgia, Father Connolly, now don't let me forget.

Cornelia's voice made short turns and tilted over and crashed. "Oh, Mother, oh, Mother, oh, Mother. . . ."

"I'm not going, Cornelia. I'm taken by surprise. I can't go."

You'll see Hapsy again. What about her? "I thought you'd never come." Granny made a long journey outward, looking for Hapsy. What if I don't find her? What then? Her heart sank down and down, there was no bottom to death, she couldn't come the the end of it. The blue light from Cornelia's lampshade drew into a tiny point in the center of her brain, it flickered and winked like an eye, quietly it fluttered and dwindled. Granny lay curled down within herself, amazed and watchful, staring at the point of light that was herself; her body was now only a deeper mass of shadow in an endless darkness and this darkness would curl around the light and swallow it up. God, give a sign!

For the second time there was no sign. Again no bridegroom and the priest in the house. She could not remember any other sorrow because this grief wiped them all away. Oh, no, there's nothing more cruel than this — I'll never forgive it. She stretched herself with a deep breath and blew out the light.

REYNOLDS PRICE

Uncle Grant

SUPPOSING HE COULD KNOW I have thought of him all this week. Supposing I was not three thousand miles from northeast North Carolina and supposing he had not been dead six years and I could find him and say, "I have thought of you all this week" — then he would be happy. Supposing though he was alive and I was still here in England — in Oxford whose light and color and trees and even grass would be strange to him as the moon (as they are to me) — and supposing he heard I had thought of him. It would go more or less like this. He would be in my aunt's kitchen in a straight black chair near the stove, having finished his breakfast. My aunt would have finished before he started and by then would be spreading beds or sweeping the porch, in her nightdress still. So he would be alone — his natural way, the way he had spent, say, sixty per cent of his life, counting sleep. His back would be straight as the chair, but his body would lean to the left, resting. The way he rested was to feel out the table beside him with his left elbow (an apple-green table with red oilcloth for a cover) and finding a spot, press down and then lay his head, his *face*, in his hand. His long right arm would lie on his hollow flank, the fingers hinged on the knee, and his legs would be clasped, uncrossed not to wrinkle the starched khaki trousers and ending in high-top shoes that, winter or summer, would be slashed into airy patterns, clean as the day they were bought, just ventilated with a razor blade. His white suspenders would rise from his waist to his shoulders, crossing the starched gray shirt (never with a tie but always buttoned at the neck and when he was dressed, pinned with a dull gold bar), but his face would be covered, his eyes. Only the shape of his skull would be clear — narrow and long, pointed at the chin, domed at the top — and the color of the skin that covered it, unbroken by a single hair except sparse brows, the color of a penny polished down by years of thumbs till Lincoln's face is a featureless shadow but with red life running beneath. That way he would be resting — not waiting, just resting as if he had worked when all he had done was wake at six and reach to his radio and lie on till seven, hearing music and thinking, then shaving and dressing and spreading his bed and stepping through the yard to the kitchen to eat what my aunt cooked (after she fired the stove if it was winter) — and he would rest till half-past eight when the cook would come and say towards him "Mr. Grant" (they were not good friends) and towards my aunt down the hall, "Miss Ida, here's you a letter," having stopped at the post office on her way. My aunt would come and stand by the stove and read with lips moving silent and then say, "Look, Uncle Grant. Here's a letter from Reynolds." He would look up squinting while she read out something like, " 'Tell Uncle Grant I am thinking about him this week,' " but before she could read any more, he would slap his flank and spring to his feet, rocking in his lacework shoes, opening and shutting his five-foot-ten like a bellows, and flicking at his ears — "Great God A-mighty! Where *is* Reynolds?" When she said "England" he would say, "Over yonder with them Hitalians and he been thinking about Grant? Great God A-mighty!" and then trail off into laughing and then for a long time to come into smiling. He would be happy that whole day and it is a fact — there is no one alive or dead I could have made happier with eight or ten words.

But he is dead and the reason I have thought of him these few days is strange — not because I remembered some joke on him and certainly not from seeing his likeness in the blue-black Negroes of the Oxford streets but because I went in a store to buy postcards and saw a card from the Berlin Museum — on a black background an Egyptian head, the tall narrow skull rocked back on the stalky neck, the chin offered out like a flickering tongue, the waving lips set in above (separate as if they were carved by a better man), the ears with their heavy lobes pinned closed to the skull, and the black-rimmed sockets holding no eyes at all. I looked on, not knowing why, and turned the card over. The head was Amenhotep IV, pharaoh of Egypt in the eighteenth dynasty who canceled the worship of bestial gods and changed his name to Akhnaton, "it pleases Aton," the one true god, the streaming disc, the sun. I bought the card and left the shop and walked ten yards and said to myself in the street what I suddenly knew, "It's the one picture left of Uncle Grant."

His full name as far as we knew was Grant Terry, and he said he was born near Chatham, Virginia which is some hundred miles to the left of Richmond. (There are still white Terrys near there from whom his family would have taken its name.) He never knew his age but in 1940 when he heard of Old Age Assistance and wanted it (you had to show proof you were sixty-five), my father took him to our doctor who said, "I'll certify him — sure — but if those Welfare Workers took a look at his eyes, they wouldn't need *my* guarantee. He's well past seventy." So assuming he was seventy-five in 1940, that would make him born around 1865 — maybe born into freedom and named for a general his parents heard of who set them free — but we didn't know about his youth, what he did to live when he was growing in the years after the war. There was nothing much he could have done but farm for somebody — chopping or picking cotton or ginning cotton or sawing pine timber or at best tending somebody's yard. We did know he had a wife named Ruth who gave him a son named Felix. It is the one thing I recall him telling me from his past (and he told me more than once, never with tears and sometimes with laughing at the end as if it was just his best true story) — "When I left my home in Virginia to come down here, I said to Ruth and my boy, 'I'll see you in Heaven if I don't come back.'" And he never went back.

He came south eighty miles to North Carolina. He told my father he came in a road gang hired by a white contractor to pave the Raleigh streets, but he never said when he came — not to me anyhow, not to anybody still alive. He never said why he came to Macon either. (The streets of Macon are still not paved). Maybe he had done his Raleigh work and meant to head back to Ruth and Felix but never got farther than sixty miles, stopping in Macon, population two hundred, in Warren County which touches the Virginia line. Or maybe he came to Macon with a railroad gang. (That seems a fair guess. He always called Macon a "seaport town." It was more than a hundred miles from the sea. What he meant was Seaboard Railway — the Norfolk-to-Raleigh tracks split Macon.) Anyhow, he was there by the time I was born in 1933 though he wasn't attached to us, and his work by then — whatever it had been before — was growing things. He planted people's flowers and hoed them, raked dead leaves and burned them, and tended lawns — what lawns there were in Macon where oaktree shade and white sand soil discouraged grass — and then he began tending me.

Not that I needed much tending. My mother was always there and my aunt down the road, and a Negro girl named Millie Mae looked after me in the morning. But sometimes in the evening my parents went visiting or to a picture show (not often, it being the deep Depression), and then Uncle Grant would sit by me while I slept. I don't know why they selected him, *trusted* him, when my aunt could have kept me or Millie Mae. Maybe they thought he could make me grow. (When he first came to Macon and asked for work and somebody said, "What can you do?" he said, "I can make things grow" so they gave him a chance, and he proved it the rest of his life — till my father could say, "Uncle Grant could stick a Coca-Cola bottle in the ground and raise you an ice-cold drink by sunup tomorrow." And God knew I needed growing — I had mysterious convulsions till I was four, sudden blue twitching rigors that rushed me unconscious into sight of death every three or four months.) The best reason though would be that, having no friends of his own, he had taken to me, and there is a joke which seems to show that. One evening when I was nearly two, my parents left me with him, saying they would be back late and that he could sleep in an army cot in my room. But they came back sooner than they expected, and when they drove up under the trees, instead of the house being dark and quiet, there was light streaming from my bedroom and mouth-harp music and laughing enough for a party. In surprise they crept to the porch and peeped in. My high-railed iron bed was by the window, and I was in it in outing pajamas but not lying down — facing Uncle Grant who was standing on the floor playing harp music while I danced in time and laughed. Then he knocked out the spit and passed the harp to me, and I blew what I could while he clapped hands. And then they stopped it — not being angry but saying I had better calm down and maybe Uncle Grant shouldn't pass the harp to me in case of germs (I had already caught gingivitis from chewing a brass doorknob) — and that was our first joke on him.

It went on like that another year — him working the yard off and on and staying with me odd evenings — and then my father changed jobs (*got* a job after six years of failing to sell insurance to wiped-out farmers) and we left Macon, going west a hundred miles to Asheboro, still in North Carolina, where we lived in a small apartment. Uncle Grant of course stayed on in Macon — he still wasn't ours and we had no lawn of our own, no room for him — but before long my father sent bus fare to my aunt and asked her to put Uncle Grant on the bus (Uncle Grant couldn't read), and soon he arrived for his first visit. He spent the nights in a Negro boardinghouse and the days and evenings in our kitchen. There was nothing he could do to help except wash dishes (he couldn't cook), but help wasn't what my father wanted. He wanted just to talk and every evening after supper, he stayed in the kitchen and talked to Uncle Grant till almost time to sleep. I was too young then to listen — or if I listened, to remember the things they said. They laughed a good deal though — I remember that — and the rest of the time they talked about the past. My mother says they did but *she* didn't listen, and now they are dead and nobody knows why they sat there night after night at a hard kitchen table under a bare light bulb, talking on and on, and laughing. Unless they loved each other — meaning there would come times when they needed to meet, and they never explained the need to themselves. My father would just send bus fare through my aunt or there would be a letter from her saying Uncle Grant was ready for a visit and had asked her to say he was coming and we would go meet the bus, my father and I — five or six times in the two years we lived in three small rooms.

Then we bought two acres of land in the country near Asheboro and built a house. Or began to. The land needed clearing first — of loblolly pines and blackjack oaks and redbugs and snakes — so Uncle Grant came and spent the weekdays supervising that. He spent the nights at the same boardinghouse and as far as we knew went nowhere and had no Negro friends, but he spent his Sundays with us. We would pick him up in the car after church — my father and I — and drive out to look at our land. He would tell us what trees had gone that week and beg our pardon for, say, sacrificing a dogwood that had stood in the carpenters' path. But what I remember about those mornings — I was five — are two things he did which changed my mind. One Sunday when the clearing had just begun, the three of us were walking around the land — I in shorts and what I called Jesus-sandals — and as we came to a pile of limbs and weeds, six feet of black snake streamed out. It was May and black snakes go crazy in May so he headed for me and reared on his tail to fight. My father and I were locked in stiff surprise, but before the snake could lash at me, Uncle Grant took one step sideways like lightning and grabbed the snake's tail and cracked him on the air like a leather whip. Then we all breathed deep and looked and laughed at two yards of limp dead snake in Uncle Grant's hand. The way that changed my mind was to make me see Uncle Grant, not as the nurse who sat with me nights or talked on and on to my father, but as a fearless hero to imitate, and I never saw him in the old tame way again, not for eight or nine years. Then another Sunday morning we were walking — the land was clear by this time and building had started, but there wasn't a blade of grass, only mud and thousands of rocks that looked identical to me — and Uncle Grant leaned down quick as he had for the snake and came up with a little rock and handed it to me. It was a perfect Indian arrowhead, and in my joy I said, "How in the world did you see it?" and he said, "I'm three parts Indian myself" which deepened the feeling I had had for him since the snake and also made our two rocky acres something grand — a hunting ground of the Occoneechees or a campsite or even, I hoped, a battlefield (though we never found a second head to prove it).

When the house was finished and we moved in, he came with us. There was one small room off the kitchen where the furnace was, and his bed was there and a little low table to carry the things he owned — in the daytime his shaving equipment and his extra shirt, and at night his precious belongings — an Ingersoll watch and a pocket knife. In the daytime he worked to grow us a lawn, and gradually, single-handed, he grew us a beauty. And once it was strong, he began to cut it — with a small hand sickle and his pocket knife. We had a lawn mower and he tried to use it but stopped, saying rocks were too plentiful still — the real reason being he could cut grass better, cut it *right*, by hand and if that meant bending to the ground all day at age about seventy-five and trimming two acres with a three-inch blade, then that was all right. It was what he could do, in spring and summer. In the fall he raked leaves, not waiting till the trees were bare and taking them all at once but raking all day every day. It was one of our jokes on him (a true joke — they were all true) that we once saw him run a few yards and catch a dead leaf as it fell, in the air, and grind it to dust in his hand. In the evening after us he ate at the kitchen counter and washed all our dishes and then went into his room and sat on his bed and looked at picture magazines. Sometimes my father would sit with him and I would fly in and out, but most of the time he sat in silence, thinking whatever his private thoughts were, till we gave him a radio.

That was Christmas 1939 and there wasn't much to hear except black war news, but nothing we gave him ever pleased him more. Not that he had seemed unhappy before — I don't think he thought about happiness — but now he would sit there on into the night. I would sit beside him long as my mother allowed in the dark (the only light was the radio dial), hearing our favorite things which were short-wave programs in German and Spanish with Morse Code bursting in like machine-gun fire to make us laugh. We didn't understand a word and my father who thought we were fools would step to the door and shake his head at us in the dark, but Uncle Grant would slap his thigh and say, *"Listen* to them Hitalians, Mr. Will!" *Hitalians* was what he called all foreigners, and "Great God A-mighty" was his favorite excited expression, the one he used every time some Spaniard would speed up the news or "The Star-Spangled Banner" would play so before long of course I was saying it too — age six. At first I just said it with him when he laughed, but once I slipped and said it in front of my mother, and she asked him not to curse around me and made me stay out of his room for a while. With me being punished my father filled the gap by spending more time in the furnace room, and it was then the jokes piled up. Despite all the war news, he would have a new joke every evening — my father, that is, on Uncle Grant. One night for instance after they had sat an hour listening, they switched off the radio to let it cool and to talk. They talked quite awhile till my father said, "Let's switch it on. It's time for the midnight news" so they did, and there was the news, waiting for them. When it had finished and music had begun, Uncle Grant said, "When does they sleep, Mr. Will?" My father said, "Who?" and he said — pointing through the dark to the radio — "Them little peoples in yonder." My father whose work was electrical supplies explained about waves in the air without wires and Uncle Grant nodded. But some time later when they had sat up extra-late, Uncle Grant asked if it wasn't bedtime. My father took the hint but was slow about leaving — standing in the door, hearing the end of some program — so Uncle Grant stood and unbuttoned his collar, then thought and switched off the radio. My father said, "How come you did that?" and he said, "I can't undress with them little peoples watching, Mr. Will." So my father never tried explaining again.

Then after three years we lost the house and all that grass and had to move to another apartment in Asheboro. By then I had a year-old brother named Bill so again there was no room for Uncle Grant and nothing for him to do if there had been, and my father explained it a month in advance — that much as we wanted him around, we couldn't keep paying him three dollars a week just to wash dishes and that if he stayed on in Asheboro he would have to find someplace to sleep and hire-out to other people to pay his rent. He told my father he would think it over, and he thought that whole last month, asking no advice, sitting by himself most evenings as I was in school and busy and my father was ashamed in his presence, and giving no sign of his plans till the day we moved. He helped that day by packing china and watching how the movers treated our furniture, and when everything had gone except his few belongings, my father said, "Where are you going, Uncle Grant?" He said, "I'm sleeping in that boardinghouse till I get you all's windows washed. Then I'm going to Macon on the bus. I ain't hiring-out in this town." (Asheboro was a stocking-mill town.) My father said, "You might break your radio on the bus. Wait till Sunday and I'll carry you." Uncle Grant said, "I been studying that — where am I going to plug in a radio in Macon? You keep it here and if I wants it I'll let you know." My father said, "Maybe when I get a little money I can trade it in on a battery set," and he said "Maybe you can" and two days later went to Macon by bus, saying he would stay with a Negro named Rommie Watson till he found a house. But somewhere in the hundred miles, for some reason, he changed his mind and when the bus set him down, he walked to my aunt's back door and asked could he sleep in her old smokehouse till he found a place of his own? She knew of course why we turned him loose so she told him Yes, and he swept it out and slept on an army cot, coming to her kitchen for meals but not eating well, not looking for a house of his own, not saying a word about work. My aunt finally asked him was he all right, and he said, "I will be soon as I get my bearings." In about two weeks he came in to breakfast with the cot rolled under his arm and his bag of belongings. When he had eaten he said he had found a house at the far end of Macon — a one-room house under oak trees in the yard of a Negro church. Then he left and was gone all day, all night, but my aunt looked out in the morning and there he was, trimming her bushes, having got some sort of bearings, enough to last two years.

We had turned him loose in 1942. He lived on thirteen years and he never let us take hold again. We stayed in Asheboro three years after he left — two years in that apartment and a year in a good-sized house — but he didn't come to visit in all that time. I don't know whether we asked him and if we did, what reason he gave for refusing. He just didn't come and he might have said he was too old. But he worked for my aunt every day, strong as ever, still trimming what he grew with a pocket knife, and the only way he showed age was by not taking supper in my aunt's kitchen. In summer he would stop about six, in winter about five — before dark — and put up his tools and come to the back door, and my aunt would give him cold biscuits and sometimes a little jar of syrup or preserves, and he would walk home a mile and a half and spend his evenings by a kerosene lamp, alone. But that was no change for him, being by himself.

What *was* a change was that after he had been back in Macon two years, he fell in some sort of love with a girl named Katie. She was not from Macon but had come there as cook to a cousin of ours who returned so she had no Negro friends either, and though she was no more than twenty, she began to sit with him some evenings. My aunt didn't know if they got beyond sitting, but she didn't worry much, not at first. Uncle Grant was pushing eighty and it seemed at first that Katie was good to him in ways that made him happy. My aunt *did* say to him once, "Uncle Grant, don't let that girl take your money away," and he said, "No'm. Every penny I lends her, she pay me back." But then it turned bad. After six months or so Katie began taking him to Warrenton on Saturdays (the county seat, five miles away), and they would drink fifty-cent wine called "Sneaky Pete," and every week he would have the few hairs shaved off his head (to hide them from Katie as they were white). For a while he managed to keep his drinking to Saturdays and to be cold-sober when he turned up for Sunday breakfast so my aunt didn't complain but finally he slipped. One Sunday he came in late — about nine — walking straight and of course dressed clean but old around the eyes and with his hat still on. He said "Good morning" and sat by the green kitchen table. My aunt said the same and, not really noticing, gave him a dish of corn flakes. He ate a few spoonfuls in silence. Then he sprang to the floor and slapped his flank and said, "What is the meaning of *this*?" — so loud she could smell the wine and pointing at his bowl. My aunt went over and there was a needle in his food. Thinking fast, she laughed and said, "Excuse me, Uncle Grant. I was sewing in here this week and somebody came to the door, and I stuck the needle in the cereal box, and it must have worked through." That was the truth and, sober, he would have known it, but he stood there rocking a little and then said, "Somebody trying to kill me is all *I* know." My aunt said, "If you are that big a fool, you can leave my house" so he stood another minute and then he left.

That was in late October — he had just started raking leaves. His shame kept him home the following day — and for two months to come. My aunt reckoned he would come back when he got hungry but he didn't. What food he got he bought from his neighbors or maybe Katie sneaked him things from our cousin's kitchen, but he didn't show up at my aunt's, and every leaf fell and thousands of acorns, and she finally hired boys to clear them. He still hadn't showed up by Christmas when we arrived for three days. That was the first we knew of his shame. My father said, "To be sure, he'll show up to see me," but my aunt said, "You are the *last* one he wants to see, feeling like he does," and my father saw she was right. We had brought him a box of Brown Mule chewing tobacco. He surely knew that — we gave him that every Christmas — and we waited but he didn't come. When we left on the 27th my father gave my aunt the Brown Mule and told her to save it till Uncle Grant showed up. She said in that case it would be bone-dry by the time he got it.

But for once she was wrong. About two weeks later in a hard cold spell his house burned down in the night from an overheated stove. My aunt heard that from her cook in the morning and heard that he got out unharmed with the clothes on his back so she packed a lard bucket with food and set our tobacco on top and sent it by the cook to where he was, which was at some neighbor's. The cook came back and said he thanked her and that afternoon he came. My aunt was nodding but the cook waked her and said, "Mr. Grant's out yonder on the porch, Miss Ida." She went and told him she was sorry to hear of his trouble and what was he going to do now? He said, "I don't hardly know but could I just sleep in the smokehouse till I get my bearings?" She thought and said, "Yes, if you'll stay there without having company." He knew who she meant and nodded and spent the rest of the day cleaning the smokehouse and getting the woodstove fit to use.

He stayed there without having company, working on the yard by day and on the smokehouse by night. It was just one room, twice as tall as wide, with pine walls and floor. He scrubbed every board — cold as it was — and when they were dry, tacked newspapers around the walls high as he could reach to keep out wind. And as winter passed he kept finding things to do to that one room till it looked as if he took it to be his home. So when spring came my aunt hired a carpenter, and he put plasterboard on the walls and linoleum underfoot and a lock on the door. Then she took back the army cot and bought an old iron bed and a good felt mattress and gave Uncle Grant a key to the door, saying, "This is your key. I'll keep the spare one in case you lose it." But he never lost it and he lived on there, having got the bearings, somehow or other, that lasted the rest of his life.

We moved back to Warren County in 1945. My father got a job that let him live in Warrenton (or travel from there, selling freezers to farmers), and we lived in a hotel apartment, still with no yard of our own. But Sunday afternoons we would drive the five miles to Macon for supper with my aunt. When we got there we would sit an hour and talk, and then my father would rise and say he was stepping out back to see Uncle Grant and who wanted to come? That was a signal for me to say "Me," and for a year or so I said it and followed him to the smokehouse. Uncle Grant would have been waiting all afternoon and talk would begin by him asking me about school and what I was doing. I was twelve and wasn't doing much but keeping a diary so my answers wouldn't take long, and he would turn to my father, and they would begin where they left off the week before in the circles of remembering and laughing. Old as I was, I still didn't listen, but soon as they got underway, I would stand and walk round the room, reading the papers on the walls till I knew them by heart. (What I *did* hear was, week after week, my father offering to take Uncle Grant on one of his Virginia business trips and detour to Chatham so he could look up Felix his son and Ruth his wife if she was alive. Uncle Grant would say, "That's a good idea. Let me know when you fixing to go." But he never went. He rode with my father a number of times — down into South Carolina and as far west as Charlotte — but whenever they set the date for a trip to Virginia and the date drew near, Uncle Grant would find yard work that couldn't wait or get sick a day or two with rheumatism.) But a year of such Sundays passed, and I slowed down on the smokehouse visits. My father would rise as before and ask who was going with him to Uncle Grant's, and more and more my brother volunteered, not me. He was going on six, the age I had been when Uncle Grant cracked the snake and found me the arrowhead and we listened to Hitalian news together, so he stepped into whatever place Uncle Grant kept for me and gradually filled more and more of it. But not all, never all, because every time my father came back from a visit he would say, "Uncle Grant asked after you. Step out yonder and speak to him, son." I would look up from what I was doing — seventh-grade arithmetic or a Hardy Boys mystery — and say, "Soon as I finish this," and of course before I finished, it would be dark and supper would be ready. But I always saw him after supper when he came in to eat and to wash our dishes — little fidgety meetings with nothing to talk about but how he was feeling and with gaps of silence getting longer and longer till I would say "Goodbye" and he would say "All right" and I would hurry out. (Occasionally though, he would move some way that detained me — by dropping the dishrag, say, and old as he was, stooping for it in a flash that recalled him reaching bare-handed for the snake to save me — and I would find things to say or look on awhile at his slow body, seeing how grand he had been and knowing how happy I could make him, just waiting around.)

It went on like that till the summer of 1947. Then we moved again — sixty miles, to Raleigh, into a house with two good yards and a steam-heated basement room — and as my father arranged, Uncle Grant followed in a day or so. He had not volunteered to follow, even when my father described the basement room and the grass and privet hedge that, since it was August, were nearly out of hand, so my father asked him — "Would you come up and help us get straight?" and he said, "I'll ask Miss Ida can I take off a week." She gave him the week and we gave him the fare and he came. He started next morning at the ankle-high grass, and by sundown he had cut a patch about twenty feet square and sat in the kitchen, bolt-upright but too tired to eat. My father saw the trouble and saw a way out — he said, "I am driving to Clinton tomorrow. Come on and keep me company in this heat." Uncle Grant accepted, not mentioning grass. And none of us mentioned it again. When they got back from Clinton two evenings later, he spent one night, and the next day he went to Macon for good. Busy as my father was, he took Uncle Grant by car and spent a night at my aunt's. Then he came back to Raleigh and at supper that evening said, "He is older than I counted on him being. He won't last long. So I bought him a battery radio to keep him company."

He was maybe eighty-two when he tackled our new lawn and lost. My father was forty-seven. Uncle Grant lasted eight years, working on my aunt's yard till eight months before he died (no slower than ever and with nothing but a boy to rake up behind him), spending his evenings with nothing but his battery radio (Katie having drunk herself jobless and vanished), complaining of nothing but sometimes numb feet, asking for nothing but Brown Mule tobacco (and getting that whenever we visited, especially at Christmas). My father lasted six.

He died in February, 1954 — my father. Cancer of the lung with tumors the size of bird eggs clustered in his throat which nobody noticed till he thought he had bronchitis and called on a doctor. It went very quickly — twenty-one days — and my aunt didn't tell Uncle Grant till she had to. Hoping for the best, she had seen no reason to upset him in advance, but when we phoned her that Sunday night, she put on her coat and went to the smokehouse and knocked. Uncle Grant cracked the door and seeing it was her (she had never called on him after dark before), said, "What's wrong, Miss Ida?" She stood on the doorstep — half of a granite millstone — and said, "Will Price is dead." The heat of his room rushed past her into the dark, and directly he said, "Sit down, Miss Ida," pointing behind him to his single chair. She was my *mother's* sister but she stepped in and sat on his chair, and he sat on the edge of his mattress. Some radio music played on between them, and according to her, he never asked a question but waited. So when she got breath enough, she said the funeral was Tuesday and that he could ride down with her and her son if he wanted to. He thought and said, "Thank you, no'm. I better set here," and she went home to bed. In the morning after his breakfast, he stepped to her bedroom door and called her out and handed her three dollar bills to go towards flowers and she took them. He didn't work all that day or come in again for food so she sent his supper by the cook who reported he wasn't sick, but before she left Tuesday morning for Raleigh, he was stripping ivy off the lightninged oak, too busy to do more than wave goodbye as the car rolled down to the road.

He just never mentioned my father, that was all — for his own reasons, never spoke my father's name in anybody's hearing again. My aunt came back from the funeral and gave him a full description, and he said, "It sounds mighty nice," and ever after that if she brought up the subject — remembering some joke of my father's for instance — he would listen and laugh a little if that was expected but at the first break, get up and leave the room. He went on speaking of others who were someway gone — Ruth his wife and Felix his son and once or twice even Katie — but never my father, not even the last time I saw him.

That was Christmas of 1954 and by then he was flat on his back in a Welfare Home near Warrenton, had been there nearly four months. Six months after my father's death, his feet and legs went back on him totally. He couldn't stand for more than ten minutes without going numb from his waist down, and one night he fell, going to the smokehouse from supper — on his soft grass — so he took his bed, and when he didn't come to breakfast, my aunt went out and hearing of the fall, asked her doctor to come. He came and privately told her nothing was broken — it was poor circulation which would never improve, and didn't she want him to find Uncle Grant a place with nurses? There was nothing she could do but agree, being old herself, and the doctor found space in the house of a woman named Sarah Cawthon who tended old Negroes for the Welfare Department. Then my aunt asked Uncle Grant if going there wasn't the wise thing for him — where he could rest with attention and regular meals and plenty of company and his radio and where she could visit him Saturdays, headed for Warrenton? He thought and said "Yes'm, it is," and she bought him two suits of pajamas and a flannel robe (he had always slept in long underwear), and they committed him early in September — her and her son — as the end of summer slammed down.

We didn't visit Macon in a body that Christmas. My mother wasn't up to it so we spent the day in Raleigh, but early on the 26th I drove to Macon to deliver our gifts and collect what was waiting for us. I stayed with my aunt most of the day, and her children and grandchildren came in for dinner, but after the eating, things got quiet and people took pains not to speak of the past, and at four o'clock I loaded up and said goodbye. My aunt followed me to the car and kissed me and said, "Aren't you going to stop by Sarah Cawthon's and see Uncle Grant?" I looked at the sky to show it was late, and she said, "It won't take long and nobody God made will appreciate it more." So I stopped by and knocked on the holly-wreathed door and Sarah Cawthon came. I said I would like to see Grant Terry, and she said, "Yes sir. Who is calling?" I smiled at that and said "Reynolds Price." — "Mr. Will Price's boy?" — "His oldest boy." She smiled too and said he was waiting for me and headed for a back bedroom. I paused at the door and she went ahead, flicking on the light, saying, "Mr. Grant, here's you a surprise." Then she walked out and I walked in, and the first thing I noticed was his neck. He was sitting up in bed in his clean pajamas. They were buttoned to the top, but they had no collar and his neck was bare. That was the surprise. I had just never seen it before, not down to his shoulders, and the sight of it now — so lean and long but the skin drawn tight — surprised me. *He* was not surprised. He had known *some* Price would turn up at Christmas, and seeing it was me, he laughed, "Great God A-mighty, Reynolds, you bigger than me." (I was twenty-one. I had reached my full growth some time before, but he still didn't say "*Mr.* Reynolds.") Then he pointed to a corner of the room where a two-foot plastic Christmas tree stood on a table, hung with a paper chain but no lights. There were two things under the tree on tissue paper — some bedroom shoes from my aunt and the box of Brown Mule my mother had mailed without telling me — and he said, "I thank you for my present," meaning the tobacco which he had not opened. I noticed when he laughed that his teeth were gone and remembered my aunt commenting on the strangeness of that — how his teeth had vanished since he took his bed, just dissolved with nobody's help. So the Brown Mule was useless, like the shoes. He never stood up any more, he said. But that was the nearest he came to speaking of his health, and I didn't ask questions except to say did he have a radio? He said "Two" and pointed to his own battery set on the far side of him and across the room to one by an empty bed. I asked whose that was and he said, "Freddy's. The Nigger that sleeps yonder." I asked where was Freddy now and he said, "Spending some time with his family, thank God. All that ails him is his water." But before he explained Freddy's symptoms, Sarah Cawthon returned with orange juice for both of us and a slice of fruitcake for me. Then she smoothed the sheets around Uncle Grant and said to him, "Tell Mr. Reynolds your New Year's resolution." He said, "What you driving at?" So she told me — "Mr. Grant's getting baptized for New Year. He's been about to run me crazy to get him baptized — ain't you, Mr. Grant?" He didn't answer, didn't look at her or me but down at his hands on the sheet, and she went on — "Yes, sir, he been running me *crazy* to get him baptized, old as he is, so I have arranged it for New Year's Day with my preacher. I got a big old trough in the back yard, and we are bringing that in the kitchen and spreading a clean sheet in it and filling it up with nice warm water, and *under* he's going — ain't you, Mr. Grant?" Still looking down, he said he would think it over. She said, "Well, of course you are and we wish Mr. Reynolds could be here to see it, don't we?" Then she took our glasses and left. When her steps had faded completely, he looked up at me and said, "I ain't going to be baptized in no hog trough." I said I was sure it wasn't a hog trough, but if he didn't want to be dipped, I saw no reason why he should. He said, "It ain't *me* that wants it. It's that woman. She come in here — last week, I believe — and asked me was I baptized and I said, 'No, not to my knowledge' so she said, 'Don't you know you can't get to Heaven and see your folks till you baptized?'" He waited a moment and asked me, "Is that the truth?" And straight off I said, "No. You'll see everybody you want to see, I'm sure. Give them best wishes from me!" He laughed, "I'll do that thing," then was quiet a moment, and not looking at me, said, "There *is* two or three I hope to meet, but I ain't studying the rest." Then he looked and said, "You're sure about that? — what you just now told me?" and again not waiting I said I was sure so he smiled, and I reckoned I could leave. I stepped to his window and looked out at what was almost night — "Uncle Grant, I better be heading home." He said, "Thank you, sir" (not saying what for), and I stopped at the foot of his bed and asked what I had to ask, what my father would have asked — "Is there any little thing I can do for you?" He said "Not a thing." I said, "You are not still worried about being baptized, are you?" and he said, "No, you have eased my mind. I can tell that woman *my* mind is easy, and if she want to worry, that's *her* red wagon." I laid my hand on the ridge of sheet that was his right foot — "If you need anything, tell Aunt Ida, and she'll either get it or let us know." He said, "I won't need nothing." Then I stepped to the door and told him "Goodbye," and he said, "Thank you" again (still not saying what for) and — grinning — that he would see me in Heaven if not any sooner. I grinned too and walked easy down Sarah Cawthon's hall and made it to the door without being heard and got in the car and started the sixty miles to Raleigh in full night alone, wondering part of the way (maybe fifteen minutes), "Have I sent him to Hell with my theology?" but knowing that was just a joke and smiling to myself and driving on, thinking gradually of my own business, not thinking of him at all, not working back to what he had been in previous days, feeling I had no reasons.

And went on till late last week — nearly seven years — not thinking of him more than, say fifteen seconds at a stretch, not even when he died just before his afternoon nap, the May after I saw him in December. Freddy his roommate told my aunt, "I was making another police dog and he died" — Freddy made dogs to sell, out of socks and knitting wool — and she and her son handled the funeral. We didn't go, my part of the family (my mother had a job by then and I was deep in college exams and my brother was too young to drive), but my mother sent flowers and they buried him at Mount Zion Church which he never attended, a mile from my aunt's, not in a Welfare coffin but in one she paid for, in a grave I have never seen.

Yet because of an accident — stopping to buy postcards — I have spent a week, three thousand miles from home, thinking of nothing but him, working back to what he may have been, to what we knew anyhow, finding I knew a good deal, finding *reasons*, and thinking how happy he would be if he could know, how long he would laugh, rocking in his lacework shoes, if he heard what reminded me of him (a Hitalian face on a card — Amenhotep IV, pharaoh of Egypt in the eighteenth dynasty who fathered six daughters but no son on Nefertiti his queen and canceled the worship of hawks and bulls and changed his name to Akhnaton, "it pleases Aton," the single god, the sun that causes growth) — and him the son of Negro slaves, named Grant maybe for the Union general (a name he could not recognize or write), who grew up near Chatham, Virginia, and made his one son Felix on a woman named Ruth and left them both to go south to work and somehow settled in Macon near us, finally with us (claiming he could make things grow, which he could), and tended me nights when I was a baby and our yard when we had one and for his own reasons loved my father and was loved by him and maybe loved me, *trusted* me enough to put his salvation in my hands that last day I saw him (him about ninety and me twenty-one) and believed what I said — that in Heaven he would meet the few folks he missed — and claimed he would see me there. And this is the point, this is what I know after this last week — that final joke, if it *was* a joke (him saying he would see me in Heaven), whoever it was on, it was not on him.

ELIZABETH SPENCER

First Dark

WHEN TOM BEAVERS STARTED coming back to Richton, Mississippi, on weekends, after the war was over, everybody in town was surprised and pleased. They had never noticed him much before he paid them this compliment; now they could not say enough nice things. There was not much left in Richton for him to call family — just his aunt who had raised him, Miss Rita Beavers, old as God, ugly as sin, deaf as a post. So he must be fond of the town, they reasoned; certainly it was a pretty old place. Far too many young men had left it and never come back at all.

He would drive in every Friday night from Jackson, where he worked. All weekend, his Ford, dusty of flank, like a hard-ridden horse, would sit parked down the hill near Miss Rita's old wire front gate, which sagged from the top hinge and had worn a span in the ground. On Saturday morning, he would head for the drugstore, then the post office; then he would be observed walking here and there around the streets under the shade trees. It was as though he were looking for something.

He wore steel taps on his heels, and in the still the click of them on the sidewalks would sound across the big front lawns and all the way up to the porches of the houses, where two ladies might be sitting behind a row of ferns. They would identify him to one another, murmuring in their fine little voices, and say it was just too bad there was nothing here for young people. It was just a shame they didn't have one or two more old houses, here, for a Pilgrimage — look how Natchez had waked up.

One Saturday morning in early October, Tom Beavers sat at the counter in the drugstore and reminded Totsie Poteet, the drugstore clerk, of a ghost story. Did he remember the strange old man who used to appear to people who were coming into Richton along the Jackson road at twilight — what they called "first dark"?

"Sure I remember," said Totsie. "Old Cud'n Jimmy Wiltshire used to tell us about him every time we went 'possum hunting. I could see him plain as I can see you, the way he used to tell it. Tall, with a top hat on, yeah, and waiting in the weeds alongside the road ditch, so'n you couldn't tell if he wasn't taller than any mortal man could be, because you couldn't tell if he was standing down in the ditch or not. It would look like he just grew up out of the weeds. Then he'd signal to you."

"Them that stopped never saw anybody," said Tom Beavers, stirring his coffee. "There were lots of folks besides Mr. Jimmy that saw him."

"There was, let me see . . ." Totsie enumerated others — some men, some women, some known to drink, others who never touched a drop. There was no way to explain it. "There was that story the road gang told. Do you remember, or were you off at school? It was while they were straightening the road out to the highway — taking the curves out and building a new bridge. Anyway, they said that one night at quitting time, along in the winter and just about dark, this old guy signaled to some of 'em. They said they went over and he asked them to move a bulldozer they had left across the road, because he had a wagon back behind on a little dirt road, with a sick nigger girl in it. Had to get to the doctor and this was the only way. They claimed they knew didn't nobody live back there on that little old road, but niggers can come from anywhere. So they moved the bulldozer and cleared back a whole lot of other stuff, and waited and waited. Not only didn't no wagon ever come, but the man that had stopped them, he was gone, too. They was right shook up over it. You never heard that one?"

"No, I never did." Tom Beavers said this with his eyes looking up over his coffee cup, as though he sat behind a hand of cards. His lashes and brows were heavier than was ordinary, and worked as a veil might, to keep you away from knowing exactly what he was thinking.

"They said he was tall and had a hat on." The screen door flapped to announce a customer, but Totsie kept on talking. "But whether he was a white man or a real light-colored nigger they couldn't say. Some said one and some said another. I figured they'd been pulling on the jug a little earlier than usual. You know why? I never heard of *our* ghost *saying* nothing. Did you, Tom?"

He moved away on the last words, the way a clerk will, talking back over his shoulder and ahead of him to his new customer at the same time, as though he had two voices and two heads. "And what'll it be today, Miss Frances?"

The young woman standing at the counter had a prescription already out of her bag. She stood with it poised between her fingers, but her attention was drawn toward Tom Beavers, his coffee cup, and the conversation she had interrupted. She was a girl whom no ordinary description would fit. One would have to know first of all who she was: Frances Harvey. After that, it was all right for her to be a little odd-looking, with her reddish hair that curled back from her brow, her light eyes, and her high, pale temples. This is not the material for being pretty, but in Frances Harvey it was what could sometimes be beauty. Her family home was laden with history that nobody but the Harveys could remember. ~~It would have been on a~~ ~~Pilgrimage if Richton had had one.~~ Frances still lived in it, looking after an invalid mother.

"What were you-all talking about?" she wanted to know.

"About that ghost they used to tell about," said Totsie, holding out his hand for the prescription. "The one people used to see just outside of town, on the Jackson road."

"Buy why?" she demanded. "Why were you talking about him?"

"Tom, here —" the clerk began, but Tom Beavers interrupted him.

"I was asking because I was curious," he said. He had been studying her from the corner of his eye. Her face was beginning to show the wear of her mother's long illness, but that couldn't be called change. Changing was something she didn't seem to have done, her own style being the only one natural to her.

"I was asking," he went on, "because I saw him." He turned away from her somewhat too direct gaze and said to Totsie Poteet, whose mouth had fallen open, "It was where the new road runs close to the old road, and as far as I could tell he was right on the part of the old road where people always used to see him."

"But when?" Frances Harvey demanded.

"Last night," he told her. "Just around first dark. Driving home."

A wealth of quick feeling came up in her face. "So did I! Driving home from Jackson! I saw him, too!"

For some people, a liking for the same phonograph record or for Mayan archaeology is enough of an excuse to get together. Possibly, seeing the same ghost was no more than that. Anyway, a week later, on Saturday at first dark, Frances Harvey and Tom Beavers were sitting together in a car parked just off the highway, near the spot where they agreed the ghost had appeared. The season was that long, peculiar one between summer and fall, and there were so many crickets and tree frogs going full tilt in their periphery that their voices could hardly be distinguished from the background noises, though they both would have heard a single footfall in the grass. An edge of autumn was in the air at night, and Frances had put on a tweed jacket at the last minute, so the smell of moth balls was in the car, brisk and most unghostlike.

But Tom Beavers was not going to forget the value of the ghost, whether it put in an appearance or not. His questions led Frances into reminiscence.

"No, I never saw him before the other night," she admitted. "The Negroes used to talk in the kitchen, and Regina and I — you know my sister Regina — would sit there listening, scared to go and scared to stay. Then finally going to bed upstairs was no relief, either, because sometimes Aunt Henrietta was visiting us, and *she'd* seen it. Or if she wasn't visiting us, the front room next to us, where she stayed, would be empty, which was worse. There was no way to lock ourselves in, and besides, what was there to lock out? We'd lie all night like two sticks in bed, and shiver. Papa finally had to take a hand. He called us in and sat us down and said that the whole thing was easy to explain — it was all automobiles. What their headlights did with the dust and shadows out on the Jackson road. 'Oh, but Sammie and Jerry!' we said, with great big eyes, sitting side by side on the sofa, with our tennis shoes flat on the floor."

"Who were Sammie and Jerry?" asked Tom Beavers.

"Sammie was our cook. Jerry was her son, or husband, or something. Anyway, they certainly didn't have cars. Papa called them in. They were standing side by side by the bookcase, and Regina and I were on the sofa — four pairs of big eyes, and Papa pointing his finger. Papa said, 'Now, you made up these stories about ghosts, didn't you?' 'Yes, sir,' said Sammie. 'We made them up.' 'Yes, sir,' said Jerry. 'We sho did.' 'Well, then, you can just stop it,' Papa said. 'See how peaked these children look?' Sammie and Jerry were terribly polite to us for a week, and we got in the car and rode up and down the Jackson road at first dark to see if the headlights really did it. But we never saw anything. We didn't tell Papa, but headlights had nothing whatever to do with it."

"You had your own *car* then?" He couldn't believe it.

"Oh no!" She was emphatic. "We were too young for that. Too young to drive, really, but we did anyway."

She leaned over to let him give her cigarette a light, and saw his hand tremble. Was he afraid of the ghost or of her? She would have to stay away from talking family.

Frances remembered Tommy Beavers from her childhood — a small boy going home from school down a muddy side road alone, walking right down the middle of the road. His old aunt's house was at the bottom of a hill. It was damp there, and the yard was always muddy, with big fat chicken tracks all over it, like Egyptian writing. How did Frances know? She could not remember going there, ever. Miss Rita Beavers was said to order cold ham, mustard, bread, and condensed milk from the grocery store. "I doubt if that child ever has anything hot," Frances's mother had said once. He was always neatly dressed in the same knee pants, high socks, and checked shirt, and sat several rows ahead of Frances in study hall, right in the middle of his seat. He was three grades behind her; in those days, that much younger seemed very young indeed. What had happened to his parents? There was some story, but it was not terribly interesting, and, his people being of no importance, she had forgotten.

"I think it's past time for our ghost," she said. "He's never out so late at night."

"He gets hungry, like me," said Tom Beavers. "Are you hungry, Frances?"

They agreed on a highway restaurant where an orchestra played on weekends. Everyone went there now.

From the moment they drew up on the graveled entrance, cheerful lights and a blare of music chased the spooks from their heads. Tom Beavers ordered well and danced well, as it turned out. Wasn't there something she had heard about his being "smart"? By "smart," Southerners mean intellectual, and they say it in an almost condescending way, smart being what you are when you can't be anything else, but it is better, at least, than being nothing. Frances Harvey had been away enough not to look at things from a completely Southern point of view, and she was encouraged to discover that she and Tom had other things in common besides a ghost, though all stemming, perhaps, from the imagination it took to see one.

They agreed about books and favorite movies and longing to see more plays. She sighed that life in Richton was so confining, but he assured her that Jackson could be just as bad; *it* was getting to be like any Middle Western city, he said, while Richton at least had a sense of the past. This was the main reason, he went on, gaining confidence in the jumble of commonplace noises — dishes, music, and a couple of drinkers chattering behind them — that he had started coming back to Richton so often. He wanted to keep a connection with the past. He lived in a modern apartment, worked in a soundproof office — he could be in any city. But Richton was where he had been born and raised, and nothing could be more old-fashioned. Too many people seemed to have their lives cut in two. He was earnest in desiring that this should not happen to him.

"You'd better be careful," Frances said lightly. Her mood did not incline her to profound conversation. "There's more than one ghost in Richton. You may turn into one yourself, like the rest of us."

"It's the last thing I'd think of you," he was quick to assure her.

Had Tommy Beavers really said such a thing, in such a natural, charming way? Was Frances Harvey really so pleased? Not only was she pleased but, feeling warmly alive amid the music and small lights, she agreed with him. She could not have agreed with him more.

"I hear that Thomas Beavers has gotten to be a very attractive man," Frances Harvey's mother said unexpectedly one afternoon.

Frances had been reading aloud — Jane Austen this time. Theirs was one house where the leather-bound sets were actually read. In Jane Austen, men and women seesawed back and forth for two or three hundred pages until they struck a point of balance; then they got married. She had just put aside the book, at the end of a chapter, and risen to lower the shade against the slant of afternoon sun. "Or so Cud'n Jennie and Mrs. Giles Antley and Miss Fannie Stapleton have been coming and telling you," she said.

"People talk, of course, but the consensus is favorable," Mrs. Harvey said. "Wonders never cease; his mother ran away with a brush salesman. But nobody can make out what he's up to, coming back to Richton."

"Does he have to be 'up to' anything?" Frances asked.

"Men are always up to something," said the old lady at once. She added, more slowly, "In Thomas's case, maybe it isn't anything it oughtn't to be. They say he reads a lot. He may just have taken up with some sort of idea."

Frances stole a long glance at her mother's face on the pillow. Age and illness had reduced the image of Mrs. Harvey to a kind of caricature, centered on a mouth that Frances could not help comparing to that of a fish. There was a tension around its rim, as though it were outlined in bone, and the underlip even stuck out a little. The mouth ate, it took medicine, it asked for things, it gasped when breath was short, it commented. But when it commented, it ceased to be just a mouth and became part of Mrs. Harvey, that witty tyrant with the infallible memory for the right detail, who was at her terrible best about men.

"And what could he be thinking of?" she was wont to inquire when some man had acted foolishly. No one could ever defend accurately the man in question, and the only conclusion was Mrs. Harvey's; namely, that he wasn't thinking, if, indeed, he could. Although she had never been a belle, never a flirt, her popularity with men was always formidable. She would be observed talking marathons with one in a corner, and could you ever be sure, when they both burst into laughter, that they had not just exchanged the most shocking stories? "Of course, *he* —" she would begin later, back with the family, and the masculinity that had just been encouraged to strut and preen a little was quickly shown up as idiotic. Perhaps Mrs. Harvey hoped by this method to train her daughters away from a lot of sentimental nonsense that was their birthright as pretty Southern girls in a house with a lawn that moonlight fell on and that was often lit also by Japanese lanterns hung for parties. "Oh, he's not like that, Mama!" the little girls would cry. They were already alert for heroes who would ride up and cart them off. "Well, then, you watch," she would say. Sure enough, if you watched, she would be right.

Mrs. Harvey's younger daughter, Regina, was a credit to her mother's long campaign; she married well. The old lady, however, never tired of pointing out behind her son-in-law's back that his fondness for money was ill-concealed, that he had the longest feet she'd ever seen, and that he sometimes made grammatical errors.

Her elder daughter, Frances, on a trip to Europe, fell in love, alas! The gentleman was of French extraction but Swiss citizenship, and Frances did not marry him, because he was already married — that much filtered back to Richton. In response to a cable, she had returned home one hot July in time to witness her father's wasted face and last weeks of life. That same September, the war began. When peace came, Richton wanted to know if Frances Harvey would go back to Europe. Certain subtly complicated European matters, little understood in Richton, seemed to be obstructing Romance; one of them was probably named Money. Meanwhile, Frances's mother took to bed, in what was generally known to be her last illness.

So no one crossed the ocean, but eventually Tom Beavers came up to Mrs. Harvey's room one afternoon, to tea.

Though almost all her other faculties were seriously impaired, in ear and tongue Mrs. Harvey was as sound as a young beagle, and she could still weave a more interesting conversation than most people who go about every day and look at the world. She was of the old school of Southern lady talkers; she vexed you with no ideas, she tried to protect you from even a moment of silence. In the old days, when a bright company filled the downstairs rooms, she could keep the ball rolling amongst a crowd. Everyone — all the men especially — got their word in, but the flow of things came back to her. If one of those twenty-minutes-to-or-after silences fell — and even with her they did occur — people would turn and look at her daughter Frances. "And what do you think?" some kind-eyed gentleman would ask. Frances did not credit that she had the sort of face people would turn to, and so did not know how to take advantage of it. What did she think? Well, to answer that honestly took a moment of reflection — a fatal moment, it always turned out. Her mother would be up instructing the maid, offering someone an ashtray or another goody, or remarking outright, "Frances if so timid. She never says a word."

Tom Beavers and stayed not only past teatime ~~that day~~ but for a drink as well. Mrs. Harvey was induced to take a glass of sherry, and now her bed became her enormous throne. Her keenest suffering as an invalid was occasioned by the absence of men. "What is a house without a man in it?" she would often cry. From her eagerness to be charming to Frances's guest that afternoon, it seemed that she would have married Tom Beavers herself if he had asked her. The amber liquid set in her small four-sided glass glowed like a jewel, and her diamond flashed; she had put on her best ring for the company. What a pity no longer to show her ankle, that delicious bone, so remarkably slender for so ample a frame.

Since the time had flown so, they all agreed enthusiastically that Tom should wait downstairs while Frances got ready to go out to dinner with him. ~~He was hardly past the stair landing before the old lady was seized by such a fit of coughing that she could hardly speak. "It's been — it's been too much — too much for me!" she gasped out.~~ *dressed for dinner, mother*

~~But after~~ Frances had found the proper sedative for her, she was calmed, and insisted on having her say.

"Thomas Beavers has a good job with an insurance company in Jackson," she informed her daughter, as though Frances were incapable of finding out anything for herself. "He makes a good appearance. He is the kind of man" — she paused — "who would value a wife of good family." ~~She stopped, panting for breath. It was this~~ complimenting a man behind his back that was too much for her — as much out of character, and hence ~~as much of~~ a strain, as if she had got out of bed and ~~tried to~~ tap-dance.

"Heavens, Mama," Frances said, and almost giggled.

At this, the old lady, thinking the girl had made light of her suitor, half screamed at her, "Don't be so critical, Frances! You can't be so critical of men!"

and fell into an even more terrible spasm of coughing. Frances had to lift her from the pillow and hold her straight until the fit passed and her breath returned. Then Mrs. Harvey's old, dry, crooked, ineradicably feminine hand was laid on her daughter's arm, and when she spoke again she shook the arm to emphasize her words.

"When your father knew he didn't have long to live," she whispered, "we discussed whether to send for you or not. You know you were his favorite, Frances. 'Suppose our girl is happy over there,' he said. 'I wouldn't want to bring her back on my account.' I said you had to have the right to choose whether to come back or not. You'd never forgive us, I said, if you didn't have the right to choose."

Frances could visualize this very conversation taking place between her parents; she could see them, decorous and serious, talking over the fact of his approaching death as though it were a piece of property for agreeable disposition in the family. She could never remember him without thinking, with a smile, how he used to come home on Sunday from church (he being the only one of them who went) and how, immediately after hanging his hat and cane in the hall, he would say, "Let all things proceed in orderly progression to their final confusion. How long before dinner?" No, she had had to come home. Some humor had always existed between them — her father and her — and humor, of all things, cannot be betrayed.

"I meant to go back," said Frances now. "But there was the war. At first I kept waiting for it to be over. I still wake up at night sometimes thinking, I wonder how much longer before the war will be over. And then —" She stopped short. For the fact was that her lover had been married to somebody else, and her mother was the very person capable of pointing that out to her. Even in the old lady's present silence she heard the unspoken thought, and got up nervously from the bed, loosing herself from the hand on her arm, smoothing her reddish hair where it was inclined to straggle. "And then he wrote me that he had gone back to his wife. Her family and his had always been close, and the war brought them back together. This was in Switzerland — naturally, he couldn't stay on in Paris during the war. There were the children, too — all of them were Catholic. Oh, I do understand how it happened."

Mrs. Harvey turned her head impatiently on the pillow. She dabbed at her moist upper lip with a crumpled linen handkerchief; her diamond flashed once in motion. "War, religion, wife, children — yes. But men do what they want to."

Could anyone make Frances as angry as her mother could? "Believe what you like then! You always know so much better than I do. *You* would have managed things somehow. Oh, you would have had your way!"

"Frances," said Mrs. Harvey, "I'm an old woman." The hand holding her handkerchief fell wearily, and her eyelids dropped shut. "If you should want to marry Thomas Beavers and bring him here, I will accept it. There will be no distinctions. Next, I suppose, we will be having his old deaf aunt for tea. I hope she has a hearing aid. I haven't got the strength to holler at her."

"I don't think any of these plans are necessary, Mama."

The eyelids slowly lifted. "None?"

"None."

Mrs. Harvey's breathing was as audible as a voice. She spoke, at last, without scorn, honestly. "I cannot bear the thought of leaving you alone. You, nor the house, nor your place in it — alone. I foresaw Tom Beavers here! What has he got that's better than you and this place? I knew he would come!"

Terrible as her mother's meanness was, it was not half so terrible as her love. Answering nothing, explaining nothing, Frances stood without giving in. She trembled, and tears ran down her cheeks. The two women looked at each other helplessly across the darkening room.

In the car, later that night, Tom Beavers asked, "Is your mother trying to get rid of me?" They had passed an unsatisfactory evening, and he was not going away without knowing why.

"No, it's just the other way around," said Frances, in her candid way. "She wants you so much she'd like to eat you up. She wants you in the house. Couldn't you tell?"

"She once chased me out of the yard," he recalled.

"Not really!"

They turned into Harvey Street (that was actually the name of it), and when he had drawn the car up before the dark front steps, he related the incident. He told her that Mrs. Harvey had been standing just there in the yard, talking to some visitor who was leaving by inches, the way ladies used to — ten minutes' more talk for every forward step. He, a boy not more than nine, had been crossing a corner of the lawn where a faint path had already been worn; he had had nothing to do with wearing the path and had taken it quite innocently and openly. "You, boy!" Mrs. Harvey's fan was an enormous painted thing. She had furled it with a clack so loud he could still hear it. "You don't cut through my yard again! Now, you stop where you are and you go all the way back around by the walk, and don't you ever do that again." He went back and all the way around. She was fanning comfortably as he passed. "Old Miss Rita Beavers' nephew," he heard her say, and though he did not speak of it now to Frances, Mrs. Harvey's rich tone had been as stuffed with wickedness as a fruitcake with goodies. In it you could have found so many things: that, of course, he didn't know any better, that he was poor, that she knew his first name but would not deign to mention it, that she meant him to understand all this and more. Her fan was probably still somewhere in the house, he reflected. If he ever opened the wrong door, it might fall from above and brain him. It seemed impossible that nowadays he could even have the chance to open the wrong door in the Harvey house. With its graceful rooms and big lawn, its camellias and magnolia trees, the house had been one of the enchanted castles of his childhood, and Frances and Regina Harvey had been two princesses running about the lawn one Saturday morning drying their hair with big white towels and not noticing when he passed.

There was a strong wind that evening. On the way home, Frances and Tom had noticed how the night was streaming, but whether with mist or dust or the smoke from some far-off fire in the dry winter woods they could not tell. As they stood on the sidewalk, the clouds raced over them, and moonight now and again came through. A limb rubbed against a high cornice. Inside the screened area of the porch, the swing jangled in its iron chains. Frances's coat blew about her, and her hair blew. She felt herself to be no different from anything there that the wind was blowing on, her happiness of no relevance in the dark torrent of nature.

"I can't leave her, Tom. But I can't ask you to live with her, either. Of all the horrible ideas! She'd make demands, take all my time, laugh at you behind your back — she has to run everything. You'd hate me in a week."

He did not try to pretty up the picture, because he had a feeling that it was all too accurate. Now, obviously, was the time she should go on to say there was no good his waiting around through the years for her. But hearts are not noted for practicality, and Frances stood with her hair blowing, her hands stuck in her coat pockets, and did not go on to say anything. Tom pulled her close to him — in, as it were, out of the wind.

"I'll be coming by next weekend, just like I've been doing. And the next one, too," he said. "We'll just leave it that way, if it's O.K. with you."

"Oh yes, it is, Tom!" Never so satisfied to be weak, she kissed him and ran inside.

He stood watching on the walk until her light flashed on. Well, he had got what he was looking for; a connection with the past, he had said. It was right upstairs, a splendid old mass of dictatorial female flesh, thinking about him. Well, they could go on, he and Frances, sitting on either side of a sickbed, drinking tea and sipping sherry with streaks of gray broadening their brows, while the familiar seasons came and went. So he thought. Like Frances, he believed that the old lady had a stranglehold on life.

Suddenly, in March, Mrs. Harvey died.

A heavy spring funeral, with lots of roses and other scented flowers in the house, is the worst kind of all. There is something so recklessly fecund about a south Mississippi spring that death becomes just another word in the dictionary, along with swarms of others, and even so pure and white a thing as a gardenia has too heavy a scent and may suggest decay. Mrs. Harvey, amid such odors, sank to rest with a determined pomp, surrounded by admiring eyes.

While Tom Beavers did not "sit with the family" at this time, he was often observed with the Harveys, and there was whispered speculation among those who were at the church and the cemetery that the Harvey house might soon come into new hands, "after a decent interval." No one would undertake to judge for a Harvey how long an interval was decent.

Frances suffered from insomnia in the weeks that followed, and at night she wandered about the spring-swollen air of the old house, smelling now spring and now death. "Let all things proceed in orderly progression to their final confusion." She had always thought that the final confusion referred to death, but now she began to think that it could happen any time; that final confusion, having found the door ajar, could come into a house and show no inclination to leave. The worrisome thing, the thing it all came back to, was her mother's clothes. They were numerous, expensive, and famous, and Mrs. Harvey had never discarded any of them. If you opened a closet door, hatboxes as big as crates towered above your head. The shiny black trim of a great shawl stuck out of a wardrobe door just below the lock. Beneath the lid of a cedar chest, the bright eyes of a tippet were ready to twinkle at you. And the jewels! Frances's sister had restrained her from burying them all on their mother, and had even gone off with a wad of them tangled up like fishing tackle in an envelope, on the ground of promises made now and again in the course of the years.

("Regina," said Frances, "what else were you two talking about besides jewelry?" "I don't remember," said Regina, getting mad.

"Frances makes me so mad," said Regina to her husband as they were driving home. "I guess I can love Mama and jewelry, too. Mama certainly loved *us* and jewelry, too.")

One afternoon, Frances went out to the cemetery to take two wreaths sent by somebody who had "just heard." She drove out along the winding cemetery road, stopping the car a good distance before she reached the gate, in order to walk through the woods. The dogwood was beautiful that year. She saw a field where a house used to stand but had burned down; its cedar trees remained, and two bushes of bridal wreath marked where the front gate had swung. She stopped to admire the clusters of white bloom massing up through the young, feathery leaf and stronger now than the leaf itself. In the woods, the redbud was a smoke along shadowy ridges, and the dogwood drifted in layers, like snow suspended to give you all the time you needed to wonder at it. But why, she wondered, do they call it bridal *wreath*? It's not a wreath but a little bouquet. Wreaths are for funerals, anyway. As if to prove it, she looked down at the two she held, one in each hand. She walked on, and such complete desolation came over her that it was more of a wonder than anything in the woods — more, even, than death.

As she returned to the car from the two parallel graves, she met a thin, elderly, very light-skinned Negro man in the road. He inquired if she would mind moving her car so that he could pass. He said that there was a sick colored girl in his wagon, whom he was driving in to the doctor. He pointed out politely that she had left her car right in the middle of the road. "Oh, I'm terribly sorry," said Frances, and hurried off toward the car.

That night, reading late in bed, she thought, I could have given her a ride into town. No wonder they talk about us up North. A mile into town in a wagon! She might have been having a baby. She became conscience-stricken about it — foolishly so, she realized, but if you start worrying about something in a house like the one Frances Harvey lived in, in the dead of night, alone, you will go on worrying about it until dawn. She was out of sleeping pills.

She remembered having bought a fresh box of sedatives for her mother the day before she died. She got up and went into her mother's closed room, where the bed had been dismantled for airing, its wooden parts propped along the walls. On the closet shelf she found the shoe box into which she had packed away the familiar articles of the bedside table. Inside she found the small enameled-cardboard box, with the date and prescription inked on the cover in Totsie Poteet's somewhat prissy handwriting, but the box was empty. She was surprised, for she realized that her mother could have used only one or two of the pills. Frances was so determined to get some sleep that she searched the entire little store of things in the shoe box quite heartlessly, but there were no pills. She returned to her room and tried to read, but could not, and so smoked instead and stared out at the dawn-blackening sky. The house sighed. She could not take her mind off the Negro girl. If she died . . . When it was light, she dressed and got into the car.

In town, the postman was unlocking the post office to sort the early mail. "I declare," he said to the rural mail carrier who arrived a few minutes later, "Miss Frances Harvey is driving herself crazy. Going back out yonder to the cemetery, and it not seven o'clock in the morning."

"Aw," said the rural deliveryman skeptically, looking at the empty road.

"That's right. I was here and seen her. You wait there, you'll see her come back. She'll drive herself nuts. Them old maids like that, left in them old houses — crazy and sweet, or crazy and mean, or just plain crazy. They just ain't locked up like them that's down in the asylum. That's the only difference."

"Miss Frances Harvey ain't no more than thirty-two, -three years old."

"Then she's just got more time to get crazier in. You'll see."

one   some time later

~~That day was~~ Friday, ~~and~~ Tom Beavers, ~~back from Jackson,~~ came up Frances Harvey's sidewalk, as usual, at exactly a quarter past seven in the evening. ~~Frances was not "going out" yet, and Regina had telephoned her long distance to say that "in all probability" she should not be receiving gentlemen "in." "What would Mama say?" Regina asked. Frances said she didn't know, which was not true, and went right on cooking dinners for Tom~~ every weekend.

In the dining room that night, ~~she~~ sat across one corner of the long table from ~~Tom.~~ The useless length of polished cherry stretched away from them into the shadows as sadly as a road. Her plate pushed back, her chin resting on one palm, Frances stirred her coffee and said, "I don't know what on earth to do with all of

Mama's clothes. I can't give them away, I can't sell them, I can't burn them, and the attic is full already. What can I do?"

"You look better tonight," said Tom.

"I slept," said Frances. "I slept and slept. From early this morning until just 'while ago. I never slept so well."

Then she told him about the Negro near the cemetery the previous afternoon, and how she had driven back out there as soon as dawn came, and found him again. He had been walking across the open field near the remains of the house that had burned down. There was no path to him from her, and she had hurried across ground uneven from old plowing and covered with the kind of small, tender grass it takes a very skillful mule to crop. "Wait!" she had cried. "Please wait!" The Negro had stopped and waited for her to reach him. "Your daughter?" she asked, out of breath.

"Daughter?" he repeated.

"The colored girl that was in the wagon yesterday. She was sick, you said, so I wondered. I could have taken her to town in the car, but I just didn't think. I wanted to know, how is she? Is she very sick?"

He had removed his old felt nigger hat as she approached him. "She a whole lot better, Miss Frances. She going to be all right now." Then he smiled at her. He did not say thank you, or anything more. Frances turned and walked back to the road and the car. And exactly as though the recovery of the Negro girl in the wagon had been her own recovery, she felt the return of a quiet breath and a steady pulse, and sensed the blessed stirring of a morning breeze. Up in her room, she had barely time to draw an old quilt over her before she fell asleep.

"When I woke, I knew about Mama," she said now to Tom. By the deepened intensity of her voice and eyes, it was plain that this was the important part. "It isn't right to say I *knew*," she went on, "because I had known all the time — ever since last night. I just realized it, that's all. I realized she had killed herself. It had to be that."

He listened soberly through the story about the box of sedatives. "But why?" he asked her. "It maybe looks that way, but what would be her reason for doing it?"

"Well, you see —" Frances said, and stopped.

Tom Beavers talked quietly on. "She didn't suffer. With what she had, she could have lived five, ten, who knows how many years. She was well cared for. Not hard up, I wouldn't say. Why?"

The pressure of his questioning could be insistent, and her trust in him, even if he was nobody but old Miss Rita Beavers' nephew, was well-nigh complete. "Because of you and me," she said, finally. "I'm certain of it, Tom. She didn't want to stand in our way. She never knew how to express love, you see." Frances controlled herself with an effort.

He did not reply, ~~but~~ sat industriously balancing a match folder on the tines of an unused serving fork. Anyone who has passed a lonely childhood in the company of an old deaf aunt is not inclined to doubt things hastily, and Tom Beavers would not have said he disbelieved anything Frances had told him. In fact, it seemed only too real to him. Almost before his eyes, that imperial, practical old hand went fumbling for the pills in the dark. But there had been much more to it than just love, he reflected. Bitterness, too, and pride, and control. And humor, perhaps, and the memory of a frightened little boy chased out of the yard by a twitch of her fan. Being invited to tea was one thing; suicide was quite another. Times had certainly changed, he thought.

But, of course, he could not say that he believed it, either. There was only Frances to go by. The match folder came to balance and rested on the tines. He glanced up at her, and a chill walked up his spine, for she was too serene. Cheek on palm, a lock of reddish hair fallen forward, she was staring at nothing with the absorbed silence of a child, or of a sweet, silver-haired old lady engaged in memory. Soon he might find that more and more of her was vanishing beneath this placid surface.

He himself did not know what he had seen that Friday evening so many months ago — what the figure had been that stood forward from the roadside at the tilt of the curve and urgently waved an arm to him. By the time he had braked and backed, the man had disappeared. Maybe it had been somebody drunk (for Richton had plenty of those to offer), walking it off in the cool of the woods at first dark. No such doubts had occurred to Frances. And what if he told her now the story Totsie had related of the road gang and the sick Negro girl in the wagon? Another labyrinth would open before her; she would never get out.

In Richton, the door to the past was always wide open, and what came in through it and went out of it had made people "different." But it scarcely ever happens, even in Richton, that one is able to see the precise moment when fact becomes faith, when life turns into legend, and people start to bend their finest loyalties to make themselves bemused custodians of the grave. Tom Beavers saw that moment now, in the profile of this dreaming girl, and he knew there was no time to lose.

He dropped the match folder into his coat pocket. "I think we should be leaving, Frances."

"Oh well, I don't know about going out yet," she said. "People criticize you so. Regina even had the nerve to telephone. Word had got all the way to her that you came here to have supper with me and we were alone in the house. When I tell the maid I want biscuits made up for two people, she looks like 'What would yo' mama say?'"

"I mean," he said, "I think it's time we left for good."

"And never come back?" It was exactly like Frances to balk at going to a movie but seriously consider an elopement.

"Well, never is a long time. I like to see about Aunt Rita every once in a great while. She can't remember from one time to the next whether it's two days or two years since I last came."

She glanced about the walls and at the furniture, the pictures, and the silver. "But I thought you would want to live here, Tom. It never occurred to me. I know it never occurred to Mama . . . This house . . . It can't be just left."

"It's a fine old house," he agreed. "But what would you do with all your mother's clothes?"

Her freckled hand remained beside the porcelain cup for what seemed a long time. He waited and made no move toward her; he felt her uncertainty keenly, but he believed that some people should not be startled out of a spell.

"It's just as you said," he went on finally. "You can't give them away, you can't sell them, you can't burn them, and you can't put them in the attic, because the attic is full already. So what are you going to do?"

Between them, the single candle flame achieved a silent altitude. Then, politely, as on any other night, though shaking back her hair in a decided way, she said, "Just let me get my coat, Tom."

She locked the door when they left, and put the key under the mat — a last obsequy to the house. Their hearts were bounding ahead faster than they could walk down the sidewalk or drive off in the car, and, mindful, perhaps, of what happened to people who did, they did not look back.

Had they done so, they would have seen that the Harvey house was more beautiful than ever. All unconscious of its rejection by so mere a person as Tom Beavers, it seemed, instead, to have got rid of what did not suit it, to be free, at last, to enter with abandon the land of mourning and shadows and memory.

PETER TAYLOR

In the Miro District

WHAT I MOST OFTEN think about when I am lying awake in the night, or when I am taking a long automobile trip alone, is my two parents and my maternal grandfather. I used to suppose, after I had first got to be a grown man and had first managed to get away from Tennessee, that those two parents of mine thrusting my grandfather's company upon me as they did when I was growing up, and my company upon him when he was growing very old, and their asking the two of us to like it, though we possessed the very opposite natures, was but that couple's ruthless method of disposing of the two of us, child and aging parent, in one blow. But I can see now — from the vantage point of my own late middle age — that there was really no ruthlessness in it on their part. Because I realize that living their busy, genteel, contented life together in the 1920s they didn't have the slightest conception of what that old man my grandfather was like. Or of what that boy, their son, was like either. (Of what the one's past life had been or of what the other's would be like in the future.) They weren't people to speculate about what other people and other times were "like." They knew only that what they did was what everybody else still did about grandfathers and grandsons in or about the year 1925 — in and around Nashville, Tennessee.

The fact is, my two parents were destined to go to their graves never suspecting that they had put a grandfather and a grandson in so false a position with each other that the boy and the old man would one day have to have it out between them. Indeed, they would go to their graves never suspecting that long before either of them had ever given a serious thought to dying, Grandfather and I had already had it out between us quite brutally and fatefully and had it out, as a matter of fact, in the front hall of their house in Acklen Park, in Nashville.

It happened the summer when my grandfather was seventy-nine and I had just turned eighteen. Any real pretense at companionship between the old man and me came to an abrupt and unhappy end that summer. It left me with complications of feeling that nothing else had ever done. For my grandfather, of course, whose story this is meant to be — more than mine — it did something considerably worse than leave him with complications of feeling.

What actually happened was that he turned up at our house in Acklen Park one day in July, driving his Dodge touring car and wearing his gabardine topcoat and his big straw hat, arrived there unheralded and unannounced, as he himself was fond of saying, and let himself in our front door with his own key, the key which, despite his protests, my two parents always insisted upon his having. And what he found inside the house that day was not a clean-cut young boy whom he had watched growing up and whom his daughter and son-in-law — away then on a short summer trip — had left at home to see after the premises. He found, instead, a disheveled, disreputable-looking young fellow of eighteen summers who was hardly recognizable to his own grandfather, a boy who had just now frantically pulled on his clothes and who instead of occupying his parents' house alone was keeping a young girl in the house with him, a girl whom he had hurriedly hidden — at the first sound of his grandfather's tires in the driveway — hidden, as a matter of fact, in the big oak wardrobe of the downstairs bedroom which his visiting grandfather was always expected to occupy. The ensuing confrontation between the grandfather and the grandson seemed on its surface to be accidental and something that might finally be forgotten by both of them. But it was not quite so simple as that. . . . Neither the old man nor his grandson was every quite the same after that day — not the same with each other and probably not the same within themselves. Whatever their old relationship had been, it was over forever.

To me it seems natural that I should think about all of this whenever I am lying awake at night or when I am behind the wheel of my car on some endless highway. The memory of it raises questions in my mind that there seem to be no answers to; and those are inevitably the questions one entertains at such times. I find myself wondering why, in that quaint Tennessee world I grew up in, it was so well established that grandfathers and grandsons were to be paired off and held answerable to each other for companionship; why it was that an old graybeard and a towheaded little boy, in that day and age, were expected to be more companionable even than fathers and sons are told today they ought to be. For it really is my recollection that anywhere one turned in that world one was apt to see a bent old man and a stiff-necked little boy — trudging along a country road together or plodding along the main street of a town. The world I am speaking of isn't the hard-bitten, monkey-trial world of East Tennessee that everybody knows about, but a gentler world in Middle Tennessee and more particularlyy the little region around Nashville, which was known fifty years ago as the Nashville Basin and which in still earlier times, to the first settlers — our ancestors — was known somewhat romantically perhaps, and ironically, and incorrectly even, as the Miro District.

I must digress here to say something about why that region around Nashville was so designated, because it has something or other to do with this story. My grandfather, who did not take Nashville so seriously as my parents did, was fond of referring to the city itself as the Miro District (because he said only an antique Spanish name could do justice to the grandeur which Nashvillians claimed for themselves). According to Grandfather this region had originally been so called in honor of one Don Estevan Miro, last of the Spanish governors of Spanish Louisiana, and according to this same knowledgeable grandfather of mine, the entire state of Tennessee had once been claimed to be a rightful part of that province by both the French and the Spanish, in their day as its rulers. He used often to say to me, all irony about grandeur aside, that knowing such odd pieces of history about the place where one lived made the life one lived there seem less boring. He didn't couch it quite that way. He would not, of course, have used the word *boring*. It wasn't in his vocabulary. But there is no doubt that's what he meant. And I used to try to imagine why it was that when he was scouting through the low ground or hill country west of the Tennessee River during the Civil War, it made the War seem less hateful to him at times and less scary and less boring for him to know — or to believe — that the Spanish and the French had once held title to what was by then his own country or that the Indians had once held that land sacred, or for him to realize whenever he came in to Nashville that the site of the old citadel itself, Fort Nashborough, had once actually been known merely as Frenchman's Lick.

My grandfather, when I first remember him, lived over in the next county from us, forty miles west of Nashville. But he was always and forever driving over for those visits of his — visits of three or four days, or longer — transporting himself back and forth from Hunt County to Nashville in his big tan touring car, with the canvas top put back in almost all weather, and usually wearing a broad-brimmed hat — a straw in summer, a felt in winter — and an ankle-length gabardine topcoat no matter what the season was.

He was my maternal grandfather and was known to everyone as Major Basil Manley. Seeing Major Manley like that at the wheel of his tan touring car, swinging into our driveway, it wasn't hard to imagine how he had once looked riding horseback or muleback through the wilds of West Tennessee when he was a young boy in Forrest's cavalry, or how he had looked, for that matter, in 1912, nearly half a century after he had ridden with General Forrest, at the time when he escaped from a band of hooded nightriders who had kidnapped him then — him and his law partner (and who had murdered his law partner before his eyes, on the banks of Bayou du Chien, near Reelfoot Lake).

Even when I was a very small boy, I always dreaded the sight of him out there in our driveway in his old car when he was arriving for a visit. I hated the first sound of his tires in the gravel as he came wheeling up to the house and then suddenly bore down on the brakes at the foot of our front porch steps. I dreaded him not because I was frightened by his coming or by the history of his violent exploits, which I knew about from an early time, but because I was aware always of the painful hours that he and I, who had nothing in common and for whom all our encounters were a torture, would be expected to put in together.

The old man had always had a way of turning up, you see — even when I was little more than an infant — just when it suited *me* least, when I had *other* plans which might include almost anything else in the world but the presence of a grandfather with whom it was intended I should be companionable. Sometimes he would go directly into our back yard, if it were summertime, without even removing his hat or his gabardine coat. He would plant one of the canvas yard chairs on the very spot where I had been building a little airfield or a horse farm in the grass. Then he would throw himself down into the chair and undo his collar button and remove his starched collar — he seldom wore a tie in those days — and next he would pull his straw hat down over his face and begin his inevitable dialogue with me without our having exchanged so much as a glance or a how-do-you-do. It used to seem to me he only knew I was there with him because he knew I was required to be there. "I guess you've been behaving yourself," he said from under his hat, "the way a Nashville boy ought to behave himself." . . . And, of course, I knew well enough what was meant by that. It meant I was some kind of effeminate city boy who was never willing to visit his grandfather alone in the country and who could never comprehend what it would be to ride muleback through the wilds of West Tennessee — either in pursuit of Yankee marauders or in flight from hooded nightriders. Looking up at the old man from the grass beside his chair (or from the carpet beside his platform rocker if we were settled in his downstairs bedroom), I thought to myself — thought this, or something like it — Someday you and I will have to have it out between us. I shall have to show you how it is with me and how I could never be what you are. . . . I often looked up at him, wanting — I know now — to say something that would insult him and make him leave me alone or make him take his walking stick to me. The trouble was, of course — and I seemed to have sensed this before I was school age even — that we couldn't understand or care anything about each other. Something in each of us forbade it. It was as though we faced each other across the distasteful present, across a queer, quaint world that neither of us felt himself a part of.

When I looked up at him while we were talking, often out in the back yard but more often in his room, I could never think exactly what it was about him that I hated or if I really hated him at all. Yet many a time I had that shameful feeling of wanting to insult him. And so I got into the habit of trying to see him as my two parents saw him. That's the awful part, really. I would look at him until I saw him as I knew they saw him: an old country granddaddy who came to town not wearing a tie and with only a bright gold collar button shining where a tie ought to have been in evidence. It seems shocking to me nowadays how well I knew at that

tender age just how my parents did surely see such an old man and, indeed, how
they saw all else in the world about us. They saw everything in terms of Acklen
Park in the city of Nashville in the Nashville Basin in Middle Tennessee in the old
Miro District as it had come to be in the first quarter of the twentieth century. I
suppose it was my knowing how Mother and Father saw the other grandfathers
who did actually live with *their* families in the Acklen Park neighborhood that
made me know for certain how they saw Major Basil Manley. To them, those other
grandfathers seemed all elegance while he seemed all roughness. Those others
lived quietly with their sons and daughters while he insisted upon living apart and
in a country that was only on the periphery of Middle Tennessee. Those other
grandfathers were a part of the families who had taken them in. (They had
managed to become so or perhaps had always been so.) When you saw one of
those other grandfathers out walking with a little grandson along West End
Avenue, it was apparent at once that the two of them were made of the same clay
or at least that their mutual aim in life was to make it appear to the world that they
were. Sometimes the old man and the little boy walked along West End hand in
hand or sometimes with their arms about each other, the old man's arm on the little
boy's shoulder, the little boy's arm about the old man's waist. It is a picture that
comes into my mind almost every day that I live.

This ancient and well-established practice of pairing off young with old so
relentlessly and so exclusively had, I think — or *has* — as one of its results in
Nashville the marvel that men over fifty whom one meets there nowadays are
likely to seem much too old-fashioned to be believed in almost — much too stiff
in their manner to be taken seriously at all. They seem to be putting on an act. It is
as if they are trying to *be* their grandfathers. Either that or these grandsons of
Confederate veterans are apt to have become pathetic old roués and alcoholics,
outrageously profane, and always willing to talk your ear off in the Country Club
bar — usually late at night — about how far they have fallen away from their
ideals, about how very different they are from the men their grandfathers were. To
hear them talk, one would actually suppose none of them ever had a father. One
gets the impression that they only had elegant grandfathers, born before 1860.
What is more to the point, though, is that this business of pairing off bent old
men with stiff-necked little boys plainly had its effect, too, upon the old men —
the old grandfathers themselves. For when finally they reached extreme old age
either they became absurd martinets, ordering the younger men and boys in their
families about in their quavery old voices (and often getting laughed at behind
their backs) or some among these very same old men who had once stood firm at
Missionary Ridge or had fought in the trenches before Petersburg or, like Grandfather Manley, had ridden with General Forrest became toward the very end as
thoroughly domesticated as any old woman — could be seen fussing about the
house like some old spinster great-aunt, rearranging the furniture or washing up

little stacks of dishes, forever petting and hugging the young people in the family
or clucking and fretting and even weeping softly whenever the young people didn't
behave themselves as they ought to do.

My Grandfather Manley was an exception to all of this, and I had been fully
aware of the fact long before the time he caught me and my girl staying in his
room. He was an exception in the first place because he refused from the very start
to move into the same house with my mother and father — at the time when he
was widowed — or even, for that matter, to come and live in the same town with
us. He had resisted making that fatal mistake which so many of his contemporaries
made — of moving in with their children. He was clearly different from them in a
number of other respects, too, but it must have been that first, firm refusal of his
to move in with us that allowed him to think for a few years that he could
altogether escape the ignominious fate — of the one kind or the other — which his
contemporaries had to endure.

He did not turn into an old woman and he did not try to play the martinet.
Except for those relatively brief visits of his, he was free of the rules and mores of
my parents' Nashville life. After three or four days spent mostly in my company,
he would be off again to his farm in Hunt County and to the "primitive" life he
lived there. If it was hard for anyone to see why he insisted on living in Hunt
County when he could have lived so comfortably in Nashville, I at any rate
thanked God on my knees that he had made that choice and prayed that he would
never change his mind. For the most part, he went on living in the drafty,
unheated farmhouse that he and his father before him had been born in. And on a
farm where both cotton and tobacco had once been the money crops, but where
truck farming had now become more profitable. There was no prestige or tradition
about the kind of farming he did over there. (It was somehow felt an embarrassment that he raised only tomatoes, strawberries, corn. It amounted to *truck*
farming, though we did not even say the word.) And certainly there was no
romance about the place itself. That is to say, his farm and the county it was in
were considered somewhat beyond the pale, not being in the handsome, bluegrass,
limestone country where livestock farms — and particularly horse farms — made
the landscape a joy to look upon and where the people had always held themselves
well above other mortal Tennesseeans. He preferred to go on living over there
even after my father had bought our fine house in Acklen Park and set aside the
room there for his exclusive occupancy.

It will be useful at this point to explain that before that day when I hid my girl
in the wardrobe, there actually had been two other serious and quite similar face-
offs between my grandfather and me, and useful that I give some account of those
earlier confrontations. They both took place in the very same year as the fateful
one in the front hall. And on both of those occasions Grandfather stayed on in the
house afterward, just as if nothing out of the ordinary had happened. This was so

despite there having been more violent interplay between us — verbal and otherwise — in those two encounters than there was destined to be in the last.

The first of them was in April of that year. My parents were not out of town that time. Rather, my father was in the hospital to undergo an operation on his prostate gland. He went into the hospital on the Sunday afternoon before the Monday morning when the operation was scheduled. Possibly he and my mother regarded the operation more apprehensively than they should have. My mother managed to obtain a room next to his in the hospital. She went in with him on Sunday in order to be near him during that night. My grandfather had of course been notified of the circumstances. Mother had even made a long-distance telephone call from Nashville to Huntsboro. And since Grandfather declined still to have a telephone in his house or to let the lines to other houses go across his land, he had had to be fetched by a messenger from his farm to Central's office on the town square.

That was on Saturday afternoon, and Mother had hoped he might come to Nashville on Sunday and stay in the house — presumably to keep me company — at least until Father was safely through the operation. But the old man was offended by everything about the situation. He resented being sent for and brought to the telephone office. He resented having to hear Mother's indelicate news in the presence of Central herself (a local girl and a cousin of ours). And the worst of it was, so he said on the telephone to Mother, he didn't believe in the seriousness of the operation. Actually, when Mother and Father had previously mentioned to him the possibility of such surgery, he had insisted that no such operation "existed" and that the doctor was pulling Father's leg. I was told this afterward by my father — long afterward — who said the old man had clearly resented such an unseemly subject's being referred to in his presence by his daughter or even by his son-in-law.

Anyhow, my mother told me that Grandfather would not be coming to stay with me on Sunday. I don't know whether or not she believed it. And I cannot honestly say for sure whether or not *I* believed he wasn't coming. I know only that on that Sunday afternoon, after my parents had left for the hospital, I telephoned two of my friends, two Acklen Park boys who would be graduating with me from Wallace School that June, and invited them to come over and to bring with them whatever they might have managed to filch from their fathers' liquor closets. Actually, it was only my way of informing them of what I had in mind for that Sunday afternoon and evening, because I knew where the key to Father's closet was and knew there was more than enough bourbon whiskey there to suffice for three boys on their first real binge. Since this was an opportunity we had all been contemplating for some time, my invitation was only a matter of form.

I heard Grandfather Manley in the driveway at about half past six. In fact I had lost track of time by then. We had been gulping down our whiskey as though it were lemonade. I could hardly stand on my feet when he came into the breakfast room, where we were seated about the table. I had made a stab at getting up when

I first heard his car outside. My intention was to meet him, as usual, in the front hall. But as soon as I had got halfway up I felt a little sick. I knew I would be too unsteady on my feet to effect my usual sort of welcome in the hall, which would have entailed my taking his bag to his room for him and helping him off with his topcoat. Instead, I was still seated at the table when he stepped into the breakfast-room doorway. I did manage to rise from my chair then, scraping it crazily along the linoleum floor, which, at any rate, was more than the other two boys managed. And I faced him across the gold pocket watch that he was now holding out in his open palm like a piece of incriminating evidence. Although I say I faced him across the watch, his eyes were not really on me when he spoke but on the other boys at the table. "It's more than half an hour past my suppertime," he said. "I generally eat at six." That is how I can account for the time it was. Drunk as my two friends assuredly were and difficult as they undoubtedly found it to rise, they did, when Grandfather said that about suppertime, manage to rise somehow from their chairs and without a word of farewell went stumbling out through the kitchen and out of the house.

Grandfather then turned and went to his room, giving me an opportunity to put away the liquor and the glasses. Or I suppose that was his purpose. Perhaps he had only gone to remove his topcoat and his hat. When he came back, I had not stirred but still sat there with one hand on the quart bottle, fully intending to pour myself another drink. I had waited, I think, with the intention of pouring it in his presence. Looking at me, he said, "It's a fine sort of company you are keeping nowadays here in Nashville." At that I took up the bottle and began pouring whiskey into my glass.

"They're my friends," I said, not looking at him. He stepped over to the table, seized the bottle by its neck with one hand, and took hold of my glass with the other. But I held on firmly to each — did so for several moments, that is. Together we were supporting both glass and bottle in mid-air. And then it must have been simultaneously that each of us relinquished his hold on both. The glass fell to the table, crashing and breaking into small pieces and splashing its contents over the tabletop. The bottle landed sidewise on the table, spewing out whiskey on Grandfather Manley's trousers, then rolled onto the floor, coming to rest there, unbroken but altogether empty. Immediately Grandfather Manley said, "Now you get that mess cleaned up." And he went off through the house to his room again.

His command had literally a sobering effect upon me, as probably nothing else could have done — more so, certainly, than the breakage and spillage had. Though I was feeling unsteady, I did clean up the tabletop and I wiped up the floor. I decided to take the fragments of glass and the empty bottle out to the garbage can in the alley. I didn't want my mother to see any of it and to raise questions when she came home on Monday. As I was returning from the garbage can to the house through the dark back yard, I had sudden guilt feelings about my mother and father, visualizing them in the hospital, Father lying in the white bed and Mother sitting in a straight chair beside him. I knew that I had to go to my grandfather's room and take whatever satisfaction I could from the scolding I fancied he would surely give me.

I found him in his room, seated in his platform rocker, which like all the other furniture in the room was made of golden oak — with caning in the seat and back. He sat in it as if it were a straight chair, with one of his long, khaki-clad legs crossed stiffly over the other and one high-topped brown shoe sticking out assertively into the room. All the furniture in the room was furniture which he had brought there, at my mother's urging, from his house in Hunt County. It was in marked contrast with the rest of the furniture in our house. Mother had said, however, that he would feel more comfortable and at home with his own things in the room, and that he would be more likely to take real possession of it — which, after all, was what she and Father hoped for. I suspect they thought that would be a first step toward moving him in to live with us. In the end, Mother was actually disappointed at the particular pieces he chose to bring. But there will be a time later on for me to say more about that.

Anyway, there he was in his rocker, already divested of his starched collar and of the vest he always wore under his gabardine coat. His suspenders were loosened and hanging down over the arms of the chair. And he had lit his first cigarette of the evening. (He had given up his pipe at the time of his escape from the nightriders and had taken up cigarettes, instead, because he said they gave more relief to his nerves. He had given up his beard and mustache then, too, because he couldn't forget how awful they had smelt to him when he had been hiding in the swamp for days on end and under stagnant water for many hours of the time.) I came into the room and stood before him, my back to the great golden-oak folding bed, which, when it was folded away against the wall, as it was now, could easily be mistaken for a large wardrobe like the one I was facing on the other side of the room, and matching it almost exactly in size, bulk, and color. I stood there in silence for several moments, waiting for him to begin the kind of dressing-down which he had never given me and which if he could have given me then might have made all the difference in the world in our future relation — and perhaps our lives.

For a while he said nothing. Then he said, "I don't want any supper tonight. If the cook left something, you'd better go eat it. Because if you *can* eat, it will likely do you good!" There was no note of sympathy in his voice, only an acknowledgment of my condition. But I could tell there was going to be no dressing-down, either. It was going to be just like always before when we had been left alone together.

"I can't eat anything," I said. And I began to feel that I was going to be actively ill. But somehow I was able to control and overcome that feeling. Then I began to feel drunk again, as drunk as I had been when he first came in on us. I slumped down onto a leather ottoman and sat with my elbows on my knees, still

looking at him. It was just as it had always been before. We had nothing to say to
each other — nothing we *could* say. And thinking about all the times we had been
left together like this when I was a little boy, it seemed to me that I had always
been somewhat drunk whenever he and I had had to talk, and had always been
unable to make any sense at all. "Tell me what it was like," I suddenly began now
in a too loud voice. "Tell me what it was like to be kidnapped by those nightriders
. . . out in Lake County." He sat forward in his chair as if so astonished by what I
had said that he would have to come to his feet. But still he didn't get up, and I
went on. "And what it was like . . . to see Captain Tyree hanged before your very
eyes." I was hesitating and stammering as I spoke. I had never before said
anything like this to him. In the past, you see, when we had been wanting a topic,
I had always pressed him to tell me about the Civil War — not because I cared
much about the War but because, as I realize now but didn't understand then, it
was what my parents cared about and were always telling me I ought to get him to
talk about. But he didn't want to talk about the War. Not in a serious way. He
would say, "There's little to tell, God knows," and put me off with a slapstick
anecdote or two, about shooting a man's hat off during the raid on Memphis,
outside the Gayoso Hotel, or about meeting General Forrest on a backcountry road
when, as a boy of sixteen and riding bareback on a mule, he was on his way to
enlist in Forrest's own critter company, how General Forrest and some other
officers had forced him off the road and into a muddy ditch and didn't even look
back at him until he yelled out after them every filthy kind of thing he could think
of. "But since I was a mite small for my age," he would say, "they must have
mistook me for some local farm boy. Only Forrest himself ever looked back —
looked back with that sickly grin of his." And then he was sure to end that
anecdote saying, "Likely I'm the onliest man or boy who ever called Bedford
Forrest a son-of-a-bitch and lived."

That was not, of course, the kind of war story I wanted. My father, who read
Civil War history, would, in my presence, try to draw the old man out on the
subject, asking him about Forrest's strategy or whether or not the War might have
been won if Jeff Davis had paid more attention to the "Western Theatre." And all
Grandfather Manley would say was: "I don't know about any of that. I don't know
what it matters."

But that Sunday night in his room, instead of plaguing him to talk about the War
as I had always previously tended to do, I took the opposite tack. And I think I
could not have stopped myself from going on even if I had wanted to. As I rattled
on, I felt my grandfather looking at me uncertainly, as though he were not sure
whether it was I or he that was drunk. "Tell me about your kidnapping," I said,
actually wavering on the big leather ottoman as I spoke, and my voice rising and
lowering — quite beyond my control. "Or tell me about the earthquake in 1811
that your old daddy used to tell you about, that made the Mississippi River run
upstream and formed Reelfoot Lake, and how you imagined when you were lost in

the swamp and half out of your head that you could see the craters and fissures from the earthquake still there." Suddenly Grandfather lit his second cigarette, got up from his chair, and went over and stood by a window. I suppose it occurred to him that I was mocking him, though I couldn't have said, myself, whether or not I was. "You're all worked up," he said. "And it's not just that whiskey in you. Your mother's got you all worked up about this damnable operation of your dad's."

"Tell me what it was like," I began again. In my confused and intoxicated state, my whole system seemed determined to give it all back to him — all the scary stories I had listened to through all the years about the nightriders of Reelfoot Lake. I can hear myself clearly even now, sometimes speaking to him in a singsongy voice more like a child's voice than the ordinary man's voice I had long since acquired. "Tell me what it was like to wake up in the Walnut Log Hotel at Samburg, Tennessee. . . . Tell me what it was like to lie in your bed in that shackly, one-story, backwoods hotel and have it come over you that it was no dream, that hooded men on horseback filled the yard outside, each with a blazing pine-knot torch, that there really was at every unglazed window of your room the raw rim of a shotgun barrel."

I hear myself going on and on that Sunday night. As I babbled away, it was not just that night but every night that I had ever been alone in the house with him. I had the sensation of retching or of actually vomiting, not the whiskey I had in my stomach but all the words about the nightriders I had ever had from him and had not known how to digest — words I had not ever wanted to hear. My confusion was such that some of the time I did not know at all what I was saying. I knew only that this was the beginning of my freedom from him. And I had no notion of why it should be so. Only now and then a vague thought or an image took shape for me — of him as the young soldier on horseback or of the War itself that he would not reveal to us, that he always substituted talk about the nightriders for. But now I would not have to have any of the nightrider business again. I was giving it all back. And as I did so, how nerve-racking my voice was, almost beyond endurance — to me no less than to my grandfather, he who sat before me in the bright light he had now put on in the room, wearing his rough country clothes, his blue shirt and khaki trousers, blinking his veiny eyelids at me, not really listening any longer to what I said. He was thinking then, as I knew he had always thought: *You don't want to hear such stuff as that. Not from me, you don't. You just want to hear yourself sketching in my old stories, giving them back to me. It makes me feel good. It helps you hide your feelings or whatever it is you've always wished to hide.* He sat before me blinking and thinking, one process, or one rhythm at any rate. And not really listening to me at all.

But I couldn't stop myself, any more than he could stop me with his blinking or with the twisting back and forth of his weak chin and lean jaw. The twisting was somehow offensive to me. It was something I had seen him do to other people who troubled or annoyed him in some way. It was almost as if he were chewing tobacco and looking for a place to spit — which is something he liked to boast he had never done. And I heard my awful childlike voice going on. It was as though it were not mine and as though I were someone hidden on the far side of the room from us in the big oak wardrobe where I would one day hide that girl. But my voice persisted. I went on and on, so nervous as I looked into his white-blue eyes that I feared I should burst into tears, or, worse still, into silly, little-boy laughter.

"Tell how they ordered you and Marcus Tyree out of your beds though you each slept with a revolver at your side, ordered you up from the straw mattresses on those homemade bedsteads and required the two of you to get fully dressed, even to putting on your starched collars and your black shoestring ties, and then escorted you both on muleback, at gunpoint, out to the edge of the bayou."

But he said nothing. He only kept on blinking at me. And the bright light had little or nothing to do with it. In recent years he had always blinked at me. (When I was fourteen, when I was sixteen, when I was eighteen. Those were the years when it got to be unbearable.) Each time we met, I pressed him to tell me tales about his war exploits and the suffering he endured. ("Ask him!" my father had said to me. "Ask him!" my mother had said to me.) That was what set him blinking usually. He distrusted all garrulous young people. Most of all, those who asked questions. *Why have you never waited and allowed me to speak for myself? I knew he was thinking, but didn't say. And why is it you've never opened your mouth to me about yourself?*

He had always thought I was hiding something. Tonight his suspicion was so strong I could hear it in his breathing. I went on and on. "Tell me again how you, alone, escaped! How the nightriders made a bonfire on the banks of the bayou and put a rope around Captain Tyree's neck, torturing him, pulling him up and letting him down until finally he said, 'Gentlemen, you're killing me.' And then one of the men said, 'That's what we aim to do, Captain.' And they yanked him up for the last time. How a moment later, when all eyes were on the strung-up body of your friend, your law partner, your old comrade-in-arms from the War days and with whom you had come there only as 'two friends of the court' to settle old land disputes made not by any man on earth but by an earthquake a hundred years before almost to the day, how at that moment, really in one of your wicked explosions of temper — afterward it was your rage you remembered most clearly — you vowed to survive (vowed it in your rage) and yourself bring to justice those squatters-turned-outlaws. And seeing your one chance to escape, you, in your saving rage, dived into the brackish water of the Bayou du Chien — you a man of sixty and more even then. Tell me how . . . you hid under the log floating in the bayou (somebody made a gavel from its wood for you later) and how in the pre-dawn dark they filled the dead log you were under full of buckshot, supposing it was you that was dead out there, supposing it was your body they saw floating, drifting sluggishly in the Bayou du Chien toward Reelfoot

Lake. But all the while —"

Before I finished, he had begun to laugh his sardonic courtroom laugh, which was more like an old piece of farm machinery that needed oiling than like most human laughter. It was a laugh that was famous for having destroyed the case of many a courtroom lawyer in Hunt County — more frequently than any argument or rhetoric he had ever employed. I had heard him laugh that way at our dinner table, too, when my father had expressed some opinion or theory that Grandfather had not agreed with but that he knew he could not refute with logic. And I went on long after I knew that any use there might have been in my performance that day was over. Long after I had realized that if my performance were going to have any effect, it had already been had. At some point I could see that he was no longer listening and that, after all, the victory of this engagement was somehow his. Finally I was silenced by his silence. Now he had come back from the window and sat down in the chair again and was smiling his wickedest courtroom smile at me. His green eyes seemed very bright, and I could tell that for a few moments at least my singsongy recounting of his experiences had stirred his memory. I felt that if I encouraged him — and if he permitted himself — he would even now take up where I had left off and describe one more time his ten days of wandering in the swamp after his escape and then perhaps his finally reaching a logging road on high ground and there lapping up water like an Indian out of the hoofprints of horses because he knew it was rainwater and pure, and then the ride to Tiptonville, concealed under the hay in a farmer's wagon bed.

And at last the trial of the nine nightriders.

He loved to dwell upon the fact that all nine men were proved to be previously convicted criminals, not downtrodden backwoodsmen whose livelihood in fishing and hunting the government and the big landowners of Lake County wished to take away. Perhaps he went over all that in his mind for a few moments, but what his wicked smile and the light in his eyes spoke of was a victory he was reveling in at that present moment. My long spiel about the nightrider trouble had reflected the many times I had had to listen to his account of it. And to him, I somehow understood in a flash of insight, it meant above all else what was perhaps dearest to his soul of all things during those years. It meant how many times he had successfully avoided reminiscing about the War. In retrospect I can see that it had become almost mechanical with him to answer any requests I made for stories about the War with stories about his adventures at Reelfoot Lake. For a number of years, I think, he had tried to distract me with just any of his old stories about hunting bear or deer or about lawsuits he had had that took him into tough communities where he had sometimes to fight his way out of the courtroom and sometimes share a bed in a country hotel with a known murderer whom he was defending. But for a time there had been no variations to his response. I did not know then, and do not know now, at what moment he took a vow to never talk about the Civil War and his own experiences in it, whether he unconsciously and gradually began to avoid the subject with members of his family — after he had already ceased talking about it with anybody else. But from his smile that day and his laughter, which I had only before heard him direct at my parents, I began to sense that he regarded me chiefly as their agent and that yielding to me in my pressing him to tell me about his war would be the first chink in his armor of resistance to my parents and could end with nothing less than their bringing him into Nashville and into our house to live.

At last he got up from his chair again. He was no longer smiling at me but clearly he was no longer angry with me, either. And at the end, when he dismissed me from his room, it occurred to me that seeing an eighteen-year-old boy drunk was nothing new to a man of his experience in the rough sort of world he came along in and that my pilfering my father's whiskey while he was in the hospital seemed to him almost a natural and inevitable mistake for a boy my age to have made. "You've had a hard day," he said — rather sternly but not more so than if he had been correcting me about some show of bad manners. "Get yourself a night's sleep, and we'll go to the hospital tomorrow to see how your dad is making out. Seems to me he and your mama's got you so worked up there's no telling what you *might* have done if I hadn't shown up as I did, unheralded and unannounced."

It was hardly six weeks later that we had our second run-in. He came in to Nashville on Decoration Day, when, of course, the Confederate veterans always held their most elaborate services and celebrations out at the State Fairground. Father and Mother had gone to Memphis to visit Father's sister out there over the Decoration Day weekend. They wouldn't have planned to go, so they said, except that Grandfather as usual swore he was never again going to attend a Confederate Reunion of any kind. He had been saying for years that all the reunions amounted to were occasions to promote everybody to a higher rank. He acknowledged that once upon a time he had been a party to this practice. He had been so for many years, in fact. But enough was enough. It was one thing to promote men like himself who had been private soldiers to the rank of captain and major but quite another to make them colonels and generals. They had voted him his majority back in the years before his kidnapping by the nightriders. But since the experience of that abduction by those murderous backwoodsmen, he had never attended another Confederate Reunion. For more than a dozen years now he had insisted that it would not be possible for him to pass in through the Fairground gates on any Decoration Day without being sure to come out with the rank of colonel. He could not countenance that. And he could not countenance that gathering of men each year to repeat and enlarge upon reminiscences of something that he was beginning to doubt had ever had any reality.

From the first moment after I had put my parents on the train for Memphis, I think I knew how that weekend was going to go. I would not have admitted it to myself and didn't admit it for many years afterward. I suspect, too, that from the time some weeks earlier when he had heard of my parents' plan to go to Memphis — that is, assuming that he would not be coming in for the Reunion — Grandfather must also have had some idea of how it might go. Looking back, it seems almost as if he and I were plotting the whole business together.

It didn't of course seem that way at the time. Naturally, I can only speculate on how it seemed for him, but he had made more than one visit to Nashville since the day he found me there drinking with my friends, and I had observed a decided change in him — in his attitude toward me, that is. On one occasion he had offered me a cigarette, which was the next thing, it seemed to me then, to offering me a drink. I knew of course that Grandfather had, at one time or another, used tobacco in most of its forms. And we all knew, as a matter of fact, that when he closed the door to his room at night he nearly always poured himself a drink — poured it into a little collapsible tumbler that, along with his bottle of sourmash, he had brought with him in his Gladstone bag. His drinking habits had never been exactly a secret, though he seldom made any direct reference to them except in certain stories he told. And whatever changes there were in his style during his very last years, his drinking habits never changed at all — not, I believe, from the time when he was a young boy in the Confederate Army until the day he died.

It is true that I often smelt liquor on his breath when he arrived at our house for a visit, but I believe that was because he made a habit of having a quick one when he stopped — along the way — to rest and to relieve himself at the roadside. Moreover, that was only like the drink he had in his room at night — for his nerves. I believe the other drinking he had done in his lifetime consisted entirely of great bouts he had sometimes had with groups of men on hunting trips, often as not in that very region around Reelfoot Lake where he had witnessed the torture and strangulation of his old comrade-in-arms and law partner and where he had later wandered for ten nights in the swampy woodland thereabout (he had regarded it as unsafe to travel by day and unsafe to knock on any cabin door, lest it be the hideaway of one of the nightriders), wandered without food and without fresh water to drink, and suffering sometimes from hallucinations.

I feel that I must digress again here in order to say a few things about those hallucinations he had, which must actually have been not unlike delirium tremens, and about impressions that I myself had of that country around the Lake when I visited it as a child. Actually, as a very young child — no more than three or four years old — I had been taken on a duck-hunting trip to the Lake with Father and Grandfather and a party of other men from Hunt County. I didn't go out with them, of course, when, decked out in their grass hats and grass skirts and capes — for camouflage — they took up their positions in the marshlands. I was left in the hunting lodge on the lake's edge in the care of the Negro man who had been brought along to do the cooking. I don't remember much about the days or the nights of that expedition. I must have passed them comfortably and happily enough. All I remember clearly is what seemed the endless and desolate periods of time I spent during the early-morning hours and the twilight hours of each day of our stay there, all alone in the lodge with Thomas, the cook. As I sat alone on the screened porch, which went all the way round that little batten-board lodge (of no more than three or four rooms and a loft) and listened to Thomas's doleful singing in the kitchen, all I could see in any direction was the dark water of the lake on one side and of the bayou on the other, with the cypress stumps and other broken trees rising lugubriously out of the water and the mysterious, deep woods of the bottom lands beyond on the horizon. It seemed to me that I could see for miles. And the fact was, the lodge being built high upon wooden pilings, it was indeed possible to see great distances across the lake, which was five miles wide in places.

During those hours on the screened porch I would think about the tales I had heard the men tell the night before when they were gathered around the iron stove and when I was going off to sleep on my cot in a far corner of the room. I suppose the men must have been having their drinks then. But I can't say that I remember the smell of alcohol. All the smells there in that place were strange to me, though — the smell of the water outside, the smell of the whitewash on the vertical boarding on the lodge, and the smell of the musty rooms inside the lodge which stood empty most of the year. The tales the men told were often connected with the nightrider trouble. Others were old tales about the New Madrid Earthquake that had formed the Lake more than a hundred years before. Some of the men told old folk tales about prehistoric monsters that rose up out of the lake in the dark of the moon.

I don't recall my father's contributing to this talk. My memory is that he sat somewhat outside the circle, looking on and listening appreciatively to the talk of those older men, most of whom had probably never been outside the state of Tennessee, unless it was to go a little way up into Kentucky for whiskey. But my Grandfather Manley contributed his full share. And everyone listened to him with close attention. He spoke with an authority about the Lake, of course, that none of the others quite had. When those other men told their stories about prehistoric monsters rising from the lake, one felt almost that Grandfather when he emerged from his ten days in the swampland, according to his own account, must have looked and smelt like just such a prehistoric monster. To me the scariest of his talk was that about some of the hallucinations he had, hallucinations about the hooded men mounted on strange animals charging toward him like the horsemen of the apocalypse. But almost as frightening as his own reminiscences were the accounts he had heard or read of that earthquake that made the lake.

The earthquake had begun on December 16, 1811, and the sequence of shocks was felt as far away as Detroit and Baltimore and Charleston, South Carolina. Upriver, at New Madrid, Missouri, nearly the whole town crumbled down the bluffs and into the river. The shocks went on for many days — even for several months — and in between the shocks the earth vibrated and sometimes trembled for hours on end "like the flesh of a beef just killed." Men and women and children, during the first bad shocks, hung on to trees like squirrels. In one case a tree "infested with people" was seen to fall across a newly made ravine, and the poor wretches hung there for hours until there was a remission in the earth's undulation. Whole families were seen to disappear into round holes thirty feet wide, and the roaring of the upheaval was so loud that their screams could not be heard.

Between Memphis and St. Louis the river foamed and in some places the current was observed to have reversed and run upstream for several hours. Everywhere the quake was accompanied by a loud, hoarse roaring. And on land, where fissures and craters appeared, a black liquid was ejected sometimes to a height of fifteen feet and subsequently fell in a black shower, mixed with the sand which it had forced along with it. In other places the earth burst open, and mud, water, sandstone, and coal were thrown up the distance of thirty yards. Trees everywhere were blown up, cracking and splitting and falling by the thousands at a time. It was reported that in one place the black liquid oozed out of the ground to the height of the belly of a horse. Grandfather had heard or read somewhere that John James Audubon had been caught in some of the later, less violent shocks and that his horse died of fright with him sitting it. Numbers of people died, of course, on the river as well as on the land, and many of those who survived were never afterward regarded as possessing their right senses.

Among the hallucinations that my grandfather had while wandering in the low ground after his escape was that that earthquake of a hundred years before — almost to the day of the month — had recurred or commenced again, or that he was living in that earlier time when the whole earth seemed to be convulsed and its surface appeared as it must have in primordial times. And he imagined that he was there on that frontier in company with the ragged little bands of Frenchmen and Spaniards and newly arrived American settlers, all of whose settlements had vanished into the earth, all of them in flight, like so many Adams and Eves, before the wrath of their Maker.

My father told me more than one time — again, long after I was grown — that it was only after Grandfather Manley had had a few drinks and was off somewhere with a group of men that he would describe the times of wandering in the swamps and describe his hallucinations about the earthquake. And I myself heard him speak of those hallucinations, when I was at the lodge with them and was supposed to be asleep in my cot, heard him speak of them as though they were real events he had experienced and heard him say that his visions of the earthquake were like a glimpse into the eternal chaos we live in, a glimpse no man should be permitted, and that after that, all of his war experiences seemed small and insignificant matters — as nothing. And it was after that, of course, that he could never bring himself to go back to those reunions and take part in those reminiscences with the other old soldiers of events so much magnified by them each year or take part in their magnification of their own roles by advancing themselves in rank each year.

Grandfather could only confide those feelings of his to other men. He would only confide them when he had a little whiskey in him. And what is important, too, is that he only drank alone or in the company of other men. He abhorred what my father and mother had come to speak of in the 1920s as social drinking. Drinking liquor was an evil and was a sign of weakness, he would have said, and just because one indulged in it oneself was no reason to pretend to the world that there was virtue in it. *That* to him was hypocrisy. Drinking behind closed doors or in a secluded hunting lodge, though one denounced it in public as an evil practice, signified respect for the public thing, which was more important than one's private character. It signified genuine humility.

And so it was, I must suppose, that he in some degree approved of the kind of drinking bout he had caught me in. And his approval, I suppose, spoiled the whole effect for me. It put me in the position, as I understand it now, of pretending to be like the man I felt myself altogether unlike and alien to.

And so it was that the circumstances he found me in were quite different on that inevitable Decoration Day visit of his. My parents were no sooner aboard the train for Memphis, that Friday night, than I had fetched a certain acquaintance of mine named Jeff Patterson — he was older than I and had finished his second year at Vanderbilt — and together we had picked up two girls we knew who lived on Eighth Avenue, near the Reservoir. We went dancing at a place out on Nine Mile Hill. We were joined there by two other couples of our acquaintance, and later the eight of us came back to Acklen Park. (I must say that I was much more experienced with girls by that age than I was with liquor.) We had had other, similar evenings at the house of the parents of the two other boys who joined us that night, but until then I had never been so bold as to use my parents' house for such purposes.

The girls we had with us were not the kind of girls such a boy as I was would spend any time with nowadays. That is why this part of the story may be difficult for people of a later generation to understand. With one's real girl, in those days, a girl who attended Ward Belmont school and who was enrolled in Miss Amy Lowe's dancing classes, one might neck in the back seat of a car. The girl might often respond too warmly and want to throw caution to the wind. But it was one's own manliness that made one overcome one's impulse to possess her and, most of all, overcome her impulse to let herself be possessed before taking the marriage vow. I am speaking of decent boys and girls of course and I acknowledge that even among decent or "nice" young people of that day there were exceptions to the rule. One knew of too many seven-month babies to have any doubt of that. Still, from the time one was fourteen or fifteen in Nashville, one had to know girls of various sorts and one had to have a place to take girls of the "other sort." No one of my generation would have been shocked by the events of that evening. The four couples went to bed — and finally slept — in the four bedrooms on the second floor of my parents' house in Acklen Park. As I have indicated, I had never before brought such a party to our house, and I gave no thought to how I would clean up the place afterward or how I would conceal what had gone on there.

It was only a few minutes past seven the next morning when I heard Grandfather's car outside in the driveway. I was at once electrified and paralyzed by the sound. Lying there in my own bed with that girl beside me, and with the other couples still asleep in the other rooms, I had a vision of our big, two-story brick house as it appeared from the outside that May morning, saw the details of the stone coigns at the four corners of the house, the heavy green window blinds and the keystones above the windows, even the acanthus leaves in the capitals of the columns on the front porch. I saw it all through my grandfather's sharp little eyes as he turned into the gravel driveway, and saw through his eyes not only my parents' car, which I had carelessly left out of the garage, but the cars also of the two other boys who had joined us, all three cars sitting out there in the driveway on Sunday morning, as if to announce to him that some kind of party — and even *what* kind of party, probably — was going on inside.

He didn't step into his room to set down his Gladstone bag. I heard him drop it on the floor in the front hall and then I heard his quick footstep on the long stairway. Then I heard him opening the doors to all the bedrooms. (We *had* had the decency to close ourselves off in separate rooms.) He opened my door last, by design I suppose. I was lying on my stomach and I didn't even lift my head to look at him. But I knew exactly how he would appear there in the doorway, still wearing his long coat and his summer straw hat. That was the last thought or the last vision I indulged in before I felt the first blow of his walking stick across my buttocks. At last he had struck me! That was what I thought to myself. At last we might begin to understand one another and make known our real feelings, each about the other.

By the time I felt the second blow from his stick I had realized that between the two blows he delivered me he had struck one on the buttocks of the girl beside me. Already I had begun to understand that his striking me didn't have quite the kind of significance I had imagined. By the time he had struck the girl a second time she had begun screaming. I came up on my elbows and managed to clamp my hand over her mouth to keep the neighbors from hearing her. He left us then. And over his shoulder as he went striding from the room he said, "I want you to get these bitches out of this house and to do so in one hell of a hurry!" He went back into the hallway, and then when I had scrambled out of bed I saw him, to my baffling chagrin and unaccountable sense of humilitation, hurrying into the other rooms, first one and then another, and delivering blows to the occupants of those other beds. Some of the others, I suppose, had heard him crack the door to their rooms earlier and had crawled out of bed before he got there. But I heard him and saw him wielding his stick against Jeff Patterson's backsides and against the little bottom of the girl beside him. Finally — still wearing his hat and his gabardine coat, mind you — he passed through the hall again and toward the head of the stair. I was standing in the doorway to my room by then, but still clad only in my underwear shorts. As he went down the stairsteps he glanced back at me and spoke again: "You get those bitches out of your mother's house and you do it in one hell of a hurry."

Even before I was able to pull on my clothes, all four of the girls were fully dressed and scurrying down the stairs, followed immediately by the three boys. I came to the head of the stairs and stood there somewhat bemused, looking down. The girls had gone off into the front rooms downstairs in search of certain of their possessions. I heard them calling to each other desperately, "I left my lipstick right here on this table!" And, "Oh God, where's my purse?" And, "Where in the world are my pumps?" I realized then that one of them had gone down the stairs barefoot, and simultaneously I saw Grandfather Manley moving by the foot of the stairs and toward the living room.

I descended slowly, listening to the voices in the front room. First there had come a little shriek from one of the girls when Grandfather entered. Then I heard his voice reassuring them. By the time I reached the living-room doorway he was assisting them in their search, whereas the three boys only stood by, watching. It was he himself who found that little purse. Already the four girls seemed completely at ease. He spoke to them gently and without contempt or even condescension. The girl who had been my date left with the others, without either of us raising the question of whether or not I might see her home. As they went out through the wide front door the four girls called out, "Goodbye!" in cheerful little voices. I opened my mouth to respond, but before I could make a sound I heard Grandfather answering, "Goodbye, girls." And it came over me that it had been to him, not me, they were calling goodbye. When he and I were alone in the hall, he said, "And now I reckon you realize what we've got to do. We've got to do something about those sheets."

It is a fact that he and I spent a good part of that day doing certain clean-up jobs and employing the electric iron here and there. I can't say it drew us together, though, or made any sort of bond between us. Perhaps that's what he imagined the result would be. But I never imagined so for a moment. I knew that one day there was something he would have to know about me that he couldn't forgive. Though he and I were of the same blood, we had parted company, so to speak, before I was born even, and there was some divisive thing between us that could never be overcome. Perhaps I felt that day that it was my parents, somehow, who would forever be a wall between us, and that once any people turned away from what he was, as they had done, then that — whatever it was he was — was lost to them and to their children and their children's children forever. But I cannot say definitely that I felt anything so certain or grand that day. I cannot say for sure what I felt except that when he spoke with such composure and assurance to those girls in my parents' living room, I felt that there was nothing in the world he didn't know and hadn't been through.

As he and I worked away at cleaning up the bedrooms that morning, I asked myself if his knowing so well how to speak to those girls and if the genuine sympathy and even tenderness that he clearly felt toward them meant perhaps that his insistence upon living alone in that old house over in Hunt County suggested there were girls or women in his life still. Whatever else his behavior that day meant, it meant that the more bad things I did and the worse they were, then the better he would think he understood me and the more alike he would think we were. But I knew there was yet something I could do that would show him how different we were and that until I had made him grasp that, I would not begin to discover what, since I wasn't and couldn't be like him, I *was* like. Or if, merely as a result of being born when I was and where I was, at the very tail end of something, I was like nothing else at all, only incomparably without a character of my own.

In July, Mother and Father went up to Beersheba Springs, on the Cumberland Plateau, for a few days' relief from the hot weather. Beersheba was an old-fashioned watering place, the resort in past times of Episcopal bishops, Louisiana planters, and the gentry of Middle Tennessee. By the 1920s only a select few from the Nashville Basin kept cottages there and held sway at the old hotel. It was the kind of summer spot my parents felt most comfortable in. It had never had the dash of Tate Springs or the homey atmosphere of Monteagle, but it was older than either of those places and had had since its beginning gambling tables, horses, and dancing. Behind the porticoed hotel on the bluff's edge the old slave quarters were still standing, as was also the two-story brick garçonnière, reached by a covered walkway from the hotel. There was an old graveyard overgrown with box and red cedar, enclosed by a rock wall and containing old gravestones leaning at precarious angles but still bearing good Tennessee-Virginia names like Burwell and Armistead. Farther along the bluff and farther back on the plateau were substantial cottages and summer houses, a good number of them built of squared chestnut logs and flanked by handsome limestone end-chimneys. The ancient and unreconstructed atmosphere of the place had its attraction even for Grandfather Manley, and my parents had persuaded him to accompany them on their holiday there.

He drove in to Nashville and then, still in his own car, followed Mother and Father in their car to Beersheba Springs, which was seventy or eighty miles southeast of Nashville, on the edge of the Plateau and just above what used to be known as the Highland Rim. It seemed a long way away. There was no question in my mind of the old man's turning up in Nashville this time. I looked forward with pleasure to a few days of absolute freedom — from my parents, from my grandfather, and even from the servants, who were always given a holiday whenever my parents were out of town. I was in such relaxed good spirits when

Father and Mother and Grandfather Manley had departed that I went up to my room — though it was not yet noon — and took a nap on my bed. I had no plans made for this period of freedom except to see even more than usual of a Ward Belmont girl with whom I had been having dates during most of that winter and spring and whom my parents, as an indication of their approval of my courting a girl of her particular family, had had to dinner at our house several times and even on one occasion when my grandfather was there. She was acknowledged by my family and by everyone else to be my girl, and by no one more expressly than by the two of us — by the girl herself, that is, and by myself.

I was awakened from my nap just before noon that day, by the ringing of the telephone in the upstairs hall. And it so happened that the person calling was none other than she whom I would have most wished to hear from. It was not usual for such a girl to telephone any boy, not even her acknowledged favorite. I have to say that as soon as I heard her voice I experienced once of those moments I used often to have in my youth, of seeming to know how everything was going to go. I can't blame myself for how things did go during the next twenty-four hours and can't blame the girl, either. Since this is not the story of our romance, it will suffice to say that though our romance did not endure for long after that time, these events were not necessarily the cause for its failure. The girl herself has prospered in life quite as much as I have. And no doubt she sometimes speaks of me nowadays, wherever in the world she is living, as "a boy I went with in Nashville," without ever actually mentioning my name. At any rate, when she telephoned that day she said she was *very much* upset about something and wanted *very much* to see me at once. She apologized for calling. She would not have been so brash, she said, except that since I told her of my parents' plans she knew I would probably be at home alone. The circumstance about which she was upset was that since her parents, too, were out of town, her two older sisters were planning "an awful kind of party" that she could not possibly have any part in. She wanted me to help her decide what she must do.

My parents had taken our family car to Beersheba, and so it was that she and I had to meet on foot, halfway between Acklen Park and her home, which was two or three miles away, out in the Belle Meade section. And it ended, of course, after several hours of earnest talk about love and life — exchanged over milkshakes in a place called Candy Land and on the benches in the Japanese Garden in Centennial Park — ended, that is, by our coming to my house and telephoning her sisters that she had gone to spend the night with a classmate from Ward Belmont. The inevitability of its working out so is beyond question in my mind. At least, in retrospect it is. Certainly both of us had known for many days beforehand that both sets of parents would be out of town; and certainly the very passionate kind of necking which we had been indulging in that summer, in the darkness of my father's car and in the darkness of her father's back terrace, had become almost intolerable to us. But we could honestly say to ourselves that we had made no plans for that weekend. We were able to tell ourselves afterward that it was just something that happened. And I was able to tell myself for many years afterward — I cannot deny it categorically even today — that I would not have consented to our coming to my house if I had thought there were the remotest possibility of Grandfather Manley's turning up there.

And yet, though I can tell myself so, there will always be a certain lingering doubt in my mind. And even after it was clear to both of us that we would sleep together that night, her sense of propriety was still such that she refused to go up to the second floor of my house. Even when I led her into Grandfather Manley's room, she did not realize or did not acknowledge to herself that it was a bedroom we were in. I suppose she had never before seen anything quite like the furniture there. "What a darling room!" she exclaimed when I had put on the floor lamp beside the golden-oak rocker. And when I pulled down the great folding bed, even in the dim lamplight I could see that she blushed. Simultaneously almost, I caught a glimpse of myself in the mirror of the oak bureau and I cannot deny that I thought with certain glee in that moment of my grandfather or deny that I felt a certain premonition of events.

My first thought when I heard his car outside the next afternoon was, We are in *his* room! We are in *his* bed! I imagined that that was what was going to disturb him most. The fact was we had been in and out of his bed I don't know how many times by then. We had not only made love there in a literal sense, and were so engaged when he arrived, but we had during various intervals delighted each other there in the bed with card games and even checkers and Parcheesi, with enormous quantities of snacks which the cook had left for me in the refrigerator, and finally with reading aloud to each other from volumes of poetry and fiction which I fetched from my room upstairs. If there had been any sense of wrongdoing in our heads the previous afternoon, regarding such preoccupations as would be ours during those two days, it had long since been dispelled by the time that old man my grandfather arrived — dispelled for both of us, and not just that time but probably for all future time. (As for myself, I know that I never again in all the years since have had any taste for taking my pleasure with such females as those Eighth Avenue-Reservoir girls — in the casual, impersonal way that one does with such females of any class or age.)

When I told her there beside me that it was the tires of my grandfather's car she and I had heard skidding in the gravel and that it was now his quick, light step on the porch steps that I recognized, she seized me by the wrist and whispered, "Even if he knows I'm here, I don't want him to see me, and I don't want to see him. You have to hide me! Quickly!" By the time we had pushed up the folding bed, there was already the sound of his key in the front door. There was nothing for it, if she were to be hidden, but to hide her in the wardrobe.

"Over there," I said, "If you're sure you want to. But it's his room. He's apt to find you."

"Don't you let him," she commanded.

"You put on your clothes," was all I could say. I was pulling on my own trousers. And now she was running on tiptoe toward the wardrobe, with nothing on at all, carrying all her clothing and a pillow and blanket from the bed, all in a bundle clutched before her. She opened the wardrobe door, tossed everything in before her, and then hopped in on top of it. I followed her over there, buttoning my trousers and trying to get into my shirt. As I took a last step forward to close the door on her, I realized that, except for her and the bundle of clothing she was crouched on, the wardrobe was entirely empty. There were no possessions of Grandfather's in it. I thought to myself, Perhaps he never opens the wardrobe, even. And as I closed the door I saw to my delight that my brave girl, huddled there inside the wardrobe, wasn't by any means shedding tears but was smiling up at me. And I think I knew then for the first time in my life how wonderful it is to be in love and how little anything else in the world matters. And I found myself smiling back at her with hardly an awareness of the fact that she hadn't a piece of clothing on her body. And I actually delayed closing the door long enough to put the palm of my hand to my mouth and throw her a kiss.

Then, having observed the emptiness of the wardrobe, I glanced over at the oak bureau and wondered if it weren't entirely empty, too. I was inspired by that thought to quickly gather up my books, along with a bread wrapper and a jam jar, a kitchen knife, a couple of plates and glasses, and also my own shoes and socks, and to stuff them all inside a drawer of the bureau. On opening the heavy top drawer I found I was not mistaken. The drawer was empty and with no sign of its ever having been used by Grandfather — perhaps not since the day when the furniture had first been brought from Hunt County and Mother had put down the white paper in it for lining.

Already I had heard Grandfather Manley calling my name out in the front hall. It was something I think he had never done before when arriving at the house. His choosing to do so had given me the extra time I had needed. When I closed the big bureau drawer I looked at myself in the wide mirror above it, and I was almost unrecognizable even to myself. I was sweating profusely. My hair was uncombed. I had not shaved in two days. My trousers and shirt were all wrinkles. But I heard my grandfather calling me a second time and knew I had to go out there.

When I stepped, barefoot, into his view I could tell from his expression that he saw me just as I had seen myself and that I was barely recognizable to him. He was standing at the foot of the stairs, from which point he had been calling my name. No doubt my face showed him how astonished I was to have him call out to me on coming into the house — at the informality and open friendliness of it. No doubt for a minute or so he supposed that accounted wholly for my obvious consternation. He actually smiled at me. It was rather a sickly grin, though, like General Forrest's, the smile of a man who isn't given to smiling. And yet there was an undeniable warmth in his smile and in the total expression on his face. "I couldn't abide another day of Beersheba Springs," he said. "The swells over there are too rich for my blood. I thought I would just slip by here on my way home and see what kind of mischief you might be up to."

Clearly what he said was intended to amuse me. And just as clearly he meant that he preferred whatever low life he might find me engaged in to the high life led by my parents' friends at Beersheba. Presently, though, he could deceive himself no longer about my extraordinary appearance and my nervous manner's indication that something was wrong.

"What the matter, son?" he said.

"Nothing's the matter," I said belligerently.

The very friendliness of his demeanor somehow made me resent more bitterly than ever before his turning up at so inconvenient a moment. This was my real life he had come in on and was interfering with. Moreover, he had intruded this time with real and unconcealed feelings of his own. I could not permit him, at that hour of my life, to make me the object of his paternal affection. I was a grown man now and was in love with a girl who was about to be disgraced in his eyes. How could there be anything between him and me? His life, whether or not it was in any way his fault, had kept him from knowing what love of our sort was. He might know everything else in the world, including every other noble feeling which I could never be able to experience. He might be morally correct about everything else in the world, but he was not morally correct about love between a man and a woman. This was what I felt there in the hall that afternoon. I was aware of how little I had to base my judgment on. It was based mostly on the nothing that had ever been said about women in all the stories he had told me. In all the stories about the nightriders, for instance, there was no incident about his reunion with his wife, my grandmother, afterward. And I never heard him speak of her by her first name. Even now I wonder how we ever know about such men and their attitude toward women. In our part of the world we were all brought up on tales of the mysterious ways of Thomas Jefferson, whose mother and wife were scarcely mentioned in his writings, and Andrew Jackson and Sam Houston, whose reticence on the subject of women is beyond the comprehension of most men nowadays. Did they have too much respect for women? Were they perhaps, for all their courage in other domains, afraid of women or afraid of their own compelling feelings about women? I didn't think all of this, of course, as I faced Grandfather Manley there in the hall, but I believe I felt it. It seemed to me that his generation and my own were a thousand years apart.

"What's the matter, son?" he said.

"Nothing's the matter," I said.

There was nothing more for either of us to say. He began to move toward me and in the direction of his room. "Why don't you wait a minute," I said, "before you go into your room?"

His little eyes widened, and after a moment he said, "It ain't my room, y'know.

I only stay in it."

"Yes," I said, "but I've been reading in there. Let me go clear up my books and things." I had no idea but to delay him. I said, "Maybe you should go out to the kitchen and get something to eat."

But he walked right past me, still wearing his hat and coat, of course, and still carrying his little Gladstone bag. When he had passed into his room and I had followed him in there, he said, "I see no books and things."

"No," I said, "I hid them in the bureau drawer. I didn't know whether you would like my being in here."

He looked at me skeptically. I went over and opened the drawer and took out my books and my shoes and socks. Then I closed the drawer, leaving everything else in it. But he came and opened the drawer again. And he saw the plates and other things. "What else are you hiding?" he asked. No doubt he had heard the knives and the plates rattling about when I closed the drawer. Then he turned and walked over to the wardrobe. I ran ahead of him and placed myself against the door. "You've got one of those bitches of yours hidden in there, I reckon," he said.

"No, sir," I said, trying to look him straight in the eye.

"Then what is it?" he said. And he began blinking his eyes, not because I was staring into them but because he was thinking. "Are you going to tell me, or am I going to find out for myself?"

Suddenly I said, "It's my girl in there." We were both silent for a time, staring into each other's eyes. "And you've no right to open the door on her," I finally said. "Because she's not dressed."

"You're lying," he came back at me immediately. "I don't believe you for a minute." He left me and went to the folding bed and pulled it down. He set his bag on the bed and he poked at the jumble of sheets with his cane. Then he stood there, looking back at me for several moments. He still had not removed his straw hat and had not unbuttoned his coat. Finally he began moving across the room toward me. He stood right before me, looking me in the eye again. Then, with almost no effort, he pushed me aside and opened the wardrobe door.

She still hadn't managed to get into her clothes but she was hugging the pillow and had the blanket half pulled over her shoulder. I think he may have recognized her from the one time he had met her at dinner. Or maybe, I thought to myself, he was just such an old expert that he could tell what kind of girl she was from one glance at her. Anyway, he turned on me a look cold and fierce and so articulate that I imagined I could hear the words his look expressed: "So this is how bad you really are?" Then he went directly over to the bed, took up his bag and his cane, left the room, and left the house without speaking to me again.

When I had heard the front door close I took the leather ottoman across the room and sat on it, holding hands with that brave and quiet girl who, with the door wide open now, remained crouching inside the wardrobe. When finally we heard him drive out of the driveway we smiled at each other and kissed. And I thought to myself again that his generation and ours were a thousand years apart, or ten thousand.

I thought of course that when Grandfather Manley left Acklen Park he would continue on his way to Hunt County. But that was not the case. Or probably he did go to Hunt County, after all, and then turned around and went back to Beersheba Springs from there. Because he arrived at Beersheba at about eleven o'clock that night, and it would be difficult to explain how he was dressed as he was unless he had made a trip home and changed into the clothes he arrived in. He left Acklen Park about four in the afternoon, and from that time through the remaining ten years of his life he was never again seen wearing the old gabardine coat or either of his broad-brimmed hats. When he arrived at Beersheba, Mother and Father were sitting on the front gallery of the hotel with a group of friends. They were no doubt rocking away in the big rockers that furnished the porch, talking about the bridge hands they had held that evening, and enjoying the view of the moonlight valley below Cumberland Mountain.

When they saw him drive up, the car was unmistakable of course. But the man who emerged from it was not unmistakable. Major Basil Manley was dressed in a black serge suit, and in the starched collar of his white shirt he wore a black shoestring tie. I can describe his attire in such detail because from that day I never saw him in any other. That is, except on Decoration Day in those later years, when he invariably appeared in Confederate uniform. And in which uniform, at his own request, he was finally buried, not at Huntsboro and not in the family graveyard, but at Mount Olivet Cemetery, at Nashville. My father's account of his arrival on the hotel porch is memorable to me because it is the source of a great discovery which I felt I had made. My parents didn't recognize him for a certainty until he had passed along the shadowy brick walkway between the hovering boxwoods and stepped up on the porch. And then, significantly, both of them went to him and kissed him on the cheek, first my mother and then my father. And all the while, as my father described it, Major Manley stood there, ramrod straight, his cheeks wet with tears, like an old general accepting total defeat with total fortitude.

And what I understood for certain when I heard about that ceremony of theirs was that it had, after all, been their battle all along, his and theirs, not his and mine. I, after all, had only been the pawn of that gentle-seeming couple who were his daughter and son-in-law and who were my parents. It is almost unbelievable the changes that took place in Grandfather from that day. He grew his beard again, which was completely white now, of course. It hid his lean jaw and weak chin, making him very handsome, and was itself very beautiful in its silky whiteness against his black suit and black shoestring tie. The following year — the very next May — he began attending the Confederate Reunions again. And of course he was promptly promoted to the rank of colonel. Yet he did hold out against ever wearing the insignia of that rank, until he was in his coffin and it was put on him by other hands. So far as I knew he never allowed anyone — not even the other veterans — to address him other than as Major Manley. And in the fall after he had first appeared in his new role at Beersheba Springs, he began coming in to Nashville more often than ever. I was not at home that fall, since that was my first year away at college, but when I would go home for a weekend and find him there or find that he had been there, I would observe some new object in his room, an old picture of my grandmother as a girl, bare-shouldered and with dark curls about her face, the picture in its original oval frame. Other family pictures soon appeared, too. And there was a handsome washbasin and pitcher, and there were some of his favorite books, like Ramsay's *Annals of Tennessee* and lawbooks that had belonged to his father, my great-grandfather. And then, very soon, he began to bring in small pieces of furniture that were unlike the golden-oak pieces already there.

When my mother had first urged Grandfather Manley to come live with us, it was just after my grandmother died and before we had moved into the big house in Acklen Park. He had said frankly then that he thought he would find it too cramped in our little house on Division Street. But when they bought the new house, they had done so with an eye to providing accommodations that would be agreeable to an old man who might before many years not like to climb stairs and who, at any rate, was known to be fond of his privacy. They consulted with a number of their friends who had the responsibility for aging parents. It was a bond they were now going to share with those friends or a bond which they aspired to, anyway. In those days in Nashville, having a Confederate veteran around the place was comparable to having a peacock on the lawn or, if not that, at least comparable to having one's children in the right schools. It was something anybody liked to have. It didn't matter, I suppose, what rank the veteran was, since he was certain to be promoted as the years passed. The pressure on Major Manley to move in with his daughter and son-in-law was gentle always, but it was constant and it was enduring. One of the most compelling reasons given him was that they wanted him to get to know his only grandson and that they wanted the grandson to have the benefit of growing up in the house with him. Well, when the new house was bought and he was shown that room on the first floor which was to be reserved perpetually for him whenever he might choose to come and occupy it, and when he was urged to furnish it with whatever pieces he might wish to bring in from Hunt County, he no doubt felt he could not absolutely reject the invitation. And he no doubt had unrealistic dreams about some kind of rapport that might develop between him and the son of this daughter and son-in-law of his. I don't remember the day it happened of course, but it must have come as a considerable shock and disappointment to Mother when a truck hired in Huntsboro arrived, bearing not the rosewood half-canopied bed from her mother's room at home, or the cannonball four-poster from the guest room there, but the fold-away golden-oak piece that came instead, and the other golden-oak pieces that arrived instead of the walnut and mahogany pieces she had had in mind. Yet no complaint was made to the old man. (His daughter and son-in-law were much too gentle for that.) The golden oak had come out of the downstairs "office" in the old farmhouse, which he had furnished when he first got married and moved in with his own parents. No doubt he thought it most appropriate for any downstairs bedroom, even in Acklen Park. The main object was to get him to occupy the room. And, after his fashion, this of course was how he had occupied it through the years.

But by Christmas of the year he and I had our confrontations he had, piece by piece, moved all new furnishings into the room and had disposed of all the golden oak. The last piece he exchanged was the folding bed for the walnut cannonball bed. When I came home at Christmas, there was the big four-poster filling the room, its mattress so high above the floor (in order to accommodate the trundle bed) that a set of walnut bed steps was required for Grandfather to climb into or out of it. And before spring came the next year Grandfather had closed his house in Hunt County and taken up permanent residence in Acklen Park. He lived there for the rest of his life, participating in my parents' lively social activities, talking freely about his Civil War experiences, even telling the ladies how he courted my grandmother during that time, and how sometimes he would slip away from his encampment, make a dash for her father's farm, and spy on her from the edge of a wood without ever letting her know he had been in the neighborhood.

Such anecdotes delighted the Nashville ladies and the Nashville gentlemen, too. But often he would talk seriously and at length about the War itself — to the great and special delectation of both my parents — describing for a room full of people the kind of lightning warfare that Forrest carried on, going on late into the evening sometimes, describing every little crossroads skirmish from Between The Rivers to Shiloh, pausing now and then for a little parenthetical explanation, for the ladies, of such matters as the difference between tactics and strategy. Sometimes he would display remarkable knowledge of the grand strategy of the really great battles of the War, of Shiloh and Vicksburg, of Stone River, Franklin, and Chickamauga, and of other battles that he had no part in. When he had a sufficiently worthy audience he would even speculate about whether or not the War in the West might have been won if Bragg had been removed from his command or whether the whole War mightn't have been won if President Davis had not viewed it so narrowly from the Richmond point of view. Or he would raise the question of what might have happened if Lee had been allowed to go to the Mountains.

I heard my parents' accounts of all such talk of his. But I heard some of it myself, too. The fall after I had graduated from Wallace School, I went away to the University of the South, at Sewanee. My father had gone to Vanderbilt because he had been a Methodist, and Vanderbilt was the great Methodist university in those days. But he and Mother, under the influence of one of his aunts, had become Episcopalian before I was born even. And so there was never any idea but that I should go to Sewanee. I liked being at Sewanee and liked being away from

Nashville for the first time in my life. The University of course was full of boys from the various states of the Deep South. I very soon made friends there with boys from Mississippi and Louisiana and South Carolina. And since Nashville was so close by, I used to bring some of them home with me on weekends or on short holidays. They of course had never seen Grandfather Manley the way he had been before. And they couldn't imagine his being different from the way he was then. He would gather us around him sometimes in the evening and talk to us about the War Between the States. The boys loved to listen to him. They really adored him and made over him and clamored for him to tell certain stories over and over again. I enjoyed it, too, of course. He seemed quite as strange and interesting an old character to me as he did to them. And sometimes when I would ask him a question, just the way the others did, he would answer me with the same politeness he showed them, and at those times I would have the uneasy feeling that he wasn't quite certain whether it was I or one of the others who was his grandson, whether I was not perhaps merely one of the boys visiting, with the others, from Sewanee.

EUDORA WELTY

A Worn Path

IT WAS DECEMBER — a bright frozen day in the early morning. Far out in the country there was an old Negro woman with her head tied in a red rag, coming along a path through the pinewoods. Her name was Phoenix Jackson. She was very old and small and she walked slowly in the dark pine shadows, moving a little from side to side in her steps, with the balanced heaviness and lightness of a pendulum in a grandfather clock. She carried a thin, small cane made from an umbrella, and with this she kept tapping the frozen earth in front of her. This made a grave and persistent noise in the still air, that seemed meditative like the chirping of a solitary little bird.

She wore a dark striped dress reaching down to her shoe tops, and an equally long apron of bleached sugar sacks, with a full pocket: all neat and tidy, but every time she took a step she might have fallen over her shoelaces, which dragged from her unlaced shoes. She looked straight ahead. Her eyes were blue with age. Her skin had a pattern all its own of numberless branching wrinkles and as though a whole little tree stood in the middle of her forehead, but a golden color ran underneath, and the two knobs of her cheeks were illumined by a yellow burning under the dark. Under the red rag her hair came down on her neck in the frailest of ringlets, still black, and with an odor like copper.

Now and then there was a quivering in the thicket. Old Phoenix said, "Out of my way, all you foxes, owls, beetles, jack rabbits, coons and wild animals! . . . Keep out from under these feet, little bob-whites. . . . Keep the big wild hogs out of my path. Don't let none of those come running my direction. I got a long way." Under her small black-freckled hand her cane, limber as a buggy whip, would switch at the brush as if to rouse up any hiding things.

On she went. The woods were deep and still. The sun made the pine needles almost too bright to look at, up where the wind rocked. The cones dropped as light as feathers. Down in the hollow was the mourning dove — it was not too late for him.

The path ran up a hill. "Seem like there is chains about my feet, time I get this far," she said, in the voice of argument old people keep to use with themselves. "Something always take a hold of me on this hill — pleads I should stay."

After she got to the top she turned and gave a full, severe look behind her where she had come. "Up through pines," she said at length. "Now down through oaks."

Her eyes opened their widest, and she started down gently. But before she got to the bottom of the hill a bush caught her dress.

Her fingers were busy and intent, but her skirts were full and long, so that before she could pull them free in one place they were caught in another. It was not possible to allow the dress to tear. "I in the thorny bush," she said. "Thorns, you doing your appointed work. Never want to let folks pass, no sir. Old eyes thought you was a pretty little *green* bush."

Finally, trembling all over, she stood free, and after a moment dared to stoop for her cane.

"Sun so high!" she cried, leaning back and looking, while the thick tears went over her eyes. "The time getting all gone here."

At the foot of this hill was a place where a log was laid across the creek.

"Now comes the trial," said Phoenix.

Putting her right foot out, she mounted the log and shut her eyes. Lifting her skirt, leveling her cane fiercely before her, like a festival figure in some parade, she began to march across. Then she opened her eyes and she was safe on the other side.

"I wasn't as old as I thought," she said.

But she sat down to rest. She spread her skirts on the bank around her and folded her hands over her knees. Up above her was a tree in a pearly cloud of mistletoe. She did not dare to close her eyes, and when a little boy brought her a plate with a slice of marble-cake on it she spoke to him. "That would be acceptable," she said. But when she went to take it there was just her own hand in the air.

So she left that tree, and had to go through a barbed-wire fence. There she had to creep and crawl, spreading her knees and stretching her fingers like a baby trying to climb the steps. But she talked loudly to herself: she could not let her dress be torn now, so late in the day, and she could not pay for having her arm or her leg sawed off if she got caught fast where she was.

At last she was safe through the fence and risen up out in the clearing. Big dead trees, like black men with one arm, were standing in the purple stalks of the withered cotton field. There sat a buzzard.

"Who you watching?"

In the furrow she made her way along.

"Glad this not the season for bulls," she said, looking sideways, "and the good

Lord made his snakes to curl up and sleep in the winter. A pleasure I don't see no two-headed snake coming around that tree, where it come once. It took a while to get by him, back in the summer."

She passed through the old cotton and went into a field of dead corn. It whispered and shook and was taller than her head. "Through the maze now," she said, for there was no path.

Then there was something tall, black, and skinny there, moving before her.

At first she took it for a man. It could have been a man dancing in the field. But she stood still and listened, and it did not make a sound. It was as silent as a ghost.

"Ghost," she said sharply, "who be you the ghost of? For I have heard of nary death close by."

But there was no answer — only the ragged dancing in the wind.

She shut her eyes, reached out her hand, and touched a sleeve. She found a coat and inside that an emptiness, cold as ice.

"You scarecrow," she said. Her face lighted. "I ought to be shut up for good," she said with laughter. "My senses is gone. I too old. I the oldest people I ever know. Dance, old scarecrow," she said, "while I dancing with you."

She kicked her foot over the furrow, and with mouth drawn down, shook her head once or twice in a little strutting way. Some husks blew down and whirled in streamers about her skirts.

Then she went on, parting her way from side to side with the cane, through the whispering field. At last she came to the end, to a wagon track where the silver grass blew between the red ruts. The quail were walking around like pullets, seeming all dainty and unseen.

"Walk pretty," she said. "This the easy place. This the easy going."

She followed the track, swaying through the quiet bare fields, through the little strings of trees silver in their dead leaves, past cabins silver from weather, with the doors and windows boarded shut, all like old women under a spell sitting there. "I walking in their sleep," she said, nodding her head vigorously.

In a ravine she went where a spring was silently flowing through a hollow log. Old Phoenix bent and drank. "Sweet-gum makes the water sweet," she said, and drank more. "Nobody know who made this well, for it was here when I was born."

The track crossed a swampy part where the moss hung as white as lace from every limb. "Sleep on, alligators, and blow your bubbles." Then the track went into the road.

Deep, deep the road went down between the high green-colored banks. Overhead the live-oaks met, and it was as dark as a cave.

A black dog with a lolling tongue came up out of the weeds by the ditch. She was meditating, and not ready, and when he came at her she only hit him a little with her cane. Over she went in the ditch, like a little puff of milkweed.

Down there, her senses drifted away. A dream visited her, and she reached her hand up, but nothing reached down and gave her a pull. So she lay there and presently went to talking. "Old woman," she said to herself, "that black dog come up out of the weeds to stall your off, and now there he sitting on his fine tail, smiling at you."

A white man finally came along and found her — a hunter, a young man, with his dog on a chain.

"Well, Granny!" he laughed. "What are you doing there?"

"Lying on my back like a June-bug waiting to be turned over, mister," she said, reaching up her hand.

He lifted her up, gave her a swing in the air, and set her down. "Anything broken, Granny?"

"No sir, them old dead weeds is springy enough," said Phoenix, when she had got her breath. "I thank you for your trouble."

"Where do you live, Granny?" he asked, while the two dogs were growling at each other.

"Away back yonder, sir, behind the ridge. You can't even see it from here."

"On your way home?"

"No sir, I going to town."

"Why, that's too far! That's as far as I walk when I come out myself, and I get something for my trouble." He patted the stuffed bag he carried, and there hung down a little closed claw. It was one of the bob-whites, with its beak hooked bitterly to show it was dead. "Now you go on home, Granny!"

"I bound to go to town, mister," said Phoenix. "The time come around."

He gave another laugh, filling the whole landscape. "I know you old colored people! Wouldn't miss going to town to see Santa Claus!"

But something held old Phoenix very still. The deep lines in her face went into a fierce and different radiation. Without warning, she had seen with her own eyes a flashing nickel fall out of the man's pocket onto the ground.

"How old are you, Granny?" he was saying.

"There is no telling, mister," she said, "no telling."

Then she gave a little cry and clapped her hands and said, "Git on away from here, dog! Look! Look at that dog!" She laughed as if in admiration. "He ain't scared of nobody. He a big black dog." She whispered, "Sic him!"

"Watch me get rid of that cur," said the man. "Sic him, Pete! Sic him!"

Phoenix heard the dogs fighting, and heard the man running and throwing sticks. She even heard a gunshot. But she was slowly bending forward by that time, further and further forward, the lids stretched down over her eyes, as if she were doing this in her sleep. Her chin was lowered almost to her knees. The yellow palm of her hand came out from the fold of her apron. Her fingers slid down and along the ground under the piece of money with the grace and care they would have in lifting an egg from under a setting hen. Then she slowly straightened up, she stood erect, and the nickel was in her apron pocket. A bird flew by. Her lips moved. "God watching me the whole time. I come to stealing."

The man came back, and his own dog panted about them. "Well, I scared him off that time," he said, and then he laughed and lifted his gun and pointed it at Phoenix.

She stood straight and faced him.

"Doesn't the gun scare you?" he said, still pointing it.

"No, sir, I seen plenty go off closer by, in my day, and for less than what I done," she said, holding utterly still.

He smiled, and shouldered the gun. "Well, Granny," he said, "you must be a hundred years old, and scared of nothing. I'd give you a dime if I had any money with me. But you take my advice and stay home, and nothing will happen to you."

"I bound to go on my way, mister," said Phoenix. She inclined her head in the red rag. Then they went in different directions, but she could hear the gun shooting again and again over the hill.

She walked on. The shadows hung from the oak trees to the road like curtains. Then she smelled wood-smoke, and smelled the river, and she saw a steeple and the cabins on their steep steps. Dozens of little black children whirled around her. There ahead was Natchez shining. Bells were ringing. She walked on.

In the paved city it was Christmas time. There were red and green electric lights strung and criss-crossed everywhere, and all turned on in the daytime. Old Phoenix would have been lost if she had not distrusted her eyesight and depended on her feet to know where to take her.

She paused quietly on the sidewalk where people were passing by. A lady came along in the crowd, carrying an armful of red-, green- and silver-wrapped presents; she gave off perfume like the red roses in hot summer, and Phoenix stopped her.

"Please, missy, will you lace up my shoe?" She held up her foot.

"What do you want, Grandma?"

"See my shoe," said Phoenix. "Do all right for out in the country, but wouldn't look right to go in a big building."

"Stand still then, Grandma," said the lady. She put her packages down on the sidewalk beside her and laced and tied both shoes tightly.

"Can't lace 'em with a cane," said Phoenix. "Thank you, missy. I doesn't mind asking a nice lady to tie up my shoe, when I gets out on the street."

Moving slowly and from side to side, she went into the big building, and into a tower of steps, where she walked up and around and around until her feet knew to stop.

She entered a door, and there she saw nailed up on the wall the document that had been stamped with the gold seal and framed in the gold frame, which matched the dream that was hung up in her head.

"Here I be," she said. There was a fixed and ceremonial stiffness over her body.

"A charity case, I suppose," said an attendant who sat at the desk before her.

But Phoenix only looked above her head. There was sweat on her face, the wrinkles in her skin shone like a bright net.

"Speak up, Grandma," the woman said. "What's your name? We must have your history, you know. Have you been here before? What seems to be the trouble with you?"

Old Phoenix only gave a twitch to her face as if a fly were bothering her.

"Are you deaf?" cried the attendant.

But then the nurse came in.

"Oh, that's just old Aunt Phoenix," she said. "She doesn't come for herself — she has a little grandson. She makes these trips just as regular as clockwork. She lives away back off the Old Natchez Trace." She bent down. "Well, Aunt Phoenix, why don't you just take a seat? We won't keep you standing after your long trip." She pointed.

The old woman sat down, bolt upright in the chair.

"Now, how is the boy?" asked the nurse.

Old Phoenix did not speak.

"I said, how is the boy?"

But Phoenix only waited and stared straight ahead, her face very solemn and withdrawn into rigidity.

"Is his throat any better?" asked the nurse. "Aunt Phoenix, don't you hear me? Is your grandson's throat any better since the last time you came for the medicine?"

With her hands on her knees, the old woman waited, silent, erect and motionless, just as if she were in armor.

"You mustn't take up our time this way, Aunt Phoenix," the nurse said. "Tell us quickly about your grandson, and get it over. He isn't dead, is he?"

At last there came a flicker and then a flame of comprehension across her face, and she spoke.

"My grandson. It was my memory had left me. There I sat and forgot why I made my long trip."

"Forgot?" The nurse frowned. "After you came so far?"

Then Phoenix was like an old woman begging a dignified forgiveness for waking up frightened in the night. "I never did go to school, I was too old at the Surrender," she said in a soft voice. "I'm an old woman without an education. It was my memory fail me. My little grandson, he is just the same, and I forgot it in the coming."

"Throat never heals, does it?" said the nurse, speaking in a loud, sure voice to old Phoenix. By now she had a card with something written on it, a little list. "Yes. Swallowed lye. When was it? — January — two-three years ago—"

Phoenix spoke unasked now. "No, missy, he not dead, he just the same. Every little while his throat begin to close up again, and he not able to swallow. He not get his breath. He not able to help himself. So the time come around, and I go on another trip for the soothing medicine."

"All right. The doctor said as long as you came to get it, you could have it," said the nurse. "But it's an obstinate case."

"My little grandson, he sit up there in the house all wrapped up, waiting by himself," Phoenix went on. "We is the only two left in the world. He suffer and it don't seem to put him back at all. He got a sweet look. He going to last. He wear a little patch quilt and peep out holding his mouth open like a little bird. I remembers so plain now. I not going to forget him again, no, the whole enduring time. I could tell him from all the others in creation."

"All right." The nurse was trying to hush her now. She brought her a bottle of medicine. "Charity," she said, making a check mark in a book.

Old Phoenix held the bottle close to her eyes, and then carefully put it into her pocket.

"I thank you," she said.

"It's Christmas time, Grandma," said the attendant. "Could I give you a few pennies out of my purse?"

"Five pennies is a nickel," said Phoenix stiffly.

"Here's a nickel," said the attendant.

Phoenix rose carefully and held out her hand. She received the nickel and then fished the other nickel out of her pocket and laid it beside the new one. She stared at her palm closely, with her head on one side.

Then she gave a tap with her cane on the floor.

"This is what come to me to do," she said. "I going to the store and buy my child a little windmill they sells, made out of paper. He going to find it hard to believe there such a thing in the world. I'll march myself back where he waiting, holding it straight up in this hand."

She lifted her free hand, gave a little nod, turned around, and walked out of the doctor's office. Then her slow step began on the stairs, going down.

THOMAS WOLFE

Chickamauga

ON THE SEVENTH DAY of August, 1861, I was nineteen years of age. If I live to the seventh day of August this year I'll be ninety-five years old. And the way I feel this mornin' I intend to live. Now I guess you'll have to admit that that's goin' a good ways back.

I was born up at the Forks of the Toe River in 1842. Your grandpaw, boy, was born at the same place in 1828. His father, and mine too, Bill Pentland — *your* great-grandfather, boy — moved into that region way back right after the Revolutionary War and settled at the Forks of Toe. The real Indian name fer hit was Estatoe, but the white men shortened hit to Toe, and hit's been known as Toe River ever since.

Of course hit was all Indian country in those days. I've heared that the Cherokees helped Bill Pentland's father build the first house he lived in, where some of us was born. I've heared, too, that Bill Pentland's grandfather came from Scotland back before the Revolution, and that thar was three brothers. That's all the Pentlands that I ever heared of in this country. If you ever meet a Pentland anywheres you can rest assured he's descended from one of those three.

Well, now, as I was tellin' you, upon the seventh day of August, 1861, I was nineteen years of age. At seven-thirty in the mornin' of that day I started out from home and walked the whole way in to Clingman. Jim Weaver had come over from Big Hickory where he lived the night before and stayed with me. And now he went along with me. He was the best friend I had. We had growed up alongside of each other: now we was to march alongside of each other fer many a long and weary mile — how many neither of us knowed that mornin' when we started out.

Hit was a good twenty mile away from where we lived to Clingman, and I reckon young folks nowadays would consider twenty mile a right smart walk. But fer people in those days hit wasn't anything at all. All of us was good walkers. Why Jim Weaver could keep goin' without stoppin' all day long.

Jim was big and I was little, about the way you see me now, except that I've shrunk up a bit, but I could keep up with him anywheres he went. We made hit into Clingman before twelve o'clock — hit was a hot day, too — and by three o'clock that afternoon we had both joined up with the Twenty-ninth. That was my regiment from then on, right on to the end of the war. Anyways, I was an enlisted man that night, the day that I was nineteen years of age, and I didn't see my home again fer four long years.

Your Uncle Bacchus, boy, was already in Virginny: we knowed he was thar because we'd had a letter from him. He joined up right at the start with the Fourteenth. He'd already been at First Manassas and I reckon from then on he didn't miss a big fight in Virginny fer the next four years, except after Antietam where he got wounded and was laid up fer four months.

Even way back in those days your Uncle Bacchus had those queer religious notions that you've heared about. The Pentlands are good people, but everyone who ever knowed 'em knows they can go queer on religion now and then. That's the reputation that they've always had. And that's the way Back was. He was a Russellite even in those days: accordin' to his notions the world was comin' to an end and he was goin' to be right in on hit when hit happened. That was the way he had hit figgered out. He was always prophesyin' and predictin' even back before the war, and when the war came, why Back just knowed that this was hit.

Why law! He wouldn't have missed that war fer anything. Back didn't go to war because he wanted to kill Yankees. He didn't want to kill nobody. He was as tender-hearted as a baby and as brave as a lion. Some fellers told hit on him later how they'd come on him at Gettysburg, shootin' over a stone wall, and his rifle bar'l had got so hot he had to put hit down and rub his hands on the seat of his pants because they got so blistered. He was singin' hymns, they said, with tears a-streamin' down his face — that's the way they told hit, anyway — and every time he fired he'd sing another verse. And I reckon he killed plenty because when Back had a rifle in his hands he didn't miss.

But he was a good man. He didn't want to hurt a fly. And I reckon the reason that he went to war was because he thought he'd be at Armageddon. That's the way he had hit figgered out, you know. When the war came, Back said: "Well, this is hit, and I'm a-goin' to be thar. The hour has come," he said, "when the Lord is goin' to set up His kingdom here on earth and separate the sheep upon the right hand and the goats upon the left — jest like hit was predicted long ago — and I'm a-goin' to be thar when hit happens."

Well, we didn't ask him which side *he* was goin' to be on, but we all knowed which side without havin' to ask. Back was goin' to be on the *sheep* side — that's the way *he* had hit figgered out. And that's the way he had hit figgered out right up to the day of his death ten years ago. He kept prophesyin' and predictin' right up to the end. No matter what happened, no matter what mistakes he made, he kept right on predictin'. First he said the war was goin' to be the Armageddon day. And when that didn't happen he said hit was goin' to come along in the eighties. And when hit didn't happen then he moved hit up to the nineties. And when the war broke out in 1914 and the whole world had to go, why Bacchus knowed that *that* was hit.

And no matter how hit all turned out, Back never would give in or own up he was wrong. He'd say he'd made a mistake in his figgers somers, but that he'd found out what hit was and that next time he'd be right. And that's the way he was up to the time he died.

I had to laugh when I heared the news of his death, because of course, accordin' to Back's belief, after you die nothin' happens to you for a thousand years. You jest lay in your grave and sleep until Christ comes and wakes you up. So that's why I had to laugh. I'd-a-give anything to've been there the next mornin' when Back woke up and found himself in heaven. I'd've give anything just to've seen the expression on his face. I may have to wait a bit but I'm goin' to have some fun with him when I see him. But I'll bet you even then he won't give in. He'll have some reason fer hit, he'll try to argue he was right but that he made a little mistake about hit somers in his figgers.

But Back was a good man — a better man than Bacchus Pentland never lived. His only failin' was the failin' that so many Pentlands have — he went and got queer religious notions and he wouldn't give them up.

Well, like I say then, Back was in the Fourteenth. Your Uncle Sam and Uncle George was with the Seventeenth, and all three of them was in Lee's army in Virginny. I never seed nor heared from either Back or Sam fer the next four years. I never knowed what had happened to them or whether they was dead or livin' until I got back home in '65. And of course I never heared from George again until they wrote me after Chancellorsville. And then I knowed that he was dead. They told hit later when I came back home that hit took seven men to take him. They asked him to surrender. And then they had to kill him because he wouldn't be taken. That's the way he was. He never would give up. When they got to his dead body they told how they had to crawl over a whole heap of dead Yankees before they found him. And then they knowed hit was George. That's the way he was, all right. He never would give in.

He is buried in the Confederate cemetery at Richmond, Virginny. Bacchus went through thar more than twenty years ago on his way to the big reunion up at Gettysburg. He hunted up his grave and found out where he was.

That's where Jim and me thought that we'd be too. I mean with Lee's men, in Virginny. That's where we thought that we was goin' when we joined. But, like I'm goin' to tell you now, hit turned out different from the way we thought.

Bob Saunders was our Captain; L. C. McIntyre our Major; and Leander Briggs the Colonel of our regiment. They kept us thar at Clingman fer two weeks. Then they marched us into Altamont and drilled us fer the next two months. Our drillin' ground was right up and down where Parker Street now is. In those days thar was nothing thar but open fields. Hit's all built up now. To look at hit today you'd never know thar'd ever been an open field thar. But that's where hit was, all right.

Late in October we was ready and they moved us on. The day they marched us out, Martha Patton came in all the way from Zebulon to see Jim Weaver before we went away. He'd known her fer jest two months; he'd met her the very week we joined up and I was with him when he met her. She came from out along Cane River. Thar was a camp revival meetin' goin' on outside of Clingman at the time, and she was visitin' this other gal in Clingman while the revival lasted; and that was how Jim Weaver met her. We was walkin' along one evenin' toward sunset and we passed this house where she was stayin' with this other gal. And both of them was settin' on the porch as we went past. The other gal was fair, and she was dark: she had black hair and eyes, and she was plump and sort of little, and she had the pertiest complexion, and the pertiest white skin and teeth you ever seed; and when she smiled there was a dimple in her cheeks.

Well, neither of us knowed these gals, and so we couldn't stop and talk to them, but when Jim saw the little 'un he stopped short in his tracks like he was shot, and then he looked at her so hard she had to turn her face. Well, then, we walked on down the road a piece and then Jim stopped and turned and looked again, and when he did, why, sure enough, he caught *her* lookin' at him too. And then her face got red — she looked away again.

Well that was where she landed him. He didn't say a word, but Lord! I felt him jerk there like a trout upon the line — and I knowed right then and thar she had him hooked. We turned and walked on down the road a ways, and then he stopped and looked at me and said:

"Did you see that gal back thar?"

"Do you mean the light one or the dark one?"

"You know damn good and well which one I mean," said Jim.

"Yes, I seed her — what about her?" I said.

"Well, nothin' — only I'm a-goin' to marry her," he said.

I knowed then that she had him hooked. And yet I never believed at first that hit would last. Fer Jim had had so many gals — I'd never had a gal in my whole life up to that time, but Lord! Jim would have him a new gal every other week. We had some fine-lookin' fellers in our company, but Jim Weaver was the handsomest feller that you ever seed. He was tall and lean and built just right, and he carried himself as straight as a rod: he had black hair and coal-black eyes, and when he looked at you he could burn a hole through you. And I reckon he'd burned a hole right through the heart of many a gal before he first saw Martha Patton. He could have had his pick of the whole lot — a born lady-killer if you ever seed one — and that was why I never thought that hit'd last.

And maybe hit was a pity that hit did. Fer Jim Weaver until the day that he met Martha Patton had been the most happy-go-lucky feller that you ever seed. He didn't have a care in the whole world — full of fun — ready fer anything and into every kind of devilment and foolishment. But from that moment on he was a different man. And I've always thought that maybe hit was a pity that hit hit him when hit did — that hit had to come jest at that time. If hit had only come a few years later — if hit could only have waited till the war was over! He'd wanted to go so much — he'd looked at the whole thing as a big lark — but now! Well she had him, and he had her: the day they marched us out of town he had her promise, and in his watch he had her picture and a little lock of her black hair, and as they marched us out, and him beside me, we passed her, and she looked at him, and I felt him jerk again and knowed the look she gave him had gone through him like a knife.

From that time on he was a different man; from that time on he was like a man in hell. Hit's funny how hit all turns out — how none of hit is like what we expect. Hit's funny how war and a little black-haired gal will change a man — but that's the story that I'm goin' to tell you now.

The nearest rail head in those days was eighty mile away at Locust Gap. They marched us out of town right up the Fairfield Road along the river up past Crestville, and right across the Blue Ridge there, and down the mountain. We made Old Stockade the first day's march and camped thar fer the night. Hit was twenty-four miles of marchin' right across the mountain, with the roads the way they was in those days, too. And let me tell you, fer new men with only two months' trainin' that was doin' good.

We made Locust Gap in three days and a half, and I wish you'd seed the welcome that they gave us! People were hollerin' and shoutin' the whole way. All the women folk and childern were lined up along the road, bands a-playin', boys runnin' along beside us, good shoes, new uniforms, the finest-lookin' set of fellers that you *ever* seed — Lord! you'd a-thought we was goin' to a picnic from the way hit looked. And I reckon that was the way most of us felt about hit, too. We thought we was goin' off to have a lot of fun. If anyone had knowed what he was in fer or could a-seed the passel o'scarecrows that came limpin' back barefoot and half naked four years later, I reckon he'd a-thought twice before he 'listed up.

Lord, when I think of hit! When I try to tell about hit thar jest ain't words enough to tell what hit was like. And when I think of the way I was when I joined up — and the way I was when I came back four years later! When I went away I was an ignorant country boy, so tender-hearted that I wouldn't harm a rabbit. And when I came back after the war was over I could a-stood by and seed a man murdered right before my eyes with no more feelin' than I'd have had fer a stuck hog. I had no more feelin' about human life than I had fer the life of a sparrer. I'd seed a ten-acre field so thick with dead men that you could have walked all over hit without steppin' on the ground a single time.

And that was where I made my big mistake. If I'd only knowed a little more, if I'd only waited jest a little longer after I got home, things would have been all right. That's been the big regret of my whole life. I never had no education. I never had a chance to git one before I went away. And when I came back I could a-had my schoolin' but I didn't take hit. The reason was I never knowed no better: I'd seed so much fightin' and killin' that I didn't care fer nothin'. I jest felt dead and numb like all the brains had been shot out of me. I jest wanted to git me a little patch of land somewheres and settle down and fergit about the world.

That's where I made my big mistake. I didn't wait long enough. I got married too soon, and after that the children came and hit was root, hawg, or die: I had to grub fer hit. But if I'd only waited jest a little while hit would have been all right. In less'n a year hit all cleared up. I got my health back, pulled myself together and got my feet back on the ground, and had more mercy and understandin' in me, jest on account of all the sufferin' I'd seen, than I ever had. And as fer my head, why hit was better than hit ever was: with all I'd seen and knowed I could a-got a schoolin' in no time. But you see I wouldn't wait. I didn't think that hit'd ever come back. I was jest sick of livin'.

But as I say — they marched us down to Locust Gap in less'n four days' time, and then they put us on the cars fer Richmond. We got to Richmond on the mornin' of one day, and up to that very moment we had thought that they was sendin' us to join Lee's army in the north. But the next mornin' we got our orders — and they was sendin' us out west. They had been fightin' in Kentucky: we was in trouble thar; they sent us out to stop the Army of the Cumberland. And that was the last I ever saw of old Virginny. From that time on we fought it out thar in the west and south. That's where we was, the Twenty-ninth, from then on to the end.

We had no real big fights until the spring of '62. And hit takes a fight to make a soldier of a man. Before that, thar was skirmishin' and raids in Tennessee and in Kentucky. That winter we seed hard marchin' in the cold and wind and rain. We learned to know what hunger was, and what hit was to have to draw your belly in to fit your rations. I reckon by that time we knowed hit wasn't goin' to be a picnic like we thought that hit would be. We was a-learnin' all the time, but we wasn't soldiers yet. It takes a good big fight to make a soldier, and we hadn't had one yet. Early in '62 we almost had one. They marched us to the relief of Donelson — but law! They had taken her before we got thar — and I'm goin' to tell you a good story about that.

U. S. Grant was thar to take her, and we was marchin' to relieve her before old Butcher could git in. We was seven mile away, and hit was comin' on to sundown — we'd been marchin' hard. We got the order to fall out and rest. And that was when I heared the gun and knowed that Donelson had fallen. Thar was no sound of fightin'. Everything was still as Sunday. We was settin' thar aside the road and then I heared a cannon boom. Hit boomed five times, real slow like — Boom! — Boom! — Boom! — Boom! — Boom! And the moment that I heared hit, I had a premonition. I turned to Jim and I said: "Well, thar you are! That's Donelson — and she's surrendered!"

Cap'n Bob Saunders heared me, but he wouldn't believe me and he said:

"You're wrong!"

"Well," said Jim, "I hope to God he's right. I wouldn't care if the whole damn war had fallen through. I'm ready to go home."

"Well, he's wrong," said Captain Bob, "and I'll bet money on hit that he is."

Well, I tell you, that jest suited me. That was the way I was in those days — right from the beginnin' of the war to the very end. If thar was any fun or devilment goin' on, any card playin' or gamblin', or any other kind of foolishness, I was right in on hit. I'd-a-bet a man that red was green or that day was night, and if a gal had looked at me from a persimmon tree, why, law! I reckon I'd a-clumb the tree to get her. That's jest the way hit was with me all through the war. I never made a bet or played a game of cards in my life before the war or after hit was over, but while the war was goin' on I was ready fer anything.

"How much will you bet?" I said.

"I'll bet you a hundred dollars even money," said Bob Saunders, and no sooner got the words out of his mouth than the bet was on.

We planked the money down right thar and gave hit to Jim to hold the stakes. Well, sir, we didn't have to wait half an hour before a feller on a horse came ridin' up and told us hit was no use goin' any farther — Fort Donelson had fallen.

"What did I tell you?" I said to Cap'n Saunders, and I put the money in my pocket.

Well, the laugh was on him then. I wish you could a-seen the expression on his face — he looked mighty sheepish, I tell you. But he admitted hit, you know, he had to own up.

"You were right," he said. "You won the bet. But — I'll tell you what I'll do!" He put his hand into his pocket and pulled out a roll of bills. "I've got a hundred dollars left — and with me hit's all or nothin'! We'll draw cards fer this last hundred, mine against yorn — high card wins!"

Well, I was ready fer him. I pulled out my hundred, and I said, "Git out the deck!"

So they brought the deck out then and Jim Weaver shuffled hit and held hit while we drawed. Bob Saunders drawed first and he drawed the eight of spades. When I turned my card up I had one of the queens.

Well, sir, you should have seen the look upon Bob Saunders' face. I tell you what, the fellers whooped and hollered till he looked like he was ready to crawl through a hole in the floor. We all had some fun with him, and then, of course, I gave the money back. I never kept a penny in my life I made from gamblin'.

But that's the way hit was with me in those days — I was ready fer hit — fer anything. If any kind of devilment or foolishness came up I was right in on hit with the ringleaders.

Well then, Fort Donelson was the funniest fight that I was ever in because hit was all fun fer me without no fightin'. And that jest suited me. And Stone

Mountain was the most peculiar fight that I was in because — well, I'll tell you a strange story and you can figger fer yourself if you ever heared about a fight like *that* before.

Did you ever hear of a battle in which one side never fired a shot and yet won the fight and did more damage and more destruction to the other side than all the guns and cannon in the world could do? Well, that was the battle of Stone Mountain. Now, I was in a lot of battles. But the battle of Stone Mountain was the queerest one of the whole war.

I'll tell you how hit was.

We was up on top of the Mountain and the Yankees was below us tryin' to drive us out and take the Mountain. We couldn't git our guns up thar, we didn't try to — we didn't *have* to git our guns up thar. The only gun I ever seed up thar was a little brass howitzer that we pulled up with ropes, but we never fired a shot with hit. We didn't git a chance to use hit. We no more'n got hit in position before a shell exploded right on top of hit and split that little howitzer plumb in two. Hit jest fell into two parts: you couldn't have made a neater job of hit if you'd cut hit down the middle with a saw. I'll never fergit that little howitzer and the way they split hit plumb in two.

As for the rest of the fightin' on our side, hit was done with rocks and stones. We gathered together a great pile of rocks and stones and boulders all along the top of the Mountain, and when they attacked we waited and let 'em have it.

The Yankees attacked in three lines, one after the other. We waited until the first line was no more'n thirty feet below us — until we could see the whites of their eyes, as the sayin' goes — and then we let 'em have hit. We jest rolled those boulders down on 'em, and I tell you what, hit was an awful thing to watch. I never saw no worse destruction than *that* with guns and cannon during the whole war.

You could hear 'em screamin' and hollerin' until hit made your blood run cold. They kept comin' on and we mowed 'em down by the hundreds. We mowed 'em down without firin' a single shot. We crushed them, wiped them out — jest by rollin' those big rocks and boulders down on them.

There was bigger battles in the war, but Stone Mountain was the queerest one I ever seed.

Fort Donelson came early in the war, and Stone Mountain came later toward the end. And one was funny and the other was peculiar, but thar was fightin' in between that wasn't neither one. I'm goin' to tell you about that.

Fort Donelson was the first big fight that we was in — and as I say, we wasn't really in hit because we couldn't git to her in time. And after Donelson that spring, in April, thar was Shiloh. Well — all that I can tell you is, we was thar on time at Shiloh. Oh Lord, I reckon that we was! Perhaps we had been country boys before, perhaps some of us still made a joke of hit before — but after Shiloh we wasn't country boys no longer. We didn't make a joke about hit after Shiloh. They wiped the smile off of our faces at Shiloh. And after Shiloh we was boys no longer: we was vet'ran men.

From then on hit was fightin' to the end. That's where we learned what hit was like — at Shiloh. From then on we knowed what hit would be until the end.

Jim got wounded thar at Shiloh. Hit wasn't bad — not bad enough to suit him anyways — fer he wanted to go home fer good. Hit was a flesh wound in the leg, but hit was some time before they could git to him, and he was layin' out thar on the field and I reckon that he lost some blood. Anyways, he was unconscious when they picked him up. They carried him back and dressed his wound right thar upon the field. They cleaned hit out, I reckon, and they bandaged hit — thar was so many of 'em they couldn't do much more than that. Oh, I tell you what, in those days thar wasn't much that they could do. I've seen the surgeons workin' underneath an open shed with meatsaws, choppin' off the arms and legs and throwin' 'em out thar in a pile like they was sticks of wood, sometimes without no chloroform or nothin', and the screamin' and the hollerin' of the men was enough to make your head turn gray. And that was as much as anyone could do. Hit was live or die and take your chance — and thar was so many of 'em wounded so much worse than Jim that I reckon he was lucky they did anything fer him at all.

I heared 'em tell about hit later, how he come to, a-layin' stretched out thar on an old dirty blanket on the bare floor, and an army surgeon seed him lookin' at his leg all bandaged up and I reckon thought he'd cheer him up and said: "Oh, that ain't nothin' — you'll be up and fightin' Yanks again in two weeks' time."

Well, with that, they said, Jim got to cursin' and a-takin' on something terrible. They said the language he used was enough to make your hair stand up on end. They said he screamed and raved and reached down thar and jerked that bandage off and said — "Like hell I will!" They said the blood spouted up thar like a fountain, and they said that army doctor was so mad he throwed Jim down upon his back and sat on him and he took that bandage, all bloody as hit was, and he tied it back around his leg again and he said: "Goddam you, if you pull that bandage off again, I'll let you bleed to death."

And Jim, they said, came ragin' back at him until you could have heared him fer a mile, and said: "Well, by God, I don't care if I do; I'd rather die than stay here any longer."

They say they had hit back and forth thar until Jim got so weak he couldn't talk no more. I know that when I come to see him a day or two later he was settin' up and I asked him: "Jim, how is your leg? Are you hurt bad?"

And he answered: "Not bad enough. They can take the whole damn leg off," he said, "as far as I'm concerned, and bury hit here at Shiloh if they'll only let me go back home and not come back again. Me and Martha will git along somehow," he said. "I'd rather be a cripple the rest of my life than have to come back and fight in this damn war."

Well, I knowed he meant hit too. I looked at him and seed how much he meant hit, and I knowed thar wasn't anything that I could do. When a man begins to talk that way, thar hain't much you can say to him. Well, sure enough, in a week or two, they let him go upon a two months' furlough and he went limpin' away upon a crutch. He was the happiest man I ever seed. "They gave me two months' leave," he said, "but if they jest let me git back home old Bragg'll have to send his whole damn army before he gits me out of thar again."

Well, he was gone two months or more, and I never knowed what happened — whether he got ashamed of himself when his wound healed up all right, or whether Martha talked him out of hit. But he was back with us again by late July — the grimmest, bitterest-lookin' man you ever seed. He wouldn't talk to me about hit, he wouldn't tell me what had happened, but I knowed from that time on he'd never draw his breath in peace until he left the army and got back home fer good.

Well, that was Shiloh, that was the time we didn't miss, that was where we lost our grin, where we knowed at last what hit would be until the end.

I've told you of three battles now, and one was funny, one was strange, and one was — well, one showed us what war and fightin' could be like. But I'll tell you a fourth one now. And the fourth one was the greatest of the lot.

We seed some big fights in the war. And we was in some bloody battles. But the biggest fight we fought was Chickamauga. The bloodiest fight I ever seed was Chickamauga. Thar was big battles in the war, but thar never was a fight before, thar'll never be a fight again, like Chickamauga. I'm goin' to tell you how hit was at Chickamauga.

All through the spring and summer of that year Old Rosey follered us through Tennessee.

We had him stopped the year before, the time we whupped him at Stone's River at the end of '62. We tard him out so bad he had to wait. He waited thar six months at Murfreesboro. But we knowed he was a-comin' all the time. Old Rosey started at the end of June and drove us out of Shelbyville. We fell back on Tullahoma in rains the like of which you never seed. The rains that fell the last week in June that year was terrible. But Rosey kept a-comin' on.

He drove us out of Tullahoma too. We fell back across the Cumberland, we pulled back behind the mountain, but he follered us.

I reckon thar was fellers that was quicker when a fight was on, and when they'd seed just what hit was they had to do. But when it came to plannin' and a-figgerin', Old Rosey Rosecrans took the cake. Old Rosey was a fox. Fer sheer natural cunnin' I never knowed the beat of him.

While Bragg was watchin' him at Chattanooga to keep him from gittin' across the Tennessee, he sent some fellers forty mile up stream. And then he'd march 'em back and forth and round the hill and back in front of us again where we could look at 'em, until you'd a-thought that every Yankee in the world was there.

But law! All that was just a dodge! He had fellers a-sawin' and a-hammerin', a buildin' boats, a-blowin' bugles and a-beatin' drums, makin' all the noise they could — you could hear 'em over yonder gittin' ready — and all the time Old Rosey was fifty mile or more down stream, ten mile *past* Chattanooga, a-fixin' to git over way down thar. That was the kind of feller Rosey was.

We reached Chattanooga early in July and waited fer two months. Old Rosey hadn't caught up with us yet. He still had to cross the Cumberland, push his men and pull his trains across the ridges and through the gaps before he got to us. July went by, we had no news of him. "Oh Lord!" said Jim, "perhaps he ain't a-comin'!" I knowed he was a-comin', but I let Jim have his way.

Some of the fellers would git used to hit. A feller'd git into a frame of mind where he wouldn't let hit worry him. He'd let termorrer look out fer hitself. That was the way hit was with me.

With Jim hit was the other way around. Now that he knowed Martha Patton he was a different man. I think he hated the war and army life from the moment that he met her. From that time he was livin' only fer one thing — to go back home and marry that gal. When mail would come and some of us was gittin' letters he'd be the first in line; and if she wrote him why he'd walk away like someone in a dream. And if she failed to write he'd jest go off somers and set down by himself: he'd be in such a state of misery he didn't want to talk to no one. He got the reputation with the fellers fer bein' queer — unsociable — always a-broodin' and a-frettin' about somethin' and a-wantin' to be left alone. And so, after a time, they let him be. He wasn't popular with most of them — but they never knowed what was wrong, they never knowed that he wasn't really the way they thought he was at all. Hit was jest that he was hit so desperate hard, the worst-in-love man that I ever seed. But law! I knowed! I knowed what was the trouble from the start.

Hit's funny how war took a feller. Before the war I was the serious one, and Jim had been the one to play.

I reckon that I'd had to work too hard. We was so poor. Before the war hit almost seemed I never knowed the time I didn't have to work. And when the war came, why I only thought of all the fun and frolic I was goin' to have; and then at last, when I knowed what hit was like, why I was used to hit and didn't care.

I always could git used to things. And I reckon maybe that's the reason that I'm here. I wasn't one to worry much, and no matter how rough the goin' got I always figgered *I* could hold out if the others could. I let termorrer look out fer hitself. I reckon that you'd have to say I was an optimist. If things got bad, well, I always figgered that they could be worse; and if they got so bad they couldn't be no worse, why then I'd figger that they couldn't last this way ferever, they'd have to git some better sometime later on.

I reckon toward the end thar, when they got so bad we didn't think they'd ever git no better, I'd reached the place where I jest didn't care. I could still lay down and go to sleep and not worry over what was goin' to come termorrer, because I never *knowed* what was to come and so I didn't let hit worry me. I reckon you'd have to say that was the Pentland in me — our belief in what we call predestination.

Now, Jim was jest the other way. Before the war he was happy as a lark and thought of nothin' except havin' fun. But then the war came and hit changed him so you wouldn't a-knowed he was the same man.

And, as I say, hit didn't happen all at once. Jim was the happiest man I ever seed that mornin' that we started out from home. I reckon he thought of the war as we all did, as a big frolic. We gave hit jest about six months. We figgered we'd be back by then, and of course all that jest suited Jim. I reckon that suited all of us. It would give us all a chance to wear a uniform and to see the world, to shoot some Yankees and to run 'em north, and then to come back home and lord it over those who hadn't been and be a hero and court the gals.

That was the way hit looked to us when we set out from Zebulon. We never thought about the winter. We never thought about the mud and cold and rain. We never knowed what hit would be to have to march on an empty belly, to have to march barefoot with frozen feet and with no coat upon your back, to have to lay down on bare ground and try to sleep with no coverin' above you, and thankful half the time if you could find dry ground to sleep upon, and too tard the rest of hit to care. We never knowed or thought about such things as these. We never knowed how hit would be there in the cedar thickets beside Chickamauga Creek. And if we had a-knowed, if someone had a-told us, why I reckon that none of us would a-cared. We was too young and ignorant to care. And as fer *knowin'* — law! The only trouble about *knowin'* is that you've got to know what knowin's *like* before you know what knowin' *is*. Thar's no one that can tell you. You've got to know hit fer yourself.

Well, like I say, we'd been fightin' all this time and still thar was no sign of the war endin'. Old Rosey jest kept a-follerin' us and — "Lord!" Jim would say, "will it never end?"

I never knowed myself. We'd been fightin' fer two years, and I'd given over knowin' long ago. With Jim hit was different. He'd been a-prayin' and a-hopin' from the first that soon hit would be over and that he could go back and get that gal. And at first, fer a year or more, I tried to cheer him up. I told him that it couldn't last forever. But after a while hit wasn't no use to tell him that. He wouldn't believe me any longer.

Because Old Rosey kept a-comin' on. We'd whup him and we'd stop him fer a while, but then he'd git his wind, he'd be on our trail again, he'd drive us back. — "Oh Lord!" said Jim, "will hit never stop?"

That summer I been tellin' you about, he drove us down through Tennessee. He drove us out of Shelbyville, and we fell back on Tullahoma, to the passes of the hills. When we pulled back across the Cumberland I said to Jim: "Now we've got him. He'll have to cross the mountains now to git at us. And when he does, we'll have him. That's all that Bragg's been waitin' fer. We'll whup the daylights out of him this time," I said, "and after that thar'll be nothin' left of him. We'll be home by Christmas, Jim — you wait and see."

And Jim just looked at me and shook his head and said: "Lord, Lord, I don't believe this war'll ever end!"

Hit wasn't that he was afraid — or, if he was, hit made a wildcat of him in the fightin'. Jim could get fightin' mad like no one else I ever seed. He could do things, take chances no one else I ever knowed would take. But I reckon hit was jest because he was so desperate. He hated hit so much. He couldn't git used to hit the way the others could. He couldn't take hit as hit came. Hit wasn't so much that he was afraid to die. I guess hit was that he was still so full of livin'. He didn't want to die because he wanted to live so much. And he wanted to live so much because he was in love.

. . . So, like I say, Old Rosey finally pushed us back across the Cumberland. We was in Chattanooga in July, and fer a few weeks hit was quiet thar. But all the time I knowed that Rosey would keep comin' on. We got wind of him again along in August. He had started after us again. He pushed his trains across the Cumberland, with the roads so bad, what with the rains, his wagons sunk down to the axle hubs. But he got 'em over, came down in the valley, then across the ridge, and early in September he was on our heels again.

We cleared out of Chattanooga on the eighth. And our tail end was pullin' out at one end of the town as Rosey came in through the other. We dropped down around the mountain south of town and Rosey thought he had us on the run again.

But this time he was fooled. We was ready fer him now, a-pickin' out our spot and layin' low. Old Rosey follered us. He sent McCook around down toward the south to head us off. He thought he had us in retreat but when McCook got thar we wasn't thar at all. We'd come down south of town and taken our positions along Chickamauga Creek. McCook had gone too far. Thomas was follerin' us from the north and when McCook tried to git back to join Thomas, he couldn't pass us, fer we blocked the way. They had to fight us or be cut in two.

We was in position on the Chickamauga on the seventeenth. The Yankees streamed in on the eighteenth, and took their position in the woods a-facin' us. We had our backs to Lookout Mountain and the Chickamauga Creek. The Yankees had their line thar in the woods before us on a rise, with Missionary Ridge behind them to the east.

The Battle of Chickamauga was fought in a cedar thicket. That cedar thicket, from what I knowed of hit, was about three miles long and one mile wide. We fought fer two days all up and down that thicket and to and fro across hit. When the fight started that cedar thicket was so thick and dense you could a-took a butcher knife and drove hit in thar anywheres and hit would a-stuck. And when that fight was over that cedar thicket had been so destroyed by shot and shell you could a-looked in thar anywheres with your naked eye and seed a black snake run a hundred yards away. If you'd a-looked at that cedar thicket the day after that fight was over you'd a-wondered how a hummin' bird the size of your thumbnail could a-flown through thar without bein' torn into pieces by the fire. And yet more than half of us who went into that thicket came out of hit alive and told the tale. You wouldn't have thought that hit was possible. But I was thar and seed hit, and hit was.

A little after midnight — hit may have been about two o'clock that mornin', while we lay there waitin' for the fight we knowed was bound to come next day — Jim woke me up. I woke up like a flash — you got used to hit in those days — and though hit was so dark you could hardly see your hand a foot away, I knowed his face at once. He was white as a ghost and he had got thin as a rail in that last year's campaign. In the dark his face looked white as paper. He dug his hand into my arm so hard hit hurt. I roused up sharp-like; then I seed him and knowed who hit was.

"John!" he said — "John!" — and he dug his fingers in my arm so hard he made hit ache — "John! I've seed him! He was here again!"

I tell you what, the way he said hit made my blood run cold. They say we Pentlands are a superstitious people, and perhaps we are. They told hit how they saw my brother George a-comin' up the hill one day at sunset, how they all went out upon the porch and waited fer him, how everyone, the children and the grown-ups alike, all seed him as he clumb the hill, and how he passed behind a tree and disappeared as if the ground had swallered him — and how they got the news ten days later that he'd been killed at Chancellorsville on that very day and hour. I've heared these stories and I know the others all believe them, but I never put no stock in them myself. And yet, I tell you what! The sight of that white face and those black eyes a-burnin' at me in the dark — the way he said hit and the way hit was — fer I could feel the men around me and hear somethin' movin' in the wood — I heared a trace chain rattle and hit was enough to make your blood run cold! I grabbed hold of him — I shook him by the arm — I didn't want the rest of 'em to hear — I told him to hush up —

"John, he was here!" he said.

I never asked him what he meant — I knowed too well to ask. It was the third time he'd seed hit in a month — a man upon a horse. I didn't want to hear no more — I told him that hit was a dream and I told him to go back to sleep.

"I tell you, John, hit was no dream!" he said. "Oh John, I heared hit — and I heared his horse — and I seed him sittin' thar as plain as day — and he never said a word to me — he jest sat thar lookin' down, and then he turned and rode away into the woods. . . . John, John, I heared him and I don't know what hit means!"

Well, whether he seed hit or imagined hit or dreamed hit, I don't know. But the sight of his black eyes a-burnin' holes through me in the dark made me feel almost as if I'd seed hit too. I told him to lay down by me — and still I seed his eyes ablazin' thar. I know he didn't sleep a wink the rest of that whole night. I closed my eyes and tried to make him think that I was sleepin' but hit was no use — we lay thar wide awake. And both of us was glad when mornin' came.

The fight began upon our right at ten o'clock. We couldn't find out what was happenin': the woods thar was so close and thick we never knowed fer two days what had happened, and we didn't know fer certain then. We never knowed how many we was fightin' or how many we had lost. I've heared them say that even Old Rosey himself didn't know jest what had happened when he rode back into town next day, and didn't know that Thomas was still standin' like a rock. And if Old Rosey didn't know no more than this about hit, what could a common soldier know? We fought back and forth across that cedar thicket fer two days, and thar was times when you would be right up on top of them before you even knowed that they was thar. And that's the way the fightin' went — the bloodiest fightin' that was ever knowed, until that cedar thicket was soaked red with blood, and thar was hardly a place left in thar where a sparrer could have perched.

And as I say, we heared 'em fightin' out upon our right at ten o'clock, and then the fightin' came our way. I heared later that this fightin' started when the Yanks come down to the Creek and run into a bunch of Forrest's men and drove 'em back. And then they had hit back and forth until they got drove back themselves, and that's the way we had hit all day long. We'd attack and then they'd throw us back, then they'd attack and we'd beat them off. And that was the way hit went from mornin' till night. We piled up there upon their left: they mowed us down with canister and grape until the very grass was soakin' with our blood, but we kept comin' on. We must have charged a dozen times that day — I was in four of 'em myself. We fought back and forth across that wood until there wasn't a piece of hit as big as the palm of your hand we hadn't fought on. We busted through their right at two-thirty in the afternoon and got way over past the Widder Glenn's, where Rosey had his quarters, and beat 'em back until we got the whole way cross the Lafayette Road and took possession of the road. And then they drove us out again. And we kept comin' on, and both sides were still at hit after darkness fell.

We fought back and forth across that road all day with first one side and then tother holdin' hit until that road hitself was soaked in blood. They called that road the Bloody Lane, and that was jest the name fer hit.

We kept fightin' fer an hour or more after hit had gotten dark, and you could see the rifles flashin' in the woods, but then hit all died down. I tell you what, that night was somethin' to remember and to marvel at as long as you live. The fight had set the wood afire in places, and you could see the smoke and flames and hear the screamin' and the hollerin' of the wounded until hit made your blood run cold. We got as many as we could — but some we didn't even try to git — we jest let 'em lay. It was an awful thing to hear. I reckon many a wounded man was jest left to die or burn to death because we couldn't git 'em out.

You could see the nurses and the stretcher-bearers movin' through the woods, and each side huntin' fer hits dead. You could see them movin' in the smoke an' flames, an' you could see the dead men layin' there as thick as wheat, with their corpse-like faces an' black powder on their lips, an' a little bit of moonlight comin' through the trees, and all of hit more like a nightmare out of hell than anything I ever knowed before.

But we had other work to do. All through the night we could hear the Yanks a-choppin' and a-thrashin' round, and we knowed that they was fellin' trees to block us when we went fer them next mornin'. Fer we knowed the fight was only jest begun. We figgered that we'd had the best of hit, but we knowed no one had won the battle yet. We knowed the second day would beat the first.

Jim knowed hit too. Poor Jim, he didn't sleep that night — he never seed the man upon the horse that night — he jest sat there, a-grippin' his knees and starin', and a-sayin': "Lord God, Lord God, when will hit ever end?"

Then mornin' came at last. This time we knowed jest where we was and what hit was we had to do. Our line was fixed by that time. Bragg knowed at last where Rosey had his line, and Rosey knowed where he was. So we waited there, both sides, till mornin' came. Hit was a foggy mornin' with mist upon the ground. Around ten o'clock when the mist began to rise, we got the order and we went chargin' through the wood again.

We knowed the fight was goin' to be upon the right — upon our right, that is — on Rosey's left. And we knowed that Thomas was in charge of Rosey's left. And we all knowed that hit was easier to crack a flint rock with your teeth than to make old Thomas budge. But we went after him, and I tell you what, that was a fight! The first day's fight had been like playin' marbles when compared to this.

We hit old Thomas on his left at half-past ten, and Breckenridge came sweepin' round and turned old Thomas's flank and came in at his back, and then we had hit hot and heavy. Old Thomas whupped his men around like he would crack a rawhide whup and drove Breckenridge back around the flank again, but we was back on top of him before you knowed the first attack was over.

The fight went ragin' down the flank, down to the center of Old Rosey's army and back and forth across the left, and all up and down old Thomas's line. We'd hit him right and left and in the middle, and he'd come back at us and throw us back again. And we went ragin' back and forth thar like two bloody lions with that cedar thicket so tore up, so bloody and so thick with dead by that time, that hit looked as if all hell had broken loose in thar.

Rosey kept a-whuppin' men around off of his right, to help old Thomas on the left to stave us off. And then we'd hit old Thomas left of center and we'd bang him in the middle and we'd hit him on his left again, and he'd whup those Yankees back and forth off of the right into his flanks and middle as we went fer him, until we run those Yankees ragged. We had them gallopin' back and forth like kangaroos, and in the end that was the thing that cooked their goose.

The worst fightin' had been on the left, on Thomas's line, but to hold us thar they'd thinned their right out and had failed to close in on the center of their line. And at two o'clock that afternoon when Longstreet seed the gap in Wood's position on the right, he took five brigades of us and poured us through. That whupped them. That broke their line and smashed their whole right all to smithereens. We went after them like a pack of ragin' devils. We killed 'em and we took 'em by the thousands, and those we didn't kill and take right thar went streamin' back across the Ridge as if all hell was at their heels.

That was a rout if ever I heared tell of one! They went streamin' back across the Ridge — hit was each man fer himself and the devil take the hindmost. They caught Rosey comin' up — he rode into them — he tried to check 'em, face 'em round, and get 'em to come on again — hit was like tryin' to swim the Mississippi upstream on a boneyard mule! They swept him back with them as if he'd been a wooden chip. They went streamin' into Rossville like the rag-tag of creation — the worst whupped army that you ever seed, and Old Rosey was along with all the rest!

He knowed hit was all up with him, or thought he knowed hit, for everybody told him the Army of the Cumberland had been blowed to smithereens and that hit was a general rout. And Old Rosey turned and rode to Chattanooga, and he was a beaten man. I've heared tell that when he rode up to his headquarters thar in Chattanooga they had to help him from his horse, and that he walked into the house all dazed and fuddled-like, like he never knowed what had happened to him — and that he jest sat thar struck dumb and never spoke.

This was at four o'clock of that same afternoon. And then the news was brought to him that Thomas was still thar upon the field and wouldn't budge. Old Thomas stayed thar like a rock. We'd smashed the right, we'd sent it flyin' back across the Ridge, the whole Yankee right was broken into bits and streamin' back to Rossville for dear life. Then we bent old Thomas back upon his left. We thought we had him, he'd have to leave the field or else surrender. But old Thomas turned and fell back along the Ridge and put his back against the wall thar, and he wouldn't budge.

Longstreet pulled us back at three o'clock when we had broken up the right and sent them streamin' back across the Ridge. We thought that hit was over then. We moved back stumblin' like men walkin' in a dream. And I turned to Jim — I put my arm around him, and I said: "Jim, what did I say? I knowed hit, we've licked 'em and this is the end!" I never even knowed if he heared me. He went stumblin' on beside me with his face as white as paper and his lips black with the powder of the cartridge-bite, mumblin' and mutterin' to himself like someone talkin' in a dream. And we fell back to position, and they told us all to rest. And we leaned thar on our rifles like men who hardly knowed if they had come out of that hell alive or dead.

"Oh Jim, we've got 'em and this is the end!" I said.

He leaned thar swayin' on his rifle, starin' through the wood. He jest leaned and swayed thar, and he never said a word, and those great eyes of his a-burnin' through the wood.

"Jim, don't you hear me?" — and I shook him by the arm. "Hit's over, man! We've licked 'em and the fight is over! — Can't you understand?"

And then I heared them shoutin' on the right, the word came down the line again, and Jim — poor Jim! — he raised his head and listened, and "Oh God!" he said, "we've got to go again!"

Well, hit was true. The word had come that Thomas had lined up upon the Ridge, and we had to go fer him again. After that I never exactly knowed what happened. Hit was like fightin' in a bloody dream — like doin' somethin' in a nightmare — only the nightmare was like death and hell. Longstreet threw us up that hill five times, I think, before darkness came. We'd charge up to the very muzzles of their guns, and they'd mow us down like grass, and we'd come stumblin' back — or what was left of us — and form again at the foot of the hill, and then come on again. We'd charge right up the Ridge and drive 'em through the gap and fight 'em with cold steel, and they'd come back again and we'd brain each other with the butt end of our guns. Then they'd throw us back and we'd re-form and come on after 'em again.

The last charge happened jest at dark. We came along and stripped the ammunition off the dead — we took hit from the wounded — we had nothin' left ourselves. Then we hit the first line — and we drove them back. We hit the second and swept over them. We were goin' up to take the third and last — they waited till they saw the color of our eyes before they let us have hit. Hit was like a river of red-hot lead had poured down on us: the line melted thar like snow. Jim stumbled and spun round as if somethin' had whupped him like a top. He fell right toward me, with his eyes wide open and the blood a-pourin' from his mouth. I took one look at him and then stepped over him like he was a log. Thar was no more to see or think of now — no more to reach — except that line. We reached hit and they let us have hit — and we stumbled back.

And yet we knowed that we had won a victory. That's what they told us later — and we knowed hit must be so because when daybreak came next mornin' the Yankees was all gone. They had all retreated into town, and we was left there by the Creek at Chickamauga in possession of the field.

I don't know how many men got killed. I don't know which side lost the most. I only know you could have walked across the dead men without settin' foot upon the ground. I only know that cedar thicket which had been so dense and thick two days before you could've drove a knife into hit and hit would of stuck, had been so shot to pieces that you could've looked in thar on Monday mornin' with your naked eye and seed a black snake run a hundred yards away.

I don't know how many men we lost or how many of the Yankees we may have killed. The Generals on both sides can figger all that out to suit themselves. But I know that when that fight was over you could have looked in thar and wondered how a hummin' bird could've flown through that cedar thicket and come out alive. And yet that happened, yes, and something more than hummin' birds — fer men came out, alive.

And on that Monday mornin', when I went back up the Ridge to where Jim lay, thar just beside him on a little torn piece of bough, I heard a redbird sing. I turned Jim over and got his watch, his pocket-knife, and what few papers and belongin's that he had, and some letters that he'd had from Martha Patton. And I put them in my pocket.

And then I got up and looked around. It all seemed funny after hit had happened, like something that had happened in a dream. Fer Jim had wanted so desperate hard to live, and hit had never mattered half so much to me, and now I was a-standin' thar with Jim's watch and Martha Patton's letters in my pocket and a-listenin' to that little redbird sing.

And I would go all through the war and go back home and marry Martha later on, and fellers like poor Jim was layin' thar at Chickamauga Creek.

Hit's all so strange now when you think of hit. Hit all turned out so different from the way we thought. And that was long ago, and I'll be ninety-five years old if I am livin' on the seventh day of August, of this present year. Now that's goin' back a long ways, hain't hit? And yet hit all comes back to me as clear as if hit happened yesterday. And then hit all will go away and be as strange as if hit happened in a dream.

But I have been in some big battles I can tell you. I've seen strange things and been in bloody fights. But the biggest fight that I was ever in — the bloodiest battle anyone has ever fought — was at Chickamauga in that cedar thicket — at Chickamauga Creek in that great war.

RICHARD WRIGHT

The Man Who Was Almost a Man

DAVE STRUCK OUT ACROSS the fields, looking homeward through paling light. Whut's the use talkin wid em niggers in the field? Anyhow, his mother was putting supper on the table. Them niggers can't understan nothing. One of these days he was going to get a gun and practice shooting, then they couldn't talk to him as though he were a little boy. He slowed, looking at the ground. Shucks, Ah ain scareda them even ef they are biggern me! Aw, Ah know whut Ahma do. Ahm going by ol Joe's sto n git that Sears Roebuck catlog n look at them guns. Mebbe Ma will lemme buy one when she gits mah pay from ol man Hawkins. Ahma beg her t gimme some money. Ahm ol ernough to hava gun. Ahm seventeen. Almost a man. He strode, feeling his long loose-jointed limbs. Shucks, a man oughta hava little gun aftah he done worked hard all day.

He came in sight of Joe's store. A yellow lantern glowed on the front porch. He mounted steps and went through the screen door, hearing it bang behind him. There was a strong smell of coal oil and mackerel fish. He felt very confident until he saw fat Joe walk in through the rear door, then his courage began to ooze.

"Howdy, Dave! Whutcha want?"

"How yuh, Mistah Joe? Aw, Ah don wanna buy nothing. Ah jus wanted t see ef yuhd lemme look at tha catlog erwhile."

"Sure! You wanna see it here?"

"Nawsuh. Ah wans t take it home wid me. Ah'll bring it back termorrow when Ah come in from the fiels."

"You plannin on buying something?"

"Yessuh."

"Your ma lettin you have your own money now?"

"Shucks. Mistah Joe, Ahm gittin t be a man like anybody else!"

Joe laughed and wiped his greasy white face with a red bandanna.

"Whut you plannin on buyin?"

Dave looked at the floor, scratched his head, scratched his thigh, and smiled. Then he looked up shyly.

"Ah'll tell yuh, Mistah Joe, ef yuh promise yuh won't tell."

"I promise."

"Waal, Ahma buy a gun."

"A gun? Whut you want with a gun?"

"Ah wanna keep it."

"You ain't nothing but a boy. You don't need a gun."

"Aw, lemme have the catlog, Mistah Joe. Ah'll bring it back."

Joe walked through the rear door. Dave was elated. He looked around at barrels of sugar and flour. He heard Joe coming back. He craned his neck to see if he were bringing the book. Yeah, he's got it. Gawddog, he's got it!

"Here, but be sure you bring it back. It's the only one I got."

"Sho, Mistah Joe."

"Say, if you wanna buy a gun, why don't you buy one from me? I gotta gun to sell."

"Will it shoot?"

"Sure it'll shoot."

"Whut kind is it?"

"Oh, it's kinda old . . . a left-hand Wheeler. A pistol. A big one."

"Is it got bullets in it?"

"It's loaded."

"Kin Ah see it?"

"Where's your money?"

"Whut yuh wan fer it?"

"I'll let you have it for two dollars."

"Just two dollahs? Shucks, Ah could buy tha when Ah git mah pay."

"I'll have it here when you want it."

"Awright, suh. Ah be in fer it."

He went through the door, hearing it slam again behind him. Ahma git some money from Ma n buy me a gun! Only two dollahs! He tucked the thick catalogue under his arm and hurried.

"Where yuh been, boy?" His mother held a steaming dish of black-eyed peas.

"Aw, Ma, Ah jus stopped down the road t talk wid the boys."

"Yuh know bettah t keep suppah waitin."

He sat down, resting the catalogue on the edge of the table.

"Yuh git up from there and git to the well n wash yosef! Ah ain feedin no hogs in mah house!"

She grabbed his shoulder and pushed him. He stumbled out of the room, then came back to get the catalogue.

"Whut this?"

"Aw, Ma, it's jusa catlog."

"Who yuh git it from?"

"From Joe, down at the sto."

"Waal, thas good. We kin use it in the outhouse."

"Naw, Ma." He grabbed for it. "Gimme ma catlog, Ma."

She held onto it and glared at him.

"Quit hollerin at me! Whut's wrong wid yuh? Yuh crazy?"

"But Ma, please. It ain mine! It's Joe's! He tol me t bring it back t im termorrow."

She gave up the book. He stumbled down the back steps, hugging the thick book under his arm. When he had splashed water on his face and hands, he groped back to the kitchen and fumbled in a corner for the towel. He bumped into a chair; it clattered to the floor. The catalogue sprawled at his feet. When he had dried his eyes he snatched up the book and held it again under his arm. His mother stood watching him.

"Now, ef yuh gonna act a fool over that ol book, Ah'll take it n burn it up."

"Naw, Ma, please."

"Waal, set down n be still!"

He sat down and drew the oil lamp close. He thumbed page after page, unaware of the food his mother set on the table. His father came in. Then his small brother.

"Whutcha got there, Dave?" his father asked.

"Jusa catlog," he answered, not looking up.

"Yeah, here they is!" His eyes glowed at blue-and-black revolvers. He glanced up, feeling sudden guilt. His father was watching him. He eased the book under the table and rested it on his knees. After the blessing was asked, he ate. He scooped up peas and swallowed fat meat without chewing. Buttermilk helped to wash it down. He did not want to mention money before his father. He would do much better by cornering his mother when she was alone. He looked at his father uneasily out of the edge of his eye.

"Boy, how come yuh don quit foolin wid tha book n eat yo suppah?"

"Yessuh."

"How you n ol man Hawkins gitten erlong?"

"Suh?"

"Can't yuh hear? Why don yuh lissen? Ah ast yu how wuz yuh n ol man Hawkins gittin erlong?"

"Oh, swell, Pa. Ah plows mo lan than anybody over there."

"Waal, yuh oughta keep yo mind on whut yuh doin."

"Yessuh."

He poured his plate full of molasses and sopped it up slowly with a chunk of cornbread. When his father and brother had left the kitchen, he still sat and looked again at the guns in the catalogue, longing to muster courage enough to present his case to his mother. Lawd, ef Ah only had tha pretty one! He could almost feel the slickness of the weapon with his fingers. If he had a gun like that he would polish it and keep it shining so it would never rust. N Ah'd keep it loaded, by Gawd!

"Ma?" His voice was hesitant.

"Hunh?"

"Ol man Hawkins give yuh mah money yit?"

"Yeah, but ain no usa yuh thinking bout throwin nona it erway. Ahm keepin tha money sos yuh kin have cloes t go to school this winter."

He rose and went to her side with the open catalogue in his palms. She was washing dishes, her head bent low over a pan. Shyly he raised the book. When he spoke, his voice was husky, faint.

"Ma, Gawd knows Ah wans one of these."

"One of whut?" she asked, not raising her eyes.

"One of these," he said again, not daring even to point. She glanced up at the page, then at him with wide eyes.

"Nigger, is yuh gone plumb crazy?"

"Aw, Ma—"

"Git outta here! Don yuh talk t me bout no gun! Yuh a fool!"

"Ma, Ah kin buy one fer two dollahs."

"Not ef Ah knows it, yuh ain!"

"But yuh promised me one—"

"Ah don care whut Ah promised! Yuh ain nothing but a boy yit!"

"Ma, ef yuh lemme buy one Ah'll *never* ast yuh fer nothing no mo."

"Ah tol yuh t git outta here! Yuh ain gonna toucha penny of tha money fer no gun! Thas how come Ah has Mistah Hawkins t pay yo wages t me, cause Ah knows yuh ain got no sense."

"But, Ma, we needa gun. Pa ain got no gun. We needa gun in the house. Yuh kin never tell whut might happen."

"Now don yuh try to maka fool outta me, boy! Ef we did hava gun, yuh wouldn't have it!"

He laid the catalogue down and slipped his arm around her waist.

"Aw, Ma, Ah done worked hard alla summer n ain ast yuh fer nothin, is Ah, now?"

"Thas whut yuh spose t do!"

"But Ma, Ah wans a gun. Yuh kin lemme have two dollahs outta mah money. Please, Ma. I kin give it to Pa . . . Please, Ma! Ah loves yuh, Ma."

When she spoke her voice came soft and low.

"Whut yu wan wida gun, Dave? Yuh don need no gun. Yuh'll git in trouble. N ef yo pa jus thought Ah let yuh have money t buy a gun he'd hava fit."

"Ah'll hide it, Ma. It ain but two dollahs."

"Lawd, chil, whut's wrong wid yuh?"

"Ain nothin wrong, Ma. Ahm almos a man now. Ah wans a gun."

"Who gonna sell yuh a gun?"

"Ol Joe at the sto."

"N it don cos but two dollahs?"

"Thas all, Ma. Jus two dollahs. Please, Ma."

She was stacking the plates away; her hands moved slowly, reflectively. Dave kept an anxious silence. Finally, she turned to him.

"Ah'll let yuh git tha gun ef yuh promise me one thing."

"Whut's tha, Ma?"

"Yuh bring it straight back t me, yuh hear? It be fer Pa."

"Yessum! Lemme go now, Ma."

She stooped, turned slightly to one side, raised the hem of her dress, rolled down the top of her stocking, and came up with a slender wad of bills.

"Here," she said. "Lawd knows yuh don need no gun. But yer pa does. Yuh bring it right back t me, yuh hear? Ahma put it up. Now ef yuh don, Ahma have yuh pa lick yuh so hard yuh won fergit it."

"Yessum."

He took the money, ran down the steps, and across the yard.

"Dave! Yuuuuuh Daaaaave!"

He heard, but he was not going to stop now. "Naw, Lawd!"

The first movement he made the following morning was to reach under his pillow for the gun. In the gray light of dawn he held it loosely, feeling a sense of power. Could kill a man with a gun like this. Kill anybody, black or white. And if he were holding his gun in his hand, nobody could run over him; they would have to respect him. It was a big gun, with a long barrel and a heavy handle. He raised and lowered it in his hand, marveling at its weight.

He had not come straight home with it as his mother had asked; instead he had stayed out in the fields, holding the weapon in his hand, aiming it now and then at some imaginary foe. But he had not fired it; he had been afraid that his father might hear. Also he was not sure he knew how to fire it.

To avoid surrendering the pistol he had not come into the house until he knew that they were all asleep. When his mother had tiptoed to his bedside late that night and demanded the gun, he had first played possum; then he had told her that the gun was hidden outdoors, that he would bring it to her in the morning. Now he lay turning it slowly in his hands. He broke it, took out the cartridges, felt them, and then put them back.

He slid out of bed, got a long strip of old flannel from a trunk, wrapped the gun in it, and tied it to his naked thigh while it was still loaded. He did not go in to breakfast. Even though it was not yet daylight, he started for Jim Hawkins' plantation. Just as the sun was rising he reached the barns where the mules and plows were kept.

"Hey! That you, Dave?"

He turned. Jim Hawkins stood eying him suspiciously.

"What're yuh doing here so early?"

"Ah didn't know Ah wuz gittin up so early, Mistah Hawkins. Ah wuz fixin t hitch up ol Jenny n take her t the fiels."

"Good. Since you're so early, how about plowing that stretch down by the woods?"

"Suits me, Mistah Hawkins."

"O.K. Go to it!"

He hitched Jenny to a plow and started across the fields. Hot dog! This was just what he wanted. If he could get down by the woods, he could shoot his gun and nobody would hear. He walked behind the plow, hearing the traces creaking, feeling the gun tied tight to his thigh.

When he reached the woods, he plowed two whole rows before he decided to take out the gun. Finally, he stopped, looked in all directions, then untied the gun and held it in his hand. He turned to the mule and smiled.

"Know whut this is, Jenny? Naw, yuh wouldn know! Yuhs jusa ol mule! Anyhow, this is a gun, n it kin shoot, by Gawd!"

He held the gun at arm's length. Whut t hell, Ahma shoot this thing! He looked at Jenny again.

"Lissen here, Jenny! When Ah pull this ol trigger, Ah don wan yuh t run n acka fool now!"

Jenny stood with head down, her short ears pricked straight. Dave walked off about twenty feet, held the gun far out from him at arm's length, and turned his head. Hell, he told himself, Ah ain afraid. The gun felt loose in his fingers; he waved it wildly for a moment. Then he shut his eyes and tightened his forefinger. Bloom! A report half deafened him and he thought his right hand was torn from his arm. He heard Jenny whinnying and galloping over the field, and he found himself on his knees, squeezing his fingers hard between his legs. His hand was numb; he jammed it into his mouth, trying to warm it, trying to stop the pain. The gun lay at his feet. He did not quite know what had happened. He stood up and stared at the gun as though it were a living thing. He gritted his teeth and kicked the gun. Yuh almos broke mah arm! He turned to look for Jenny; she was far over the fields, tossing her head and kicking wildly.

"Hol on there, ol mule!"

When he caught up with her she stood trembling, walling her big white eyes at him. The plow was far away; the traces had broken. Then Dave stopped short, looking, not believing. Jenny was bleeding. Her left side was red and wet with blood. He went closer. Lawd, have mercy! Wondah did Ah shoot this mule? He grabbed for Jenny's mane. She flinched, snorted, whirled, tossing her head.

"Hol on now! Hol on."

Then he saw the hole in Jenny's side, right between the ribs. It was round, wet, red. A crimson stream streaked down the front leg, flowing fast. Good Gawd! Ah wuzn't shootin at tha mule. He felt panic. He knew he had to stop that blood, or Jenny would bleed to death. He had never seen so much blood in all his life. He chased the mule for half a mile, trying to catch her. Finally she stopped, breathing hard, stumpy tail half arched. He caught her mane and led her back to where the plow and gun lay. Then he stooped and grabbed handfuls of damp black earth and tried to plug the bullet hole. Jenny shuddered, whinnied, and broke from him.

"Hol on! Hol on now!"

He tried to plug it again, but blood came anyhow. His fingers were hot and sticky. He rubbed dirt into his palms, trying to dry them. Then again he attempted to plug the bullet hole, but Jenny shied away, kicking her heels high. He stood helpless. He had to do something. He ran at Jenny; she dodged him. He watched a red stream of blood flow down Jenny's leg and form a bright pool at her feet.

"Jenny . . . Jenny," he called weakly.

His lips trembled. She's bleeding t death! He looked in the direction of home, wanting to go back, wanting to get help. But he saw the pistol lying in the damp black clay. He had a queer feeling that if he only did something, this would not be; Jenny would not be there bleeding to death.

When he went to her this time, she did not move. She stood with sleepy, dreamy eyes; and when he touched her she gave a low-pitched whinny and knelt to the ground, her front knees slopping in blood.

"Jenny . . . Jenny . . ." he whispered.

For a long time she held her neck erect; then her head sank, slowly. Her ribs swelled with a mighty heave and she went over.

Dave's stomach felt empty, very empty. He picked up the gun and held it gingerly between his thumb and forefinger. He buried it at the foot of a tree. He took a stick and tried to cover the pool of blood with dirt — but what was the use? There was Jenny lying with her mouth open and her eyes walled and glassy. He could not tell Jim Hawkins he had shot his mule. But he had to tell something. Yeah, Ah'll tell em Jenny started gittin wil n fell on the joint of the plow. . . . But that would hardly happen to a mule. He walked across the field slowly, head down.

It was sunset. Two of Jim Hawkins' men were over near the edge of the woods digging a hole in which to bury Jenny. Dave was surrounded by a knot of people, all of whom were looking down at the dead mule.

"I don't see how in the world it happened," said Jim Hawkins for the tenth time.

The crowd parted and Dave's mother, father, and small brother pushed into the center.

"Where Dave?" his mother called.

"There he is," said Jim Hawkins.

His mother grabbed him.

"Whut happened, Dave? Whut yuh done?"

"Nothin."

"C mon, boy, talk," his father said.

Dave took a deep breath and told the story he knew nobody believed.

"Waal," he drawled. "Ah brung ol Jenny down here sos Ah could do mah plowin. Ah plowed bout two rows, just like yuh see." He stopped and pointed at the long rows of upturned earth. "Then somethin musta been wrong wid ol Jenny. She wouldn ack right a-tall. She started snortin n kickin her heels. Ah tried t hol her, but she pulled erway, rearin n goin in. Then when the point of the plow was stickin up in the air, she swung erroun n twisted herself back on it . . . She stuck herself n started t bleed. N fo Ah could do anything, she wuz dead."

"Did you ever hear of anything like that in all your life?" asked Jim Hawkins.

There were white and black standing in the crowd. They murmured. Dave's mother came close to him and looked hard into his face. "Tell the truth, Dave," she said.

"Looks like a bullet hole to me," said one man.

"Dave, whut yuh do wid the gun?" his mother asked.

The crowd surged in, looking at him. He jammed his hands into his pockets, shook his head slowly from left to right, and backed away. His eyes were wide and painful.

"Did he hava gun?" asked Jim Hawkins.

"By Gawd, Ah tol yuh tha wuz a gun wound," said a man, slapping his thigh.

His father caught his shoulders and shook him till his teeth rattled.

"Tell whut happened, yuh rascal! Tell whut . . ."

Dave looked at Jenny's stiff legs and began to cry.

"Whut yuh do wid tha gun?" his mother asked.

"Whut wuz he doin wida gun?" his father asked.

"Come on and tell the truth," said Hawkins. "Ain't nobody going to hurt you . . ."

His mother crowded close to him.

"Did yuh shoot tha mule, Dave?"

Dave cried, seeing blurred white and black faces.

"Ahh ddinn gggo tt sshooot hher . . . Ah ssswear ffo Gawd Ahh ddin. . . . Ah wuz a-tryin t sssee ef the old gggun would sshoot —"

"Where yuh git the gun from?" his father asked.

"Ah got it from Joe, at the sto."

"Where yuh git the money?"

"Ma give it t me."

"He kept worryin me, Bob. Ah had t. Ah tol im t bring the gun right back t me . . . It was fer yuh, the gun."

"But how yuh happen to shoot that mule?" asked Jim Hawkins.

"Ah wuzn shootin at the mule, Mistah Hawkins. The gun jumped when Ah pulled the trigger . . . N fo Ah knowed anythin Jenny was there a-bleedin."

Somebody in the crowd laughed. Jim Hawkins walked close to Dave and looked into his face.

"Well, looks like you have bought you a mule, Dave."

"Ah swear fo Gawd, Ah didn go t kill the mule, Mistah Hawkins!"

"But you killed her!"

All the crowd was laughing now. They stood on tiptoe and poked heads over one another's shoulders.

"Well, boy, looks like yuh done bought a dead mule! Hahaha!"

"Ain tha ershame."

"Hohohohoho."

Dave stood, head down, twisting his feet in the dirt.

"Well, you needn't worry about it, Bob," said Jim Hawkins to Dave's father. "Just let the boy keep on working and pay me two dollars a month."

"Whut yuh wan fer yo mule, Mistah Hawkins?"

Jim Hawkins screwed up his eyes.

"Fifty dollars."

"Whut yuh do wid tha gun?" Dave's father demanded.

Dave said nothing.

"Yuh wan me t take a tree n beat yuh till yuh talk!"

"Nawsuh!"

"Whut yuh do wid it?"

"Ah throwed it erway."

"Where?"

"Ah . . . Ah throwed it in the creek."

"Waal, c mon home. N firs thing in the mawnin git to tha creek n fin tha gun."

"Yessuh."

"Whut yuh pay fer it?"

"Two dollahs."

"Take tha gun n git yo money back n carry it t Mistah Hawkins, yuh hear? N don fergit Ahma lam you black bottom good fer this! Now march yosef on home, suh!"

Dave turned and walked slowly. He heard people laughing. Dave glared, his eyes welling with tears. Hot anger bubbled in him. Then he swallowed and stumbled on.

That night Dave did not sleep. He was glad that he had gotten out of killing the mule so easily, but he was hurt. Something hot seemed to turn over inside him each time he remembered how they had laughed. He tossed on his bed, feeling his hard pillow. N Pa says he's gonna beat me . . . He remembered other beatings, and his back quivered. Naw, naw, Ah sho don wan im t beat me tha way no mo. Dam em all! Nobody ever gave him anything. All he did was work. They treat me like a mule, n then they beat me. He gritted his teeth. N Ma had t tell on me.

Well, if he had to, he would take old man Hawkins that two dollars. But that meant selling the gun. And he wanted to keep that gun. Fifty dollars for a dead mule.

He turned over, thinking how he had fired the gun. He had an itch to fire it again. Ef other men kin shoota gun, by Gawd, Ah kin! He was still, listening. Mebbe they all sleepin now. The house was still. He heard the soft breathing of his brother. Yes, now! He would go down and get that gun and see if he could fire it! He eased out of bed and slipped into overalls.

The moon was bright. He ran almost all the way to the edge of the woods. He stumbled over the ground, looking for the spot where he had buried the gun. Yeah, here it is. Like a hungry dog scratching for a bone, he pawed it up. He puffed his black cheeks and blew dirt from the trigger and barrel. He broke it and found four cartridges unshot. He looked around; the fields were filled with silence and moonlight. He clutched the gun stiff and hard in his fingers. But, as soon as he wanted to pull the trigger, he shut his eyes and turned his head. Naw, Ah can't shoot wid mah eyes closed n mah head turned. With effort he held his eyes open; then he squeezed. *Blooooom!* He was stiff, not breathing. The gun was still in his hands. Dammit, he'd done it! He fired again. *Blooooom!* He smiled. *Blooooom! Blooooom! Click, click.* There! It was empty. If anybody could shoot a gun, he could. He put the gun into his hip pocket and started across the fields.

When he reached the top of a ridge he stood straight and proud in the moonlight, looking at Jim Hawkins' big white house, feeling the gun sagging in his pocket. Lawd, ef Ah had just one mo bullet Ah'd taka shot at tha house. Ah'd like t scare ol man Hawkins jusa little . . . Jusa enough t let im know Dave Saunders is a man.

To his left the road curved, running to the tracks of the Illinois Central. He jerked his head, listening. From far off came a faint *hoooof-hoooof; hoooof-hoooof; hoooof-hoooof.* . . . He stood rigid. Two dollahs a mont. Les see now . . . Tha means it'll take bout two years. Shucks! Ah'll be dam!

He started down the road, toward the tracks. Yeah, here she comes! He stood beside the track and held himself stiffly. Here she comes, erroun the ben . . . C mon, yuh slow poke! C mon! He had his hand on his gun; something quivered in his stomach. Then the train thundered past, the gray and brown box cars rumbling and clinking. He gripped the gun tightly; then he jerked his hand out of his pocket. Ah betcha Bill wouldn't do it! Ah betcha . . . The cars slid past, steel grinding upon steel. Ahm ridin yuh ternight, so hep me Gawd! He was hot all over. He hesitated just a moment; then he grabbed, pulled atop of a car, and lay flat. He felt his pocket; the gun was still there. Ahead the long rails were glinting in the moonlight, stretching away, away to somewhere, somewhere where he could be a man . . .

• POETRY •

MODERN SOUTHERN POETRY BEGAN at a time — the early 1920's — when the very proximity of the two words, modern and Southern, often struck against each other as crushingly as two wheels engaged in opposite directions. In fact, the working through of the incongruities presented by the simultaneous claims of modern change and a Southern community rooted, for good or ill, in stubborn traditions, provided the intellectual context and the dramatic form of many of the first poems of the modern South. Many of them trace out inner debates of what can be recognized now as typically Southern divisions, and they were all written by members of the group known as the Fugitives. The Fugitives included John Crowe Ransom, Donald Davidson, Allen Tate, Robert Penn Warren, and several others — for the most part teachers and students — who by the mid-1920's had turned Vanderbilt University in Nashville into a capital of modern poetry and poetic theory.

By the end of the twenties the Fugitives had disbanded, though they did join together under another banner when they wrote some of the polemical essays collected in the Agrarian manifesto *I'll Take My Stand* in 1930. It has sometimes mistakenly been suggested that the Agrarian essays and the Fugitive poems by the same men represent two different impulses, and should not be confused. It may have taken different forms, but the impulse behind them was the same, part of a single continuous effort to understand themselves as modern Southern artists. Every other major Southern writer after them has undergone a version of the same conscious experience.

By the time *I'll Take My Stand* was published, modern Southern literature had become an affair of individuals, not groups, scattered all over the South, and has remained so throughout the century. The best known members of the Fugitives — Ransom, Tate, and especially the remarkable Robert Penn Warren — must finally be considered in terms of individual careers and individual voices since, in each case, a large number of their poems stand outside and beyond their Fugitive associations. But because the Fugitives were the first Southerners to address the special dilemma of the modern Southern writer — bound by time and place to two different worlds — it is only natural that they should always be treated first of all as a group, a community of poets who more than any single figure ushered in the age of modern Southern letters.

The Fugitives were above all modern poets, and when they began writing their poetry and publishing their journal *The Fugitive* (1922-25), they were concerned primarily with breaking away from the long-stiffened literary styles that had dominated Southern poetry and fiction since the end of the Civil War. Trained in the classics and increasingly aware of other modern poets in the United States and abroad, they insisted on well-crafted poems whose commitments were demandingly aesthetic and intellectual. In agreement with the prescriptions of T. S. Eliot, a sort of city cousin from St. Louis, who had described in his essay "Tradition and the Individual Talent" (1919) a community of poets past and present bound together by the sole kinship of having written permanent poems, the Fugitives found their models elsewhere than in Southern literature. The pious, sentimental, and nostalgic modes of nineteenth-century Southern verse were condemned from the beginning. As *The Fugitive*'s first editorial manifesto proclaimed: *"The Fugitive flees from nothing faster than from the high-caste Brahmins of the Old South."*

It is worth noting that even in this last statement, the direction of the flight depends on a definition of what is being rejected, and in this case the rejection concerns not the South as a whole but only a certain brand of Southern attitude. If the first impulse of the Fugitives thrust them into the wide world of modern aesthetic commitments, there was always the knowledge that they were emerging from a region that was archaic in many ways; and they were discriminate enough to realize that not all of those ways were merely old-fashioned and useless.

From the beginning, the Fugitives used their poetry as a means of testing some of these Southern archaisms for their permanent value. That they recognized value where they found it did not make their Southern allegiances easy and certain, but even as they developed their own ironic brand of a modern poetic idiom they often clung to home ground for the main source of their imagery and the central arena for their struggles of belief and doubt. Most of their Southern poems take the form of speculative self-debates, where nothing is finally resolved, but in all of them the very engagement of debatable Southern identity with exacting, original poetic language gives the impression of mutual reinforcement. At the very least, the engagement usually plants a highly rarefied intellectual activity in a definite physical existence. As John Crowe Ransom claimed in his essay "Poets Without Laurels," these were modern poems, but they were also human documents. The tangled guidelines of self-direction, and the inescapable magnetic pull of the Southern soil could make them both. Certainly nowhere in their poetry is there any desire to dismiss the South altogether. They could speculate on it, and mark its failings, but they could not willingly repudiate everything that had made them what they were. And they ended by discovering in a common Southern background values that they were unable to find anywhere else.

It is important to remember that for all their metaphysical wit, ironic acrobatics, and collector's passion for the telling word no matter how exotic it might sound, the Fugitives were always Southern realists. Like every other Southern poet after them, direct personal experience takes precedence over the required received myth. Their initial rejection of the "Old South" centered on an Old South literature that all too often misrepresented reality in favor of inflated poetic diction. The example of William Gilmore Sims describing an alligator as "yonder Cayman, in his natural home,/ The mammoth lizard, all his armor on" which "Slumbers half-buried in the sedgy grass" could be repeated on an on just by turning the pages in any anthology of nineteenth-century verse. At least John Crowe Ransom's "amphibious crocodile" had "toes/ Which stank of bayous."

As Southern realists, the Fugitives were alert to the slightest romantic evasion that was even more common in Southern poetry than in Southern fiction. And as modern poets, they held themselves critically apart from modern society. Equally wary of the misleading language of the Southern literary past and the misplaced values of the Southern present, especially its too eager imitation of Northern business and industry, they countered with a microscopic awareness of a word's meaning and a constant search for Southern values they could live by.

Not surprisingly, the meaning of Southern history entered into their poetry early on, and is as pervasive there as it is in Southern fiction of the same period. Here again, certain phrases in T. S. Eliot's "Tradition and the Individual Talent" must have touched a sympathetic Southern nerve. When Eliot writes about obtaining tradition only by "great labor," when he defines the main instrument of that labor as "a historical sense" that "involves a perception, not only of the pastness of the past, but of its presence," we are reminded of Allen Tate's explanation for modern Southern literature: "With the war of 1914-1918, the South reentered the world — but gave a backward glance as it slipped over the border: that backward glance gave us the Southern renascense, a literature conscious of the past in the present." What Eliot urged as the right attitude toward the poetry of the past, the Fugitives applied also to Southern history, and to its special relation to the modern Southern mind.

The backward glance did not end with the Fugitive movement, but has remained an initiation rite for most Southern writers, including the young contemporary poets. Robert Penn Warren, no longer young but still a leading contemporary, even though his career stretches back to a full participation in the Fugitive movement, has recently evoked this peculiarly Southern introduction to the world in "Old-Time Childhood in Kentucky":

> Strange, into the past I first grew. I handled
>   the old bullet-mold.
> I drew out a saber, touched an old bayonet, I dreamed
> Of the death-scream. Old spurs I tried on.
> The first great General Jackson had ridden just north
>   to our state

To make a duel legal — or avoid the law.
It was all for honor. He said: "I would have killed him
Even with his hot lead in my heart." This for honor.

                                                                    I longed

To understand. I said the magic word.
I longed to say it aloud, to be heard.

For the Fugitives, of course, the major event of the Southern past was the Civil
War. If affected each of them in different ways, but for all of them the War's
dramatic turbulence of honor and defeat generated a public myth so pervasive and
full of meaning that it became part of each poet's private sense of himself. Three of
their past-haunted Southern poems dealing directly or indirectly with the War
come immediately to mind: John Crowe Ransom's "Antique Harvesters," Donald
Davidson's "Lee in the Mountains," and the archetypal modern Southern poem,
Allen Tate's "Ode to the Confederate Dead."

In each of these the collective myth of the South magnified by the War is
individualized by a particular manner and poetic voice. Ransom's "Southern
poem," as he was fond of calling it, offers an admiring look at the traditional rural
South, transfigured into a "Proud Lady" by a defeat that would ruin for decades
her abundant rich soil. Ransom is ironic enough to suggest that the traditional
Southern rituals are out-of-phase, drifting into Southern dream and mythology; but
he is convinced it is a mythology with meaning. That it has become antiquated
should not obscure its archaic truth; that its appreciation requires a difficult effort
only increases the value of the harvest.

Donald Davidson's "Lee in the Mountains" takes the backward look out of the
present altogether in his dramatic monologue of Robert E. Lee reflecting on the
War — and on his Virginia land and family — as he goes through his tasks of
president of Washington College in the Shenandoah Valley after his surrender. But
oddly enough, Davidson's Lee is as indecisive as any modern Fugitive. He shifts
from the painful loss of his father, to his mother's voice with its "murmuring
distillation/ Of old Virginia times now faint and gone," to a vision of the Southern
countryside ripening in peace, to a painful memory of his surrender and the
humiliation that followed, to a short-lived day-dream of a new call to arms, and
ends with a resigned description of his own trapped solitude in the mountains. His
final sermon to God's will — a combination of faith and fatalism — represents a
basic religious motif in the post-War Southern mind.

Tate's "Ode to the Confederate Dead" assumes a much more modern attitude
than either the Ransom or the Davidson poem. In it, a modern Southern poet
stands outside a Confederate cemetery and meditates on his relationship to the
dead soldiers. A recent commentator has suggested that the protagonist fails to
identify himself with the heroic faith of the Confederates because of a weakness of

creative imagination. But the thrust of the poem is that modern man does have his creative imagination, but very little else. It avails him little solace when it is empty of will and purpose.

The modern Southerner is able to recreate the exact scene and feeling of the soldier before battle, but as Tate himself has explained, the vision cannot be sustained. Opposed to the "active faith" of the older Southerner — especially those who have died young — the modern is left with "fragmentary chaos." His mind is so sensitive to the power of time to reduce all human purpose to dust that a naturalistic invasion of the spirit dogs him whenever he tries to formulate a belief. The use of "Ode" in the title is ironic, as Tate also explained, since communal celebrations depend on collective faith.

Finally, the modern Southern poet can neither dwell morbidly on the past, nor can he continually renew the dead spirit of the Confederacy. Despite the powerful pull of the past, he must "leave now/ The shut gate and the decomposing wall" and live, unsatisfactorily but necessarily, alone with his imagination and a compulsion to weigh everything in the balance of an absolute finality.

The decision taken by Tate's modern poet has not been shared by all the Southern poets who have followed, but it does represent a general shift away from the collective myths of Southern history to a more individual sense of each poet's separate Southern past. The War — and the burden of history — no longer plays a large role in the Southern poet's immediate experience, but in a century of enormous changes and migrations, he frequently looks back to a personal past of an older South identified in his imagination with a permanent home. Almost every contemporary Southern poet continues to return to private images of family and landscapes as measures of what has been lost or gained.

Loss, in almost every case, is the dominant conclusion. Often these private images are personal portraits, ghosts who seem more alive than the living: A.R. Ammons's "Nelly Myers" and James Applewhite's dead grandfather who "kept the old ways in changing times." Often, too, the very character of local landscapes is a measure of painful loss, tormenting the memory now that it has disappeared for good. In Wendell Berry's philosophical meditations on the archaic rituals of farming, the land and the farmer blend together in a single lineage that in this century has too often contributed to its own demise: "One lifetime of our history/Ruined it."

In many contemporary Southern poems, emblematic scenes of the rural life of the child confront the man who has long since grown up and left the farm. Not surprisingly, some of the most powerful descriptions of animal life have been written by Southern poets, but none of them are mere descriptions. In A.R. Ammons's "Coon Song," "Silver," and "Mule Song," in Fred Chappell's "Awakening to Music," in Robert Penn Warren's "English Cocker: Old and Blind," in James Dickey's "A Dog Sleeping on my Feet," they are ways of dramatizing man's own metamorphic, kin-seeking animal spirit.

Despite certain shared themes, and despite a shared tendency toward the retrospective monologue, modern Southern poetry after the Fugitives resists almost any statement — however vague — of collective resemblances. Poetry has become the most private of literary genres, and the combination of private life and the vast range and variety of local Southern experience over the last fifty years should cut short any general introduction, and simply let each poet speak directly for himself. Yet there is one area of modern Southern poetry where a few generalities might be risked, and that is the change that has taken place in the poet's attitude toward Southern language.

The Fugitives did address distinctive Southern experiences, especially the stubborn theme of Southern history, and they did describe more faithfully than ever before certain domestic Southern scenes. But in most cases, they expressed themselves in a language that was neutral in its regional, even national, associations. The English of John Crowe Ransom or Allen Tate is rich, precise, allusive, and packed with etymological wit, but it is usually an English derived from the literary English of favorite poets out of the English tradition. Though for the most part they did not live abroad in any permanent sense, they were attracted by Europe, and influenced by the general movement toward a rediscovery of European culture by Americans such as Henry James, Ezra Pound, and T.S. Eliot. Even as they repossessed themselves of the meaning of the South, as far as their literary vocabulary was concerned, they were more than lightly touched by the winds of expatriotism. Rarely does the common colloquial South make its voices heard.

It is difficult to know when the change occured, or who, if anyone, was responsible. The Fugitives were certainly familiar with all the different varieties of Southern speech, according to region, class, education, and race. Robert Penn Warren in a long early poem, "The Ballad of Billie Potts," is capable of basing much of the narrative on ripe country idiom and on a convincing dialect of the Southern frontier. But "The Ballad of Billie Potts" is a period piece. The great change toward what constitutes "poetic" language for the Southern poet comes somewhere between the end of the Fugitive movement and the best of the contemporary Southern poets, somewhere in the years just before and after World War II. Gradually there was a movement away from a single proper level of the poetic voice toward what would eventually become an openness to all kinds of language.

As poetry became more personal, more dedicated to the presentation of the individual consciousness of the poet, the language one heard and used everyday — or remembered out of the poet's past — was bound to find its way in the poetry. And of course the spectacular rediscovery of the Southern vernacular in the fiction of the period would have helped turn the poet's attention to the rich accumulation of image and word stored up in traditional rural speech. But of the many reasons that come to mind as partial explanations for this change, two are particularly appealing: the role of Southern music, especially the country song, both by black and white singers, and the simple proposition that for the contemporary Southern poet the rural South, even though it has receded, is never far from the university.

Southern music of the twentieth century has been the most original expression of a popular tradition in modern times. Not only have the old songs and ballads been kept alive by local singers all over the South, but new songs are continually being written. Southern musicians such as Norman Blake, the Red Clay Ramblers, and Beausoleil, just to mention a choice few, are reminders that the Southern musical tradition is an active and creative one.

The words of a song should not be divorced from its music, but even so it has to be acknowledged that a great deal of what is permanent in Southern poetry is to be found in its lyrics. Robert Penn Warren has made the convincing claim that the Southern blues comprised "one of the few unique contributions . . . that America has made to the world of art." In the blues and the modern country song, the simple, direct force of the local image could not help but affect the Southern poet's attitude toward the sounds and phrases he heard every day.

About the same time the Fugitives were publishing their anthology of Fugitive poems — in 1928 — white country music of the South was beginning to gain national attention. Jimmy Rogers and the Carter Family were starting their careers, and in the next decades the songs of early country music stars such as Roy Acuff and Hank Williams were reminders, if reminders were needed, that the American South was one of the few regions in the world where the individual living artist and the traditional forms continued to meet on equal terms. Southern jazz had already influenced an entire generation of American artists, but for the Southern poet, the country song and the remarkable performances of the blues singers must have been daily keys for opening up the poetic resources of Southern speech. Of course what was heard on the radio in the 1930's and 1940's was only a small part of the enormous variety of Southern song that could be heard locally all over the South. Anyone who has listened to Roscoe Holcomb or Sleepy John Estes or Blind Willie Johnson — and if anyone has not, do it, by all means, before the day is over — can sense that the generation of poets growing up in the modern South was never too far from the sounds of vigorous poetry.

In a recent recollection of his beginnings as a poet, Robert Penn Warren gives a good account of the various influences working on a young Southern poet. Describing the first poems he wrote at college, he remembers: "Now I began trying this and that. Sometimes something coming out of my country summers at my bookish old grandfather's remote farm — the sound of some tenant farmer picking his box, at night, in the distance, and singing a ballad, a lantern-lit revival (white or black) and the wail of a hardened sinner struck down by God A-mighty in the "straw pen," a lynching, or the sound of a "holler" musical in the distance, from some Negro man cabin-bound after a day in the tobacco field. But sometimes something echoed from Blake or Marvell. It is hard to find out who you are." If the last sentence points to a persistent theme of self-discovery in almost all modern poetry, the easy juxtaposition of oral and musical traditions — secular and sacred — with the literary tradition of English poetry is characteristically Southern.

Warren — and most of the other Southern poets who write today — is at home on the farm and in the university. And since the majority of Southern poets write in a personal mode, using a single poetic voice to address an individual experience made up of all sorts of private and public roles, they are able to accommodate — in fact, must accommodate — all the kinds of language they have ever used, as farmers, or as literary scholars and teachers. In a poet such as Fred Chappell, for example, no single "level" of discourse dominates. The farm, the small-town garage, the bus stop, the honky-tonk bar, the church steps, the front porch, and the university library, are all equally valuable verbal sources. What counts is the expressive power of the word, and its faithfulness to the poet's complete experience. The language used must reflect a multitude of different familiarities.

Of course, the dual context of farm and university attachments has been a factor in Southern poetry from the beginning of the Southern literary revival. The Fugitives were associated with universities all their lives, and several of them — Ransom, Tate, and Warren — have written some of the most influential criticism of their time. Largely because of their academic culture and calling, they almost singlehandedly raised the standards of Southern poetry by insisting on the intellectual depth and formal craftsmanship of the individual work. Each poem, as far as possible, must be independent and complete, based, again as far as possible, on permanent dramatic truths. The university after the Fugitives continued to play an important role in shaping and encouraging the writing of poetry, especially the many fine university journals that have for many years reached beyond native interest and influence. The cultivated comparisons and the intellectual commitments have therefore become habitual, but they have been deeply enriched by language and perceptions from outside the university walls. Even today, the two communities, traditions, and wisdoms — one academic, the other popular — counterbalance rather than oppose each other. Certainly in the selection that follows, Southern poets demonstrate a combination of speculative boldness and compelling home truths that are rare in contemporary poetry elsewhere.

For many years, the reputation of modern Southern literature has been dominated by fiction, with poetry, especially in the years immediately after the Fugitive movement, only rarely inspired by notably Southern claims. After World War II, and especially in recent years, however, there has been a revival of poetic interest in the matter of the South, and today Southern poetry is as vigorous an expression of the modern South as the short story. Part of the revival, in fact, may owe something to a natural confederacy between the two genres. V.S. Pritchett has remarked that the short story can be defined as a narrative brought to life by the spark of a poetic impulse. In much of the best Southern poetry, there seems to be a reciprocal desire to quicken the poem with the movement of narration. Robert Penn Warren has written some of the best long narrative poems of the century. And to give a single example from a young contemporary, Dave Smith's brilliant "The Colors of Our Age: Pink and Black" — in which the key phrase "malignant innocence" may be a kindred echo of Allen Tate's striking conjunction "malignant purity" in "Ode to the Confederate Dead" — is a retrospective monologue that narrates a crime of racism as powerfully and as directly as Tate's own "The Swimmers." Certainly dramatic power and a direct engagement of social reality are no longer the exclusive property of Southern fiction. Perhaps Southern poetry was longer in realizing the full potential of the South as an immense and momentous literary theater, but as these poems should prove, it can stand today as one of the most vivid achievements of the modern Southern tradition.

A. R. AMMONS

Nelly Myers

    I think of her
            while having a bowl of wheatflakes
(why? we never had wheatflakes
or any cereal then
except breakfast grits)
            and tears come to my eyes
and I think that I will die
because

            the bright, clear days when she was with me
and when we were together
(without caring that we were together)

can never be restored:
            my love wide-ranging
     I mused with clucking hens
and brought in from summer storms
at midnight the thrilled cold chicks
          and dried them out
            at the fireplace
and got up before morning
unbundled them from the piles of rags and
  turned them into the sun:

          I cannot go back
           I cannot be with her again

             and my love included the bronze
sheaves of broomstraw
she would be coming across the fields with
before the household was more than stirring out to pee

and there she would be coming
    as mysteriously from a new world
and she was already old when I was born but I love
the thought of her hand
wringing the tall tuft of dried grass

      and I cannot see her beat out the fuzzy bloom
again
readying the straw for our brooms at home,
I can never see again the calm sentence of her mind
    as she
measured out brooms for the neighbors and charged
a nickel a broom:

I think of her
    but cannot remember how I thought of her
as I grew up: she was not a member of the family:
I knew she was not my mother
         not an aunt, there was nothing
visiting about her: she had her room,
    she kept her bag of money
(on lonely Saturday afternoons
    you could sometimes hear the coins
spilling and spilling into her apron):
    she never went away, she was Nelly Myers, we
    called her Nel,
small, thin, her legs wrapped from knees to ankles
in homespun bandages: she always had the soreleg
        and sometimes
red would show at the knee, or the ankle would swell
and look hot
    (and sometimes the cloths would
dwindle,
    the bandages grow thin, the bowed legs look
pale and dry — I would feel good then,
    maybe for weeks
      there would seem reason of promise,
    though she rarely mentioned her legs
and was rarely asked about them): she always went,

legs red or white, went, went

through the mornings before sunrise
       covering the fields and
woods
looking for huckleberries
or quieting some wild call to move and go
    roaming the woods and acres of daybreak
and there was always a fire in the stove
when my mother rose (which was not late):

    my grandmother, they say, took her in
when she was a stripling run away from home
(her mind was not perfect
    which is no bar to this love song
        for her smile was sweet,
   her outrage honest and violent)
and they say that after she worked all day her relatives
would throw a handful of dried peas into her lap
        for her supper
and she came to live in the house I was born in the
northwest room of:

oh I will not end my grief
    that she is gone, I will not end my singing;
my songs like blueberries
felt-out and black to her searching fingers before light
welcome her
wherever her thoughts ride with mine, now or in any time
    that may come
when I am gone; I will not end visions of her naked feet
in the sandpaths: I will hear her words
    "Applecandy" which meant Christmas.
"Lambesdamn" which meant Goddamn (she was forthright
    and didn't go to church
    and nobody wondered if she should

and I agree with her the Holcomb pinegrove bordering our
field was
more hushed and lovelier than cathedrals
    not to mention country churches with unpainted boards
and so much innocence as she carried in her face
has entered few churches in one person)

and her exclamation "Founshy-day!" I know no meaning
for but knew she was using it right:

and I will not forget how though nearly deaf
she heard the tender blood in lips of children
and knew the hurt
    and knew what to do:

and I will not forget how I saw her last, tied in a chair
lest she rise to go
and fall
        for how innocently indomitable
  was her lust
and how her legs were turgid with still blood as she sat
and how real her tears were as I left
    to go back to college (damn all colleges):
    oh where her partial soul, as others thought,
roams roams my love
mother, not my mother, grandmother, not my grandmother,
slave to our farm's work, no slave I would not stoop to:
I will not end my grief, earth will not end my grief,
I move on, we move on, some scraps of us together,
    and my broken soul leaning toward her to be touched,
listening to be healed.

Coon Song

I got one good look
    in the raccoon's eyes
        when he fell from the tree
came to his feet
    and perfectly still
        seized the baying hounds
in his dull fierce stare,
    in that recognition all
        decision lost,
choice irrelevant, before the
    battle fell
        and the unwinding
of his little knot of time began:

                    Dostoevsky would think
it important if the coon
        could choose to
                be back up the tree:
or if he could choose to be
        wagging by a swamp pond,
                dabbling at scuttling
crawdads: the coon may have
        dreamed in fact of curling
                into the holed-out gall
of a fallen oak some squirrel
        had once brought
                high into the air
clean leaves to: but

                reality can go to hell
is what the coon's eyes said to me:
        and said how simple
                the solution to my
problem is: it needs only
        not to be: I thought the raccoon
                felt no anger,
saw none; cared nothing for cowardice,
        bravery; was in fact
                bored at
knowing what would ensue:
        the unwinding, the whirling growls,
                exposed tenders,
the wet teeth — a problem to be
        solved, the taut-coiled vigor
                of the hunt
ready to snap loose:

                you want to know what happened,
you want to hear me describe it,
        to placate the hound's-mouth
                slobbering in your own heart:
I will not tell you: actually the coon
        possessing secret knowledge
                pawed dust on the dogs
and they disappeared, yapping into

nothingness, and the coon went
            down to the pond
and washed his face and hands and beheld
    the world: maybe he didn't:
            I am no slave that I
should entertain you, say what you want
        to hear, let you wallow in
            your silt: one two three four five:
one two three four five six seven eight nine ten:

            (all this time I've been
                counting spaces
while you were thinking of something else)
        mess in your own sloppy silt:
            the hounds disappeared
yelping (the way you would at extinction)
        into — the order
    breaks up here — immortality:
I know that's where you think the brave
        little victims should go:
            I do not care what
you think: I do not care what you think:
        I do not care what you
            think: one two three four five
six seven eight nine ten: here we go
    round the here-we-go-round, the
            here-we-go-round, the here-we-
go-round: coon will end in disorder at the
    teeth of hounds: the situation
            will get him:
spheres roll, cubes stay put: now there
    one two three four five
        are two philosophies:
here we go round the mouth-wet of hounds:

        what I choose
        is youse:
        baby

JAMES APPLEWHITE

My Grandfather's Funeral

I knew the dignity of the words:
"As for man, his days are as grass,
As a flower of the field so he flourisheth;
For the wind passeth, and he is gone" —
But I was not prepared for the beauty
Of the old people coming from the church,
Nor for the suddenness with which our slow
Procession came again in sight of the awakening
Land, as passing white houses, Negroes
In clothes the colors of the earth they plowed,
We turned to see bushes and rusting roofs
Flicker past one way, the stretch of fields
Plowed gray or green with rye flow constant
On the other, away to unchanging pines
Hovering over parallel boles like
Dreams of clouds.

           At the cemetery the people
Surprised me again, walking across
The wave of winter-bleached grass and stones
Toward his grave; grotesques, yet perfect
In their pattern: Wainwright's round head,
His bad shoulder hunched and turning
That hand inward, Luby Paschal's scrubbed
Square face, lips ready to whistle to
A puppy, his wife's delicate ankles
Angling a foot out, Norwood Whitley
Unconsciously rubbing his blue jaw,
Locking his knees as if wearing boots —
The women's dark blue and brocaded black,
Brown stockings on decent legs supporting

Their infirm frames carefully over
The wintry grass that called them down,
Nell Overman moving against the horizon
With round hat and drawn-back shoulders —
Daring to come and show themselves
Above the land, to face the death
Of William Henry Applewhite,
Whose name was on the central store
He owned no more, who was venerated,
Generous, a tyrant to his family
With his ally, the God of Moses and lightning
(With threat of thunderclouds rising in summer
White and ominous over level fields);
Who kept bright jars of mineral water
On his screened, appled backporch, who prayed
With white hair wispy in the moving air,
Who kept the old way in changing times,
Who killed himself plowing in his garden.
I seemed to see him there, above
The bleached grass in the new spring light,
Bowed to his handplow, bent-kneed, impassive,
Toiling in the sacrament of seasons.

Tobacco Men

Late fall finishes the season for marketing:
Auctioneers babble to growers and buyers.
Pick-ups convoy on half-flat tires, tobacco
Piled in burlap sheets, like heaped-up bedding
When share-cropper families move on in November.

No one remembers the casualties
Of July's fighting against time in the sun.
Boys bend double for sand lugs, bowed
Like worshippers before the fertilized stalks.
The rubber-plant leaves glared savagely as idols.

It is I, who fled such fields, who must
Reckon up losses: Walter fallen out from heat,
Bud Powell nimble along rows as a scat-back

But too light by September, L. G. who hoisted up a tractor
To prove he was better, while mud hid his feet —
I've lost them in a shimmer that makes the rows move crooked.

Wainwright welded the wagons, weighed three
Hundred pounds, and is dead. Rabbit was mechanic
When not drunk, and Arthur best ever at curing.
Good ol' boys together — maybe all three still there,
Drinking in a barn, their moonshine clearer than air
Under fall sky impenetrable as a stone named for azure.

I search for your faces in relation
To a tobacco stalk I can see,
One fountain of up-rounding leaf.
It looms, expanding, like an oak.
Your faces form fruit where branches are forking.
Like the slow-motion explosion of a thunderhead,
It is sucking the horizon to a bruise.

A cloud's high forehead wears ice.

Drinking Music

I

Cornstalks and arrowheads, wood rot cleanly as wash
Hung in wind. They are covered by this roof as I think:
The losers, the fallen, the kind who go under, faces
As familiar as Civil War casualties to the soil's imagination.
Whiskey workers with no front teeth, men from down home,
With leather boots made by the *Georgia Giant,* denim or khaki
Their only other clothes, the dye scrubbed away
By brush in fields and seasons of laundry
So a sand white cotton shines through.

They stand for the showing of true colors, on soil
Instilled with the sun's going down, which crests up
At evening in a brick hue of broom sedge, clots below
In sweet potatoes succulent as blood.

Their ears give over to a jukebox excuse poured
Slow as molasses. Hank Williams' whiskey forgiveness.
The twang has a body like tenderloin and turnips.
Paul Junior Taylor, with your Budweiser belly,
Your shoulders muscled wide like a tackle's,
I wonder what it's done with you now.

II

The broom sedge fields were ruddy from sunset.
Cold whiskey is the color of straw.
Sky ain't hardly kept no color at all,
And Lord I'm lonely for the ground.
I'm far from home but near.
I'm high, so high and low. Sweet chariot.

The song is red, like what men eat.
Sky is clear as the ninety proof shine they drink.
Lord, Lord, a man is a funny piece of meat.
Their boots print fields that understand their feet.

WENDELL BERRY

Where

The field mouse flickers
once upon his shadow,
is gone. The watcher is left
in all silence, as after
thunder, or threat. And then
in the top of the sycamore
the redbird opens again
his clear song: *Even
so. Even so.*
Divided by little songs
these silences keep folding
back upon themselves
like long cloths put away.
They are all of the one
silence that precedes
and follows us. Too much
has fallen silent here.
There are names that rest
as silent on their stone
as fossils in creek ledges.
There are those who sleep
in graves no one remembers;
there is no language here,
now, to speak their names.

Too much of our history
will seem to have taken place
in the halls of capitals,
where the accusers have
mostly been guilty, and so
have borne witness to nothing.

Whole lives of work are buried
under leaves of thickets,
hands fallen from helves.
What was memory is dust
now, and many a story
told in shade or by the fire
is gone with the old light.
On the courthouse shelves
the facts lie mute
upon their pages, useless
nearly as the old boundary
marks — "Beginning on
the bank of the Kentucky River
at the mouth of Cane Run
at a hackberry" (1865) —
lost in the silence of
old days and voices. And yet
the land and the mind
bear the marks of a history
that they do not record.

The mind still hungers
for its earth, its bounded
and open space, the term
of its final assent. It keeps
the vision of an independent
modest abundance. It dreams
of cellar and pantry filled,
the source well husbanded.
And yet it learns care
reluctantly, and late.
It suffers plaintively from
its obligations. Long
attention to detail
is a cross it bears only
by congratulating itself.
It would like to hurry up
and get more than it needs
of several pleasant things.
It dreads all the labors
of common decency.
It recalls, with disquieting

sympathy, the motto
of a locally renowned
and long dead kinsman: "Never
set up when you can lay down."

The land bears the scars
of minds whose history
was imprinted by no example
of a forebearing mind, corrected,
beloved. A mind cast loose
in whim and greed makes
nature its mirror, and the garden
falls with the man. Great trees
once crowded this bottomland,
so thick that when they were felled
a boy could walk a mile
along their trunks and never
set foot to ground. Where
that forest stood, the fields
grew fine crops of hay:
men tied the timothy heads
together across their horses'
withers; the mountains upstream
were wooded then, and the river
in flood renewed its fields
like the Nile. Given
a live, husbandly tradition,
that abundance might
have lasted. It did not.
One lifetime of our history
ruined it. The slopes
of the watershed were stripped
of trees. The black topsoil
washed away in the tracks
of logger and plowman.
The creeks, that once ran clear
after the heaviest rains,
ran muddy, dried in summer.
From year to year watching
from his porch, my grandfather
saw a barn roof slowly
come into sight above

a neighboring ridge as plows
and rains wore down the hill.
This little has been remembered.
For the rest, one must go
and ponder in the silence
of documents, or decipher
on the land itself the healed
gullies and the unhealed,
the careless furrows drawn
over slopes too steep to plow
where the scrub growth
stands in vision's failure now.

Such a mind is as much
a predicament as such
a place. And yet a knowledge
is here that tenses the throat
as for song: the inheritance
of the ones, alive or once
alive, who stand behind
the ones I have imagined,
who took into their minds
the troubles of this place,
blights of love and race,
but saw a good fate here
and willingly paid its cost,
kept it the best they could,
thought of its good,
and mourned the good they lost.

Work Song

1. *A Lineage*
By the fall of years I learn how it has been
With Jack Beechum, Mat Feltner, Elton Penn,

And their kind, men made for their fields.
I see them stand their ground, bear their yields,

Swaying in all weathers in their long rows,
In the dance that fleshes desire and then goes

Down with the light. They have gone as they came,
And they go. They go by a kind of will. They claim

In the brevity of their strength an ancient joy.
"Make me know it! Hand it to me, boy!"

2. A Vision
If we will have the wisdom to survive,
to stand like slow-growing trees
on a ruined place, renewing, enriching it,
if we will make our seasons welcome here,
asking not too much of earth or heaven,
then a long time after we are dead
the lives our lives prepare will live
here, their houses strongly placed
upon the valley sides, fields and gardens
rich in the windows. The river will run
clear, as we will never know it,
and over it, birdsong like a canopy.
On the levels of the hills will be
green meadows, stock bells in noon shade.
On the steeps where greed and ignorance cut down
the old forest, an old forest will stand,
its rich leaf-fall drifting on its roots.
The veins of forgotten springs will have opened.
Families will be singing in the fields.
In their voices they will hear a music
risen out of the ground. They will take
nothing from the ground they will not return,
whatever the grief at parting. Memory,
native to this valley, will spread over it
like a grove, and memory will grow
into legend, legend into song, song
into sacrament. The abundance of this place,
the songs of its people and its birds,
will be health and wisdom and indwelling
light. This is no paradisal dream.
Its hardship is its possibility.

3. *A Beginning*
October's completing light falls
on the unfinished patterns of my year.
The sun is yellow in a smudge
of public lies we no longer try
to believe. Speech finally drives us
to silence. Power has weakened us.
Comfort wakens us in fear. We are
a people who must decline or perish.
I have let my mind at last bend down
where human vision begins its rise
in the dark of seeds, wombs of beasts.
It has carried my hands to roots
and foundings, to the mute urging
that in human care clears the field
and turns it green. It reaches
the silence at the tongue's root
in which speech begins. In early mist
I walk in these reopening fields
as in a forefather's dream. In dream
and sweat the fields have seasoning.
Let my words then begin in labor.
Let me sing a work song
and an earth song. Let the song of light
fall upon me as it may.
The end of this is not in sight.
And I come to the waning of the year
weary, the way long.

The Slip

for Donald Davie

The river takes the land, and leaves nothing.
Where the great slip gave way in the bank
and an acre disappeared, all human plans
dissolve. An aweful clarification occurs
where a place was. Its memory breaks
from what is known now, begins to drift.
Where cattle grazed and trees stood, emptiness

widens the air for birdflight, wind, and rain.
As before the beginning, nothing is there.
Human wrong is in the cause, human
ruin in the effect — but no matter;
all will be lost, no matter the reason.
Nothing, having arrived, will stay.
The earth, even, is like a flower, so soon
passeth it away. And yet this nothing
is the seed of all — the clear eye
of Heaven, where all the worlds appear.
Where the imperfect has departed, the perfect
begins its struggle to return. The good gift
begins again its descent. The maker moves
in the unmade, stirring the water until
it clouds, dark beneath the surface,
stirring and darkening the soul until pain
perceives new possibility. There is nothing
to do but learn and wait, return to work
on what remains. Seed will sprout in the scar.
Though death is in the healing, it will heal.

In Rain

1.
I go in under foliage
light with rain-light
in the hill's cleft,
and climb, my steps
silent as flight
on the wet leaves.
Where I go, stones
are wearing away
under the sky's flow.

2.
The path I follow
I can hardly see
it is so faintly trod
and overgrown.
At times, looking,

I fail to find it
among dark trunks, leaves
living and dead. And then
I am alone, the woods
shapeless around me.
I look away, my gaze
at rest among leaves,
and then I see the path
again, a dark way going on
through the light.

3.
In a mist of light
falling with the rain
I walk this ground
of which dead men
and women I have loved
are part, as they
are part of me. In earth,
in blood, in mind,
the dead and living
into each other pass,
as the living pass
in and out of loves
as stepping to a song.
The way I go is
marriage to this place,
grace beyond chance,
love's braided dance
covering the world.

4.
Marriages to marriages
are joined, husband and wife
are plighted to all
husbands and wives,
any life has all lives
for its delight.
Let the rain come,
the sun, and then the dark,
for I will rest
in an easy bed tonight.

DAVID BOTTOMS

Shooting Rats at the Bibb County Dump

Loaded on beer and whiskey, we ride
to the dump in carloads
to turn our headlights across the wasted field,
freeze the startled eyes of rats against mounds of rubbish.

Shot in the head, they jump only once, lie still
like dead beer cans.
Shot in the gut or rump, they writhe and try to burrow
into garbage, hide in old truck tires,
rusty oil drums, cardboard boxes scattered across the mounds,
or else drag themselves on forelegs across our beams of light
toward the darkness at the edge of the dump.

It's the light they believe kills.
We drink and load again, let them crawl
for all they're worth into the darkness we're headed for.

Under the Boathouse

Out of my clothes, I ran past the boathouse
to the edge of the dock
and stood before the naked silence of the lake,
on the drive behind me, my wife
rattling keys, calling for help with the grill,
the groceries wedged into the trunk.
Near the tail end of her voice, I sprang
from the homemade board, bent body
like a hinge, and speared the surface,
cut through water I would not open my eyes in,
to hear the junked depth pop in both ears

as my right hand dug into silk and mud,
my left clawed around a pain.
In a fog of rust I opened my eyes to see
what had me, and couldn't, but knew
the fire in my hand and the weight of the thing
holding me under, knew the shock of all
things caught by the unknown
as I kicked off the bottom like a frog,
my limbs doing fearfully strange strokes,
lungs collapsed in a confusion of bubbles,
all air rising back to its element.
I flailed after it, rose toward the bubbles
breaking on light, then felt down my arm
a tug running from a taut line.
Halfway between the bottom of the lake
and the bottom of the sky, I hung like a buoy
on a short rope, an effigy
flown in an underwater parade,
and imagined myself hanging there forever,
a curiosity among fishes, a bait hanging up
instead of down. In the lung-ache,
in the loud pulsing of temples, what gave first
was something in my head, a burst
of colors like the blind see, and I saw
against the surface a shadow like an angel
quivering in a dead-man's float,
then a shower of plastic knives and forks
spilling past me in the lightened water, a can
of barbequed beans, a bottle of A.1., napkins
drifting down like white leaves,
heavenly litter from the world I struggled toward.
What gave then was something on the other end,
and my hand rose on its own and touched my face.
Into the splintered light under the boathouse,
the loved suffocating air hovering over the lake,
the cry of my wife leaning dangerously
over the dock, empty grocery bags at her feet,
I bobbed with a hook through the palm of my hand.

Under the Vulture-Tree

We have all seen them circling pastures,
have looked up from the mouth of a barn, a pine clearing,
the fences of our own backyards, and have stood
amazed by the one slow wing beat, the endless dihedral drift.
But I had never seen so many so close, hundreds,
every limb of the dead oak feathered black,

and I cut the engine, let the river grab the jon boat
and pull it toward the tree.
The black leaves shined, the pink fruit blossomed
red, ugly as a human heart.
Then, as I passed under their dream, I saw for the first time
it's soft countenance, the raw fleshy jowls
wrinkled and generous, like the faces of the very old
who have grown to empathize with everything.

And I drifted away from them, slow, on the pull of the river,
reluctant, looking back at their roost,
calling them what I'd never called them, what they are,
those dwarfed transfiguring angels,
who flock to the side of the poisoned fox, the mud turtle
crushed on the shoulder of the road,
who pray over the leaf-graves of the anonymous lost,
with mercy enough to consume us all and give us wings.

FRED CHAPPELL

The Autumn Bleat of the Weathervane Trombone

The Guernseys lift calm brows in the thistly pasture,
What must they think? that some distuneful lovesick
Paramour is moofully wooing? Cows,
Don't sweat it, it's only Fred with his battered sliphorn
Woodshedding a Bach partita on the barn roof.
This edgy October breeze is a freshener,
Don't let it teeter me to lose my toehold,
I'll tumble in the cowlot and bruise my brass.
Johann, thou shouldst be living at this hour,
You'd bust a gusset; if only the Philharmonic
Were here to listen, they'd hire me in a trice.
Is this the way Teagarden started, think you?
He must've started *some*where, so must I,
So must we all.
       First winter's behind the mountain.

Like the spirit-shapes of great gold plums
The blown tones of the yellow trombone float
Over the fields, their wobble takes on shimmer,
There's something in air in love with rounded notes,
The goldenrod's a-groan at the globed beauty,
These are the dreams of seeds, aspirations
Of sheeted mica, Ideal Forms of creek-glint,
Sennet and tucket of beech-leaf in its glowing,
Embers of poplar within the sun-warm crowns,
The eyes-in-air of blissful Guernseys, glass eyes
Full of the hands the little yellow hands
Of autumn drifting where they drift in blue,
Blue first-cool, the bluegold music of autumn,
Half sleep, half harmless fire, halved buttermoons,
Bring me my trombone of burning gold, bring me

My harrowing desire, bring me power
To float the cool blue air at the hinge of the year,
These notes not purely born, no, but take
A purity from air and field and sky
As they boat the wind-alleys like happy balloons,
Impure world taking purest shape in the
Bubbles of breath Bach-blown, O those golden
Fermatas, can you see them nudge and brother
The last yellow tomatoes sunning themselves
On the wilted vine, and snuggling down with the pumpkins
And bloodfire bellybloated candyroasters,
The thirty-second notes in tricky clusters
Like bunches of grapes are bunches of blue grapes,
And the chromatic eighth-notes emerge like apples,
Late-sweet streaky slightly flattened apples,
The solid apples that build their nests as high
As ever Earth can reach in the waltzing tip
Of the gnarly witchyfingered ragbark tree,
The tree in the pasture where the Guernseys wait for windfall
Patiently as the Ice Age at the Pole
Because they know an early Boreas
(Rapacious snaketailed) will bring the plunkers down,
O Susan Susan you should've been there when
The cows ate up the apples,
There's nothing quite so *musically* percussive
As the molar gronchle of apple in cow-maw,
And it wasn't was it? only apples they crunched
But some loose sixteenth-notes of J. S. Bach
Mixed in with apples shining in pasture grass,
And let's suppose that now they think this tree
The Tree of Knowledge, they've tasted the apples of music,
Talismans, and shall they ever be the same?
Hell no. They dance all night till the barns come home.

The sun is hatching the world, what new creature
Will emerge? So what, I'm hatching the barn,
I'm your setting hen with the baroquest cluck,
And what new creature will emerge? Aren't barns
The larval stages of dragons, clattery shaleskins?
Before the Fall goes down we everyone
Of us shall be new animals as strange as snow.

Yellow yellow is the color of time. The land
Is bearing itself to rainbow's end, pot
Of gold overfloods the burnt-off delta of summer,
What a dazzle of driftage, what dribble of daft
Storms the skin of the eye, I'm surfeit to bursting,
Have mercy, October, my eyes have eaten all,
I'm rich to the ears, my buttons are each in danger,
O take this table away I've gluttoned on honey,
Honey the heavy gold of time bronze bees
Have hived in the apple belly of the sun
Where all the Hallelujah candles are lit
And the Birthday Boy is momentarily
Expected, is being garnered in like corn.
In the afterlife of Sun I'll meet George Garrett,
The Golden Wiseacre, and what you think he'll tell us,
Uncle Body? — A lie, of course, some furious
Giggly tale of sex & sin & salvation,
We'll laugh our mortality to death, we'll laugh
Our frailty off . . . My fancy anyhow's
That poets after the loud labor of their lives
Are gathered to the sun, they speak in flame
Forever without erasure, they lie a lot,
Where else could all that hot and light come from?
They'll all be there, Adcock and Applewhite,
Whitehead and Tate and Jackson and Watson and Keens,
Morgan, Root, and Cherry, and Godalmighty
The very thought of it makes my ears hammer.
Trapped in a burning eternity with a herd
Of poets, what kind of fate is that for a handsome
Lad like Truly-yours-ole-Fred?

Corkscrewing
The wind, there goes a leaf of tulip poplar,
Saffron mittshape, one poet's been cast from heaven,
It's too much love of earth that draws him thither,
Bondage of toadstool, the sere the yellow leaf
IIis fate is sealed, he drives to mineral
Where the tree may root him out again,
The flesh the earth is suits me fine, Nirvana
A sterile and joyless blasphemy.
Give me back my blood, there's mud in it.

O yes, Uncle Body, I'll fly with thee to rootlet
And root, we'll swim come spring the tree's resounding
River-trunk, and fan our flashy shape
In green out where the squirrels are whittling toothpicks.
Take corpus after death? I wouldn't mind,
Identity can stuff it but give me Stuff,
This world's longest loaf of dirt's the staff
Of life, O Death come unbaptize me soon,
My grandfather and I never uncovered
The final source of West Fork Pigeon River,
Wonder does it burst from the solid rock
Or comes it blubbering up from the eyes of dead men?
Whichever never mind, we want to see.

Wind-river, river of flesh, spirit-river,
Fever-stream, all these the Ocean of Earth.
Let's disport it, you and I.
Can hardly wait to swim from Singapore
To Hermeneutics and through the Dardanelles
To Transcendentalism, back through the Straits
Of Hegel right on to Greasy Branch close by
Wind Mountain, look out! the perilous Falls
Of Relativity, whew that was close,
Huh-oh now we're utterly becalmed,
The existentialist Dead Sea's a mush
Of murk, help help I'm boring, ah all right,
Here the pure sweet waters of Music open
Upon a picnic wilderness of light.
Around the World in Eighty Tractates aboard
The good ship Wittgenstein, how's that grab you,
Uncle Body? How now? Asleep again,
Old lunker? Never Aquinas rages your blood,
Never up for a sweaty set of Spinoza,
Never wanted to hike with me the slopes
Of stony Heidegger? Come on, we'll pitch
Our tent tonight under the shadow of Plato.
Where's your sense of landscape got to?
If you don't take care, old hoss, Spirit's gonna
Leave you lonesome behind, then where'll you be?

No don't tell me, I never wanted to know.

But the cleanest way to travel would be to ride
One of these untenable trombone tones
Out upon the bluebleached air, forgetless
Air of crystal, steering the golden note
Over the yellowing fields until in tang
It disappears, dream-bubble's slient pop,
And lets us slide the efferevescent atoms
All by ourselves, look Ma I'm flying no hands.
No feets no nothing. Nothing but eyes and taste buds
Skating the Mirror of Blazing Razors, the Eyeball
Of the Clarity of Transcendental Acids,
Lindy would envy our *Spirit of St. Francis,*
We could fly from here to Chuang Hzu's dream.

A Wilson cloud chamber I think it now,
This globe of sunswept blue, this blueblown
Note aloft in its hour of polished silk,
A chamber alert to every Cosmic Ray,
Every sizzle-streak of energy
Indeterminate unreckonable,
Every little tic in the lymph of the world;
For music reflects refracts makes visible
The hail of impulse Nature keeps tossing over
Her shoulder, sprinkle of feckless seed, heat,
Light, ray-quiver, sound, every wealth.
Entropy too keeps coming by, of course,
But nothing here except when the trombone note,
Sighing, deflates like a golden bubblegum.

I've got a slightly different Big Bang theory:
In the beginning was the Trombone — somewhere,
Somehow — and on its own it blew a true
And bluesy A, and here came rolling that note
Through Chaos, vibrato rich and round as a grape
Of Concord, O what a parable note was sounded!,
And us, we innocent children, we kinds of germs
Of music, on the outer skin of that note crawling
In helpless wonderment. And that's our fate,
We've got to tune and turn the music ever.
So I'll straddle the barn and lip the exercises,

Improve my embouchure and wiggle my slide
Till I get a somewhat humaner-looking lover
Than these bored Guernseys. Girls! girls!
Where are you? Don't you hear Fred's lonesome trombone
Mating call from the highest point in the valley?
You wouldn't let the music of this world die.

Would you?

Awakening to Music

      I don't forget head down
striding the raw ridges, snowbit,
knuckles red burning knots of ice
in my pockets, wind turning funnels of snow-stuff,
and cursing as I bulled along
a whiteface heifer who must have daintily
tiptoed through
the curlicues of busted barbwire
and loped excited away in sparkling cold
to skirmish my father's neighbors' fields
or maybe the whole wide silly world
in a sharp wind getting sharper always
at the awkward hour, dawn
bleaching to ash or dark coming on with
no one abroad to ask of
about stray cows.

      Till finally we met.
This coquette, tossing her rag-curled
forehead, tossing the silky string
of lucid snot pearly from chin to knees
like a Charleston necklace.
                  "Come home now,
Daisy"; and she'd ballhoot
the rocky road with a racket like a marble
rolling down a washboard, leaving
a breath-white ghost I blinked at.

I'd curse to melt the snow in air.

Sometimes:
       with hands frost-grained
from the bucket bail I'd clutch the brood-warm
teats and God help us how she'd kick a shapely
leg as sudden as a door blown shut.
Or just as quick in August when
thistle-thorns embedded in the udders.

      Sickness worst of all.
The little Jersey down in the smelly straw,
eyes back, brown eyes enfolding flame-blue
eggs in the light of a Coleman fizzing
like seltzer, and Doc McGreavy lying down
in warm embrace, ear
to guttering lungs, choosing without having to look
the iron and glass in the lumpy black bag.
The terrible births: my throat wire-taut,
hand stiff, while Doc plunged shoulder-deep
in flesh-muck, a one-armed swimmer.

      Yet even so the main thing:
was every morning the cuddling when my head
went into her toasty flank, the grandest magic helmet
breathing and her red belly
rubbing my intimate right shoulder,
and milk-squirt slicing through the foam
like yard on yard of brocade piling up.

That was how I came from sleep to another sleep,
came into a warm swamp-broad sleep,
warm rain on heart-shaped leaves and dozing orchids,
came to the pulsing green fountain where music is born.

And all those years I went clothed in this sleep,
odor and warmth
of cows blanketed about my head.

How would I get it back? Go to blood
again, sleep the light green sleep?
How can I wake, not waking to music?

Here

Burdened with diadem, the
Queen Anne's lace overhangs the ditch.
The lace is full of eyes, cold eyes
That draw a cold sky into their spheres.
The ditch twinkles now the rain has stopped.
And the ground begins to puff and suck
With little holes. A man could live down here forever,
Where his blood is.

Humility

In the necessary field among the round
Warm stones we bend to our gleaning.
The brown earth gives in to our hands, and straw
By straw burns red aslant the vesper light.

The village behind the graveyard tolls softly, begins
To glow with new-laid fires. The children
Quiet their shouting, and the martins slide
Above the cows at the warped pasture gate.

They set the tinware out on checkered oilcloth
And the thick-mouthed tumblers on the right-hand side.
The youngest boy whistles the collie to his dish
And lifts down the dented milk pail:

This is the country we return to when
For a moment we forget ourselves,
When we watch the sleeping kitten quiver
After long play, or rain comes down warm.

Here we might choose to live always, here where
Ugly rumors of ourselves do not reach,
Where in the whisper-light of the kerosene lamp
The deep Bible lies open like a turned-down bed.

DONALD DAVIDSON

Joe Clisby's Song

What did my old song say?
Something of youth and desire
And summer passing away;
Yet love is a durable fire
  And will stay.

Must I think a tune like this
Was never made for a time
That reads only lust in a kiss
And shreds the magic of rhyme
  To hit-or-miss?

By old Bethel burying-ground
In moonlight passed along
True lovers as ever were found
Who plaited hearts in a song
  Where their voices wound.

Nettie Long and I,
Burt Whitson with his Ruth,
Walked and sang to the high
Church steeple as if youth
  Could never go by.

And we walked and sang to the low
Ranks of the good dead people
As if to come or go
Was a fine tune that a steeple
  And they would know.

For the old folks that lie there

We knew were singers all.
They could get a song by ear
And had a fiddle at call
    And friends near.

If you would join their song
But fear to raise the sound,
Come walk with Nettie Long
And me, by the burying-ground.
    You'll take no wrong.

Burt Whitson and his Ruth
And many couples more
Can tune the lips of youth
As they did mine before
    To sing the truth.

Lee in the Mountains

1865-1870

Walking into the shadows, walking alone
Where the sun falls through the ruined boughs of locusts
Up to the president's office....
                            Hearing the voices
Whisper, *Hush, it is General Lee!* And strangely
Hearing my own voice say, *Good morning, boys.*
(Don't get up. You are early. It is long
Before the bell. You will have long to wait
On these cold steps....)
                            The young have time to wait.
But soldiers' faces under their tossing flags
Lift no more by any road or field,
And I am spent with old wars and new sorrow.
Walking the rocky path, where steps decay
And the paint cracks and grass eats on the stone.
It is not General Lee, young men....
It is Robert Lee in a dark civilian suit who walks,
An outlaw fumbling for the latch, a voice
Commanding in a dream where no flag flies.

My father's house is taken and his hearth
Left to the candle-drippings where the ashes
Whirl at a chimney-breath on the cold stone.
I can hardly remember my father's look, I cannot
Answer his voice as he calls farewell in the misty
Mounting where riders gather at gates.
He was old then — I was a child — his hand
Held out for mine, some daybreak snatched away,
And he rode out, a broken man. Now let
His lone grave keep, surer than cypress roots,
The vow I made beside him. God too late
Unseals to certain eyes the drift
Of time and the hopes of men and a sacred cause.
The fortune of the Lees goes with the land
Whose sons will keep it still. My mother
Told me much. She sat among the candles,
Fingering the *Memoirs,* now so long unread.
And as my pen moves on across the page
Her voice comes back, a murmuring distillation
Of old Virginia times now faint and gone,
The hurt of all that was and cannot be.

Why did my father write? I know he saw
History clutched as a wraith out of blowing mist
Where tongues are loud, and a glut of little souls
Laps at the too much blood and the burning house.
He would have his say, but I shall not have mine.
What I do is only a son's devoir
To a lost father. Let him only speak.
The rest must pass to men who never knew
(But on a written page) the strike of armies,
And never heard the long Confederate cry
Charge through the muzzling smoke or saw the bright
Eyes of the beardless boys go up to death.
It is Robert Lee who writes with his father's hand —
The rest must go unsaid and the lips be locked.

If all were told, as it cannot be told —
If all the dread opinion of the heart
Now could speak, now in the shame and torment
Lashing the bound and trampled States —

If a word were said, as it cannot be said —
I see clear waters run in Virginia's Valley
And in the house the weeping of young women
Rises no more. The waves of grain begin.
The Shenandoah is golden with new grain.
The Blue Ridge, crowned with a haze of light,
Thunders no more. The horse is at plough. The rifle
Returns to the chimney crotch and the hunter's hand.
And nothing else than this? Was it for this
That on an April day we stacked our arms
Obedient to a soldier's trust? To lie
Ground by heels of little men,
Forever maimed, defeated, lost, impugned?
And was I then betrayed? Did I betray?

If it were said, as still as it might be said —
If it were said, and a word should run like fire,
Like living fire into the roots of grass,
The sunken flag would kindle on wild hills,
The brooding hearts would waken, and the dream
Stir like a crippled phantom under the pines,
And this torn earth would quicken into shouting
Beneath the feet of ragged bands —
                                        The pen
Turns to the waiting page, the sword
Bows to the rust that cankers and the silence.

Among these boys whose eyes lift up to mine
Within gray walls where droning wasps repeat
A hollow reveille, I still must face,
Day after day, the courier with his summons
Once more to surrender, now to surrender all.
Without arms or men I stand, but with knowledge only
I face what long I saw, before others knew,
When Pickett's men streamed back, and I heard the tangled
Cry of the Wilderness wounded, bloody with doom.

The mountains, once I said, in the little room
At Richmond, by the huddled fire, but still
The President shook his head. The mountains wait,
I said, in the long beat and rattle of siege

At cratered Petersburg. Too late
We sought the mountains and those people came.
And Lee is in mountains now, beyond Appomattox,
Listening long for voices that never will speak
Again; hearing the hoofbeats come and go and fade
Without a stop, without a brown hand lifting
The tent-flap, or a bugle call at dawn,
Or ever on the long white road the flag
Of Jackson's quick brigades. I am alone,
Trapped, consenting, taken at last in mountains.

It is not the bugle now, or the long roll beating.
The simple stroke of a chapel bell forbids
The hurtling dream, recalls the lonely mind.
Young men, the God of your fathers is a just
And merciful God Who in this blood once shed
On your green altars measures out all days,
And measures out the grace
Whereby alone we live;
And in His might He waits,
Brooding within the certitude of time,
To bring this lost forsaken valor
And the fierce faith undying
And the love quenchless
To flower among the hills to which we cleave,
To fruit upon the mountains whither we flee,
Never forsaking, never denying
His children and His children's children forever
Unto all generations of the faithful heart.

JAMES DICKEY

A Dog Sleeping on My Feet

Being his resting place,
I do not even tense
The muscles of a leg
Or I would seem to be changing.
Instead, I turn the page
Of the notebook, carefully not

Remembering what I have written,
For now, with my feet beneath him
Dying like embers,
The poem is beginning to move
Up through my pine-prickling legs
Out of the night wood,

Taking hold of the pen by my fingers.
Before me the fox floats lightly,
On fire with his holy scent.
All, all are running.
Marvelous is the pursuit,
Like a dazzle of nails through the ankles,

Like a twisting shout through the trees
Sent after the flying fox
Through the holes of logs, over streams
Stock-still with the pressure of moonlight.
My killed legs,
My legs of a dead thing, follow,

Quick as pins, through the forest,
And all rushes on into dark
And ends on the brightness of paper.

When my hand, which speaks in a daze
The hypnotized language of beasts,
Shall falter, and fail

Back into the human tongue,
And the dog gets up and goes out

To wander the dawning yard,
I shall crawl to my human bed
And lie there smiling at sunrise,
With the scent of the fox

Burning my brain like an incense,
Floating out of the night wood,
Coming home to my wife and my sons
From the dream of an animal,
Assembling the self I must wake to,
Sleeping to grow back my legs.

Cherrylog Road

Off Highway 106
At Cherrylog Road I entered
The '34 Ford without wheels,
Smothered in kudzu,
With a seat pulled out to run
Corn whiskey down from the hills.

And then from the other side
Crept into an Essex
With a rumble seat of red leather
And then out again, aboard
A blue Chevrolet, releasing
The rust from its other color,

Reared up on three building blocks.
None had the same body heat;
I changed with them inward, toward
The weedy heart of the junkyard,
For I knew that Doris Holbrook

Would escape from her father at noon

And would come from the farm
To seek parts owned by the sun
Among the abandoned chassis,
Sitting in each in turn
As I did, leaning forward
As in a wild stock-car race

In the parking lot of the dead.
Time after time, I climbed in
And out the other side, like
An envoy or movie star
Met at the station by crickets.
A radiator cap raised its head,

Become a real toad or a kingsnake
As I neared the hub of the yard,
Passing through many states,
Many lives, to reach
Some grandmother's long Pierce-Arrow
Sending platters of blindness forth

From its nickel hubcaps
And spilling its tender upholstery
On sleepy roaches,
The glass panel in between
Lady and colored driver
Not all the way broken out,

The back-seat phone
Still on its hook.
I got in as though to exclaim,
"Let us go to the orphan asylum,
John: I have some old toys
For children who say their prayers."

I popped with sweat as I thought
I heard Doris Holbrook scrape
Like a mouse in the southern-state sun
That was eating the paint in blisters
From a hundred car tops and hoods.

She was tapping like code,

Loosening the screws,
Carrying off headlights,
Sparkplugs, bumpers,
Cracked mirrors and gear-knobs,
Getting ready, already,
To go back with something to show

Other than her lips' new trembling
I would hold to me soon, soon,
Where I sat in the ripped back seat
Talking over the interphone,
Praying for Doris Holbrook
To come from her father's farm

And to get back there
With no trace of me on her face
To be seen by her red-haired father
Who would change, in the squalling barn,
Her back's pale skin with a strop,
Then lay for me

In a bootlegger's roasting car
With a string-triggered 12-gauge shotgun
To blast the breath from the air.
Not cut by the jagged windshields,
Through the acres of wrecks she came
With a wrench in her hand,

Through dust where the blacksnake dies
Of boredom, and the beetle knows
The compost has no more life.
Someone outside would have seen
The oldest car's door inexplicably
Close from within:

I held her and held her and held her,
Convoyed at terrific speed
By the stalled, dreaming traffic around us,
So the blacksnake, stiff
With inaction, curved back

Into life, and hunted the mouse

With deadly overexcitement,
The beetles reclaimed their field
As we clung, glued together,
With the hooks of the seat springs
Working through to catch us red-handed
Amidst the gray, breathless batting

That burst from the seat at our backs.
We left by separate doors
Into the changed, other bodies
Of cars, she down Cherrylog Road
And I to my motorcycle
Parked like the soul of the junkyard

Restored, a bicycle fleshed
With power, and tore off
Up Highway 106, continually
Drunk on the wind in my mouth,
Wringing the handlebar for speed,
Wild to be wreckage forever.

False Youth: Two Seasons (Winter)

Through an ice storm in Nashville I took a student home,
Sliding off the road twice or three times; for this
She asked me in. She was a living-in-the-city
Country girl   who on her glazed porch broke off
An icicle, and bit through its blank bone: brought me
Into another life   in the shining-skinned clapboard house
Surrounded by a world where creatures could not stand,
Where people broke hip after hip. At the door my feet
Took hold, and at the fire I sat down with her blind
Grandmother. All over the double room were things
That would never freeze, but would have taken well
To ice: long tassels hanging from lamps   curtains
Of beads   a shawl on the mantel   all endless things
To touch   untangle   all things intended to be
Inexhaustible to hands. She sat there, fondling

What was in reach   staring into the fire with me
Never batting a lid. I talked to her easily   eagerly
Of my childhood   my mother whistling in her heartsick bed
My father grooming his gamecocks. She rocked, fingering
The lace on the arm of the chair   changing its pattern
Like a game of chess. Before I left, she turned and raised
Her hands, and asked me to bend down. An icicle stiffened
In my stomach   as she drew on my one lock of hair
Feeling the individual rare strands   not pulling any
Out. I closed my eyes as she put her fingertips lightly
On them   and saw, behind sight   something in me   fire
Swirl in a great shape like a fingerprint   like none other
In the history of the earth   looping   holding its wild lines
Of human force. Her forefinger   then her keen nail
Went all the way along the deep middle line of my brow
Not guessing but knowing   quivering   deepening
Whatever I showed by it. She said, you must laugh a lot
Or be in the sun, and I began to laugh quietly against
The truth, so she might feel what the line she followed
Did then. Her hands fell   and she said to herself, My God,
To have a growing boy. You cannot fool the blind, I knew
As I battled for air   standing   laughing a lot as she
Said I must do   squinting also as in the brightest sun
In Georgia   to make good   to make good the line in my head.
She lifted her face like a swimmer; the fire swarmed
On my false, created visage   as she rocked and took up
The tassel of a lamp. Some kind of song may have passed
Between our closed mouths as I headed   into the ice.
My face froze with the vast world of time   in a smile
That has never left me since my thirty-eighth year
When I skated like an out-of-shape bear to my Chevrolet
And spun my wheels on glass: that time when age was caught
In a thaw in a ravelling room   when I conceived of my finger
Print as a shape of fire   and of youth as a lifetime search
For the blind.

RANDALL JARRELL

A Girl in a Library

An object among dreams, you sit here with your shoes off
And curl your legs up under you; your eyes
Close for a moment, your face moves toward sleep . . .
You are very human.
                              But my mind, gone out in tenderness,
Shrinks from its object with a thoughtful sigh.
This is a waist the spirit breaks its arm on.
The gods themselves, against you, struggle in vain.
This broad low strong-boned brow; these heavy eyes;
These calves, grown muscular with certainties;
This nose, three medium-sized pink strawberries
— But I exaggerate. In a little you will leave:
I'll hear, half squeal, half shriek, your laugh of greeting —
Then, *decrescendo*, bars of that strange speech
In which each sound sets out to seek each other,
Murders its own father, marries its own mother,
And ends as one grand transcendental vowel.

(Yet for all I know, the Egyptian Helen spoke so.)
As I look, the world contracts around you:
I see Brünnhilde had brown braids and glasses
She used for studying; Salome straight brown bangs,
A calf's brown eyes, and sturdy light-brown limbs
Dusted with cinnamon, an apple-dumpling's . . .
Many a beast has gnawn a leg off and got free,
Many a dolphin curved up from Necessity —
The trap has closed about you, and you sleep.
If someone questioned you, *What doest thou here?*
You'd knit your brows like an orangoutang
(But not so sadly; not so thoughtfully)
And answer with a pure heart, guilelessly:

I'm studying. . . .
                          If only you were not!
Assignments,
             recipes,
                   the *Official Rulebook*
Of Basketball — ah, let them go; you needn't mind.
The soul has no assignments, neither cooks
Nor referees: it wastes its time.
                        It wastes its time.
Here in this enclave there are centuries
For you to waste: the short and narrow stream
Of Life meanders into a thousand valleys
Of all that was, or might have been, or is to be.
The books, just leafed through, whisper endlessly . . .
Yet it is hard. One sees in your blurred eyes
The "uneasy half-soul" Kipling saw in dogs'.
One sees it, in the glass, in one's own eyes.
In rooms alone, in galleries, in libraries,
In tears, in searchings of the heart, in staggering joys
We memorize once more our old creation,
Humanity: with what yawns the unwilling
Flesh puts on its spirit, O my sister!

So many dreams! And not one troubles
Your sleep of life? no self stares shadowily
From these worn hexahedrons, beckoning
With false smiles, tears? . . .
                    Meanwhile Tatyana
Larina (gray eyes nickel with the moonlight
That falls through the willows onto Lensky's tomb;
Now young and shy, now old and cold and sure)
Asks, smiling: "But what is she dreaming of, fat thing?"
I answer: She's not fat. She isn't dreaming.
She purrs or laps or runs, all in her sleep;
Believes, awake, that she is beautiful;
She never dreams.
               Those sunrise-colored clouds
Around man's head — that inconceivable enchantment
From which, at sunset, we come back to life
To find our graves dug, families dead, selves dying:
Of all this, Tanya, she is innocent.
For nineteen years she's faced reality:

They look alike already.
                           They say, man wouldn't be
The best thing in this world — and isn't he? —
If he were not too good for it. But she
— She's good enough for it.
                           And yet sometimes
Her sturdy form, in its pink strapless formal,
Is as if bathed in moonlight — modulated
Into a form of joy, a Lydian mode;
This Wooden Mean's a kind, furred animal
That speaks, in the Wild of things, delighting riddles
To the soul that listens, trusting . . .
                           Poor senseless Life:
When, in the last light sleep of dawn, the messenger
Comes with his message, you will not awake.
He'll give his feathery whistle, shake you hard,
You'll look with wide eyes at the dewy yard
And dream, with calm slow factuality:
"Today's Commencement. My bachelor's degree
In Home Ec., my doctorate of philosophy
In Phys. Ed.
               [Tanya, they won't even *scan*]
Are waiting for me. . . ."
                           Oh, Tatyana,
The Angel comes: better to squawk like a chicken
Than to say with truth, "But I'm a *good* girl,"
And Meet his Challenge with a last firm strange
Uncomprehending smile; and — then, then! — see
The blind date that has stood you up: your life.
(For all this, if it isn't, perhaps, life,
Has yet, at least, a language of its own
Different from the books'; worse than the books'.)
And yet, the ways we miss our lives are life.
Yet . . . yet . . .
               to have one's life add up to *yet!*

You sigh a shuddering sigh. Tatyana murmurs,
"Don't cry, little peasant"; leaves us with a swift
"Good-bye, good-bye . . . Ah, don't think ill of me . . ."
Your eyes open: you sit here thoughtlessly.

I love you — and yet — and yet — I love you.

Don't cry, little peasant. Sit and dream.
One comes, a finger's width beneath your skin,
To the braided maidens singing as they spin;
There sound the shepherd's pipe, the watchman's rattle
Across the short dark distance of the years.
I am a thought of yours: and yet, you do not think . . .
The firelight of a long, blind, dreaming story
Lingers upon your lips; and I have seen
Firm, fixed forever in your closing eyes,
The Corn King beckoning to his Spring Queen.

DONALD JUSTICE

Women in Love

It always comes, and when it comes they know.
To will it is enough to take them there.
The knack is this, to fasten and not let go.

Their limbs are charmed; they cannot stay or go.
Desire is limbo — they're unhappy there.
It always comes, and when it comes they know.

Their choice of hells would be the one they know.
Dante describes it, the wind circling there.
The knack is this, to fasten and not let go.

The wind carries them where they want to go,
And that seems cruel to strangers passing there.
It always comes, and when it comes they know
The knack is this, to fasten and not let go.

Tales from a Family Album

How shall I speak of doom, and ours in special,
But as of something altogether common?
No house of Atreus ours, too humble surely,
The family tree a simple chinaberry
Such as springs up in Georgia in a season.
(Under it sags the farmer's broken wagon.)
Nor may I laud it much for shade or beauty,
But praise that tree for being prompt to flourish,
Despite the worm and weather out of heaven.

I publish of my folk how they have prospered
With something in the eyes, perhaps inherent,
Or great-winged nose, bespeaking an acquaintance
Not casual and not recent with a monster,
Citing, as an example of some courage,
That aunt, long gone, who kept one in a birdcage
Thirty-odd years in shape of a green parrot,
Nor overcame her fears, yet missed no feeding,
Thrust in the crumbs with thimbles on her fingers.

I had an uncle, long of arm and hairy,
Who seldom spoke in any lady's hearing
For fear his tongue should light on aught unseemly,
Yet he could treat most kindly with us children
Touching that beast, wholly imaginary,
Which, hunting once, his hounds had got the wind of.
And even of this present generation
There is a cousin of no great removal
On whom the mark is printed of a forepaw.

How shall I speak of doom and not the shadow
Caught in the famished cheeks of those few beauties
My people boast of, being flushed and phthisic?
Of my own childhood I remember dimly
One who died young, though as a hag most toothless,
Her fine hair wintry, from a hard encounter
By moonlight in a dark wood with a stranger,
Who had as well been unicorn or centaur
For all she might recall of him thereafter.

There was a kinsman took up pen and paper
To write our history, at which he perished,
Calling for water and the holy wafer,
Who had, till then, resisted all persuasion.
I pray your mercy on a leaf so shaken,
And mercy likewise on these other fallen,
Torn from the berry-tree in heaven's fashion,
For there was something in their way of going
Put doom upon my tongue and bade me utter.

The Grandfathers

Why will they never sleep?
JOHN PEALE BISHOP

Why will they never sleep,
The old ones, the grandfathers?
Always you find them sitting
On ruined porches, deep
In the back country, at dusk,
Hawking and spitting.
They might have sat there forever,
Tapping their sticks,
Peevish, discredited gods.
Ask the lost traveler how,
At road-end, they will fix
You maybe with the cold
Eye of a snake or a bird
And answer not a word,
Only these blank, oracular
Headshakes or headnods.

ETHERIDGE KNIGHT

The Idea of Ancestry

1

Taped to the wall of my cell are 47 pictures: 47 black
faces: my father, mother, grandmothers (1 dead), grandfathers (both dead), brothers, sisters, uncles, aunts,
cousins (1st & 2nd), nieces, and nephews. They stare
across the space at me sprawling on my bunk. I know
their dark eyes, they know mine. I know their style,
they know mine. I am all of them, they are all of me;
they are farmers, I am a thief, I am me, they are thee.

I have at one time or another been in love with my mother,
1 grandmother, 2 sisters, 2 aunts (1 went to the asylum),
and 5 cousins. I am now in love with a 7 yr old niece
(she sends me letters written in large block print, and
her picture is the only one that smiles at me).

I have the same name as 1 grandfather, 3 cousins, 3 nephews,
and 1 uncle. The uncle disappeared when he was 15, just took
off and caught a freight (they say). He's discussed each year
when the family has a reunion, he causes uneasiness in
the clan, he is an empty space. My father's mother, who is 93
and who keeps the Family Bible with everybody's birth dates
(and death dates) in it, always mentions him. There is no
place in her Bible for "whereabouts unknown."

2

Each fall the graves of my grandfathers call me, the brown
hills and red gullies of mississippi send out their electric
messages, galvanizing my genes. Last yr / like a salmon quitting

the cold ocean-leaping and bucking up his birthstream / I
hitchhiked my way from L.A. with 16 caps in my pocket and a
monkey on my back. And I almost kicked it with the kinfolks.
I walked barefooted in my grandmother's backyard / I smelled the
    old
land and the woods / I sipped cornwhiskey from fruit jars with the
    men /
I flirted with the women / I had a ball till the caps ran out
and my habit came down. That night I looked at my grandmother
and split / my guts were screaming for junk / but I was almost
contented / I had almost caught up with me.
(The next day in Memphis I cracked a croaker's crib for a fix).

This yr there is a gray stone wall damming my stream, and when
the falling leaves stir my genes, I pace my cell or flop on my bunk
and stare at 47 black faces across the space. I am all of them,
they are all of me, I am me, they are thee, and I have no children
to float in the space between.

WILLIAM MILLS

Southern Vortex

This Louisiana sun
Draws bits and pieces
In a hot focus.
The foreman has sent me off
From the others to chip paint,
And the heat and white shell glare
Of this lonesome tank farm
May have cooked my head to hallucinations,
May be keeping me from
Understanding this vortex:
Green tanks, scraggled trees,
And one woodpecker,
Grinding out the way.

The Exclusion Principle

Somewhere in my fortieth year
And a cold Sunday
I try to explain
How the exclusion principle
Has left me with three friends
None in the place where I live.
Childless,
Three degrees and three books,
I, who never could understand hard thoughts,
Fidgit if certainty lasts
Longer than a Methodist sermon,
Am lately preoccupied
With an abandoned topcoat
On a chair's back
In a hotel with wooden floors.

Pity

She asked me twice
Didn't I kill the
Catfish
Before I took the pliers
And stripped his hide.
I said no,
You'd have to break his neck.
I, now uneasy,
Blood bright on my fingers
Saw her wince,
The whiskered fish
Twisting.
Looks like torture that way,
She said,
And I said look
If you ask that question
It leads to another.
This is the way it's done.

JOHN CROWE RANSOM

Bells for John Whiteside's Daughter

There was such speed in her little body,
And such lightness in her footfall,
It is no wonder her brown study
Astonishes us all.

Her wars were bruited in our high window.
We looked among orchard trees and beyond
Where she took arms against her shadow,
Or harried unto the pond

The lazy geese, like a snow cloud
Dripping their snow on the green grass,
Tricking and stopping, sleepy and proud,
Who cried in goose, Alas,

For the tireless heart within the little
Lady with rod that made them rise
From their noon apple-dreams and scuttle
Goose-fashion under the skies!

But now go the bells, and we are ready,
In one house we are sternly stopped
To say we are vexed at her brown study,
Lying so primly propped.

The Equilibrists

Full of her long white arms and milky skin
He had a thousand times remembered sin.
Alone in the press of people traveled he,
Minding her jacinth, and myrrh, and ivory.

Mouth he remembered: the quaint orifice
From which came heat that flamed upon the kiss,
Till cold words came down spiral from the head.
Grey doves from the officious tower illsped.

Body: it was a white field ready for love,
On her body's field, with the gaunt tower above,
The lilies grew, beseeching him to take,
If he would pluck and wear them, bruise and break.

Eyes talking: Never mind the cruel words,
Embrace my flowers, but not embrace the swords.
But what they said, the doves came straightway flying
And unsaid: Honor, Honor, they came crying.

Importunate her doves. Too pure, too wise,
Clambering on his shoulder, saying, Arise,
Leave me now, and never let us meet,
Eternal distance now command thy feet.

Predicament indeed, which thus discovers
Honor among thieves, Honor between lovers.
O such a little word is Honor, they feel!
But the grey word is between them cold as steel.

At length I saw these lovers fully were come
Into their torture of equilibrium;
Dreadfully had forsworn each other, and yet
They were bound each to each, and they did not forget.

And rigid as two painful stars, and twirled
About the clustered night their prison world,
They burned with fierce love always to come near,
But honor beat them back and kept them clear.

Ah, the strict lovers, they are ruined now!
I cried in anger. But with puddled brow
Devising for those gibbeted and brave
Came I descanting: Man, what would you have?

For spin your period out, and draw your breath,
A kinder saeculum begins with Death.
Would you ascend to Heaven and bodiless dwell?
Or take your bodies honorless to Hell?

In Heaven you have heard no marriage is,
No white flesh tinder to your lecheries,
Your male and female tissue sweetly shaped
Sublimed away, and furious blood escaped.

Great lovers lie in Hell, the stubborn ones
Infatuate of the flesh upon the bones;
Stuprate, they rend each other when they kiss,
The pieces kiss again, no end to this.

But still I watched them spinning, orbited nice.
Their flames were not more radiant than their ice.
I dug in the quiet earth and wrought the tomb
And made these lines to memorize their doom: —

EPITAPH

Equilibrists lie here; stranger, tread light;
Close, but untouching in each other's sight;
Mouldered the lips and ashy the tall skull.
Let them lie perilous and beautiful.

Antique Harvesters

(SCENE: *Of the Mississippi the bank sinister, and of the Ohio the bank sinister.*)

Tawny are the leaves turned but they still hold,
And it is harvest; what shall this land produce?
A meager hill of kernels, a runnel of juice;
Declension looks from our land, it is old.
Therefore let us assemble, dry, grey, spare,
And mild as yellow air.

"I hear the croak of a raven's funeral wing."
The young men would be joying in the song

Of passionate birds; their memories are not long.
What is it thus rehearsed in sable? "Nothing."
Trust not but the old endure, and shall be older
Than the scornful beholder.

We pluck the spindling ears and gather the corn.
One spot has special yield? "On this spot stood
Heroes and drenched it with their only blood."
And talk meets talk, as echoes from the horn
Of the hunter — echoes are the old man's arts,
Ample are the chambers of their hearts.

Here come the hunters, keepers of a rite;
The horn, the hounds, the lank mares coursing by
Straddled with archetypes of chivalry;
And the fox, lovely ritualist, in flight
Offering his unearthly ghost to quarry;
And the fields, themselves to harry.

Resume, harvesters. The treasure is full bronze
Which you will garner for the Lady, and the moon
Could tinge it no yellower than does this noon;
But grey will quench it shortly — the field, men, stones.
Pluck fast, dreamers; prove as you amble slowly
Not less than men, not wholly.

Bare the arm, dainty youths, bend the knees
Under bronze burdens. And by an autumn tone
As by a grey, as by a green, you will have known
Your famous Lady's image; for so have these;
And if one say that easily will your hands
More prosper in other lands,

Angry as wasp-music be your cry then:
"Forsake the Proud Lady, of the heart of fire,
The look of snow, to the praise of a dwindled choir,
Song of degenerate specters that were men?
The sons of the fathers shall keep her, worthy of
What these have done in love."

True, it is said of our Lady, she ageth.
But see, if you peep shrewdly, she hath not stooped;

Take no thought of her servitors that have drooped,
For we are nothing; and if one talk of death —
Why, the ribs of the earth subsist frail as a breath
If but God wearieth.

Vision by Sweetwater

Go and ask Robin to bring the girls over
To Sweetwater, said my Aunt; and that was why
It was like a dream of ladies sweeping by
The willows, clouds, deep meadowgrass, and the river.

Robin's sisters and my Aunt's lily daughter
Laughed and talked, and tinkled light as wrens
If there were a little colony all hens
To go walking by the steep turn of Sweetwater.

Let them alone, dear Aunt, just for one minute
Till I go fishing in the dark of my mind:
Where have I seen before, against the wind,
These bright virgins, robed and bare of bonnet,

Flowing with music of their strange quick tongue
And adventuring with delicate pace by the stream, —
Myself a child, old suddenly at the scream
From one of the white throats which it hid among?

Two in August

Two that could not have lived their single lives
As can some husbands and wives
Did something strange: they tensed their vocal cords
And attacked each other with silences and words
Like catapulted stones and arrowed knives.

Dawn was not yet; night is for loving or sleeping,
Sweet dreams or safekeeping;
Yet he of the wide brows that were used to laurel
And she, the famed for gentleness, must quarrel.
Furious both of them, and scared, and weeping.

How sleepers groan, twitch, wake to such a mood
Is not well understood,
Nor why two entities grown almost one
Should rend and murder trying to get undone,
With individual tigers in their blood.

She in terror fled from the marriage chamber
Circuiting the dark rooms like a string of amber
Round and round and back,
And would not light one lamp against the black,
And heard the clock that clanged: Remember, Remember.

And he must tread barefooted the dim lawn,
Soon he was up and gone;
High in the trees the night-mastered birds were crying
With fear upon their tongues, no singing nor flying
Which are their lovely attitudes by dawn.

Whether those bird-cries were of heaven or hell
There is no way to tell;
In the long ditch of darkness the man walked
Under the hackberry trees where the birds talked
With words too sad and strange to syllable.

JAMES SEAY

It All Comes Together Outside
the Restroom in Hogansville

It was the hole for looking in
only I looked out
in daylight that broadened
as I brought my eye closer.
First there was a '55 Chevy
shaved and decked like old times
but waiting on high-jacker shocks.
Then a sign that said J. D. Hines Garage.
In J. D.'s door was an empty Plymouth
with the windows down and the radio on.
A black woman was singing in Detroit
in a voice that brushed against the face
like the scarf
turning up in the wrong suitcase
long ago after everything came to grief.
What was inside we can only imagine —
men I guess trying to figure what would make it
work again. Beyond them
beyond the cracked engine blocks and thrown pistons
beyond that failed restroom
etched with our acids beyond that American Oil Station
beyond the oil on the ground
the mobile homes all over Hogansville
beyond our longing
all Georgia was green.
I'd had two for the road
a cheap enough thrill
and I wanted to think
I could take only what aroused me.
The interstate to Atlanta was wide open.
I wanted a different life.

So did J. D. Hines. So did the voice on the radio.
So did the man or woman
who made the hole in the window.
The way it works is this:
we devote ourselves to an image
we can't live with and try to kill
anything that suggests it could be otherwise.

Grabbling in Yokna Bottom

The hungry come in a dry time
To muddy the water of this swamp river
And take in ncts what fish or eel
Break surface to suck at this world's air.

But colder blood backs into the water's wood —
Gills the silt rather than rise to light —
And who would eat a cleaner meat
Must grabble in the hollows of underwater stumps and roots,

Must cram his arm and hand beneath the scum
And go by touch where eye cannot reach,
Must seize and bring to light
What scale or slime is touched —

Must in that instant — on touch —
Without question or reckoning
Grab up what wraps itself cold-blooded
Around flesh or flails the water to froth,

Or else feel the fish slip by,
Or learn that the loggerhead's jaw is thunder-deaf,
Or that the cottonmouth's fangs burn like heated needles
Even under water.

The well-fed do not wade this low river.

No Man's Good Bull

No man's good bull grazes wet clover
And leaves the pasture as he came.
My uncle's prize Angus was bloated
And breathing hard by afternoon
On the day he got into our clover pasture
Before the sun could burn the dew away.
He bellowed death from the field
As we grappled to hold his legs and head;
Our vet inserted a trocar between his ribs,
        let the whelming gas escape,
And to show us the nature of that gas
Put a match to the valve . . . a blue flame caught
     and the animal bolted from us,
Heading into the woods along the river bottom,
Turning only to test the new fire
        of his black side.

Each night we see his flame, blue and soft
           beside the river,
As he steals in before dawn
To plunge his head into wet clover,
Graze his fill,
     blaze up,
And answer that which lows to him in heat.
We watch him burn —
        hoof, hide, and bone.

DAVE SMITH

The Tire Hangs in the Yard

1.
First it was the secret place where I went to dream, end
of the childhood road, deep-tracked, the dark
behind my best friend's house, blackberry
thickets of darkness, and later
where we stared, with our girls, into the sky.

Past the hedgerow and the house-stolen field, past
the wing-shooting of crow remembered, I drive
bathed by green dashlight and the sun's
blood glinting on leaves just parted, then see

again the dead end, the dying woods, that stillness still
ticking like throat-rattle — and Jesus Christ
look at the beer cans, the traffic, even
hung on a berry vine somebody's rubber,

and wouldn't you know it that tire still hangs.

2.
In the Churchland Baptist Church the hot ivy hung, smelling
of dust, all mouths lifting their black holes
like a tire I kept dreaming. Clenched
by mother and father who stank sweetly in sweat,

I sang and sang until the black ceiling
of our house seemed to bellow with storm
and the tire skulled against my eyes
in time with the great clock in the far hall.

Hanging in darkness, like genitals, it made me listen.

3.

Years pass and memory's pendulum swings to changeless shame:
one summer night I came to fistfight Jim Jenrett,
whose house she came to and she no more now
than a frail hand on my cheek, and I
am beer-brave and nearly wild with all
the dozen piling from cars. Jesus,
look at us in the ghost-flare of headlights,
pissing, taunting, boy-shadows all right,
and me in the tire spinning my childish words.

We pass also, and are blind, into the years like trees
holding their scars, half-healed, the dark where Jim,
dunned by our words, goes out
near dawn and steps in the tire
and shies up the electric extension cord, noosed,
by the rope whose tire, burdened, ticks slowly.

4.

Ghost-heart of this place, of dreams, I give you a shove
and sure enough I hear the tick and all that was
is, and a girl straightening her skirt walks
smack against you and screams. You know
who laughs, smoking in the dark, don't you?

There are no headlights now, only the arc of blackness
gathering the hung world in its gullet. Blink
and maybe he's there, his great feet jammed
halfway in the hole of your heart,
gone halfway.

5.

Where do they go who once were with us on this dream road,
who flung themselves like seed under berry-
black nights, the faces black-clustered,
who could lean down and tell us
what love is and mercy and why now

I imagine a girl, mouth open in the sexual O, her hair
gone dull as soap scum, the husband grunting
as his fist smacks again, the scream

not out yet, nor the promise
she could never love anyone else.

I climb in the tire, swinging like a secret in the dark
woods surrounded by the homelights of strangers.
She swore she loved me best.

In the church I imagined this place left forever behind
but it's with me as I try to see the road begin.
Blackberries on both sides blackly hang.
Tall trees, in blackness, lean back at me.
When will they come, the headlights washing
over me like revelation, in cars
ticking and swirling?

Once when my mother could not find me, they came here.
Said "So this is it, the place." It was dark,
or nearly, and they said I might have died.
I asked them what being dead was like.
Like going blind or flying at night.

I shove my foot at the dirt and swing in absolute black.
The whine of the rope is like a distant scream.
I think, so this is it. Really it.

— for Robert Penn Warren

The Colors of Our Age: Pink and Black

That year the war went on, nameless, somewhere,
but I felt no war in my heart,
not even the shotgun's ba-bam
at the brown blur of quail.
I abandoned brothers and fathers,
the slow march through marsh
and soybean nap where
at field's end the black shacks
noiselessly squatted under strings
of smoke. I wore flags of pink:
shirts, cuff links, belt, stitching.

Black pants noosed my ankles
into scuffed buck shoes.
I whistled Be-Bop-a-Lula
below a hat like Gene Vincent's.
My uniform for the light, and girls.

Or one girl, anyway, whose name I licked
like candy, for it was deliciously
pink as her sweater. Celia,
slow, drawling, and honey-haired,
whose lips hold in the deep mind
our malignant innocence of joy.
Among my children, on the first
of October, I sit for supper,
feet bare, tongue numb with smoke,
to help them sort out my history's
hysterical photographs. In pink
hands they take us up, fearless,
as we are funny and otherworldly.

Just beyond our sill two late hummingbirds,
black and white, fight for the feeder's
red, time-stalled one drop.
They dart in, drink, are gone,
and small hands part before me
an age of look-alikes, images
in time like a truce-wall
I stare over. The hot, warping
smell of concrete comes, fear
bitter as tear gas rakes
a public parking lot. Midtown
Shopping Center, Portsmouth, Va.,
the *Life* caption says, ink
faded only slightly, paper yellowing.

Everyone is here, centered, in horror
like Lee Oswald's stunned Ranger.
A 1958 Ford Victoria, finned,
top down and furred dice hung,
seems ready to leap in the background.
The black teenager, no name given,
glares at the lens in distraction.

Half-crouched, he shows no teeth,
is shirtless, finely muscled,
his arms extended like wings.
White sneakers with red stars
make him pigeon-toed, alert.
His fingers spread at his thighs
like Wilt Chamberlain trying
to know what moves and not look.

Three girls lean behind him, *Norcom H.S.*
stenciled on one who wears a circle
pin, another a ring and chain.
Their soft chocolate faces appear
glazed, cheeks like Almond Joys.
They face the other side, white,
reared the opposite direction,
barbered heads, ears, necks.
In between, a new shiny hammer
towers like an icon lifted
to its highest trajectory.
A Klan ring sinks into flesh,
third finger, left hand,
cuddling the hammer handle.

This man's shirt is white, soiled,
eagle-shaped, and voluminous. Collar up.
Each detail enters my eye like grit
from long nights without sleep.
I might have been this man, risen,
a small-town hero gone gimpy
with hatred of anyone's black eyes.
I watch the hummingbirds feint
and watch my children dismiss them,
focusing hammer and then a woman
tattooed under the man's scarred
and hairless forearm. The scroll
beneath the woman says *Freedom*.
Above her head, in dark letters
shaped like a school name on
my son's team jacket: *Seoul, 1954*.
When our youngest asks, I try
to answer: A soldier, a war . . .

"Was that black man the enemy?"

I watch the feeder's tiny eye-round
drop, perfect as a breast
under the sweater of a girl
I saw go down, scuttling
like a crab, low, hands no use
against whatever had come to beat
into her silky black curls.
Her eyes were like quick birds
when the hammer nailed
her boyfriend's skull. Sick,
she flew against Penney's wall,
our hands trying to slap her sane.
In the Smarte Shop, acidly,
the mannequins smiled
in disbelief. Then I was
yanked from the light, a door

opened. I fell, as in memory I fall
to a time before that time.
Celia and I had gone to a field,
blanket spread, church done,
no one to see, no one expected.
But the black shack door opened,
the man who'd been wordless,
always, spoke, his words intimate
as a brother's, but banging out.
He grinned, he laughed, he wouldn't
stop. I damned his lippy face
but too late. He wiggled
his way inside my head.
He looked out, kept looking
from car window, school mirror,
from face black and tongue
pink as the clothes he wore.

Often enough Celia shrieked for joy,
no place too strange or obscene
for her, a child of the South,
manic for the black inside.
When he fell, she squeezed

my hand and more, her lips came
fragrant at my ear. I see them
near my face, past the hammer.
But what do they say? Why, now,
do I feel the insuck of breath
as I begin to run — and from her?
Children, I lived there and wish
I could tell you this is only
a moment fading and long past.

But in Richmond, Charlotte, God knows
where else, by the ninth green,
at the end of a flagstone pathway
under pine shadow, a Buick waits
and I wait, heart hammering,
bearing the done and the undone,
unforgiven, wondering in what
year, in what terrible hour,
the summons will at last come.
That elegant card in the hand
below the seamless, sealed face —
when it calls whoever I am
will I stand for once and not run?
Or be whistled back, what I was, hers?

Out here, supper waiting, I watch my son
slip off, jacketed, time, place,
ancestors of no consequence to him,
no more than pictures a man carries
(unless a dunk-shot inscribed).
For him, we are the irrelevance of age.
Who, then, will tell him of wars,
of faces that gather in his face
like shadows? For Christ's sake
look, I call to him, or you will
have to wait, somewhere, with us.
There I am, nearest the stranger
whose hammer moves quicker
than the Lord's own hand. I am
only seventeen. I don't smoke.
That's my friend Celia, kissing me.
We don't know what we're doing.

We're wearing pink and black.
She's dead now, I think.

· DABNEY · STUART

The Soup Jar

Its metal top refused my father's twisting;
He tried warm water, a dishcloth, the heel of a shoe,
But couldn't budge its stubborn *status quo.*
It had stood its ground, longer than he, rusting.

I had to help. Gripped the jar while he cursed
Into place the tricky gadget guaranteed
To open anything, then gave it all he had.
I jerked my hand, and a hunk of glass, back when it burst.

Someone else tied my tourniquet. He paled
And had to sit down. Seven stitches later
We cleaned the floor and had another dish for supper.
Alone, he got nothing. It took us both to fail.

Weeks after, my world spun around that jar
And I saw it, and him, through angry tears.
Now it seems, recalled through these shattered years,
So small a thing — some broken glass, a scar.

Mining in Killdeer Alley

for Nathan

One, and then another, they settled before me
            like flakes of air,
Halfway up the hill, their splayed toes sketching
Shadows, the grass tufts, gravel, merging;
They came down from their marvelous fluency
To wobble on dumb stilts

Like earthbound creatures, hindered by strangeness.
The shadows were blue and voluminous, and their toes lost,
And the pronouns confused, and they shied and took flight
Again as I drove the rest of the way up the hill.
When I entered the house
And called my wife to the window they were back,

                          settled,

Settled into the dark; and in the Blue Ridge morning
They parted, again, for my descent.

                   They were there
Every day the last seven months before the gift,
Feathering my passage
Like wings, their angled wings, her shoulder blades
As she bent awkwardly before the sink, mornings,
In the ninth month.

So that my father, who we thought was dying,
Could see him, we carried his newborn grandson
Up the back stairs of the hospital. The light was broken
All over the blanket, and our child swam in his glasses
With pieces of that broken light.

                 Their russet throats,
The sun shattered in the gravel,

              the gray veins
Of his impeccable wrist,

          Lord, for the life of me.

When we brought him home they had flown away.

No Yellow Jackets on the Mountain

                          for Mike Martin

Friendship turns. And turns again. Another name
For history, the mimes of history

                  end-
less

    exercises, webs of language
Preceding us, spun brotherhoods into which we fall
As we are born, learning to speak to each other.

Ten years ago you stopped chasing
The cities of the Western world as if they were women,
Abandoned the mazes of strasses and allées
And freight yards, and came back to Virginia
To build a cabin on Big Walker Mountain.
Since then I've climbed it a half dozen times
To speak with you, passing
The trail's forks and the forked trees, one tree
Writhing upward past its fractured limb, above
The bloodroot and wintergreen, until
I can dream it so clearly the whole ascent
Seems part of the talk itself, composed
— except for the light beyond the unsettled leaves
Casting these flickered shadows — as a poem
Is composed.
                    And yet
The light in a poem
Is like no other light, nor like itself,
Shining as it does through a network
Which is also its source.
                              Can poetry
Glow in the dark, then? With darkness?
Can a friend? What kind of luminous mesh
Is strong enough to sustain the complexities
Of friendship? What is sufficient?
                                    Your life
Seems to crumble
Like rotted wood to the touch.
One day the wind will rise
And disperse it over the mountain:
Have you wished for this from the beginning?
                                        I remember
Your hand burrowing in a chestnut stump,
Fingering the cool loam, then suddenly withdrawn,
Already swelling with the hidden sting.
                              And today
I climb the mountain again, leaning
Against its pitch, listing
Past broken
Causes, twisted
Growth, wanting again

To give it up, turn back, missing
The highwire joy that keeps a man
Working at these heights from letting go.

I rest on a rock. I find myself

Staring down at the valley, my eyes
Filled with the railroad tracks' dazzling
Twin silver, playing their usual trick
Of joining beyond sight, denying themselves.

Meanwhile, the blue shadows on the leaving trees,
The early petals, fallen, the predictable transactions,
Departures, a mountain cabin
— paper littering a table, a heated stone —
These are never sufficient, but they remain
Clues to places, or a place:
They too reflect a light.

● ALLEN ● TATE

Ode to the Confederate Dead

Row after row with strict impunity
The headstones yield their names to the element,
The wind whirrs without recollection;
In the riven troughs the splayed leaves
Pile up, of nature the casual sacrament
To the seasonal eternity of death;
Then driven by the fierce scrutiny
Of heaven to their election in the vast breath,
They sough the rumour of mortality.

Autumn is desolation in the plot
Of a thousand acres where these memories grow
From the inexhaustible bodies that are not
Dead, but feed the grass row after rich row.
Think of the autumns that have come and gone! —
Ambitious November with the humors of the year,
With a particular zeal for every slab,
Staining the uncomfortable angels that rot
On the slabs, a wing chipped here, an arm there:
The brute curiosity of an angel's stare
Turns you, like them, to stone,
Transforms the heaving air
Till plunged to a heavier world below
You shift your sea-space blindly
Heaving, turning like the blind crab.

Dazed by the wind, only the wind
The leaves flying, plunge

You know who have waited by the wall
The twilight certainty of an animal,

Those midnight restitutions of the blood
You know — the immitigable pines, the smoky frieze
Of the sky, the sudden call: you know the rage,
The cold pool left by the mounting flood,
Of muted Zeno and Parmenides.
You who have waited for the angry resolution
Of those desires that should be yours tomorrow,
You know the unimportant shrift of death
And praise the vision
And praise the arrogant circumstance
Of those who fall
Rank upon rank, hurried beyond decision —
Here by the sagging gate, stopped by the wall.

   Seeing, seeing only the leaves
   Flying, plunge and expire

Turn your eyes to the immoderate past,
Turn to the inscrutable infantry rising
Demons out of the earth — they will not last.
Stonewall, Stonewall, and the sunken fields of hemp,
Shiloh, Antietam, Malvern Hill, Bull Run.
Lost in that orient of the thick-and-fast
You will curse the setting sun.

   Cursing only the leaves crying
   Like an old man in a storm

You hear the shout, the crazy hemlocks point
With troubled fingers to the silence which
Smothers you, a mummy, in time.

                 The hound bitch
Toothless and dying, in a musty cellar
Hears the wind only.

            Now that the salt of their blood
Stiffens the saltier oblivion of the sea,
Seals the malignant purity of the flood,
What shall we who count our days and bow
Our heads with a commemorial woe
In the ribboned coats of grim felicity,

What shall we say of the bones, unclean,
Whose verdurous anonymity will grow?
The ragged arms, the ragged heads and eyes
Lost in these acres of the insane green?
The gray lean spiders come, they come and go;
In a tangle of willows without light
The singular screech-owl's tight
Invisible lyric seeds the mind
With the furious murmur of their chivalry.

We shall say only the leaves
Flying, plunge and expire

We shall say only the leaves whispering
In the improbable mist of nightfall
That flies on multiple wing;
Night is the beginning and the end
And in between the ends of distraction
Waits mute speculation, the patient curse
That stones the eyes, or like the jaguar leaps
For his own image in a jungle pool, his victim.
What shall we say who have knowledge
Carried to the heart? Shall we take the act
To the grave? Shall we, more hopeful, set up the
       grave
In the house? The ravenous grave?

                             Leave now
The shut gate and the decomposing wall:
The gentle serpent, green in the mulberry bush,
Riots with his tongue through the hush —
Sentinel of the grave who counts us all!

The Oath

It was near evening, the room was cold
Half dark; Uncle Ben's brass bullet-mould
And powder-horn and Major Bogan's face
Above the fire in the half-light plainly said:
There's naught to kill but the animated dead.

Horn nor mould nor major follows the chase.
Being cold I urged Lytle to the fire
In the blank twilight with not much left untold
By two old friends when neither's a great liar.
We sat down evenly in the smoky chill.
There's precious little to say between day and dark,
Perhaps a few words on the implacable will
Of time sailing like a magic barque
Or something as fine for the amenities,
Till dusk seals the window, the fire grows bright,
And the wind saws the hill with a swarm of bees.
Now meditating a little on the firelight
We heard the darkness grapple with the night
And give an old man's valedictory wheeze
From his westward breast between his polar jaws;
Then Lytle asked: Who are the dead?
Who are the living and the dead?
And nothing more was said.
So I, leaving Lytle to that dream,
Decided what it is in time that gnaws
The ageing fury of a mountain stream
When suddenly as an ignorant mind will do
I thought I heard the dark pounding its head
On a rock, crying: *Who are the dead?*
Then Lytle turned with an oath — By God it's true!

The Swimmers

SCENE: *Montgomery County,*
Kentucky, July 1911

Kentucky water, clear springs: a boy fleeing
  To water under the dry Kentucky sun,
  His four little friends in tandem with him, seeing

Long shadows of grapevine wriggle and run
  Over the green swirl; mullein under the ear
  Soft as Nausicaä's palm; sullen fun

Savage as childhood's thin harmonious tear:

O fountain, bosom source undying-dead
Replenish me the spring of love and fear

And give me back the eye that looked and fled
When a thrush idling in the tulip tree
Unwound the cold dream of the copperhead.

— Along the creek the road was winding; we
Felt the quicksilver sky. I see again
The shrill companions of that odyssey:

Bill Eaton, Charlie Watson, "Nigger" Layne
The doctor's son, Harry Duèsler who played
The flute; and Tate, with water on the brain.

Dog-days: the dusty leaves where rain delayed
Hung low on poison-oak and scuppernong,
And we were following the active shade

Of water, that bells and bickers all night long.
"No more'n a mile," Layne said. All five stood still.
Listening, I heard what seemed at first a song;

Peering, I heard the hooves come down the hill.
The posse passed, twelve horse; the leader's face
Was worn as limestone on an ancient sill.

Then, as sleepwalkers shift from a hard place
In bed, and rising to keep a formal pledge
Descend a ladder into empty space,

We scuttled down the bank below a ledge
And marched stiff-legged in our common fright
Along a hog-track by the riffle's edge:

Into a world where sound shaded the sight
Dropped the dull hooves again; the horsemen came
Again, all but the leader. It was night

Momently and I feared: eleven same
Jesus-Christers unmembered and unmade,
Whose Corpse had died again in dirty shame.

The bank then levelling in a speckled glade,
  We stopped to breathe above the swimming-hole;
  I gazed at its reticulated shade

Recoiling in blue fear, and felt it roll
  Over my ears and eyes and lift my hair
  Like seaweed tossing on a sunk atoll.

I rose again. Borne on the copper air
  A distant voice green as a funeral wreath
  Against a grave: "That dead nigger there."

The melancholy sheriff slouched beneath
  A giant sycamore; shaking his head
  He plucked a sassafras twig and picked his teeth:

"We come too late." He spoke to the tired dead
  Whose ragged shirt soaked up the viscous flow
  Of blood in which It lay discomfited.

A butting horse-fly gave one ear a blow
  And glanced off, as the sheriff kicked the rope
  Loose from the neck and hooked it with his toe

Away from the blood. — I looked back down the slope:
  The friends were gone that I had hoped to greet. —
  A single horseman came at a slow lope

And pulled up at the hanged man's horny feet;
  The sheriff noosed the feet, the other end
  The stranger tied to his pommel in a neat

Slip-knot. I saw the Negro's body bend
  And straighten, as a fish-line cast transverse
  Yields to the current that it must subtend.

The sheriff's Goddamn was a murmured curse
  Not for the dead but for the blinding dust
  That boxed the cortège in a cloudy hearse

And dragged it towards our town. I knew I must

Not stay till twilight in that silent road;
    Sliding my bare feet into the warm crust,

I hopped the stonecrop like a panting toad
    Mouth open, following the heaving cloud
    That floated to the court-house square its load

Of limber corpse that took the sun for shroud.
    There were three figures in the dying sun
    Whose light were company where three was crowd.

My breath crackled the dead air like a shotgun
    As, sheriff and the stranger disappearing,
    The faceless head lay still. I could not run

Or walk, but stood. Alone in the public clearing
    This private thing was owned by all the town,
    Though never claimed by us within my hearing.

ALICE WALKER

Burial

I

They have fenced in the dirt road
that once led to Wards Chapel
A.M.E. church,
and cows graze
among the stones that
mark my family's graves.
The massive oak is gone
from out the church yard,
but the giant space is left
unfilled;
despite the two-lane blacktop
that slides across
the old, unalterable
roots.

II

Today I bring my own child here;
to this place where my father's
grandmother rests undisturbed
beneath the Georgia sun,
above her the neatstepping hooves
of cattle.
Here the graves soon grow back into the land.
Have been known to sink. To drop open without
warning. To cover themselves with wild ivy,

blackberries. Bittersweet and sage.
No one knows why. No one asks.
When Burning Off Day comes, as it does
some years,
the graves are haphazardly cleared and snakes
hacked to death and burned sizzling
in the brush. . . . The odor of smoke, oak
leaves, honeysuckle.
Forgetful of geographic resolutions as birds,
the farflung young fly South to bury
the old dead.

III

The old women move quietly up
and touch Sis Rachel's face.
"Tell Jesus I'm coming," they say.
"Tell Him I ain't goin' to *be*
long."

My grandfather turns his creaking head
away from the lavender box.
He does not cry. But looks afraid.
For years he called her "Woman";
shortened over the decades to
"'Oman."
On the cut stone for "'Oman's" grave
he did not notice
they had misspelled her name.

(The stone reads *Racher Walker* — not "Rachel" —
Loving Wife, Devoted Mother.)

IV

As a young woman, who had known her? Tripping
eagerly, "loving wife," to my grandfather's
bed. Not pretty, but serviceable. A hard
worker, with rough, moist hands. Her own two
babies dead before she came.

Came to seven children,
To aprons and sweat.
Came to quiltmaking,
Came to canning and vegetable gardens
big as fields.
Came to fields to plow.
Cotton to chop.
Potatoes to dig.
Came to multiple measles, chickenpox,
and croup.
Came to water from springs.
Came to leaning houses one story high.
Came to rivalries. Saturday night battles.
Came to straightened hair, Noxzema, and
feet washing at the Hardshell Baptist church.
Came to zinnias around the woodpile.
Came to grandchildren not of her blood
whom she taught to dip snuff without
sneezing.

Came to death blank, forgetful of it all.

When he called her "'Oman" she no longer
listened. Or heard, or knew, or felt.

V

It is not until I see my first grade teacher
review her body that I cry.
Not for the dead, but for the gray in my
first grade teacher's hair. For memories
of before I was born, when teacher and
grandmother loved each other; and later
above the ducks made of soap and the orange-
legged chicks Miss Reynolds drew over
my own small hand
on paper with wide blue lines.

VI

Not for the dead, but for memories. None of
them sad. But seen from the angle of her
death.

ROBERT PENN WARREN

Evening Hawk

From plane of light to plane, wings dipping through
Geometries and orchids that the sunset builds,
Out of the peak's black angularity of shadow, riding
The last tumultuous avalanche of
Light above pines and the guttural gorge,
The hawk comes.

            His wing
Scythes down another day, his motion
Is that of the honed steel-edge, we hear
The crashless fall of stalks of Time.

The head of each stalk is heavy with the gold of our error.

Look! Look! he is climbing the last light
Who knows neither Time nor error, and under
Whose eye, unforgiving, the world, unforgiven, swings
Into shadow.

         Long now,
The last thrush is still, the last bat
Now cruises in his sharp hieroglyphics. His wisdom
Is ancient, too, and immense. The star
Is steady, like Plato, over the mountain.

If there were no wind we might, we think, hear
The earth grind on its axis, or history
Drip in darkness like a leaking pipe in the cellar.

English Cocker: Old and Blind

With what painful deliberation he comes down the stair,
At the edge of each step one paw suspended in air,
And distrust. Does he thus stand on a final edge
Of the world? Sometimes he stands thus, and will not budge,

With a choking soft whimper, while monstrous blackness is whirled
Inside his head, and outside too, the world
Whirling in blind vertigo. But if your hand
Merely touches his head, old faith comes flooding back — and

The paw descends. His trust is infinite
In you, who are, in his eternal night,
Only a frail scent subject to the whim
Of wind, or only a hand held close to him

With a dog biscuit, or, in a sudden burst
Of temper, the force that jerks that goddamned, accurst
Little brute off your bed. But remember how you last saw
Him hesitate in his whirling dark, one paw

Suspended above the abyss at the edge of the stair,
And remember that musical whimper, and how, then aware
Of a sudden sweet heart-stab, you knew in him
The kinship of all flesh defined by a halting paradigm.

The Corner of the Eye

The poem is just beyond the corner of the eye.
You cannot see it — not yet — but sense the faint gleam,

Or stir. It may be like a poor little shivering fieldmouse,
One tiny paw lifted from snow while, far off, the owl

Utters. Or like breakers, far off, almost as soundless as dream.
Or the rhythmic rasp of your father's last breath, harsh

As the grind of a great file the blacksmith sets to hoof.
Or the whispering slither the torn morning newspaper makes,

Blown down an empty slum street in New York, at midnight,
Past dog shit and garbage cans, while the full moon,

Phthisic and wan, above the East River, presides
Over that last fragment of history which is

Our lives. Or the foggy glint of old eyes of
The sleepless patient who no longer wonders

If he will once more see in that window the dun-
Bleached dawn that promises what. Or the street corner

Where always, for years, in passing you felt, unexplained, a pang
Of despair, like nausea, till one night, late, late on that spot

You were struck stock-still and again remembered — felt
Her head thrust to your shoulder, she clinging, while you

Mechanically pat the fur coat, hear sobs, and stare up
Where tall buildings, frailer than reed-stalks, reel among stars.

Yes, something there at eye-edge lurks, hears ball creak in socket,
Knows, before you do, tension of muscle, change

Of blood pressure, heart-heaves of sadness, foot's falter, for
It has stalked you all day, or years, breath rarely heard, fangs dripping.

And now, any moment, great hindquarters may hunch, ready —
Or is it merely a poem, after all?

The Place

From shelving cliff-darkness, green arch and nave
Skyward aspire, translucently, to heights
Where tattered gold tags of sunlight twirl, swing,
Or downward sift to the upturned eye. Upward,
The eye probes infinite distance, infinite
Light, while foot, booted, tangled in fern,

Grips stone. Fern
Bleeds on stone.

       This
Is the hour of the unbounded loneliness. This
Is the hour of the self's uncertainty
Of self. This is the hour when
Prayer might be a possibility, if
It were. This
Is the hour when what is remembered is
Forgotten. When
What is forgotten is remembered, and
You are not certain which is which.
But tell me:

      How had you ever forgotten that spot
Where once wild azalea bloomed? And what there passed? And forgotten
That truth may lurk in irony? How,
Alone in a dark piazza, as the cathedral clock
Announced 3 A.M. to old tiles of the starless city, could you bear
To remember the impossible lie, told long before, elsewhere?
But a lie you had found all too possible.

Self is the cancellation of self, and now is the hour.
Self is the mutilation of official meanings, and this is the place.
You hear water of minor musical utterance
On stone, but from what direction?
You hear, distantly, a bird-call you cannot identify.
Is the shadow of the cliff creeping upon you?
You are afraid to look at your watch.

You think of the possibility of lying on stone,
Among fern fronds, and waiting
For the shadow to find you.
The stars would not be astonished
To catch a glimpse of the form through interstices
Of leaves now black as enameled tin. Nothing astounds the stars.
They have long lived. And you are not the first
To come to such a place seeking the most difficult knowledge.

Old Photograph of the Future

That center of attention — an infantile face
That long years ago showed, no doubt, pink and white —
Now faded, and in the photograph only a trace
Of grays, not much expression in sight.

That center of attention, swathed in a sort of white dress,
Is precious to the woman who, pretty and young,
Leans with a look of surprised blessedness
At the mysterious miracle forth-sprung.

In the background somewhat, the masculine figure
Looms, face agleam with achievement and pride.
In black coat, derby at breast, he is quick to assure
You the world's in good hands — lay your worries aside.

The picture is badly faded. Why not?
Most things show wear around seventy-five,
And that's the age this picture has got.
The man and woman no longer, of course, live.

They lie side by side in whatever love survives
Under green turf, or snow, and that child, years later, stands there
While old landscapes blur and he in guilt grieves
Over nameless promises unkept, in undefinable despair.

Muted Music

As sultry as the cruising hum
Of a single fly lost in the barn's huge, black
Interior, on a Sunday afternoon, with all the sky
Ablaze outside — so sultry and humming
Is memory when in barn-shade, eyes shut,
You lie in hay, and wonder if that empty, lonely,
And muted music was all the past was, after all.
Does the past now cruise your empty skull like
That blundering buzz at barn-height — which is dark

Except for the window at one gable, where
Daylight is netted gray with cobwebs, and the web
Dotted and sagged with blunderers that once could cruise and hum.

What do you really know
Of that world of decision and
Action you once strove in? What
Of that world where now
Light roars, while you, here, lulled, lie
In a cunningly wrought and mathematical

Box of shade, and try, of all the past, to remember
Which was *what, what, which*. Perhaps
That sultry hum from the lone bumbler, cruising high
In shadow, is the only sound that truth can make,
And into that muted music you soon sink
To hear at last, at last, what you have strained for
All the long years, and sometimes at dream-verge thought

You heard — the song the moth sings, the babble
Of falling snowflakes (in a language
No school has taught you), the scream
Of the reddening bud of the oak tree

As the bud bursts into the world's brightness.

Covered Bridge

Another land, another age, another self
Before all had happened that has happened since
And is now arranged on the shelf
Of memory in a sequence that I call Myself.

How can you think back and know
Who was the boy, sleepless, who lay
In a moonless night of summer, but with star-glow
Gemming the dewy miles, and acres, you used to go?

You think of starlight on the river, star
By star declaring its motionless, holy self,

You wondered if reflection was seen by the sky's star.

Long, long ago, some miles away,
There was an old covered bridge across that stream,
And if impact of hoof or wheel made the loose board sway,
That echo wandered the landscape, night or day.

But if by day, the human bumble and grind
Absorbed the sound, or even birdsong
Interfered in its fashion, and only at night might you find
That echo filling the vastness of your mind,

Till you wondered what night, long off, you would set hoof
On those loose boards and then proceed
To trot through the caverning dark beneath that roof.
Going where? Just going. That would be enough.

Then silence would wrap that starlit land,
And you would sleep — who now do not sleep
As you wonder why you cannot understand
What pike, highway, or path has led you from land to land,

From year to year, to lie in what strange room,
Where to prove identity you now lift up
Your own hand — scarcely visible in that gloom.

Old-Time Childhood in Kentucky

When I was a boy I saw the world I was in.
I saw it for what it was. Canebrakes with
Track beaten down by bear paw. Tobacco,
In endless rows, the pink inner flesh of black fingers
Crushing to green juice tobacco worms plucked
From a leaf. The great trout,
Motionless, poised in the shadow of his
Enormous creek-boulder.
But the past and the future broke on me, as I got older.

Strange, into the past I first grew. I handled the old bullet-mold.

I drew out a saber, touched an old bayonet, I dreamed
Of the death-scream. Old spurs I tried on.
The first great General Jackson had ridden just north to our state
To make a duel legal — or avoid the law.
It was all for honor. He said: "I would have killed him
Even with his hot lead in my heart." This for honor. I longed
To understand. I said the magic word.
I longed to say it aloud, to be heard.

I saw the strategy of Bryce's Crossroads, saw
The disposition of troops at Austerlitz, but knew
It was far away, long ago. I saw
The marks of the old man's stick in the dust, heard
The old voice explaining. His eyes weren't too good,
So I read him books he wanted. Read him
Breasted's *History of Egypt*. Saw years uncoil like a snake.
I built a pyramid with great care. There interred
Pharaoh's splendor and might.
Excavation next summer exposed that glory to man's sight.

At a cave mouth my uncle showed me crinoid stems,
And in limestone skeletons of the fishy form of some creature.
"All once under water," he said, "no saying the millions
Of years." He walked off, the old man still with me. "Grandpa,"
I said, "what do you do, things being like this?" "All you can,"
He said, looking off through treetops, skyward. "Love
Your wife, love your get, keep your word, and
If need arises die for what men die for. There aren't
Many choices.
And remember that truth doesn't always live in the number of voices."

He hobbled away. The woods seemed darker. I stood
In the encroachment of shadow. I shut
My eyes, head thrown back, eyelids black.
I stretched out the arm on each side, and, waterlike,
Wavered from knees and hips, feet yet firm-fixed, it seemed,
On shells, in mud, in sand, in stone, as though
In eons back I grew there in that submarine
Depth and lightlessness, waiting to discover
What I would be, might be, after ages — how many? — had rolled over.

Mortal Limit

I saw the hawk ride updraft in the sunset over Wyoming.
It rose from coniferous darkness, past gray jags
Of mercilessness, past whiteness, into the gloaming
Of dream-spectral light above the last purity of snow-snags.

There — west — were the Tetons. Snow-peaks would soon be
In dark profile to break constellations. Beyond what height
Hangs now the black speck? Beyond what range will gold eyes see
New ranges rise to mark a last scrawl of light?

Or, having tasted that atmosphere's thinness, does it
Hang motionless in dying vision before
It knows it will accept the mortal limit,
And swing into the great circular downwardness that will restore

The breath of earth? Of rock? Of rot? Of other such
Items, and the darkness of whatever dream we clutch?

Three Darknesses

I

There is some logic here to trace, and I
Will try hard to find it. But even as I begin, I
Remember one Sunday morning, festal with springtime, in
The zoo of Rome. In a natural, spacious, grassy area,
A bear, big as a grizzly, erect, indestructible,
Unforgiving as God, as rhythmic as
A pile-driver — right-left, right-left —
Slugged at an iron door. The door,
Heavy, bolted, barred, must have been
The entrance to a dark enclosure, a cave,
Natural or artificial. Minute by minute, near, far,
Wheresoever we wandered, all Sunday morning,
With the air full of colored balloons trying to escape
From children, the ineluctable
Rhythm continues. You think of the
Great paws like iron on iron. Can iron bleed?

Since my idiot childhood the world has been
Trying to tell me something. There is something
Hidden in the dark. The bear
Was trying to enter into the darkness of wisdom.

II

Up Black Snake River, at anchor in
That black tropical water, we see
The cormorant rise — cranky, graceless,
Ungeared, unhinged, one of God's more cynical
Improvisations, black against carmine of sunset. He
Beats seaward. The river gleams blackly west, and thus
The jungle divides on a milk-pale path of sky toward the sea.
Nothing human is visible. Each of us lies looking
Seaward. Ice melts in our glasses. We seem ashamed
Of conversation. Asia is far away. The radio is not on.
The grave of my father is far away. Our host
Rises silently, is gone. Later we see him,
White helmet in netting mystically swathed,
As he paddles a white skiff into the tangled
Darkness of a lagoon. There moss hangs. Later,
Dark now, we see the occasional stab of his powerful
Light back in the darkness of trunks rising
From the side lagoon, the darkness of moss suspended.
We think of the sound a snake makes
As it slides off a bough — the slop, the slight swish,
The blackness of water. You
Wonder what your host thinks about
When he cuts the light and drifts on the lagoon of midnight.
Though it is far from midnight. Upon his return,
He will, you know,
Lie on the deck-teak with no word. Your hostess
Had gone into the cabin. You hear
The pop of a wine cork. She comes back. The wine
Is breathing in darkness.

III

The nurse is still here. Then
She is not here. You
Are here but are not sure
It is you in the sudden darkness. No matter.
A damned nuisance, but trivial —
The surgeon has just said that. A dress rehearsal,
You tell yourself, for
The real thing. Later. Ten years? Fifteen?
Tomorrow, only a dry run. At
5 A.M. they will come. Your hand reaches out in darkness
To the TV button. It is an old-fashioned western.
Winchester fire flicks white in the dream-night.
It has something to do with vice and virtue, and the vastness
Of moonlit desert. A stallion, white and flashing, slips,
Like spilled quicksilver, across
The vastness of moonlight. Black
Stalks of cacti, like remnants of forgotten nightmares, loom
Near at hand. Action fades into distance, but
You are sure that virtue will triumph. Far beyond
All the world, the mountains lift. The snow peaks
Float into moonlight. They float
In that unnamable altitude of white light. God
Loves the world. For what it is.

JAMES WHITEHEAD

About a Year After He Got Married He Would Sit Alone in an Abandoned Shack in a Cotton Field Enjoying Himself

I'd sit inside the abandoned shack all morning
Being sensitive, a fair thing to do
At twenty-three, my first son born, and burning
To get my wife again. The world was new
And I was nervous and wonderfully depressed.

The light on the cotton flowers and the child
Asleep at home was marvelous and blessed,
And the dust in the abandoned air was mild
As sentimental poverty. I'd scan
Or draw the ragged wall the morning long.

Newspaper for wallpaper sang but didn't mean.
Hard thoughts of justice were beyond my ken.
Lord, forgive young men their gentle pain,
Then bring them stones. Bring their play to ruin.

He Records a Little Song for a Smoking Girl

Smoking all that much has got her eyes
Pinched and a little lined — so the misery
Of cigarettes deserves a song. Prize
For doing anything, catastrophe
In small doses, smoke cuts into a face
Almost as deep as Benzedrine and booze.

Still she's a lovely girl in every place
Because she is so young. O she will lose
Her surfaces of head in love and time
Though all the rest stay smooth and be close-pored.

Her legs would make a blind man smile, and rime —
Her belly and the thing in sweet accord
Years from now will cry. Forgive, forgive
My cigarettes, I swallowed smoke alive.

A Local Man Doesn't Like the Music

Those tunes don't recollect one memory
I ever had. Not one could call my name.
And when the music isn't company
It's time to go and time to change your mind.

I've been dissatisfied. My pretty wives
Were decent, warm, and wrong. My sons have played
It smarter than I did. My daughters' lives
Are better than their mothers'. They are good.

I love them all, but I don't love them well.
I've been dissatisfied to be alone,
The one sure way to make your bed in hell.

I'll change my mind. I'll like to where I've gone,
Whatever trailer park or motel room.
Alone or with some girl, I'll write a song.

MILLER
WILLIAMS

A Poem for Emily

Small fact and fingers and farthest one from me,
a hand's width and two generations away,
in this still present I am fifty three.
You are not yet a full day.

When I am sixty three, when you are ten,
and you are neither closer nor as far,
your arms will fill with what you know by then,
the arithmetic and love we do and are.

When I by blood and luck am eighty six
and you are some place else and thirty three
believing in sex and god and politics
with children who look not at all like me,

some time I know you will have read them this
so they will know I love them and say so
and love their mother. Child, whatever is
is always or never was. Long ago,

a day I watched a while beside your bed,
I wrote this down, a thing that might be kept
a while, to tell you what I would have said
when you were who knows what and I was dead
which is I stood and loved you while you slept.

After the Revolution for Jesus the Associate Professor Prepares His Final Remarks

What the blind lost when radio
gave way to TV,
what the deaf lost when movies
stopped spelling out words and spoke,
was a way back in. Always, this desire
to be inside again, when the doors are closed.

On the other side of the doors
our friends and parents and grandparents
work and eat and read books and make sense and love.

The thought of being disconnected
from history or place can empty the heart;
we are most afraid,
whatever else we fear,
of feeling the memory go, and of exile.
And death, which is both at once.

Still, as our lives
are the inhalations and exhalations of gods
we ought not fear those things we know will come
and ought not hope for what we know will not.
The dogs that waited for soldiers to come home
from Phillipi, New Guinea, Pennsylvania,
are all dead now whether or not the men
came back to call them.
There is no constancy but a falling away
with only love as a temporary stay
and not much assurance of that.

The desert religions are founded on sandy ways
to set ourselves free from that endless tumbling downward.
Thus we endow ourselves with gods of purpose,
the purposes of gods, and do their battles.

We are sent to war for money, but we go for god.

Prison is no place for living
but for reliving lives.
I remember a quarrel of students
proving, reproving the world;
a woman taking love
she didn't want, but needed
like a drowning swimmer
thrown a strand of barbed wire
by a kind stranger standing on the shore.

Imperfect love in that imperfect world
seemed elegant and right.
Now the old air that shaped itself to our bodies
will take the forms of others.
They will laugh with this air and pass it through their bodies
but days like ours
they will not come again to this poor planet.

I am reinventing our days together.
A man should be careful with words
at a time like this,
but lies have some attraction over the truth;
there is something in deceitful words
that sounds good to the ear.

The first layer of paint conceals the actor;
the second conceals the paint.
By which sly truth we have come to where we are.

I can hear brief choirs of rifles.
Inside my head
naked women wander toward my bed.
How gently they lie there, loving themselves to sleep.

What do we know that matters that Aeschylus did not know?

I do believe in God, the Mother and Father,
Maker of possibility, distance and dust,
who may never come to judge or quicken the dead
but does abide. We live out our lives
inside the body of God,

a heretic and breathing universe
that feeds on the falling of sparrows
and the crumbling of nations,
the rusting away of metal
and the rotting of wood.
I will be eaten by God.
There is nothing to fear.
To die, the singers believe, is to go home.
Where should I go, going home? Lord, I am here.

CHARLES WRIGHT

Northhanger Ridge

Half-bridge over nothingness,
White sky of the palette knife; blot orange,
Vertical blacks; blue, birdlike,
Drifting up from the next life,
The heat-waves, like consolation, wince —
One cloud, like a trunk, stays shut
Above the horizon; off to the left, dream-wires,
Hill-snout like a crocodile's.

Or so I remember it,
Their clenched teeth in their clenched mouths,
Their voices like shards of light,
Brittle, unnecessary.
Ruined shoes, roots, the cabinet of lost things:
This is the same story,
Its lips in flame, its throat a dark water,
The page stripped of its meaning.

Sunday, and Father Dog is turned loose:
Up the long road the children's feet
Snick in the dust like raindrops; the wind
Excuses itself and backs off; inside, heat
Lies like a hand on each head;
Slither and cough. Now Father Dog
Addles our misconceptions, points, preens,
His finger a white flag, run up, run down.

Bow-wow and arf, the Great Light;
O, and the Great Yes, and the Great No;
Redemption, the cold kiss of release,
&c.; sentences, sentences.

(Meanwhile, docile as shadows, they stare
From their four corners, looks set:
No glitter escapes
This evangelical masonry.)

Candleflame; vigil and waterflow:
Like dust in the night the prayers rise:
From 6 to 6, under the sick Christ,
The children talk to the nothingness,
Crossrack and wound; the dark room
Burns like a coal, goes
Ash to the touch, ash to the tongue's tip;
Blood turns in the wheel:

Something drops from the leaves; the drugged moon
Twists and turns in its sheets; sweet breath
In a dry corner, the black widow reknits her dream.
Salvation again declines,
And sleeps like a skull in the hard ground,
Nothing for ears, nothing for eyes;
It sleeps as it's always slept, without
Shadow, waiting for nothing.

— *Bible Camp, 1949*

Dead Color

I lie for a long time on my left side and my right side
And eat nothing,
                but no voice comes on the wind
And no voice drops from the cloud.
Between the grey spiders and the orange spiders,
                  no voice comes on the wind . . .

Later, I sit for a long time by the waters of Har,
And no face appears on the face of the deep.

Meanwhile, the heavens assemble their dark map.
The traffic begins to thin.
Aphids munch on the sweet meat of the lemon trees.

The lawn sprinklers rise and fall . . .

And here's a line of brown ants cleaning a possum's skull.
And here's another, come from the opposite side.

Over my head, star-pieces dip in their yellow scarves toward
    their black desire.

Windows, rapturous windows!

• DRAMA •

THE DRAMA OF THE South, which had its beginnings in such plays as "The Octoroon: or, Life in Louisiana ," "The Recruiting Officer," and "The Orphan," was nurtured both in the salons and theaters of Richmond, New Orleans, and Charleston; now, however, it is largely identified with plays written by William Faulkner, Paul Green, Lillian Hellman, Beth Henley, DuBose Heyward, Carson McCullers, Tennessee Williams, and Thomas Wolfe. Of these, the most important, without doubt, is Tennessee Williams, who was born in 1911 in Columbus, Mississippi, though he lived in St. Louis, Memphis, New Orleans, and New York, among other places. His plays, famous for their intense psychological conflicts not easily camouflaged by pressed gabardine suits or flouncy chiffons, often reveal, as he put it, dynamic, transformed truths; these plays are crucibles where superficial gentility and one-dimensional living are severely tested. In the production notes to "The Glass Menagerie," for example, Williams states that the "straight realistic play with its genuine Frigidaire and its authentic ice-cubes, its characters who speak exactly as its audience speaks, corresponds to the academic landscape and has the same virtue of a photographic likeness. Everyone should know nowadays the unimportance of the photographic in art: that truth, life, or reality is an organic thing which the poetic imagination can represent or suggest, in essence, only through transformation, through changing into other forms than those which were merely present in appearance."

The audience in the Civic Theatre in Chicago on December 26, 1944, applauded the palpable evidence of these ideas as they witnessed Williams's first commercially successful play, "The Glass Menagerie." Though the play takes place in the apartment overlooking an unnamed alley in St. Louis, Williams emphasizes that the first scene occurs in memory and is therefore nonrealistic; yet, it is through the evocation of the Mississippi Delta by Amanda Wingfield, the mother of Laura, a crippled young woman with one leg shorter than the other, who lacks, much to the chagrin of her mother, the companionship of gentlemen callers, that the Old South of *Gone With the Wind* hovers over the dreary present of the 1930's with its intruding reminders of Bertesgaden, Chamberlain, and Guernica. Jim O'Connor, a friend of Laura's brother, pays a visit to the Wingfields and has a warm, honest conversation with Laura; he has no intention, however, of pursuing a relationship with her because he is engaged to someone else. As they talk, Laura is embar-

rassed to mention that they had gone to the same high school (she was romantically called by him in those days "Blue Roses" because of her bout with
pleurosis), but as time passes it becomes clear that she is able, in her own way, to
read the handwriting on the wall — she is "peculiar" and "cripple" (words that
are offensive to her mother) — in spite of the fact that ironically she has not been
able to master the Gregg shorthand diagram and a typewriter keyboard chart that
visually dominate the scene. Williams encapsulates Laura in a haunting world of
glass figurines and she herself is "like a piece of translucent glass touched by
light, given a momentary radiance, not actual, not lasting." Similar to one of the
glass unicorns that loses its horn, Laura's world remains fragmented, isolated, and
fragile.

Three years later, on December 3, 1947 at the Barrymore Theatre, Williams's
place in the history of American theater was confirmed with the opening of "A
Streetcar Named Desire," directed by Elia Kazan, and starring Marlon Brando as
Stanley Kowalski, Kim Hunter as Stella, Karl Malden as Mitch, and Jessica Tandy
as Blanche DuBois. Like Amanda Wingfield, Blanche transports with her to
steamy New Orleans nostalgic memories of Belle Reve, the decaying family home
that she had been forced to sell. Yet, unlike "The Glass Menagerie," this play
emerges from a violently passionate love relationship within the bonds of marriage. As the outsider, Blanche partially tries to disguise the brute force she
encounters when visiting Stella and Stanley by covering a naked light bulb with a
colored paper lantern, a ploy no more successful than her frequent trips to the
bathroom where she takes nips from a bottle of liquor and relaxes in prolonged hot
baths. To a large extent, the theme of this play is reflected in the section of Hart
Crane's "The Broken Tower" that Williams quoted as an epigraph to the play:

> And so it was I entered the broken world
> To trace the visionary company of love, its voice
> An instant in the mind (I know not whither hurled)
> But not for long to hold each desperate choice.

Indeed this world is a broken one where the values of a pregnant woman hoping to
start a family are in direct contrast with those of her desolate, nymphomaniac
sister, who leaves the stage pathetically disoriented with a wispy sentence that has
entered the consciousness of the theater-going public: "Whoever you are — I have
always depended on the kindness of strangers."

Following the production of "Summer and Smoke" (1948), the novel, *The
Roman Spring of Mrs. Stone* (1950), the productions of "The Rose Tattoo" (1951)
and of "Camino Real" (1953, directed by Elia Kazan, and revived under José
Quintero's direction in 1960), "Cat on a Hot Tin Roof" was produced at the
Morosco Theatre in New York City on March 24, 1955, likewise under the
direction of Elia Kazan; it won for Williams his third New York Critics' Circle

Award and his second Pulitzer Prize. In this play set in a plantation on the Mississippi Delta, Brick and Maggie, who have no children and whose married sexual life has long ceased, are vying with Brick's brother and sister-in-law and their brood of "no-neck monsters" for the affection (and property) of Big Daddy, whose spastic colon is thought to be symptomatic of a cancerous condition. Neither Big Daddy nor Brick are satisfied husbands, and while Big Mama apparently accepts her status, Maggie definitely wants to improve her lot, even to the extent of announcing at the end of the play that she is pregnant when she is not. She tells Brick: " . . . life has got to be allowed to continue even after the *dream* of life is — all — over . . . ." Brick, however, has a different philosophy: "Mendacity is a system that we live in. Liquor is one way out an' death's the other . . . ." Greed, homosexuality, unhappy marriages, mendacity, and sibling rivalry are some of the themes that Williams develops in this play, one that despite its popularity is artistically less successful than some of his others.

William's reputation, however, does not rest simply on a handful of plays: his dramatic vision was sustained over many years and includes such well-known plays as "Orpheus Descending" (1957), "Sweet Bird of Youth" (1959), "Period of Adjustment" (1960), "The Night of the Iguana" (1961), "The Milk Train Doesn't Stop Here Anymore" (1962), "Small Craft Warnings" (1972), in addition to many one-act plays, ten of which were performed in two programs at the Lucille Lorter Theatre in New York City in the summer of 1986. Some of these plays anticipate, as several critics have noted, the later, full-length dramas. "The Long Goodbye" (1940), for instance, the story of a young writer and his family in St. Louis, prefigures "The Glass Menagerie," while the aging, self-deluding belle in "Portrait of a Madonna" (1944) foreshadows Blanche DuBois of "A Streetcar Named Desire" and Alma Winemiller of "Summer and Smoke" (1948, and revived in 1952 under José Quintero's direction) — the latter a part made famous by Geraldine Page. Williams has a penchant for exposing his characters constantly to glaring realities that test both their mettle and their capacity to cope, and though some withdraw into a twilight world of illusion, others adapt in ways that seem to suggest that the world is not entirely blocked or closed.

From one perspective, Lillian Hellman's "The Little Foxes," which opened at the National Theatre in New York City on February 15, 1939, with Tallulah Bankhead and Frank Conroy playing Regina and Horace Giddens (Bette Davis played Regina in the 1941 film version), has a close affinity with "Cat on a Hot Tin Roof," in that both plays deal with a rich husband/father, who happens to be sick, and whose family is concerned about how his wealth will be distributed after his death. In "The Little Foxes," Hellman focuses her play on the dominating personality of Regina, who, unlike Big Mama, is able to coerce her brothers, Ben and Oscar, so that she, not they, will benefit from her husband's wealth. The title, from the Song of Solomon 2:15 ("Take us the foxes, the little foxes, that spoil the vines, for our vines have tender grapes"), suggests that the South is being ravaged by greedy entrepreneurs who are more interested in making money than in acting as stewards of their land and culture.

The action of this play takes place at the turn of the century in an unspecified Southern locale and reveals a more aggressive South than the stereotypical view, particularly in the lack of love and friendship between and among the various Hubbards and Giddens. Oscar, for example, married Birdie mainly to acquire her family's plantation, and they even bandy about the idea that their conniving son, Leo, might marry Alexandra, Regina and Horace's only daughter. When William Marshall, a Chicago industrialist, wants to set up a cotton mill, he agrees to do so providing the Hubbards can finance fifty-one percent of the cost. Shrewdly Regina tells her two brothers that her husband, who has been away at Johns Hopkins Hospital in Baltimore, might be holding out for a larger share of the ownership; in addition, she lets it be known that her cooperation in securing his portion of the money will cost them forty percent of their shares.

After Horace returns home and learns that Leo has stolen negotiable bonds from him, he says, to the astonishment of Regina, that he will not prosecute Leo, but will merely say that the bonds were a loan and that he will add a coda to his will indicating that these bonds will constitute her only inheritance from him. Regina threatens her brothers as her husband, off stage, goes through his final agony: "And if he doesn't live I shall want seventy-five percent in exchange for the bonds." Yet as Alexandra, perhaps an autobiographical portrait of Hellman, insinuates, Regina is able to outmaneuver everyone but herself; Alexandra replies to her mother's invitation that they sleep in the same room with the question, "Are you afraid, Mama?" which at once challenges this Southern family about the disvalues they have embraced as well as suggests that Alexandra, who is about to leave the family home, is more mature than her mother and is not about to repeat her mistakes.

Though George Jean Nathan praised this play for not betraying "an inch of compromise, not a sliver of a sop to the comfortable acquiescence of Broadway or Piccadilly, not the slightest token that its author had anything in her purpose but writing the truest and most honest play on her theme that it was possible for her to write," he does not deal with the heavily episodic nature of the play, nor with the problems posed by the prolonged absence of Horace. Of Hellman's twelve plays, her reputation rests primarily not only on this play, but on "The Children's Hour" (1934), about two headmistresses accused of being lesbians, and on "Toys in the Attic" (1960), about a man who collapses under the weight of the "love" of the women in his life. Neither of these three plays reveals, however, the high political drama that took place in Hellman's life, most poignantly captured in *Scoundrel Time* (1976) and in the "Julia" section of *Pentimento* (1973), later made into a movie (1977).

An inspiration to many Southern men and women of letters has been Paul Green, professor and playwright, whose early work dates from the days of World

War I. In 1920, for example, The Carolina Players of the University of North Carolina at Chapel Hill produced five of Green's one-act plays. In 1926, his first full drama, winner of a Pulitzer Prize, "In Abraham's Bosom," was first presented by the Provincetown Players in their Greenwich Village Theatre in New York City beginning on December 30, and followed by other successful plays, including "The House of Connelly" (1931) and "Johnny Johnson" (1936), with music by Kurt Weill.

Subtitled "The Tragedy of a Southern Negro," "In Abraham's Bosom" featured a black cast and won the generous support of Brooks Atkinson: " 'In Abraham's Bosom' is penetrating, unswerving tragedy . . . and surely one of the most pungent folk dramas of the American stage." The protagonist, Abe, the son of a black woman and a white slave-owner, Colonel McCranie, educates himself and hopes eventually to educate his people by starting a school. Yet Abe's dream is short-lived and his lot in life quickly worsens. Fortunately, with a building rented from his white half-brother, Lonnie McCranie, Abe rekindles his spirit and starts organizing once again a school, only to have his efforts quashed by the Klan. In a fit of rage, Abe kills Lonnie, not without some provocation however on Lonnie's part. In turn, Abe is killed by a mob. Like his namesake, it would seem that Abe's mission in life is to go to a new land and receive the inheritance promised him by the Lord, who becomes his final refuge: "Blast me, Lord, in your thunder and lightning, if it is your will! Catch me away in the whirlwind, for I'm a sinner. Your will, your will, not mine." Abe's family shares in his death; tragically, Abe has sacrificed his son, Douglass — another Isaac. Abe is no new Abraham Lincoln inaugurating a new age for Southern blacks. The audience never witnesses Abe's apotheosis, which, if it is ever to occur, is delayed to some future time, as suggested by the biblical legend upon which the axis of the play rotates.

Green's plays still continue to delight thousands of theater goers every year. In 1937, "The Lost Colony," a symphonic drama (a term Green mentioned in his essay "Nationwide Drama" and which meant "the organic and interwoven uses of music, dance mime, folksong, pageantry, masks, etc., in telling the dramatic tale"), was first produced at Roanoke Island in North Carolina and still attracts crowds every summer. Other symphonic dramas followed, including "The Highland Call" (1939), "The Common Glory" (1947), "Faith of Our Fathers" (1950), "Wilderness Road" (1955), "The Founders" (1957), "The Confederacy" (1958), "Stephen Foster" (1959), "Cross and Sword" (1965), "Texas" (1966), and "Trumpet in the Land" (1970). Such pageants have and continue to be rousing reminders of America's past, and though some might find a certain sameness about them, they provide a type of popular entertainment that entire families can enjoy and profit from.

With only two plays to her credit, "The Member of the Wedding" (based on her novel) and "The Square Root of Wonderful" (1957), in addition to Edward Albee's adaptation of "The Ballad of a Sad Café" (1963), Carson McCullers has taken her rightful place as an important American playwright. Her play "The Member of the Wedding," starring Ethel Waters, Julie Harris, and Brandon de Wilde, opened in previews on December 22, 1949, in Philadelphia, and moved to New York City where it opened on January 5th at the Empire Theatre. In young Frankie Addams (a.k.a. F. Jasmine Addams, as she prefers), we see the dilemmas facing a young, distraught teenager (12 years old, 5' 5¾" tall), as she tries to project herself as an adult, especially as an integral part of Janis and Jarvis's wedding party. Her aspirations, her naïveté, her expectations lack the experiential wisdom of an older person, and thus her tragic-comic environment prompts her to meet and consult with others who might be a source of consolation, let alone genuine advice. Particularly in her conversations with Bernice, whether they be about Honey, who committed suicide in jail, or about Bernice's five-year marriage to Ludie, Frankie does achieve in the third act a muted epiphany: "Now for the first time I realize that the world is certainly — a sudden place." Surprisingly, the play's central focus is not the wedding as such, much as that might be hinted at by the title, but rather both the ordinary and the extraordinary events that seem to hover just beyond Frankie's grasp and which, somehow or other, she has to integrate into her life.

Neither Thomas Wolfe's "Welcome to Our City," published in *Esquire*, October 1957, which deals with a group of businessmen trying to reclaim black housing, only to find they have a race riot on their hands, nor his "Mannerhouse" (1948), a play about the Civil War, has entered into the mainstream of American theater. Likewise, William Faulkner's "The Marionettes" (written for a University of Mississippi theatrical group in 1920) and "Requiem for a Nun" (1959), known primarily because of the author's importance in American letters, have not achieved lasting popularity. "Requiem," however, is significant in the Faulkner canon because it deals with major themes in Faulkner's literature, as embodied in the dilemma of Temple Drake, a white woman, who must decide whether or not to succumb to intense sexual feelings or try to live out a charade in polite Southern society. The murder of her child by a black servant is indicative of the depth of her dilemma. Violence, passion, life in a confined community, and sexual freedom are also integral to Dubose Heyward's *Porgy* (1925), better known in the American folk opera version, "Porgy and Bess" (1935), with George Gershwin's music and lyrics by Ira Gershwin and DuBose Heyward. Life on Catfish Row is an endless series of triumphs and defeats, of calms and hurricanes, of births and deaths, and Porgy's desire to be with Bess, despite his handicap, reveals that in Heyward's imagination, certain blacks, driven by love and determination, are ready to leave an isolated world and seek their fortune elsewhere. "Summertime," "It Takes a Long Pull," "I'm on My Way," "A Woman is a Sometime Thing," "Where Is My Bess?," and "I Got Plenty O' Nuttin'" bring together theme and place in a poignant manner; the music and lyrics capture the rhythms, color, movement, aspirations, and dreams of a people long oppressed from both inside and outside pressures, and who long to find more than a bittersweet modicum of happiness.

The Southern dramatic tradition has gradually shifted gears in more recent years. Beth Henley's "Crimes of the Heart," "The Miss Firecracker Contest" (1982), and her one-act play "Am I Blue" (1982), show the influence that T.V. sitcoms have had on the legitimate theater. In "Crimes of the Heart," which won the 1981 Pulitzer Prize and the New York Drama Critics' Circle Award, for example, the three MaGrath sisters, Babe, Lenny, and Meg, share with one another in the MaGrath kitchen in Hazlehurst, Mississippi, their private disasters, reminiscent of the situations that the characters of Flannery O'Connor and Eudora Welty find themselves in. Woven together are elements of the Gothic, the ridiculous, and repressed, and the irrepressible. In "Pump Boys and Dinettes" (1981), featuring combinations of country pop, soft rock, and Southern Gospel music that recount the trials and tribulations of those who work in a gas station and at the Double Cupp Diner in Frog Level, South Carolina, twelve of the nineteen songs were written by Jim Wann, who also did a musical revue with Bland Simpson about Jesse James entitled "Diamond Studs." In addition, The Red Clay Ramblers of Chapel Hill, North Carolina, have provided the music for Sam Shepherd's play, "A Lie of the Mind" (1985). Tommy Thompson, Michael Craver, and Jack Herrick, the Ramblers' music director, contributed original songs, including "Run Sister Run," "Home Is Where the Heart Is," and "Can't Live Without 'em Blues." Their music has given contemporary theater a dimension that has long been part of Southern culture; such music, heard mainly at fiddlers' conventions in Virginia and North Carolina, traces its roots back to Elizabethan folk tunes.

Unlike other genres, especially the novel and the short story, drama in the South has not progressed in a manner that can be easily diagrammed or traced. Rather, it has tended to reflect the dynamics at work in the larger cultural American scene; this is partially because playwrights with national and international ambitions are very conscious of their audiences and must, willy-nilly, recognize the expectations of Broadway. Such adaptation and flexibility is not surprising in that popular cultural patterns have always greatly influenced the structure of drama and the manner in which plays are staged. Yet, with the recent growth of regional theaters across the country, and the South is no exception, a mood and environment is being created whereby playwrights are being encouraged to look once again to their regional roots to explore what is dramatically universal. What are they likely to discover? That which has been theirs all along: a strong family tradition with conflicting values; marvelous, idiomatic speech patterns; a vibrant love of music that has very deep roots, and a tough honesty that shines through any social pretensions.

CARSON McCULLERS

The Member of the Wedding

CHARACTERS

BERENICE SADIE BROWN
FRANKIE ADDAMS
JOHN HENRY WEST
JARVIS
JANICE
MR. ADDAMS
MRS. WEST
HELEN FLETCHER
DORIS
SIS LAURA
T. T. WILLIAMS
HONEY CAMDEN BROWN
BARNEY MacKEAN

TIME: *August, 1945*
PLACE: *A small Southern town*

ACT ONE — A late afternoon in August
ACT TWO — Afternoon of the next day
ACT THREE
   Scene One — The wedding day — afternoon of the
next day following Act Two

Scene Two	4 A.M. the following morning
Scene Three	Late afternoon, in the following November

ACT ONE

A part of a Southern back yard and kitchen. At stage left there is a scuppernong arbor. A sheet, used as a stage curtain, hangs raggedly at one side of the arbor. There is an elm tree in the yard. The kitchen has in the center a table with chairs. The walls are drawn with child drawings. There is a stove to the right and a small coal heating stove with coal scuttle in rear center of kitchen. The kitchen opens on the left into the yard. At the interior right a door leads to a small inner room. A door at the left leads into the front hall. The lights go on dimly, with a dreamlike effect, gradually revealing the family in the yard and Berenice Sadie Brown in the kitchen. Berenice, the cook, is a stout, motherly Negro woman with an air of great capability and devoted protection. She is about forty-five years old. She has a quiet, flat face and one of her eyes is made of blue glass. Sometimes, when her socket bothers her, she dispenses with the false eye and wears a black patch. When we first see her she is wearing the patch and is dressed in a simple print work dress and apron.

Frankie, a gangling girl of twelve with blonde hair cut like a boy's, is wearing shorts and a sombrero and is standing in the arbor gazing adoringly at her brother Jarvis and his fiancée Janice. She is a dreamy, restless girl, and periods of energetic activity alternate with a rapt attention to her inward world of fantasy. She is thin and awkward and very much aware of being too tall. Jarvis, a good-looking boy of twenty-one, wearing an army uniform, stands by Janice. He is awkward when he first appears because this is his betrothal visit. Janice, a young, pretty, fresh-looking girl of eighteen or nineteen is charming but rather ordinary, with brown hair done up in a small knot. She is dressed in her best clothes and is anxious to be liked by her new family. Mr. Addams, Frankie's father, is a deliberate and absent-minded man of about forty-five. A widower of many years, he has become set in his habits. He is dressed conservatively, and there is about him an old-fashioned look and manner. John Henry, Frankie's small cousin, aged seven, picks and eats any scuppernongs he can reach. He is a delicate, active boy and wears gold-rimmed spectacles which give him an oddly judicious look. He is blond and sunburned and when we first see him he is wearing a sun-suit and is barefooted.

[*Berenice Sadie Brown is busy in the kitchen.*]

JARVIS: Seems to me like this old arbor has shrunk. I remember when I was a child it used to seem absolutely enormous. When I was Frankie's age, I had a vine swing here. Remember, Papa?

FRANKIE: It don't seem so absolutely enormous to me, because I am so tall.

JARVIS: I never saw a human grow so fast in all my life. I think maybe we ought to tie a brick to your head.

FRANKIE [*hunching down in obvious distress*]: Oh, Jarvis! Don't.

JANICE: Don't tease your little sister. I don't think Frankie is too tall. She probably won't grow much more. I had the biggest portion of my growth by the time I was thirteen.

FRANKIE: But I'm just twelve. When I think of all the growing years ahead of me, I get scared.

[*Janice goes to Frankie and puts her arms around her comfortingly. Frankie stands rigid, embarrassed and blissful.*]

JANICE: I wouldn't worry.

[*Berenice comes from the kitchen with a tray of drinks. Frankie rushes eagerly to help her serve them.*]

FRANKIE: Let me help.

BERENICE: Them two drinks is lemonade for you and John Henry. The others got liquor in them.

FRANKIE: Janice, come sit on the arbor seat. Jarvis, you sit down too.

[*Jarvis and Janice sit close together on the wicker bench in the arbor. Frankie hands the drinks around, then perches on the ground before Janice and Jarvis and stares adoringly at them.*]

FRANKIE: It was such a surprise when Jarvis wrote home you are going to be married.

JANICE: I hope it wasn't a bad surprise.

FRANKIE: Oh, Heavens no! [*with great feeling*] As a matter of fact ... [*She strokes Janice's shoes tenderly and Jarvis' army boot.*] If only you knew how I feel.

MR. ADDAMS: Frankie's been bending my ears ever since your letter came, Jarvis. Going on about weddings, brides, grooms, etc.

JANICE: It's lovely that we can be married at Jarvis' home.

MR. ADDAMS: That's the way to feel, Janice. Marriage is a sacred institution.

FRANKIE: Oh, it will be beautiful.

JARVIS: Pretty soon we'd better be shoving off for Winter Hill. I have to be back in barracks tonight.

FRANKIE: Winter Hill is such a lovely, cold name. It reminds me of ice and snow.

JANICE: You know it's just a hundred miles away, darling.

JARVIS: Ice and snow indeed! Yesterday the temperature on the parade ground reached 102.

[*Frankie takes a palmetto fan from the table and fans first Janice, then Jarvis.*]

JANICE: That feels so good, darling. Thanks.

FRANKIE: I wrote you so many letters, Jarvis, and you never, never would answer me. When you were stationed in Alaska, I wanted so much to hear about Alaska. I sent you so many boxes of home-made candy, but you never answered me.

JARVIS: Oh, Frankie. You know how it is...

FRANKIE [*sipping her drink*]: You know this lemonade tastes funny. Kind of sharp and hot. I believe I got the drinks mixed up.

JARVIS: I was thinking my drink tasted mighty sissy. Just plain lemonade — no liquor at all.

[*Frankie and Jarvis exchange their drinks. Jarvis sips his.*]

JARVIS: This is better.

FRANKIE: I drank a lot. I wonder if I'm drunk. It makes me feel like I had four legs instead of two. I think I'm drunk. [*She gets up and begins to stagger around in imitation of drunkenness.*] See! I'm drunk! Look, Papa how drunk I am! [*Suddenly she turns a handspring; then there is a blare of music from the club house gramophone off to the right.*]

JANICE: Where does the music come from? It sounds so close.

FRANKIE: It is. Right over there. They have club meetings and parties with boys on Friday nights. I watch them here from the yard.

JANICE: It must be nice having your club house so near.

FRANKIE: I'm not a member now. But they are holding an election this afternoon, and maybe I'll be elected.

JOHN HENRY: Here comes Mama.

[*Mrs. West, John Henry's mother, crosses the yard from the right. She is a vivacious, blonde woman of about thirty-three. She is dressed in sleazy, rather dowdy summer clothes.*]

MR. ADDAMS: Hello, Pet. Just in time to meet our new family member.

MRS. WEST: I saw you out here from the window.

JARVIS [*rising, with Janice*]: Hi, Aunt Pet. How is Uncle Eustace?

MRS. WEST: He's at the office.

JANICE [*offering her hand with the engagement ring on it*]: Look Aunt Pet. May I call you Aunt Pet?

MRS. WEST [*hugging her*]: Of course, Janice. What a gorgeous ring!

JANICE: Jarvis just gave it to me this morning. He wanted to consult his father and get it from his store, naturally.

MRS. WEST: How lovely.

MR. ADDAMS: A quarter carat — not too flashy but a good stone.

MRS. WEST [*to Berenice, who is gathering up the empty glasses*]: Berenice, what have you and Frankie been doing to my John Henry? He sticks over here in your kitchen morning, noon and night.

BERENICE: We enjoys him and Candy seems to like it over here.

MRS. WEST: What on earth do you do to him?

BERENICE: We just talks and passes the time of day. Occasionally plays cards.

MRS. WEST: Well, if he gets in your way just shoo him home.

BERENICE: Candy don't bother nobody.

JOHN HENRY [*walking around barefooted in the arbor*]: These grapes are so squelchy when I step on them.

MRS. WEST: Run home, darling, and wash your feet and put on your sandals.

JOHN HENRY: I like to squelch on the grapes.

[*Berenice goes back to the kitchen.*]

JANICE: That looks like a stage curtain. Jarvis told me how you used to write plays and act in them out here in the arbor. What kind of shows do you have?

FRANKIE: Oh, crook shows and cowboy shows. This summer I've had some cold shows — about Esquimos and explorers — on account of the hot weather.

JANICE: Do you ever have romances?

FRANKIE: Naw ... [with bravado] I had crook shows for the most part. You see I never believed in love until now. [*Her look lingers on Janice and Jarvis. She hugs Janice and Jarvis, bending over them from the back of the bench.*]

MRS. WEST: Frankie and this little friend of hers gave a performance of "The Vagabond King" out here last spring.

[*John Henry spreads out his arms and imitates the heroine of the play from memory, singing in his high childish voice.*]

JOHN HENRY: Never hope to bind me. Never hope to know. [speaking] Frankie was the king-boy. I sold the tickets.

MRS. WEST: Yes, I have always said that Frankie has talent.

FRANKIE: Aw, I'm afraid I don't have much talent.

JOHN HENRY: Frankie can laugh and kill people good. She can die, too.

FRANKIE [*with some pride*]: Yeah, I guess I die all right.

MR. ADDAMS: Frankie rounds up John Henry and those smaller children, but by the time she dresses them in the costumes, they're worn out and won't act in the show.

JARVIS [*looking at his watch*]: Well, it's time we shove off for Winter Hill — Frankie's land of icebergs and snow — where the temperature goes up to 102.

[*Jarvis takes Janice's hand. He gets up and gazes fondly around the yard and the arbor. He pulls her up and stands with his arm around her, gazing around him at the arbor and the yard.*]

JARVIS: It carries me back — this smell of mashed grapes and dust. I remember all the endless summer afternoons of my childhood. It does carry me back.

FRANKIE: Me too. It carries me back, too.

MR. ADDAMS [*putting one arm around Janice and shaking Jarvis' hand*]: Merciful Heavens! It seems I have two Methuselahs in my family! Does it carry you back to your childhood too, John Henry?

JOHN HENRY: Yes, Uncle Royal.

MR. ADDAMS: Son, this visit was a real pleasure. Janice, I'm mighty pleased to see my boy has such lucky judgment in choosing a wife.

FRANKIE: I hate to think you have to go. I'm just now realizing you're here.

JARVIS: We'll be back in two days. The wedding is Sunday.

[*The family move around the house toward the street. John Henry enters the kitchen through the back door. There are the sounds of "good-byes" from the front yard.*]

JOHN HENRY: Frankie was drunk. She drank a liquor drink.

BERENICE: She just made out like she was drunk — pretended.

JOHN HENRY: She said, "Look, Papa, how drunk I am," and she couldn't walk.

FRANKIE'S VOICE: Good-bye, Jarvis. Good-bye Janice.

JARVIS' VOICE: See you Sunday.

MR. ADDAMS' VOICE: Drive carefully, son. Good-bye Janice.

JANICE'S VOICE: Good-bye and thanks, Mr. Addams. Good-bye, Frankie darling.

ALL THE VOICES: Good-bye! Good-bye!

JOHN HENRY: They are going now to Winter Hill.

[*There is the sound of the front door opening, then of steps in the hall. Frankie enters through the hall.*]

FRANKIE: Oh, I can't understand it! The way it all just suddenly happened.

BERENICE: Happened? Happened?

FRANKIE: I have never been so puzzled.

BERENICE: Puzzled about what?

FRANKIE: The whole thing. They are so beautiful.

BERENICE [*after a pause*]: I believe the sun done fried your brains.

JOHN HENRY [*whispering*]: Me too.

BERENICE: Look here at me. You jealous.

FRANKIE: Jealous?

BERENICE: Jealous because your brother's going to be married.

FRANKIE [*slowly*]: No. I just never saw any two people like them. When they walked in the house today it was so queer.

BERENICE: You jealous. Go and behold yourself in the mirror. I can see from the color of your eyes.

[*Frankie goes to the mirror and stares. She draws up her left shoulder, shakes her head, and turns away.*]

FRANKIE [*with feeling*]: Oh! They were the two prettiest people I ever saw. I just can't understand how it happened.

BERENICE: Whatever ails you? — actin' so queer.

FRANKIE: I don't know. I bet they have a good time every minute of the day.

JOHN HENRY: Less us have a good time.

FRANKIE: Us have a good time? Us? [*She rises and walks around the table.*]

BERENICE: Come on. Less have a game of three-handed bridge.

[*They sit down to the table, shuffle the cards, deal, and play a game.*]

FRANKIE: Oregon, Alaska, Winter Hill, the wedding. It's all so queer.

BERENICE: I can't bid, never have a hand these days.

FRANKIE: A spade.

JOHN HENRY: I want to bid spades. That's what I was going to bid.

FRANKIE: Well, that's your tough luck. I bid them first.

JOHN HENRY: Oh, you fool jackass! It's not fair!

BERENICE: Hush quarreling, you two [*She looks at both their hands.*] To tell the truth, I don't think either of you got such a grand hand to fight over the bid about. Where is the cards? I haven't had no kind of a hand all week.

FRANKIE: I don't give a durn about it. It is immaterial with me. [*There is a long pause. She sits with her head propped on her hand, her legs wound around each other.*] Let's talk about them — and the wedding.

BERENICE: What you want to talk about?

FRANKIE: My heart feels them going away — going farther and farther away — while I am stuck here by myself.

BERENICE: You ain't here by yourself. By the way, where's your Pa?

FRANKIE: He went to the store. I think about them, but I remembered them more as a feeling than as a picture.

BERENICE: A feeling?

FRANKIE: They were the two prettiest people I ever saw. Yet it was like I couldn't see all of them I wanted to see. My brains couldn't gather together quick enough to take it all in. And then they were gone.

BERENICE: Well stop commenting about it. You don't have your mind on the game.

FRANKIE [*playing her cards, followed by John Henry*]: Spades are trumps and you got a spade. I have some of my mind on the game.

[*John Henry puts his donkey necklace in his mouth and looks away.*]

FRANKIE: Go on, cheater.

BERENICE: Make haste.

JOHN HENRY: I can't. It's a king. The only spade I got is a king, and I don't want to play my king under Frankie's ace. And I'm not going to do it either.

FRANKIE [*throwing her cards down on the table*]: See, Berenice, he cheats!

BERENICE: Play your king, John Henry. You have to follow the rules of the game.

JOHN HENRY: My king. It isn't fair.

FRANKIE: Even with this trick, I can't win.

BERENICE: Where is the cards? For three days I haven't had a decent hand. I'm beginning to suspicion something. Come on less us count these old cards.

FRANKIE: We've worn these old cards out. If you would eat these old cards, they would taste like a combination of all the dinners of this summer together with a sweaty-handed, nasty taste. Why, the jacks and the queens are missing.

BERENICE: John Henry, how come you do a thing like that? So that's why you asked for the scissors and stole off quiet behind the arbor. Now Candy, how come you took our playing cards and cut out the pictures?

JOHN HENRY: Because I wanted them. They're cute.

FRANKIE: See? He's nothing but a child. It's hopeless. Hopeless!

BERENICE: Maybe so.

FRANKIE: We'll just have to put him out of the game. He's entirely too young. [*John Henry whimpers.*]

BERENICE: Well, we can't put Candy out of the game. We gotta have a third to play. Besides, by the last count he owes me close to three million dollars.

FRANKIE: Oh, I am sick unto death. [*She sweeps the cards from the table, then gets up and begins walking around the kitchen. John Henry leaves the table and picks up a large blonde doll on the chair in the corner.*] I wish they'd taken me with them to Winter Hill this afternoon. I wish tomorrow was Sunday instead of Saturday.

BERENICE: Sunday will come.

FRANKIE: I doubt it. I wish I was going somewhere for good. I wish I had a hundred dollars and could just light out and never see this town again.

BERENICE: It seems like you wish for a lot of things.

FRANKIE: I wish I was somebody else except me.

JOHN HENRY [*holding the doll*]: You serious when you gave me the doll a while ago?

FRANKIE: It gives me a pain just to think about them.

BERENICE: It is a known truth that gray-eyed peoples are jealous.

[*There are sounds of children playing in the neighboring yard.*]

JOHN HENRY: Let's go out and play with the children.

FRANKIE: I don't want to.

JOHN HENRY: There's a big crowd, and they sound like they having a mighty good time. Less go.

FRANKIE: You got ears. You heard me.

JOHN HENRY: I think maybe I better go home.

FRANKIE: Why, you said you were going to spend the night. You just can't eat dinner and then go off in the afternoon like that.

JOHN HENRY: I know it.

BERENICE: Candy, Lamb, you can go home if you want to.

JOHN HENRY: But less go out, Frankie. They sound like they having a lot of fun.

FRANKIE: No, they're not. Just a crowd of ugly, silly children. Running and hollering and running and hollering. Nothing to it.

JOHN HENRY: Less go!

FRANKIE: Well, then I'll entertain you. What do you want to do? Would you like for me to read to you out of The Book of Knowledge, or would you rather do something else?

JOHN HENRY: I rather do something else. [*He goes to the back door, and looks into the yard. Several young girls of thirteen or fourteen, dressed in clean print frocks, file slowly across the back yard.*] Look. Those big girls.

FRANKIE: [*running out into the yard*]: Hey, there. I'm mighty glad to see you. Come on in.

HELEN: We can't. We were just passing through to notify our new member.

FRANKIE [*overjoyed*]: Am I the new member?

DORIS: No, you're not the one the club elected.

FRANKIE: Not elected?

HELEN: Every ballot was unanimous for Mary Littlejohn.

FRANKIE: Mary Littlejohn! You mean that girl who just moved in next door? That pasty fat girl with those tacky pigtails? The one who plays the piano all day long?

DORIS: Yes. The club unanimously elected Mary.

FRANKIE: Why, she's not even cute.

HELEN: She is too; and, furthermore, she's talented.

FRANKIE: I think it's sissy to sit around the house all day playing classical music.

DORIS: Why, Mary is training for a concert career.

FRANKIE: Well, I wish to Jesus she would train somewhere else.

DORIS: You don't have enough sense to appreciate a talented girl like Mary.

FRANKIE: What are you doing in my yard? You're never to set foot on my Papa's property again. [*Frankie shakes Helen.*] Son-of-a-bitches. I could shoot you with my Papa's pistol.

JOHN HENRY [*shaking his fists*]: Son-of-a-bitches.

FRANKIE: Why didn't you elect me? [*She goes back into the house.*] Why can't I be a member?

JOHN HENRY: Maybe they'll change their mind and invite you.

BERENICE: I wouldn't pay them no mind. All my life I've been wantin' things that I ain't been gettin'. Anyhow those club girls is fully two years older than you.

FRANKIE: I think they have been spreading it all over town that I smell bad. When I had those boils and had to use that black bitter-smelling ointment, old Helen Fletcher asked me what was that funny smell I had. Oh, I could shoot every one of them with a pistol.

[*Frankie sits with her head on the table. John Henry approaches and pats the back of Frankie's neck.*]

JOHN HENRY: I don't think you smell bad. You smell sweet, like a hundred flowers.

FRANKIE: The son-of-a-bitches. And there was something else. They were telling nasty lies about married people. When I think of Aunt Pet and Uncle Eustace! And my own father! The nasty lies! I don't know what kind of fool they take me for.

BERENICE: That's what I tell you. They too old for you.

[*John Henry raises his head, expands his nostrils and sniffs at himself. Then Frankie goes into the interior bedroom and returns with a bottle of perfume.*]

FRANKIE: Boy! I bet I use more perfume than anybody else in town. Want some on you, John Henry? You want some, Berenice? [*She sprinkles perfume.*]

JOHN HENRY: Like a thousand flowers.

BERENICE: Frankie, the whole idea of a club is that there are members who are included and the non-members who are not included. Now what you ought to do is to round you up a club of your own. And you could be the president yourself. [*There is a pause.*]

FRANKIE: Who would I get?

BERENICE: Why, those little children you hear playing in the neighborhood.

FRANKIE: I don't want to be the president of all those little young left-over people.

BERENICE: Well, then enjoy your misery. That perfume smells so strong it makes me sick.

[*John Henry plays with the doll at the kitchen table and Frankie watches.*]

FRANKIE: Look here at me, John Henry. Take off those glasses. [*John Henry takes off his glasses.*] I bet you don't need those glasses. [*She points to the coal scuttle.*] What is this?

JOHN HENRY: The coal scuttle.

FRANKIE [*taking a shell from the kitchen shelf*]: And this?

JOHN HENRY: The shell we got at Saint Peter's Bay last summer.

FRANKIE: What is that little thing crawling around on the floor?

JOHN HENRY: Where?

FRANKIE: That little thing crawling around near your feet.

JOHN HENRY: Oh. [*He squats down.*] Why, it's an ant. How did that get in here.

FRANKIE: If I were you I'd just throw those glasses away. You can see good as anybody.

BERENICE: Now quit picking with John Henry.

FRANKIE: They don't look becoming. [*John Henry wipes his glasses and puts them back on.*] He can suit himself. I was only telling him for his own good. [*She walks restlessly around the kitchen.*] I bet Janice and Jarvis are members of a lot of clubs. In fact, the army is kind of like a club.

[*John Henry searches through Berenice's pocketbook.*]

BERENICE: Don't root through my pocketbook like that, Candy. Ain't a wise policy to search folk's pocketbooks. They might think you trying to steal their money.

JOHN HENRY: I'm looking for your new glass eye. Here it is. [*He hands Berenice the glass eye.*] You got two nickels and a dime.

[*Berenice takes off her patch, turns away and inserts the glass eye.*]

BERENICE: I ain't used to it yet. The socket bothers me. Maybe it don't fit properly.

JOHN HENRY: The blue glass eye looks very cute.

FRANKIE: I don't see why you had to get that eye. It has a wrong expression — let alone being blue.

BERENICE: Ain't anybody ask your judgment, wise-mouth.

JOHN HENRY: Which one of your eyes do you see out of the best?

BERENICE: The left eye, of course. The glass eye don't do me no seeing good at all.

JOHN HENRY: I like the glass eye better. It is so bright and shiny — a real pretty eye. Frankie, you serious when you gave me this doll a while ago?

FRANKIE: Janice and Jarvis. It gives me this pain just to think about them.

BERENICE: It is a known truth that gray-eyed people are jealous.

FRANKIE: I told you I wasn't jealous. I couldn't be jealous of one of them without being jealous of them both. I 'sociate the two of them together. Somehow they're just so different from us.

BERENICE: Well, I were jealous when my foster-brother, Honey, married Clorina. I sent a warning I could tear the ears off her head. But you see I didn't. Clorina's got ears just like anybody else. And now I love her.

FRANKIE [*stopping her walking suddenly*]: J.A. — Janice and Jarvis. Isn't that the strangest thing?

BERENICE: What?

FRANKIE: J.A. — Both their names begin with "J.A."

BERENICE: And? What about it?

FRANKIE [*walking around the kitchen table*]: If only my name was Jane. Jane or Jasmine.

BERENICE: I don't follow your frame of mind.

FRANKIE: Jarvis and Janice and Jasmine. See?

BERENICE: No. I don't see.

FRANKIE: I wonder if it's against the law to change your name. Or add to it.

BERENICE: Naturally. It's against the law.

FRANKIE [*impetuously*]: Well, I don't care. F. Jasmine Addams.

JOHN HENRY [*approaching with the doll*]: You serious when you give me this? [*He pulls up the doll's dress and pats her.*] I will name her Belle.

FRANKIE: I don't know what went on in Jarvis' mind when he brought me that doll. Imagine bringing me a doll! I had counted on Jarvis bringing me something from Alaska.

BERENICE: Your face when you unwrapped that package was a study.

FRANKIE: John Henry, quit pickin' at the doll's eyes. It makes me so nervous. You hear me! [*He sits the doll up.*] In fact, take the doll somewhere out of my sight.

JOHN HENRY: Her name is Lily Belle.

[*John Henry goes out and props the doll up on the back steps. There is the sound of an unseen Negro singing from the neighboring yard.*]

FRANKIE [*going to the mirror*]: The big mistake I made was to get this close crew cut. For the wedding, I ought to have long brunette hair. Don't you think so?

BERENICE: I don't see how come brunette hair is necessary. But I warned you about getting your head shaved off like that before you did it. But nothing would do but you shave it like that.

FRANKIE [*stepping back from the mirror and slumping her shoulders*]: Oh, I am so worried about being so tall. I'm twelve and five-sixth years old and already five feet five and three-fourths inches tall. If I keep on growing like this until I'm twenty-one, I figure I will be nearly ten feet tall.

JOHN HENRY [*re-entering the kitchen*]: Lily Belle is taking a nap on the back steps. Don't talk so loud, Frankie.

FRANKIE [*after a pause*]: I doubt if they ever get married or go to a wedding. Those freaks.

BERENICE: Freaks. What freaks you talking about?

FRANKIE: At the fair. The ones we saw there last October.

JOHN HENRY: Oh, the freaks at the fair! [*He holds out an imaginary skirt and begins to skip around the room with one finger resting on the top of his head.*] Oh, she was the cutest little girl I ever saw. I never saw anything so cute in my whole life. Did you, Frankie?

FRANKIE: No. I don't think she was cute.

BERENICE: Who is that he's talking about?

FRANKIE: That little old pin-head at the fair. A head no bigger than an orange. With the hair shaved off and a big pink bow at the top. Bow was bigger than the head.

JOHN HENRY: Shoo! She was too cute.

BERENICE: That little old squeezed-looking midget in them little trick evening clothes. And that giant with the hang-jaw face and them huge loose hands. And that morphidite! Half man — half woman. With that tiger skin on one side and that spangled skirt on the other.

JOHN HENRY: But that little-headed girl was cute.

FRANKIE: And that wild colored man they said came from a savage island and ate those real live rats. Do you think they make a very big salary?

BERENICE: How would I know? In fact, all them freak folks down at the fair every October just gives me the creeps.

FRANKIE [*after a pause, and slowly*]: Do I give you the creeps?

BERENICE: You?

FRANKIE: Do you think I will grow into a freak?

BERENICE: You? Why certainly not, I trust Jesus!

FRANKIE [*going over to the mirror, and looking at herself*]: Well, do you think I will be pretty?

BERENICE: Maybe. If you file down them horns a inch or two.

FRANKIE [*turning to face Berenice, and shuffling one bare foot on the floor*]: Seriously.

BERENICE: Seriously, I think when you fill out you will do very well. If you behave.

FRANKIE: But by Sunday, I want to do something to improve myself before the wedding.

BERENICE: Get clean for a change. Scrub your elbows and fix yourself nice. You will do very well.

JOHN HENRY: You will be all right if you file down them horns.

FRANKIE [*raising her right shoulder and turning from the mirror*]: I don't know what to do. I just wish I would die.

BERENICE: Well, die then!

JOHN HENRY: Die.

FRANKIE [*suddenly exasperated*]: Go home! [*There is a pause.*] You heard me! [*She makes a face at him and threatens him with the fly swatter. They run twice around the table.*] Go home! I'm sick and tired of you, you little midget.

[*John Henry goes out, taking the doll with him.*]

BERENICE: Now what makes you act like that? You are too mean to live.

FRANKIE: I know it. [*She takes a carving knife from the table drawer.*] Something about John Henry just gets on my nerves these days. [*She puts her left ankle over her right knee and begins to pick with the knife at a splinter in her foot.*] I've got a splinter in my foot.

BERENICE: That knife ain't the proper thing for a splinter.

FRANKIE: It seems to me that before this summer I used always to have such a good time. Remember this spring when Evelyn Owen and me used to dress up in costumes and go down town and shop at the five-and-dime? And how every Friday night we'd spend the night with each other either at her house or here? And then Evelyn Owen had to go and move away to Florida. And now she won't even write to me.

BERENICE: Honey, you are not crying, is you? Don't that hurt you none?

FRANKIE: It would hurt anybody else except me. And how the wisteria in town was so blue and pretty in April but somehow it was so pretty it made me sad. And how Evelyn and me put on that show the Glee Club did at the High School Auditorium? [*She raises her head and beats time with the knife and her fist on the table, singing loudly with sudden energy.*] Sons of toil and danger! Will you serve a stranger! And bow down to Burgundy! [*Berenice joins in on "Burgundy." Frankie pauses, then begins to pick her foot again, humming the tune sadly.*]

BERENICE: That was a nice show you children copied in the arbor. You will meet another girl friend you like as well as Evelyn Owen. Or maybe Mr. Owen will move back into town. [*There is a pause.*] Frankie, what you need is a needle.

FRANKIE: I don't care anything about my old feet. [*She stomps her foot on the floor and lays down the knife on the table.*] It was just so queer the way it happened this afternoon. The minute I laid eyes on the pair of them I had this funny feeling. [*She goes over and picks up a saucer of milk near the cat-hole in the back of the door and pours the milk in the sink.*] How old were you, Berenice, when you married your first husband?

BERENICE: I were thirteen years old.

FRANKIE: What made you get married so young for?

BERENICE: Because I wanted to.

FRANKIE: You never loved any of your four husbands but Ludie.

BERENICE: Ludie Maxwell Freeman was my only true husband. The other ones were just scraps.

FRANKIE: Did you marry with a veil every time?

BERENICE: Three times with a veil.

FRANKIE [*pouring milk into the saucer and returning the saucer to the cat-hole*]: If only I just knew where he is gone. Ps,ps,ps ... Charles, Charles.

BERENICE: Quit worrying yourself about that old alley cat. He's gone off to hunt a friend.

FRANKIE: To hunt a friend?

BERENICE: Why certainly. He roamed off to find himself a lady friend.

FRANKIE: Well, why don't he bring his friend home with him? He ought to know I would be only too glad to have a whole family of cats.

BERENICE: You done seen the last of that old alley cat.

FRANKIE [*crossing the room*]: I ought to notify the police force. They will find Charles.

BERENICE: I wouldn't do that.

FRANKIE [*at the telephone*]: I want the police force, please ... Police force? ... I am notifying you about my cat ... Cat! He's lost. He is almost pure Persian.

BERENICE: As Persian as I is.

FRANKIE: But with short hair. A lovely color of gray with a little white spot on his throat. He answers to the name of Charles, but if he don't answer to that, he might come if you call "Charlina." ... My name is Miss F. Jasmine Addams and the address is 124 Grove Street.

BERENICE [*giggling as Frankie re-enters*]: Gal, they going to send around here and tie you up and drag you off to Milledgeville. Just picture them fat blue police chasing tomcats around alleys and hollering. "Oh Charles! Oh come here, Charlina!" Merciful Heavens.

FRANKIE: Aw, shut up!

[*Outside a voice is heard calling in a drawn-out chant, the words almost indistinguishable: "Lot of okra, peas, fresh butter beans ..."*]

BERENICE: The trouble with you is that you don't have no sense of humor no more.

FRANKIE: [*disconsolately*]: Maybe I'd be better off in jail.

[*The chanting voice continues and an ancient Negro woman, dressed in a clean*

print dress with several petticoats, the ruffle of one of which shows, crosses the
yard. She stops and leans on a gnarled stick.]

FRANKIE: Here comes the old vegetable lady.

BERENICE: Sis Laura is getting mighty feeble to peddle this hot weather.

FRANKIE: She is about ninety. Other old folks lose their faculties, but she found
some faculty. She reads futures, too.

BERENICE: His, Sis Laura. How is your folks getting on?

SIS LAURA: We ain't much, and I feels my age these days. Want any peas
today? [*She shuffles across the yard.*]

BERENICE: I'm sorry, I still have some left over from yesterday. Good-bye, Sis
Laura.

SIS LAURA: Good-bye. [*She goes off behind the house to the right, continuing*
her chant.]

[*When the old woman is gone Frankie begins walking around the kitchen.*]

FRANKIE: I expect Janice and Jarvis are almost to Winter Hill by now.

BERENICE: Sit down. You make me nervous.

FRANKIE: Jarvis talked about Granny. He remembers her very good. But when I
try to remember Granny, it is like her face is changing — like a face seen under
water. Jarvis remembers Mother too, and I don't remember her at all.

BERENICE: Naturally! Your mother died the day that you were born.

FRANKIE [*standing with one foot on the seat of the chair, leaning over the chair*
back and laughing]: Did you hear what Jarvis said?

BERENICE: What?

FRANKIE [*after laughing more*]: They were talking about whether to vote for C.
P. MacDonald. And Jarvis said, "Why I wouldn't vote for that scoundrel if he was
running to be dogcatcher." I never heard anything so witty in my life. [*There is a*
silence during which Berenice watches Frankie, but does not smile.] And you
know what Janice remarked. When Jarvis mentioned about how much I've grown,
she said she didn't think I looked so terribly big. She said she got the major
portion of her growth before she was thirteen. She said I was the right height and
had acting talent and ought to go to Hollywood. She did, Berenice.

BERENICE: O.K. All right! She did!

FRANKIE: She said she thought I was a lovely size and would probably not grow
any taller. She said all fashion models and movie stars ...

BERENICE: She did not. I heard her from the window. She only remarked that
you probably had already got your growth. But she didn't go on and on like that or
mention Hollywood.

FRANKIE: She said to me ...

BERENICE: She said to you! This is a serious fault with you, Frankie. Somebody
just makes a loose remark and then you cozen it in your mind until nobody would
recognize it. Your Aunt Pet happened to mention to Clorina that you had sweet
manners and Clorina passed it on to you. For what it was worth. Then next thing I

know you are going all around and bragging how Mrs. West thought you had the finest manners in town and ought to go to Hollywood, and I don't know what-all you didn't say. And that is a serious fault.

FRANKIE: Aw, quit preaching at me.

BERENICE: I ain't preaching. It's the solemn truth and you know it.

FRANKIE: I admit it a little. [*She sits down at the table and puts her forehead on the palms of her hands. There is a pause, and then she speaks softly.*] What I need to know is this. Do you think I made a good impression?

BERENICE: Impression?

FRANKIE: Yes.

BERENICE: Well, how would I know?

FRANKIE: I mean, how did I act? What did I do?

BERENICE: Why, you didn't do anything to speak of.

FRANKIE: Nothing?

BERENICE: No. You just watched the pair of them like they was ghosts. Then, when they talked about the wedding, them ears of yours stiffened out the size of cabbage leaves...

FRANKIE [*raising her hand to her ear*]: They didn't!

BERENICE: They did.

FRANKIE: Some day you are going to look down and find that big fat tongue of yours pulled out by the roots and laying there before you on the table.

BERENICE: Quit talking so rude.

FRANKIE [*after a pause*]: I'm so scared I didn't make a good impression.

BERENICE: What of it? I got a date with T. T. and he's supposed to pick me up here. I wish him and Honey would come on. You make me nervous.

[*Frankie sits miserably, her shoulders hunched. Then with a sudden gesture she bangs her forehead on the table. Her fists are clenched and she is sobbing.*]

BERENICE: Come on. Don't act like that.

FRANKIE [*her voice muffled*]: They were so pretty. They must have such a good time. And they went away and left me.

BERENICE: Sit up. Behave yourself.

FRANKIE: They came and went away, and left me with this feeling.

BERENICE: Hosee! I bet I know something. [*She begins tapping with her heel: one, two, three — bang! After a pause, in which the rhythm is established, she begins singing.*] Frankie's got a crush! Frankie's got a crush! Frankie's got a crush on the *wedding!*

FRANKIE: Quit!

BERENICE: Frankie's got a crush! Frankie's got a crush!

FRANKIE: You better quit! [*She rises suddenly and snatches up the carving knife.*]

BERENICE: You lay down that knife.

FRANKIE: Make me. [*She bends the blade slowly.*]

BERENICE: Lay it down, *Devil*. [*There is a silence.*] Just throw it! You just! [*After a pause Frankie aims the knife carefully at the closed door leading to the bedroom and throws it. The knife does not stick in the wall.*]

FRANKIE: I used to be the best knife thrower in this town.

BERENICE: Frances Addams, you goin' to try that stunt once too often.

FRANKIE: I warned you to quit pickin' with me.

BERENICE: You are not fit to live in a house.

FRANKIE: I won't be living in this one much longer; I'm going to run away from home.

BERENICE: And a good riddance to a big old bag of rubbage.

FRANKIE: You wait and see. I'm leaving town.

BERENICE: And where do you think you are going?

FRANKIE [*gazing around at the walls*]: I don't know.

BERENICE: You're going crazy. That's where you going.

FRANKIE: No. [*solemnly*] This coming Sunday after the wedding, I'm leaving town. And I swear to Jesus by my two eyes I'm never coming back here any more.

BERENICE [*going to Frankie and pushing her damp bangs back from her forehead*]: Sugar? You serious?

FRANKIE [*exasperated*]: Of course! Do you think I would stand here and say that swear and tell a story? Sometimes, Berenice, I think it takes you longer to realize a fact than it does anybody who ever lived.

BERENICE: But you say you don't know where you going. You going, but you don't know where. That don't make no sense to me.

FRANKIE [*after a long pause in which she again gazes around the walls of the room*]: I feel just exactly like somebody has peeled all the skin off me. I wish I had some good cold peach ice cream. [*Berenice takes her by the shoulders.*]

[*During the last speech, T. T. Williams and Honey Camden Brown have been approaching through the back yard. T. T. is a large and pompous-looking Negro man of about fifty. He is dressed like a church deacon, in a black suit with a red emblem in the lapel. His manner is timid and over-polite. Honey is a slender, limber Negro boy of about twenty. He is quite light in color and he wears loud-colored, snappy clothes. He is brusque and there is about him an odd mixture of hostility and playfulness. He is very high-strung and volatile. They are trailed by John Henry. John Henry is dressed for the afternoon in a clean white linen suit, white shoes and socks. Honey carries a horn. They cross the back yard and knock at the back door. Honey holds his hand to his head.*]

FRANKIE: But every word I told you was the solemn truth. I'm leaving here after the wedding.

BERENICE [*taking her hands from Frankie's shoulders and answering the door*]: Hello, Honey and T. T. I didn't hear you coming.

T.T.: You and Frankie too busy discussing something. Well, your foster-brother, Honey, got into a ruckus standing on the sidewalk in front of the Blue Moon Café.

Police cracked him on the haid.

BERENICE [*turning on the kitchen light*]: What! [*She examines Honey's head.*] Why, it's a welt the size of a small egg.

HONEY: Times like this I feel like I got to bust loose or die.

BERENICE: What were you doing?

HONEY: Nothing. I was just passing along the street minding my own business when this drunk soldier came out of the Blue Moon Café and ran into me. I looked at him and he gave me a push. I pushed him back and he raised a ruckus. This white M.P. came up and slammed me with his stick.

T. T.: It was one of those accidents can happen to any colored person.

JOHN HENRY [*reaching for the horn*]: Toot some on your horn, Honey.

FRANKIE: Please blow.

HONEY [*to John Henry, who has taken the horn*]: Now, don't bother my horn, Butch.

JOHN HENRY: I want to toot it some.

[*John Henry takes the horn, tries to blow it, but only succeeds in slobbering in it. He holds the horn away from his mouth and sings: "Too-ty-toot, too-ty-toot." Honey snatches the horn away from him and puts it on the sewing table.*]

HONEY: I told you not to touch my horn. You got it full of slobber inside and out. It's ruined! [*He loses his temper, grabs John Henry by the shoulders and shakes him hard.*]

BERENICE [*slapping Honey*]: Satan! Don't you dare touch that little boy! I'm going to stomp out your brains!

HONEY: You ain't mad because John Henry is a little boy. It's because he's a white boy. John Henry knows he needs a good shake. Don't you, Butch?

BERENICE: Ornery — no good!

[*Honey lifts John Henry and swings him, then reaches in his pocket and brings out some coins.*]

HONEY: John Henry, which would you rather have — the nigger money or the white money?

JOHN HENRY: I rather have the dime. [*He takes it.*] Much obliged. [*He goes out and crosses the yard to his house.*]

BERENICE: You troubled and beat down and try to take it out on a little boy. You and Frankie just alike. The club girls don't elect her and she turns on John Henry too. When folks are lonesome and left out, they turn so mean. T. T. do you wish a small little quickie before we start?

T. T. [*looking at Frankie and pointing toward her*]: Frankie ain't no tattle-tale. Is you? [*Berenice pours a drink for T. T.*]

FRANKIE [*disdaining his question*]: That sure is a cute suit you got on, Honey. Today I heard somebody speak of you as Lightfoot Brown. I think that's such a grand nickname. It's on account of your travelling — to Harlem, and all the different places where you have run away, and your dancing. Lightfoot! I wish somebody would call me Lightfoot Addams.

BERENICE: It would suit me better if Honey Camden had brick feets. As it is, he keeps me so anxious-worried. C'mon, Honey and T. T. Let's go! [*Honey and T. T. go out.*]

FRANKIE: I'll go out into the yard.

[*Frankie, feeling excluded, goes out into the yard. Throughout the act the light in the yard has been darkening steadily. Now the light in the kitchen is throwing a yellow rectangle in the yard.*]

BERENICE: Now Frankie, you forget all that foolishness we were discussing. And if Mr. Addams don't come home by good dark, you go over to the Wests'. Go play with John Henry.

HONEY AND T. T. [*from outside*]: So long!

FRANKIE: So long, you all. Since when have I been scared of the dark? I'll invite John Henry to spend the night with me.

BERENICE: I thought you were sick and tired of him.

FRANKIE: I am.

BERENICE [*kissing Frankie*]: Good night, Sugar!

FRANKIE: Seems like everybody goes off and leaves me. [*She walks towards the West's yard, calling, with cupped hands.*] — John Henry. John Henry.

JOHN HENRY'S VOICE: What do you want, Frankie?

FRANKIE: Come over and spend the night with me.

JOHN HENRY'S VOICE: I can't.

FRANKIE: Why?

JOHN HENRY: Just because.

FRANKIE: Because why? [*John Henry does not answer.*] I thought maybe me and you could put up my Indian tepee and sleep out here in the yard. And have a good time. [*There is still no answer.*] Sure enough. Why don't you stay and spend the night?

JOHN HENRY [*quite loudly*]: Because, Frankie. I don't want to.

FRANKIE [*angrily*]: Fool Jackass! Suit yourself! I only asked you because you looked so ugly and so lonesome.

JOHN HENRY [*skipping toward the arbor*]: Why, I'm not a bit lonesome.

FRANKIE [*looking at the house*]: I wonder when that Papa of mine is coming home. He always comes home by dark. I don't want to go into that empty, ugly house all by myself.

JOHN HENRY: Me neither.

FRANKIE [*standing with outstretched arms, and looking around her*]: I think something is wrong. It's too quiet. I have a peculiar warning in my bones. I bet you a hundred dollars it's going to storm.

JOHN HENRY: I don't want to spend the night with you.

FRANKIE: A terrible, terrible dog-day storm. Or maybe even a cyclone.

JOHN HENRY: Huh.

FRANKIE: I bet Jarvis and Janice are now at Winter Hill. I see them just plain as I see you. Plainer. Something is wrong. It is too quiet.

[*A clear horn begins to play a blues tune in the distance.*]

JOHN HENRY: Frankie?

FRANKIE: Hush! It sounds like Honey.

[*The horn music becomes jazzy and spangling, then the first blues tune is repeated. Suddenly, while still unfinished, the music stops. Frankie waits tensely.*]

FRANKIE: He has stopped to bang the spit out of his horn. In a second he will finish. [*after a wait*] Please, Honey, go on finish!

JOHN HENRY [*softly*]: He done quit now.

FRANKIE [*moving restlessly*]: I told Berenice that I was leavin' town for good and she did not believe me. Sometimes I honestly think she is the biggest fool that ever drew breath. You try to impress something on a big fool like that, and it's just like talking to a block of cement. I kept on telling and telling and telling her. I told her I had to leave this town for good because it is inevitable. Inevitable.

[*Mr. Addams enters the kitchen from the house, calling: "Frankie, Frankie."*]

MR. ADDAMS [*calling from the kitchen door*]: Frankie, Frankie.

FRANKIE: Yes, Papa.

MR. ADDAMS [*opening the back door*]: You had supper?

FRANKIE: I'm not hungry.

MR. ADDAMS: Was a little later than I intended, fixing a timepiece for a railroad man. [*He goes back through the kitchen and into the hall, calling: "Don't leave the yard!"*]

JOHN HENRY: You want me to get the weekend bag?

FRANKIE: Don't bother me, John Henry. I'm thinking.

JOHN HENRY: What you thinking about?

FRANKIE: About the wedding. About my brother and the bride. Everything's been so sudden today. I never believed before about the fact that the earth turns at the rate of about a thousand miles a day. I didn't understand why it was that if you jumped up in the air you wouldn't land in Selma or Fairview or somewhere else instead of the same back yard. But now it seems to me I feel the world going around very fast. [*Frankie begins turning around in circles with arms outstretched. John Henry copies her. They both turn.*] I feel it turning and it makes me dizzy.

JOHN HENRY: I'll stay and spend the night with you.

FRANKIE [*suddenly stopping her turning*]: No. I just now thought of something.

JOHN HENRY: You just a little while ago was begging me.

FRANKIE: I know where I'm going.

[*There are sounds of children playing in the distance.*]

JOHN HENRY: Let's go play with the children, Frankie.

FRANKIE: I tell you I know where I'm going. It's like I've known it all my life.

Tomorrow I will tell everybody.

JOHN HENRY: Where?

FRANKIE [*dreamily*]: After the wedding I'm going with them to Winter Hill. I'm going off with them after the wedding.

JOHN HENRY: You serious?

FRANKIE: Shush, just now I realized something. The trouble with me is that for a long time I have been just an "I" person. All other people can say "we." When Berenice says "we" she means her lodge and church and colored people. Soldiers can say "we" and mean the army. All people belong to a "we" except me.

JOHN HENRY: What are we going to do?

FRANKIE: Not to belong to a "we" makes you too lonesome. Until this afternoon I didn't have a "we," but now after seeing Janice and Jarvis I suddenly realize something.

JOHN HENRY: What?

FRANKIE: I know that the bride and my brother are the "we" of me. So I'm going with them, and joining with the wedding. This coming Sunday when my brother and the bride leave this town, I'm going with the two of them to Winter Hill. And after that to whatever place that they will ever go. [*There is a pause.*] I love the two of them so much and we belong to be together. I love the two of them so much because they are the *we* of me.

[*The curtain falls.*]

ACT TWO

The scene is the same: the kitchen of the Addams home. Berenice is cooking. John Henry sits on the stool, blowing soap bubbles with a spool. It is the afternoon of the next day.

[*The front door slams and Frankie enters from the hall.*]

BERENICE: I been phoning all over town trying to locate you. Where on earth have you been?

FRANKIE: Everywhere. All over town.

BERENICE: I been so worried. I got a good mind to be seriously mad with you. Your Papa came home to dinner today. He was mad when you didn't show up. He's taking a nap now in his room.

FRANKIE: I walked up and down Main Street and stopped in almost every store. Bought my wedding dress and silver shoes. Went around by the mills. Went all over the complete town and talked to nearly everybody in it.

BERENICE: What for, pray tell me?

FRANKIE: I was telling everybody about the wedding and my plans. [*She takes off her dress and remains barefooted in her slip.*]

BERENICE: You mean just people on the street? [*She is creaming butter and sugar for cookies.*]

FRANKIE: Everybody. Storekeepers. The monkey and monkey-man. A soldier. Everybody. And you know the soldier wanted to join with me and asked me for a date this evening. I wonder what you do on dates.

BERENICE: Frankie, I honestly believe you have turned crazy on us. Walking all over town and telling total strangers this big tale. You know in your soul this mania of yours is pure foolishness.

FRANKIE: Please call me F. Jasmine. I don't wish to have to remind you any more. Everything good of mine has got to be washed and ironed so I can pack them in the suitcase. [*She brings in a suitcase and opens it.*] Everybody in town believes that I'm going. All except Papa. He's stubborn as an old mule. No use arguing with people like that.

BERENICE: Me and Mr. Addams has some sense.

FRANKIE: Papa was bent over working on a watch when I went by the store. I asked him could I buy the wedding clothes and he said charge them at Mac-Dougals. But he wouldn't listen to any of my plans. Just sat there with his nose to the grindstone and answered with — kind of grunts. He never listens to what I say. [*There is a pause.*] Sometimes I wonder if Papa loves me or not.

BERENICE: Course he loves you. He is just a busy widowman — set in his ways.

FRANKIE: Now I wonder if I can find some tissue paper to line this suitcase.

BERENICE: Truly, Frankie, what makes you think they want you taggin' along with them? Two is company and three is a crowd. And that's the main thing about a wedding. Two is company and three is a crowd.

FRANKIE: You wait and see.

BERENICE: Remember back to the time of the flood. Remember Noah and the Ark.

FRANKIE: And what has that got to do with it?

BERENICE: Remember the way he admitted them creatures.

FRANKIE: Oh, shut up your big old mouth!

BERENICE: Two by two. He admitted them creatures two by two.

FRANKIE [*after a pause*]: That's all right. But you wait and see. They will take me.

BERENICE: And if they don't?

FRANKIE [*turning suddenly from washing her hands at the sink*]: If they don't, I will kill myself.

BERENICE: Kill yourself, how?

FRANKIE: I will shoot myself in the side of the head with the pistol that Papa keeps under his handkerchiefs with Mother's picture in the bureau drawer.

BERENICE: You heard what Mr. Addams said about playing with that pistol. I'll just put this cookie dough in the icebox. Set the table and your dinner is ready. Set John Henry a plate and one for me. [*Berenice puts the dough in the ice-box.*

Frankie hurriedly sets the table. Berenice takes dishes from the stove and ties a napkin around John Henry's neck.] I have heard of many a peculiar thing. I have knew men to fall in love with girls so ugly that you wonder if their eyes is straight.

JOHN HENRY: Who?

BERENICE: I have knew women to love veritable satans and thank Jesus when they put their split hooves over the threshold. I have knew boys to take it into their heads to fall in love with other boys. You know Lily Mae Jenkins.

FRANKIE: I'm not sure. I know a lot of people.

BERENICE: Well, you either know him or you don't know him. He prisses around in a girl's blouse with one arm akimbo. Now this Lily Mae Jenkins fell in love with a man name Juney Jones. A man, mind you. And Lily Mae turned into a girl. He changed his nature and his sex and turned into a girl.

FRANKIE: What?

BERENICE: He did. To all intents and purposes. [*Berenice is sitting in the center chair at the table. She says grace.*] Lord, make us thankful for what we are about to receive to nourish our bodies. Amen.

FRANKIE: It's funny I can't think who you are talking about. I used to think I knew so many people.

BERENICE: Well, you don't need to know Lily Mae Jenkins. You can live without knowing him.

FRANKIE: Anyway, I don't believe you.

BERENICE: I ain't arguing with you. What was we speaking about?

FRANKIE: About peculiar things.

BERENICE: Oh, yes. As I was just now telling you I have seen many a peculiar thing in my day. But one thing I never knew and never heard about. No, siree. I never in all my days heard of anybody falling in love with a wedding. [*There is a pause.*] And thinking it all over I have come to a conclusion.

JOHN HENRY: How? How did that boy change into a girl? Did he kiss his elbow? [*He tries to kiss his elbow.*]

BERENICE: It was just one of them things, Candy Lamb. Yep, I have come to the conclusion that what you ought to be thinking about is a beau. A nice little white boy beau.

FRANKIE: I don't want any beau. What would I do with one? Do you mean something like a soldier who would maybe take me to the Idle Hour?

BERENICE: Who's talking about soldiers? I'm talking about a nice little white boy your own age. How 'bout that little old Barney next door?

FRANKIE: Barney MacKean! That nasty Barney!

BERENICE: Certainly! You could make out with him until somebody better comes along. He would do.

FRANKIE: You are the biggest crazy in this town.

BERENICE: The crazy calls the sane crazy.

[*Barney MacKean, a boy of twelve, shirtless and wearing shorts, and Helen*

Fletcher, a girl of twelve or fourteen, cross the yard from the left, go through the arbor and out on the right. Frankie and John Henry watch them from the window.]

FRANKIE: Yonder's Barney now with Helen Fletcher. They are going to the alley behind the Wests' garage. They do something bad back there. I don't know what it is.

BERENICE: If you don't know what it is, how come you know it is bad?

FRANKIE: I just know it. I think maybe they look at each other and peepee or something. They don't let anybody watch them.

JOHN HENRY: I watched them once.

FRANKIE: What do they do?

JOHN HENRY: I saw. They don't peepee.

FRANKIE: Then what do they do?

JOHN HENRY: I don't know what it was. But I watched them. How many of them did you catch, Berenice? Them beaus?

BERENICE: How many? Candy Lamb, how many hairs is in this plait? You're talking to Miss Berenice Sadie Brown.

FRANKIE: I think you ought to quit worrying about beaus and be content with T.T. I bet you are forty years old.

BERENICE: Wise-mouth. How do you know so much? I got as much right as anybody else to continue to have a good time as long as I can. And as far as that goes, I'm not so old as some peoples would try and make out. I ain't changed life yet.

JOHN HENRY: Did they all treat you to the picture show, them beaus?

BERENICE: To the show, or one thing or another. Wipe off your mouth.

[*There is the sound of piano tuning.*]

JOHN HENRY: The piano tuning man.

BERENICE: Ye Gods, I seriously believe this will be the last straw.

JOHN HENRY: Me too.

FRANKIE: It makes me sad. And jittery too. [*She walks around the room.*] They tell me that when they want to punish the crazy people in Milledgeville, they tie them up and make them listen to piano tuning. [*She puts the empty coal scuttle on her head and walks around the table.*]

BERENICE: We could turn on the radio and drown him out.

FRANKIE: I don't want the radio on. [*She goes into the interior room and takes off her dress, speaking from inside.*] But I advise you to keep the radio on after I leave. Some day you will very likely hear us speak over the radio.

BERENICE: Speak about what, pray tell me?

FRANKIE: I don't know exactly what about. But probably some eye witness account about something. We will be asked to speak.

BERENICE: I don't follow you. What are we going to eye witness? And who will ask us to speak?

JOHN HENRY [*excitedly*]: What, Frankie? Who is speaking on the radio?

FRANKIE: When I said *we*, you thought I meant you and me and John Henry West. To speak over the world radio. I have never heard of anything so funny since I was born.

JOHN HENRY [*climbing up to kneel on the seat of the chair*]: Who? What?

FRANKIE: Ha! Ha! Ho! Ho! Ho! Ho!

[*Frankie goes around punching things with her fist, and shadow boxing. Berenice raises her right hand for peace. Then suddenly they all stop. Frankie goes to the window, and John Henry hurries there also and stands on tiptoe with his hands on the sill. Berenice turns her head to see what has happened. The piano is still. Three young girls in clean dresses are passing before the arbor. Frankie watches them silently at the window.*]

JOHN HENRY [*softly*]: The club of girls.

FRANKIE: What do you son-of-a-bitches mean crossing my yard? How many times must I tell you not to set foot on my Papa's property?

BERENICE: Just ignore them and make like you don't see them pass.

FRANKIE: Don't mention those crooks to me.

[*T. T. and Honey approach by way of the back yard. Honey is whistling a blues tune.*]

BERENICE: Why don't you show me the new dress? I'm anxious to see what you selected. [*Frankie goes into the interior room. T. T. knocks on the door. He and Honey enter.*] Why T. T. what you doing around here this time of day?

T. T.: Good afternoon, Miss Berenice. I'm here on a sad mission.

BERENICE [*startled*]: What's wrong?

T. T.: It's about Sis Laura Thompson. She suddenly had a stroke and died.

BERENICE: What! Why she was by here just yesterday. We just ate her peas. They in my stomach right now, and her lyin' dead on the cooling board this minute. The Lord works in strange ways.

T. T.: Passed away at dawn this morning.

FRANKIE [*putting her head in the doorway*]: Who is it that's dead?

BERENICE: Sis Laura, Sugar. That old vegetable lady.

FRANKIE [*unseen, from the interior room*]: Just to think — she passed by yesterday.

T. T.: Miss Berenice, I'm going around to take up a donation for the funeral. The policy people say Sis Laura's claim has lapsed.

BERENICE: Well, here's fifty cents. The poor old soul.

T. T.: She was brisk as a chipmunk to the last. The Lord had appointed the time for her. I hope I go that way.

FRANKIE [*from the interior room*]: I've got something to show you all. Shut your eyes and don't open them until I tell you. [*She enters the room dressed in an orange satin evening dress with silver shoes and stockings.*] These are the wedding clothes. [*Berenice, T. T. and John Henry stare.*]

JOHN HENRY: Oh, how pretty!

FRANKIE: Now tell me your honest opinion. [*There is a pause.*] What's the matter? Don't you like it, Berenice?

BERENICE: No. It don't do.

FRANKIE: What do you mean? It don't do.

BERENICE: Exactly that. It just don't do. [*She shakes her head while Frankie looks at the dress.*]

FRANKIE: But I don't see what you mean. What is wrong?

BERENICE: Well, if you don't see it I can't explain it to you. Look there at your head, to begin with. [*Frankie goes to the mirror.*] You had all your hair shaved off like a convict and now you tie this ribbon around this head without any hair. Just looks peculiar.

FRANKIE: But I'm going to wash and try to stretch my hair tonight.

BERENICE: Stretch your hair! How you going to stretch your hair? And look at them elbows. Here you got on a grown woman's evening dress. And that brown crust on your elbows. The two things just don't mix. [*Frankie, embarrassed, covers her elbows with her hands. Berenice is still shaking her head.*] Take it back down to the store.

T. T.: The dress is too growny looking.

FRANKIE: But I can't take it back. It's bargain basement.

BERENICE: Very well then. Come here. Let me see what I can do.

FRANKIE [*going to Berenice, who works with the dress*]: I think you're just not accustomed to seeing anybody dressed up.

BERENICE: I'm not accustomed to seein' a human Christmas tree in August.

JOHN HENRY: Frankie's dress looks like a Christmas tree.

FRANKIE: Two-faced Judas! You just now said it was pretty. Old double-faced Judas! [*The sounds of piano tuning are heard again.*] Oh, that piano tuner!

BERENICE: Step back a little now.

FRANKIE [*looking in the mirror*]: Don't you honestly think it's pretty? Give me your candy opinion.

BERENICE: I never knew anybody so unreasonable! You ask me my candy opinion, I give you my candy opinion. You ask me again, and I give it to you again. But what you want is not my honest opinion, but my good opinion of something I know is wrong.

FRANKIE: I only want to look pretty.

BERENICE: Pretty is as pretty does. Ain't that right, T. T.? You will look well enough for anybody's wedding. Excepting your own.

[*Mr. Addams enters through the hall door.*]

MR. ADDAMS: Hello, everybody. [*to Frankie*] I don't want you roaming around the streets all morning and not coming home at dinner time. Looks like I'll have to tie you up in the back yard.

FRANKIE: I had business to tend to. Papa, look!

MR. ADDAMS: What is it, Miss Picklepriss?

FRANKIE: Sometimes I think you have turned stone blind. You never even noticed my new dress.

MR. ADDAMS: I thought it was a show costume.

FRANKIE: Show costume! Papa, why is it you don't ever notice what I have on or pay any serious mind to me? You just walk around like a mule with blinders on, not seeing or caring.

MR. ADDAMS: Never mind that now. [to T. T. and Honey] I need some help down at my store. My porter failed me again. I wonder if you or Honey could help me next week.

T. T.: I will if I can, sir, Mr. Addams. What days would be convenient for you, sir?

MR. ADDAMS: Say Wednesday afternoon.

T. T.: Now, Mr. Addams, that's one afternoon I promised to work for Mr. Finny, sir. I can't promise anything, Mr. Addams. But if Mr. Finny change his mind about needing me, I'll work for you, sir.

MR. ADDAMS: How about you, Honey?

HONEY [shortly]: I ain't got the time.

MR. ADDAMS: I'll be so glad when the war is over and you biggety, worthless niggers get back to work. And, furthermore, you *sir* me! Hear me?

HONEY [reluctantly]: Yes, — sir.

MR. ADDAMS: I better go back to the store now and get my nose down to the grindstone. You stay home, Frankie. [He goes out through the hall door.]

JOHN HENRY: Uncle Royal called Honey a nigger. Is Honey a nigger?

BERENICE: Be quiet now, John Henry. [to Honey] Honey, I got a good mind to shake you till you spit. Not saying *sir* to Mr. Addams, and acting so impudent.

HONEY: T. T. said sir enough for a whole crowd of niggers. But for folks that calls me nigger, I got a real good nigger razor. [He takes a razor from his pocket. Frankie and John Henry crowd close to look. When John Henry touches the razor Honey says:] Don't touch it, Butch, it's sharp. Liable to hurt yourself.

BERENICE: Put up that razor, Satan! I worry myself sick over you. You going to die before your appointed span.

JOHN HENRY: Why is Honey a nigger?

BERENICE: Jesus knows.

HONEY: I'm so tensed up. My nerves been scraped with a razor. Berenice, loan me a dollar.

BERENICE: I ain't handing you no dollar, worthless, to get high on them reefer cigarettes.

HONEY: Gimme, Berenice, I'm so tensed up and miserable. The nigger hole. I'm sick of smothering in the nigger hole. I can't stand it no more.

[Relenting, Berenice gets her pocketbook from the shelf, opens it, and takes out some change.]

BERENICE: Here's thirty cents. You can buy two beers.

HONEY: Well, thankful for tiny, infinitesimal favors. I better be dancing off now.

T. T.: Same here. I still have to make a good deal of donation visits this afternoon. [*Honey and T. T. go to the door.*]

BERENICE: So long, T. T. I'm counting on you for tomorrow and you too, Honey.

FRANKIE and JOHN HENRY: So long.

T. T.: Good-bye, you all. Good-bye. [*He goes out, crossing the yard.*]

BERENICE: Poor ole Sis Laura. I certainly hope that when my time comes I will have kept up my policy. I dread to think the church would ever have to bury me. When I die.

JOHN HENRY: Are you going to die, Berenice?

BERENICE: Why, Candy, everybody has to die.

JOHN HENRY: Everybody? Are you going to die, Frankie?

FRANKIE: I doubt it. I honestly don't think I'll ever die.

JOHN HENRY: What is "die"?

FRANKIE: It must be terrible to be nothing but black, black, black.

BERENICE: Yes, baby.

FRANKIE: How many dead people do you know? I know six dead people in all. I'm not counting my mother. There's William Boyd who was killed in Italy. I knew him by sight and name. An' that man who climbed poles for the telephone company. An' Lou Baker. The porter at Finny's place who was murdered in the alley back of Papa's store. Somebody drew a razor on him and the alley people said that his cut throat shivered like a mouth and spoke ghost words to the sun.

JOHN HENRY: Ludie Maxwell Freeman is dead.

FRANKIE: I didn't count Ludie; it wouldn't be fair. Because he died just before I was born. [*to Berenice*] Do you think very frequently about Ludie?

BERENICE: You know I do. I think about the five years when me and Ludie was together, and about all the bad times I seen since. Sometimes I almost wish I had never knew Ludie at all. It leaves you too lonesome afterward. When you walk home in the evening on the way from work, it makes a little lonesome quinch come in you. And you take up with too many sorry men to try to get over the feeling.

FRANKIE: But T. T. is not sorry.

BERENICE: I wasn't referring to T. T. He is a fine upstanding colored gentleman, who has walked in a state of grace all his life.

FRANKIE: When are you going to marry with him?

BERENICE: I ain't going to marry with him.

FRANKIE: But you were just now saying . . .

BERENICE: I was saying how sincerely I respect T. T. and sincerely regard T. T. [*There is a pause.*] But he don't make me shiver none.

FRANKIE: Listen, Berenice, I have something queer to tell you. It's something that happened when I was walking around town today. Now I don't exactly know how to explain what I mean.

BERENICE: What is it?

FRANKIE [*now and then pulling her bangs or lower lip*]: I was walking along and I passed two stores with a alley in between. The sun was frying hot. And just as I passed this alley, I caught a *glimpse* of something in the corner of my left eye. A dark double shape. And this glimpse brought to my mind — so sudden and clear — my brother and the bride that I just stood there and couldn't hardly bear to look and see what it was. It was like they were there in that alley, although I knew that they are in Winter Hill almost a hundred miles away. [*There is a pause.*] Then I turn slowly and look. And you know what was there? [*There is a pause.*] It was just two colored boys. That was all. But it gave me such a queer feeling.

[*Berenice has been listening attentively. She stares at Frankie, then draws a package of cigarettes from her bosom and lights one.*]

BERENICE: Listen at me! Can you see through these bones in my forehead? [*She points to her forehead.*] Have you, Frankie Addams, been reading my mind? [*There is a pause.*] That's the most remarkable thing I ever heard of.

FRANKIE: What I mean is that . . .

BERENICE: I know what you mean. You mean right here in the corner of your eye. [*She points to her eye.*] You suddenly catch something there. And this cold shiver run all the way down you. And you whirl around. And you stand there facing Jesus knows what. But not Ludie, not who you want. And for a minute you feel like you been dropped down a well.

FRANKIE: Yes. That is it. [*Frankie reaches for a cigarette and lights it, coughing a bit.*]

BERENICE: Well, that is mighty remarkable. This is a thing been happening to me all my life. Yet just now is the first time I ever heard it put into words. [*There is a pause.*] Yes, that is the way it is when you are in love. A thing known and not spoken.

FRANKIE [*patting her foot*]: Yet I always maintained I never believed in love. I didn't admit it and never put any of it in my shows.

JOHN HENRY: I never believed in love.

BERENICE: Now I will tell you something. And it is to be a warning to you. You hear me, John Henry. You hear me, Frankie.

JOHN HENRY: Yes. [*He points his forefinger.*] Frankie is smoking.

BERENICE [*squaring her shoulders*]: Now I am here to tell you I was happy. There was no human woman in all the world more happy than I was in them days. And that includes everybody. You listening to me, John Henry? It includes all the queens and millionaires and first ladies of the land. And I mean it includes people of all color. You hear me, Frankie? No human woman in all the world was happier than Berenice Sadie Brown.

FRANKIE: The five years you were married to Ludie.

BERENICE: From that autumn morning when I first met him on the road in front of Campbell's Filling Station until the very night he died, November, the year 1933.

FRANKIE: The very year and the very month I was born.

BERENICE: The coldest November I ever seen. Every morning there was frost and puddles were crusted with ice. The sunshine was pale yellow like it is in winter time. Sounds carried far away, and I remember a hound dog that used to howl toward sundown. And everything I seen come to me as a kind of sign.

FRANKIE: I think it is a kind of sign I was born the same year and the same month he died.

BERENICE: And it was a Thursday towards six o'clock. About this time of day. Only November. I remember I went to the passage and opened the front door. Dark was coming on; the old hound was howling far away. And I go back in the room and lay down on Ludie's bed. I lay myself down over Ludie with my arms spread out and my face on his face. And I pray that the Lord would contage my strength to him. And I ask the Lord let it be anybody, but not let it be Ludie. And I lay there and pray for a long time. Until night.

JOHN HENRY: How? [*in a higher, wailing voice*] How, Berenice?

BERENICE: That night he died. I tell you he died. Ludie! Ludie Freeman! Ludie Maxwell Freeman died! [*She hums.*]

FRANKIE [*after a pause*]: It seems to me I feel sadder about Ludie than any other dead person. Although I never knew him. I know I ought to cry sometimes about my mother, or anyhow Granny. But it looks like I can't. But Ludie — maybe it was because I was born so soon after Ludie died. But you were starting out to tell some kind of a warning.

BERENICE [*looking puzzled for a moment*]: Warning? Oh, yes! I was going to tell you how this thing we was talking about applies to me. [*As Berenice begins to talk Frankie goes to a shelf above the refrigerator and brings back a fig bar to the table.*] It was the April of the following year that I went one Sunday to the church where the congregation was strange to me. I had my forehead down on the top of the pew in front of me, and my eyes were open — not peeping around in secret, mind you, but just open. When suddenly this shiver ran all the way through me. I had caught sight of something from the corner of my eye. And I looked slowly to the left. There on the pew, just six inches from my eyes, was this *thumb*.

FRANKIE: What thumb?

BERENICE: Now I have to tell you. There was only one small portion of Ludie Freeman which was not pretty. Every other part about him was handsome and pretty as anyone would wish. All except this right thumb. This one thumb had a mashed, chewed appearance that was not pretty. You understand?

FRANKIE: You mean you suddenly saw Ludie's thumb when you were praying?

BERENICE: I mean I seen *this* thumb. And as I knelt there just staring at this thumb, I begun to pray in earnest. I prayed out loud! Lord, manifest! Lord, manifest!

FRANKIE: And did He — manifest?

BERENICE: Manifest, my foot! [*spitting*] You know who that thumb belonged to?

FRANKIE: Who?

BERENICE: Why, Jamie Beale. That big old no-good Jamie Beale. It was the first time I ever laid eyes on him.

FRANKIE: Is that why you married him? Because he had a mashed thumb like Ludie's?

BERENICE: Lord only knows. I don't. I guess I felt drawn to him on account of that thumb. And then one thing led to another. First thing I know I had married him.

FRANKIE: Well, I think that was silly. To marry him just because of that thumb.

BERENICE: I'm not trying to dispute with you. I'm just telling you what actually happened. And the very same thing occurred in the case of Henry Johnson.

FRANKIE: You mean to sit there and tell me Henry Johnson had one of those mashed thumbs too?

BERENICE: No. It was not the thumb this time. It was the coat. [*Frankie and John Henry look at each other in amazement. After a pause Berenice continues.*] Now when Ludie died, them policy people cheated me out of fifty dollars so I pawned everything I could lay hands on, and I sold my coat and Ludie's coat. Because I couldn't let Ludie be put away cheap.

FRANKIE: Oh! Then you mean Henry Johnson bought Ludie's coat and you married him because of it?

BERENICE: Not exactly. I was walking down the street one evening when I suddenly seen this shape appear before me. Now the shape of this boy ahead of me was so similar to Ludie through the shoulders and the back of the head that I almost dropped dead there on the sidewalk. I followed and run behind him. It was Henry Johnson. Since he lived in the country and didn't come into town, he had chanced to buy Ludie's coat and from the back view it looked like it was Ludie's ghost or Ludie's twin. But how I married him I don't exactly know, for, to begin with, it was clear that he did not have his share of sense. But you let a boy hang around and you get fond of him. Anyway, that's how I married Henry Johnson.

FRANKIE: He was the one went crazy on you. Had eatin' dreams and swallowed the corner of the sheet. [*There is a pause.*] But I don't understand the point of what you was telling. I don't see how that about Jamie Beale and Henry Johnson applies to me.

BERENICE: Why, it applies to everybody and it is a warning.

FRANKIE: But how?

BERENICE: Why, Frankie, don't you see what I was doing? I loved Ludie and he was the first man I loved. Therefore I had to go and copy myself forever afterward. What I did was to marry off little pieces of Ludie whenever I come across them. It was just my misfortune they all turned out to be the wrong pieces. My intention was to repeat me and Ludie. Now don't you see?

FRANKIE: I see what you're driving at. But I don't see how it is a warning applied to me.

BERENICE: You don't! Then I'll tell you. [*Frankie does not nod or answer. The piano tuner plays an arpeggio.*] You and that wedding tomorrow. That is what I am warning about. I can see right through them two gray eyes of yours like they was glass. And what I see is the saddest piece of foolishness I ever knew.

JOHN HENRY [*in a low voice*]: Gray eyes is glass.

[*Frankie tenses her brows and looks steadily at Berenice.*]

BERENICE: I see what you have in mind. Don't think I don't. You see something unheard of tomorrow, and you right in the center. You think you going to march to the preacher right in between your brother and the bride. You think you going to break into that wedding, and then Jesus knows what else.

FRANKIE: No. I don't see myself walking to the preacher with them.

BERENICE: I see through them eyes. Don't argue with me.

JOHN HENRY [*repeating softly*]: Gray eyes is glass.

BERENICE: But what I'm warning is this. If you start out falling in love with some unheard-of thing like that, what is going to happen to you? If you take a mania like this, it won't be the last time and of that you can be sure. So what will become of you? Will you be trying to break into weddings the rest of your days?

FRANKIE: It makes me sick to listen to people who don't have any sense. [*She sticks her fingers in her ears and hums.*]

BERENICE: You just settin' yourself this fancy trap to catch yourself in trouble. And you know it.

FRANKIE: They will take me. You wait and see.

BERENICE: Well, I been trying to reason seriously. But I see it is no use.

FRANKIE: You are just jealous. You are just trying to deprive me of all the pleasure of leaving town.

BERENICE: I am just trying to head this off. But I still see it is no use.

JOHN HENRY: Gray eyes is glass.

[*The piano is played to the seventh note of the scale and this is repeated.*]

FRANKIE [*singing*]: Do, ray, mee, fa, sol, la, tee, do. Tee. Tee. It could drive you wild. [*She crosses to the screen door and slams it.*] You didn't say anything about Willis Rhodes. Did he have a mashed thumb or a coat or something? [*She returns to the table and sits down.*]

BERENICE: Lord, now that really was something.

FRANKIE: I only know he stole your furniture and was so terrible you had to call the Law on him.

BERENICE: Well, imagine this! Imagine a cold bitter January night. And me laying all by myself in the big parlor bed. Alone in the house because everybody else had gone for the Saturday night. Me, mind you, who hates to sleep in a big empty bed all by myself at any time. Past twelve o'clock on this cold, bitter January night. Can you remember winter time, John Henry? [*John Henry nods.*]

Imagine! Suddenly there comes a sloughing sound and a tap, tap, tap. So Miss Me
. . . [*She laughs uproariously and stops suddenly, putting her hand over her
mouth.*]

FRANKIE: What? [*leaning closer across the table and looking intently at
Berenice*] What happened?

[*Berenice looks from one to the other, shaking her head slowly. Then she speaks
in a changed voice.*]

BERENICE: Why, I wish you would look yonder. I wish you would look. [*Frankie
glances quickly behind her, then turns back to Berenice.*]

FRANKIE: What? What happened?

BERENICE: Look at them two little pitchers and them four big ears. [*Berenice
gets up suddenly from the table.*] Come on, chillin, less us roll out the dough for
the cookies tomorrow. [*Berenice clears the table and begins washing dishes at the
sink.*]

FRANKIE: If it's anything I mortally despise, it's a person who starts out to tell
something and works up people's interest, and then stops.

BERENICE [*still laughing*]: I admit it. And I am sorry. But it was just one of
them things I suddenly realized I couldn't tell you and John Henry.

[*John Henry skips up to the sink.*]

JOHN HENRY [*singing*]: Cookies! Cookies! Cookies!

FRANKIE: You could have sent him out of the room and told me. But don't think
I care a particle about what happened. I just wish Willis Rhodes had come in
about that time and slit your throat. [*She goes out into the hall.*]

BERENICE [*still chuckling*]: That is a ugly way to talk. You ought to be ashamed.
Here, John Henry, I'll give you a scrap of dough to make a cookie man.

[*Berenice gives John Henry some dough. He climbs up on a chair and begins to
work with it. Frankie enters with the evening newspaper. She stands in the
doorway, then puts the newspaper on the table.*]

FRANKIE: I see in the paper where we dropped a new bomb — the biggest one
dropped yet. They call it a atom bomb. I intend to take two baths tonight. One
long soaking bath and scrub with a brush. I'm going to try to scrape this crust off
my elbows. Then let out the dirty water and take a second bath.

BERENICE: Hooray, that's a good idea. I will be glad to see you clean.

JOHN HENRY: I will take two baths.

[*Berenice has picked up the paper and is sitting in a chair against the pale
white light of the window. She holds the newspaper open before her and her
head is twisted down to one side as she strains to see what is printed there.*]

FRANKIE: Why is it against the law to change your name?

BERENICE: What is that on your neck? I thought it was a head you carried on that
neck. Just think. Suppose I would suddenly up and call myself Mrs. Eleanor
Roosevelt. And you would begin naming yourself Joe Louis. And John Henry here
tried to pawn himself off as Henry Ford.

FRANKIE: Don't talk childish; that is not the kind of changing I mean. I mean from a name that doesn't suit you to a name you prefer. Like I changed from Frankie to F. Jasmine.

BERENICE: But it would be a confusion. Suppose we all suddenly change to entirely different names. Nobody would ever know who anybody was talking about. The whole world would go crazy.

FRANKIE: I don't see what that has to do with it.

BERENICE: Because things accumulate around your name. You have a name and one thing after another happens to you and things have accumulated around the name.

FRANKIE: But what has accumulated around my old name? [*Berenice does not reply.*] Nothing! See! My name just didn't mean anything. Nothing ever happened to me.

BERENICE: But it will. Things will happen.

FRANKIE: What?

BERENICE: You pin me down like that and I can't tell you truthfully. If I could, I wouldn't be sitting here in this kitchen right now, but making a fine living on Wall Street as a wizard. All I can say is that things will happen. Just what, I don't know.

FRANKIE: Until yesterday, nothing ever happened to me.

[*John Henry crosses to the door and puts on Berenice's hat and shoes, takes her pocketbook and walks around the table twice.*]

BERENICE: John Henry, take off my hat and my shoes and put up my pocketbook. Thank you very much. [*John Henry does so.*]

FRANKIE: Listen, Berenice. Doesn't it strike you as strange that I am I and you are you? Like when you are walking down a street and you meet somebody. And you are you. And he is him. Yet when you look at each other, the eyes make a connection. Then you go off one way. And he goes off another way. You go off into different parts of town, and maybe you never see each other again. Not in your whole life. Do you see what I mean?

BERENICE: Not exactly.

FRANKIE: That's not what I mean to say anyway. There are all these people here in town I don't even know by sight or name. And we pass alongside each other and don't have any connection. And they don't know me and I don't know them. And now I'm leaving town and there are all these people I will never know.

BERENICE: But who do you want to know?

FRANKIE: Everybody. Everybody in the world.

BERENICE: Why, I wish you would listen to that. How about people like Willis Rhodes? How about them Germans? How about them Japanese?

[*Frankie knocks her head against the door jamb and looks up at the ceiling.*]

FRANKIE: That's not what I mean. That's not what I'm talking about.

BERENICE: Well, what *is* you talking about?

[*A child's voice is heard outside, calling: "Batter up! Batter up!"*]

JOHN HENRY: Less play out, Frankie.

FRANKIE: No. You go. [*after a pause*] This is what I mean.

[*Berenice waits, and when Frankie does not speak again, says:*]

BERENICE: What on earth is wrong with you?

FRANKIE [*after a long pause, then suddenly, with hysteria*]: Boyoman! Manoboy! When we leave Winter Hill we're going to more places than you ever thought about or even knew existed. Just where we will go first I don't know, and it don't matter. Because after we go to that place we're going on to another. Alaska, China, Iceland, South America. Travelling on trains. Letting her rip on motorcycles. Flying around all over the world in airplanes. Here today and gone tomorrow. All over the world. It's the damn truth. Boyoman! [*She runs around the table.*]

BERENICE: Frankie!

FRANKIE: And talking of things happening. Things will happen so fast we won't hardly have time to realize them. Captain Jarvis Addams wins highest medals and is decorated by the President. Miss F. Jasmine Addams breaks all records. Mrs. Janice Addams elected Miss United Nations in beauty contest. One thing after another happening so fast we don't hardly notice them.

BERENICE: Hold still, fool.

FRANKIE [*her excitement growing more and more intense*]: And we will meet them. Everybody. We will just walk up to people and know them right away. We will be walking down a dark road and see a lighted house and knock on the door and strangers will rush to meet us and say: "Come in! Come in!" We will know decorated aviators and New York people and movie stars. We will have thousands and thousands of friends. And we will belong to so many clubs that we can't even keep track of all of them. We will be members of the whole world. Boyoman! Manoboy!

[*Frankie has been running round and round the table in wild excitement and when she passes the next time Berenice catches her slip so quickly that she is caught up with a jerk.*]

BERENICE: *Is* you gone raving wild? [*She pulls Frankie closer and puts h   arm around her waist.*] Sit here in my lap and rest a minute. [*Frankie sits in Ber nice's lap. John Henry comes close and jealously pinches Frankie.*] Leave Frankie alone. She ain't bothered you.

JOHN HENRY: I'm sick.

BERENICE: Now no, you ain't. Be quiet and don't grudge your cousin a little bit love.

JOHN HENRY [*hitting Frankie*]: Old mean bossy Frankie.

BERENICE: What she doing so mean right now? She just laying here wore out. [*They continue sitting. Frankie is relaxed now.*]

FRANKIE: Today I went to the Blue Moon — this place that all the soldiers are so fond of and I met a soldier — a red-headed boy.

BERENICE: What is all this talk about the Blue Moon and soldiers?

FRANKIE: Berenice, you treat me like a child. When I see all these soldiers milling around town I always wonder where they came from and where they are going.

BERENICE: They were born and they going to die.

FRANKIE: There are so many things about the world I do not understand.

BERENICE: If you did understand you would be God. Didn't you know that?

FRANKIE: Maybe so. [*She stares and stretches herself on Berenice's lap, her long legs sprawled out beneath the kitchen table.*] Anyway, after the wedding I won't have to worry about things any more.

BERENICE: You don't have to now. Nobody requires you to solve the riddles of the world.

FRANKIE [*looking at newspaper*]: The paper says that this new atom bomb is worth twenty thousand tons of T.N.T.

BERENICE: Twenty thousand tons? And there ain't but two tons of coal in the coal house — all that coal.

FRANKIE: The paper says the bomb is a very important science discovery.

BERENICE: The figures these days have got too high for me. Read in the paper about ten million peoples killed. I can't crowd that many peoples in my mind's eye.

JOHN HENRY: Berenice, is the glass eye your mind's eye?

[*John Henry has climbed up on the back rungs of Berenice's chair and has been hugging her head. He is now holding her ears.*]

BERENICE: Don't yank my head back like that, Candy. Me and Frankie ain't going to float up through the ceiling and leave you.

FRANKIE: I wonder if you have ever thought about this? Here we are — right now. This very minute. Now. But while we're talking right now, this minute is passing. And it will never come again. Never in all the world. When it is gone, it is gone. No power on earth could bring it back again.

JOHN HENRY [*beginning to sing*]:

I sing because I'm happy,
I sing because I'm free,
For His eye is on the sparrow,
And I know He watches me.

BERENICE [*singing*]:

Why should I feel discouraged?
Why should the shadows come?
Why should my heart be lonely,

Away from heaven and home?
For Jesus is my portion,
My constant friend is He,
For His eye is on the sparrow,
And I know He watches me.
So, I sing because I'm happy.

[*John Henry and Frankie join on the last three lines.*]

I sing because I'm happy
I sing because I'm free,
For His eye is on the sparrow,
And I know he watches . . .

BERENICE: Frankie, you got the sharpest set of human bones I ever felt.
[*The curtain falls.*]

ACT THREE

SCENE ONE

The scene is the same: the kitchen. It is the day of the wedding. When the curtain rises Berenice, in her apron, and T. T. Williams in a white coat have just finished preparations for the wedding refreshments. Berenice has been watching the ceremony through the half-open door leading into the hall. There are sounds of congratulations off-stage, the wedding ceremony having just finished.

BERENICE [*to T. T. Williams*]: Can't see much from this door. But I can see Frankie. And her face is a study. And John Henry's chewing away at the bubble gum that Jarvis bought him. Well, sounds like it's all over. They crowding in now to kiss the bride. We better take this cloth off the sandwiches. Frankie said she would help you serve.

T. T.: From the way she's been acting, I don't think we can count much on her.

BERENICE: I wish Honey was here. I'm so worried about him since what you told me. It's going to storm. It's a mercy they didn't decide to have the wedding in the back yard like they first planned.

T. T.: I thought I'd better not minch the matter. Honey was in a bad way when I saw him this morning.

BERENICE: Honey Camden don't have too large a share of judgment as it is, but when he gets high on them reefers, he's got no more judgment than a four-year-old child. Remember that time he swung at the police and nearly got his eyes beat out?

T. T.: Not to mention six months on the road.

BERENICE: I haven't been so anxious in all my life. I've got two people scouring Sugarville to find him. [*in a fervent voice*] God, you took Ludie but please watch over my Honey Camden. He's all the family I got.

T. T.: And Frankie behaving this way about the wedding. Poor little critter.

BERENICE: And the sorry part is that she's perfectly serious about all this foolishness. [*Frankie enters the kitchen through the hall door.*] Is it all over? [*T. T. crosses to the ice box with sandwiches.*]

FRANKIE: Yes. And it was such a pretty wedding I wanted to cry.

BERENICE: You told them yet?

FRANKIE: About my plans — no, I haven't yet told them.

[*John Henry comes in and goes out.*]

BERENICE: Well, you better hurry up and do it, for they going to leave the house right after the refreshments.

FRANKIE: Oh, I know it. But something just seems to happen to my throat; every time I tried to tell them, different words came out.

BERENICE: What words?

FRANKIE: I asked Janice how come she didn't marry with a veil. [*with feeling*] Oh, I'm so embarrassed. Here I am all dressed up in this tacky evening dress. Oh, why didn't I listen to you! I'm so ashamed.

[*T. T. goes out with a platter of sandwiches.*]

BERENICE: Don't take everything so strenuous like.

FRANKIE: I'm going in there and tell them now! [*She goes.*]

JOHN HENRY [*coming out of the interior bedroom, carrying several costumes*]: Frankie sure gave me a lot of presents when she was packing the suitcase. Berenice, she gave me all the beautiful show costumes.

BERENICE: Don't set so much store by all those presents. Come tomorrow morning and she'll be demanding them back again.

JOHN HENRY: And she even gave me the shell from the Bay. [*He puts the shell to his ear and listens.*]

BERENICE: I wonder what's going on up there. [*She goes to the door and opens it and looks through.*]

T. T. [*returning to the kitchen*]: They all complimenting the wedding cake. And drinking the wine punch.

BERENICE: What's Frankie doing? When she left the kitchen a minute ago she was going to tell them. I wonder how they'll take this total surprise. I have a feeling like you get just before a big thunder storm.

[*Frankie enters, holding a punch cup.*]

BERENICE: You told them yet?

FRANKIE: There are all the family around and I can't seem to tell them. I wish I had written it down on the typewriter beforehand. I try to tell them and the words just — die.

BERENICE: The words just die because the very idea is so silly.

FRANKIE: I love the two of them so much. Janice put her arms around me and said she had always wanted a little sister. And she kissed me. She asked me again what grade I was in in school. That's the third time she's asked me. In fact, that's the main question I've been asked at the wedding.

[*John Henry comes in, wearing a fairy costume, and goes out. Berenice notices Frankie's punch and takes it from her.*]

FRANKIE: And Jarvis was out in the street seeing about this car he borrowed for the wedding. And I followed him out and tried to tell him. But while I was trying to reach the point, he suddenly grabbed me by the elbows and lifted me up and sort of swung me. He said: "Frankie, the lankie, the alaga fankie, the tee-legged, toe-legged, bow-legged Frankie." And he gave me a dollar bill.

BERENICE: That's nice.

FRANKIE: I just don't know what to do. I have to tell them and yet I don't know how to.

BERENICE: Maybe when they're settled, they will invite you to come and visit with them.

FRANKIE: Oh no! I'm going *with* them.

[*Frankie goes back into the house. There are louder sounds of voices from the interior. John Henry comes in again.*]

JOHN HENRY: The bride and groom are leaving. Uncle Royal is taking their suitcases out to the car.

[*Frankie runs to the interior room and returns with her suitcase. She kisses Berenice.*]

FRANKIE: Good-bye, Berenice. Good-bye, John Henry. [*She stands a moment and looks around the kitchen.*] Farewell, old ugly kitchen. [*She runs out.*]

[*There are sounds of good-byes as the wedding party and the family guests move out of the house to the sidewalk. The voices get fainter in the distance. Then, from the front sidewalk there is the sound of disturbance. Frankie's voice is heard, diminished by distance, although she is speaking loudly.*]

FRANKIE'S VOICE: That's what I am telling you. [*Indistinct protesting voices are heard.*]

MR. ADDAMS' VOICE [*indistinctly*]: Now be reasonable, Frankie.

FRANKIE'S VOICE [*screaming*]: I have to go. Take me! Take me!

JOHN HENRY [*entering excitedly*]: Frankie is in the wedding car and they can't get her out. [*He runs out but soon returns.*] Uncle Royal and my Daddy are having to haul and drag old Frankie. She's holding onto the steering wheel.

MR. ADDAMS' VOICE: You march right along here. What in the world has come into you? [*He comes into the kitchen with Frankie who is sobbing.*] I never heard of such an exhibition in my life. Berenice, you take charge of her.

[*Frankie flings herself on the kitchen chair and sobs with her head in her arms on the kitchen table.*]

JOHN HENRY: They put old Frankie out of the wedding. They hauled her out of the wedding car.

MR. ADDAMS [*clearing his throat*]: That's sufficient, John Henry. Leave Frankie alone. [*He puts a caressing hand on Frankie's head.*] What makes you want to leave your old papa like this? You've got Janice and Jarvis all upset on their wedding day.

FRANKIE: I love them so!

BERENICE [*looking down the hall*]: Here they come. Now please be reasonable, Sugar.

[*The bride and groom come in. Frankie keeps her face buried in her arms and does not look up. The bride wears a blue suit with a white flower corsage pinned at the shoulder.*]

JARVIS: Frankie, we came to tell you good-bye. I'm sorry you're taking it like this.

JANICE: Darling, when we are settled we want you to come for a nice visit with us. But we don't yet have any place to live. [*She goes to Frankie and caresses her head. Frankie jerks.*] Won't you tell us good-bye now?

FRANKIE [*with passion*]: We! When you say *we*, you only mean you and Jarvis. And I am not included. [*She buries her head in her arms again and sobs.*]

JANICE: Please, darling, don't make us unhappy on our wedding day. You know we love you.

FRANKIE: See! *We* — when you say we, I am not included. It's not fair.

JANICE: When you come visit us you must write beautiful plays, and we'll all act in them. Come, Frankie, don't hide your sweet face from us. Sit up. [*Frankie raises her head slowly and stares with a look of wonder and misery.*] Good-bye, Frankie, darling.

JARVIS: So long, now, kiddo.

[*They go out and Frankie still stares at them as they go down the hall. She rises, crosses towards the door and falls on her knees.*]

FRANKIE: Take me! Take me!

[*Berenice puts Frankie back on her chair.*]

JOHN HENRY: They put Frankie out of the wedding. They hauled her out of the wedding car.

BERENICE: Don't tease your cousin, John Henry.

FRANKIE: It was a frame-up all around.

BERENICE: Well, don't bother no more about it. It's over now. Now cheer up.

FRANKIE: I wish the whole world would die.

BERENICE: School will begin now in only three more weeks and you'll find another bosom friend like Evelyn Owen you so wild about.

JOHN HENRY [*seated below the sewing maching*]: I'm sick, Berenice. My head hurts.

BERENICE: No you're not. Be quiet, I don't have the patience to fool with you.

FRANKIE [*hugging her hunched shoulders*]: Oh, my heart feels so cheap!

BERENICE: Soon as you get started in school and have a chance to make these here friends, I think it would be a good idea to have a party.

FRANKIE: Those baby promises rasp on my nerves.

BERENICE: You could call up the society editor of the *Evening Journal* and have the party written up in the paper. And that would make the fourth time your name has been published in the paper.

FRANKIE [*with a trace of interest*]: When my bike ran into that automobile, the paper called me Fankie Addams, F-A-N-K-I-E. [*She puts her head down again.*]

JOHN HENRY: Frankie, don't cry. This evening we can put up the teepee and have a good time.

FRANKIE: Oh, hush up your mouth.

BERENICE: Listen to me. Tell me what you would like and I will try to do it if it is in my power.

FRANKIE: All I wish in the world, is for no human being ever to speak to me as long as I live.

BERENICE: Bawl, then, misery.

[*Mr. Addams enters the kitchen, carrying Frankie's suitcase, which he sets in the middle of the kitchen floor. He cracks his finger joints. Frankie stares at him resentfully, then fastens her gaze on the suitcase.*]

MR. ADDAMS: Well, it looks like the show is over and the monkey's dead.

FRANKIE: You think it's over, but it's not.

MR. ADDAMS: You want to come down and help me at the store tomorrow? Or polish some silver with the shammy rag? You can even play with those old watch springs.

FRANKIE [*still looking at her suitcase*]: That's my suitcase I packed. If you think it's all over, that only shows how little you know. [*T. T. comes in.*] If I can't go with the bride and my brother as I was meant to leave this town, I'm going anyway. Somehow, anyhow, I'm leaving town. [*Frankie raises up in her chair.*] I can't stand this existence — this kitchen — this town — any longer! I will hop a train and go to New York. Or hitch rides to Hollywood, and get a job there. If worse comes to worse, I can act in comedies. [*She rises.*] Or I could dress up like a boy and join the Merchant Marines and run away to sea. Somehow, anyhow, I'm running away.

BERENICE: Now quiet down —

FRANKIE [*grabbing the suitcase and running into the hall*]: Please, Papa, don't try to capture me.

[*Outside the wind starts to blow.*]

JOHN HENRY [*from the doorway*]: Uncle Royal, Frankie's got your pistol in her suitcase.

[*There is the sound of running footsteps and of the screen door slamming.*]

BERENICE: Run catch her.

[*T. T. and Mr. Addams rush into the hall, followed by John Henry.*]

MR. ADDAMS' VOICE: Frankie! Frankie! Frankie!

[*Berenice is left alone in the kitchen. Outside the wind is higher and the hall door is blown shut. There is a rumble of thunder, then a loud clap. Thunder and flashes of lightning continue. Berenice is seated in her chair, when John Henry comes in.*]

JOHN HENRY: Uncle Royal is going with my Daddy, and they are chasing her in our car. [*There is a thunder clap.*] The thunder scares me, Berenice.

BERENICE [*taking him in her lap*]: Ain't nothing going to hurt you.

JOHN HENRY: You think they're going to catch her?

BERENICE [*putting her hand to her head*]: Certainly. They'll be bringing her home directly. I've got such a headache. Maybe my eye socket and all these troubles.

JOHN HENRY [*with his arms around Berenice*]: I've got a headache, too. I'm sick, Berenice.

BERENICE: No you ain't. Run along, Candy. I ain't got the patience to fool with you now.

[*Suddenly the lights go out in the kitchen, plunging it in gloom. The sound of wind and storm continues and the yard is a dark storm-green.*]

JOHN HENRY: Berenice!

BERENICE: Ain't nothing. Just the lights went out.

JOHN HENRY: I'm scared.

BERENICE: Stand still, I'll just light a candle. [*muttering*] I always keep one around, for such like emergencies. [*She opens a drawer.*]

JOHN HENRY: What makes the lights go out so scarey like this?

BERENICE: Just one of them things, Candy.

JOHN HENRY: I'm scared too. Where's Honey?

BERENICE: Jesus knows I'm scared too. With Honey snow-crazy and loose like this — and Frankie run off with a suitcase and her Papa's pistol. I feel like every nerve been picked out of me.

JOHN HENRY [*holding out his seashell and stroking Berenice*]: You want to listen to the ocean?

[*The curtain falls.*]

SCENE TWO

The scene is the same. There are still signs in the kitchen of the wedding: punch glasses and the punch bowl on the drainboard. It is four o'clock in the morning. As the curtain rises, Berenice and Mr. Addams are alone in the kitchen. There is a crepuscular glow in the yard.

MR. ADDAMS: I never was a believer in corporal punishment. Never spanked Frankie in my life, but when I lay my hands on her . . .

BERENICE: She'll show up soon — but I know how you feel. What with worrying about Honey Camden, John Henry's sickness and Frankie, I've never lived through such a anxious night. [*She looks through the window. It is dawning now.*]

MR. ADDAMS: I'd better go and find out the last news of John Henry, poor baby. [*He goes through the hall door.*]

[*Frankie comes into the yard and crosses to the arbor. She looks exhausted and almost beaten. Berenice has seen her from the window, rushes into the yard and grabs her by the shoulders and shakes her.*]

BERENICE: Frankie Addams, you ought to be skinned alive. I been so worried.

FRANKIE: I've been so worried too.

BERENICE: Where have you been this night? Tell me everything.

FRANKIE: I will, but quit shaking me.

BERENICE: Now tell me the A and the Z of this.

FRANKIE: When I was running around the dark scarey streets, I begun to realize that my plans for Hollywood and the Merchant Marines were child plans that would not work. I hid in the alley behind Papa's store, and it was dark and I was scared. I opened the suitcase and took out Papa's pistol. [*She sits down on her suitcase.*] I vowed I was going to shoot myself. I said I was going to count three and on three pull the trigger. I counted one — two — but I didn't count three — because at the last minute, I changed my mind.

BERENICE: You march right along with me. You going to bed.

FRANKIE: Oh, Honey Camden!

[*Honey Camden Brown, who has been hiding behind the arbor, has suddenly appeared.*]

BERENICE: Oh, Honey, Honey. [*They embrace.*]

HONEY: Shush, don't make any noise; the law is after me.

BERENICE [*in a whisper*]: Tell me.

HONEY: Mr. Wilson wouldn't serve me so I drew a razor on him.

BERENICE: You kill him?

HONEY: Didn't have no time to find out. I been runnin' all night.

FRANKIE: Lightfoot, if you drew a razor on a white man, you'd better not let them catch you.

BERENICE: Here's six dolla's. If you can get to Fork Falls and then to Atlanta. But be careful slippn' through the white folks' section. They'll be combing the county looking for you.

HONEY [*with passion*]: Don't cry, Berenice.

BERENICE: Already I feel that rope.

HONEY: Don't you dare cry. I know now all my days have been leading up to this minute. No more "boy this — boy that" — no bowing, no scraping. For the first time, I'm free and it makes me happy. [*He begins to laugh hysterically.*]

BERENICE: When they catch you, they'll string you up.

HONEY [*beside himself, brutally*]: Let them hang me — I don't care. I tell you I'm glad. I tell you I'm happy. [*He goes out behind the arbor.*]

FRANKIE [*calling after him*]: Honey, remember you are Lightfoot. Nothing can stop you if you want to run away.

[*Mrs. West, John Henry's mother, comes into the yard.*]

MRS. WEST: What was all that racket? John Henry is critically ill. He's got to have perfect quiet.

FRANKIE: John Henry's sick, Aunt Pet?

MRS. WEST: The doctor say he has meningitis. He must have perfect quiet.

BERENICE: I haven't had time to tell you yet. John Henry took sick sudden last night. Yesterday afternoon when I complained of my head, he said he had a headache too and thinking he copies me I said, "Run along, I don't have the patience to fool with you." Looks like a judgment on me. There won't be no more noise, Mrs. West.

MRS. WEST: Make sure of that. [*She goes away.*]

FRANKIE [*putting her arm around Berenice*]: Oh, Berenice, what can we do?

BERENICE [*stroking Frankie's head*]: Ain't nothing we can do but wait.

FRANKIE: The wedding — Honey — John Henry — so much has happened that my brain can't hardly gather it in. Now for the first time I realize that the world is certainly — a sudden place.

BERENICE: Sometimes sudden, but when you are waiting, like this, it seems so slow.

[*The curtain falls.*]

SCENE THREE

The scene is the same: the kitchen and arbor. It is months later, a November day, about sunset. The arbor is brittle and withered. The elm tree is bare except for a few ragged leaves. The yard is tidy and the lemonade stand and sheet stage curtain are now missing. The kitchen is neat and bare and the furniture has been removed. Berenice, wearing a fox fur, is sitting in a chair with an old suitcase and doll at her feet. Frankie enters.

FRANKIE: Oh, I am just mad about these Old Masters.

BERENICE: Humph!

FRANKIE: The house seems so hollow. Now that the furniture is packed. It gives me a creepy feeling in the front. That's why I came back here.

BERENICE: Is that the only reason why you came back here?

FRANKIE: Oh, Berenice, you know. I wish you hadn't given quit notice just because Papa and I are moving into a new house with Uncle Eustace and Aunt Pet out in Limewood.

BERENICE: I respect and admire Mrs. West but I'd never get used to working for her.

FRANKIE: Mary is just beginning this Rachmaninoff Concerto. She may play it for her debut when she is eighteen years old. Mary playing the piano and the whole orchestra playing at one and the same time, mind you. Awfully hard.

BERENICE: Ma-ry Littlejohn.

FRANKIE: I don't know why you always have to speak her name in a tinged voice like that.

BERENICE: Have I ever said anything against her? All I said was that she is too lumpy and marshmallow white and it makes me nervous to see her just setting there sucking them pigtails.

FRANKIE: Braids. Furthermore, it is no use our discussing a certain party. You could never possibly understand it. It's just not in you.

[*Berenice looks at her sadly, with faded stillness, then pats and strokes the fox fur.*]

BERENICE: Be that as it may. Less us not fuss and quarrel this last afternoon.

FRANKIE: I don't want to fuss either. Anyway, this is not our last afternoon. I will come and see you often.

BERENICE: No, you won't, baby. You'll have other things to do. Your road is already strange to me.

[*Frankie goes to Berenice, pats her on the shoulder, then takes her fox fur and examines it.*]

FRANKIE: You still have the fox fur that Ludie gave you. Somehow this little fur looks so sad — so thin and with a sad little fox-wise face.

BERENICE [*taking the fur back and continuing to stroke it*]: Got every reason to be sad. With what has happened in these two last months. I just don't know what I have done to deserve it. [*She sits, the fur in her lap, bent over with her forearms on her knees and her hands limply dangling.*] Honey gone and John Henry, my little boy gone.

FRANKIE: You did all you could. You got poor Honey's body and gave him a Christian funeral and nursed John Henry.

BERENICE: It's the way Honey died and the fact that John Henry had to suffer so. Little soul!

FRANKIE: It's peculiar — the way it all happened so fast. First Honey caught and hanging himself in the jail. Then later in that same week, John Henry died and then I met Mary. As the irony of fate would have it, we first got to know each other in front of the lipstick and cosmetics counter at Woolworth's. And it was the week of the fair.

BERENICE: The most beautiful September I ever seen. Countless white and yellow butterflies flying around them autumn flowers — Honey dead and John Henry suffering like he did and daisies, golden weather, butterflies — such strange death weather.

FRANKIE: I never believed John Henry would die. [*There is a long pause. She looks out the window.*] Don't it seem quiet to you in here? [*There is another, longer pause.*] When I was a little child I believed that out under the arbor at night there would come three ghosts and one of the ghosts wore a silver ring. [*whispering*] Occasionally when it gets so quiet like this I have a strange feeling. It's like John Henry is hovering somewhere in this kitchen — solemn looking and ghost-grey.

A BOY'S VOICE [*from the neighboring yard*]: Frankie, Frankie.

FRANKIE [*calling to the boy*]: Yes, Barney. [*to Berenice*] Clock stopped. [*She shakes the clock.*]

THE BOY'S VOICE: Is Mary there?

FRANKIE [*to Berenice*]: It's Barney MacKean. [*to the boy, in a sweet voice*] Not yet. I'm meeting her at five. Come on in, Barney, won't you?

BARNEY: Just a minute.

FRANKIE [*to Berenice*]: Barney puts me in mind of a Greek god.

BERENICE: What? Barney put you in mind of a what?

FRANKIE: Of a Greek god. Mary remarked that Barney reminded her of a Greek god.

BERENICE: It looks like I can't understand a thing you say no more.

FRANKIE: You know, those old-timey Greeks worship those Greek gods.

BERENICE: But what has that got to do with Barney MacKean?

FRANKIE: On account of the figure.

[*Barney MacKean, a boy of thirteen, wearing a football suit, bright sweater and cleated shoes, runs up the back steps into the kitchen.*]

BERENICE: Hi, Greek god Barney. This afternoon I saw your inititals chalked down on the front sidewalk. M.L. loves B.M.

BARNEY: If I could find out who wrote it, I would rub it out with their faces. Did you do it, Frankie?

FRANKIE [*drawing herself up with sudden dignity*]: I wouldn't do a kid thing like that. I even resent you asking me. [*She repeats the phrase to herself in a pleased undertone.*]. Resent you asking me.

BARNEY: Mary can't stand me anyhow.

FRANKIE: Yes she can stand you. I am her most intimate friend. I ought to know. As a matter of fact she's told me several lovely compliments about you. Mary and I are riding on the moving van to our new house. Would you like to go?

BARNEY: Sure.

FRANKIE: O.K. You will have to ride back with the furniture 'cause Mary and I are riding on the front seat with the driver. We had a letter from Jarvis and Janice this afternoon. Jarvis is with the Occupation Forces in Germany and they took a vacation trip to Luxembourg. [*She repeats in a pleased voice:*] Luxembourg. Berenice, don't you think that's a lovely name?

BERENICE: It's kind of a pretty name, but it reminds me of soapy water.

FRANKIE: Mary and I will most likely pass through Luxembourg when we — are going around the world together.

[*Frankie goes out followed by Barney and Berenice sits in the kitchen alone and motionless. She picks up the doll, looks at it and hums the first two lines of "I Sing Because I'm Happy." In the next house the piano is heard again, as the curtain falls.*]

TENNESSEE WILLIAMS

The Glass Menagerie

SCENE: *An Alley in St. Louis*

Part I. Preparation for a Gentleman Caller.
Part II. The Gentleman calls.

Time: Now and the Past.

THE CHARACTERS:

AMANDA WINGFIELD (*the mother*)
A little woman of great but confused vitality clinging frantically to another time and place. Her characterization must be carefully created, not copied from type. She is not paranoiac, but her life is paranoia. There is much to admire in Amanda, and as much to love and pity as there is to laugh at. Certainly she has endurance and a kind of heroism, and though her foolishness makes her unwittingly cruel at times, there is tenderness in her slight person.

LAURA WINGFIELD (*her daughter*)
Amanda, having failed to establish contact with reality, continues to live vitally in her illusions, but Laura's situation is even graver. A childhood illness has left her crippled, one leg slightly shorter than the other, and held in a brace. This defect need not be more than suggested on the stage. Stemming from this, Laura's separation increases till she is like a piece of her own glass collection, too exquisitely fragile to move from the shelf.

TOM WINGFIELD (*her son*)

And the narrator of the play. A poet with a job in a warehouse. His nature is not remorseless, but to escape from a trap he has to act without pity.

JIM O'CONNOR (*the gentlman caller*)

A nice, ordinary, young man.

SCENE ONE

The Wingfield apartment is in the rear of the building, one of those vast hive-like conglomerations of cellular living-units that flower as warty growths in over-crowded urban centers of lower middle-class population and are symptomatic of the impulse of this largest and fundamentally enslaved section of American society to avoid fluidity and differentiation and to exist and function as one interfused mass of automatism.

The apartment faces an alley and is entered by a fire escape, a structure whose name is a touch of accidental poetic truth, for all of these huge buildings are always burning with the slow and implacable fires of human desperation. The fire escape is part of what we see — that is, the landing of it and steps descending from it.

The scene is memory and is therefore nonrealistic. Memory takes a lot of poetic license. It omits some details; others are exaggerated, according to the emotional value of the articles it touches, for memory is seated predominantly in the heart. The interior is therefore rather dim and poetic.

At the rise of the curtain, the audience is faced with the dark, grim rear wall of the Wingfield tenement. This building is flanked on both sides by dark, narrow alleys which run into murky canyons of tangled clotheslines, garbage cans, and the sinister latticework of neighboring fire escapes. It is up and down these side alleys that exterior entrances and exits are made during the play. At the end of Tom's opening commentary, the dark tenement wall slowly becomes transparent and reveals the interior of the ground-floor Wingfield apartment.

Nearest the audience is the living room, which also serves as a sleeping room for Laura, the sofa unfolding to make her bed. Just beyond, separated from the living room by a wide arch or second proscenium with transparent faded portieres (or second curtain), is the dining room. In an old-fashioned whatnot in the living room are seen scores of transparent glass animals. A blown-up photograph of the father hangs on the wall of the living room, to the left of the archway. It is the face of a very handsome young man in a doughboy's First World War cap. He is gallantly smiling, ineluctably smiling, as if to say "I will be smiling forever."

Also hanging on the wall, near the photograph, are a typewriter keyboard chart and a Gregg shorthand diagram. An upright typewriter on a small table stands beneath the charts.

The audience hears and sees the opening scene in the dining room through both the transparent fourth wall of the building and the transparent gauze portieres of the dining-room arch. It is during this revealing scene that the fourth wall slowly ascends, out of sight. This transparent exterior wall is not brought down again until the very end of the play, during Tom's final speech.

The narrator is an undisguised convention of the play. He takes whatever license with dramatic convention is convenient to his purposes.

Tom enters, dressed as a merchant sailor, and strolls across to the fire escape. There he stops and lights a cigarette. He addresses the audience.

TOM: Yes, I have tricks in my pocket, I have things up my sleeve. But I am the opposite of a stage magician. He gives you illusion that has the appearance of truth. I give you truth in the pleasant disguise of illusion.

To begin with, I turn back time. I reverse it to that quaint period, the thirties, when the huge middle class of America was matriculating in a school for the blind. Their eyes had failed them, or they had failed their eyes, and so they were having their fingers pressed forcibly down on the fiery Braille alphabet of a dissolving economy.

In Spain there was revolution. Here there was only shouting and confusion. In Spain there was Guernica. Here there were disturbances of labor, sometimes pretty violent, in otherwise peaceful cities such as Chicago, Cleveland, Saint Louis . . . This is the social background of the play.

[*Music begins to play.*]

The play is memory. Being a memory play, it is dimly lighted, it is sentimental, it is not realistic. In memory everything seems to happen to music. That explains the fiddle in the wings.

I am the narrator of the play, and also a character in it. The other characters are my mother, Amanda, my sister, Laura, and a gentleman caller who appears in the final scenes. He is the most realistic character in the play, being an emissary from a world of reality that we were somehow set apart from. But since I have a poet's weakness for symbols, I am using this character also as a symbol; he is the long-delayed but always expected something that we live for.

There is a fifth character in the play who doesn't appear except in this larger-than-life-size photograph over the mantel. This is our father who left us a long time ago. He was a telephone man who fell in love with long distances; he gave up his job with the telephone company and skipped the light fantastic out of town . . . The last we heard of him was a picture postcard from Mazatlan, on the Pacific coast of Mexico, containing a message of two words: "Hello — Goodbye!" and no address.

I think the rest of the play will explain itself. . .

[*Amanda's voice becomes audible through the portieres.*]

[*Legend on screen: "Ou sont les neiges."*]

[*Tom divides the portieres and enters the dining room. Amanda and Laura are seated at a drop-leaf table. Eating is indicated by gestures without food or utensils. Amanda faces the audience. Tom and Laura are seated in profile. The interior has lit up softly and through the scrim we see Amanda and Laura seated at the table.*]

AMANDA [*calling*]: Tom?

TOM: Yes, Mother.

AMANDA: We can't say grace until you come to the table!

TOM: Coming, Mother. [*He bows slightly and withdraws, reappearing a few moments later in his place at the table.*]

AMANDA [*to her son*]: Honey, don't *push* with your *fingers*. If you have to push with something, the thing to push with is a crust of bread. And chew — chew! Animals have secretions in their stomachs which enable them to digest food without mastication, but humans beings are supposed to chew their food before they swallow it down. Eat food leisurely, son, and really enjoy it. A well-cooked meal has lots of delicate flavors that have to be held in the mouth for appreciation. So chew your food and give your salivary glands a chance to function!

[*Tom deliberately lays his imaginary fork down and pushes his chair back from the table.*]

TOM: I haven't enjoyed one bite of this dinner because of your constant directions on how to eat it. It's you that make me rush through meals with your hawklike attention to every bite I take. Sickening — spoils my appetite — all this discussion of — animals' secretion — salivary glands — mastication!

AMANDA [*lightly*]: Temperament like a Metropolitan star!

[*Tom rises and walks toward the living room.*]

You're not excused from the table.

TOM: I'm getting a cigarette.

AMANDA: You smoke too much.

[*Laura rises.*]

LAURA: I'll bring in the blanc mange.

[*Tom remains standing with his cigarette by the portieres.*]

AMANDA: [*rising*]: No, sister, no, sister — you be the lady this time and I'll be the darky.

LAURA: I'm already up.

AMANDA: Resume your seat, little sister — I want you to stay fresh and pretty — for gentlemen callers!

LAURA [*sitting down*]: I'm not expecting any gentlemen callers.

AMANDA [*crossing out to the kitchenette, airly*]: Sometimes they come when they are least expected! Why, I remember one Sunday afternoon in Blue Mountain —.

[*She enters the kitchenette.*]

TOM: I know what's coming!

LAURA: Yes. But let her tell it.

TOM: Again?

LAURA: She loves to tell it.

[*Amanda returns with a bowl of dessert*].

AMANDA: One Sunday afternoon in Blue Mountain — your mother received — *seventeen!* — gentlemen callers! Why, sometimes there weren't chairs enough to accommodate them all. We had to send the nigger over to bring in folding chairs from the parish house.

TOM [*remaining at the portieres*]: How did you entertain those gentlemen callers?

AMANDA: I understood the art of conversation!

TOM: I bet you could talk.

AMANDA: Girls in those days *knew* how to talk, I can tell you.

TOM: Yes?

[*Image on screen:* Amanda as a girl on a porch, greeting callers.]

AMANDA: They knew how to entertain their gentlemen callers. It wasn't enough for a girl to be possessed of a pretty face and a graceful figure — although I wasn't slighted in either respect. She also needed to have a nimble wit and a tongue to meet all occasions.

TOM: What did you talk about?

AMANDA: Things of importance going on in the world! Never anything coarse or common or vulgar.

[*She addresses Tom as though he were seated in the vacant chair at the table though he remains by the portieres. He plays this scene as though reading from a script.*]

My callers were gentlemen — all! Among my callers were some of the most prominent young planters of the Mississippi Delta — planters and sons of planters!

[*Tom motions for music and a spot of light on Amanda. Her eyes lift, her face glows, her voice becomes rich and elegiac.*]

[*Screen legend:* "Ou sont les neiges d'antan?"]

There was young Champ Laughlin who later became vice-president of the Delta Planters Bank. Hadley Stevenson who was drowned in Moon Lake and left his widow one hundred and fifty thousand in Government bonds. There were the Cutrere brothers, Wesley and Bates. Bates was one of my bright particular beaux!

He got in a quarrel with that wild Wainwright boy. They shot it out on the floor of Moon Lake Casino. Bates was shot through the stomach. Died in the ambulance on his way to Memphis. His widow was also well provided-for, came into eight or ten thousand acres, that's all. She married him on the rebound — never loved her — carried my picture on him the night he died! And there was that boy that every girl in the Delta had set her cap for! That beautiful brilliant young Fitzhugh boy from Greene County!

TOM: What did he leave his widow?

AMANDA: He never married! Gracious, you talk as though all of my old admirers had turned up their toes to the daisies!

TOM: Isn't this the first you've mentioned that still survives?

AMANDA: That Fitzhugh boy went North and made a fortune — came to be known as the Wolf of Wall Street! He had the Midas touch, whatever he touched turned to gold! And I could have been Mrs. Duncan J. Fitzhugh, mind you! But — I picked your *father!*

LAURA [*rising*]: Mother, let me clear the table.

AMANDA: No, dear, you go in front and study your typewriter chart. Or practice your shorthand a little. Stay fresh and pretty! — It's almost time for our gentlemen callers to start arriving. [*She flounces girlishly toward the kitchenette*] How many do you suppose we're going to entertain this afternoon?

[*Tom throws down the paper and jumps up with a groan.*]

LAURA [*alone in the dining room*]: I don't believe we're going to receive any, Mother.

AMANDA [*reappearing, airily*]: What? No one — not one? You must be joking! [*Laura nervously echoes her laugh. She slips in a fugitive manner through the half-open portieres and draws them gently behind her. A shaft of very clear light is thrown on her face against the faded tapestry of the curtains. Faintly the music of "The Glass Menagerie" is heard as she continues, lightly:*]

Not one gentleman caller? It can't be true! There must be a flood, there must have been a tornado!

LAURA: It isn't a flood, it's not a tornado, Mother. I'm just not popular like you were in Blue Mountain. . . .

[*Tom utters another groan. Laura glances at him with a faint, apologetic smile. Her voice catches a little:*]

Mother's afraid I'm going to be an old maid.

[*The scene dims out with the "Glass Menagerie" music.*]

SCENE TWO

On the dark stage the screen is lighted with the image of blue roses. *Gradually Laura's figure becomes apparent and the screen goes out. The music subsides.*

Laura is seated in the delicate ivory chair at the small clawfoot table. She wears a dress of soft violet material for a kimono — her hair is tied back from her forehead with a ribbon. She is washing and polishing her collection of glass. Amanda appears on the fire escape steps. At the sound of her ascent, Laura catches her breath, thrusts the bowl of ornaments away, and seats herself stiffly before the diagram of the typewriter keyboard as though it held her spellbound. Something has happened to Amanda. It is written in her face as she climbs to the landing: a look that is grim and hopeless and a little absurd. She has on one of those cheap or imitation velvety-looking cloth coats with imitation fur collar. Her hat is five or six years old, one of those dreadful cloche hats that were worn in the late Twenties, and she is clutching an enormous black patent-leather pocketbook with nickel clasps and initials. This is her full-dress outfit, the one she usually wears to the D.A.R. Before entering she looks through the door. She purses her lips, opens her eyes very wide, rolls them upward and shakes her head. Then she slowly lets herself in the door. Seeing her mother's expression Laura touches her lips with a nervous gesture.

LAURA: Hello, Mother, I was — [*She makes a nervous gesture toward the chart on the wall. Amanda leans against the shut door and stares at Laura with a martyred look.*]

AMANDA: Deception? Deception? [*She slowly removes her hat and gloves, continuing the sweet suffering stare. She lets the hat and gloves fall on the floor — a bit of acting.*]

LAURA [*shakily*]: How was the D.A.R. meeting?

[*Amanda slowly opens her purse and removes a dainty white handkerchief which she shakes out delicately and delicately touches to her lips and nostrils.*]
Didn't you go to the D.A.R. meeting, Mother?

AMANDA [*faintly, almost inaudibly*]: —No. —No. [*then more forcibly:*] I did not have the strength — to go to the D.A.R. In fact, I did not have the courage! I wanted to find a hole in the ground and hide myself in it forever! [*She crosses slowly to the wall and removes the diagram of the typewriter keyboard. She holds it in front of her for a second, staring at it sweetly and sorrowfully — then bites her lips and tears it in two pieces.*]

LAURA [*faintly*]: Why did you do that, Mother?

[*Amanda repeats the same procedure with the chart of the Gregg Alphabet.*]
Why are you —

AMANDA: Why? Why? How old are you, Laura?

LAURA: Mother, you know my age.

AMANDA: I thought that you were an adult; it seems that I was mistaken. [*She crosses slowly to the sofa and sinks down and stares at Laura.*]

LAURA: Please don't stare at me, Mother.

[*Amanda closes her eyes and lowers her head. There is a ten-second pause.*]

AMANDA: What are we going to do, what is going to become of us, what is the future?

[*There is another pause.*]

LAURA: Has something happened, Mother?

[*Amanda draws a long breath, takes out the handkerchief again, goes through the dabbing process.*]

Mother, has — something happened?

AMANDA: I'll be all right in a minute, I'm just bewildered — [*She hesitates.*] — by life. . . .

LAURA: Mother, I wish that you would tell me what's happened!

AMANDA: As you know, I was supposed to be inducted into my office at the D.A.R. this afternoon.

[*Screen image:* A swarm of typewriters.]

But I stopped off at Rubicam's Business College to speak to your teachers about your having a cold and ask them what progress they thought you were making down there.

LAURA: Oh. . . .

AMANDA: I went to the typing instructor and introduced myself as your mother. She didn't know who you were. "Wingfield," she said, "We don't have any such student enrolled at the school!"

I assured her she did, that you had been going to classes since early in January.

"I wonder," she said, "If you could be talking about that terribly shy little girl who dropped out of school after only a few days' attendance?"

"No," I said, "Laura, my daughter, has been going to school every day for the past six weeks!"

"Excuse me," she said. She took the attendance book out and there was your name, unmistakably printed, and all the dates you were absent until they decided that you had dropped out of school.

I still said, "No, there must have been some mistake! There must have been some mix-up in the records!"

And she said, "No — I remember her perfectly now. Her hands shook so that she couldn't hit the right keys! The first time we gave a speed test, she broke down completely — was sick at the stomach and almost had to be carried into the wash room! After that morning she never showed up any more. We phoned the house but never got any answer" — While I was working at Famous-Barr, I suppose, demonstrating those —

[*She indicates a brassiere with her hands.*]

Oh! I felt so weak I could barely keep on my feet! I had to sit down while they got me a glass of water! Fifty dollars' tuition, all of our plans — my hopes and ambitions for you — just gone up the spout, just gone up the spout like that.

[*Laura draws a long breath and gets awkwardly to her feet. She crosses to the*

Victrola and winds it up.]
What are you doing?

LAURA: Oh! [*She releases the handle and returns to her seat.*]

AMANDA: Laura, where have you been going when you've gone out pretending that you were going to business college?

LAURA: I've just been going out walking.

AMANDA: That's not true.

LAURA: It is. I just went walking.

AMANDA: Walking? Walking? In winter? Deliberately courting pneumonia in that light coat? Where did you walk to, Laura?

LAURA: All sorts of places — mostly in the park.

AMANDA: Even after you'd started catching that cold?

LAURA: It was the lesser of two evils, Mother.

[*Screen image:* Winter scene in a park.]

I couldn't go back there. I — threw up — on the floor!

AMANDA: From half past seven till after five every day you mean to tell me you walked around in the park, because you wanted to make me think that you were still going to Rubicam's Business College?

LAURA: It wasn't as bad as it sounds. I went inside places to get warmed up.

AMANDA: Inside where?

LAURA: I went in the art museum and the bird houses at the Zoo. I visited the penguins every day! Sometimes I did without lunch and went to the movies. Lately I've been spending most of my afternoons in the Jewel Box, that big glass house where they raise the tropical flowers.

AMANDA: You did all this to deceive me, just for deception? [*Laura looks down.*] Why?

LAURA: Mother, when you're disappointed, you get that awful suffering look on your face, like the picture of Jesus' mother in the museum!

AMANDA: Hush!

LAURA: I couldn't face it.

[*There is a pause. A whisper of strings is heard. Legend on screen:* "The Crust of Humility."]

AMANDA [*hopelessly fingering the huge pocketbook*]: So what are we going to do the rest of our lives? Stay home and watch the parades go by? Amuse ourselves with the glass menagerie, darling? Eternally play those worn-out phonograph records your father left as a painful reminder of him? We won't have a business career — we've given that up because it gave us nervous indigestion! [*She laughs wearily.*] What is there left but dependency all our lives? I know so well what becomes of unmarried women who aren't prepared to occupy a position. I've seen such pitiful cases in the South — barely tolerated spinsters living upon the grudging patronage of sister's husband or brother's wife! — stuck away in some little mousetrap of a room — encouraged by one in-law to visit another — little

birdlike women without any nest — eating the crust of humility all their life!
Is that the future that we've mapped out for ourselves? I swear it's the only
alternative I can think of! [*She pauses.*] It isn't a very pleasant alternative, is it!
[*She pauses again.*] Of course — some girls *do marry.*

[*Laura twists her hands nervously.*]
Haven't you ever liked some boy?

LAURA: Yes, I liked one once. [*She rises.*] I came across his picture a while ago.

AMANDA [*with some interest*]: He gave you his picture?

LAURA: No, it's in the yearbook.

AMANDA [disappointed]: Oh — a high school boy.

[*Screen image:* Jim as the high school hero bearing a silver cup.]

LAURA: Yes. His name was Jim. [*She lifts the heavy annual from the claw-foot
table.*] Here he is in *The Pirates of Penzance.*

AMANDA [*absently*]: The what?

LAURA: The operetta the senior class put on. He had a wonderful voice and we
sat across the aisle from each other Mondays, Wednesdays and Fridays in the Aud.
Here he is with the silver cup for debating! See his grin?

AMANDA [*absently*]: He must have had a jolly disposition.

LAURA: He used to call me — Blue Roses.

[*Screen image:* Blue roses.]

AMANDA: Why did he call you such a name as that?

LAURA: When I had that attack of pleurosis — he asked me what was the matter
when I came back. I said pleurosis — he thought that I said Blue Roses! So that's
what he always called me after that. Whenever he saw me, he'd holler, "Hello,
Blue Roses!" I didn't care for the girl that he went out with. Emily Meisenbach.
Emily was the best-dressed girl at Soldan. She never struck me, though, as being
sincere . . . It says in the Personal Section — they're engaged. That's — six years
ago! They must be married by now.

AMANDA: Girls that aren't cut out for business careers usually wind up married
to some nice man. [*She gets up with a spark of revival.*] Sister, that's what you'll
do!

[*Laura utters a startled, doubtful laugh. She reaches quickly for a piece of glass.*]

LAURA: But, Mother —

AMANDA: Yes? [*She goes over to the photograph.*]

LAURA [*in a tone of frightened apology*]: I'm — crippled!

AMANDA: Nonsense! Laura, I've told you never, never to use that word. Why,
you're not crippled, you just have a little defect — hardly noticeable, even! When
people have some slight disadvantage like that, they cultivate other things to make
up for it — develop charm — and vivacity — and — *charm!* That's all you have to
do! [*She turns again to the photograph.*] One thing your father had *plenty of* —
was *charm!*

[*The scene fades out with music.*]

SCENE THREE

Legend on screen: "After the fiasco —"
Tom speaks from the fire escape landing.

TOM: After the fiasco at Rubicam's Business College, the idea of getting a gentleman caller for Laura began to play a more and more important part in Mother's calculations. It became an obsession. Like some archetype of the universal unconscious, the image of the gentleman caller haunted our small apartment. . . .

[*Screen image:* A young man at the door of a house with flowers.]

An evening at home rarely passed without some allusion to this image, this specter, this hope. . . . Even when he wasn't mentioned, his presence hung in Mother's preoccupied look and in my sister's frightened, apologetic manner — hung like a sentence passed upon the Wingfields!

Mother was a woman of action as well as words. She began to take logical steps in the planned direction. Late that winter and in the early spring — realizing that extra money would be needed to properly feather the nest and plume the bird — she conducted a vigorous campaign on the telephone, roping in subscribers to one of those magazines for matrons called *The Homemaker's Companion,* the type of journal that features the serialized sublimations of ladies of letters who think in terms of delicate cuplike breasts, slim, tapering waists, rich, creamy thighs, eyes like wood smoke in autumn, fingers that soothe and caress like strains of music, bodies as powerful as Etruscan sculpture.

[*Screen image:* The cover of a glamor magazine.]

[*Amanda enters with the telephone on a long extension cord. She is spotlighted in the dim stage.*]

AMANDA: Ida Scott? This is Amanda Wingfield! We *missed* you at the D.A.R. last Monday! I said to myself: She's probably suffering with that sinus condition! How is that sinus condition?

Horrors! Heaven have mercy! — You're a Christian martyr, yes, that's what you are, a Christian martyr.

Well, I just now happened to notice that your subscription to the *Companion's* about to expire! Yes, it expires with the next issue, honey! — just when that wonderful new serial by Bessie Mae Hopper is getting off to such an exciting start. Oh, honey, it's something that you can't miss! You remember how *Gone with the Wind* took everybody by storm? You simply couldn't go out if you hadn't read it. All everybody *talked* was Scarlett O'Hara. Well, this is a book that critics already compare to *Gone with the Wind.* It's the *Gone with the Wind* of the post-World-War generation! — What? — Burning? — Oh, honey, don't let them burn, go take a look in the oven and I'll hold the wire! Heavens — I think she's hung up!

[*The scene dims out.*]

[*Legend on screen:* "You think I'm in love with Continental Shoemakers?"]

[*Before the lights come up again, the violent voices of Tom and Amanda are heard. They are quarreling behind the portieres. In front of them stands Laura with clenched hands and panicky expression. A clear pool of light is on her figure throughout this scene.*]

TOM: What in Christ's name am I —

AMANDA [*shrilly*]: Don't you use that —

TOM: — supposed to do!

AMANDA: — expression! Not in my —

TOM: Ohhh!

AMANDA: — presence! Have you gone out of your senses?

TOM: I have, that's true, *driven* out!

AMANDA: What is the matter with you, you — big — big — IDIOT!

TOM: Look! — I've got *no thing,* no single thing —

AMANDA: Lower your voice!

TOM: — in my life here that I can call my OWN! Everything is —

AMANDA: Stop that shouting!

TOM: Yesterday you confiscated my books! You had the nerve to —

AMANDA: I took that horrible novel back to the library — yes! That hideous book by that insane Mr. Lawrence.

[*Tom laughs wildly.*]

I cannot control the output of diseased minds or people who cater to them —

[*Tom laughs still more wildly.*]

BUT I WON'T ALLOW SUCH FILTH BROUGHT INTO MY HOUSE! No, no, no, no, no!

TOM: House, house! Who pays rent on it, who makes a slave of himself to —

AMANDA [*fairly screeching*]: Don't you DARE to —

TOM: No, no, *I* mustn't say things! *I've* got to just —

AMANDA: Let me tell you —

TOM: I don't want to hear any more!

[*He tears the portieres open. The dining-room area is lit with a turgid smoky red glow. Now we see Amanda; her hair is in metal curlers and she is wearing a very old bathrobe, much too large for her slight figure, a relic of the faithless Mr. Wingfield. The upright typewriter now stands on the drop-leaf table, along with a wild disarray of manuscripts. The quarrel was probably precipitated by Amanda's interruption of Tom's creative labor. A chair lies overthrown on the floor. Their gesticulating shadows are cast on the ceiling by the fiery glow.*]

AMANDA: You *will* hear more, you —

TOM: No, I won't hear more, I'm going out!

AMANDA: You come right back in —

TOM: Out, out, out! Because I'm —

AMANDA: Come back here, Tom Wingfield! I'm not through talking to you!

TOM: Oh, go —

LAURA [*desperately*]: — Tom!

AMANDA: You're going to listen, and no more insolence from you! I'm at the end of my patience!

[*He comes back toward her.*]

TOM: What do you think I'm at? Aren't I supposed to have any patience to reach the end of, Mother? I know, I know. It seems unimportant to you, what I'm *doing* — what I *want* to do — having a little *difference* between them! You don't think that —

AMANDA: I think you've been doing things that you're ashamed of. That's why you act like this. I don't believe that you go every night to the movies. Nobody goes to the movies night after night. Nobody in their right minds goes to the movies as often as you pretend to. People don't go to the movies at nearly midnight, and movies don't let out at two A.M. Come in stumbling. Muttering to yourself like a maniac! You get three hours' sleep and then go to work. Oh, I can picture the way you're doing down there. Moping, doping, because you're in no condition.

TOM [*wildly*]: No, I'm in no condition!

AMANDA: What right have you got to jeopardize your job? Jeopardize the security of us all? How do you think we'd manage if you were —

TOM: Listen! You think I'm crazy about the *warehouse*? [*He bends fiercely toward her slight figure*] You think I'm in love with the Continental Shoemakers? You think I want to spend fifty-five *years* down there in that — *celotex interior!* with — *fluorescent* — *tubes!* Look! I'd rather somebody picked up a crowbar and battered out my brains — than go back mornings! I *go!* Every time you come in yelling that Goddamn *"Rise and Shine!" "Rise and Shine!"* I say to myself, "How *lucky dead* people are!" But I get up. I *go!* For sixty-five dollars a month I give up all that I dream of doing and being *ever!* And you say self — *self's* all I ever think of. Why, listen, if self is what I thought of, Mother, I'd be where he is — GONE! [*He points to his father's picture.*] As far as the system of transportation reaches! *He starts past her. She grabs his arm.*] Don't grab at me, Mother!

AMANDA: Where are you going?

TOM: I'm going to the *movies!*

AMANDA: I don't believe that lie!

[*Tom crouches toward her, overtowering her tiny figure. She backs away, gasping.*]

TOM: I'm going to opium dens! Yes, opium dens, dens of vice and criminals' hangouts, Mother. I've joined the Hogan Gang, I'm a hired assassin, I carry a tommy gun in a violin case! I run a string of cat houses in the Valley! They call me Killer, Killer Wingfield, I'm leading a double-life, a simple, honest warehouse worker by day, by night a dynamic *czar* of the *underworld, Mother.* I go to gambling casinos, I spin away fortunes on the roulette table! I wear a patch over one eye and a false mustache, sometimes I put on green whiskers. On those occasions they call me — *El Diablo!* Oh, I could tell you many things to make you sleepless! My enemies plan to dynamite this place. They're going to blow us all sky-high some night! I'll be glad, very happy, and so will you! You'll go up, up on a broomstick, over Blue Mountain with seventeen gentlemen callers! You ugly — babbling old — *witch. . . .*

[He goes through a series of violent, clumsy movements, seizing his overcoat, lunging to the door, pulling it fiercely open. The women watch him, aghast. His arm catches in the sleeve of the coat as he struggles to pull it on. For a moment he is pinioned by the bulky garment. With an outraged groan he tears the coat off again, splitting the shoulder of it, and hurls it across the room. It strikes against the shelf of Laura's glass collection, and there is a tinkle of shattering glass. Laura cries out as if wounded.]

[Music.]

[Screen legend: "The Glass Menagerie."*]*

LAURA *[shrilly]: My glass!* — menagerie. . . . *[She covers her face and turns away.]*

[But Amanda is still stunned and stupefied by the "ugly witch" so that she barely notices this occurrence. Now she recovers her speech.]

AMANDA *[in an awful voice]*: I won't speak to you — until you apologize!

[She crosses through the portieres and draws them together behind her. Tom is left with Laura. Laura clings weakly to the mantel with her face averted. Tom stares at her stupidly for a moment. Then he crosses to the shelf. He drops awkwardly on this knees to collect the fallen glass, glancing at Laura as if he would speak but couldn't.]

["The Glass Menagerie" music steals in as the scene dims out.]

SCENE FOUR

The interior of the apartment is dark. There is a faint light in the alley. A deep-voiced bell in a church is tolling the hour of five.

Tom appears at the top of the alley. After each solemn boom of the bell in the tower, he shakes a little noisemaker or rattle as if to express the tiny spasm of man in contrast to the sustained power and dignity of the Almighty. This and the unsteadiness of his advance make it evident that he has been drinking. As he climbs the few steps to the fire escape landing light steals up inside. Laura appears in the front room in a nightdress. She notices that Tom's bed is empty. Tom fishes in his pockets for his door key, removing a motley assortment of articles in the search, including a shower of movie ticket stubs and an empty bottle. At last he finds the key, but just as he is about to insert it, it slips from his fingers. He strikes a match and crouches below the door.

TOM [*bitterly*]: One crack — and it falls through!
[*Laura opens the door.*]
LAURA: Tom! Tom, what are you doing?
TOM: Looking for a door key.
LAURA: Where have you been all this time?
TOM: I have been to the movies.
LAURA: All this time at the movies?
TOM: There was a very long program. There was a Garbo picture and a Mickey Mouse and a travelogue and a newsreel and a preview of coming attractions. And there was an organ solo and a collection for the Milk Fund — simultaneously — which ended up in a terrible fight between a fat lady and an usher!
LAURA [*innocently*]: Did you have to stay through everything?
TOM: Of course! And, oh, I forgot! There was a big stage show! The headliner on this stage show was Malvolio the Magician. He performed wonderful tricks, many of them, such as pouring water back and forth between pitchers. First it turned to wine and then it turned to beer and then it turned to whisky. I know it was whisky it finally turned into because he needed somebody to come up out of the audience to help him, and I came up — both shows! It was Kentucky Straight Bourbon. A very generous fellow, he gave souvenirs. [*He pulls from his back pocket a shimmering rainbow-colored scarf.*] He gave me this. This is his magic scarf. You can have it, Laura. You wave it over a canary cage and you get a bowl of goldfish. You wave it over the goldfish bowl and they fly away canaries. . . . But the wonderfullest trick of all was the coffin trick. We nailed him into a coffin and he got out of the coffin without removing one nail. [*He has come inside.*] There is a trick that would come in handy for me — get me out of this two-by-four situation! [*He flops onto the bed and starts removing his shoes.*]
LAURA: Tom — shhh!
TOM: What're you shushing me for?
LAURA: You'll wake up Mother.
TOM: Goody, goody! Pay 'er back for all those "Rise an' Shines." [*He lies down, groaning.*] You know it don't take much intelligence to get yourself into a nailed-up coffin, Laura. But who in hell ever got himself out of one without removing one nail?
[*As if in answer the father's grinning photograph lights up. The scene dims out.*]
[*Immediately following, the church bell is heard striking six. At the sixth stroke the alarm clock goes off in Amanda's room, and after a few moments we hear her calling: "Rise and Shine! Rise and Shine! Laura, go tell your brother to rise and shine!"*]

TOM [*sitting up slowly*]: I'll rise — but I won't shine.

[*The light increases.*]

AMANDA: Laura, tell your brother his coffee is ready.

[*Laura slips into the front room.*]

LAURA: Tom! — It's nearly seven. Don't make Mother nervous.

[*He stares at her stupidly.*]

[*beseechingly:*] Tom, speak to Mother this morning. Make up with her, apologize, speak to her!

TOM: She won't to me. It's her that started not speaking.

LAURA: If you just say you're sorry she'll start speaking.

TOM: Her not speaking — is that such a *tragedy*?

LAURA: Please — please!

AMANDA [*calling from the kitchenette*]: Laura, are you going to do what I asked you to do, or do I have to get dressed and go out myself?

LAURA: Going, going — soon as I get on my coat!

[*She pulls on a shapeless felt hat with a nervous, jerky movement, pleadingly glancing at Tom. She rushes awkwardly for her coat. The coat is one of Amanda's, inaccurately made-over, the sleeves too short for Laura.*]

Butter and what else?

AMANDA [*entering from the kitchenette*]: Just butter. Tell them to charge it.

LAURA: Mother, they make such faces when I do that.

AMANDA: Sticks and stones can break our bones, but the expression on Mr. Garfinkel's face won't harm us! Tell your brother his coffee is getting cold.

LAURA [*at the door*]: Do what I asked you, will you, will you, Tom?

[*He looks sullenly away.*]

AMANDA: Laura, go now or just don't go at all!

LAURA [*rushing out*]: Going — going!

[*A second later she cries out. Tom springs up and crosses to the door. Tom opens the door.*]

TOM: Laura?

LAURA: I'm all right. I slipped, but I'm all right.

AMANDA [*peering anxiously after her*]: If anyone breaks a leg on those fire-escape steps, the landlord ought to be sued for every cent he possesses! [*She shuts the door. Now she remembers she isn't speaking to Tom and returns to the other room.*]

[*As Tom comes listlessly for his coffee, she turns her back to him and stands rigidly facing the window on the gloomy gray vault of the areaway. Its light on her face with its aged but childish features is cruelly sharp, satirical as a Daumier print.*]

[*The music of "Ave Maria," is heard softly.*]

[*Tom glances sheepishly but sullenly at her averted figure and slumps at the table. The coffee is scalding hot; he sips it and gasps and spits it back in the cup. At his gasp, Amanda catches her breath and half turns. Then she catches herself and turns back to the window. Tom blows on his coffee, glancing sidewise at his mother. She clears her throat. Tom clears his. He starts to rise, sinks back down again, scratches his head, clears his throat again. Amanda coughs. Tom raises his cup in both hands to blow on it, his eyes staring over the rim of it at his mother for several moments. Then he slowly sets the cup down and awkwardly and hesitantly rises from the chair.*]

TOM [*hoarsely*]: Mother. I — I apologize, Mother.

[*Amanda draws a quick, shuddering breath. Her face works grotesquely. She breaks into childlike tears.*]

I'm sorry for what I said, for everything that I said, I didn't mean it.

AMANDA [*sobbingly*]: My devotion has made me a witch and so I make myself hateful to my children!

TOM: *No, you don't.*

AMANDA: I worry so much, don't sleep, it makes me nervous!

TOM [*gently*]: I understand that.

AMANDA: I've had to put up a solitary battle all these years. But you're my right-hand bower! Don't fall down, don't fail!

TOM [*gently*]: I try, Mother.

AMANDA [*with great enthusiasm*]: Try and you will *succeed!* [*The notion makes her breathless.*] Why, you — you're just *full* of natural endowments! Both of my children — they're *unusual* children! Don't you think I know it? I'm so — *proud!* Happy and — feel I've — so much to be thankful for but — promise me one thing, son!

TOM: What, Mother?

AMANDA: Promise, son, you'll — never be a drunkard!

TOM [*turns to her grinning*]: I will never be a drunkard, Mother.

AMANDA: That's what frightened me so, that you'd be drinking! Eat a bowl of Purina!

TOM: Just coffee, Mother.

AMANDA: Shredded wheat biscuit?

TOM: No. No, Mother, just coffee.

AMANDA: You can't put in a day's work on an empty stomach. You've got ten minutes — don't gulp! Drinking too-hot liquids makes cancer of the stomach. . . . Put cream in.

TOM: No, thank you.

AMANDA: To cool it.

TOM: No! No, thank you, I want it black.

AMANDA: I know, but it's not good for you. We have to do all that we can to build ourselves up. In these trying times we live in, all that we have to cling to is — each other. . . . That's why it's so important to — Tom, I — I sent out your sister so I could discuss something with you. If you hadn't spoken I would have spoken to you. [*She sits down.*]

TOM [*gently*]: What is it, Mother, that you want to discuss?

AMANDA: *Laura!*

[*Tom puts his cup down slowly.*]

[*Legend on screen:* "Laura." *Music: "The Glass Menagerie."*]

TOM: — Oh. — Laura . . .

AMANDA [*touching his sleeve*]: You know how Laura is. So quiet but — still water runs deep! She notices things and I think she — broods about them.

[*Tom looks up.*]

A few days ago I came in and she was crying.

TOM: What about?

AMANDA: You.

TOM: Me?

AMANDA: She has an idea that you're not happy here.

TOM: What gave her that idea?

AMANDA: What gives her any idea? However, you do act strangely. I — I'm not criticizing, understand *that!* I know your ambitions do not lie in the warehouse, that like everybody in the whole wide world — you've had to — make sacrifices, but — Tom — Tom — life's not easy, it calls for — Spartan endurance! There's so many things in my heart that I cannot describe to you! I've never told you but I — *loved* your father. . . .

TOM [*gently*]: I know that, Mother.

AMANDA: And you — when I see you taking after his ways! Staying out late — and — well, you *had* been drinking the night you were in that — terrifying condition! Laura says that you hate the apartment and that you go out nights to get away from it! Is that true, Tom?

TOM: No. You say that there's so much in your heart that you can't describe to me. That's true of me, too. There's so much in my heart that I can't describe to *you!* So let's respect each other's —

AMANDA: But, why — *why,* Tom — are you always so *restless?* Where do you *go* to, nights?

TOM: I — go to the movies.

AMANDA: Why do you go to movies so much, Tom?

TOM: I go to the movies because — I like adventure. Adventure is something I don't have much of at work, so I go to the movies.

AMANDA: But, Tom, you go to the movies *entirely* too *much!*

TOM: I like a lot of adventure.

[*Amanda looks baffled, then hurt. As the familiar inquisition resumes, Tom becomes hard and impatient again. Amanda slips back into her querulous attitude toward him.*]

[*Image on screen: A sailing vessel with Jolly Roger.*]

AMANDA: Most young men find adventure in their careers.

TOM: Then most young men are not employed in a warehouse.

AMANDA: The world is full of young men employed in warehouses and offices and factories.

TOM: Do all of them find adventure in their careers?

AMANDA: They do or they do without it! Not everybody has a craze for adventure.

TOM: Man is by instinct a lover, a hunter, a fighter, and none of those instincts are given much play at the warehouse!

AMANDA: Man is by instinct! Don't quote instinct to me! Instinct is something that people have got away from! It belongs to animals! Christian adults don't want it!

TOM: What do Christian adults want, then, Mother?

AMANDA: Superior things! Things of the mind and the spirit! Only animals have to satisfy instincts! Surely your aims are somewhat higher than theirs! Than monkeys — pigs —

TOM: I reckon they're not.

AMANDA: You're joking. However, that isn't what I wanted to discuss.

TOM [*rising*]: I haven't much time.

AMANDA [*pushing his shoulders*]: Sit down.

TOM: You want me to punch in red at the warehouse, Mother?

AMANDA: You have five minutes. I want to talk about Laura.

[*Screen legend:* "Plans and Provisions."]

TOM: All right! What about Laura?

AMANDA: We have to be making some plans and provisions for her. She's older than you, two years, and nothing has happened. She just drifts along doing nothing. It frightens me terribly how she just drifts along.

TOM: I guess she's the type that people call home girls.

AMANDA: There's no such type, and if there is, it's a pity! That is unless the home is hers, with a husband!

TOM: What?

AMANDA: Oh, I can see the handwriting on the wall as plain as I see the nose in front of my face! It's terrifying! More and more you remind me of your father! He was out all hours without explanation! — Then *left! Goodbye!* And me with the bag to hold. I saw that letter you got from the Merchant Marine. I know what you're dreaming of. I'm not standing here blindfolded. [*She pauses.*] Very well, then. Then *do* it! But not till there's somebody to take your place.

TOM: What do you mean?

AMANDA: I mean that as soon as Laura has got somebody to take care of her, married, a home of her own, independent — why, then you'll be free to go wherever you please, on land, on sea, whichever way the wind blows you! But until that time you've got to look out for your sister. I don't say me because I'm old and don't matter! I say for your sister because she's young and dependent.

I put her in business college — a dismal failure! Frightened her so it made her sick at the stomach. I took her over to the Young People's League at the church. Another fiasco. She spoke to nobody, nobody spoke to her. Now all she does is fool with those pieces of glass and play those worn-out records. What kind of a life is that for a girl to lead?

TOM: What can I do about it?

AMANDA: Overcome selfishness! Self, self, self is all that you ever think of!

[*Tom springs up and crosses to get his coat. It is ugly and bulky. He pulls on a cap with earmuffs.*]

Where is your muffler? Put your wool muffler on!

[*He snatches it angrily from the closet, tosses it around his neck and pulls both ends tight.*]

Tom! I haven't said what I had in mind to ask you.

TOM: I'm too late to —

AMANDA [*catching his arm — very importunately; then shyly*]: Down at the warehouse, aren't there some — nice young men?

TOM: No!

AMANDA: There *must* be — *some*. . .

TOM: Mother — [*He gestures.*]

AMANDA: Find out one that's clean-living — doesn't drink and ask him out for sister!

TOM: What?

AMANDA: For *sister!* To *meet!* Get *acquainted!*

TOM [*stamping to the door*]: Oh, my *go-osh!*

AMANDA: Will you?

[*He opens the door. She says, imploringly:*]

Will you?

[*He starts down the fire escape.*]

Will you? *Will* you, dear?

TOM [*calling back*]: Yes!

[*Amanda closes the door hesitantly and with a troubled but faintly hopeful expression.*]

[*Screen image: The cover of a glamor magazine.*]

[*The spotlight picks up Amanda at the phone.*]

AMANDA: Ella Cartwright? This is Amanda Wingfield! How are you honey? How is that kidney condition?

[*There is a five-second pause.*]

Horrors!

[*There is another pause.*]

You're a Christian martyr, yes, honey, that's what you are, a Christian martyr! Well, I just now happened to notice in my little red book that your subscription to the *Companion* has just run out! I knew that you wouldn't want to miss out on the wonderful serial starting in this new issue. It's by Bessie Mae Hopper, the first thing she's written since *Honeymoon for Three*. Wasn't that a strange and interesting story? Well, this one is even lovelier, I believe. It has a sophisticated, society background. It's all about the horsey set on Long Island!

[*The light fades out.*]

SCENE FIVE

Legend on the screen: "Annunciation."

Music is heard as the light slowly comes on.

It is early dusk of a spring evening. Supper has just been finished in the Wingfield apartment. Amanda and Laura, in light colored dresses, are removing dishes from the table in the dining room, which is shadowy, their movements formalized almost as a dance or ritual, their moving forms as pale and silent as moths. Tom, in white shirt and trousers, rises from the table and crosses toward the fire escape.

AMANDA [*as he passes her*]: Son, will you do me a favor?

TOM: What?

AMANDA: Comb your hair! You look so pretty when your hair is combed.

[*Tom slouches on the sofa with the evening paper. Its enormous headline reads: "Franco Triumphs."*]

There is only one respect in which I would like you to emulate your father.

TOM: What respect is that?

AMANDA: The care he always took of his appearance. He never allowed himself to look untidy.

[*He throws down the paper and crosses to the fire escape.*]

Where are you going?

TOM: I'm going out to smoke.

AMANDA: You smoke too much. A pack a day at fifteen cents a pack. How much would that amount to in a month? Thirty times fifteen is how much, Tom? Figure it out and you will be astounded at what you could save. Enough to give you a night-school course in accounting at Washington U.! Just think what a wonderful thing that would be for you, son!

[*Tom is unmoved by the thought.*]

TOM: I'd rather smoke. [*He steps out on the landing, letting the screen door slam.*]

AMANDA [*sharply*]: I know! That's the tragedy of it. . . . [*Alone, she turns to look at her husband's picture.*]

[*Dance music: "The World Is Waiting for the Sunrise!"*]

TOM [*to the audience*]: Across the alley from us was the Paradise Dance Hall.

On evenings in spring the windows and doors were open and the music came outdoors. Sometimes the lights were turned out except for a large glass sphere that hung from the ceiling. It would turn slowly about and filter the dusk with delicate rainbow colors. Then the orchestra played a waltz or a tango, something that had a slow and sensuous rhythm. Couples would come outside, to the relative privacy of the alley. You could see them kissing behind ash pits and telephone poles. This was the compensation for lives that passed like mine, without any change or adventure. Adventure and change were imminent in this year. They were waiting around the corner for all these kids. Suspended in the mist over Berchtesgaden, caught in the folds of Chamberlain's umbrella. In Spain there was Guernica! But here there was only hot swing music and liquor, dance halls, bars, and movies, and sex that hung in the gloom like a chandelier and flooded the world with brief, deceptive rainbows. . . . All the world was waiting for bombardments!

[*Amanda turns from the picture and comes outside.*]

AMANDA [*sighing*]: A fire escape landing's a poor excuse for a porch. [*She spreads a newspaper on a step and sits down, gracefully and demurely as if she were settling into a swing on a Mississippi veranda.*] What are you looking at?

TOM: The moon.

AMANDA: Is there a moon this evening?

TOM: It's rising over Garfinkel's Delicatessen.

AMANDA: So it is! A little silver slipper of a moon. Have you made a wish on it yet?

TOM: Um-hum.

AMANDA: What did you wish for?

TOM: That's a secret.

AMANDA: A secret, huh? Well, I won't tell mine either. I will be just as mysterious as you.

TOM: I bet I can guess what yours is.

AMANDA: Is my head so transparent?

TOM: You're not a sphinx.

AMANDA: No, I don't have secrets. I'll tell you what I wished for on the moon. Success and happiness for my precious children! I wish for that whenever there's a moon, and when there isn't a moon, I wish for it, too.

TOM: I thought perhaps you wished for a gentleman caller.

AMANDA: Why do you say that?

TOM: Don't you remember asking me to fetch one?

AMANDA: I remember suggesting that it would be nice for your sister if you brought home some nice young man from the warehouse. I think that I've made that suggestion more than once.

TOM: Yes, you have made it repeatedly.

AMANDA: Well?

TOM: We are going to have one.

AMANDA: *What?*

TOM: A gentleman caller!

[*The annunication is celebrated with music.*]

[*Amanda rises.*]

[*Image on screen:* A caller with a bouquet.]

AMANDA: You mean you have asked some nice young man to come over?

TOM: Yep. I've asked him to dinner.

AMANDA: You really did?

TOM: I did!

AMANDA: You did, and did he — *accept?*

TOM: He did!

AMANDA: Well, well — well, well! That's — lovely!

TOM: I thought that you would be pleased.

AMANDA: It's definite then?

TOM: Very definite.

AMANDA: Soon?

TOM: Very soon.

AMANDA: For heaven's sake, stop putting on and tell me some things, will you?

TOM: What things do you want me to tell you?

AMANDA: *Naturally* I would like to know when he's *coming!*

TOM: He's coming tomorrow.

AMANDA: *Tomorrow?*

TOM: Yep. Tomorrow.

AMANDA: But, Tom!

TOM: Yes, Mother?

AMANDA: Tomorrow gives me no time!

TOM: Time for what?

AMANDA: Preparations! Why didn't you phone me at once, as soon as you asked him, the minute that he accepted? Then, don't you see, I could have been getting ready!

TOM: You don't have to make any fuss.

AMANDA: Oh, Tom, Tom, Tom, of course I have to make a fuss! I want things nice, not sloppy! Not thrown together. I'll certainly have to do some fast thinking, won't I?

TOM: I don't see why you have to think at all.

AMANDA: You just don't know. We can't have a gentleman caller in a pigsty! All my wedding silver has to be polished, the monogrammed table linen ought to be laundered! The windows have to be washed and fresh curtains put up. And how about clothes! We have to *wear* something, don't we?

TOM: Mother, this boy is no one to make a fuss over!

AMANDA: Do you realize he's the first young man we've introduced to your sister? It's terrible, dreadful, disgraceful that poor little sister has never received a single gentleman caller! Tom, come inside! [*She opens the screen door.*]

TOM: What for?

AMANDA: I want to ask you some things.

TOM: If you're going to make such a fuss, I'll call it off, I'll tell him not to come!

AMANDA: You certainly won't do anything of the kind. Nothing offends people worse than broken engagements. It simply means I'll have to work like a Turk! We won't be brilliant, but we will pass inspection. Come on inside.

[*Tom follows her inside, groaning.*]

Sit down.

TOM: Any particular place you would like me to sit?

AMANDA: Thank heavens I've got that new sofa! I'm, also making payments on a floor lamp I'll have sent out! And put the chintz covers on, they'll brighten things up! Of course I'd hoped to have these walls re-papered. . . . What is the young man's name?

TOM: His name is O'Connor.

AMANDA: That, of course, means fish — tomorrow is Friday! I'll have that salmon loaf — with Durkee's dressing! What does he do? He works at the warehouse?

TOM: Of course! How else would I —

AMANDA: Tom, he — doesn't drink?

TOM: Why do you ask me that?

AMANDA: Your father *did!*

TOM: Don't get started on that!

AMANDA: He *does* drink, then?

TOM: Not that I know of!

AMANDA: Make sure, be certain! The last thing I want for my daughter's a boy who drinks!

TOM: Aren't you being a little premature? Mr. O'Connor has not yet appeared on the scene!

AMANDA: But will tomorrow. To meet your sister, and what do I know about his character? Nothing! Old maids are better off than wives of drunkards!

TOM: Oh, my God!

AMANDA: Be still!

TOM [*leaning forward to whisper*]: Lots of fellows meet girls whom they don't marry!

AMANDA: Oh, talk sensibly, Tom — and don't be sarcastic! [*She has gotten a hairbrush.*]

TOM: What are you doing?

AMANDA: I'm brushing that cowlick down! [*She attacks his hair with the brush.*] What is this young man's position at the warehouse?

TOM [*submitting grimly to the brush and the interrogation*]: This young man's position is that of a shipping clerk, Mother.

AMANDA: Sounds to me like a fairly responsible job, the sort of job *you* would be in if you just had more *get up*. What is his salary? Have you any idea?

TOM: I would judge it to be approximately eighty-five dollars a month.

AMANDA: Well — not princely, but —

TOM: Twenty more than I make.

AMANDA: Yes, how well I know! But for a family man, eight-five dollars a month is not much more than you can just get by on. . . .

TOM: Yes, but Mr. O'Connor is not a family man.

AMANDA: He might be, mightn't he? Some time in the future?

TOM: I see. Plans and provisions.

AMANDA: You are the only young man that I know of who ignores the fact that the future becomes the present, the present the past, and the past turns into everlasting regret if you don't plan for it!

TOM: I will think that over and see what I can make of it.

AMANDA: Don't be supercilious with your mother! Tell me some more about this — what do you call him?

TOM: James D. O'Connor. The D. is for Delaney.

AMANDA: Irish on *both* sides! *Gracious!* And doesn't drink?

TOM: Shall I call him up and ask him right this minute?

AMANDA: The only way to find out about those things is to make discreet inquiries at the proper moment. When I was a girl in Blue Mountain and it was suspected that a young man drank, the girl whose attentions he had been receiving, if any girl *was,* would sometimes speak to the minister of his church, or rather her father would if her father was living, and sort of feel him out on the young man's character. That is the way such things are discreetly handled to keep a young woman from making a tragic mistake!

TOM: Then how did you happen to make a tragic mistake?

AMANDA: That innocent look of your father's had everyone fooled! He *smiled —* the world was *enchanted!* No girl can do worse than put herself at the mercy of a handsome appearance! I hope that Mr. O'Connor is not too good-looking.

TOM: No, he's not too good-looking. He's covered with freckles and hasn't too much of a nose.

AMANDA: He's not right-down homely, though?

TOM: Not right-down homely. Just medium homely, I'd say.

AMANDA: Character's what to look for in a man.

TOM: That's what I've always said, Mother.

AMANDA: You've never said anything of the kind and I suspect you would never give it a thought.

TOM: Don't be so suspicious of me.

AMANDA: At least I hope he's the type that's up and coming.

TOM: I think he really goes in for self-improvement.

AMANDA: What reason have you to think so?

TOM: He goes to night school.

AMANDA [*beaming*]: Splendid! What does he do, I mean study?

TOM: Radio engineering and public speaking!

AMANDA: Then he has visions of being advanced in the world! Any young man who studies public speaking is aiming to have an executive job some day! And radio engineering? A thing for the future! Both of these facts are very illuminating. Those are the sort of things that a mother should know concerning any young man who comes to call on her daughter. Seriously or — not.

TOM: One little warning. He doesn't know about Laura. I didn't let on that we had dark ulterior motives. I just said, why don't you come and have dinner with us? He said okay and that was the whole conversation.

AMANDA: I bet it was! You're eloquent as an oyster. However, he'll know about Laura when he gets here. When he sees how lovely and sweet and pretty she is, he'll thank his lucky stars he was asked to dinner.

TOM: Mother, you mustn't expect too much of Laura.

AMANDA: What do you mean?

TOM: Laura seems all those things to you and me because she's ours and we love her. We don't even notice she's crippled any more.

AMANDA: Don't say crippled! You know that I never allow that word to be used!

TOM: But face facts, Mother. She is and — that's not all —

AMANDA: What do you mean "not all"?

TOM: Laura is very different from other girls.

AMANDA: I think the difference is all to her advantage.

TOM: Not quite all — in the eyes of others — strangers — she's terribly shy and lives in a world of her own and those things make her seem a little peculiar to people outside the house.

AMANDA: Don't say peculiar.

TOM: Face the facts. She is.

[*The dance ball music changes to a tango that has a minor and somewhat ominous tone.*]

AMANDA: In what way is she peculiar — may I ask?

TOM [*gently*]: She lives in a world of her own — a world of little glass ornaments, Mother. . . .

[*He gets up. Amanda remains holding the brush, looking at him, troubled.*] She plays old phonograph records and — that's about all — [*He glances at himself in the mirror and crosses to the door.*]

AMANDA [*sharply*]: Where are you going?

TOM: I'm going to the movies. [*He goes out the screen door.*]

AMANDA: Not to the movies, every night to the movies! [*She follows quickly to the screen door.*] I don't believe you always go to the movies!

[*He is gone. Amanda looks worriedly after him for a moment. Then vitality and*]

optimism return and she turns from the door, crossing to the portieres.]
Laura, Laura!

[*Laura answers from the kitchenette.*]

LAURA: Yes, Mother.

AMANDA: Let those dishes go and come in front!

[*Laura appears with a dish towel. Amanda speaks to her gaily.*]
Laura, come here and make a wish on the moon!

[*Screen image:* The Moon.]

LAURA [*entering*]: Moon — moon?

AMANDA: A little silver slipper of a moon. Look over your left shoulder, Laura,
and make a wish!

[*Laura looks faintly puzzled as if called out of sleep. Amanda seizes her
shoulders and turns her at an angle by the door.*]
Now! Now, darling, *wish!*

LAURA: What shall I wish for, Mother?

AMANDA [*her voice trembling and her eyes suddenly filling with tears*]: Happiness! Good fortune!

[*The sound of the violin rises and the stage dims out.*]

SCENE SIX

*The light comes up on the fire escape landing. Tom is leaning against the grill,
smoking.*

[*Screen image:* The high school hero.]

TOM: And so the following evening I brought Jim home to dinner. I had known Jim
slightly in high school. In high school Jim was a hero. He had tremendous Irish
good nature and vitality with the scrubbed and polished look of white chinaware.
He seemed to move in a continual spotlight. He was a star in basketball, captain of
the debating club, president of the senior class and the glee club and he sang the
male lead in the annual light operas. He was always running or bounding, never
just walking. He seemed always at the point of defeating the law of gravity. He
was shooting with such velocity through his adolescence that you would logically
expect him to arrive at nothing short of the White House by the time he was thirty.
But Jim apparently ran into more interference after his graduation from Soldan.
His speed had definitely slowed. Six years after he left high school he was holding
a job that wasn't much better than mine.

[*Screen image:* The Clerk.]

He was the only one at the warehouse with whom I was on friendly terms. I was
valuable to him as someone who could remember his former glory, who had seen
him win basketball games and the silver cup in debating. He knew of my secret

practice of retiring to a cabinet of the washroom to work on poems when business was slack in the warehouse. He called me Shakespeare. And while the other boys in the warehouse regarded me with suspicious hostility, Jim took a humorous attitude toward me. Gradually his attitude affected the others, their hostility wore off and they also began to smile at me as people smile at an oddly fashioned dog who trots across their path at some distance.

I knew that Jim and Laura had known each other at Soldan, and I had heard Laura speak admiringly of his voice. I didn't know if Jim remembered her or not. In high school Laura had been as unobtrusive as Jim had been astonishing. If he did remember Laura, it was not as my sister, for when I asked him to dinner, he grinned and said, "You know, Shakespeare, I never thought of you as having folks!"

He was about to discover that I did. . . .

[*Legend on screen:* "The accent of a coming foot."]

[*The light dims out on Tom and comes up in the Wingfield living room — a delicate lemony light. It is about five on a Friday evening of late spring which comes "scattering poems in the sky."*]

[*Amanda has worked like a Turk in preparation for the gentleman caller. The results are astonishing. The new floor lamp with its rose silk shade is in place, a colored paper lantern conceals the broken light fixture in the ceiling, new billowing white curtains are at the windows, chintz covers are on the chairs and sofa, a pair of new sofa pillows make their initial appearance. Open boxes and tissue paper are scattered on the floor.*]

[*Laura stands in the middle of the room with lifted arms while Amanda crouches before her, adjusting the hem of a new dress, devout and ritualistic. The dress is colored and designed by memory. The arrangement of Laura's hair is changed; it is softer and more becoming. A fragile, unearthly prettiness has come out in Laura: she is like a piece of translucent glass touched by light, given a momentary radiance, not actual, not lasting.*]

AMANDA [*impatiently*]: Why are you trembling?

LAURA: Mother, you've made me so nervous!

AMANDA: How have I made you nervous?

LAURA: By all this fuss! You make it seem so important!

AMANDA: I don't understand you, Laura. You couldn't be satisfied with just sitting home, and yet whenever I try to arrange something for you, you seem to resist it. [*She gets up.*] Now take a look at yourself. No, wait! Wait just a moment — I have an idea!

LAURA: What is it now?

[*Amanda produces two powder puffs which she wraps in handkerchiefs and stuffs in Laura's bosom.*]

LAURA: Mother, what are you doing?

AMANDA: They call them "Gay Deceivers"!

LAURA: I won't wear them!

AMANDA: You will!

LAURA: Why should I?

AMANDA: Because, to be painfully honest, your chest is flat.

LAURA: You make it seem like we were setting a trap.

AMANDA: All pretty girls are a trap, a pretty trap, and men expect them to be.

[*Legend on screen:* "A pretty trap."]

Now look at yourself, young lady. This is the prettiest you will ever be! [*She stands back to admire Laura.*] I've got to fix myself now! You're going to be surprised by your mother's appearance!

[*Amanda crosses through the portieres, humming gaily. Laura moves slowly to the long mirror and stares solemnly at herself. A wind blows the white curtains inward in a slow, graceful motion and with a faint, sorrowful sighing.*]

AMANDA [*from somewhere behind the portieres*]: It isn't dark enough yet.

[*Laura turns slowly before the mirror with a troubled look.*]

[*Legend on screen:* "This is my sister: Celebrate her with strings!" *Music plays.*]

AMANDA [*laughing, still not visible*]: I'm going to show you something. I'm going to make a spectacular appearance!

LAURA: What is it, Mother?

AMANDA: Possess your soul in patience — you will see! Something I've resurrected from that old trunk! Styles haven't changed so terribly much after all. . . . [*She parts the portieres.*] Now just look at your mother! [*She wears a girlish frock of yellowed voile with a blue silk sash. She carries a bunch of jonquils — the legend of her youth is nearly revived. Now she speaks feverishly:*] This is the dress in which I led the cotillion. Won the cakewalk twice at Sunset Hill, wore one Spring to the Governor's Ball in Jackson! See how I sashayed around the ballroom, Laura? [*She raises her skirt and does a mincing step around the room.*] I wore it on Sundays for my gentlemen callers! I had it on the day I met your father. . . . I had malaria fever all that Spring. The change of climate from East Tennessee to the Delta — weakened resistance. I had a little temperature all the time — not enough to be serious — just enough to make me restless and giddy! Invitations poured in — parties all over the Delta! "Stay in bed," said Mother, "you have a fever!" — but I just wouldn't. I took quinine but kept on going, going! Evenings, dances! Afternoons, long, long rides! Picnics — lovely! So lovely, that country in May — all lacy with dogwood, literally flooded with jonquils! That was the spring I had the craze for jonquils. Jonquils became an absolute obsession. Mother said, "Honey, there's no more room for jonquils." And still I kept on bringing in more jonquils. Whenever, wherever I saw them, I'd say, "Stop! Stop! I see jonquils!" I made the young men help me gather the jonquils! It was a joke, Amanda and her jonquils. Finally there were no more vases to hold them, every available space was filled with jonquils. No vases to hold them? All right, I'll hold them myself! And then I — [*She stops in front of the picture. Music plays.*] met your father! Malaria fever and jonquils and then — this — boy. . . . [*She switches on the rose-colored lamp.*] I hope they get here before it starts to rain. [*She crosses the room and places the jonquils in a bowl on the table.*] I gave your brother a little extra change so he and Mr. O'Connor could take the service car home.

LAURA [*with an altered look*]: What did you say his name was?

AMANDA: O'Connor.

LAURA: What is his first name?

AMANDA: I don't remember. Oh, yes, I do. It was — Jim!

[*Laura sways slightly and catches hold of a chair.*]

[*Legend on screen:* "Not Jim!"]

LAURA [*faintly*]: Not — Jim!

AMANDA: Yes, that was it, it was Jim! I've never known a Jim that wasn't nice!

[*The music becomes ominous.*]

LAURA: Are you sure his name is Jim O'Connor?

AMANDA: Yes. Why?

LAURA: Is he the one that Tom used to know in high school?

AMANDA: He didn't say so. I think he just got to know him at the warehouse.

LAURA: There was a Jim O'Connor we both knew in high school — [*then, with effort*] If that is the one that Tom is bringing to dinner — you'll have to excuse me, I won't come to the table.

AMANDA: What sort of nonsense is this?

LAURA: You asked me once if I'd ever liked a boy. Don't you remember I showed you this boy's picture?

AMANDA: You mean the boy you showed me in the yearbook?

LAURA: Yes, that boy.

AMANDA: Laura, Laura, were you in love with that boy?

LAURA: I don't know, Mother. All I know is I couldn't sit at the table if it was him!

AMANDA: It won't be him! It isn't the least bit likely. But whether it is or not, you will come to the table. You will not be excused.

LAURA: I'll have to be, Mother.

AMANDA: I don't intend to humor your silliness, Laura. I've had too much from you and your brother, both! So just sit down and compose yourself till they come. Tom has forgotten his key so you'll have to let them in, when they arrive.

LAURA [*panicky*]: Oh, Mother — *you* answer the door!

AMANDA [*lightly*]: I'll be in the kitchen — busy!

LAURA: Oh, Mother, please answer the door, don't make me do it!

AMANDA [*crossing into the kitchenette*]: I've got to fix the dressing for the salmon. Fuss, fuss — silliness! — over a gentleman caller!

[*The door swings shut. Laura is left alone.*]

[*Legend on screen:* "Terror!"]

[*She utters a low moan and turns off the lamp — sits stiffly on the edge of the sofa, knotting her fingers together.*]

[*Legend on screen:* "The Opening of a Door!"]

[*Tom and Jim appear on the fire escape steps and climb to the landing. Hearing their approach, Laura rises with a panicky gesture. She retreats to the portieres. The doorbell rings. Laura catches her breath and touches her throat. Low drums sound.*]

AMANDA [*calling*]: Laura, sweetheart! The door!

[*Laura stares at it without moving.*]

JIM: I think we just beat the rain.

TOM: Uh-huh. [*He rings again, nervously. Jim whistles and fishes for a cigarette.*]

AMANDA [*very, very gaily*]: Laura, that is your brother and Mr. O'Connor! Will you let them in, darling?

[*Laura crosses toward the kitchenette door.*]

LAURA [*breathlessly*]: Mother — you go to the door!

[*Amanda steps out of the kitchenette and stares furiously at Laura. She points imperiously at the door.*]

LAURA: Please, please!

AMANDA [*in a fierce whisper*]: What is the matter with you, you silly thing?

LAURA [*desperately*]: Please, you answer it, *please!*

AMANDA: I told you I wasn't going to humor you, Laura. Why have you chosen this moment to lose your mind?

LAURA: Please, please, please, you go!

AMANDA: You'll have to go to the door because I can't!

LAURA [*despairingly*]: I can't either!

AMANDA: *Why?*

LAURA: I'm *sick!*

AMANDA: I'm sick, too — of your nonsense! Why can't you and your brother be normal people? Fantastic whims and behavior!

[*Tom gives a long ring.*]

Preposterous goings on! Can you give me one reason — [*She calls out lyrically.*] *Coming! Just one second!* — why you should be afraid to open a door? Now you answer it, Laura!

LAURA: Oh, oh, oh . . . [*She returns through the portieres, darts to the Victrola, winds it frantically and turns it on.*]

AMANDA: Laura Wingfield, you march right to that door!

LAURA: *Yes — yes, Mother!*

[*A faraway, scratchy rendition of "Dardanella" softens the air and gives her strength to move through it. She slips to the door and draws it cautiously open. Tom enters with the caller, Jim O'Connor.*]

TOM: Laura, this is Jim. Jim, this is my sister, Laura.

JIM [*stepping inside*]: I didn't know that Shakespeare had a sister!

LAURA [*retreating, stiff and trembling, from the door*]: How — how do you do?

JIM [*heartily, extending his hand*]: Okay!

[*Laura touches it hesitantly with hers.*]

JIM: You hand's *cold*, Laura!

LAURA: Yes, well — I've been playing the Victrola. . . .

JIM: Must have been playing classical music on it! You ought to play a little hot swing music to warm you up!

LAURA: Excuse me — I haven't finished playing the Victola. . . . [*She turns awkwardly and hurries into the front room. She pauses a second by the Victrola. Then she catches her breath and darts through the portieres like a frightened deer.*]

JIM [*grinning*]: What was the matter?

TOM: Oh — with Laura? Laura is — terribly shy.

JIM: Shy, huh? It's unusual to meet a shy girl nowadays. I don't believe you ever mentioned you had a sister.

TOM: Well, now you know. I have one. Here is the *Post Dispatch*. You want a piece of it?

JIM: Uh-huh.

TOM: What piece? The comics?

JIM: Sports! [*He glances at it.*] Ole Dizzy Dean is on his bad behavior.

TOM [*uninterested*]: Yeah? [*He lights a cigarette and goes over to the fire-escape door.*]

JIM: Where are *you* going?

TOM: I'm going out on the terrace.

JIM [*going after him*]: You know, Shakespeare — I'm going to sell you a bill of goods!

TOM: What goods?

JIM: A course I'm taking.

TOM: Huh?

JIM: In public speaking! You and me, we're not the warehouse type.

TOM: Thanks — that's good news. But what has public speaking got to do with it?

JIM: It fits you for — executive positions!

TOM: Awww.

JIM: I tell you it's done a helluva lot for me.

[*Image on screen:* Executive at his desk.]

TOM: In what respect?

JIM: In every! Ask yourself what is the difference between you an' me and men in the office down front? Brains? — No! — Ability? — No! Then what? Just one little thing —

TOM: What is that one little thing?

JIM: Primarily it amounts to — social poise! Being able to square up to people and hold your own on any social level!

AMANDA [*from the kitchenette*]: Tom?

TOM: Yes, Mother?

AMANDA: Is that you and Mr. O'Connor?

TOM: Yes, Mother.

AMANDA: Well, you just make yourselves comfortable in there.

TOM: Yes, Mother.

AMANDA: Ask Mr. O'Connor if he would like to wash his hands.

JIM: Aw, no — no — thank you — I took care of that at the warehouse. Tom —

TOM: Yes?

JIM: Mr. Mendoza was speaking to me about you.

TOM: Favorably?

JIM: What do you think?

TOM: Well —

JIM: You're going to be out of a job if you don't wake up.

TOM: I am waking up —

JIM: You show no signs.

TOM: The signs are interior.

[*Image on the screen:* The sailing vessel with the Jolly Roger again.]

TOM: I'm planning to change. [*He leans over the fire-escape rail, speaking with quiet exhilaration. The incandescent marquees and signs of the first-run movie houses light his face from across the alley. He looks like a voyager.*] I'm right at the point of committing myself to a future that doesn't include the warehouse and Mr. Mendoza or even a night-school course in public speaking.

JIM: What are you gassing about?

TOM: I'm tired of the movies.

JIM: Movies!

TOM: Yes, movies! Look at them — [*a wave toward the marvels of Grand Avenue*] All of those glamorous people — having adventures — hogging it all, gobbling the whole thing up! You know what happens? People go to the *movies* instead of *moving!* Hollywood characters are supposed to have all the adventures for everybody in America, while everybody in America sits in a dark room and watches them have them! Yes, until there's a war. That's when adventure becomes available to the masses! *Everyone's* dish, not only Gable's! Then the people in the dark room come out of the dark room to have some adventures themselves — goody, goody! It's our turn now, to go to the South Sea Island — to make a safari — to be exotic, far-off! But I'm not patient. I don't want to wait till then. I'm tired of the *movies* and I am *about* to *move!*

JIM [*incredulously*]: Move?

TOM: Yes.

JIM: When?

TOM: Soon!

JIM: Where? Where?

[*The music seems to answer the question, while Tom thinks it over. He searches in his pockets.*]

TOM: I'm starting to boil inside. I know I seem dreamy, but inside — well, I'm boiling! Whenever I pick up a shoe, I shudder a little thinking how short life is and what I am doing! Whatever that means, I know it doesn't mean shoes — except as something to wear on a traveler's feet! [*He finds what he has been searching for in his pockets and holds out a paper to Jim.*] Look —

JIM: What?

TOM: I'm a member.

JIM [*reading*]: The Union of Merchant Seamen.

TOM: I paid my dues this month, instead of the light bill.

JIM: You will regret it when they turn the lights off.

TOM: I won't be here.

JIM: How about your mother?

TOM: I'm like my father. The bastard son of a bastard! Did you notice how he's grinning in his picture in there! And he's been absent going on sixteen years!

JIM: You're just talking, you drip. How does your mother feel about it?

TOM: Shhh! Here comes Mother! Mother is not acquainted with my plans!

AMANDA [*coming through the portieres*]: Where are you all?

TOM: On the terrace, Mother.

[*They start inside. She advances to them. Tom is distinctly shocked at her appearance. Even Jim blinks a little. He is making his first contact with girlish Southern vivacity and in spite of the night-school course in public speaking is somewhat thrown off the beam by the unexpected outlay of social charm. Certain responses are attempted by Jim but are swept aside by Amanda's gay laughter and chatter. Tom is embarrassed but after the first shock Jim reacts very warmly. He grins and chuckles, is altogether won over.*]

[*Image on screen:* Amanda as a girl]

AMANDA [*coyly smiling, shaking her girlish ringlets*]: Well, well, well, so this is Mr. O'Connor. Introductions entirely unnecessary. I've heard so much about you from my boy. I finally said to him, Tom — good gracious! — why don't you bring this paragon to supper? I'd like to meet this nice young man at the warehouse! — instead of just hearing him sing your praises so much! I don't know why my son is so stand-offish — that's not Southern behavior!

Let's sit down and — I think we could stand a little more air in here! Tom, leave the door open. I felt a nice fresh breeze a moment ago. Where has it gone to? Mmm, so warm already! And not quite summer, even. We're going to burn up when summer really gets started. However, we're having — we're having a very light supper. I think light things are better fo' this time of year. The same as light clothes are. Light clothes an' light food are what warm weather calls fo'. You know our blood gets so thick during th' winter — it takes a while fo' us to *adjust* ou'selves! — when the season changes . . . It's come so quick this year. I wasn't prepared. All of a sudden — heavens! Already summer! I ran to the trunk an' pulled out this light dress — terribly old! Historical almost! But feels so good — so good an' co-ol, y'know. . . .

TOM: Mother —

AMANDA: Yes, honey?

TOM: How about — supper?

AMANDA: Honey, you go ask Sister if supper is ready! You know that Sister is in full charge of supper! Tell her you hungry boys are waiting for it. [*to Jim*] Have you met Laura?

JIM: She —

AMANDA: Let you in? Oh, good, you've met already! It's rare for a girl as sweet an' pretty as Laura to be domestic! But Laura is, thank heavens, not only pretty but also very domestic. I'm not at all. I never was a bit. I never could make a thing but angel-food cake. Well, in the South we had so many servants. Gone, gone, gone. All vestige of gracious living! Gone completely! I wasn't prepared for what the future brought me. All of my gentlemen callers were sons of planters and so of course I assumed that I would be married to one and raise my family on a large piece of land with plenty of servants. But man proposes — and woman accepts the proposal! To vary that old, old saying a little bit — I married no planter! I married a man who worked for the telephone company! That gallantly smiling gentleman over there! [*She points to the picture.*] A telephone man who — fell in love with long-distance! Now he travels and I don't even know where! But what am I going on for about my — tribulations? Tell me yours — I hope you don't have any! Tom?

TOM [*returning*]: Yes, Mother?

AMANDA: Is supper nearly ready?

TOM: It looks to me like supper is on the table.

AMANDA: Let me look — [*She rises prettily and looks through the portieres.*] Oh, lovely! But where is Sister?

TOM: Laura is not feeling well and she says that she thinks she'd better not come to the table.

AMANDA: What? Nonsense! Laura? Oh, Laura!

LAURA [*from the kitchenette, faintly*]: Yes, Mother.

AMANDA: You really must come to the table. We won't be seated until you come to the table! Come in, Mr. O'Connor. You sit over there, and I'll. . . . Laura? Laura Wingfield! You're keeping us waiting, honey! We can't say grace until you come to the table!

[*The kitchenette door is pushed weakly open and Laura comes in. She is obviously quite faint, her lips trembling, her eyes wide and staring. She moves unsteadily toward the table.*]

[*Screen legend:* "Terror!"]

[*Outside a summer storm is coming on abruptly. The white curtains billow inward at the windows and there is a sorrowful murmur from the deep blue dusk.*]

[*Laura suddenly stumbles; she catches at a chair with a faint moan.*]

TOM: Laura!

AMANDA: Laura!

[*There is a clap of thunder.*]

[*Screen legend:* "Ah!"]

[*despairingly*] Why, Laura, you *are* ill, darling! Tom, help your sister into the living room, dear! Sit in the living room, Laura — rest on the sofa. Well! [*to Jim as Tom helps his sister to the sofa in the living room*] Standing over the hot stove made her ill! I told her that it was just too warm this evening, but —

[*Tom comes back to the table.*]

Is Laura all right now?

TOM: Yes.

AMANDA: What *is* that? Rain? A nice cool rain has come up! [*She gives Jim a frightened look.*] I think we may — have grace — now . . .

[*Tom looks at her stupidly.*] Tom, honey — you say grace!

TOM: Oh . . . "For these and all thy mercies —"

[*They bow their heads, Amanda stealing a nervous glance at Jim. In the living room Laura, stretched on the sofa, clenches her hand to her lips, to hold back a shuddering sob.*]

God's Holy Name be praised —

[*The scene dims out.*]

SCENE SEVEN

It is half an hour later. Dinner is just being finished in the dining room, Laura is still huddled upon the sofa, her feet drawn under her, her head resting on a pale blue pillow, her eyes wide and mysteriously watchful. The new floor lamp with its shade of rose-colored silk gives a soft, becoming light to her face, bringing out the fragile, unearthly prettiness which usually escapes attention. From outside there is a steady murmur of rain, but it is slackening and soon stops; the air outside becomes pale and luminous as the moon breaks through the clouds. A moment after the curtain rises, the lights in both rooms flicker and go out.

JIM: Hey, there, Mr. Light Bulb!

[*Amanda laughs nervously.*]

[*Legend on screen:* "Suspension of a public service."]

AMANDA: Where was Moses when the lights went out? Ha-ha. Do you know the answer to that one, Mr. O'Connor?

JIM: No, Ma'am, what's the answer?

AMANDA: In the dark!

[*Jim laughs appreciatively.*]

Everybody sit still. I'll light the candles. Isn't it lucky we have them on the table? Where's a match? Which of you gentlemen can provide a match?

JIM: Here.

AMANDA: Thank you, Sir.

JIM: Not at all, Ma'am!

AMANDA [*as she lights the candles*]: I guess the fuse has burnt out. Mr. O'Connor, can you tell a burnt-out fuse? I know I can't and Tom is a total loss when it comes to mechanics.

[*They rise from the table and go into the kitchenette, from where their voices are heard.*]

Oh, be careful you don't bump into something. We don't want our gentleman caller to break his neck. Now wouldn't that be a fine howdy-do?

JIM: Ha-ha! Where is the fuse box?

AMANDA: Right here next to the stove. Can you see anything?

JIM: Just a minute.

AMANDA: Isn't electricity a mysterious thing? Wasn't it Benjamin Franklin who tied a key to a kite? We live in such a mysterious universe, don't we? Some people say that science clears up all the mysteries for us. In my opinion it only creates more! Have you found it yet?

JIM: No, Ma'am. All these fuses look okay to me.

AMANDA: Tom!

TOM: Yes, Mother?

AMANDA: That light bill I gave you several days ago. The one I told you we got the notices about?

[*Legend on screen:* "Ha!"]

TOM: Oh — yeah.

AMANDA: You didn't neglect to pay it by any chance?

TOM: Why, I —

AMANDA: Didn't! I might have known it!

JIM: Shakespeare probably wrote a poem on that light bill, Mrs. Wingfield.

AMANDA: I might have known better than to trust him with it! There's such a high price for negligence in this world!

JIM: Maybe the poem will win a ten-dollar prize.

AMANDA: We'll just have to spend the remainder of the evening in the nineteenth century, before Mr. Edison made the Mazda lamp!

JIM: Candlelight is my favorite kind of light.

AMANDA: That shows you're romantic! But that's no excuse for Tom. Well, we got through dinner. Very considerate of them to let us get through dinner before they plunged us into everlasting darkness, wasn't it, Mr. O'Connor?

JIM: Ha-ha!

AMANDA: Tom, as a penalty for your carelessness you can help me with the dishes.

JIM: Let me give you a hand.

AMANDA: Indeed you will not!

JIM: I ought to be good for something.

AMANDA: Good for something? [*Her tone is rhapsodic.*] *You?* Why, Mr. O'Connor, nobody, *nobody's* given me this much entertainment in years — as you have!

JIM: Aw, now, Mrs. Wingfield!

AMANDA: I'm not exaggerating, not one bit! But Sister is all by her lonesome. You go keep her company in the parlor! I'll give you this lovely old candelabrum that used to be on the altar at the Church of the Heavenly Rest. It was melted a little out of shape when the church burnt down. Lightning struck it one spring. Gypsy Jones was holding a revival at the time and he intimated that the church was destroyed because the Episcopalians gave card parties.

JIM: Ha-ha.

AMANDA: And how about you coaxing Sister to drink a little wine? I think it would be good for her! Can you carry both at once?

JIM: Sure. I'm Superman!

AMANDA: Now, Thomas, get into this apron!

[*Jim comes into the dining room, carrying the candelabrum, its candles lighted, in one hand and a glass of wine in the other. The door of the kitchenette swings closed on Amanda's gay laughter; the flickering light approaches the portieres. Laura sits up nervously as Jim enters. She can hardly speak from the almost intolerable strain of being alone with a stranger.*]

[*Screen legend:* "I don't suppose you remember me at all!"]

[*At first, before Jim's warmth overcomes her paralyzing shyness, Laura's voice is thin and breathless, as though she had just run up a steep flight of stairs. Jim's attitude is gently humorous. While the incident is apparently unimportant, it is to Laura the climax of her secret life.*]

JIM: Hello there, Laura.

LAURA [*faintly*]: Hello.

[*She clears her throat.*]

JIM: How are you feeling now? Better?

LAURA: Yes. Yes, thank you.

JIM: This is for you. A little dandelion wine. [*He extends the glass toward her with extravagant gallantry.*]

LAURA: Thank you.

JIM: Drink it — but don't get drunk!

[*He laughs heartily. Laura takes the glass uncertainly; she laughs shyly.*] Where shall I set the candles?

LAURA: Oh — oh, anywhere . . .

JIM: How about here on the floor? Any objections?

LAURA: No.

JIM: I'll spread a newspaper under to catch the drippings. I like to sit on the floor. Mind if I do?

LAURA: Oh, no.

JIM: Give me a pillow?

LAURA: What?

JIM: A pillow!

LAURA: Oh . . . [*She hands him one quickly.*]

JIM: How about you? Don't you like to sit on the floor?

LAURA: Oh — yes.

JIM: Why don't you, then?

LAURA: I — will.

JIM: Take a pillow!

[*Laura does. She sits on the floor on the other side of the candelabrum. Jim crosses his legs and smiles engagingly at her.*] I can't hardly see you sitting way over there.

LAURA: I can — see you.

JIM: I know, but that's not fair, I'm in the limelight.

[*Laura moves her pillow closer.*]

Good! Now I can see you! Comfortable?

LAURA: Yes.

JIM: So am I. Comfortable as a cow! Will you have some gum?

LAURA: No, thank you.

JIM: I think that I will indulge, with your permission. [*He musingly unwraps a stick of gum and holds it up.*] Think of the fortune made by the guy that invented the first piece of chewing gum. Amazing, huh? The Wrigley Building is one of the sights of Chicago — I saw it when I went up to the Century of Progress. Did you take in the Century of Progress?

LAURA: No, I didn't.

JIM: Well, it was quite a wonderful exposition. What impressed me most was the Hall of Science. Gives you an idea of what the future will be in America, even more wonderful than the present time is! [*There is a pause. Jim smiles at her.*] Your brother tells me you're shy. Is that right, Laura?

LAURA: I — don't know.

JIM: I judge you to be an old-fashioned type of girl. Well, I think that's a pretty good type to be. Hope you don't think I'm being too personal — do you?

LAURA [*hastily, out of embarrassment*]: I believe I *will* take a piece of gum, if you — don't mind. [*clearing her throat*] Mr. O'Connor, have you — kept up with your singing?

JIM: Singing? Me?

LAURA: Yes. I remember what a beautiful voice you had.

JIM: When did you hear me sing?

[*Laura does not answer, and in the long pause which follows a man's voice is heard singing offstage.*]

VOICE:

O blow, ye winds, heigh-ho,
A-roving I will go!
I'm off to my love
With a boxing glove —
Ten thousand miles away!

JIM: You say you've heard me sing?

LAURA: Oh, yes! Yes, very often . . . I — don't suppose — you remember me — at all?

JIM [*smiling doubtfully*]: You know I have an idea I've seen you before. I had that idea soon as you opened the door. It seemed almost like I was about to remember your name. But the name that I started to call you — wasn't a name! And so I stopped myself before I said it.

LAURA: Wasn't it — Blue Roses?

JIM [*springing up, grinning*]: Blue Roses! My gosh, yes — Blue Roses! That's what I had on my tongue when you opened the door! Isn't it funny what tricks your memory plays? I didn't connect you with high school somehow or other. But that's where it was; it was high school. I didn't even know you were Shakespeare's sister! Gosh, I'm sorry.

LAURA: I didn't expect you to. You — barely knew me!

JIM: But we did have a speaking acquaintance, huh?

LAURA: Yes, we — spoke to each other.

JIM: When did you recognize me?

LAURA: Oh, right away!

JIM: Soon as I came in the door?

LAURA: When I heard your name I thought it was probably you. I knew that Tom used to know you a little in high school. So when you came in the door — well, then I was — sure.

JIM: Why didn't you *say* something, then?

LAURA [*breathlessly*]: I didn't know what to say, I was — too surprised!

JIM: For goodness' sakes! You know, this sure is funny!

LAURA: Yes! Yes, isn't it, though . . .

JIM: Didn't we have a class in something together?

LAURA: Yes, we did.

JIM: What class was that?

LAURA: It was — singing — chorus!

JIM: Aw!

LAURA: I sat across the aisle from you in the Aud.

JIM: Aw.

LAURA: Mondays, Wednesdays, and Fridays.

JIM: Now I remember — you always came in late.

LAURA: Yes, it was so hard for me, getting upstairs. I had that brace on my leg — it clumped so loud!

JIM: I never heard any clumping.

LAURA [*wincing at the recollection*]: To me is sounded like — thunder!

JIM: Well, well, well, I never even noticed.

LAURA: And everybody was seated before I came in. I had to walk in front of all those people. My seat was in the back row. I had to go clumping all the way up the aisle with everyone watching!

JIM: You shouldn't have been self-conscious.

LAURA: I know, but I was. It was always such a relief when the singing started.

JIM: Aw, yes, I've placed you now! I used to call you Blue Roses. How was it that I got started calling you that?

LAURA: I was out of school a little while with pleurosis. When I came back you asked me what was the matter. I said I had pleurosis — you thought I said *Blue Roses*. That's what you always called me after that!

JIM: I hope you didn't mind.

LAURA: Oh, no — I liked it. You see, I wasn't acquainted with many — people

. . . .

JIM: As I remember you sort of stuck by yourself.

LAURA: I — I — never have had much luck at — making friends.

JIM: I don't see why you wouldn't.

LAURA: Well, I — started out badly.

JIM: You mean being —

LAURA: Yes, it sort of — stood between me —

JIM: You shouldn't have let it!

LAURA: I know, but it did, and —

JIM: You were shy with people!

LAURA: I tried not to be but never could —

JIM: Overcome it?

LAURA: No, I — I never could!

JIM: I guess being shy is something you have to work out of kind of gradually.

LAURA [*sorrowfully*]: Yes — I guess it —

JIM: Takes time!

LAURA: Yes —

JIM: People are not so dreadful when you know them. That's what you have to remember! And everybody has problems, not just you, but practically everybody has got some problems. You think of yourself as having the only problems, as being the only one who is disappointed. But just look around you and you will see lots of people as disappointed as you are. For instance, I hoped when I was going to high school that I would be further along at this time, six years later, than I am now. You remember that wonderful write-up I had in *The Torch*?

LAURA: Yes! [*She rises and crosses to the table.*]

JIM: It said I was bound to succeed in anything I went into!

[*Laura returns with the high school yearbook.*]

Holy Jeez! *The Torch!*

[*He accepts it reverently. They smile across the book with mutual wonder. Laura crouches beside him and they begin to turn the pages. Laura's shyness is dissolving in his warmth.*]

LAURA: Here you are in *The Pirates of Penzance*!

JIM [*wistfully*]: I sang the baritone lead in that operetta.

LAURA [*raptly*]: So — *beautifully!*

JIM [*protesting*]: Aw —

LAURA: Yes, yes — beautifully — beautifully!

JIM: You heard me?

LAURA: All three times!

JIM: No!

LAURA: Yes!

JIM: All three performances?

LAURA [*looking down*]: Yes.

JIM: Why?

LAURA: I — wanted to ask you to — autograph my program. [*She takes the program from the back of the yearbook and shows it to him.*]

JIM: Why didn't you ask me to?

LAURA: You were always surrounded by your own friends so much that I never had a chance to.

JIM: You should have just —

LAURA: Well, I — thought you might think I was —

JIM: Thought I might think you was — what?

LAURA: Oh —

JIM [*with reflective relish*]: I was beleaguered by females in those days.

LAURA: You were terribly popular!

JIM: Yeah —

LAURA: You had such a — friendly way —

JIM: I was spoiled in high school.

LAURA: Everybody — liked you!

JIM: Including you?

LAURA: I — yes, I — did, too — [*She gently closes the book in her lap.*]

JIM: Well, well, well! Give me that program, Laura.

[*She hands it to him. He signs it with a flourish.*]

There you are — better late than never!

LAURA: Oh, I — what a — surprise!

JIM: My signature isn't worth very much right now. But some day — maybe — it will increase in value! Being disappointed is one thing and being discouraged is something else. I am disappointed but I am not discouraged. I'm twenty-three years old. How old are you?

LAURA: I'll be twenty-four in June.

JIM: That's not old age!

LAURA: No, but —

JIM: You finished high school?

LAURA [*with difficulty*]: I didn't go back.

JIM: You mean you dropped out?

LAURA: I made bad grades in my final examinations. [*She rises and replaces the book and the program on the table. Her voice is strained.*] How is — Emily Meisenbach getting along?

JIM: Oh, that kraut-head!

LAURA: Why do you call her that?

JIM: That's what she was.

LAURA: You're not still — going with her?

JIM: I never see her.

LAURA: It said in the "Personal" section that you were — engaged!

JIM: I know, but I wasn't impressed by that — propaganda!

LAURA: It wasn't — the truth?

JIM: Only in Emily's optimistic opinion!

LAURA: Oh —

[*Legend:* "What have you done since high school?"]

[*Jim lights a cigarette and leans indolently back on his elbows smiling at Laura with a warmth and charm which lights her inwardly with altar candles. She remains by the table, picks up a piece from the glass menagerie collection, and turns it in her hands to cover her tumult.*]

JIM [*after several reflective puffs on his cigarette*]: What have you done since high school?

[*She seems not to hear him.*]

Huh?

[*Laura looks up.*]

I said what have you done since high school, Laura?

LAURA: Nothing much.

JIM: You must have been doing something these six long years.

LAURA: Yes.

JIM: Well, then, such as what?

LAURA: I took a business course at business college —

JIM: How did that work out?

LAURA: Well, not very — well — I had to drop out, it gave me — indigestion —

[*Jim laughs gently.*]

JIM: What are you doing now?

LAURA: I don't do anything — much. Oh, please don't think I sit around doing nothing! My glass collection takes up a good deal of time. Glass is something you have to take good care of.

JIM: What did you say — about glass?

LAURA: Collection I said — I have one — [*She clears her throat and turns away again, acutely shy.*]

JIM [*abruptly*]: You know what I judge to be the trouble with you? Inferiority complex! Know what that is? That's what they call it when someone low-rates himself! I understand it because I had it, too. Although my case was not so aggravated as yours seems to be. I had it until I took up public speaking, developed my voice, and learned that I had an aptitude for science. Before that time I never thought of myself as being outstanding in any way whatsoever! Now I've never made a regular study of it, but I have a friend who says I can analyze people better than doctors that make a profession of it. I don't claim that to be necessarily true, but I can sure guess a person's psychology, Laura! [*He takes out his gum.*] Excuse me, Laura. I always take it out when the flavor is gone. I'll use this scrap of paper to wrap it in. I know how it is to get it stuck on a shoe. [*He wraps the gum in paper and puts it in his pocket.*] Yep — that's what I judge to be your principal trouble. A lack of confidence in yourself as a person. You don't have the proper amount of faith in yourself. I'm basing that fact on a number of your remarks and also on certain observations I've made. For instance that clumping you thought was so awful in high school. You say that you even dreaded to walk into class. You see what you did? You dropped out of school, you gave up an education because of a clump, which as far as I know was practically non-existent! A little physical defect is what you have. Hardly noticeable even! Magnified thousands of times by imagination! You know what my strong advice to you is? Think of yourself as *superior* in some way!

LAURA: In what way would I think?

JIM: Why, man alive, Laura! Just look about you a little. What do you see? A world full of common people! All of 'em born and all of 'em going to die! Which of them has one-tenth of your good points! Or mine! Or anyone else's, as far as that goes — gosh! Everybody excels in some one thing. Some in many! [*He unconsciously glances at himself in the mirror.*] All you've got to do is discover in *what!* Take me, for instance. [*He adjusts his tie at the mirror.*] My interest happens to lie in electro-dynamics. I'm taking a course in radio engineering at night school, Laura, on top of a fairly responsible job at the warehouse. I'm taking that course and studying public speaking.

LAURA: Ohhhh.

JIM: Because I believe in the future of television! [*turning his back to her.*] I wish to be ready to go up right along with it. Therefore I'm planning to get in on the ground floor. In fact I've already made the right connections and all that remains is for the industry itself to get under way! Full steam — [*His eyes are starry.*] *Knowledge* — Zzzzzp! *Money* — Zzzzzzp! — *Power!* That's the cycle democracy is built on!

[*His attitude is convincingly dynamic. Laura stares at him, even her shyness eclipsed in her absolute wonder. He suddenly grins.*]

I guess you think I think a lot of myself!

LAURA: No — o-o-o, I —

JIM: Now how about you? Isn't there something you take more interest in than anything else?

LAURA: Well, I do — as I said — have my — glass collection —

[*A peal of girlish laughter rings from the kitchenette.*]

JIM: I'm not right sure I know what you're talking about. What kind of glass is it?

LAURA: Little articles of it, they're ornaments mostly! Most of them are little animals made out of glass, the tiniest little animals in the world. Mother calls them a glass menagerie! Here's an example of one, if you'd like to see it! This one is one of the oldest. It's nearly thirteen.

[*Music:* "The Glass Menagerie."]

[*He stretches out his hand.*]

Oh, be careful — if you breathe, it breaks!

JIM: I'd better not take it. I'm pretty clumsy with things.

LAURA: Go on, I trust you with him! [*She places the piece in his palm.*] There now — you're holding him gently! Hold him over the light, he loves the light! You see how the light shines through him?

JIM: It sure does shine!

LAURA: I shouldn't be partial, but he is my favorite one.

JIM: What kind of thing is this one supposed to be?

LAURA: Haven't you noticed the single horn on his forehead?

JIM: A unicorn, huh?

LAURA: Mmmm-hmmm!

JIM: Unicorns — aren't they extinct in the modern world?

LAURA: I know!

JIM: Poor little fellow, he must feel sort of lonesome.

LAURA [*smiling*]: Well, if he does, he doesn't complain about it. He stays on a shelf with some horses that don't have horns and all of them seem to get along nicely together.

JIM: How do you know?

LAURA [*lightly*]: I haven't heard any arguments among them!

JIM [*grinning*]: No arguments, huh? Well, that's a pretty good sign! Where shall I set him?

LAURA: Put him on the table. They all like a change of scenery once in a while!

JIM: Well, well, well, well — [*He places the glass piece on the table, then raises his arms and stretches.*] Look how big my shadow is when I stretch!

LAURA: Oh, oh, yes — it stretches across the ceiling!

JIM [*crossing to the door*]: I think it's stopped raining. [*He opens the fire-escape door and the background music changes to a dance tune.*] Where does the music come from?

LAURA: From the Paradise Dance Hall across the alley.

JIM: How about cutting the rug a little, Miss Wingfield?

LAURA: Oh, I —

JIM: Or is your program filled up? Let me have a look at it. [*He grasps an imaginary card.*] Why, every dance is taken! I'll just have to scratch some out.

[*Waltz music:* "La Golondrina."]

Ahhh, a waltz! [*He executes some sweeping turns by himself, then holds his arms toward Laura.*]

LAURA [*breathlessly*]: I — can't dance!

JIM: There you go, that inferiority stuff!

LAURA: I've never danced in my life!

JIM: Come on, try!

LAURA: Oh, but I'd step on you!

JIM: I'm not made out of glass.

LAURA: How — how — how do we start?

JIM: Just leave it to me. You hold your arms out a little.

LAURA: Like this?

JIM [*taking her in his arms*]: A little big higher. Right. Now don't tighten up, that's the main thing about it — relax.

LAURA [*laughing breathlessly*]: It's hard not to.

JIM: Okay.

LAURA: I'm afraid you can't budge me.

JIM: What do you bet I can't? [*He swings her into motion.*]

LAURA: Goodness, yes, you can!

JIM: Let yourself go, now, Laura, just let yourself go.

LAURA: I'm —

JIM: Come on!

LAURA: — trying!

JIM: Not so stiff — easy does it!

LAURA: I know but I'm —

JIM: Loosen th' backbone! There now, that's a lot better.

LAURA: Am I?

JIM: Lots, lots better! [*He moves her about the room in a clumsy waltz.*]

LAURA: Oh, my!

JIM: Ha-ha!

LAURA: Oh, my goodness!

JIM: Ha-ha-ha!

[*They suddently bump into the table, and the glass piece on it falls to the floor. Jim stops the dance.*]

What did we hit on?

LAURA: Table.

JIM: Did something fall off it? I think —

LAURA: Yes.

JIM: I hope it wasn't the little glass horse with the horn!

LAURA: Yes. [*She stoops to pick it up.*]

JIM: Aw, aw, aw. Is it broken?

LAURA: Now it is just like all the other horses.

JIM: It's lost its —

LAURA: Horn! It doesn't matter. Maybe it's a blessing in disguise.

JIM: You'll never forgive me. I bet that that was your favorite piece of glass.

LAURA: I don't have favorites much. It's no tragedy, Freckles. Glass breaks so easily. No matter how careful you are. The traffic jars the shelves and things fall off them.

JIM: Still I'm awfully sorry that I was the cause.

LAURA [*smiling*]: I'll just imagine he had an operation. The horn was removed to make him feel less — freakish!

[*The both laugh.*]

Now he will feel more at home with the other horses, the ones that don't have horns. . . .

JIM: Ha-ha, that's very funny! [*Suddenly he is serious.*] I'm glad to see that you have a sense of humor. You know — you're — well — very different! Surprisingly different from anyone else I know! [*His voice becomes soft and hesitant with a genuine feeling.*] Do you mind me telling you that?

[*Laura is abashed beyond speech.*]

I mean it in a nice way —

[*Laura nods shyly, looking away.*]

You make me feel sort of — I don't know how to put it! I'm usually pretty good at expressing things, but — this is something that I don't know how to say!

[*Laura touches her throat and clears it — turns the broken unicorn in her hands. His voice becomes softer.*]

Has anyone ever told you that you were pretty?

[*There is a pause, and the music rises slightly. Laura looks up slowly, with wonder, and shakes her head.*]

Well you are! In a very different way from anyone else. And all the nicer because of the difference, too.

[*His voice becomes low and husky. Laura turns away, nearly faint with the novelty of her emotions.*]

I wish that you were my sister. I'd teach you to have some confidence in yourself. The different people are not like other people, but being different is nothing to be ashamed of. Because other people are not such wonderful people. They're one hundred times one thousand. You're one times one! They walk all over the earth. You just stay here. They're common as — weeds, but — you — well, you're — *Blue Roses!*

[*Image on screen:* Blue Roses.]

[*The music changes.*]

LAURA: But blue is wrong for — roses. . . .

JIM: It's right for you! You're — pretty!

LAURA: In what respect am I pretty?

JIM: In all respects — believe me! Your eyes — your hair — are pretty! Your hands are pretty! [*He catches hold of her hand.*] You think I'm making this up because I'm invited to dinner and have to be nice. Oh, I could do that! I could put on an act for you, Laura, and say lots of things without being very sincere. But this time I am. I'm talking to you sincerely. I happened to notice you had this inferiority complex that keeps you from feeling comfortable with people. Somebody needs to build your confidence up and make you proud instead of shy and turning away and — blushing. Somebody — ought to — *kiss* you, Laura!

[*His hand slips slowly up her arm to her shoulder as the music swells tumultuously. He suddenly turns her about and kisses her on the lips. When he releases her, Laura sinks on the sofa with a bright, dazed look. Jim backs away and fishes in his pocket for a cigarette.*]

[*Legend on screen:* "A Souvenir."]

Stumblejohn!

[*He lights the cigarette, avoiding her look. There is a peal of girlish laughter from Amanda in the kitchenette. Laura slowly raises and opens her hand. It still contains the little broken glass animal. She looks at it with a tender, bewildered expression.*]

Stumblejohn! I shouldn't have done that — that was way off the beam. You don't smoke, do you?

[*She looks up, smiling, not hearing the question. He sits beside her rather gingerly. She looks at him speechlessly — waiting. He coughs decorously and moves a little farther aside as he considers the situation and senses her feelings, dimly, with perturbation. He speaks gently.*]

Would you — care for a — mint?

[*She doesn't seem to hear him but her look grows brighter even.*]

Peppermint? Life Saver? My pocket's a regular drugstore — wherever I go . . . . [*He pops a mint in his mouth. Then he gulps and decides to make a clean breast of it. He speaks slowly and gingerly.*] Laura, you know, if I had a sister like you, I'd do the same thing as Tom. I'd bring out fellows and — introduce her to them. The right type of boys — of a type to — appreciate her. Only — well — he made a mistake about me. Maybe I've got no call to be saying this. That may not have been the idea in having me over. But what if it was? There's nothing wrong about that. The only trouble is that in my case — I'm not in a situation to — do the right thing. I can't take down your number and say I'll phone. I can't call up next week and — ask for a date. I thought I had better explain the situation in case you — misunderstood it and — I hurt your feelings. . . .

[*There is a pause. Slowly, very slowly, Laura's look changes, her eyes returning slowly from his to the glass figure in her palm. Amanda utters another gay laugh in the kitchenette.*]

LAURA [*faintly*]: You — won't — call again?

JIM: No, Laura, I can't. [*He rises from the sofa.*] As I was just explaining, I've — got strings on me. Laura, I've — been going steady! I go out all the time with a girl named Betty. She's a home-girl like you, and Catholic, and Irish, and in a great many ways we — get along fine. I met her last summer on a moonlight boat trip up the river to Alton, on the *Majestic*. Well — right away from the start it was — love!

[*Legend:* Love!]

[*Laura sways slightly forward and grips the arm of the sofa. He fails to notice, now enrapt in his own comfortable being.*]

Being in love has made a new man of me!

[*Leaning stiffly forward, clutching the arm of the sofa, Laura struggles visibly with her storm. But Jim is oblivious; she is a long way off.*]

The power of love is really pretty tremendous! Love is something that — changes the whole world, Laura!

[*The storm abates a little and Laura leans back. He notices her again.*]

It happened that Betty's aunt took sick, she got a wire and had to go to Centralia. So Tom — when he asked me to dinner — I naturally just accepted the invitation, not knowing that you — that he — that I — [*He stops awkwardly.*] Huh — I'm a stumblejohn!

[*He flops back on the sofa. The holy candles on the altar of Laura's face have been snuffed out. There is a look of almost infinite desolation. Jim glances at her uneasily.*]

I wish that you would — say something.

[*She bites her lip which was trembling and then bravely smiles. She opens her hand again on the broken glass figure. Then she gently takes his hand and raises it level with her own. She carefully places the unicorn in the palm of his hand, then pushes his fingers closed upon it.*]

What are you — doing that for? You want me to have him? Laura?

[*She nods.*]

What for?

LAURA: A — souvenir. . . .

[*She rises unsteadily and crouches beside the Victrola to wind it up.*]

[*Legend on screen:* "Things have a way of turning out so badly!" *Or image:* "Gentleman caller waving goodbye — gaily."]

[*At this moment Amanda rushes brightly back into the living room. She bears a pitcher of fruit punch in an old-fashioned cut-glass pitcher, and a plate of macaroons. The plate has a gold border and poppies painted on it.*]

AMANDA: Well, well, well! Isn't the air delightful after the shower? I've made you children a little liquid refreshment.

[*She turns gaily to Jim.*] Jim, do you know that song about lemonade?

"Lemonade, lemonade

Made in the shade and stirred with a spade —

Good enough for any old maid!"

JIM [*uneasily*]: Ha-ha! No — I never heard it.

AMANDA: Why, Laura! You look so serious!

JIM: We were having a serious conversation.

AMANDA: Good! Now you're better acquainted!

JIM [*uncertainly*]: Ha-ha! Yes.

AMANDA: You modern young people are much more serious-minded than my generation. I was so gay as a girl!

JIM: You haven't changed, Mrs. Wingfield.

AMANDA: Tonight I'm rejuvenated! The gaiety of the occasion, Mr. O'Connor. [*She tosses her head with a peal of laughter, spilling some lemonade.*] Oooo! I'm baptizing myself!

JIM: Here — let me —

AMANDA [*setting the pitcher down*]: There now. I discovered we had some maraschino cherries. I dumped them in, juice and all!

JIM: You shouldn't have gone to that trouble, Mrs. Wingfield.

AMANDA: Trouble, trouble? Why, it was loads of fun! Didn't you hear me cutting up in the kitchen? I bet your ears were burning! I told Tom how outdone with him I was for keeping you to himself so long a time! He should have brought you over much, much sooner! Well, now that you've found your way, I want you to be a very frequent caller! Not just occasional but all the time! Oh, we're going to have a lot of gay times together! I see them coming! Mmm, just breathe that air! So fresh, and the moon's so pretty! I'll skip back out — I know where my place is when young folks are having a — serious conversation!

JIM: Oh, don't go out, Mrs. Wingfield. The fact of the matter is I've got to be going.

AMANDA: Going, now? You're joking! Why it's only the shank of the evening, Mr. O'Connor!

JIM: Well, you know how it is.

AMANDA: You mean you're a young workingman and have to keep workingmen's hours. We'll let you off early tonight. But only on the condition that next time you stay later. What's the best night for you? Isn't Saturday night the best night for you workingmen?

JIM: I have a couple of time-clocks to punch, Mrs. Wingfield. One at morning, another at night!

AMANDA: My, but you *are* ambitious! You work at night, too?

JIM: No, Ma'am, not work but — Betty!

[*He crosses deliberately to pick up his hat. The band at the Paradise Dance Hall goes into a tender waltz.*]

AMANDA: Betty? Betty? Who's — Betty!

[*There is an ominous cracking sound in the sky.*]

JIM: Oh, just a girl. The girl I go steady with!

[*He smiles charmingly. The sky falls.*]

[*Legend:* "The Sky Falls."]

AMANDA [*a long-drawn exhalation*]: Ohhhh . . . Is it a serious romance, Mr. O'Connor?

JIM: We're going to be married the second Sunday in June.

AMANDA: Ohhhh — how nice! Tom didn't mention that you were engaged to be married.

JIM: The cat's not out of the bag at the warehouse yet. You know how they are. They call you Romeo and stuff like that. [*He stops at the oval mirror to put on his hat. He carefully shapes the brim and the crown to give a discreetly dashing effect.*] It's been a wonderful evening, Mrs. Wingfield. I guess this is what they mean by Southern hospitality.

AMANDA: It really wasn't anything at all.

JIM: I hope it don't seem like I'm rushing off. But I promised Betty I'd pick her up at the Wabash depot, an' by the time I get my jalopy down there her train'll be in. Some women are pretty upset if you keep 'em waiting.

AMANDA: Yes, I know — the tyranny of women! [*She extends her hand.*] Goodbye, Mr. O'Connor. I wish you luck — and happiness — and success! All three of them, and so does Laura! Don't you, Laura?

LAURA: Yes!

JIM [*taking Laura's hand*]: Goodbye, Laura. I'm certainly going to treasure that souvenir. And don't you forget the good advice I gave you. [*He raises his voice to a cheery shout.*] So long, Shakespeare! Thanks again, ladies. Good night!

[*He grins and ducks jauntily out. Still bravely grimacing, Amanda closes the door on the gentleman caller. Then she turns back to the room with a puzzled expression. She and Laura don't dare to face each other. Laura crouches beside the Victrola to wind it.*]

AMANDA [*faintly*]: Things have a way of turning out so badly. I don't believe that I would play the Victrola. Well, well — well! Our gentleman caller was engaged to be married! [*She raises her voice.*] Tom!

TOM [*from the kitchenette*]: Yes, Mother?

AMANDA: Come in here a minute. I want to tell you something awfully funny.

TOM [*entering with a macaroon and a glass of the lemonade*]: Has the gentleman caller gotten away already?

AMANDA: The gentleman caller has made an early departure. What a wonderful joke you played on us!

TOM: How do you mean?

AMANDA: You didn't mention that he was engaged to be married.

TOM: Jim? Engaged?

AMANDA: That's what he just informed us.

TOM: I'll be jiggered! I didn't know about that.

AMANDA: That seems very peculiar.

TOM: What's peculiar about it?

AMANDA: Didn't you call him your best friend down at the warehouse?

TOM: He is, but how did I know?

AMANDA: It seems extremely peculiar that you wouldn't know your best friend was going to be married!

TOM: The warehouse is where I work, not where I know things about people!

AMANDA: You don't know things anywhere! You live in a dream; you manufacture illusions!

[*He crosses to the door.*]

Where are you going?

TOM: I'm going to the movies.

AMANDA: That's right, now that you've had us make such fools of ourselves. The effort, the preparations, all the expense! The new floor lamp, the rug, the clothes for Laura! All for what? To entertain some other girl's fiancé! Go to the movies, go! Don't think about us, a mother deserted, an unmarried sister who's crippled and has no job! Don't let anything interfere with your selfish pleasure! Just go, go, go — to the movies!

TOM: All right, I will! The more you shout about my selfishness to me the quicker I'll go, and I won't go to the movies!

AMANDA: Go, then! Go to the moon — you selfish dreamer!

[*Tom smashes his glass on the floor. He plunges out on the fire escape, slamming the door. Laura screams in fright. The dance-hall music becomes louder. Tom stands on the fire escape, gripping the rail. The moon breaks through the storm clouds, illuminating his face.*]

[*Legend on screen: "And so goodbye . . ."*]

[*Tom's closing speech is timed with what is happening inside the house. We see, as though through soundproof glass, that Amanda appears to be making a comforting speech to Laura, who is huddled upon the sofa. Now that we cannot hear the mother's speech, her silliness is gone and she has dignity and tragic beauty. Laura's hair hides her face until, at the end of the speech, she lifts her head to smile at her mother. Amanda's gestures are slow and graceful, almost dancelike, as she comforts her daughter. At the end of her speech she glances a moment at the father's picture — then withdraws through the portieres. At the close of Tom's speech, Laura blows out the candles, ending the play.*]

TOM: I didn't go to the moon, I went much further — for time is the longest distance between two places. Not long after that I was fired for writing a poem on the lid of a shoe-box. I left Saint Louis. I descended the steps of this fire escape for a last time and followed, from then on, in my father's footsteps, attempting to find in motion what was lost in space. I traveled around a great deal. The cities swept about me like dead leaves, leaves that were brightly colored but torn away from the branches. I would have stopped, but I was pursued by something. It always came upon me unawares, taking me altogether by surprise. Perhaps it was a familiar bit of music. Perhaps it was only a piece of transparent glass. Perhaps I am walking along a street at night, in some strange city, before I have found companions. I pass the lighted window of a shop where perfume is sold. The window is filled with pieces of colored glass, tiny transparent bottles in delicate colors, like bits of a shattered rainbow. Then all at once my sister touches my shoulder. I turn around and look into her eyes. Oh, Laura, Laura, I tried to leave you behind me, but I am more faithful than I intended to be! I reach for a cigarette, I cross the street, I run into the movies or a bar, I buy a drink, I speak to the nearest stranger — anything that can blow your candles out!

[*Laura bends over the candles*.]

For nowadays the world is lit by lightning! Blow out your candles, Laura — and so goodbye. . . .

[*She blows the candles out*.]

A SOUTHERN MISCELLANY

A DRIVE DOWN ALMOST any twisting road in one of the myriad hollows in Appalachia will reveal that many of the crafts so prevalent throughout the entire South in the nineteenth century still continue today. Though the diminishing number of older mountain artisans have not forgotten the art of pottery-making or glass-blowing handed down from one generation to another, the younger ones approach these traditional crafts from a more technical point of view, as their innovative and often daring designs, shapes, and colors reveal. Throughout the entire United States, there even seems to be renewed interest in the folk arts of the past as Americans (and foreigners, too, for that matter) rediscover the forms and functions of simple artifacts that have long been part of American history.

Perhaps no craft has been appreciated over the years as much as that of quilting. Quilts, made up, as they are, of diverse textures and highly prized designs, could well serve as an image for "A Southern Miscellany," this section of our anthology that stitches together important reminiscences, essays, and interviews of well-known Southern writers in an effort to provide a larger, contextual framework for the intricate patterns of their fiction, poetry, and drama. The names of the quilts, often based on geometric designs, flowers, scrolls, animals, and family stories — and, when silks, satins, velvets, and brocades became available, quilts were specially cut for making skirts and vests — would please almost anyone who enjoys riding the London tubes: Roman stripe, Dresden plate, giant tumbling blocks, fence rail, Amish diamond, birds-in-air, double wedding ring, mariner's compass, nine patch, rolling stone, North Carolina lily, robbing Peter to pay Paul, old maid's patience, schoolhouse, tree-of-life, sunshine and shadow, Lafayette's orange peel, grandmother's fan, and cross-in-square to name but a few. In all, quilts express a type of imagination that emerges, one way or another, from deep within an exuberant, communal, visual, and pragmatic psyche, as elaborately described in Eudora Welty's moving tribute to Ida M'Toy.

William Faulkner's "Mississippi," which appeared in *Holiday* magazine in April 1954, provides marvelous whole cloth for a Southern literary quilt, because it imaginatively explores the history of the South by portraying Faulkner's fictional characters — the DeSpains, the Sartorises, the Compsons, the McCaslins, the Ewells, the Snopses — as genuine, historical, representative personages who settled in the South in general and Mississippi in particular. In transforming such characters into historical types, Faulkner fuses together his fiction with verifiable Southern history, and the result is that his characters enter into our memories in such a way that we are not forced to distinguish between what "really" happened with the way he depicted it. And Faulkner's emphases on history, place, and people underscore central themes that the other writers represented in this anthology have likewise developed. In "Mississippi," Faulkner traces the successive waves of slaves and landowners, of yeomen and gentry, as seen initially through the eyes of a child who, as he grows up, eventually assumes the position of a Southern gentleman. Along the way, the young boy is juxtaposed with the Old Man, the Mississippi River, whose waters continue to be the systole and diastole of Southern lifeblood, providing the land and its inhabitants with the nourishment needed to survive. Faulkner shows, as he does likewise in *Go Down, Moses* (1942), that the Delta towns prospered because of increasing cotton and lumber traffic, while the wilderness began to shrink as man built asphalt roads and confined the bear and deer and other wild animals to vanishing, remote areas.

Ever sensitive to man's relationship to his environment, Faulkner, as the omnipresent *persona* in this essay, knew from experience that the Old Man has a mind of his own, and for centuries could fool those who lived on his banks into a sense of false security whenever he wanted. Thus, those Southerners who lived near the Mississippi, and those who were dependent on this river, had to be both respectful and resourceful as they took what they had and planned for the future, fully aware of the vicissitudes of time, place, and weather. It is fitting that Faulkner finishes this essay by dramatizing his young daughter and Mammy Caroline [Barr] quietly working together on a quilt for his daughter's hope chest: "There was electricity in [Mammy Caroline's] cabin now, but she would not use it, insisting still on the kerosene lamps which she had always known. Nor would she use the spectacles either, wearing them merely as an ornament across the brow of the immaculate white cloth — headrag — which bound her now hairless head. She did not need them: a smolder of wood ashes on the hearth winter and summer in which sweet potatoes roasted, the five-year-old white child in a miniature rocking chair at one side of it and the aged Negress, not a great deal larger, in her chair at the other, the basket bright with scraps and fragments of cloth between them and in that dim light in which the middleaged [Faulkner] himself could not have read his own name without his glasses, the two of them with infinitesimal and tedious and patient stitches annealing the bright stars and squares and diamonds into another pattern to be folded away among the cedar shavings in the trunk." This charming vignette, which soars from the warmly human to the ethereally mythic, embodies important social and moral dimensions found in some of Faulkner's major fiction, as the fire and the hearth provide a familial ambiance where people of different generations and races can communicate with one another.

This essay, in turn, provides an excellent framework in which to read Shelby Foote's three-volume history of the Civil War, a comprehensive and dramatic work by a novelist and historian who believes that there is a definite connaturality between fiction and history, as he mentions in his interview with John Jones: "No, they're not that different, writing history and writing fiction. All the same problems are there . . . . You are looking for the truth, and, as I said also, it's not a different truth, it's the same truth. You try and find out the truth, and it doesn't really make that much difference — to the person writing it, anyhow, whether you made up the facts, which you then must respect, or you found them in documents which you must respect. I never felt cramped at all while writing the history. I felt just as free as I feel when I'm writing a novel." In his own way, C. Vann Woodward confirms Foote's views in subscribing to what Robert Penn Warren wrote in "Wind and Gibbon": "History is not truth. Truth is in the telling." These historians of the South, and it would not be difficult to add many others, including T. Harry Williams, Dumas Malone, George Brown Tindall, and Joel Williamson, have revealed aspects of Southern society that have served to reinforce the views of Southern fiction writers, who invent and relate the events and truths that help mankind endure, as Faulkner phrased it in his Nobel Prize Speech (perhaps a bit bombastically), "by reminding him of the courage and honor and hope and pride and compassion and pity and sacrifice which have been the glory of his past."

Woodward, professor emeritus of history at Yale, and winner of the Bancroft and Pulitzer Prizes, and author of the important *Origins of the New South, 1877-1913* (1951) and *The Strange Career of Jim Crow* (1955) is keenly aware that modern historians, often preoccupied by sequential chronological development and prompted by a desire to find order in the affairs of mankind, must overcome the penchant to delve into the past, as R. G. Collingwood notes, and end up by cataloguing sociological fossils, identifying former societal strata, and presenting the past in the form of dioramas where the curious peer through glass windows at papier-mâché figures bending over glowing plastic fireplaces. Southerners, unlike other Americans, often feel less removed from their own historical past; for many, the imaginatively honest works of both Southern novelists and historians have reduced the textbookish quality of history that renders it distant from the immediacy of human life.

We know, however, from our collective experience of contemporary situations that Southern history, of events as distant from us as the battle of Bull Run and the surrender at Appomattox, even when studied chronologically, have both an inner and an outer dimension, and these have to be properly aligned so that our vision of them has perspective, depth, and vital meaning. Historians must go beyond an analysis of the properties of the events they are investigating to the point whereby they can appreciate the thought expressed in these events. C. Vann Woodward in *Thinking Back: The Perils of Writing History* (1986) has related the difficulties he had when he grappled with the problems linking Southern history and fiction; with a characteristic sense of largesse, he writes that Southern men and women of letters "did not encourage sociological generalization about types, classes, or races — planters, yeomen, poor whites, or slaves — but rather supported the historian's concern for the particular, the concrete, the individual. Most important of all was the proof so magnificently presented in their work that the provincial subject matter we shared was no trap of obscurity but an embarrassment of riches, a treasure of neglected opportunity." The historian's task, then, aided by the fiction writer's and the poet's imagination, challenges him to discover within himself the thought of others in such a way as to re-enact such past thought in his own mind; thus, creative evaluation and conscientious discernment become essential tools of the historian's trade. Neither Faulkner, Foote, nor Woodward has been Pollyanish in their various descriptions of the specifics of Southern fiction, culture, and history, and certainly none of them has expressed views that would foreclose on the South's future. Faulkner's highly personal conclusion to "Mississippi" could well summarize the tension that most historians and fiction writers of the South have experienced at one time or another: "Loving all of it even while he had to hate some of it because he knows now that you don't love because: you love despite; not for the virtues, but despite the faults."

For Louis D. Rubin, Jr., educator, critic of Southern literature and culture, and publisher, what united the East-Coast Southern world he grew up in was not the Mississippi, but the railroad, and in particular the Boll Weevil — the "little gas-electric locomotive coach . . . placed in service in the early 1920s." It was so named because "the black folk of the South Carolina sea-islands through which the little train passed fancied its resemblance to the bug which had moved northward and then eastward from Mexico to devastate the cotton crops." From this little train, reminiscent of the Yellow Dog in Eudora Welty's *Delta Wedding,* one could catch a glimpse of small towns and flag-stop stations — as well as of Charleston and Savannah — and sense briefly the diversity of Southern life. For Rubin, going back to Charleston after World War II was a far different experience than he had expected: "Charleston had changed in many ways, and my loyalty and attachment were really not so much to a place as to a time — to years when I had been a child and an adolescent growing up in a small Southern city. And Charleston was not that any more: this was borne in on me whenever I went back to visit." Like others who have found themselves in analogous situations, such as the young Bayard Sartoris returning home from World War I in Faulkner's *Sartoris* (1929), George Webber in Thomas Wolfe's *You Can't Go Home Again* (1940), and Laurel McKelva Hand in Eudora Welty's *The Optimist's Daughter* (1972), Rubin asks an essential question: "*Is* the South becoming the 'non-South'?" His answer is a tempered and nuanced "No." Rubin knows that the South long has had a habit of incorporating seemingly destructive elements and turning them into something creative and energizing. Each decisive step in the South's history, he notes, such as the Civil War, Reconstruction, the New South through the 1890's, the Populist revolt, World War I, the Depression, the New Deal, the downfall of King Cotton, Brown vs. Board of Education, the industrialization of the 1960's and

1970's, and even the election of Jimmy Carter, might have contributed significantly to the disappearance of the South; yet, the South continues to exist and be identified as such, even though old neighborhoods and even whole cities have undergone processes of change and development.

Faulkner in his 1956 interview with Jean Stein also highlights the importance of place and his native region, his own "little postage stamp of native soil" as he called it, and how from the late 1920's on (even though he would eventually be living in Hollywood and Charlottesville), he would never "live long enough to exhaust it, and by sublimating the actual into the apocryphal" he would have "complete liberty to use whatever talent" he might have to its fullest. Northern Mississippi "opened up a gold mine of other peoples, so I created a cosmos of my own. I can move these people around like God, not only in space but in time too." Thus, Faulkner's lifelong fidelity to Mississippi and the South as both a source and a locus for his fiction should not surprise us since most Americans identify strongly with the place where they were born and raised, even if, in fact, their hometown has so changed that they prefer to live somewhere else. One automatically associates Faulkner with Oxford, Mississippi, and his imaginary Yoknapatawpha County; Willie Morris with Yazoo, Mississippi; Walker Percy with Greenville, Mississippi, and Covington, Louisiana; Flannery O'Connor with Milledgeville, Georgia; Shelby Foote with Memphis, Tennessee, and Thomas Wolfe with Asheville, North Carolina.

Eudora Welty, who has lived all her life in Jackson, Mississippi, has written that place "absorbs our earliest notice and attention, it bestows on us our original awareness; and our critical powers spring up from the study of it and the growth of experience inside it. It perseveres in bringing us back to earth when we fly too high. It never really stops informing us, for it is forever astir, alive, changing, reflecting, like the mind of man itself. One place comprehended can make us understand other places better. Sense of place gives equilibrium; extended, it is sense of direction, too. Carried off we might be in spirit, and should be, when we are reading or writing something good; but it is the sense of place going with us still that is the ball of golden thread to carry us there and back and in every sense of the word to bring us home." One of the hallmarks of Southern fiction is that Southern writers rarely go beyond the borders of the South to find their subject matter; despite a highly mobile American society, they seem to be inveterate, determined homebodies.

This word "home," so essential in our American vocabulary and often difficult to find the exact equivalent of in other languages, is powerfully dramatized in James Agee's Pulitzer Prize-winning *A Death in the Family* (1941), most notably in the novel's preface, "Knoxville: Summer 1915." In this lyrical introduction, beautifully set to music by Samuel Barber, Agee pictures that betwitching time after dinner as families enjoy the quiet of a summer evening; some wash the dishes, others water their lawns with nozzles that create wide bells of film, while still others sit serenely on front porches and rehearse the day's activities. For Rufus, the young protagonist, his whole world is localized on a quilt in the family's back yard, and in a reflective mood he praises and blesses his existence: "By some chance, here they are, all on this earth; and who shall ever tell the sorrow of being on this earth, lying, on quilts, on the grass, in a summer evening, among the sounds of the night. May God bless my people, my uncle, my aunt, my mother, my good father, oh, remember them kindly in their time of trouble; and in the hour of their taking away." The death of Rufus's father provides a catalyst for Rufus, his sister, and his mother to regroup and find those values in their lives that can give them strength, hope, and courage to continue, and bears witness to the spiritual dimension in Southern fiction, as exemplified most dramatically in the essays and fiction of Flannery O'Connor and Walker Percy.

Rufus's situation is not unsimilar to the one young Walker Percy and his two brothers found themselves in when first their father and then their mother died, and they were subsequently taken in and adopted by their cousin, William Alexander Percy, the famous Greenville, Mississippi, poet, plantation owner, and author of *Lanterns on the Levee* (1941), a forthright and intimate chronicle that bridges two epochs. This book records the changes that took place as many saw the old ways disappear and new ways emerge that threatened and disoriented them. "Of Will Percy," Carl Sandburg once wrote, "it might be said that he is to the state of Mississippi what William Allen White is to Kansas, what Fiorello LaGuardia is to Manhattan. Each has his life story identified with, inextricably joined to, his locale and region. The deep South, the old South, new South, several Souths move across Percy's autobiography." Percy's first chapter is entitled "The Delta" and his last "Home," and in between are the moving recollections of a planter's son, his education at Sewanee and Harvard Law School, and his battles on various fronts, including those against the Ku Klux Klan and the Mississippi flood of 1927.

Spending his formative years, from fourteen to twenty-six years of age, in his uncle's house, Walker Percy had a chance to observe his uncle firsthand and assess gradually his uncle's views; it did not surprise Walker Percy that his uncle would continue to develop his views after writing *Lanterns on the Levee,* and that the Northern liberals, whom he lashed out at and who seem as difficult to locate as the Southern aristocrats in W.J. Cash's *The Mind of the South* (1941), could well have become trusted business partners and even friends had he lived long enough. Today, as Walker Percy reminds us, William Alexander Percy might find most "members of his own 'class' not exactly embattled in a heroic Götterdämmerung, not exactly fighting the good fight as he called it, but having simply left, taken off for the exurbs where, barricaded in patrolled subdivisions and country clubs and private academies, they worry about their kids and drugs."

As one of America's outstanding novelists and men of letters, Walker Percy has continued the family tradition and distinguished himself over the years as a witty and probing thinker and creative writer. Well-versed in the works of both European and American philosophic and semiotic writers, from Søren Kierkegaard to Gabriel Marcel, from Charles Sanders Peirce to Ludwig Wittgenstein, and as someone who received a medical degree but does not practice medicine, he has captured the spirit of the modern Christian wayfarer who often lives on the fringes of society, yet does not hesitate to question life's fundamental values. As Dr. Percy wrote in *The Message in the Bottle,* "The question is not whether the Good News is no longer relevant, rather whether it is possible that man is presently undergoing a temptuous restructuring of his consciousness which does not allow him to take account of the Good News." Many of the protagonists in Walker Percy's novels, including Binx Bolling, Will Barrett, and Dr. Thomas More, know that the search is the normal condition in life. And like Helen Keller, a woman who has obviously touched Walker Percy's life in many ways, he has given a spiritual vision to those of his readers who wish to correlate their complex experiences with an adequate expression of them.

As do most Americans, Southerners come in all sizes, shapes, and colors, and belong to a large number of religious denominations. A group picture of them is impossible, though they do have features that outsiders tend to recognize. One thing is for certain, however: They recognize one another and have tremendous reverence for each other, something that surpasses being polite or hospitable. Zora Neale Hurston writes that in the early part of this century many Southerners were not given to reading books, and thus some took their manner of addressing one another right out of the barnyard and woods: "When they get through with you," she wrote, "you and your whole family look like an acre of totem poles." At one point in *Dust Tracks on a Road* (1942), her autobiography, she tells of meeting a group of musicians from the North, who were ignorant of the way Southerners regard one another: "They did not know of the way an average Southern child, white or black, is raised on simile and invective. They know how to call names. It is an everyday affair to hear somebody called a mullet-headed, mule-eared, wall-eyed, hog-nosed, 'gator-faced, shad-mouthed, screw-necked, goat-bellied, pussle-gutted, camel-backed, butt-spring, battle-hammed, knock-kneed, razor-legged, box-ankled, shovel-footed, unmated so-and-so. . . ." Such epithets, however, mask an honesty, a love of metaphor, and an acceptance of one another, as only people who have been close to one another can use. And who would deny that a character description of someone else is often a self-portrait? Eudora Welty has said that for one person to call another "unforgettable" seems a trifle condescending, yet her sketch and photographs of Ida M'Toy are unforgettable. After years of serving as a practical nurse in Jackson, Mississippi, Ida M'Toy, a black woman, began selling clothes from a makeshift store in her house. Miss Welty portrays her subject as one who "despises a drab color and welcomes bright clothes with a queenly and triumphant smile, as if she acknowledges the bold brave heart that chose that . . . . Her customers, poverty-bound little cooks and maids and cotton-choppers, go away feeling that they have turned into queens. Ida has put second-hand clothes on their backs and, with all the abrupt bullying of a busy fairy, wrapped them in some glowing raiment of illusion, set them in a whirl of bedazzlement; and they skitter out with shining eyes and empty hands, with every hoarded penny spent." Perhaps it is appropriate to conclude with a picture of Ida M'Toy and her magical powers to transform and give enormous delight to others; she remains a symbol, for all to see and know, of the Southern creative imagination that, as Faulkner said, is able to arrest motion and hold it fixed so that one hundred years later "when a stranger looks at it, it moves again since it is life."

• ESSAYS •

• W. J. • CASH

from

The Mind of the South

SUCH WAS THE GENERAL picture of the South in 1932. Everybody was either ruined beyond his wildest previous fears or stood in peril of such ruin. And the general psychological reaction? First a universal bewilderment and terror, which perhaps went beyond that of the nation at large by the measure of the South's lack of training in analysis, and particularly social analysis. Men everywhere walked in a kind of daze. They clustered, at first to assure one another that all would shortly be well; then, with the passage of time, to ask questions in the pleading hope of thus being assured; but in the end they fled before the thought in one another's eyes.

And along with this there went in the case of the masses a slow wondering and questioning, and in the end a gradually developing bitterness of desperation. They had laughed at first, uneasily. But afterward, when they heard from the pulpit that it was a punishment visited upon the people from the hand of God as the penalty of their sins (and they did hear it in almost solid chorus from the ministers), they accepted it in some fashion, and, as always, without demur. Yet beneath that acceptance something else was plainly going on. More completely and helplessly in the grip of social forces than Southerners had ever been before — even more completely and helplessly perhaps than in Reconstruction and Populist times — they blamed the Yankee, in the shape of Wall Street, as their fathers before them had blamed him, muttered curses against the name of Morgan as the epitome of it. But beyond that they puzzled with furrowed brows at a vague shadow looming over them — the shadow of organized society. For the first time in the history of the South they dimly felt the thing was there, and groped to make out its shape and form and nature and to comprehend how it came to have so much power over themselves, as a child gropes to grasp the far-away woods and hills through the pane of his nursery window.

And in the last days before the coming of Roosevelt, some of them, despairing of making sense of it, were falling into the impatient mood natural to simple men when confronted with what defies their understanding and wishing that they might sweep it all aside and start again with a more readily comprehensible world; they were using the word "revolution." Very cloudy was their wishing, very far were they from the will to action, very greatly did they fall short of being the majority as yet, and very unclear was every one of them as to precisely whom and what it was he meant to rebel against. Nevertheless, there the word was, marching about in the open. I myself heard it in the most conservative communities in North Carolina, both rural and urban, and from men of sober and grave mind.

In the classes, moreover, there was something of a correlative mood. With the best of all possible worlds crumpling about their ears, the ruling orders, or at least a surprisingly large number of the people who made them up, were more nearly shocked out of the old smugness than they ever had been. For them also the shadow of organized society had swung close enough to be almost palpable, and in their turn they were fumbling for its meaning, too. Now and then one of them was actually wondering if after all it were true that noses were manifestly made for the bearing of spectacles. And many of them were exhibiting a strange humbleness of spirit — were confessing that it was possible that they, the South, America, the world, had been following false gods all during that long period of speculation in the twenties, were granting even that their leadership had perhaps not been as wise as it might have been, and that reforms were going to have to be made to set things right again. At the summit of the matter, indeed, some of them were actually — not embracing the notion of revolution, certainly, but, at the last, viewing it with the apathetic eyes of men who have looked so long on terror that they no longer feel much of anything. They were talking of it in quiet voices as something which was sure to come soon or late, unless there was a great change.

And so it fell out that no section of the country greeted Franklin Roosevelt and the New Deal with more intense and unfeigned enthusiasm than did the South. Probably, indeed, no other section greeted them with nearly so much enthusiasm.

It was obvious enough that the basic Rooseveltian ideas, with their emphasis on the social values as against the individual, and on the necessity of revising all values in the light of the conditions created by the machine and the disappearance of the frontier, ran directly contrary to the basic Southern attitudes. And moreover, the New Deal was in some respects actually to aggravate the bad conditions in the

South, or at least to seem responsible for it. Take the case of the agricultural program, for instance.

As I have already indicated, the collapse of credit consequent on the low price brought by the cotton crop of 1931, plus the naturally discouraging effect of that price itself, had resulted in a great reduction of acreage planted to cotton in 1932. But in the first year in which the New Deal curtailment and subsidy schemes came into effect — 1934 — the acreage was to go down to less than twenty-eight million acres, which represented a decline of over thirteen million acres from 1931, more than twenty million from 1926, and more than six million from even 1910! And in 1935 the figure would remain about the same. All of which meant, naturally, that unemployment among tenant farmers and sharecroppers was again enormously increased.

In industry also, first NRA, with its increased wages and shortened hours, and afterward the Wagner Labor Relations Act and the Wage and Hour Law were to have a somewhat comparable effect. For these acted on the owners of the cotton mills and those of nearly all other sorts of factories to move them to seek to dispense with as many employees as possible — in the case of the cotton mills by making the stretch-out virtually universal, and in all cases by turning increasingly to the use of machines wherever they could be made to replace labor — a tendency which has continued right on down to the present.

But the South took no cognizance of any of this. Roosevelt was hope and confidence after long despair. And more than that, he was hope and confidence riding under the banner of the Democratic Party, over what appeared then to be the emaciated corpse of the Republican Party, under whose rule catastrophe had arrived. For the South, in truth, it was almost as though the bones of Pickett and his brigade had suddenly sprung alive to go galloping up that slope at Gettysburg again and snatch victory from the Yankee's hand after all. And many and many a man felt in his inmost soul that it was really worth having endured the unfortunate Mr. Hoover for four years to have achieved at last the satisfaction of seeing the old Black Radical enemy and oppressor brought to complete rout and ignominy. I have myself heard the sentiment pointedly expressed.

Nor was it only that Roosevelt was Democracy hopeful and confident. He was also Democracy triumphant — Democracy sweeping dramatically and swiftly toward success. Probably it was in many ways only temporary and inadequate success, bought by doubtful means. But there it was for the time being, indubitably; however much it might be true that the New Deal was at least partly canceling out its own purposes in the South, as in the rest of the United States, the overwhelmingly dominant fact was that it had rescued the section — again, along with the nation at large — from the vicious circle of increasing ruin in which it had been caught from 1929 forward.

First it proceeded to save most of the bankers who were not already wholly liquidated, dead, or in jail. Usually, that was accomplished, indeed, by having the depositors agree to lose a more or less great part of their savings. Nevertheless, it wasn't long until these depositors themselves did begin to recover what was left of their wealth, whereas most of them had once despaired of ever again seeing any part of it; hence everybody was content.

And having saved the bankers and the depositors, this New Deal, with its huge spending, its wide benefit payments, and its various programs, was going on plainly to get the wheels of the whole economic machine to rolling again — with a vast creaking and reluctance, to be sure, but quite perceptibly none the less. If rural unemployment was increasing as a result of the farm programs, that fact was nothing to the majority of the rural population as against the fact that cotton would bring a peak price of nearly twelve cents in 1933, nearly fourteen cents in 1934 and 1935, and that in 1936 it would actually climb up to nearly fifteen cents. And if the devaluation of the currency made those prices somewhat illusory in reality, that fact of course went generally unnoted. When to that was added the relief programs, the very existence of the increase in unemployment was largely obscured, not only for the South in general but even for the unemployed themselves. For WPA wages or direct relief payments did more than barely make their condition tolerable for these dispossessed ones; often, in the case of the least ambitious, it actually made their whole life much more tolerable than it had ever been before.

The Democratic politicians in Washington who managed the practical distribution of relief funds, observing cannily that money spent in a section which was certain to be Democratic anyhow could have no effect for political purposes; observing also that the South had always stoutly maintained that lower wages than those paid elsewhere in the nation were justified here because of alleged lower living costs; and being pressed by the Southerners among their own ranks and by the Southern politicians in general, not to make the payments in the section large enough to "spoil" those on the relief rolls for private employment — these politicians dealt with Dixie with a striking niggardliness. WPA wages ranged from less than thirty dollars per month up to fifty or a little more, according to the state in question and the skill of the worker, but in no case much exceeded half that paid in the East, and in all cases was a great deal less than that paid in any other section of the country.

Scanty as this was, however, it generally exceeded what a sharecropper, black or white, and many tenants, could make even when they had employment and even when their whole families worked — for that matter what many day laborers, servants, and so on in the towns could make, also. For the tenant and sharecropper it had the disadvantage, certainly, that it called for working all the year round instead of less than half the time. But the hours were so short and the labor generally so light that this made little real difference. Hence it was natural enough that among the unambitious and unproud their passage from productive employment to the relief rolls was not felt as an unbearably unpleasant turn of affairs.

Similarly in industry. If the total possibility of employment was being reduced as the employers turned to a greater use of machines, that fact was blotted out of view by the consideration that the mills at last were starting up again, running with more and more regularity, that wages were back to something more like the old levels, and that hours had been reduced beyond the wildest dream ever before harbored by Southern workers. Even the cottonmill stretch-out, at bottom still bitterly hated and resented, became almost supportable for the moment.

Relief and Social Security played their part here, too: in providing refuge for the workers who remained unemployed, or in easing the fears of those who had jobs as to what would happen if the worst came about and they lost them.

And finally, not only industrialists, landowners, and labor, rural and agricultural, but the whole business community felt hopeful again. Business was increasing only inch by inch perhaps, and had a long way to go before it would be really good. Nevertheless, it was plainly on the upgrade. Even rents were beginning to rise again and the realtors, the very speculators who survived, began eagerly to conjure up visions of saving all the water in their properties yet.

Thus the South, essentially as unanalytical now as it had always been, bothered neither to observe that the New Deal ran counter to its established ideas and values or to weigh it in any wise, but took Mr. Roosevelt and all his purposes to its heart with a great burst of thanksgiving. And in the first glad relief of escape from terror and defeat, even the ruling classes carried, or seemed to carry, that mood of candor and humbleness of spirit which they had begun to show before Roosevelt to greater lengths still.

From every public platform, the politicians of the established Democratic machines, enjoying such patronage as they had never before imagined, unanimously declaimed over again every utterance of Mr. Roosevelt's; announced that the South, like the nation, had plainly been wrong in the 1920's, had too long neglected its duties to the underdog; declared their undying allegiance to every objective of the new order — seemed half to mean it; to anyone who was not acquainted with the Southern habit of making words serve for deeds, would have seemed wholly to mean it.

And the mood found echo in virtually every editorial page, including even such standpatters as the *Charlotte Observer*; in virtually everybody one met in the streets. The very bankers and many of the factory masters echoed it with no more than a few cautious reservations.

Looking at the South in those days, indeed, one might readily have concluded that at last the old pattern was on its way to conclusive break-up, that new ideas and a new tolerance were sweeping the field, and that the region as a whole, growing genuinely social-minded and realistic, was setting itself to examine its problems with clear eyes and dispassionate temper — in a word, that the old long lag between the Southern mind and the changing conditions of the Southern world was about to end. And if, having looked once, the observer had gone away and continued from afar to search in the news from the section for evidence to bear out the conclusion, he might have gone on to the present believing it to be entirely sound. For great and real changes were indubitably taking place, and others were in the making.

There was the fact, for instance, that the Southern people in most of the states were throwing off the incubus of prohibition; and in the larger towns at least, even showing a growing tendency to cast off such bonds as the old Sunday blue laws, in the teeth of the bitter-end opposition of the clergy.

What lay behind this immediately was probably the prevailing enthusiasm for Mr. Roosevelt, the desire to carry out all his suggestions to the limit. But what made it possible for even that enthusiasm to override the obstacles in the way was the fact that the great debacle in Hoover's Administration had definitely shaken the undisputed sway over politics which the ministers had formerly exercised. Southern people of all classes, perhaps more generally than the relatively more complex population of the rest of the nation, blamed and resented Mr. Hoover for all their troubles. And blaming him, they inevitably turned to remembering that it was the ministers who had led the South to abandon its historical allegiance to the Democratic Party in 1928, and so, especially in the towns, to doubting that their pronouncements on politics were always and necessarily inspired by Heaven.

Incidentally, it is interesting to note in this connection that no extensive religious revival developed in the South in the years of the depression, though the off-brand hysterical sects capitalized on it greatly to extend their membership and influence. In view of the history and tradition of the section, such revivals might reasonably have been expected to be one of the most certain reactions to the prevailing terror and despair.

But ultimately, perhaps, the new breaking of so-called moral bonds testified to more than the immediate factors I mention. To the fact that, here as everywhere, life in the town was having its cumulative effect and making inevitably for the slow dissociation of traditional concepts which no longer fitted the needs of the environment. To the slow filtering, if only at fourth hand, of the modern ideology through considerable segments of the urban population; and to the fact that in the depression period of wondering and questioning, men had sometimes turned their new doubts on other things than economics. In fine, to a still cloudy but genuine growth toward rationalistic attitudes, a certain weariness with the old feeling that the word atoned for the deed, and a developing sense that candid acceptance of innocent hedonism was a way of life better adapted to town-dwellers at least than covert indulgence behind official Puritanism — a mounting impatience with taboo for mere taboo's sake.

The thirties would also witness a further decline in lynching, though the first half of the decade threatened to prove that the practice was actually on the increase. In 1930 a total of twenty Negroes was lynched, as against seven in 1929. The next year the figure was twelve. In 1932 it dipped abruptly to six, soared to twenty-four in 1933, declined only to fifteen in 1934, mounted again to eighteen in 1935.

What explains this surge it is hard to say. The most obvious guess is that it was a reaction to the prevailing emotions of terror and despair; an attempt on the part of the harried rural white population to reassure itself by performing the old White Supremacy ritual, to achieve both relief from intolerable tensions and the old desperate, pleasurable sense of power associated with the action. But it is difficult to reconcile the assumption with the record for 1932, when these emotions were presumably at their height, or with that for the next three years, when terror and despair were certainly receding. That is, unless we are to suppose that in 1932 apathy, the issue of terror and despair, had gone so far as to benumb any effort at alleviation even by such feverish devices as lynching, and that after Mr. Roosevelt's election returning exuberance gave a fillip to the crime. Perhaps the true key to the matter is that any new reduction in the incidence of the crime was likely to remain precarious for a considerable length of time, and that the record for any one year or even several years would in a great measure depend on the law of chance as it governed the development of local incidents apt to give rise to the crime.

At any rate, such organizations as the Association of Southern women for the Prevention of Lynching and the Commission on Interracial Cooperation were greatly extending their influence even as the surge was in progress. The former had devised an effective scheme for combating the practice by appointing as observers in every county where it was possible women of high social rank, whose duty it was to find out about threatened lynchings before they happened, telephone the sheriff or police chief and urge him to do his duty by preventing the offense, and then to telephone every other important man of good will in the community and ask him to do the same. And both organizations had carried out elaborate studies of lynching, clearly demonstrating such things as that it did not protect Southern Womanhood but only endangered it. And these studies, in turn, had been picked up and passed on by the more enlightened newspapers.

In 1936, as in 1937, the number of Negroes lynched was eight. The following year saw it reduced to six. And in 1939 it dropped to three, just one fifty-fifth of that for 1892.

In the field of social legislation, again, quite remarkable things were going on, or at least things which seemed remarkable when set against the past. Thus, this period was to see child labor in the mills almost disappear, though not in commerce. Years before, indeed, it had been partly eliminated by the adoption of compulsory school laws by the states. But under the lax child labor statutes its use in the vacation period, often running to six months out of the year and even longer, had still been quite common. Now, however, these laws were generally strengthened, and in some cases, as in North Carolina, the age limit was raised to sixteen years.

All the states were adopting social security and old-age pension laws, to avail themselves of Federal *largesse*. An increasing number of the larger towns were sponsoring slum-clearance projects. And with the destruction of NRA and its labor codes by the Supreme Court, some of the states would enact laws considerably reducing the legal hours of labor for textile mills, other industries, and some branches of trade, though the merchants, often among the worst labor sweaters, universally escaped.

In the schools the growth of the modern mind and the new analysis and criticism was going steadily forward. They had been considerably crippled, of course, by the reduction in income consequent upon the depression. In truth, the more reactionary forces in the various states, and this was particularly true in North Carolina, had more or less successfully taken advantage of the prevailing mood of the depression to cut appropriations for the state universities more than was made necessary by the collapse of the general economy, in the hope of starving the new spirit out and rendering its activities impossible. At Chapel Hill there was for a while a veritable exodus of distinguished professors to more lucrative and promising jobs in the North. But the men who were most immediately valuable to the South, as Howard Odum and Frank Graham at North Carolina, generally stayed on.

And the losses of funds and great names were to a large extent counterbalanced by two other considerations. One of these was that now fairly large numbers of the young Southerners who were joining the faculties had been trained in the new attitude and viewpoint. The other was that the students were now more amenable to the thing. This generation of youth was probably the soberest-minded the South had ever known. The colleges still swarmed with those who dreamed hopefully of acquiring riches as Babbitts, of course; but the more intelligent sort were aware that they belonged to a world quite unknown to their fathers and were willing and sometimes eager to lay aside the old sentimentality and unrealism and try to understand the case.

For all their handicaps, the universities and colleges of the South were generally to become more intelligent and more useful in the thirties than they ever had been before.

The period would see the publication by the University of North Carolina Press of a mass of searching material about the South, of which the most considerable items were Howard Odum's great sociological compilation, *Southern Regions*, Rupert Vance's *Human Factors in Cotton Culture* and *Human Geography of the South*, and *These Are Our Lives*, a compilation by the Federal Writers' Project which is one of the most enlightening and moving human documents ever printed. But it is significant that it was not merely North Carolina men who wrote the books and monographs published at Chapel Hill, but men in schools scattered over all the South.

There were still plenty of Southern colleges whose only claim to respect was a football team, but they were becoming fewer as the years hurried on.

In journalism, too, the decade was to see a notable development of intelligence and realism. Under the editorial direction of Virginius Dabney, the Richmond *Times-Dispatch* developed into one of the most liberal newspapers in the nation; one which so far dared to flout the tradition of its milieu that it campaigned against the poll tax in Virginia and in 1938 supported the Wagner-Van Nuys anti-lynching bill, in both cases against the active opposition of Senators Carter Glass and Harry Flood Byrd.

For my own part, I have always been doubtful of schemes for Federal control of lynching, fearing that their net effect on the South would only be to rouse its trigger-quick dander, always so allergic to the fear of Federal coercion and so tend to increase rather than suppress the practice. But that does not change the fact that the stand of the *Times-Dispatch* was an unusually courageous sort of journalism.

In Raleigh Jonathan Daniels made the *News and Observer* equally liberal, at least on the economic and political side — sometimes waxing almost too uncritical in his eagerness to champion the underdog: surely a curious charge to bring against a Southern editor.

At Charlotte J. E. Dowd, one of the owners of the *Charlotte News*, took over the editorial reins of that once stodgy journal and made of it one of the most lively, intelligent, and enterprising in Dixie. In 1937 this paper, through a member of its staff, Cameron Shipp, carried out the most uncompromising and thorough survey of local slum conditions ever carried out in a Southern town.

The Richmond *News-Leader*, the Norfolk *Virginia-Pilot*, and the *Montgomery Advertiser* — all already distinguished for intelligence — added steadily to their reputation for liberality in the decade. In Birmingham John Temple Graves II and Osborne Zuber made the *Age-Herald* and the *News* consistently tolerant. And in Atlanta the *Constitution* and the *Journal* at least acquired a more open-mouthed attitude than had formerly been theirs.

Just as important was the fact that many of the smaller newspapers were now getting more liberal and intelligent editing. One of the happy results of the depression, from the standpoint of the welfare of the South, was that it had gone a long way toward halting the old exodus to the North of talented young men with journalistic ambitions. The development of standardized daily journalism helped to that end, also. Unable to secure jobs in the East or Middle West, they were perforce driven into service at home, and carried their brains with them. They were far from free, even where they owned their papers, and had to proceed against the prevailing prejudices with great caution; but in the course of time they gradually enlarged their latitude.

Mention of university presses, newspapers, printing, suggests something else that properly ought to be noted in this connection. The South had now begun to have a greatly flourishing literature.

All along from 1900 Ellen Glasgow had of course been exercising her irony on her native land, in a long series of tales which grew constantly more penetrating and impatient of sentimentality. And in 1925 she produced, in *Barren Ground*, what I judge to be the first real novel, as opposed to romances, the South had brought forth; certainly the first wholly genuine picture of the people who make up and always have made up the body of the South.

In the same period there was also Cabell, playing Olympian Zeus on Monument Avenue, and in both the Poictesme and Lichfield, Sill, cycles holding up a thinly hidden mirror to his fellow countrymen and their notions. That Colonel Rudolph Musgrave is a Virginian and a Southerner anyone can see. But so, I have no doubt, is Jurgen or Florian de Puysange. And the Cabell women are all concocted in very great measure out of the legend of Southern Womanhood, just as Horvendile is unmistakably related to the most celebrated character in the repertoire of the Southern pulpit.

It is true, I am sure, that these are in their essence also timeless shadows, without place save that they dwell upon something which approximates the earth. They stand in some wise for men of every race and age, at least in the Western world; the universal legend of fair women; the hoary myth of evil made splendid flesh and weary and perilous wisdom. And all of them are exhibited to us against the background of their creator's own tenderly mocking perception, are themselves sometimes for a little endowed with it. But in the shape of their personal being, in their own view of themselves and their fellows, in their peculiar tradition, they are none the less decisively Southern.

The very Cabell rhetoric is in some sense an inheritance from the Southern rhetoric of the past. That rhetoric passed through the prism of his mind, tamed to his humor and made seemly, but still wearing ineluctably upon it the stamp of its origin. And if this seems preposterous, then let the reader try to imagine it as having been fashioned by a man of any other country.

But if Miss Glasgow and Cabell had been upon the scene all these years. H. L. Mencken indulged in only rhetorical exaggeration when he wrote "The Sahara of the Bozart." At Nashville there were the Fugitive poets, and in New Orleans there was some stirring of literary activity. But save for these exceptions the literary state of the region was to be accurately measured by Thomas Dixon, Jr., whose many rabid novels, and especially *The Clansman*, which was made into the moving picture *The Birth of a Nation*, probably contributed no little to stirring up racial feeling and to the creation of the Ku Klux Klan.

But the twenties were to see a rapidly accelerating growth, which went along with and in fact constituted a part of the same essential movement toward intellectual freedom which was in evidence in the schools. In Kentucky Elizabeth

Maddox Roberts, who properly belongs to the South, produced *The Time of Man*. In South Carolina Julia Peterkin and DuBose Heyward appeared. In New York Laurence Stallings, a Georgian, contributed to *What Price Glory?* the saltiness which made it a dramatic success. In Atlanta there was Frances Newman. At Chapel Hill Paul Green wrote *In Abraham's Bosom*, and Professor Koch's students turned out their Carolina Playmakers productions in profusion, invented a new American folk drama. And besides these there were many more: Conrad Aiken, Emily Clark, with her sharp-tongued *Reviewer*, Gerald W. Johnson, Roark Bradford, Evelyn Scott, W. E. Woodward, Isa Glenn, Maristan Chapman, Clement Wood, and so on and so on.

Behind them came a swelling troop of younger men and women, eagerly following in their footsteps. The end of the decade saw Thomas Wolfe and William Faulkner tower into view almost simultaneously. The thirties opened with Erskine Caldwell's *Tobacco Road*. And thereafter the multiplication of Southern writers would go on at such a pace until in 1939 the South actually produced more books of measureable importance than any other section of the country, until anybody who fired off a gun in the region was practically certain to kill an author.

The makers of this new literature differed widely in their viewpoints and interests, of course. For instance, Mrs. Peterkin and DuBose Heyward, while exhibiting an enormous freshness in their approach to the Negro — they were the first Southern novelists to deal with him in recognizably human terms instead of those of the old convention — still retained considerable vestiges of sentimentality. Both were prone to see only the poetical or ingratiating aspects of the Negro's lot.

On the other hand, not a few of these writers — perhaps even a majority of those who came up in the twenties — showed a marked tendency to react to a new extreme, and as they sloughed off the old imperative to use their writings as a vehicle for glorifying and defending Dixie, to take more or less actively to hating and denouncing the South. Thomas Wolfe made Eugene Gant openly hate the section. And though Faulkner has denied that he has any interest in anything but the individual, there is in his works a kind of fury of portraiture, a concentration on decadence and social horrors, which is to our purpose here. The case of Caldwell is manifest. And readers of the *American Mercury* in H. L. Mencken's time as editor will recall that baiting the South in its pages was one of the favorite sports of young Southerners of literary and intellectual pretensions.

In reality they hated the South a good deal less than they said and thought. Rather, so far as their hatred was not mere vain profession designed to invite attention to their own superior perception, they hated it with the exasperated hate of a lover who cannot persuade the object of his affections to his desire. Or, perhaps more accurately, as Narcissus, growing at length analytical, might have suddenly begun to hate his image reflected in the pool.

All these men remained fundamentally Southern in their basic emotions. Intense belief in and love for the Southern legend had been bred into them as children and could not be bred out again simply by taking thought; lay ineradicably at the bottom of their minds, to set up conflict with their new habit of analysis and their new perceptions. And their hate and anger against the South was both a defense mechanism against the inner uneasiness created by that conflict and a sort of reverse embodiment of the old sentimentality itself. Thomas Wolfe almost explicitly makes Eugene Gant recognize as much.

The continuing power of the Southern heritage upon them is curious to observe. Wolfe's rhetoric, far more obviously than Cabell's, is directly descended from the old Southern line.

But that will scarcely do for Faulkner and Caldwell? These, as everyone knows, had been to school to the Middle Westerners and the Russians and to Joyce.

They had, certainly. And yet it seems to me that when you drain off the extraneous elements, the long flowing grace of Faulkner's best sentences, his loving choice of highly colored words, often plainly stuck in merely for their own sake, is — personal, yes, but also distinctly Southern. And perhaps it is not best to be too sure even about Caldwell's carefully stripped style.

When we turn from the manner of their writing to the question of its content, the matter is clearer. Growing steadily more realistic; in the case of the Caldwells and the Faulkners, sternly rooting out not only sentimentality but even sentiment or, so far as it was possible, emotion of any sort, these new Southern authors remained in some curious fashion *romantics* in their choice of materials — shall we say, romantics of the appalling. Or am I mistaken in thinking that the essence of romanticism is the disposition to deal in the more-than-life-sized, the large and heroic, the picturesque and vivid and extravagant?

Even the dullest critics have observed that Wolfe's people rise straight out of Brobdingnag, that their gestures rock the forests about Asheville. He himself once attempted to explain it on the score of his own great size. And the pedestrian, matter-of-fact realism of Dreiser or Ruth Suckow is poles away from the realism of Faulkner's decadent gentry and savage poor whites, or of Caldwell's Jeeter Lester and Ty Ty Walden and their outrageous broods.

To that it can be retorted, of course, that the South, by my own account of it, is itself an extravagant and vivid and even more-than-life-sized land. Nevertheless, I am convinced that the analysis I put forward retains a great deal of validity. Not even the South is one solid explosion of dynamite, which is about the impression you get from the Southern books of the late 1920's and the earlier thirties. This, indeed, is the chief criticism to be made of these books, at least when we attempt to regard them as a picture of the South, as everybody has done: telling the truth in detail, they fail to tell it in adequate perspective. The effect is much as though a painter had set out to do a portrait by painting only the subject's wens, warts, and chicken-pox scars.

I am inferring nothing so foolish, naturally, as that the Southern heritage was the sole determinant in shaping the writers to whom I refer, or, indeed, that the personal mind and character of the men themselves was not the primary element. Merely, the artist does not live in a vacuum, and like other men is compounded out of all his experience from birth. That Wolfe's great size had a good deal to do with the size of his Gulliverian giants seems to me eminently probable, but so also did the fact that he was a Southerner.

But I have diverged a little. To return now: the main point here is that, however much the new Southern authors might differ in their approach to their material, and regardless of what faults they might still display, nearly all of them had decisively escaped from the old Southern urge to turn the country into Never-Never Land, that nearly all of them stood, intellectually at least, pretty decisively outside the legend; and so were able to contribute to the region its first literature of any bulk and importance. And at the same time, in one measure or another, to cast light on the Southern social scene and direct attention to Southern social problems. The very concentration of the hate-and-horror school upon their chosen materials served the latter purpose admirably, regardless of their own intentions.

To which I should add that, as time passed, the hate reaction and its loud profession in some quarters tended to dwindle. It is not often to be observed in books published in the last two of three years. The calm, good-humored criticism of Jonathan Daniels's *A Southerner Discovers the South* and of the *North Georgia Review*, an able little quarterly published at Clayton, Georgia, by Lillian Smith and Paula Snelling, is now becoming generally characteristic.

The proposition that Southern writers of any importance were generally moving toward a more clear-eyed view of the Southern world even has a certain applicability to a group which might seem to stand wholly outside what I have been saying. I refer to the so-called Southern Agrarians, who made their appearance in the late twenties, with the center of their activity at Vanderbilt University in Nashville, and who were led by John Crowe Ransom, Allen Tate, and Donald Davidson.

Primarily this group was one which turned its gaze sentimentally backward. Its appearance just as the South was moving toward the crisis of the depression, just as Progress was apparently sweeping the field, just as the new critics and writers were beginning to swing lustily against the old legend and the old pattern, was significant. In a real fashion these men were mouthpieces of the fundamental, if sometimes subterranean, will of the South to hold to the old way: the spiritual heirs of Thomas Nelson Page. And their first joint declaration, *I'll Take My Stand*, was, like their earlier prose works in general, essentially a determined reassertion of the validity of the legend of the Old South, an attempt to revive and fully restore the identification of that Old South with Cloud-Cuckoo Town, or at any rate to render it as a Theocritean idyl.

But the attempt was made with enormously intellectualized arguments, which itself is evidence of how far the South had moved on its highest levels, how far the new spirit had invaded even conservative quarters like Vanderbilt. The yearning of these men toward the past had encountered and mingled with all that yearning for the past which, in Europe and America, has moved in an unbroken stream since the early-nineteenth-century revolt against Rousseau. They had read the *Summa Theologica* of St. Thomas Aquinas, were steeped in Spinoza, Hobbes, Kant, and all the philosophers; they worshipped at the shrine of Dr. John Donne (the Donne of St. Paul's deanery and the esoteric poems rather than the author of "To His Mistress Going to Bed," of course); they had been influenced in varying degree by De Maistre, John Ruskin, Ferdinand Brunetière, the neo-Catholicism of Hilaire Belloc and Gilbert Chesterton, the neo-medievalism of Belloc and Chesterton and T. S. Eliot, by Irving Babbitt and Paul Elmer Moore and Norman Foerster.

They distrusted science almost as warmly as Bishop Wilberforce had once distrusted it, felt with conviction that it assumed much too arrogantly to be on the verge of illuminating the whole of the vast range of illimitable darkness which is the mysterious universe, that its total effect on men was to make them too smug and knowing and brightly hard, to loose the old bonds without replacing them with new ones or having the capacity to replace them with new ones — perhaps not altogether without reason. They distrusted industrialism and its effect on mankind and the South even more positively, and certainly not without reason. They had more than a few doubts about democracy. Arrant individualists, they yet recoiled from the monadism which, swinging up through the centuries from the Renaissance, was flowering in the chaos of our times; felt the pressing need for the revival of values, and above everything a religious faith, which should again bind Western men, or at least some portion of them, into a unified whole.

Being poets (the old Fugitive group formed the core of the Agrarian group), they longed for a happy land into which to project their hearts' desire. Being Southerners, and so subject, subconsciously at any rate, to the old powerful drive toward idealization of the fatherland, they caught up all their wishing and all their will to think themselves back into the old certainties and projected them upon the Old South as the Arcadia in which they had once been realized, and to which return would have to be made if salvation were to be achieved.

Yet, as what I say indicates, and despite their strong tendency to preciosity, there was from the first a good deal more realism in them than in any of the earlier apologists and idealizers. Theirs was to be no close repetition of the pro-slavery argument of Harper, Dew & Company, with every shred of evidence relentlessly twisted to their purpose.

It is not true, as was foolishly charged by the Communists and others who should have known better, that they consciously inclined to Fascism. And it is not true, as Sherwood Anderson and an army of followers clamored, that all that moved them was simply the nostalgic wish to sit on cool and columned verandas, sip mint juleps, and converse exquisitely while the poor whites and the black men toiled for them in the hot, wide fields spread out against the horizon.

It is true that Allen Tate got into near-Fascist company as one of the editors of the *American Review,* though that was the result of sympathies which had nothing directly to do with Fascism. I think he was quite candid when he protested to the *Nation* that he would join the Communists if the only alternative were the Silver Shirts.

It is true also that the majority of the contributors to *I'll Take My Stand* were primarily occupied with the aristocratic notion in their examination of the Old South. And it is true, finally, that they took little account of the case of the underdog proper, the tenants and sharecroppers, industrial labor, and the Negroes as a group.

Nevertheless, they did take much account of the small landowning farmers — the yeomen. A minority of them, with John Donald Wade of Georgia University as the most eminent, was even more concerned with these people than with the planters. And practically every contributor to the book confessed openly or tacitly that the Old South was in the main more simple, plain, and recognizably human in a new country than the legend had ever had it in the past. Furthermore, it may be said that the virtues they assigned to the Old South were essentially the virtues which it indubitably possessed. Save for the fact that they insisted on making it a good bit more contemplative and deeply wise than I think it was, they are much the same virtues I have myself assigned to it at its best: honor, courage, generosity, amiability, courtesy.

Merely, the Agrarians refused to observe the faults of the Old South and the operation of its system upon the people who lived under it. And, above all, to confess that the diseases which presently afflict the South are not and cannot logically be made to be, as they maintain, solely the fault of the introduction of industrialism and commercialism, but in very great part flow directly out of the pattern laid down in the Old South itself.

As time has gone on, however, they have tended to modify their views in the direction of realism. The tendency to idealize the Old South has gone steadily on, indeed. It is to be observed plainly in such books as Allen Tate's *The Fathers* and Caroline Gordon's *None Shall Look Back.* And above all in Stark Young's *So Red the Rose.* It is more than a little ironic that the last novel was written by a man who prefers to live in New York (an Agrarian by remote control, as it were) and who serves the *New Republic* as drama critic. But the case serves brilliantly to illustrate the power of the South over its sons even when they flee from it, and is perhaps explicable enough on the theory that distance tends to heighten and not lessen romantic nostalgia.

But despite the persistence of this tendency to idealize, the movement toward realism which I mention has gone forward, too. Taxed by most of the critics with having no knowledge of the elements of sociology and economics, at which they were inclined to sneer in *I'll Take My Stand* and their early essays in the *American*

Review, the Agrarians were not long in setting out to remedy the lack, and they have gradually exhibited more respect for the facts in these fields. Moreover, they have gathered many new converts, some of whom are well versed in the social sciences and have no patience with precious nonsense about them — converts of whom the most notable is Herbert Agar of the Louisville *Courier-Journal.*

Again, when the critics pointed out their lack of awareness of the underdog in *I'll Take My Stand* and charged that Agrarianism was only a nebulous piece of poetizing about the joys of communion with the soil, without definite form or objective, they tacitly admitted the justice of the indictment by expanding their doctrine into a "program." Ever since they have spent a great deal of ink in deploring the growth of tenantry, sharecropping, absentee landlordism, and industrial proletarianism; have continually maintained that the South could never be healthy again until the land was widely distributed among small holders. In the hands of such men as Mr. Agar, the argument here has become very extensive and formidable. But it cannot be said that their "program" is yet properly such, for they have never got around to telling us precisely how the redistribution of the land is to be brought about — though that is not to be too much held against them, since the problem is obviously one of staggering difficulties.

These Agrarians have had the bad influence of encouraging smugness and sentimentality in many quarters, and even of giving these vices sanction as a sort of higher wisdom. But it is fair to say that this has probably been well balanced out by their services in puncturing the smugness of Progress, in directing attention to the evils of *laissez-faire* industrialism, in their insistence on the necessity of developing a sensible farm program for the region, and in recalling that the South must not be too much weaned away from its ancient leisureliness — the assumption that the first end of life is living itself — which, as they rightly contend, is surely one of its greatest virtues.

WILLIAM FAULKNER

Mississippi

MISSISSIPPI BEGINS IN THE lobby of a Memphis, Tennessee hotel and extends south to the Gulf of Mexico. It is dotted with little towns concentric about the ghosts of the horses and mules once tethered to the hitch-rail enclosing the county courthouse and it might almost be said to have only those two directions, north and south, since until a few years ago it was impossible to travel east or west in it unless you walked or rode one of the horses or mules; even in the boy's early manhood, to reach by rail either of the adjacent county towns thirty miles away to the east or west, you had to travel ninety miles in three different directions on three different railroads.

In the beginning it was virgin — to the west, along the Big River, the alluvial swamps threaded by black almost motionless bayous and impenetrable with cane and buckvine and cypress and ash and oak and gum; to the east, the hardwood ridges and the prairies where the Appalachian mountains died and buffalo grazed; to the south, the pine barrens and the moss-hung liveoaks and the greater swamps less of earth than water and lurking with alligators and water moccasins, where Louisiana in its time would begin.

And where in the beginning the predecessors crept with their simple artifacts, and built the mounds and vanished, bequeathing only the mounds in which the succeeding recordable Algonquian stock would leave the skulls of their warriors and chiefs and babies and slain bears, and the shards of pots, and hammer- and arrow-heads and now and then a heavy silver Spanish spur. There were deer to drift in herds alarmless as smoke then, and bear and panther and wolves in the brakes and bottoms, and all the lesser beasts — coon and possum and beaver and mink and mushrat (not muskrat: mushrat); they were still there and some of the land was still virgin in the early nineteen hundreds when the boy himself began to hunt. But except for looking occasionally out from behind the face of a white man or a Negro, the Chickasaws and Choctaws and Natchez and Yazoos were as gone as the predecessors, and the people the boy crept with were the descendants of the Sartorises and De Spains and Compsons who had commanded the Manassas and Sharpsburg and Shiloh and Chickamauga regiments, and the McCaslins and Ewells and Holstons and Hogganbecks whose fathers and grandfathers had manned them, and now and then a Snopes too because by the beginning of the twentieth century Snopeses were everywhere: not only behind the counters of grubby little side street stores patronised mostly by Negroes, but behind the presidents' desks of banks and the directors' tables of wholesale grocery corporations and in the deaconries of Baptist churches, buying up the decayed Georgian houses and chopping them into apartments and on their death-beds decreeing annexes and baptismal fonts to the churches as mementos to themselves or maybe out of simple terror.

They hunted too. They too were in the camps where the De Spains and Compsons and McCaslins and Ewells were masters in their hierarchial turn, shooting the does not only when law but the Master too said not, shooting them not even because the meat was needed but leaving the meat itself to be eaten by scavengers in the woods, shooting it simply because it was big and moving and alien, of an older time than the little grubby stores and the accumulating the compounding money; the boy a man now and in his hierarchial turn Master of the camp and coping, having to cope, not with the diminishing wilderness where there was less and less game, but with the Snopeses who were destroying that little which did remain.

These elected the Bilboes and voted indefatigably for the Vardamans, naming their sons after both; their origin was in bitter hatred and fear and economic rivalry of the Negroes who farmed little farms no larger than and adjacent to their own, because the Negro, remembering when he had not been free at all, was therefore capable of valuing what he had of it enough to struggle to retain even that little and had taught himself how to do more with less: to raise more cotton with less money to spend and food to eat and fewer or inferior tools to work with: this, until he, the Snopes, could escape from the land into the little grubby side street stores where he could live not beside the Negro but on him by marking up on the inferior meat and meal and molasses the price which he, the Negro, could not even always read.

In the beginning, the obsolescent, dispossessed tomorrow by the already obsolete: the wild Algonquian — Chickasaw and Choctaw and Natchez and Pascagoula — looking down from the tall Mississippi bluffs at the Chippeway canoe containing three Frenchmen — and had barely time to whirl and look behind him at a thousand Spaniards come overland from the Atlantic Ocean, and for a little while longer had the privilege of watching an ebb-flux-ebb-flux of alien nationalities as rapid as the magician's spill and evanishment of inconstant cards: the Frenchman for a second, then the Spaniard for perhaps two, then the Frenchman for another two and then the Spaniard again and then the Frenchman again for that last half-breath before the Anglo-Saxon, who would come to stay, to endure: the tall man roaring with Protestant scripture and boiled whiskey, Bible and jug in one hand and like as not an Indian tomahawk in the other, brawling, turbulent, uxorious and polygamous: a married invincible bachelor without destination but only motion, advancement, dragging his gravid wife and most of his mother-in-law's kin behind him into the trackless wilderness, to spawn that child behind a log-crotched rifle and then get her with another one before they moved again, and at the same time scattering his inexhaustible other seed in three hundred miles of dusky bellies: without avarice or compassion or forethought either: felling a tree which took two hundred years to grow, to extract from it a bear or a capful of wild honey.

He endured, even after he too was obsolete, the younger sons of Virginia and Carolina planters coming to replace him in wagons laden with slaves and indigo seedlings over the very roads he had hacked out with little else but the tomahawk. Then someone gave a Natchez doctor a Mexican cotton seed (maybe with the bollweevil already in it since, like the Snopes, he too has taken over the southern earth) and changed the whole face of Mississippi, slaves clearing rapidly now the virgin land lurking still (1850) with the ghosts of Murrell and Mason and Hare and the two Harpes, into plantation fields for profit where he, the displaced and obsolete, had wanted only the bear and the deer and the sweetening for his tooth. But he remained, hung on still; he is still there even in the boy's middle-age, living in a log or plank or tin hut on the edge of what remains of the fading wilderness, by and on the tolerance and sometimes even the bounty of the plantation owner to whom, in his intractable way and even with a certain dignity and independence, he is a sycophant, trapping coons and muskrats, now that the bear and the panther are almost gone too, improvident still, felling still the two-hundred-year-old tree even though it has only a coon or a squirrel in it now.

Manning, when that time came, not the Manassas and Shiloh regiments but confederating into irregular bands and gangs owning not much allegiance to anyone or anything, unified instead into the one rite and aim of stealing horses from Federal picket-lines; this in the intervals of raiding (or trying to) the plantation house of the very man to whom he had been the independent sycophant and intended to be again, once the war was over and presuming that the man came back from his Sharpsburg or Chickamauga majority, or colonelcy or whatever it had been; trying to, that is, until the major's or colonel's wife or aunt or mother-in-law, who had buried the silver in the orchard and still held together a few of the older slaves, fended him off and dispersed him, and when necessary even shot him, with the absent husband's or nephew's or son-in-law's hunting gun or dueling pistols, — the women, the indomitable, the undefeated, who never surrendered, refusing to allow the Yankee *minie*balls to be dug out of portico column or mantelpiece or lintel, who seventy years later would get up and walk out of *Gone with the Wind* as soon as Sherman's name was mentioned; irreconcilable and enraged and still talking about it long after the weary exhausted men who had fought and lost it gave up trying to make them hush: even in the boy's time the boy himself knowing about Vicksburg and Corinth and exactly where his grandfather's regiment had been at First Manassas before he remembered hearing very much about Santa Claus.

In those days (1901 and -2 and -3 and -4) Santa Claus occurred only at Christmas, not like now, and for the rest of the year children played with what they could find or contrive or make, though just as now, in '51 and -2 and -3 and -4, they still played, aped in miniature, what they had been exposed to, heard or seen or been moved by most. Which was true in the child's time and case too: the indomitable unsurrendered old women holding together still, thirty-five and forty years later, a few of the old house slaves: women too who, like the white ones, declined, refused to give up the old ways and forget the old anguishes. The child himself remembered one of them: Caroline: free these many years but who had declined to leave. Nor would she ever accept in full her weekly Saturday wages, the family never knew why unless the true reason was the one which appeared: for the simple pleasure of keeping the entire family reminded constantly that they were in arrears to her, compelling the boy's grandfather then his father and finally himself in his turn to be not only her banker but her bookkeeper too, having got the figure of eighty-nine dollars into her head somehow or for some reason, and though the sum itself altered, sometimes more and sometimes less and sometimes it would be she herself who would be several weeks in arrears, it never changed: one of the children, white or Negro, liable to appear at any time, usually when most of the family would be gathered at a meal, with the message: 'Mammy says to tell you not to forget you owe her eighty-nine dollars.'

To the child, even at that time, she seemed already older than God, calling him grandsire 'colonel' but never the child's father nor the father's brother and sister by anything but their christian names even when they themselves had become grandparents: a matriarch with a score of descendants (and probably half that many more whom she had forgotten or outlived), one of them a boy too, whether a great grandson or merely a grandson even she did not remember, born in the same week with the white child and both bearing the same (the white child's grandsire's) name, suckled at the same black breast and sleeping and eating together and playing together the game which was the most important thing the white child knew at that time since at four and five and six his world was still a female world and he had heard nothing else that he could remember: with empty spools and chips and sticks and a scraped trench filled with wellwater for the River, playing over again in miniature the War, the old irremediable battles — Shiloh and Vicksburg and Brice's Crossroads which was not far from where the child (both of them) had been born, the boy because he was white arrogating to himself the right to be the Confederate General — Pemberton or Johnston or Forrest — twice to the black child's once, else, lacking that once in three, the black one would not play at all.

Not the tall man, he was still the hunter, the man of the woods; and not the slave because he was free now; but that Mexican cotton seed which someone had given the Natchez doctor clearing the land fast now, plowing under the buffalo grass of the eastern prairies and the brier and switch-cane of the creek- and river-bottoms of the central hills and deswamping that whole vast flat alluvial Delta-shaped sweep of land along the Big River, the Old Man: building the levees to hold him off the land long enough to plant and harvest the crop: he taking another foot of scope in his new dimension for every foot man constricted him in the old: so that the steamboats carrying the baled cotton to Memphis or New Orleans seemed to crawl along the sky itself.

And little steamboats on the smaller rivers too, penetrating the Tallahatchie as far up as Wylie's Crossing above Jefferson. Though most of the cotton from that section, and on to the east to that point of no economic return where it was more expedient to continue on east to the Tombigbee and then south to Mobile, went the sixty miles overland to Memphis by mule and wagon; there was a settlement — a tavern of sorts and a smithy and a few gaunt cabins — on the bluff above Wylie's, at the exact distance where a wagon or a train of them loaded with cotton either starting or resuming the journey in the vicinity of Jefferson, would have to halt for the night. Or not even a settlement but rather a den, whose denizens lurked unseen by day in the brakes and thickets of the river bottom, appearing only at night and even then only long enough to enter the tavern kitchen where the driver of the day's cotton wagon sat unsuspecting before the fire, whereupon driver wagon mules and cotton and all would vanish: the body into the river probably and the wagon burned and the mules sold days or weeks later in a Memphis stockyard and the unidentifiable cotton already on its way to the Liverpool mill.

At the same time, sixteen miles away in Jefferson, there was a pre-Snopes, one of the tall men actually, a giant of a man in fact: a dedicated lay Baptist preacher but furious not with a furious unsleeping dream of paradise nor even for universal Order with an upper-case O, but for simple civic security. He was warned by everyone not to go in there because not only could he accomplish nothing, he would very likely lose his own life trying it. But he did go, alone, talking not of gospel nor God nor even virtue, but simply selected the biggest and boldest and by appearance anyway the most villainous there and said to him: 'I'll fight you. If you lick me, you take what money I have. If I lick you, I baptise you into my church': and battered and mauled and gouged that one into sanctity and civic virtue then challenged the next biggest and most villainous and then the next; and the following Sunday baptised the entire settlement in the river, the cotton wagons now crossing on Wylie's hand-powered ferry and passing peacefully and unchallenged on to Memphis until the railroads came and took the bales away from them.

That was in the seventies. The Negro was a free farmer and a political entity now; one, he could not sign his name, was Federal marshal at Jefferson. Afterward he became the town's official bootlegger (Mississippi was one of the first to essay the noble experiment, along with Maine), resuming — he had never really quitted it — his old allegiance to his old master and gaining his professional name, Mulberry, from the hugh old tree behind Doctor Habersham's drugstore, in the gallery-like tunnels among the roots of which he cached the bottled units of his commerce.

Soon he (the Negro) would even forge ahead in that economic rivalry with Snopes which was to send Snopes in droves into the Ku Klux Klan — not the old original one of the war's chaotic and desperate end which, measured against the desperate times, was at least honest and serious in its desperate aim, but into the later base one of the twenties whose only kinship to the old one was the old name. And a little money to build railroads with was in the land now, brought there by the man who in '66 had been a carpet-bagger but who now was a citizen; his children would speak the soft consonantless Negro tongue as the children of parents who had lived below the Potomac and Ohio Rivers since Captain John Smith, and their children would boast of their Southern heritage. In Jefferson his name was Redmond. He had found the money with which Colonel Sartoris had opened the local cottonfields to Europe by building his connecting line up to the main railroad from Memphis to the Atlantic Ocean — narrow gauge, like a toy, with three tiny locomotives like toys too, named after Colonel Sartoris's three daughters, each with its silver-plated oilcan engraved with the daughter's christian name: like toys, the standard-sized cars jacked up at the junction then lowered onto the narrow trucks, the tiny locomotive now invisible ahead of its charges so that they appeared in process of being snatched headlong among the fields they served by an arrogant plume of smoke and the arrogant shrieking of a whistle — who, after the inevitable quarrel, finally shot Colonel Sartoris dead on a Jefferson street, driven, everyone believed, to the desperate act by the same arrogance and intolerance which had driven Colonel Sartoris's regiment to demote him from its colonelcy in the fall elections after Second Manassas and Sharpsburg.

So there were railroads in the land now; now couples who had used to go overland by carriage to the River landings and the steamboats for the traditional New Orleans honeymoon, could take the train from almost anywhere. And presently pullmans too, all the way from Chicago and the Northern cities where the cash, the money was, so that the rich Northerners could come down in comfort and open the land indeed: setting up with their Yankee dollars the vast lumbering plants and mills in the southern pine section, the little towns which had been hamlets without change or alteration for fifty years, booming and soaring into cities overnight above the stump-pocked barrens which would remain until in simple economic desperation people taught themselves to farm pine trees as in other sections they had already learned to farm corn and cotton.

And Northern lumber mills in the Delta too: the mid-twenties now and the Delta booming with cotton and timber both. But mostly booming with simple money: increment a troglodyte which had fathered twin troglodytes: solvency and bankruptcy, the three of them booming money into the land so fast that the problem was how to get rid of it before it whelmed you into suffocation. Until in something almost resembling self-defense, not only for something to spend it on but to bet the increment from the simple spending on, seven or eight of the bigger Delta towns formed a baseball league, presently raiding as far away — and successfully too — for pitchers and short-stops and slugging outfielders, as the two major leagues, the boy, a young man now, making acquaintance with this league and one of the big Northern lumber companies not only coincidentally with one another but because of one another.

At this time the young man's attitude of mind was that of most of the other young men in the world who had been around twenty-one years of age in April, 1917, even though at times he did admit to himself that he was possibly using the fact that he had been nineteen on that day as an excuse to follow the avocation he was coming more and more to know would be forever his true one: to be a tramp, a harmless possessionless vagabond. In any case, he was quite ripe to make the acquaintance, which began with that of the lumber company which at the moment was taking a leisurely bankruptcy in a town where lived a lawyer who had been appointed the referee in the bankruptcy: a family friend of the young man's family and older than he, yet who had taken a liking to the young man and so invited him to come along for the ride too. His official capacity was that of interpreter, since he had a little French and the defuncting company had European connections. But no interpreting was ever done since the entourage did not go to Europe but moved instead into a single floor of a Memphis hotel, where all — including the interpreter — had the privilege of signing chits for food and theatre tickets and even the bootleg whiskey (Tennessee was in its dry mutation then) which the bellboys would produce, though not of course at the discreet and innocent-looking places clustered a few miles away just below the Mississippi state line, where roulette and dice and blackjack were available.

Then suddenly Mr Sells Wales was in it too, bringing the baseball league with him. The young man never did know what connection (if any) Mr Wales had with the bankruptcy, nor really bothered to wonder, let alone care and ask, not only because he had developed already that sense of *noblesse oblige* toward the avocation which he knew was his true one, which would have been reason enough, but because Mr Wales himself was already a legend in the Delta. Owner of a plantation measured not in acres but in miles and reputedly sole owner of one of the league baseball teams or anyway most of its players, certainly of the catcher and the base-stealing short-stop and the .340 hitting outfielder ravished or pirated it was said from the Chicago Cubs, his ordinary costume seven days a week was a two- or three-days' beard and muddy high boots and a corduroy hunting coat, the tale, the legend telling of how he entered a swank St. Louis hotel in that costume late one night and demanded a room of a dinner jacketed clerk, who looked once at the beard and the muddy boots but probably mostly at Mr Wale's face and said they were filled up: whereupon Mr Wales asked how much they wanted for the hotel and was told, superciliously, in tens of thousands, and — so told the legend — drew from his corduroy hip a wad of thousand dollar bills sufficient to have bought the hotel half again at the price stated and told the clerk he wanted every room in the building vacated in ten minutes.

That one of course was apocryphal, but the young man himself saw this one: Mr Wales and himself having a leisurely breakfast one noon in the Memphis hotel when Mr Wales remembered suddenly that his private ball club was playing one of its most important games at a town about sixty miles away at three oclock that afternoon and telephoned to the railroad station to have a special train ready for them in thirty minutes, which it was: an engine and a caboose: reaching Coahoma about three oclock with a mile still to the ball park: a man (there were no taxis at the station at that hour and few in Mississippi anywhere at that time) sitting behind the wheel of a dingy though still sound Cadillac car, and Mr Wales said:

'What do you want for it?'

'What?' the man in the car said.

'Your automobile,' Mr Wales said.

'Twelve fifty,' the man said.

'All right,' Mr Wales said, opening the door.

'I mean twelve hundred and fifty dollars,' the man said.

'All right,' Mr Wales said, then to the young man: 'Jump in.'

'Hold up here, mister,' the man said.

'I've bought it,' Mr Wales said, getting in too. 'The ball park,' he said. 'Hurry.'

The young man never saw the Cadillac again, though he became quit familiar with the engine and caboose during the next succeeding weeks while the league pennant race waxed hotter and hotter, Mr Wales keeping the special train on call in the Memphis yards as twenty-five years earlier a city-dwelling millionaire might have hacked a carriage and pair to his instant nod, so that it seemed to the young man that he would barely get back to Memphis to rest before they would be rushing once more down the Delta to another baseball game.

'I ought to be interpreting, sometime,' he said once.

'Interpret, then,' Mr Wales said. 'Interpret what this goddamn cotton market is going to do tomorrow, and we can both quit chasing this blank blank sandlot ball team.'

The cotton seed and the lumber mills clearing the rest of the Delta too, pushing what remained of the wilderness further and further southward into the V of Big River and hills. When the young man, a youth of sixteen and seventeen then, was first accepted into that hunting club of which he in his hierarchial time would be Master, the hunting grounds, haunt of deer and bear and wild turkey, could be reached in a single day or night in a mule-drawn wagon. Now they were using automobiles: a hundred miles then two hundred southward and still southward as the wilderness dwindled into the confluence of the Yazoo River and the big one, the Old Man.

The Old Man: all his little contributing streams levee-ed too, along with him, and paying none of the dykes any heed at all when it suited his mood and fancy, gathering water all the way from Montana to Pennsylvania every generation or so and rolling it down the artificial gut of his victims' puny and baseless hoping, piling the water up, not fast: just inexorable, giving plenty of time to measure his crest and telegraph ahead, even warning of the exact day almost when he would enter the house and float the piano out of it and the pictures off the walls, and even remove the house itself if it were not securely fastened down.

Inexorable and unhurried, overpassing one by one his little confluent feeders and shoving the water into them until for days their current would flow backward, upstream: as far upstream as Wylie's Crossing above Jefferson. The little rivers were dyked too but back here was the land of individualists: remnants and descendants of the tall men now taken to farming, and of Snopeses who were more than individualists: they were Snopeses, so that where the owners of the thousand-acre plantations along the Big River confederated as one man with sandbags and machines and their Negro tenants and wagehands to hold the sandboils and the cracks, back here the owner of the hundred or two hundred acre farm patrolled his section of levee with a sandbag in one hand and his shotgun in the other, lest his upstream neighbor dynamite it to save his (the upstream neighbor's) own.

Piling up the water while white man and Negro worked side by side in shifts in the mud and the rain, with automobile headlights and gasoline flares and kegs of whiskey and coffee boiling in fifty-gallon batches in scoured and scalded oil-drums; lapping, tentative, almost innocently, merely inexorable (no hurry, his) among and beneath and between and finally over the frantic sandbags, as if his whole purpose had been merely to give man another chance to prove, not to him but to man, just how much the human body could bear, stand, endure; then, having let man prove it, doing what he could have done at any time these past weeks if so minded: removing with no haste nor any particular malice or fury either, a mile or two miles of levee and coffee drums and whiskey kegs and gas flares in one sloughing collapse, gleaming dully for a little while yet among the parallel cotton middles until the fields vanished along with the roads and lanes and at last the towns themselves.

Vanished, gone beneath one vast yellow motionless expanse, out of which projected only the tops of trees and telephone poles and the decapitations of human dwelling-places like enigmatic objects placed by inscrutable and impenetrable design on a dirty mirror; and the mounds of the predecessors on which, among a tangle of moccasins, bear and horses and deer and mules and wild turkeys and cows and domestic chickens waited patient in mutual armistice; and the levees themselves, where among a jumble of uxorious flotsam the young continued to be born and the old to die, not from exposure but from simple and normal time and decay, as if man and his destiny were in the end stronger even than the river which had dispossessed him, inviolable by and invincible to, alteration.

Then, having proved that too, he — the Old Man — would withdraw, not retreat: subside, back from the land slowly and inexorably too, emptying the confluent rivers and bayous back into the old vain hopeful gut, but so slowly and gradually that not the waters seemed to fall but the flat earth itself to rise, creep in one plane back into light and air again: one constant stain of yellow-brown at one constant altitude on telephone poles and the walls of gins and houses and stores as though the line had been laid off with a transit and painted in one gigantic unbroken brush-stroke, the earth itself one alluvial inch higher, the rich dirt one inch deeper, drying into long cracks beneath the hot fierce glare of May: but not for long, because almost at once came the plow, the plowing and planting already two months late but that did not matter: the cotton man-tall once more by August and whiter and denser still by picking-time, as if the Old Man said, 'I do what I want to, when I want to. But I pay my way.'

And the boats, of course. They projected above that yellow and liquid plane and even moved upon it: the skiffs and skows of fishermen and trappers, the launches of the United States Engineers who operated the Levee Commission, and one small shallow-draught steamboat steaming in paradox among and across the cotton fields themselves, its pilot not a riverman but a farmer who knew where the submerged fences were, its masthead lookout a mechanic with a pair of pliers to cut the telephone wires to pass the smokestack through: no paradox really, since on the River it had resembled a house to begin with, so that here it looked no different from the baseless houses it steamed among, and on occasion even strained at top boiler pressure to overtake like a mallard drake after a fleeing mallard hen.

But these were not enough, very quickly not near enough; the Old Man meant business indeed this time. So now there began to arrive from the Gulf ports the shrimp trawlers and pleasure cruisers and the Coast Guard cutters whose bottoms had known only salt water and the mouths of tidal rivers, to be run still by their salt water crews but conned by the men who knew where the submerged roads and fences were for the good reason that they had been running mule-plow furrows along them or up to them all their lives, sailing among the swollen carcasses of horses and mules and deer and cows and sheep to pluck the Old Man's patient flotsam, black and white, out of trees and the roofs of gins and cotton sheds and floating cabins and the second storey windows of houses and office buildings; then — the salt-water men, to whom land was either a featureless treeless salt-marsh or a snake- and alligator-infested swamp impenetrable with trumpet vine and Spanish moss; some of whom had never even seen the earth into which were driven the spiles supporting the houses they lived in — staying on even after they were no longer needed, as though waiting to see emerge from the water what sort of country it was which bore the economy on which the people — men and women, black and white, more of black than white even, ten to one more — lived whom they had saved; seeing the land for that moment before mule and plow altered it right up to the water's receding edge, then back into the River again before the trawlers and cruisers and cutters became marooned into canted and useless rubble too along with the ruined hencoops and cowsheds and privies; back onto the Old Man, shrunken once more into his normal banks, drowsing and even innocent-looking, as if it were something else beside he who had changed, for a little time anyway, the whole face of the adjacent earth.

They were homeward bound now, passing the river towns, some of which were respectable in age when south Mississippi was a Spanish wilderness: Greenville and Vicksburg, Natchez and Grand- and Petit Gulf (vanished now and even the old site known by a different name) which had known Mason and one at least of the Harpes and from or on which Murrell had based his abortive slave insurrection intended to efface the white people from the land and leave him emperor of it, the land sinking away beyond the levee until presently you could no longer say where water began and earth stopped: only that these lush and verdant sunny savannahs would no longer bear your weight. The rivers flowed no longer west, but south now, no longer yellow or brown, but black, threading the miles of yellow salt marsh from which on an off-shore breeze mosquitoes came in such clouds that in your itching and burning anguish it would seem to you you could actually see them in faint adumbration crossing the earth, and met tide and then the uncorrupted salt: not the Gulf quite yet but at least the Sound behind the long barrier of the islands — Ship and Horn and Petit Bois, the trawler and cruiser bottoms home again now among the lighthouses and channel markers and shipyards and drying nets and processing plants for fish.

The man remembered that from his youth too: one summer spent being blown innocently over in catboats since, born and bred for generations in the north Mississippi hinterland, he did not recognise the edge of a squall until he already had one. The next summer he returned because he found that he liked that much water, this time as a hand in one of the trawlers, remembering: a four-gallon iron pot over a red bed of charcoal on the foredeck, in which decapitated shrimp boiled among handsful of salt and black pepper, never emptied, never washed and constantly renewed, so that you ate them all day long in passing like peanuts; remembering: the pre-dawn, to be broken presently by the violent near-subtropical yellow-and-crimson day almost like an audible explosion, but still dark for a little while yet, the dark ship creeping onto the shimp grounds in a soundless sternward swirl of phosphorus like a drowning tumble of fireflies, the youth lying face down on the peak staring into the dark water watching the disturbed shrimp burst outward-shooting in fiery and fading fans like the trails of tiny rockets.

He learned the barrier islands too; one of a crew of five amateurs sailing a big sloop in off-shore races, he learned not only how to keep a hull on its keel and moving but how to get it from one place to another and bring it back: so that, a professional now, living in New Orleans he commanded for pay a power launch belonging to a bootlegger (this was the twenties), whose crew consisted of a Negro cook-deckhand-stevedore and the bootlegger's younger brother: a slim twenty-one or -two year old Italian with yellow eyes like a cat and a silk shirt bulged faintly by an armpit-holstered pistol too small in calibre to have done anything but got them all killed, even if the captain or the cook had dreamed of resisting or resenting trouble if and when it came, which the captain or the cook would extract from the holster and hide at the first opportunity (not concealed really: just dropped into the oily bilge under the engine, where, even though Pete soon discovered where it would be, it was safe because he refused to thrust his hand and arm into the oil-fouled water but instead merely lay about the cockpit, sulking); taking the launch across Pontchartrain and down the Rigolets out to the Gulf, the Sound, then lying-to with no lights showing until the Coast Guard cutter (it ran almost on schedule; theirs was a job too even if it was, comparatively speaking, a hopeless one) made its fast haughty eastward rush, going, they always like to believe, to Mobile, to a dance, then by compass on to the island (it was little more than a sandspit bearing a line of ragged and shabby pines thrashing always in the windy crash and roar of the true Gulf on the other side of it) where the Caribbean schooner would bury the casks of green alcohol which the bootlegger's mother back in New Orleans would convert and bottle and label into scotch or bourbon or gin. There were a few wild cattle on the island which they would have to watch for, the Negro digging and Pete still sulking and refusing to help at all because of the pistol, and the captain watching for the charge (they couldn't risk showing a light) which every three or four trips would come — the gaunt wild half-seen shapes charging suddenly and with no warning down at them as they turned and ran through the nightmare sand and hurled themselves into the dinghy, to pull along parallel to the shore, the animals following, until they had tolled them far enough away for the Negro to go back ashore for the remaining casks. Then they would heave-to again and lie until the cutter passed back westward, the dance obviously over now, in the same haughty and imperious rush.

That was Mississippi too, though a different one from where the child had been bred; the people were Catholics, the Spanish and French blood still showed in the names and faces. But it was not a deep one, if you did not count the sea and the boats on it: a curve of beach, a thin unbroken line of estates and apartment hotels owned and inhabited by Chicago millionaires, standing back to back with another thin line, this time of tenements inhabited by Negroes and whites who ran the boats and worked in the fish-processing plants.

Then the Mississippi which the young man knew began: the fading purlieus inhabited by a people whom the young man recognised because their like was in his country too: descendants, heirs at least in spirit, of the tall men, who worked in no factories and farmed no land nor even truck patches, living not out of the earth but on its denizens: fishing guides and individual professional fishermen, trappers of muskrats and alligator hunters and poachers of deer, the land rising now, once more earth instead of half water, vista-ed and arras-ed with the long leaf pines which northern capital would convert into dollars in Ohio and Indiana and Illinois banks. Though not all of it. Some of it would alter hamlets and villages into cities and even build whole new ones almost overnight, cities with Mississippi names but patterned on Ohio and Indiana and Illinois because they were bigger than Mississippi towns, rising, standing today among the tall pines which created them, then tomorrow (that quick, that fast, that rapid) among the stumpy pockage to which they were monuments. Because the land had made its one crop: the soil too fine and light to compete seriously in cotton: until people discovered that it would grow what other soils would not: the tomatoes and strawberries and the fine cane for sugar: not the sorghum of the northern and western counties which people of the true cane country called hog-feed, but the true sweet cane which made the sugar house molasses.

Big towns, for Mississippi: cities, we called them: Hattiesburg, and Laurel, and Meridian, and Canton; and towns deriving by name from further away than Ohio: Kosciusko named after a Polish general who thought that people should be free who wanted to be, and Egypt because there was corn there when it was nowhere else in the bad lean times of the old war which the old women had still never surrendered, and Philadelphia where the Neshoba Indians whose name the county bears still remain for the simple reason that they did not mind living in peace with other people, no matter what their color or politics. This was the hills now: Jones County which old Newt Knight, its principal proprietor and first citizen or denizen, whichever you liked, seceded from the Confederacy in 1862, establishing still a third republic within the boundaries of the United States until a Confederate military force subdued him in his embattled log-castle capital; and Sullivan's Hollow: a long narrow glen where a few clans or families with North Ireland and Highland names feuded and slew one another in the old pre-Culloden fashion yet banding together immediately and always to resist any outsider in the pre-Culloden fashion too: vide the legend of the revenue officer hunting illicit whiskey stills, captured and held prisoner in a stable and worked in traces as the pair to a plow-mule. No Negro ever let darkness catch him in Sullivan's Hollow. In fact, there were few Negroes in this country at all: a narrow strip of which extended up into the young man's own section: a remote district there through which Negroes passed infrequently and rapidly and only by daylight.

It is not very wide, because almost at once there begins to the east of it the prairie country which sheds its water into Alabama and Mobile Bay, with its old tight intermarried towns and plantation houses columned and porticoed in the traditional Georgian manner of Virginia and Carolina in place of the Spanish and French influence of Natchez. These towns are Columbus and Aberdeen and West Point and Shuqualak, where the good quail shooting is and the good bird dogs are bred and trained — horses too: hunters; Dancing Rabbit is here too, where the treaty dispossessing them of Mississippi was made between the Choctaws and the United States; and in one of the towns lived a kinsman of the young man, dead now, rest him: an invincible and incorrigible bachelor, a leader of cotillions and an inveterate diner-out since any time an extra single man was needed, any hostess thought of him first.

But he was a man's man too, and even more: a young man's man, who played poker and matched glasses with the town's young bachelors and the apostates still young enough in time to still resist the wedlock; who walked not only in spats and a stick and yellow gloves and a Homburg hat, but an air of sardonic and inviolable atheism too, until at last he was forced to the final desperate resort of prayer: sitting after supper one night among the drummers in the row of chairs on the sidewalk before the Gilmer Hotel, waiting to see what (if anything) the evening would bring, when two of the young bachelors passing in a Model T Ford stopped and invited him to drive across the line into the Alabama hills for a gallon of moonshine whiskey. Which they did. But the still they sought was not in hills because these were not hills: it was the dying tail of the Appalachian mountain range. But since the Model T's engine had to be running fast anyway for it to have any headlights, going up the mountain was an actual improvement, especially after they had to drop to low gear. And coming from the generation before the motor car, it never occurred to him that coming back down would be any different until they got the gallon and had a drink from it and turned around and started back down. Or maybe it was the whiskey, he said, telling it: the little car rushing faster and faster behind a thin wash of light of about the same volume that two lightning bugs would have made, around the plunging curves which, the faster the car ran, became only the more frequent and sharp and plunging, whipping around the nearly right-angle bends with a rock wall on one hand and several hundred feet of vertical and empty night on the other, until at last he prayed; he said: 'Lord, You know I haven't worried You in over forty years, and if You'll just get me back to Columbus I promise never to bother You again.'

And now the young man, middleaged now or anyway middleaging, is back home too where they who altered the swamps and forests of his youth, have now altered the face of the earth itself; what he remembered as dense river bottom jungle and rich farm land, is now an artificial lake twenty-five miles long: a flood control project for the cotton fields below the huge earth dam, with a few more outboard-powered fishing skiffs on it each year, and at last a sailboat. On his way in to town from his home the middleaging (now a professional fiction-writer: who had wanted to remain the tramp and the possessionless vagabond of his young manhood but time and success and the hardening of his arteries had beaten him) man would pass the back yard of a doctor friend whose son was an undergraduate at Harvard. One day the undergraduate stopped him and invited him in and showed him the unfinished hull of a twenty-foot sloop, saying, 'When I get her finished, Mr Bill, I want you to help me sail her.' And each time he passed after that, the undergraduate would repeat: 'Remember, Mr Bill, I want you to help me sail her as soon as I get her in the water:' to which the middleaging would answer as always: 'Fine, Arthur. Just let me know.'

Then one day he came out of the postoffice: a voice called him from a taxicab, which in small Mississippi towns was any motor car owned by any footloose young man who liked to drive, who decreed himself a taxicab as Napoleon decreed himself emperor; in the car with the driver was the undergraduate and a young man whose father had vanished recently somewhere in the West out of the ruins of the bank of which he had been president, and a fourth young man whose type is universal: the town clown, comedian, whose humor is without viciousness and quite often witty and always funny. 'She's in the water, Mr Bill.' the undergraduate said. 'Are you ready to go now?' And he was, and the sloop was too; the undergraduate had sewn his own sails on his mother's machine; they worked her out into the lake and got her on course all tight and drawing, when suddenly it seemed to the middleaging that part of him was no longer in the sloop but about ten feet away, looking at what he saw: a Harvard undergraduate, a taxi-driver, the son of an absconded banker and a village clown and a middleaged novelist sailing a home-made boat on an artificial lake in the depths of the north Mississippi hills: and he thought that that was something which did not happen to you more than once in your life.

Home again, his native land; he was born of it and his bones will sleep in it; loving it even while hating some of it: the river jungle and the bordering hills where still a child he had ridden behind his father on the horse after the bobcat or fox or coon or whatever was ahead of the belling hounds and where he had hunted alone when he got big enough to be trusted with a gun, now the bottom of a muddy lake being raised gradually and steadily every year by another layer of beer cans and bottle caps and lost bass plugs — the wilderness, the two weeks in the woods, in camp, the rough food and the rough sleeping, the life of men and horses and hounds among men and horses and hounds, not to slay the game but to pursue it, touch and let go, never satiety — moved now even further away than that down the flat Delta so that the mile-long freight trains, visible for miles across the fields where the cotton is mortgaged in February, planted in May, harvested in September and put into the Farm Loan in October in order to pay off February's mortgage in order to mortgage next year's crop, seem to be passing two or even three of the little Indian-named hamlets at once over the very ground where, a youth now capable of being trusted even with a rifle, he had shared in the yearly ritual of Old Ben: the big old bear with one trap-ruined foot who had earned for himself a name, a designation like a living man through the legend of the deadfalls and traps he had wrecked and the hounds he had slain and the shots he had survived, until Boon Hogganbeck, the youth's father's stable foreman, ran in and killed it with a hunting knife to save a hound which he, Boon Hogganbeck, loved.

But most of all he hated the intolerance and injustice: the lynching of Negroes not for the crimes they committed but because their skins were black (they were becoming fewer and fewer and soon there would be no more of them but the evil would have been done and irrevocable because there should never have been any); the inequality: the poor schools they had then when they had any, the hovels they had to live in unless they wanted to live outdoors: who could worship the white man's God but not in the white man's church; pay taxes in the white man's courthouse but couldn't vote in it or for it; working by the white man's clock but having to take his pay by the white man's counting (Captain Joe Thoms, a Delta planter though not one of the big ones, who after a bad crop year drew a thousand silver dollars from the bank and called his five tenants one by one into the dining room where two hundred of the dollars were spread carelessly out on the table beneath the lamp, saying: 'Well, Jim, that's what we made this year.' Then the Negro: 'Gret God, Cap'n Joe, is all that mine?' And Captain Thoms: 'No, no, just half of it is yours. The other half belongs to me, remember.'); the bigotry which could send to Washington some of the senators and congressmen we sent there and which could erect in a town no bigger than Jefferson five separate denominations of churches but set aside not one square foot of ground where children could play and old people could sit and watch them.

But he loves it, it is his, remembering: the trying to, having to, stay in bed until the crack of dawn would bring Christmas and of the other times almost as good as Christmas; of being waked at three oclock to have breakfast by lamplight in order to drive by surrey into town and the depot to take the morning train for the three or four days in Memphis where he would see automobiles, and the day in 1910 when, twelve years old, he watched John Moissant land a bicycle-wheeled aileronless (you warped the whole wing-tip to bank it or hold it level) Bleriot monoplane on the infield of the Memphis race-track and knew forever after that someday he too would have to fly alone; remembering: his first sweetheart, aged eight, plump and honey-haired and demure and named Mary, the two of them sitting side by side on the kitchen steps eating ice cream; and another one, Minnie this time, granddaughter of the old hillman from whom, a man himself now, he bought moonshine whiskey, come to town at seventeen to take a job behind the soda counter of the drug store, watching her virginal and innocent and without self-consciousness pour Coca-Cola syrup into the lifted glass by hooking her thumb through the ring of the jug and swinging it back and up in one unbroken motion onto her horizontal upper arm exactly as he had seen her grandfather pour whiskey from a jug a thousand times.

Even while hating it, because for every Joe Thoms with two hundred silver dollars and every Snopes in a hooded nightshirt, somewhere in Mississippi there was this too: remembering: Ned, born in a cabin in the back yard in 1865, in the time of the middleaged's great-grandfather and had outlived three generations of them, who had not only walked and talked so constantly for so many years with the three generations that he walked and talked like them, he had two tremendous trunks filled with the clothes which they had worn — not only the blue brass-buttoned frock coat and the plug hat in which he had been the great-grandfather's and the grandfather's coachman, but the broadcloth frock coats which the great-grandfather himself had worn, and the pigeon-tailed ones of the grandfather's time and the short coat of his father's which the middleaged could remember on the backs for which they had been tailored, along with the hats in their eighty years of mutation too: so that, glancing idly up and out the library window, the middleaged would see that back, that stride, that coat and hat going down the drive toward the road, and his heart would stop and even turn over. He (Ned) was eighty-four now and in these last few years he had begun to get a little mixed up, calling the middleaged not only 'Master' but sometimes 'Master Murry', who was the middleaged's father, and 'Colonel' too, coming once a week through the kitchen and in to the parlor or perhaps found there, saying: 'Here's where I wants to lay, right here where I can be facing out that window. And I wants it to be a sunny day, so the sun can come in on me. And I wants you to preach the sermon. I wants you to take a dram of whiskey for me, and lay yourself back and preach the best sermon you ever preached.'

And Caroline too, whom the middleaged had inherited too in his hierarchial turn, nobody knowing anymore exactly how many more years than a hundred she was but not mixed up, she: who had forgotten nothing, calling the middleaged 'Memmy' still, from fifty-odd years ago when that was as close as his brothers could come to 'William'; his youngest daughter, aged four and five and six, coming in to the house and saying, 'Pappy, Mammy said to tell you not to forget you owe her eighty-nine dollars.'

'I wont,' the middleaged would say. 'What are you all doing now?'

'Piecing a quilt,' the daughter answered. Which they were. There was electricity in her cabin now, but she would not use it, insisting still on the kerosene lamps which she had always known. Nor would she use the spectacles either, wearing them merely as an ornament across the brow of the immaculate white cloth — headrag — which bound her now hairless head. She did not need them: a smolder of wood ashes on the hearth winter and summer in which sweet potatoes roasted, the five-year-old white child in a miniature rocking chair at one side of it and the aged Negress, not a great deal larger, in her chair at the other, the basket bright with scraps and fragments of cloth between them and in that dim light in which the middleaged himself could not have read his own name without his glasses, the two of them with infinitesimal and tedious and patient stitches annealing the bright stars and squares and diamonds into another pattern to be folded away among the cedar shavings in the trunk.

Then it was the Fourth of July, the kitchen was closed after breakfast so the cook and houseman could attend a big picnic; in the middle of the hot morning the aged Negress and the white child gathered green tomatoes from the garden and ate them with salt, and that afternoon beneath the mulberry tree in the back yard the two of them ate most of a fifteen-pound chilled watermelon, and that night Caroline had the first stroke. It should have been the last, the doctor thought so too. But by daylight she had rallied, and that morning the generations of her loins began to arrive, from her own seventy and eighty year old children, down through their great- and twice-great-grandchildren — faces which the middleaged had never seen before until the cabin would no longer hold them: the women and girls sleeping on the floor inside and the men and boys sleeping on the ground in front of it, Caroline herself conscious now and presently sitting up in the bed: who had forgotten nothing: matriarchial and imperial, and more: imperious: ten and even eleven oclock at night and the middleaged himself undressed and in bed, reading, when sure enough he would hear the slow quiet stockinged or naked feet mounting the back stairs; presently the strange dark face — never the same one of two nights ago or the two or three nights before that — would look in the door at him, and the quiet, courteous, never servile voice would say: 'She want the ice cream.' And he would rise and dress and drive in to the village; he would even drive through the village although he knew that everything there will have long been closed and he would do what he had done two nights ago: drive thirty miles on to the arterial highway and then up or down it until he found an open drive-in or hot-dog stand to sell him the quart of ice cream.

But that stroke was not the one; she was walking again presently, even, despite the houseman's standing order to forestall her with the automobile, all the way in to town to sit with his, the middleaging's, mother, talking, he liked to think, of the old days of his father and himself and the three younger brothers, the two of them two women who together had never weighed two hundred pounds in a house roaring with five men: though they probably didn't since women, unlike men, have learned how to live uncomplicated by that sort of sentimentality. But it was as if she knew herself that the summer's stroke was like the throat-clearing sound inside the grandfather clock preceding the stroke of midnight or of noon, because she never touched the last unfinished quilt again. Presently it had vanished, no one knew where, and as the cold came and the shortening days she began to spend more and more time in the house, not her cabin but the big house, sitting in a corner of the kitchen while the cook and houseman were about, then in the middleaging's wife's sewing room until the family gathered for the evening meal, the houseman carrying her rocking chair into the dining room to sit there while they ate: until suddenly (it was almost Christmas now) she insisted on sitting in the parlor until the meal was ready, none knew why, until at last she told them, through the wife: 'Miss Hestelle, when them niggers lays me out, I want you to make me a fresh clean cap and apron to lay in.' That was her valedictory; two days after Christmas the stroke came which was the one; two days after that she lay in the parlor in the fresh cap and apron she would not see, and the middleaging did indeed lay back and preach the sermon, the oration, hoping that when his turn came there would be someone in the world to owe him the sermon which all owed to her who had been, as he had been from infancy, within the scope and range of that fidelity and that devotion and that rectitude.

Loving all of it even while he had to hate some of it because he knows now that you dont love because: you love despite; not for the virtues, but despite the faults.

FLANNERY O'CONNOR

The Catholic Novelist in the Protestant South

IN THE PAST SEVERAL years I have gone to speak at a number of Catholic colleges, and I have been pleased to discover that fiction seems to be important to the Catholic student in a way it would not have been twenty, or even ten, years ago. In the past, Catholic imagination in this country has been devoted almost exclusively to practical affairs. Our energies have gone into what has been necessary to sustain existence, and now that our existence is no longer in doubt, we are beginning to realize that an impoverishment of the imagination means an impoverishment of the religious life as well.

I am concerned that future Catholics have a literature. I want them to have a literature that will be undeniably theirs, but which will also be understood and cherished by the rest of our countrymen. A literature for ourselves alone is a contradiction in terms. You may ask, why not simply call this literature Christian? Unfortunately, the word Christian is no longer reliable. It has come to mean anyone with a golden heart. And a golden heart would be a positive interference in the writing of fiction.

I am specifically concerned with fiction because that is what I write. There is a certain embarrassment about being a storyteller in these times when stories are considered not quite as satisfying as statements and statements not quite as satisfying as statistics; but in the long run, a people is known, not by its statements or its statistics, but by the stories it tells. Fiction is the most impure and the most modest and the most human of the arts. It is closest to man in his sin and his suffering and his hope, and it is often rejected by Catholics for the very reasons that make it what it is. It escapes any orthodoxy we might set up for it, because its dignity is an imitation of our own, based like our own on free will, a free will that operates even in the teeth of divine displeasure. I won't go far into the subject of whether such a thing as a Catholic novel is possible or not. I feel that this is a bone which has been picked bare without giving anybody any nourishment. I am simply going to assume that novelists who are deeply Catholic will write novels which you may call Catholic if the Catholic aspects of the novel are what interest you. Such a novel may be characterized in any number of other ways, and perhaps the more ways the better.

In American Catholic circles we are long on theories of what Catholic fiction should be, and short on the experience of having any of it. Once when I spoke on this subject at a Catholic university in the South, a gentleman arose and said that the concept *Catholic novel* was a limiting one and that the novelist, like Whitman, should be alien to nothing. All I could say to him was, "Well, I'm alien to a great deal." We are limited human beings, and the novel is a product of our best limitations. We write with the whole personality, and any attempt to circumvent it, whether this be an effort to rise above belief or above background, is going to result in a reduced approach to reality.

But I think that in spite of this spotty and suspect sophistication, which you find here and there among us, the American Catholic feels the same way he has always felt toward the novel: he trusts the fictional imagination about as little as he trusts anything. Before it is well on its feet, he is worrying about how to control it. The young Catholic writer, more than any other, is liable to be smothered at the outset by theory. The Catholic press is constantly broken out in a rash of articles on the failure of the Catholic novelist: the Catholic novelist is failing to reflect the virtue of hope, failing to show the Church's interest in social justice, failing to portray our beliefs in a light that will make them desirable to others. He occasionally writes well, but he always writes wrong.

We have recently gone through a period of self-criticism on the subject of Catholics and scholarship, which for the most part has taken place on a high level. Our scholarship, or lack of it, has been discussed in relation to what scholarship is in itself, and the discussion — when it has been most valuable — has been conducted by those who are scholars and who know from their own experience what the scholar is and does.

But when we talk about the Catholic failure to produce good fiction in this country, we seldom hear from anyone actively engaged in trying to produce it, and the discussion has not yielded any noticeable returns. We hear from editors, schoolteachers, moralists, and housewives; anyone living considers himself an authority on fiction. The novelist, on the other hand, is supposed to be like Mr. Jarrell's pig that didn't know what bacon was. I think, though, that it is occasionally desirable that we look at the novel — even the so-called Catholic novel — from some particular novelist's point of view.

Catholic discussions of novels by Catholics are frequently ridiculous because every given circumstance of the writer is ignored except his Faith. No one taking part in these discussions seems to remember that the eye sees what it has been given to see by concrete circumstances, and the imagination reproduces what, by some related gift, it is able to make live.

I collect articles from the Catholic press on the failures of the Catholic novelist, and recently in one of them I came upon this typical sentence: "Why not a positive novel based on the Church's fight for social justice, or the liturgical revival, or life in a seminary?"

I take it that if seminarians began to write novels about life in the seminary, there would soon be several less seminarians, but we are to assume that anybody who can write at all, and who has the energy to do some research, can give us a novel on this or any needed subject — and can make it positive.

A lot of novels do get written in this way. It is, in fact, the traditional procedure of the hack, and by some accident of God, such a novel might turn out to be a work of art, but the possibility is unlikely.

In this same article, the writer asked this wistful question: "Would it not seem in order now for some of our younger men to explore the possibilities inherent in certain positive factors which make Catholic life and the Catholic position in this country increasingly challenging?"

This attitude, which proceeds from the standpoint of what it would be good to do or have to supply a general need, is totally opposite from the novelist's own approach. No serious novelist "explores possibilities inherent in factors." Conrad wrote that the artist "descends within himself, and in that region of stress and strife, if he be deserving and fortunate, he finds the terms of his appeal."

Where you find the terms of your appeal may have little or nothing to do with what is challenging in the life of the Church at the moment. And this is particularly apparent to the Southern Catholic writer, whose imagination has been molded by life in a region which is traditionally Protestant. The two circumstances that have given character to my own writing have been those of being Southern and being Catholic. This is considered by many to be an unlikely combination, but I have found it to be a most likely one. I think that the South provides the Catholic novelist with some benefits that he usually lacks, and lacks to a conspicuous degree. The Catholic novel can't be categorized by subject matter, but only by what it assumes about human and divine reality. It cannot see man as determined; it cannot see him as totally depraved. It will see him as incomplete in himself, as prone to evil, but as redeemable when his own efforts are assisted by grace. And it will see this grace as working through nature, but as entirely transcending it, so that a door is always open to possibility and the unexpected in the human soul. Its center of meaning will be Christ; its center of destruction will be the devil. No matter how this view of life may be fleshed out, these assumptions form its skeleton.

But you don't write fiction with assumptions. The things we see, hear, smell, and touch affect us long before we believe anything at all, and the South impresses its image on us from the moment we are able to distinguish one sound from another. By the time we are able to use our imaginations for fiction, we find that our senses have responded irrevocably to a certain reality. This discovery of being bound through the senses to a particular society and a particular history, to particular sounds and a particular idiom, is for the writer the beginning of a recognition that first puts his work into real human perspective for him. What the Southern Catholic writer is apt to find, when he descends within his imagination, is not Catholic life but the life of this region in which he is both native and alien. He discovers that the imagination is not free, but bound.

For many young writers, Catholic or other, this is not a pleasant discovery. They feel that the first thing they must do in order to write well is to shake off the clutch of the region. They would like to set their stories in a region whose way of life seems nearer the spirit of what they think they have to say, or better, they would like to eliminate the region altogether and approach the infinite directly. But this is not even a possibility.

The fiction writer finds in time, if not at once, that he cannot proceed at all if he cuts himself off from the sights and sounds that have developed a life of their own in his senses. The novelist is concerned with the mystery of personality, and you cannot say much that is significant about this mystery unless the characters you create exist with the marks of a believable society about them. The larger social context is simply left out of much current fiction, but it cannot be left out by the Southern writer. The image of the South, in all its complexity, is so powerful in us that it is a force which has to be encountered and engaged. The writer must wrestle with it, like Jacob with the angel, until he has extracted a blessing. The writing of any novel worth the effort is a kind of personal encounter, an encounter with the circumstances of the particular writer's imagination, with circumstances which are brought to order only in the actual writing.

The Catholic novel that fails is usually one in which this kind of engagement is absent. It is a novel which doesn't grapple with any particular culture. It may try to make a culture out of the Church, but this is always a mistake because the Church is not a culture. The Catholic novel that fails is a novel in which there is no sense of place, and in which feeling is, by that much, diminished. Its action occurs in an abstracted setting that could be anywhere or nowhere. This reduces its dimensions drastically and cuts down on those tensions that keep fiction from being facile and slick.

The Southern writer's greatest tie with the South is through his ear, which is usually sharp but not too versatile outside his own idiom. With a few exceptions, such as Miss Katherine Anne Porter, he is not too often successfully cosmopolitan in fiction, but the fact is that he doesn't need to be. A distinctive idiom is a powerful instrument for keeping fiction social. When one Southern character speaks, regardless of his station in life, an echo of all Southern life is heard. This helps to keep Southern fiction from being a fiction of purely private experience.

Alienation was once a diagnosis, but in much of the fiction of our time it has become an ideal. The modern hero is the outsider. His experience is rootless. He can go anywhere. He belongs nowhere. Being alien to nothing, he ends up being alienated from any kind of community based on common tastes and interests. The borders of his country are the sides of his skull.

The South is traditionally hostile to outsiders, except on her own terms. She is traditionally against intruders, foreigners from Chicago or New Jersey, all those who come from afar with moral energy that increases in direct proportion to the distance from home. It is difficult to separate the virtues of this quality from the narrowness which accompanies and colors it for the outside world. It is more difficult still to reconcile the South's instinct to preserve her identity with her equal instinct to fall eager victim to every poisonous breath from Hollywood or Madison Avenue. But good and evil appear to be joined in every culture at the spine, and as far as the creation of a body of fiction is concerned, the social is superior to the purely personal. Somewhere is better than anywhere. And traditional manners, however unbalanced, are better than no manners at all.

The writer whose themes are religious particularly needs a region where these themes find a response in the life of the people. The American Catholic is short on places that reflect his particular religious life and his particular problems. This country isn't exactly cut in his image. Where he does have a place — such as the Midwestern parishes, which serve as J. F. Powers' region, or South Boston, which belongs to Edwin O'Connor — these places lack the significant features that result in a high degree of regional self-consciousness. They have no great geographical extent, they have no particularly significant history, certainly no history of defeat; they have no real peasant class, and no cultural unity of the kind you find in the South. So that no matter what the writer brings to them in the way of talents, they don't bring much to him in the way of exploitable benefits. Where Catholics do abound, they usually blend almost imperceptibly into the general materialistic background. If the Catholic faith were central to life in America, Catholic fiction would fare better, but the Church is not central to this society. The things that bind us together as Catholics are known only to ourselves. A secular society understands us less and less. It becomes more and more difficult in America to make belief believable, but in this the Southern writer has the greatest possible advantage. He lives in the Bible Belt.

It was about 1919 that Mencken called the South the Bible Belt and the Sahara of the Bozarts. Today Southern literature is known around the world, and the South is still the Bible Belt. Sam Jones' grandma read the Bible thirty-seven times on her knees. And the rural and small-town South, and even a certain level of the city South, is made up of the descendants of old ladies like her. You don't shake off their influence in even several generations.

To be great storytellers, we need something to measure ourselves against, and this is what we conspicuously lack in this age. Men judge themselves now by what they find themselves doing. The Catholic has the natural law and the teachings of the Church to guide him, but for the writing of fiction, something more is necessary.

For the purposes of fiction, these guides have to exist in a concrete form, known and held sacred by the whole community. They have to exist in the form of stories which affect our image and our judgment of ourselves. Abstractions, formulas, laws will not serve here. We have to have stories in our background. It takes a story to make a story. It takes a story of mythic dimensions, one which belongs to everybody, one in which everybody is able to recognize the hand of God and its descent. In the Protestant South, the Scriptures fill this role.

The Hebrew genius for making the absolute concrete has conditioned the Southerner's way of looking at things. That is one of the reasons why the South is a storytelling section. Our response to life is different if we have been taught only a definition of faith than if we have trembled with Abraham as he held the knife over Isaac. Both of these kinds of knowledge are necessary, but in the last four or five centuries, Catholics have overemphasized the abstract and consequently impoverished their imaginations and their capacity for prophetic insight.

Nothing will insure the future of Catholic fiction so much as the biblical revival that we see signs of now in Catholic life. The Bible is held sacred in the Church, we hear it read at Mass, bits and pieces of it are exposed to us in the liturgy, but because we are not totally dependent on it, it has not penetrated very far into our consciousness nor conditioned our reactions to experience. Unfortunately, where you find Catholics reading the Bible, you find that it is usually a pursuit of the educated, but in the South the Bible is known by the ignorant as well, and it is always that *mythos* which the poor hold in common that is most valuable to the fiction writer. When the poor hold sacred history in common, they have ties to the universal and the holy, which allows the meaning of their every action to be heightened and seen under the aspect of eternity. The writer who views the world in this light will be very thankful if he has been fortunate enough to have the South for his background, because here belief can still be made believable, even if for the modern mind it cannot be made admirable.

Religious enthusiasm is accepted as one of the South's more grotesque features, and it is possible to build upon that acceptance, however little real understanding such acceptance may carry with it. When you write about backwoods prophets, it is very difficult to get across to the modern reader that you take these people seriously, that you are not making fun of them, but that their concerns are your own and, in your judgment, central to human life. It is almost inconceivable to this reader that such could be the case. It is hard enough for him to suspend his disbelief and accept an anagogical level of action at all, harder still for him to accept its action in an obviously grotesque character. He has the mistaken notion that a concern with grace is a concern with exalted human behavior, that it is a pretentious concern. It is, however, simply a concern with the human reaction to that which, instant by instant, gives life to the soul. It is a concern with a realization that breeds charity and with the charity that breeds action. Often the nature of grace can be made plain only by describing its absence.

The Catholic writer may be immersed in the Bible himself, but if his readers and his characters are not, he does not have the instrument to plumb meaning — and specifically Christian meaning — that he would have if the biblical background were known to all. It is what writer, character, and reader share that makes it possible to write fiction at all.

The circumstances of being a Southerner, of living in a non-Catholic but religious society, furnish the Catholic novelist with some very fine antidotes to his own worst tendencies. We too much enjoy indulging ourselves in the logic that kills, in making categories smaller and smaller, in prescribing attitudes and proscribing subjects. For the Catholic, one result of the Counter-Reformation was a practical overemphasis on the legal and logical and a consequent neglect of the Church's broader tradition. The need for this emphasis has now diminished, and the Church is busy encouraging those biblical and liturgical revivals which should restore Catholic life to its proper fullness. Nevertheless the scars of this legalistic approach are still upon us. Those who are long on logic, definitions, abstractions, and formulas are frequently short on a sense of the concrete, and when they find themselves in an environment where their own principles have only a partial application to society, they are forced, not to abandon the principles, but in applying them to a different situation, to come up with fresh reactions.

I often find among Catholics a certain impatience with Southern literature, sometimes a fascinated impatience, but usually a definite feeling that with all the violence and grotesqueries and religious enthusiasm reflected in its fiction, the South — that is, the rural, Protestant, Bible Belt South — is a little beyond the pale of Catholic respect, and that certainly it would be ridiculous to expect the emergence in such soil of anything like a literature inspired by Catholic belief. But for my part, I don't think that this is at all unlikely. There are certain conditions necessary for the emergence of Catholic literature which are found nowhere else in this country in such abundance as in the Protestant South; and I look forward with considerable relish to the day when we are going to have to enlarge our notions about the Catholic novel to include some pretty odd Southern specimens.

It seems to me that the Catholic Southerner's experience of living so intimately with the division of Christendom is an experience that can give much breadth and poignance to the novels he may produce. The Catholic novelist in the South is forced to follow the spirit into strange places and to recognize it in many forms not totally congenial to him. He may feel that the kind of religion that has influenced Southern life has run hand in hand with extreme individualism for so long that there is nothing left of it that he can recognize, but when he penetrates to the human aspiration beneath it, he sees not only what has been lost to the life he observes, but more, the terrible loss to us in the Church of human faith and passion. I think he will feel a good deal more kinship with backwoods prophets and shouting fundamentalists than he will with those politer elements for whom the supernatural is an embarrassment and for whom religion has become a department of sociology or culture or personality development. His interest and sympathy may very well go — as I know my own does — directly to those aspects of Southern life where the religious feeling is most intense and where its outward forms are farthest from the Catholic, and most revealing of a need that only the Church can fill. This is not because, in the felt superiority of orthodoxy, he wishes to subtract one theology from another, but because, descending within himself to find his region, he discovers that it is with these aspects of Southern life that he has a feeling of kinship strong enough to spur him to write.

The result of these underground religious affinities will be a strange and, to many, perverse fiction, one which serves no felt need, which gives us no picture of Catholic life, or the religious experiences that are usual with us, but I believe that it will be Catholic fiction. These people in the invisible Church make discoveries that have meaning for us who are better protected from the vicissitudes of our own natures, and who are often too lazy and satisfied to make any discoveries at all. I believe that the Catholic fiction writer is free to find his subject in the invisible Church and that this will be the vocation of many of us brought up in the South. In a literature that tends naturally to extremes, as Southern literature does, we need something to protect us against the merely extreme, the merely personal, the merely grotesque, and here the Catholic, with his older tradition and his ability to resist the dissolution of belief, can make his contribution to Southern literature, but only if he realizes first that he has as much to learn from it as to give it. The Catholic novelist in the South will bolster the South's best traditions, for they are the same as his own. And the South will perhaps lead him to be less timid as a novelist, more respectful of the concrete, more trustful of the blind imagination.

The opportunities for the potential Catholic writer in the South are so great as to be intimidating. He lives in a region where there is a thriving literary tradition, and this is always an advantage to the writer, who is initially inspired less by life than by the work of his predecessors. He lives in a region which is struggling, in both good ways and bad, to preserve its identity, and this is an advantage, for his dramatic need is to know manners under stress. He lives in the Bible Belt, where belief can be made believable. He has also here a good view of the modern world. A half-hour's ride in this region will take him from places where the life has a distinctly Old Testament flavor to places where the life might be considered post-Christian. Yet all these varied situations can be seen in one glance and heard in one conversation.

I think that Catholic novelists in the future will be able to reinforce the vital strength of Southern literature, for they will know that what has given the South her identity are those beliefs and qualities which she has absorbed from the Scriptures and from her own history of defeat and violation: a distrust of the abstract, a sense of human dependence on the grace of God, and a knowledge that evil is not simply a problem to be solved, but a mystery to be endured.

If all that is missing in this scene is the practical influence of the visible

Catholic Church, the writer will find that he has to supply the lack, as best he can, out of himself; and he will do this by the way he uses his eyes. If he uses them in the confidence of his Faith, and according to the needs of what he is making, there will be nothing in life too grotesque, or too "un-Catholic," to supply the materials of his work. Certainly in a secular world, he is in a particular position to appreciate and cherish the Protestant South, to remind us of what we have and what we must keep.

• WILLIAM STYRON •

This Quiet Dust

You mought be rich as cream
And drive you coach and four-horse team,
But you can't keep de world from moverin' round
Nor Nat Turner from gainin' ground.

And your name it mought be Caesar sure
And got you cannon can shoot a mile or more,
But you can't keep de world from moverin' round
Nor Nat Turner from gainin' ground.

—Old-time Negro Song

MY NATIVE STATE OF Virginia is, of course, more than ordinarily conscious of its past, even for the South. When I was learning my lessons in the mid-1930s at a grammar school on the banks of the James River, one of the required texts was a history of Virginia — a book I can recall far more vividly than any history of the United States or of Europe I studied at a later time. It was in this work that I first encountered the name Nat Turner. The reference to Nat was brief; as a matter of fact, I do not think it unlikely that it was the very brevity of the allusion — amounting almost to a quality of haste — which captured my attention and stung my curiosity. I can no longer quote the passage exactly, but I remember that it went something like this: "In 1831, a fanatical Negro slave named Nat Turner led a terrible insurrection in Southampton County, murdering many white people. The insurrection was immediately put down, and for their cruel deeds Nat Turner and most of the other Negroes involved in the rebellion were hanged." Give or take a few harsh adjectives, this was all the information on Nat Turner supplied by that forgotten historian, who hustled on to matters of greater consequence.

I must have first read this passage when I was ten or eleven years old. At that time my home was not far from Southampton County, where the rebellion took place, in a section of the Virginia Tidewater which is generally considered part of the Black Belt because of the predominance of Negroes in the population. (When I speak of the South and Southerners here, I speak of *this* South, where Deep South attitudes prevail; it would include parts of Maryland and East Texas.) My boyhood experience was the typically ambivalent one of most native Southerners, for whom the Negro is simultaneously taken for granted and as an object of unending concern. On the one hand, Negroes are simply a part of the landscape, an unexceptional feature of the local scenery, yet as central to its character as the pinewoods and sawmills and mule teams and sleepy river estuaries that give such color and tone to the Southern geography. Unnoticed by white people, the Negroes blend with the land and somehow melt and fade into it, so that only when one reflects upon their possible absence, some magical disappearance, does one realize how unimaginable this absence would be: it would be easier to visualize a South without trees, without *any* people, without life at all. Thus at the same time, ignored by white people, Negroes impinge upon their collective subconscious to such a degree that it may be rightly said that they become the focus of an incessant preoccupation, somewhat like a monstrous, recurring dream populated by identical faces wearing expressions of inquietude and vague reproach. "Southern whites cannot walk, talk, sing, conceive of laws or justice, think of sex, love, the family, or freedom without responding to the presence of Negroes." The words are those of Ralph Ellison, and, of course, he is right.

Yet there are many Souths, and the experience of each Southerner is modified by the subtlest conditions of self and family and environment and God knows what else, and I have wondered if it has ever properly been taken into account how various this response to the presence of the Negroes can be. I cannot tell how typical my own awareness of Negroes was, for instance, as I grew up near my birthplace — a small seaside city about equally divided between black and white. My feelings seem to have been confused and blurred, tinged with sentimentality, colored by a great deal of folklore, and wobbling always between a patronizing affection, fostered by my elders, and downright hostility. Most importantly, my feelings were completely uninformed by that intimate knowledge of black people which Southerners claim as their special patent; indeed, they were based upon an almost total ignorance.

For one thing, from the standpoint of attitudes toward race, my upbringing was hardly unusual: it derived from the simple conviction that Negroes were in every respect inferior to white people and should be made to stay in their proper order in the scheme of things. At the same time, by certain Southern standards my family was enlightened: although my mother taught me firmly that the use of "lady" instead of "woman" in referring to a Negro female was quite improper, she writhed at the sight of the extremes of Negro poverty, and would certainly have thrashed me had she ever heard me use the word "nigger." Yet outside the confines of family, in the lower-middle-class school world I inhabited every day, this was a word I commonly used. School segregation, which was an ordinary fact of life for me, is devastatingly effective in accomplishing something that it was only peripherally designed to do: it prevents the awareness even of the existence of another race. Thus, whatever hostility I bore toward the Negroes was based almost entirely upon hearsay.

And so the word "nigger," which like all my schoolmates I uttered so freely and so often, had even then an idle and listless ring. How could that dull epithet carry meaning and conviction when it was applied to a people so diligently isolated from us that they barely existed except as shadows which came daily to labor in the kitchen, to haul away garbage, to rake up leaves? An unremarked paradox of Southern life is that its racial animosity is really grounded not upon friction and propinquity, but upon an almost complete lack of contact. Surrounded by a sea of Negroes, I cannot recall more than once — and then briefly, when I was five or six — ever having played with a Negro child, or ever having spoken to a Negro, except in trifling talk with the cook, or in some forlorn and crippled conversation with a dotty old grandfather angling for hardshell crabs on a lonesome Sunday afternoon many years ago. Nor was I by any means uniquely sheltered. Whatever knowledge I gained in my youth about Negroes, I gained from a distance, as if I had been watching actors in an all-black puppet show.

* * *

Such an experience has made me distrust any easy generalizations about the South, whether they are made by white sociologists or Negro playwrights, Southern politicians or Northern editors. I have come to understand at least as much about the Negro after having lived in the North. One of the most egregious of the Southern myths — one in this case propagated solely by Southerners — is that of the Southern white's boast that he "knows" the Negro. Certainly in many rural areas of the South the cultural climate has been such as to allow a mutual understanding, and even a kind of intimacy, to spring up between the races, at least in some individual instances. But my own boyhood surroundings, which were semi-urban (I suppose suburban is the best description, though the green little village on the city's outskirts where I grew up was a far cry from Levittown), and which have become the youthful environment for vast numbers of Southerners, tended almost totally to preclude any contact between black and white, especially when that contact was so sedulously proscribed by law.

Yet if white Southerners cannot "know" the Negro, it is for this very reason that the entire sexual myth needs to be reexamined. Surely a certain amount of sexual tension between the races does continue to exist, and the Southern white man's fear of sexual aggression on the part of the Negro male is still too evident to be ignored. But the nature of the growth of the urban, modern South has been such as to impose ever more effective walls between the races. While it cannot be denied that slavery times produced an enormous amount of interbreeding (with all of its totalitarianism, this was a free-for-all atmosphere far less self-conscious about carnal mingling than the Jim Crow era which began in the 1890s) and while even now there must logically take place occasional sexual contacts between the races — especially in rural areas where a degree of casual familiarity has always obtained — the monolithic nature of segregation has raised such an effective barrier between whites and Negroes that it is impossible not to believe that theories involving a perpetual sexual "tension" have been badly inflated. Nor is it possible to feel that a desire to taste forbidden fruit has ever really caused this barrier to be breached. From the standpoint of the Negro, there is indifference or uncompli-cated fear; from that of the white — segregation, the law, and, finally, indif-ference, too. When I was growing up, the older boys might crack wan jokes about visiting the Negro whorehouse street (patronized entirely, I later discovered, by Negroes plus a few Scandinavian sailors), but to my knowledge none of them ever really went there. Like Negroes in general, Negro girls were to white men phantoms, shadows. To assume that anything more than a rare and sporadic intimacy on any level has existed in the modern South between whites and Negroes is simply to deny, with a truly willful contempt for logic, the monstrous effectiveness of that apartheid which has been the Southern way of life for almost three-quarters of a century.

I have lingered on this matter only to try to underline a truth about Southern life which has been too often taken for granted, and which has therefore been overlooked or misinterpreted. Most Southern white people *cannot* know or touch black people and this is because of the deadly intimidation of a universal law. Certainly one feels the presence of this gulf even in the work of a writer as supremely knowledgeable about the South as William Faulkner, who confessed a hesitancy about attempting to "think Negro," and whose Negro characters, as marvelously portrayed as most of them are, seem nevertheless to be meticulously *observed* rather than *lived*. Thus in *The Sound and the Fury*, Faulkner's magnifi-cent Dilsey comes richly alive, yet in retrospect one feels this is a result of countless mornings, hours, days Faulkner had spent watching and listening to old Negro servants, and not because Dilsey herself is a being created from a sense of withinness: at the last moment Faulkner draws back, and it is no mere happen-stance that Dilsey, alone among the four central figures from whose points of view the story is told, is seen from the outside rather than from that intensely "inner" vantage point, the interior monologue.

Innumerable white Southerners have grown up as free of knowledge of the Negro character and soul as a person whose background is rural Wisconsin or Maine. Yet, of course, there is a difference, and it is a profound one, defining the white Southerner's attitudes and causing him to be, for better or for worse, whatever it is he is to be. For the Negro is *there*. And he is there in a way he never is in the North, no matter how great his numbers. In the South he is a perpetual and immutable part of history itself, a piece of the vast fabric so integral and necessary that without him the fabric dissolves; his voice, his black or brown face passing on a city street, the sound of his cry rising from a wagonload of flowers, his numberless procession down dusty country roads, the neat white church he has built in some pine grove with its air of grace and benison and tranquillity, his silhouette behind a mule team far off in some spring field, the wail of his blues blaring from some jukebox in a backwoods roadhouse, the sad wet faces of nursemaids and cooks waiting in the evening at city bus stops in pouring rain — the Negro is always *there*.

No wonder then, as Ellison says, the white Southerner can do virtually nothing without responding to the presence of Negroes. No wonder the white man so often grows cranky, fanciful, freakish, loony, violent: how else respond to a paradox which requires, with the full majesty of law behind it, that he deny the very reality of a people whose multitude approaches and often exceeds his own; that he disclaim the existence of those whose human presence has marked every acre of the land, every hamlet and crossroad and city and town, and whose humanity, however inflexibly denied, is daily evidenced to him like a heartbeat in loyalty and wickedness, madness and hilarity and mayhem and pride and love? The Negro may feel that it is too late to be known, and that the desire to know him reeks of outrageous condescension. But to break down the old law, to come to *know* the Negro, has become the moral imperative of every white Southerner.

II

I suspect that my search for Nat Turner, my own private attempt as a novelist to re-create and bring alive that dim and prodigious black man, has been at least a partial fulfillment of this mandate, although the problem has long since resolved itself into an artistic one — which is as it should be. In the late 1940s, having finished college in North Carolina and come to New York, I found myself again haunted by that name I had first seen in the Virginia history textbook. I had learned something more of Southern history since then, and I had become fascinated by the subject of Negro slavery. One of the most striking aspects of the institution is the fact that in the 250 years of its existence in America, it was singularly free of organized uprisings, plots, and rebellions. (It is curious that as recently as the late 1940s, scholarly insights were lagging, and I could only have suspected then what has since been made convincing by such historians as Frank Tannenbaum and Stanley Elkins: that American Negro slavery, unique in its psychological oppressiveness — the worst the world has ever known — was simply so despotic and emasculating as to render organized revolt next to impossible.) There were three exceptions: a conspiracy by the slave Gabriel Prosser and his followers near Richmond in the year 1800, the plot betrayed, the conspirators hanged; a similar conspiracy in 1822, in Charleston, South Carolina, led by a free Negro named Denmark Vesey, who also was betrayed before he could carry out his plans, and who was executed along with other members of the plot.

The last exception, of course, was Nat Turner, and he alone in the entire annals of American slavery — alone among all those "many thousand gone" — achieved a kind of triumph.

Even today, many otherwise well-informed people have never heard the name Nat Turner, and there are several plausible reasons for such an ignorance. One of these, of course, is that the study of our history — and not alone in the South — has been tendentious in the extreme, and has often avoided even an allusion to a figure like Nat, who inconveniently disturbs our notion of a slave system which, though morally wrong, was conducted with such charity and restraint that any organized act of insurrectory and murderous violence would be unthinkable. But a general ignorance about Nat Turner is even more understandable in view of the fact that so little is left of the actual record. Southampton County, which even now is off the beaten track, was at that period the remotest backwater imaginable. The relativity of time allows us elastic definitions: 1831 was yesterday. Yet the year 1831, in the Presidency of Andrew Jackson, lay in the very dawn of our modern history, three years before a railroad ever touched the soil of Virginia, a full fifteen years before the use of the telegraph. The rebellion itself was of such a cataclysmic nature as practically to guarantee confusion of the news, distortion, wild rumors, lies, and, finally, great areas of darkness and suppression; all of these have contributed to Nat's obscurity.

As for the contemporary documents themselves, only one survives: the *Confessions of Nat Turner*, a brief pamphlet of some five thousand words, transcribed from Nat's lips as he awaited trial, by a somewhat enigmatic lawyer named Thomas Gray, who published the *Confessions* in Baltimore and then vanished from sight. There are several discrepancies in Gray's transcript but it was taken down in haste, and in all major respects it seems completely honest and reliable. Those few newspaper accounts of the time, from Richmond and Norfolk, are sketchy, remote, filled with conjecture, and are thus virtually worthless. The existing county court records of Southampton remain brief and unilluminating, dull lists, a dry catalogue of names in fading ink: the white people slain, the Negroes tried and transported south, or acquitted, or convicted and hanged.

Roughly seventy years after the rebellion (in 1900, which by coincidence was the year Virginia formally adopted its first Jim Crow laws), the single scholarly book ever to be written on the affair was published — *The Southampton Insurrection*, by a Johns Hopkins Ph.D. candidate named William S. Drewry, who was an unreconstructed Virginian of decidedly pro-slavery leanings and a man so quaintly committed to the *ancien régime* that, in the midst of a description of the ghastliest part of the uprising, he was able to reflect that "slavery in Virginia was not such to arouse rebellion, but was an institution which nourished the strongest affection and piety in slave and owner, as well as moral qualities worthy of any age of civilization." For Drewry, Nat Turner was some sort of inexplicable aberration, like a man from Mars. Drewry was close enough to the event in time, however, to be able to interview quite a few of the survivors, and since he also possessed a bloodthirsty relish for detail, it was possible for him to reconstruct the chronology of the insurrection with what appears to be considerable accuracy. Drewry's book (it is of course long out of print) and Nat's *Confessions* remain the only significant sources about the insurrection. Of Nat himself, his background and early years, very little can be known. This is not disadvantageous to a novelist, since it allows him to speculate — with a freedom not accorded the historian — upon all the intermingled miseries, ambitions, frustrations, hopes, rages, and desires which caused this extraordinary black man to rise up out of those early mists of our history and strike down his oppressors with a fury of retribution unequaled before or since.

* * *

He was born in 1800, which would have made him at the time of the insurrection thirty-one years old — exactly the age of so many great revolutionaries at the decisive moment of their insurgency: Martin Luther,* Robespierre, Danton, Fidel Castro. Thomas Gray, in a footnote to the *Confessions*, describes him as having the "true Negro face" (an offhand way of forestalling an assumption that he might have possessed any white blood), and he adds that "for natural intelligence and quickness of apprehension he is surpassed by few men I have ever seen" — a lofty tribute indeed at that inflammatory instant, with antebellum racism at its most hysteric pitch. Although little is known for certain of Nat's childhood and youth, there can be no doubt that he was very precocious and that he learned not only to read and write with ease — an illustrious achievement in itself, when learning to read and write was forbidden to Negroes by law — but at an early age acquired a knowledge of astronomy, and later on experimented in making paper and gunpowder. (The resemblance here to the knowledge of the ancient Chinese is almost too odd to be true, but I can find no reason to doubt it.)

---

* See Erik Erikson's *Young Man Luther* for a brilliant study of the development of the revolutionary impulse in a young man, and the relationship of this impulse to the father-figure. Although it is best to be wary of any heavy psychoanalytical emphasis, one cannot help believing that Nat Turner's relationship with his father, like Luther's, was tormented and complicated, especially since this person could not have been his real father, who ran away when Nat was an infant, but the white man who owned and raised him.

The early decades of the nineteenth century were years of declining prosperity for the Virginia Tidewater, largely because of the ruination of the land through greedy cultivation of tobacco — a crop which had gradually disappeared from the region, causing the breakup of many of the big old plantations and the development of subsistence farming on small holdings. It was in these surroundings — a flat pastoral land of modest farms and even more modest homesteads, where it was rare to find a white man prosperous enough to own more than half a dozen Negroes, and where two or three slaves to a family was the general rule — that Nat was born and brought up, and in these surroundings he prepared himself for the apocalyptic role he was to play in history. Because of the failing economic conditions, it was not remarkable that Nat was purchased and sold several times by various owners (in a sense, he was fortunate in not having been sold off to the deadly cotton and rice plantations of South Carolina and Georgia, which was the lot of many Virginia Negroes of the period); and although we do not know much about any of these masters, the evidence does not appear to be that Nat was ill-treated, and in fact one of these owners (Samuel Turner, brother of the man whose property Nat was born) developed so strong a paternal feeling for the boy and such regard for Nat's abilities, that he took the fateful step of encouraging him in the beginnings of an education.

The atmosphere of the time and place was fundamentalist and devout to a passionate degree, and at some time during his twenties Nat, who had always been a godly person — "never owning a dollar, never uttering an oath, never drinking intoxicating liquors, and never committing a theft" — became a Baptist preacher. Compared to the Deep South, Virginia slave life was not so rigorous; Nat must have been given considerable latitude, and found many opportunities to preach and exhort the Negroes. His gifts for preaching, for prophecy, and his own magnetism seem to have been so extraordinary that he grew into a rather celebrated figure among the Negroes of the county, his influence even extending to the whites, one of whom — a poor, half-cracked, but respectable overseer named Brantley — he converted to the faith and baptized in a mill pond in the sight of a multitude of the curious, both black and white. (After this no one would have anything to do with Brantley, and he left the county in disgrace.)

At about this time Nat began to withdraw into himself, fasting and praying, spending long hours in the woods or in the swamp, where he communed with the Spirit and where there came over him, urgently now, intimations that he was being prepared for some great purpose. His fanaticism grew in intensity, and during these lonely vigils in the forest he began to see apparitions:

> I saw white spirits and black spirits engaged in battle, and the sun was darkened; the thunder rolled in the heavens and blood flowed in streams . . . I wondered greatly at these miracles, and prayed to be

informed of a certainty of the meaning thereof; and shortly afterwards, while laboring in the fields, I discovered drops of blood on the corn as though it were dew from heaven. For as the blood of Christ had been shed on this earth, and had ascended to heaven for the salvation of sinners, it was now returning to earth again in the form of dew . . . On the twelfth day of May, 1828, I heard a loud noise in the heavens, and the Spirit instantly appeared to me and said the Serpent was loosened, and Christ had laid down the yoke he had borne for the sins of men, and that I should take it on and fight against the Serpent, for the time was fast approaching when the first should be last and the last should be first . . .

Like all revolutions, that of Nat Turner underwent many worrisome hesitations, false starts, procrastinations, delays (with appropriate irony, Independence Day, 1830, had been one of the original dates selected, but Nat fell sick and the moment was put off again); finally, however, on the night of Sunday, August 21, 1831, Nat, together with five other Negroes in whom he had placed his confidence and trust, assembled in the woods near the home of his owner of the time, a carriage maker named Joseph Travis, and commenced to carry out a plan of total annihilation. The penultimate goal was the capture of the county seat, then called Jerusalem (a connotation certainly not lost on Nat, who, with the words of the prophets roaring in his ears, must have felt like Gideon himself before the extermination of the Midianites); there were guns and ammunition in Jerusalem, and with these captured it was then Nat's purpose to sweep thirty miles eastward, gathering black recruits on the way until the Great Dismal Swamp was reached — a snake-filled and gloomy fastness in which Nat believed, with probable justification, only Negroes could survive, and no white man's army could penetrate. The immediate objective, however, was the destruction of every white man, woman, and child on the ten-mile route to Jerusalem; no one was to be spared; tender infancy and feeble old age alike were to perish by the axe and the sword. The command, of course, was that of God Almighty, through the voice of his prophet Ezekiel: *"Son of Man, prophesy and say, Thus saith the Lord; Say, a sword, a sword is sharpened, and also furbished: it is sharpened to make a sore slaughter . . . Slay utterly old and young, both maids and little children, and women . . ."* It was a scheme so wild and daring that it could only have been the product of the most wretched desperation and frustrate misery of soul; and of course it was doomed to catastrophe not only for whites but for Negroes — and for black men in ways which from the vantage point of history now seem almost unthinkable.

* * *

They did their job rapidly and with merciless and methodical determination.

Beginning at the home of Travis — where five people, including a six-month-old infant, were slain in their beds — they marched from house to house on an eastward route, pillaging, murdering, sparing no one. Lacking guns — at least to begin with — they employed axes, hatchets, and swords as their tools of destruction, and swift decapitation was their usual method of dispatch. (It is interesting that the Negroes did not resort to torture, nor were they ever accused of rape. Nat's attitude toward sex was Christian and high-minded, and he had said: "We will not do to their women what they have done to ours.")

On through the first day they marched, across the hot August fields, gaining guns and ammunition, horses, and a number of willing recruits. That the insurrection was not purely racial, but perhaps obscurely pre-Marxist, may be seen in the fact that a number of dwellings belonging to poor white people were pointedly passed by. At midday on Monday their force had more than tripled, to the amount of nineteen, and nearly thirty white people lay dead. By this time, the alarm had been sounded throughout the country, and while the momentum of the insurgent band was considerable, many of the whites had fled in panic to the woods, and some of the farmers had begun to resist, setting up barricades from which they could fire back at Nat's forces. Furthermore, quite a few of the rebels had broken into the brandy cellars of the houses they had attacked and had gotten roaring drunk — an eventuality Nat had feared and had warned against. Nevertheless, the Negroes — augmented now by forty more volunteers — pressed on toward Jerusalem, continuing the attack into the next night and all through the following day, when at last obstinate resistance by the aroused whites and the appearance of a mounted force of militia troops (also, it must be suspected, continued attrition by the apple brandy) caused the rebels to be dispersed, only a mile or so from Jerusalem.

Almost every one of the Negroes was rounded up and brought to trial — a legalistic nicety characteristic of a time in which it was necessary for one to determine whether *his* slave, property, after all, worth eight or nine hundred dollars, was really guilty and deserving of the gallows. Nat disappeared immediately after the insurrection, and hid in the woods for over two months, when near-starvation and the onset of autumnal cold drove him from his cave and forced him to surrender to a lone farmer with a shotgun. Then he too was brought to trial in Jerusalem — early in November 1831 — for fomenting a rebellion in which sixty white people had perished.

* * *

The immediate consequences of the insurrection were exceedingly grim. The killing of so many white people was in itself an act of futility. It has never been determined with any accuracy how many black people, not connected with the rebellion, were slain at the hands of rampaging bands of white men who swarmed all over Southampton in the week following the uprising, seeking reprisal and vengeance. A contemporary estimate by a Richmond newspaper, which deplored this retaliation, put the number at close to two hundred Negroes, many of them free, and many of them tortured in ways unimaginably horrible. But even more important was the effect that Nat Turner's insurrection had upon the institution of slavery at large. News of the revolt spread among Southern whites with great speed: the impossible, the unspeakable had at last taken place after 200 years of the ministrations of sweet old mammies and softly murmured Yassuhs and docile compliance — and a shock wave of anguish and terror ran through the entire South. If such a nightmarish calamity happened there, would it not happen *here?* — here in Tennessee, in Augusta, in Vicksburg, in these bayous of Louisiana? Had Nat lived to see the consequences of his rebellion, surely it would have been for him the cruelest irony that his bold and desperate bid for liberty had caused only the most tyrannical new controls to be imposed upon Negroes everywhere — the establishment of patrols, further restrictions upon movement, education, assembly, and the beginning of other severe and crippling restraints which persisted throughout the slaveholding states until the Civil War. Virginia had been edging close to emancipation, and it seems reasonable to believe that the example of Nat's rebellion, stampeding many moderates in the legislature into a conviction that the Negroes could not be safely freed, was a decisive factor in the ultimate victory of the proslavery forces. Had Virginia, with its enormous prestige among the states, emancipated its slaves, the effect upon our history would be awesome to contemplate.

Nat brought cold, paralyzing fear to the South, a fear that never departed. If white men had sown the wind with chattel slavery, in Nat Turner they had reaped the whirlwind for white and black alike.

Nat was executed, along with sixteen other Negroes who had figured large in the insurrection. Most of the others were transported south, to the steaming fields of rice and cotton. On November 11, 1831, Nat was hanged from a live oak tree in the town square of Jerusalem. He went to his death with great dignity and courage. "The bodies of those executed," wrote Drewry, "with one exception, were buried in a decent and becoming manner. That of Nat Turner was delivered to the doctors, who skinned it and made grease of the flesh."

III

Not long ago, in the spring of the year, when I was visiting my family in Virginia, I decided to go down for the day to Southampton County, which is a drive of an hour and a half by car from the town where I was born and raised. Nat Turner was of course the reason for this trip, although I had nothing particular or urgent in mind. What research it was possible to do on the event I had long since done. The Southampton court records, I had already been reliably informed, would prove unrewarding. It was not a question, then, of digging out more facts, but simply a matter of wanting to savor the mood and atmosphere of a landscape I had not seen for quite a few years, since the times when as a boy I used to pass through Southampton on the way to my father's family home in North Carolina. I thought also that there might be a chance of visiting some of the historic sites connected with the insurrection, and perhaps even of retracing part of the route of the uprising through the help of one of those handsomely produced guidebooks for which the Historical Commission of Virginia is famous — guides indispensable for a trip to such Old Dominion shrines as Jamestown and Appomattox and Monticello. I became even more eager to go when one of my in-laws put me in touch by telephone with a cousin of his. This man, whom I shall call Dan Seward, lived near Franklin, the main town of Southampton, and he assured me in those broad cheery Southern tones which are like a warm embrace — and which, after long years in the chill North, are to me always so familiar, reminiscent, and therefore so unsettling, sweet, and curiously painful — that he would like nothing better than to aid me in my exploration in whatever way he could.

* * *

Dan Seward is a farmer, and prosperous grower of peanuts in a prosperous agricultural region where the peanut is the unquestioned monarch. A combination of sandy loam soil and a long growing season has made Southampton ideal for the cultivation of peanuts; over 30,000 acres are planted annually, and the crop is processed and marketed in Franklin — a thriving little town of 7,000 people — or in Suffolk and Portsmouth, where it is rendered into Planters cooking oil and stock feed and Skippy peanut butter. There are other money-making crops — corn and soybeans and cotton. The county is at the northernmost edge of the cotton belt, and thirty years ago cotton was a major source of income. Cotton has declined in importance but the average yield per acre is still among the highest in the South, and the single gin left in the county in the little village of Drewryville processes each year several thousand bales which are trucked to market down in North Carolina. Lumbering is also very profitable, owing mainly to an abundance of the loblolly pines valuable in the production of kraft wood pulp; and the Union Bag-Camp Paper Company's plant on the Blackwater river in Franklin is a huge enterprise employing over 1,600 people. But it is peanuts — the harvested vines in autumn piled up mile after mile in dumpy brown stacks like hay — which have brought money to Southampton, and a sheen of prosperity that can be seen in the freshly painted farmhouses along the monotonously flat state highway which leads into Franklin, and the new-model Dodges and Buicks parked slantwise against the curb of some crossroads hamlet, and the gaudy, eye-catching signs that advise the wisdom of a bank savings account for all those surplus funds.

The county has very much the look of the New South about it, with its airport and its shiny new motels, its insistent billboards advertising space for industrial sites, the sprinkling of housing developments with television antennas gleaming from every rooftop, its supermarkets and shopping centers and its flavor of go-getting commercialism. This is the New South, where agriculture still prevails but has joined in a vigorous union with industry, so that even the peanut when it goes to market is ground up in some rumbling engine of commerce and becomes metamorphosed into wood stain or soap or cattle feed. The Negroes, too, have partaken of this abundance — some of it, at least — for they own television sets also, and if not new-model Buicks (the Southern white man's strictures against Negro ostentation remain intimidating), then decent late-model used Fords; while in the streets of Franklin the Negro women shopping seemed on the day of my visit very proud and well-dressed compared to the shabby stooped figures I recalled from the Depression years when I was a boy. It would certainly appear that Negroes deserve some of this abundance, if only because they make up so large a part of the work force. Since Nat Turner's day the balance of population in Southampton — almost 60 per cent Negro — has hardly altered by a hair.

"I don't know anywhere that a Negro is treated better than around here," Mr. Seward was saying to the three of us, on the spring morning I visited him with my wife and my father. "You take your average person from up North, he just doesn't *know* the Negro like we do. Now for instance I have a Negro who's worked for me for years, name of Ernest. He knows if he breaks his arm — like he did a while ago, fell off a tractor — he knows he can come to me and I'll see that he's taken care of, hospital expenses and all, and I'll take care of him and his family while he's unable to work, right on down the line. I don't ask him to pay back a cent, either, that's for sure. We have a wonderful relationship, that Negro and myself. By God, I'd die for that Negro and he knows it, and he'd do the same for me. But Ernest doesn't want to sit down at my table, here in this house, and have supper with me — and he wouldn't want me in *his* house. And Ernest's got kids like I do, and he doesn't want them to go to school with my Bobby, any more than Bobby wants to go to school with *his* kids. It works both ways. People up North don't seem to be able to understand a simple fact like that."

Mr. Seward was a solidly fleshed, somewhat rangy, big-shouldered man in his early forties with an open, cheerful manner which surely did nothing to betray the friendliness with which he had spoken on the telephone. He had greeted us — total strangers, really — with an animation and uncomplicated good will that would have shamed an Eskimo; and for a moment I realized that, after years amid the granite outcroppings of New England, I had forgotten that this *was* the passionate, generous, outgoing nature of the South, no artificial display but a social gesture as natural as breathing.

* * *

Mr. Seward had just finished rebuilding his farmhouse on the outskirts of town, and he had shown us around with a pride I found understandable: there was a sparkling electric kitchen worthy of an advertisement in *Life* magazine, some handsome modern furniture, and several downstairs rooms paneled beautifully in the prodigal and lustrous hardwood of the region. It was altogether a fine, tasteful house, resembling more one of the prettier medium-priced homes in the Long Island suburbs than the house one might contemplate for a Tidewater farmer. Upstairs, we had inspected his son Bobby's room, a kid's room with books like *Pinocchio* and *The Black Arrow* and *The Swiss Family Robinson,* and here there was a huge paper banner spread across one entire wall with the crayon inscription: *"Two . . . four . . . six . . . eight! We Don't Want to Integrate!"* It was a sign which so overwhelmingly dominated the room that it could not help provoking comment, and it was this that eventually had led to Mr. Seward's reflections about *knowing* Negroes.

There might have been something vaguely defensive in his remarks but not a trace of hostility. His tone was matter-of-fact and good-natured, and he pronounced the word Negro as *nigra,* which most Southerners do with utter naturalness while intending no disrespect whatsoever, in fact quite the opposite — the mean epithet, of course, is *nigger.* I had the feeling that Mr. Seward had begun amiably to regard us as sympathetic but ill-informed outsiders, non-Southern, despite his knowledge of my Tidewater background and my father's own accent, which is thick as grits. Moreover, the fact that I had admitted to having lived in the North for fifteen years caused me, I fear, to appear alien in his eyes, *déraciné,* especially when my acculturation to Northern ways has made me adopt the long "e" and say Negro. The racial misery, at any rate, is within inches of driving us mad: how can I explain that, with all my silent disagreement with Mr. Seward's paternalism, I knew that when he said, "By God, I'd die for that Negro," he meant it?

Perhaps I should not have been surprised that Mr. Seward seemed to know very little about Nat Turner. When we got around to the subject, it developed that he had always thought that the insurrection occurred way back in the eighteenth century. Affably, he described seeing in his boyhood the "Hanging Tree," the live oak from which Nat had been executed in Courtland (Jerusalem had undergone this change of name after the Civil War), and which had died and been cut down some thirty years ago; as for any other landmarks, he regretted that he did not know of a single one. No, so far as he knew, there just wasn't anything.

For me, it was the beginning of disappointments which grew with every hour. Had I *really* been so ingenuous as to believe that I would unearth some shrine, some home preserved after the manner of Colonial Williamsburg, a relic of the insurrection at whose portal I would discover a lady in billowing satin and crinoline, who for fifty cents would shepherd me about the rooms with a gentle drawl indicating the spot where a good mistress fell at the hands of the murderous darky? The native Virginian, despite himself, is cursed with a suffocating sense of history, and I do not think it impossible that I actually suspected some such monument. Nevertheless, confident that there would be something to look at, I took heart when Mr. Seward suggested that after lunch we all drive over to Courtland, ten miles to the west. He had already spoken to a friend of his, the Sheriff of the county, who knew all the obscure byways and odd corners of Southampton, mainly because of his endless search for illegal stills; if there was a solitary person alive who might be able to locate some landmark, or could help retrace part of Nat Turner's march, it was the Sheriff. This gave me hope. For I had brought along Drewry's book and its map which showed the general route of the uprising, marking the houses by name. In the sixty years since Drewry, there would have been many changes in the landscape. But with this map oriented against the Sheriff's detailed county map, I should easily be able to pick up the trail and thus experience, however briefly, a sense of the light and shadow that played over that scene of slaughter and retribution a hundred and thirty-four years ago.

Yet it was as if Nat Turner had never existed, and as the day lengthened and afternoon wore on, and as we searched Nat's part of the county — five of us now, riding in the Sheriff's car with its huge star emblazoned on the doors, and its radio blatting out hoarse intermittent messages, and its riot gun protectively nuzzling the backs of our necks over the edge of the rear seat — I had the sensation from time to time that this Negro, who had so long occupied my thoughts, who indeed had so obsessed my imagination that he had acquired larger spirit and flesh than most of the living people I encountered day in and day out, had been merely a crazy figment of my mind, a phantom no more real than some half-recollected image from a fairy tale. For here in the back country, this horizontal land of woods and meadows where he had roamed, only a few people had heard of Nat Turner, and of those who had — among the people we stopped to make inquiries of, both white and black, along dusty country roads, at farms, at filling stations, at crossroad stores — most of them confused him, I think, with something spectral, mythic, a black Paul Bunyan who had perpetrated mysterious and nameless deeds in millennia past. They were neither facetious nor evasive, simply unaware. Others confounded him with the Civil War — a Negro general. One young Negro field hand, lounging at an Esso station, figured he was a white man. A white man, heavy-lidded and paunchy, slow-witted, an idler at a rickety store, thought him an illustrious racehorse of bygone days.

The Sheriff, a smallish, soft-speaking ruminative man, with the whisper of a smile frozen on his face as if he were perpetually enjoying a good joke, knew full well who Nat Turner was, and I could tell he relished our frustrating charade. He was a shrewd person, quick and sharp with countrified wisdom, and he soon became quite as fascinated as I with the idea of tracking down some relic of the uprising (although he said that Drewry's map was hopelessly out of date, the roads of that time now abandoned to the fields and woods, the homes burnt down or gone to ruin); the country people's ignorance he found irresistible and I think it tickled him to perplex their foolish heads, white or black, with the same old leading question: "You heard about old Nat Turner, ain't you?" But few of them had heard, even though I was sure that many had plowed the same fields that Nat had crossed, lived on land that he had passed by; and as for dwellings still standing which might have been connected with the rebellion, not one of these back-country people could offer the faintest hint or clue. As effectively as a monstrous and unbearable dream, Nat had been erased from memory.

It was late afternoon when, with a sense of deep fatigue and frustration, I suggested to Mr. Seward and the Sheriff that maybe we had better go back to Courtland and call it a day. They were agreeable — relieved, I felt, to be freed of this tedious and fruitless search — and as we headed east down a straight unpaved road, the conversation became desultory, general. We spoke of the North. The Sheriff was interested to learn that I often traveled to New York. He went there occasionally himself, he said; indeed, he had been there only the month before — "to pick up a nigger," a fugitive from custody who had been awaiting trial for killing his wife. New York was a fine place to spend the night, said the Sheriff, but he wouldn't want to live there.

As he spoke, I had been gazing out of the window, and now suddenly something caught my eye — something familiar, a brief flickering passage of a distant outline, a silhouette against the sun-splashed woods — and I asked the Sheriff to stop the car. He did, and as we backed up slowly through a cloud of dust, I recognized a house standing perhaps a quarter of a mile off the road, from this distance only a lopsided oblong sheltered by an enormous oak, but the whole tableau — the house and the glorious hovering tree and the stretch of woods beyond — so familiar to me that it might have been some home I passed every day. And of course now as recognition came flooding back, I knew whose house it was. For in *The Southampton Insurrection*, the indefatigable Drewry had included many photographs — amateurish, doubtless taken by himself, and suffering from the fuzzy offset reproduction of 1900. But they were clear enough to provide an unmistakable guide to the dwellings in question, and now as I again consulted the book I could see that this house — the monumental oak above it grown scant inches it seemed in sixty years — was the one referred to by Drewry as having belonged to Mrs. Catherine Whitehead. From this distance, in the soft clear light of a spring afternoon, it seemed most tranquil, but few houses have come to know such a multitude of violent deaths. There in the late afternoon of Monday, August 22, Nat Turner and his band had appeared, and they set upon and killed "Mrs. Catherine Whitehead, son Richard, and four daughters, and grandchild."

The approach to the house was by a rutted lane long ago abandoned and overgrown with lush weeds which make a soft, crushed, rasping sound as we rolled over them. Dogwood, white and pink, grew on either side of the lane, quite wild and wanton in lovely pastel splashes. Not far from the house a pole fence interrupted our way; the Sheriff stopped the car and we got out and stood there for a moment, looking at the place. It was quiet and still — so quiet that the sudden chant of a mockingbird in the woods was almost frightening — and we realized then that no one lived in the house. Scoured by weather, paintless, worn down to the wintry gray of bone and with all the old mortar gone from between the timbers, it stood alone and desolate above its blasted, sagging front porch, the ancient door ajar like an open wound. Although never a manor house, it had once been a spacious and comfortable country home; now in near-ruin it sagged, finished, a shell, possessing only the most fragile profile of itself. As we drew closer still we could see that the entire house, from its upper story to the cellar, was filled with thousands of shucked ears of corn — feed for the malevolent-looking little razorback pigs which suddenly appeared in a tribe at the edge of the house, eying us, grunting. Mr. Seward sent them scampering with a shied stick and a farmer's sharp "Whoo!" I looked up at the house, trying to recollect its particular role in Nat's destiny, and then I remembered.

* * *

There was something baffling, secret, irrational about Nat's own participation in the uprising. He was unable to kill. Time and time again in his confession one discovers him saying (in an offhand tone; one must dig for the implications): "I could not give the death blow, the hatchet glanced from his head," or, "I struck her several blows over the head, but I was unable to kill her, as the sword was dull . . ." It is too much to believe, over and over again; the glancing hatchet, the dull sword. It smacks rather, as in *Hamlet*, of rationalization, ghastly fear, an access of guilt, a shrinking from violence, and fatal irresolution. Alone here at this house, turned now into a huge corncrib around which pigs rooted and snorted in the silence of a spring afternoon, here alone was Nat finally able — or was he forced? — to commit a murder, and this upon a girl of eighteen named Margaret Whitehead, described by Drewry in terms perhaps not so romantic or farfetched after all, as "the belle of the county." The scene is apocalyptic — afternoon bedlam in wild harsh sunlight and August heat.

"I returned to commence the work of death, but those whom I left had not been idle; all the family were already murdered but Mrs. Whitehead and her daughter Margaret. As I came round the door I saw Will pulling Mrs. Whitehead out of the house and at the step he nearly severed her head from her body with his axe. Miss Margaret, when I discovered her, had concealed herself in the corner formed by the projection of the cellar cap from the house; on my approach she fled into the field but was soon overtaken and after repeated blows with a sword, I killed her by a blow on the head with a fence rail."

It is Nat's only murder. Why, from this point on, does the momentum of the uprising diminish, the drive and tension sag? Why, from this moment in the *Confessions*, does one sense in Nat something dispirited, listless, as if all life and juice had been drained from him, so that never again through the course of the rebellion is he even on the scene when a murder is committed? What happened to Nat in this place? Did he discover his humanity here, or did he lose it?

I lifted myself up into the house, clambering through a doorway without steps, pushing myself over the crumbling sill. The house had a faint yeasty fragrance, like flat beer. Dust from the mountains of corn lay everywhere in the deserted rooms, years and decades of dust, dust an inch thick in some places, lying in a fine gray powder like sooty fallen snow. Off in some room amid the piles of corn I could hear a delicate scrabbling and a plaintive squeaking of mice. Again it was very still, the shadow of the prodigious old oak casting a dark pattern of leaves, checkered with bright sunlight, aslant through the gaping door. As in those chilling lines of Emily Dickinson, even this lustrous and golden day seemed to find its only resonance in the memory, and perhaps a premonition, of death.

> This quiet Dust was Gentlemen and Ladies,
> And Lads and Girls;
> Was laughter and ability and sighing,
> And frocks and curls.

Outside, the Sheriff was calling in on his car radio, his voice blurred and indistinct; then the return call from the county seat, loud, a dozen incomprehensible words in an uproar of static. Suddenly it was quiet again, the only sound my father's soft voice as he chatted with Mr. Seward.

I leaned against the rotting frame of the door, gazing out past the great tree and into that far meadow where Nat had brought down and slain Miss Margaret Whitehead. For an instant, in the silence, I thought I could hear a mad rustle of taffeta, and rushing feet, and a shrill girlish piping of terror; then that day and this day seemed to meet and melt together, becoming almost one, and for a long moment indistinguishable.

. ALLEN .
TATE

A Southern Mode
of the Imagination

I

WHAT I AM ABOUT to say will be composed of obscure speculation, mere opinion, and reminiscence verging upon autobiography. But having issued this warning, and given notice to the scholars of American literature that the entire affair will be somewhat unreliable, I must allude to some of the things that I shall not try to say. I shall not discuss or "place" any of the Southern writers of the period now somewhat misleadingly called the Southern Renaissance. It was more precisely a birth, not a rebirth. The eyes of the world are on William Faulkner; for that reason I shall not talk about him. I take it to be a commonplace of literary history that no writer of Mr. Faulkner's power could emerge from a literary and social vacuum. It is a part of Mr. Faulkner's legend about himself that he did appear, like the sons of Cadmus, full grown, out of the unlettered soil of his native state, Mississippi. But we are under no obligation to take his word for it. Two other modern writers of prose-fiction, Mr. Stark Young and Miss Eudora Welty, quite as gifted as Mr. Faulkner, if somewhat below him in magnitude and power, are also natives of that backward state, where fewer people can read than in any other state in the Union. I shall not pause to explain my paradoxical conviction, shared I believe by Mr. Donald Davidson, that the very backwardness of Mississippi, and of the South as a whole, might partially explain the rise of a new literature which has won the attention not only of Americans but of the Western world.

If the Elizabethan age would still be the glory of English literature without Shakespeare, the new literature of the Southern states would still be formidable without Faulkner. I have promised not to discuss any one writer in detail, but I shall invoke certain names: Elizabeth Madox Roberts, Robert Penn Warren, Eudora Welty, Stark Young, Dubose Heyward, Ellen Glasgow, James Branch

Cabell, Katherine Anne Porter, Carson McCullers, Tennessee Williams, Thomas Wolfe, Paul Green, Caroline Gordon, Flannery O'Connor, Truman Capote, Ralph Ellison, John Crowe Ransom, Donald Davidson, Peter Taylor, Andrew Lytle. It is scarcely chauvinism on my part to point out that, with the exception of Fitzgerald and Hemingway, the region north of the Potomac and Ohio Rivers has become the stepsister of American fiction. And it has been said, so often that I almost believe it, that the American branch of the New Criticism is of Southern origin — a distinction about which my own feelings are neutral.

Before I turn to the more speculative part of this discussion, I should like to quote a paragraph written in the Reconstruction period — that is, around 1870 — by a New England novelist who had come to the South as a benign carpetbagger to observe and to improve what he observed. He was John William De Forest, of Connecticut, whose works were almost completely forgotten until about ten years ago. He was not only one of the best nineteenth-century American novelists; he was a shrewd social commentator, whose dislike of Southerners did not prevent him from seeing them more objectively than any other Northerner of his time. I quote:

Not until Southerners get rid of some of their social vanity, not until they cease talking of themselves in a spirit of self-adulation, not until they drop the idea that they are Romans and must write in the style of Cicero, will they be able to so paint life that the world shall crowd to see the picture. Meanwhile let us pray that a true Southern novelist will soon arise, for he will be able to furnish us vast amusement and some instruction. His day is passing; in another generation his material will be gone; the chivalrous Southron will be as dead as the slavery that created him.

It was not until fifty years later that De Forest's demands upon the Southern novelist were fulfilled, when the writers whose names I have listed began to appear. My own contemporaries called the nineteenth-century Ciceronian Southern style "Confederate prose," and we avoided it more assiduously than sin. Of a Southern woman novelist of the 1860's, Augusta Evans, author of *St. Elmo*, it was said that her heroines had swallowed an unabridged dictionary.

My reason for adopting the *causerie* instead of the formal discourse has a quite simple explanation. I have no talent for research; or at any rate I am like the man who, upon being asked whether he could play the violin, answered that he didn't know because he had never tried. Apart from inadequate scholarship, it would be improper of me to pretend to an objectivity, which I do not feel, in the recital of certain events, in which I have been told that I played a small part. None of us — and by us I mean not only the group of poets who with unintentional prophecy styled themselves the "Fugitives," but also our contemporaries in other Southern states — none of us, thirty-five years ago, was conscious of playing any part at all. I ought not to speak for my contemporaries, most of whom are still living and able to talk. The essays and books about us that have begun to appear give me a little less than the shock of recognition. If one does not recognize oneself, one may not unreasonably expect to recognize one's friends. One writer, Mr. John Bradbury, in a formidable book of some three hundred pages entitled *The Fugitives*, says that John Crowe Ransom taught his students, of whom I had the honor to be one, the "knowledge of good and evil." I don't recognize in this role my old friend and early master; I surmise that he has found it no less disconcerting than I do. Our initiation into the knowledge of good and evil, like everybody else's, must have been at birth; our later improvement in this field of knowledge, haphazard and extra-curricular. John Ransom taught us — Robert Penn Warren, Cleanth Brooks, Andrew Lytle and myself — Kantian aesthetics and a philosophical dualism, tinged with Christian theology, but ultimately derived from the Nicomachian ethics. I allude to my own education not because it was unique, but because it was the education of my generation in the South. But we said at that time very little about the South; an anomalous reticence in a group of men who later became notoriously sectional in point of view.

We knew we were Southerners, but this was a matter of plain denotation; just as we knew that some people were Yankees; or we knew that there were people whom — if we saw them — we would think of as Yankees; we might even have said, but only among ourselves, you understand: "He's a Yankee." Brainard Cheney told me years ago that when he was a small boy in Southern Georgia, down near the Okefenokee Swamp, the rumor spread that some Yankees were coming to town. All the little boys gathered in the courthouse square to see what Yankees looked like. This was about 1910. My boyhood, in the border state of Kentucky, was evidently more cosmopolitan. There were a few Northerners, no doubt; there were a few elderly gentlemen who had been Southern Unionists, or homemade Yankees, as they were discourteously described, who had fought in the Federal Army. One of these, old Mr. Crabb, white-haired, beak-nosed, and distinguished, frequently passed our house on his morning walk. He had an empty sleeve, and my mother said he had got his arm shot off at the Battle of Gettysburg. I knew that my grandfather had been in Pickett's charge, and I wondered idly whether he had shot it off. I do not remember whether I wished that he had.

This was our long moment of innocence, which I tried to recover in a poem many years later. And for men of my age, who missed the first World War by a few months, it was a new Era of Good Feeling between the sections. Some time before 1914 the North had temporarily stopped trying to improve us, or had at least paused to think about something else. Having just missed being sent to France in the A. E. F., I came to Vanderbilt University from a rural small-town society that had only a superficial Victorian veneer pasted over what was still an eighteenth-century way of living. It has been said that Kentucky seceded in 1865. In my boyhood, and even much later, Kentucky was more backward and Southern, socially and economically, than Tennessee or North Carolina. This preindustrial society meant, for people living in it, that one's identity had everything to do with land and material property, at a definite place, and very little to do with money. It was better for a person, however impoverished, of my name, to be identified with Tate's Creek Pike, in Fayette County, than to be the richest man in town without the identification of place. This was simple and innocent; it had little to do with what the English call *class*. Yet from whatever point of view one may look at it, it will in the end lead us towards the secret of what was rather grandiosely called, by the late W. J. Cash, the Southern Mind.

If I may bring to bear upon it an up-to-date and unSouthern adjective, it was an extroverted mind not much given to introspection. (I do not say meditation, which is something quite different.) Such irony as this mind was capable of was distinctly romantic; it came out of the sense of dislocated external relations: because people were not *where* they ought to be they could not be *who* they ought to be; for men had missed their proper role, which was to be attached to a place. Mr. Faulkner's lawyer Benbow and the Compson family, in *The Sound and the Fury,* are people of this sort; I know of no better examples than Mr. Andrew Lytle's Jack Cropleigh, in his novel *The Velvet Horn,* or the narrator of his powerful short story, "Mister McGregor." It is the irony of time and place out of joint. It was provincial or, if you will, ignorant of the world. It was the irony of social discrepancies, not the tragic irony of the peripety, or of interior change. It is premodern; it can be found in the early books of Ellen Glasgow and James Branch Cabell, as different at the surface as their books may appear to be.

But with the end of the first World War a change came about that literary historians have not yet explained; whether we shall ever understand it one cannot say. Southern literature in the second half of this century may cease to engage the scholarly imagination; the subject may eventually become academic, and buried with the last dissertation. Back in the nineteen-thirties, I believe it was precisely 1935, I wrote for the tenth anniversary issue of *The Virginia Quarterly Review* an essay entitled "The Profession of Letters in the South," which glanced at a possible explanation by analogy to another literary period. I refer to it here in order to qualify, or at any rate to extend its agreement, not, I hope, to call attention to myself. So far as that old essay is concerned, other persons have already done this for me. When I look at the index of a work of contemporary criticism (I always look there first), and see my name, I get a little nervous because the following passage has a two-to-one chance over anything else I have written, to be quoted; I quote it again:

The considerable achievement of Southerners in modern American letters must not beguile us into too much hope for the future. The Southern novelist has left his mark upon the age; but it is of the age. From the peculiarly historical consciousness of the Southern writer has come good work of a special order; but the focus of this consciousness is quite temporary. It has made possible the curious burst of intelligence that we get at a crossing of the ways, not unlike, on an infinitesimal scale, the outburst of poetic genius at the end of the sixteenth century when commercial England had already begun to crush feudal England. The Histories and Tragedies of Shakespeare record the death of the old regime, and Doctor Faustus gives up feudal order for world power.

My purpose in quoting the passage — I marvel that prose so badly written could have been quoted so much — is not to approve of the approbation it has received, but to point out that whatever rightness it may have is not right enough. It says nothing about the particular quality of the Southern writers of our time.

The quality that I have in mind, none too clearly, makes its direct impact upon the reader, even if he be the foreign reader: he knows that he is reading a Southern book. But this explains nothing, for a quality can only be pointed to or shared, not defined. Let me substitute for the word quality the phrase *mode of discourse*.

The traditional Southern mode of discourse presupposes somebody at the other end silently listening: it is the rhetorical mode. Its historical rival is the dialectical mode, or the give and take between two minds, even if one mind, like the mind of Socrates, prevail at the end. The Southerner has never been a dialectician. The ante-bellum Southerner quoted Aristotle in defense of slavery, but Plato, the dialectician, was not opposed to the "peculiar institution," and he could have been cited with equal effect in support of the South Carolinian daydream of a Greek democracy. Aristotle was chosen by the South for good reason: although the Stagirite (as the Southerners called him) was a metaphysician, the South liked the deductive method, if its application were not too abstruse, and nobody could quarrel with the arrangement, in the order of importance, of the three great Aristotelian treatises on man in society: the *Nicomachian Ethics*, the *Politics*, and the *Rhetoric*. Aristotle assumed first principles from which he — and the old Southerners after him — could make appropriate deductions about the inequalities of men. Plato reached first principles by means of dialogue, which can easily become subjective: the mind talking to itself. The Southerner always talks to somebody else, and this somebody else, after varying intervals, is given his turn; but the conversation is always among rhetoricians; that is to say, the typical Southern conversation is not going anywhere; it is not about anything. *It is about the people who are talking*, even if they never refer to themselves, which they usually don't, since conversation is only an expression of manners, the purpose of which is to make everybody happy. This may be the reason why Northerners and other uninitiated persons find the alternating, or contrapuntal, conversation of Southerners fatiguing. Educated Northerners like their conversation to be about ideas.

II

The foregoing, rather too broad distinction between dialectic and rhetoric is not meant to convey the impression that no Southerner of the past or the present was ever given to thought; nor do I wish to imply that New Englanders were so busy thinking that they wholly neglected that form of rhetoric which may be described as the manners of men talking in society. Emerson said that the "scholar is man thinking." Had Southerners of that era taken seriously the famous lecture entitled

"The American Scholar," they might have replied by saying that the gentleman is man talking. The accomplished Christian gentleman of the old South was the shadow, attenuated by evangelical Calvinism, of his Renaissance spiritual ancestor, who had been the creation of the rhetorical tradition, out of Aristotle through Cicero, distilled finally by Castiglione. By contrast, the New England sage, embodied in Ralph Waldo Emerson, took seriously what has come to be known since the Industrial Revolution as the life of the mind: an activity a little apart from life, and perhaps leading to the fashionable alienation of the "intellectual" of our time. The protective withdrawal of the New England sage into dialectical truth lurks back of Emerson's famous definition of manners as the "invention of a wise man to keep a fool at a distance." (There is little doubt of the part Emerson conceived himself as playing.) The notorious lack of self-consciousness of the ante-bellum Southerner made it almost impossible for him to define anything; least of all could he imagine the impropriety of a definition of manners. Yet had a Southern contemporary of Emerson decided to argue the question, he might have retorted that manners are not *in*ventions, but *con*ventions tacitly agreed upon to protect the fool from consciousness of his folly. I do not wholly subscribe to this Southern view; there is to be brought against it Henry Adam's unkind portrait of Rooney Lee, a son of Robert E. Lee, who soon became a Confederate officer. The younger Lee, said Adams, when they were fellow students at Harvard, seemed to have only the habit of command, and no brains. (Adams didn't say it quite so rudely, but that is what it came to.) Rooney Lee, like his famous father, was a man of action, action through the habit of command being a form of rhetoric: he acted upon the assumptions of identification by place. The Lee identification, the whole Virginian myth of the rooted man, was the model of the more homely mystique of Tate's Creek Pike in the frontier state of Kentucky, whose citizens the Virginians thought were all Davy Crocketts — a frontiersman who described himself as "half-horse and half-alligator." Virginia was the model for the entire Upper South.

Northern historians were for years puzzled that Lee and the Southern yeoman farmer fought for the South, since neither had any interest in slavery. The question was usually put in this form: Why did Lee, who never owned a slave and detested slavery, become the leader of the slavocracy? Because he was a rhetorician who would have flunked Henry Adam's examination as miserably as his son. A Southern dialectician, could he be imagined in Lee's predicament, would have tossed his loyalties back and forth and come out with an abstraction called Justice, and he would have fought in the Federal Army or not at all. The record seems to indicate that the one dialectical abstraction that Lee entertained came to him after the war: the idea of constitutional government, for which in retrospect he considered that he had fought. Perhaps he did fight for it; yet I have the temerity to doubt his word. He fought for the local community which he could not abstract into fragments. He was in the position of the man who is urged by an outsider to repudiate his family because a cousin is an embezzler, or of the man who tries to rectify his ill-use of his brother by pretending that his entire family is a bad lot. I trust that in this analogy it is clear that the brother is the Negro slave.

What Robert E. Lee has to do with Southern literature is a question that might at this point quite properly be asked. Lee has a good deal to do with it, if we are going to look at Southern literature as the rhetorical expression of a Southern Mind. But even to be conscious of the possibility of a Southern Mind could lead us into a mode of discourse radically different from that of the rhetorician. We are well on the way towards dialectics. If we say that the old Southern Mind was rhetorical we must add that our access to it must be through its public phase, which was almost exclusively political. I do not believe that the ante-bellum Southerners, being wholly committed to the rhetorical mode, were capable of the elementary detachment that has permitted modern Southerners to discern the significance of that commitment, and to relate it to other modes of discourse. For the rhetorical mode is related to the myth-making faculty, and the mythopoeic mind assumes that certain great typical actions embody human truth. The critical detachment which permits me to apply this commonplace to the Southern Mind would not, I believe, have been within the grasp of better intellects than mine in the South up to the first World War. It has been said that the failure of the old Southern leaders to understand the Northern mind (which was then almost entirely the New England mind) was a failure of intelligence. In view of the task which the South had set for itself — that is, the preservation of local self-government within a framework of republican federalism — the charge is no doubt true. The old Southerners, being wholly committed to the rhetoric of politics, could not come to grips with the dynamic forces in the North that were rapidly making the exclusively political solution of their problem obsolete: they did not understand economics. The Southern public *persona* was supported by what W. J. Cash called, in a neo-Spenglerian phrase, the "proto-Dorian" myth. This *persona* was that of the agrarian patriot, a composite image of Cincinnatus dropping the plough for the sword, and of Cicero leaving his rhetorical studies to apply them patriotically to the prosecution of Cataline. The center round which the Southern political imagination gravitated was perhaps even smaller than the communities of which the South was an aggregate. In the first place, that aggregate was not a whole; and in the second, it would follow that the community itself was not a whole. The South was an aggregate of farms and plantations, presided over by our composite agrarian hero, Cicero Cincinnatus. I can think of no better image for what the South was before 1860, and for what it largely still was until about 1914, than that of the old gentleman in Kentucky who sat every afternoon in his front yard under an old sugar tree, reading Cicero's Letters to Atticus. When the hands suckering the tobacco in the adjoining field needed orders, he kept his place in the book with his forefinger, walked out into the field, gave the orders, and then returned to his reading under the shade of the tree. He was also a lawyer, and occasionally he went to his office, which was over the feed store in the county seat, a village with a population of about four hundred people.

The center of the South, then, was the family, no less for Robert E. Lee than for the people on Tate's Creek Pike; for Virginia was a great aggregate of families that thought almost infinite ramifications of relationship was almost one family. Such a society could not be anything but political. The virtues cherished under such a regime were almost exclusively social and moral, with none of the intensively cultivated divisions of intellectual labor which are necessary to a flowering of the arts, whether literary or plastic. It is thus significant that the one original art of the South was domestic architecture, as befitted a family-centered society. It has been frequently noted that the reason why the South did not produce a great ante-bellum literature was the lack of cities as cultural centers. This was indeed a lack; but it is more important to understand why cultural centers were missing. The South did not want cultural centers; it preferred the plantation center. William Gilmore Simms argued repeatedly in the 1850's that no exclusively agrarian society had produced a great literature. Was this a failure of intelligence? I think not, if we look at the scene from the inside. After Archimedes had observed that, had he a fulcrum big enough, he could move the world, was it a failure of the Greek intelligence that it did not at once construct such a fulcrum? Were the Greek philosophers less intelligent than the late Albert Einstein and Professor Teller, who have found a way not only to move the world but perhaps to destroy it? But the plantation myth — and I use the word myth not to indicate a fantasy, but a reality — this myth, if Greek at all, was the limited Spartan myth. It was actually nearer to Republican Rome, a society which, like the South, was short in metaphysicians and great poets, and long in moralists and rhetoricians.

Mr. Lionel Trilling has said somewhere that the great writer, the spokesman of a culture, carries in himself the fundamental dialectic of that culture: the deeper conflicts of which his contemporaries are perhaps only dimly aware. There is a valuable truth in this observation. The inner strains, stresses, tensions, the shocked self-consciousness of a highly differentiated and complex society, issue in the dialectic of the high arts. The Old South, I take it, was remarkably free of this self-consciousness; the strains that it felt were external. And I surmise that had our Southern *persona*, our friend Cicero Cincinnatus, been much less simple than he was, the distractions of the sectional agitation nevertheless were so engrossing that they would have postponed almost indefinitely that self-examination which is the beginning, if not of wisdom, then at least of the arts of literature. When one is under attack, it is inevitable that one should put not only one's best foot forward but both feet, even if one of them rests upon the neck of a Negro slave. One then attributes to "those people over there" (the phrase that General Lee used to designate the Federal Army) all the evil of his own world. The defensive Southerner said that *if only* "those people over there" would let us alone, the vast Sabine Farm of the South (where men read Horace but did not think it necessary to be Horace) would perpetuate itself forever.

The complicated reasons for this Southern isolationism were, as I have tried to indicate, partly internal and partly external; but whatever the causes, the pertinent fact for any approach to the modern literary Renaissance is that the South was more isolated from 1865 to about 1920 than it had been before 1865. It was the isolationism of economic prostration, defeat, and inverted pride. And the New South of Henry W. Grady's rhetoric was just as isolated and provincial as the Old South of Thomas Nelson Page. For Grady's New South, the complete answer was the factory. (It was put into the less than distinguished verse of "The Song of the Chattahoochee," by Sidney Lanier.) I venture to think that there was more to be said for Page's Old South, even if we agree that, like Grady's New South, it was unreal: I take it that a pleasant dream is to be preferred to an actuality which imitates a nightmare. Neither the unreal dream nor the actual nightmare could lead to the conception of a complete society. If we want proof of this, we need only to look at the South today.

I should like now to return to the inadequacy of my speculations, twenty-four years ago, on the reasons for the sudden rise of the new Southern literature — a literature which, I have been told often enough to authorize the presumption, is now the center of American literature. (I do not insist upon this.) Social change must have had something to do with it, but it does not explain it. I do not hope to explain it now. I wish only to add a consideration which I have already adumbrated. If it seems narrow, technical, and even academically tenuous, it is probably not less satisfactory than the conventional attribution of literary causation to what is called the historical factor. No doubt, without this factor, without the social change, the new literature could not have appeared. One can nevertheless imagine the same consciousness of the same change around 1920, without the appearance of any literature whatever. Social change may produce a great social scientist, like the late Howard W. Odum, of North Carolina. Social upheaval will not in itself produce a poet like John Crowe Ransom or a novelist like William Faulkner.

There was another kind of change taking place at the same time, and it was decisive. The old Southern *rhetor*, the speaker who was eloquent before the audience but silent in himself, had always had at his disposal a less formal version of the rhetorical mode of discourse than the political oration. Was it not said that Southerners were the best storytellers in America? Perhaps they still are. The tall tale was the staple of Southern conversation. Augustus Baldwin Longstreet's *Georgia Scenes* is a collection of tall tales written by an accomplished gentleman for other accomplished gentlemen; this famous book is in no sense folk literature, or an expression of the late V. L. Parrington's democratic spirit. It is the art of the rhetorician applied to the anecdote, to the small typical action resembling the mediaeval *exemplum*, and it verges upon myth — the minor secular myth which just succeeds in the skirting round the suprahuman myth of religion. We have got something like this myth in *Huckleberry Finn*, which I take to be the first modern novel by a Southerner. We are now prepared by depth psychology to describe the action of *Huckleberry Finn* as not only typical, but as archetypal. What concerns me about it, for my purposes, is not whether it is a great novel (perhaps the *scale* of the action and the *range* of consciousness are too small for a great novel); what concerns me is the mode of its progression; for this mode is no longer the mode of rhetoric, the mode of the speaker reporting in person an argument or an action in which he is not dramatically involved. The action is generated inside the characters: there is internal dialogue, a conflict within the self. Mark Twain seems not to have been wholly conscious of what he had done; for he never did it again. Ernest Hemingway has said that the modern American novel comes out of *Huckleberry Finn*, and William Faulkner has paid a similar tribute. But this is not quite to the point.

Mark Twain was a forerunner who set an example which was not necessarily an influence. The feature of *Huckleberry Finn* which I have tried to discern, the shift from the rhetorical mode to the dialectical mode, had to be rediscovered by the twentieth-century novelists of the South. The example of Mark Twain was not quite fully developed and clean in outline. Most of the recent essays on *Huckleberry Finn* — by Lionel Trilling and T. S. Eliot for example — have not been able to approach the end of the novel without embarrassment. (The one exception is a perceptive essay by Mr. Leo Marx.) Huck himself is a dramatic dialectician; Tom Sawyer, who reappears at the end and resolves the action externally with the preposterous "liberation" of Nigger Jim, who is already free, is a ham Southern rhetorician of the old school. He imposes his "style" upon a reality which has no relation to it, without perception of the ironic "other possible case" which is essential to the dramatic dialectic of the arts of fiction.

Here, as I come to the end of these speculations, I must go off again into surmises and guesses. What brought about the shift from rhetoric to dialectic? The Southern fictional dialectic of our time is still close to the traditional subject matter of the old informal rhetoric — the tall tale, the anecdote, the archetypal story. The New England dialectic of the Transcendentalists, from which Hawthorne had to protect himself by remaining aloof, tended to take flight into the synthesis of pure abstraction, in which the inner struggle is resolved in an idea. The Southern dramatic dialectic of our time is being resolved, as in the novels of William Faulkner, in action. The short answer to our question: How did this change come about? is that the South not only reentered the world with the first World War; it looked round and saw for the first time since about 1830 that the Yankees were not to blame for everything. It looks like a simple discovery, and it was; that is why it was difficult to make. The Southern legend, as Malcolm Cowley has called it, of defeat and heroic frustration was taken over by a dozen or more first-rate writers and converted into a universal myth of the human condition. W. B. Yeats's great epigram points to the nature of the shift from melodramatic rhetoric to the dialectic of tragedy: "Out of the quarrel with others we make rhetoric; out of the quarrel with ourselves, poetry."

EUDORA WELTY

Place in Fiction

PLACE IS ONE OF the lesser angels that watch over the racing hand of fiction, perhaps the one that gazes benignly enough from off to one side, while others, like character, plot, symbolic meaning, and so on, are doing a good deal of wing-beating about her chair, and feeling, who in my eyes carries the crown, soars highest of them all and rightly relegates place into the shade. Nevertheless, it is this lowlier angel that concerns us here. There have been signs that she has been rather neglected of late; maybe she could do with a little petitioning.

What place has place in fiction? It might be thought so modest a one that it can be taken for granted: the location of a novel; to use a term of the day, it may make the novel "regional." The term, like most terms used to pin down a novel, means little; and Henry James said there isn't any difference between "the English novel" and "the American novel," since there are only two kinds of novels at all, the good and the bad. Of course Henry James didn't stop there, and we all hate generalities, and so does place. Yet as soon as we step down from the general view to the close and particular, as writers must and readers may and teachers well know how to, and consider what good writing may be, place can be seen, in her own way, to have a great deal to do with that goodness, if not to be responsible for it. How so?

First, with the goodness — validity — in the raw material of writing. Second, with the goodness in the writing itself — the achieved world of appearance, through which the novelist has his whole say and puts his whole case. There will still be the lady, always, who dismissed *The Ancient Mariner* on grounds of implausibility. Third, with the goodness — the worth — in the writer himself: place is where he has his roots, place is where he stands; in his experience out of which he writes, it provides the base of reference; in his work, the point of view. Let us consider place in fiction in these three wide aspects.

Wide, but of course connected — vitally so. And if in some present-day novels the connection has apparently slipped, that makes a fresh reason for us to ponder the subject of place. For novels, besides being the pleasantest things imaginable, are powerful forces on the side. Mutual understanding in the world being nearly always, as now, at low ebb, it is comforting to remember that it is through art that one country can nearly always speak reliably to another, if the other can hear at all. Art, though, is never the voice of a country; it is an even more precious thing, the voice of the individual, doing its best to speak, not comfort of any sort, indeed, but truth. And the art that speaks it most unmistakably, most directly, most variously, most fully, is fiction; in particular, the novel.

Why? Because the novel from the start has been bound up in the local, the "real," the present, the ordinary day-to-day of human experience. Where the imagination comes in is in directing the use of all this. That use is endless, and there are only four words, of all the millions we've hatched, that a novel rules out: "Once upon a time." They make a story a fairy tale by the simple sweep of the remove — by abolishing the present and the place where we are instead of conveying them to us. Of course we shall have some sort of fairy tale with us always — just now it is the historical novel. Fiction is properly at work on the here and now, or the past made here and now; for in novels *we* have to be there. Fiction provides the ideal texture through which the feeling and meaning that permeate our own personal, present lives will best show through. For in his theme — the most vital and important part of the work at hand — the novelist has the blessing of the inexhaustible subject: you and me. You and me, here. Inside that generous scope and circumference — who could ask for anything more? — the novel can accommodate practically anything on earth; and has abundantly done so. The novel so long as it be *alive* gives pleasure, and must always give pleasure, enough to stave off the departure of the Wedding Guest forever, except for that one lady.

It is by the nature of itself that fiction is all bound up in the local. The internal reason for that is surely that *feelings* are bound up in place. The human mind is a mass of associations — associations more poetic even than actual. I say, "The Yorkshire Moors," and you will say, *"Wuthering Heights,"* and I have only to murmur, "If Father were only alive —" for you to come back with "We could go to Moscow," which certainly is not even so. The truth is, fiction depends for its life on place. Location is the crossroads of circumstance, the proving ground of "What happened? Who's here? Who's coming?" — and that is the heart's field.

Unpredictable as the future of any art must be, one condition we may hazard about writing: of all the arts, it is the one least likely to cut the cord that binds it to its source. Music and dancing, while originating out of place — groves! — and perhaps invoking it still to minds pure or childlike, are no longer bound to dwell there. Sculpture exists out in empty space: that is what it commands and replies to. Toward painting, place, to be so highly visible, has had a curious and changing relationship. Indeed, wasn't it when landscape invaded painting, and painting was given, with the profane content, a narrative content, that this worked to bring on a revolution to the art? Impressionism brought not the likeness-to-life but the mystery of place onto canvas; it was the method, not the subject, that told this. Painting and writing, always the closest two of the sister arts (and in ancient Chinese days only the blink of an eye seems to have separated them), have each a still closer connection with place than they have with each other; but a difference lies in their respective requirements of it, and even further in the way they use it — the written word being ultimately as different from the pigment as the note of the scale is from the chisel.

One element, which has just been mentioned, is surely the underlying bond that connects all the arts with place. All of them celebrate its mystery. Where does this mystery lie? Is it in the fact that place has a more lasting identity than we have, and we unswervingly tend to attach ourselves to identity? Might the magic lie partly, too, in the *name* of the place — since that is what *we* gave it? Surely, once we have it named, we have put a kind of poetic claim on its existence; the claim works even out of sight — may work forever sight unseen. The Seven Wonders of the World still give us this poetic kind of gratification. And notice we do not say simply "The Hanging Gardens" — that would leave them dangling out of reach and dubious in nature; we say "The Hanging Gardens of Babylon," and there they are, before our eyes, shimmering and garlanded and exactly elevated to the Babylonian measurement.

Edward Lear tapped his unerring finger on the magic of place in the limerick. There's something unutterably convincing about that Old Person of Sparta who had twenty-five sons and one darta, and it is surely beyond question that he fed them on snails and weighed them in scales, because we know where that Old Person is *from* — Sparta! We certainly do not need further to be told his *name*. "Consider the source." Experience has ever advised us to base validity on point of origin.

Being shown how to locate, to place, any account is what does most toward *making* us believe it, not merely allowing us to, may the account be the facts or a lie; and that is where place in fiction comes in. Fiction is a lie. Never in its inside thoughts, always in its outside dress.

Some of us grew up with the china night-light, the little lamp whose lighting showed its secret and with that spread enchantment. The outside is painted with a scene, which is one thing; then, when the lamp is lighted, through the porcelain sides a new picture comes out through the old, and they are seen as one. A lamp I knew of was a view of London till it was lit; but then it was the Great Fire of London, and you could go beautifully to sleep by it. The lamp alight is the combination of internal and external, glowing at the imagination as one; and so is the good novel. Seeing that these inner and outer surfaces do lie so close together and so implicit in each other, the wonder is that human life so often separates them, or appears to, and it takes a good novel to put them back together.

The good novel should be steadily alight, revealing. Before it can hope to be that, it must of course be steadily visible from its outside, presenting a continuous, shapely, pleasing and finished surface to the eye.

The sense of a story when the visibility is only partial or intermittent is as endangered as Eliza crossing the ice. Forty hounds of confusion are after it, the black waters of disbelief open up between its steps, and no matter which way it jumps it is bound to slip. Even if it has a little baby moral in its arms, it is more than likely a goner.

The novel must get Eliza across the ice; what it means — the way it proceeds — is always in jeopardy. It must be given a surface that is continuous and unbroken, never too thin to trust, always in touch with the senses. Its world of experience must be at every step, through every moment, within reach as the world of appearance.

This makes it the business of writing, and the responsibility of the writer, to disentangle the significant — in character, incident, setting, mood, everything — from the random and meaningless and irrelevant that in real life surround and beset it. It is a matter of his selecting and, by all that implies, of changing "real" life as he goes. With each word he writes, he acts — as literally and methodically as if he hacked his way through a forest and blazed it for the word that follows. He makes choices at the explicit demand of this one present story; each choice implies, explains, limits the next, and illuminates the one before. No two stories ever go the same way, although in different hands one story might possibly go any one of a thousand ways; and though the woods may look the same from outside, it is a new and different labyrinth every time. What tells the author his way? Nothing at all but what he knows inside himself: the same thing that hints to him afterward how far he has missed it, how near he may have come to the heart of it. In a working sense, the novel and its place have become one: work has made them, for the time being, the same thing, like the explorer's tentative map of the known world.

The reason why every word you write in a good novel is a lie, then, is that it is written expressly to serve the purpose; if it does not apply, it is fancy and frivolous, however specially dear to the writer's heart. Actuality, it is true, is an even bigger risk to the novel than fancy writing is, being frequently even more confusing, irrelevant, diluted and generally far-fetched than ill-chosen words can make it. Yet somehow, the world of appearance in the novel has got to *seem* actuality. Is there a reliable solution to the problem? Place being brought to life in the round before the reader's eye is the readiest and gentlest and most honest and natural way this can be brought about, I think; every instinct advises it. The moment the place in which the novel happens is accepted as true, through it will begin to glow, in a kind of recognizable glory, the feeling and thought that inhabited the novel in the author's head and animated the whole of his work.

Besides furnishing a plausible abode for the novel's world of feeling, place has a good deal to do with making the characters real, that is, themselves, and keeping them so. The reason is simply that, as Tristram Shandy observed, "We are not made of glass, as characters on Mercury might be." Place *can* be transparent, or translucent: not people. In real life we have to express the things plainest and closest to our minds by the clumsy word and the half-finished gesture; the chances are our most usual behavior makes sense only in a kind of daily way, because it has become familiar to our nearest and dearest, and still demands their constant indulgence and understanding. It is our describable outside that defines us, willy-nilly, to others, that may save us, or destroy us, in the world; it may be our shield against chaos, our mask against exposure; but whatever it is, the move we make in the place we live has to signify our intent and meaning.

Then think how unprotected the poor character in a novel is, into whose mind the author is inviting us to look — unprotected and hence surely unbelievable! But no, the author has expressly seen to believability. Though he must know all, again he works with illusion. Just as the world of a novel is more highly selective than that of real life, so character in a novel is much more definite, less shadowy than our own, in order that we may believe in it. This is not to say that the character's scope must be limited; it is our vision of it that is guided. It is a kind of phenomenon of writing that the likeliest character has first to be enclosed inside the bounds of even greater likelihood, or he will fly to pieces. Paradoxically, the more narrowly we can examine a fictional character, the greater he is likely to loom up. We must see him set to scale in his proper world to know his size. Place, then, has the most delicate control over character too: by confining character, it defines it.

Place in fiction is the named, identified, concrete, exact and exacting, and therefore credible, gathering spot of all that has been felt, is about to be experienced, in the novel's progress. Location pertains to feeling; feeling profoundly pertains to place; place in history partakes of feeling, as feeling about history partakes of place. Every story would be another story, and unrecognizable as art, if it took up its characters and plot and happened somewhere else. Imagine *Swann's Way* laid in London, or *The Magic Mountain* in Spain, or *Green Mansions* in the Black Forest. The very notion of moving a novel brings ruder havoc to the mind and affections than would a century's alteration in its time. It is only too easy to conceive that a bomb that could destroy all trace of places as we know them, in life and through books, could also destroy all feelings as we know them, so irretrievably and so happily are recognition, memory, history, valor, love, all the instincts of poetry and praise, worship and endeavor, bound up in place. From the dawn of man's imagination, place has enshrined the spirit; as soon as man stopped wandering and stood still and looked about him, he found a god in that place; and from then on, that was where the god abided and spoke from if ever he spoke.

Feelings are bound up in place, and in art, from time to time, place undoubtedly works upon genius. Can anyone well explain otherwise what makes a given dot on the map come passionately alive, for good and all, in a novel — like one of those novae that suddenly blaze with inexplicable fire in the heavens? What brought a *Wuthering Heights* out of Yorkshire, or a *Sound and the Fury* out of Mississippi?

If place does work upon genius, how does it? It may be that place can focus the gigantic, voracious eye of genius and bring its gaze to point. Focus then means awareness, discernment, order, clarity, insight — they are like the attributes of love. The act of focusing itself has beauty and meaning; it is the act that, continued in, turns into mediation, into poetry. Indeed, as soon as the least of us stands still, that is the moment something extraordinary is seen to be going on in the world. The drama, old beyond count as it is, is no older than the first stage. Without the amphitheatre around it to persuade the ear and bend the eye upon a point, how could poetry ever have been spoken, how have been heard? Man is articulate and intelligible only when he begins to communicate inside the strict terms of poetry and reason. Symbols in the end, both are permanent forms of the act of focusing.

Surely place induces poetry, and when the poet is extremely attentive to what is there, a meaning may even attach to his poem out of the spot on earth where it is spoken, and the poem signify the more because it does spring so wholly out of its place, and the sap has run up into it as into a tree.

But we had better confine ourselves here to prose. And then, to take the most absolutely unfanciful novelist of them all, it is to hear him saying, *"Madame Bovary — c'est moi."* And we see focusing become so intent and aware and conscious in this most "realistic" novel of them all as to amount to fusion. Flaubert's work is indeed of the kind that is embedded immovably as rock in the country of its birth. If, with the slicers of any old (or new) criticism at all, you were to cut down through *Madame Bovary*, its cross section would still be the same as the cross section of that living earth, in texture, color, composition, all; which would be no surprise to Flaubert. For such fusion always means accomplishment no less conscious than it is gigantic — effort that must exist entirely as its own reward. We all know the letter Flaubert wrote when he had just found, in the morning paper, in an account of a minister's visit to Rouen, a phrase in the Mayor's speech of welcome

> which I had written the day before, textually, in my *Bovary* . . . Not only were the idea and the words the same, but even the rhythm of the style. It's things like this that give me pleasure . . . Everything one invents is true, you may be perfectly sure of that! Poetry is as precise as geometry . . . And besides, after reaching a certain point, one no longer makes any mistakes about the things of the soul. My poor Bovary, without a doubt, is suffering and weeping this very instant in twenty villages of France.

And now that we have come to the writer himself, the question of place resolves itself into the point of view. In this changeover from the objective to the subjective, wonderful and unexpected variations may occur.

Place, to the writer at work, is seen in a frame. Not an empty frame, a brimming one. Point of view is a sort of burning-glass, a product of personal experience and time; it is burnished with feelings and sensibilities, charged from moment to moment with the sun-points of imagination. It is an instrument — one of intensification; it acts, it behaves, it is temperamental. We have seen that the writer must accurately choose, combine, superimpose upon, blot out, shake up, alter the outside world for one absolute purpose, the good of his story. To do this, he is always seeing double, two pictures at once in his frame, his and the world's, a fact that he constantly comprehends; and he works best in a state of constant and subtle and unfooled reference between the two. It is his clear intention — his passion, I should say — to make the reader see only one of the pictures — the author's — under the pleasing illusion that it is the world's; this enormity is the accomplishment of a good story. I think it likely that at the moment of the writer's highest awareness of, and responsiveness to, the "real" world, his imagination's choice (and miles away it may be from actuality) comes closest to being infallible for his purpose. For the spirit of things is what is sought. No blur of inexactness, no cloud of vagueness, is allowable in good writing; from the first seeing to the last putting down, there must be steady lucidity and uncompromise of purpose. I speak, of course, of the ideal.

One of the most important things the young writer comes to see for himself is that point of view *is* an instrument, not an end in itself, that is useful as a glass, and not as a mirror to reflect a dear and pensive face. Conscientiously used, point of view will discover, explore, see through — it may sometimes divine and prophesy. Misused, it turns opaque almost at once and gets in the way of the book. And when the good novel is finished, its cooled outside shape, what Sean O'Faolàin has called "the veil of reality," has all the burden of communicating that initial, spontaneous, overwhelming, driving charge of personal inner feeling that was the novel's reason for being. The measure of this representation of life corresponds most tellingly with the novel's life expectancy: whenever its world of outside appearance grows dim or false to the eye, the novel has expired.

Establishing a chink-proof world of appearance is not only the first responsibility of the writer; it is the primary step in the technique of every sort of fiction: lyric and romantic, of course; the "realistic," it goes without saying; and other sorts as well. Fantasy itself must touch ground with at least one toe, and ghost stories must have one foot, so to speak, in the grave. The black, squat, hairy ghosts of M. R. James come right out of Cambridge. Only fantasy's stepchild, poor science-fiction, does not touch earth anywhere; and it is doubtful already if happenings entirely confined to outer space are ever going to move us, or even divert us for long. Satire, engaged in its most intellectual of exercises, must first of all establish an impeccable *locus operandi*; its premise is the kingdom where certain rules apply. The countries Gulliver visits are the systems of thought and learning Swift satirizes made visible one after the other and set in operation. But while place in satire is a purely artificial construction, set up to be knocked down, in humor place becomes its most revealing and at the same time is itself the most revealed. This is because humor, it seems to me, of all forms of fiction, entirely accepts place for what it is.

"Spotted Horses," by William Faulkner, is a good case in point. At the same time that this is just about Mr. Faulkner's funniest story, it is the most thorough and faithful picture of a Mississippi crossroads hamlet that you could ever hope to see. True in spirit, it is also true to everyday fact. Faulkner's art, which often lets him shoot the moon, tells him when to be literal too. In all its specification of detail, both mundane and poetic, in its complete adherence to social fact (which nobody knows better than Faulkner, surely, in writing today), by its unerring aim of observation as true as the sights of a gun would give, but Faulkner has no malice, only compassion; and even and also in the joy of those elements of harlequinade-fantasy that the spotted horses of the title bring in — in all that shining fidelity to place lies the heart and secret of this tale's comic glory.

Faulkner is, of course, the triumphant example in America today of the mastery of place in fiction. Yoknapatawpha County, so supremely and exclusively and majestically and totally itself, is an everywhere, but only because Faulkner's first concern is for what comes first — Yoknapatawpha, his own created world. I am not sure, as a Mississippian myself, how widely it is realized and appreciated that these works of such marvelous imaginative power can also stand as works of the carefulest and purest representation. Heightened, of course: their specialty is they are twice as true as life, and that is why it takes a genius to write them. "Spotted Horses" may not have happened yet; if it had, some others might have tried to make a story of it; but "Spotted Horses" could happen tomorrow — that is one of its glories. It could happen today or tomorrow at any little crossroads hamlet in Mississippi; the whole combination of irresistibility is there. We have the Snopses ready, the Mrs. Littlejohns ready, nice Ratliff and the Judge ready and sighing, the clowns, sober and merry, settled for the evening retrospection of it in the cool dusk of the porch; and the Henry Armstids armed with their obsessions, the little periwinkle-eyed boys armed with their indestructibility; the beautiful, overweening spring, too, the moonlight on the pear trees from which the mockingbird's song keeps returning; and the little store and the fat boy to steal and steal away at its candy. There are undoubtedly spotted horses too, in the offing — somewhere in Texas this minute, straining toward the day. After Faulkner has told it, it is easy for one and all to look back and see it.

Faulkner, simply, knew it already; it is a different kind of knowledge from Flaubert's, and proof could not add much to it. He was born knowing, or rather learning, or rather prophesying, all that and more; and having it all together at one time available while he writes is one of the marks of his mind. If there *is* any more in Mississippi than is engaged and dilated upon, and made twice as real as it used to be and applies now to the world, in the one story "Spotted Horses," then we would almost rather not know it — but I don't bet a piece of store candy that there is. In Faulkner's humor, even more measurably than in his tragedy, it is all there.

It may be going too far to say that the exactness and concreteness and solidity of the real world achieved in a story correspond to the intensity of feeling in the author's mind and to the very turn of his heart; but there lies the secret of our confidence in him.

Making reality real is art's responsibility. It is a practical assignment, then, a self-assignment: to achieve, by a cultivated sensitivity for observing life, a capacity for receiving its impressions, a lonely, unremitting, unaided, unaidable vision, and transferring this vision without distortion to it onto the pages of a novel, where, if the reader is so persuaded, it will turn into the reader's illusion. How bent on this peculiar joy we are, reader and writer, willingly to practice, willingly to undergo, this alchemy for it!

What is there, then, about place that is transferable to the pages of a novel? The best things — the explicit things: physical texture. And as place has functioned between the writer and his material, so it functions between the writer and reader. Location is the ground conductor of all the currents of emotion and belief and moral conviction that charge out from the story in its course. These charges need the warm hard earth underfoot, the light and lift of air, the stir and play of mood, the softening bath of atmosphere that give the likeness-to-life that life needs. Through the story's translation and ordering of life, the unconvincing raw material becomes the very heart's familiar. Life *is* strange. Stories hardly make it more so; with all they are able to tell and surmise, they make it more believably, more inevitably so.

I think the sense of place is as essential to good and honest writing as a logical mind; surely they are somewhere related. It is by knowing where you stand that you grow able to judge where you are. Place absorbs our earliest notice and attention, it bestows on us our original awareness; and our critical powers spring up from the study of it and the growth of experience inside it. It perseveres in bringing us back to earth when we fly too high. It never really stops informing us, for it is forever astir, alive, changing, reflecting, like the mind of man itself. One place comprehended can make us understand other places better. Sense of place gives equilibrium; extended, it is sense of direction too. Carried off we might be in spirit, and should be, when we are reading or writing something good; but it is the sense of place going with us still that is the ball of golden thread to carry us there and back and in every sense of the word to bring us home.

What can place *not* give? Theme. It can present theme, show it to the last detail — but place is forever illustrative: it is a picture of what man has done and imagined, it is his visible past, result. Human life is fiction's only theme.

Should the writer, then, write about home? It is both natural and sensible that the place where we have our roots should become the setting, the first and primary proving ground, of our fiction. Location, however, is not simply to be used by the writer — it is to be discovered, as each novel itself, in the act of writing, is discovery. Discovery does not imply that the place is new, only that we are. Place is as old as the hills. Kilroy at least has been there, and left his name. Discovery, not being a matter of writing our name on a wall, but of seeing what that wall is, and what is over it, is a matter of vision.

One can no more say, "To write stay home," than one can say, "To write leave home." It is the writing that makes its own rules and conditions for each person. And though place is home, it is for the writer writing simply *locus*. It is where the particular story he writes can be pinned down, the circle it can spin through and keep the state of grace, so that for the story's duration the rest of the world suspends its claim upon it and lies low as the story in peaceful extension, the *locus* fading off into the blue.

Naturally, it is the very breath of life, whether one writes a word of fiction or not, to go out and see what is to be seen of the world. For the artist to be unwilling to move, mentally or spiritually or physically, out of the familiar is a sign that spiritual timidity or poverty or decay has come upon him; for what is familiar will then have turned into all that is tyrannical.

One can only say: writers must always write best of what they know, and sometimes they do it by staying where they know it. But not for safety's sake. Although it is in the words of a witch — or all the more because of that — a comment of Hecate's in *Macbeth* is worth our heed. "Security/Is mortal's chiefest enemy.". In fact, when we think in terms of the spirit, which are the terms of writing, is there a conception more stupefying than that of security? Yet writing of what you know has nothing to do with security: what is more dangerous? How can you go out on a limb if you do not know your own tree? No art ever came out of not risking your neck. And risk — experiment — is a considerable part of the joy of doing, which is the lone, simple reason all writers of serious fiction are willing to work as hard as they do.

The open mind and the receptive heart — which are at last and with fortune's smile the informed mind and the experienced heart — are to be gained anywhere, any time, without necessarily moving an inch from any present address. There must surely be as many ways of seeing a place as there are pairs of eyes to see it. The impact happens in so many different ways.

It may be the stranger within the gates whose eye is smitten by the crucial thing, the essence of life, the moment or act in our long-familiar midst that will forever define it. The inhabitant who has taken his fill of a place and gone away may look back and see it for good, from afar, still there in his mind's eye like a city over the hill. It was in the New Zealand stories, written eleven thousand miles from home and out of homesickness, that Katherine Mansfield came into her own. Joyce transplanted not his subject but himself while writing about it, and it was as though he had never left it at all: there it was, still in his eye, exactly the way he had last seen it. From the Continent he wrote the life of Dublin as it was then into a book of the future, for he went translating his own language of it on and on into a country of its own, where it set up a kingdom as renowned as Prester John's. Sometimes two places, two countries, are brought to bear on each other, as in E. M. Forster's work, and the heart of the novel is heard beating most plainly, most passionately, most personally when two places are at meeting point.

There may come to be new places in our lives that are second spiritual homes — closer to us in some ways, perhaps, than our original homes. But the home tie is the blood tie. And had it meant nothing to us, any other place thereafter would have meant less, and we would carry no compass inside ourselves to find home ever, anywhere at all. We would not even guess what we had missed.

It is noticeable that those writers who for their own good reasons push out against their backgrounds nearly always passionately adopt the new one in their work. Revolt itself is a reference and tribute to the potency of what is left behind. The substitute place, the adopted country, is sometimes a very much stricter, bolder, or harsher one than the original, seldom more lax or undemanding — showing that what was wanted was structure, definition, rigidity — perhaps these were wanted, and understanding was not.

Hemingway in our time has sought out the formal and ruthless territories of the world, archaic ones often, where there are bullfight arenas, theatres of hunting and war, places with a primitive, or formidable, stripped-down character, with implacable codes, with inscrutable justices and inevitable retributions. But whatever the scene of his work, it is the *places* that never are hostile. People give pain, are callous and insensitive, empty and cruel, carrying with them no pasts as they promise no futures. But place heals the hurt, soothes the outrage, fills the terrible vacuum that these human beings make. It heals actively, and the response is given consciously, with the ardent care and explicitness, respect and delight of a lover, when fishing streams or naming over streets becomes almost something of the lover's secret language — as the careful conversations between characters in Hemingway bear hints of the secret language of hate. The response to place has the added intensity that comes with the place's not being native or taken for granted, but found, chosen; thereby is the rest more heavily repudiated. It is the response of the aficionado; the response, too, is adopted. The title "A Clean Well Lighted Place" is just what the human being is not, for Hemingway, and perhaps it is the epitome of what man would like to find in his fellowman but never has yet, says the author, and never is going to.

We see that point of view is hardly a single, unalterable vision, but a profound and developing one of great complexity. The vision itself may move in and out of its material, shuttle-fashion, instead of being simply turned on it, like a telescope on the moon. Writing is an expression of the writer's own peculiar personality, could not help being so. Yet in reading great works one feels that the finished piece transcends the personal. All writers great and small must sometimes have felt that they have become part of what they wrote even more than it still remains a part of them.

When I speak of writing from where you have put down roots, it may be said that what I urge is "regional" writing. "Regional," I think, is a careless term, as well as a condescending one, because what it does is fail to differentiate between the localized raw material of life and its outcome as art. "Regional" is an outsider's term; it has no meaning for the insider who is doing the writing, because as far as he knows he is simply writing about life. Jane Austen, Emily Brontë, Thomas Hardy, Cervantes, Turgenev, the authors of the books of the Old Testament, all confined themselves to regions, great or small — but are they regional? Then who from the start of time has not been so?

It may well be said that all work springing out of such vital impulse from its native soil has certain things in common. But what signifies is that these are not the little things that it takes a fine-tooth critic to search out, but the great things, that could not be missed or mistaken, for they are the beacon lights of literature.

It seems plain that the art that speaks most clearly, explicitly, directly and passionately from its place of origin will remain the longest understood. It is through place that we put out roots, wherever birth, chance, fate or our traveling selves set us down; but where those roots reach toward — whether in America, England or Timbuktu — is the deep and running vein, eternal and consistent and everywhere purely itself, that feeds and is fed by the human understanding. The challenge to writers today, I think, is not to disown any part of our heritage. Whatever our theme in writing, it is old and tried. Whatever our place, it has been visited by the stranger, it will never be new again. It is only the vision that can be new; but that is enough.

C. VANN WOODWARD

The Search for Southern Identity

THE TIME IS COMING, if indeed it has not already arrived, when the Southerner will begin to ask himself whether there is really any longer very much point in calling himself a Southerner. Or if he does, he might well wonder occasionally whether it is worth while insisting on the point. So long as he remains at home where everybody knows him the matter hardly becomes an issue. But when he ventures among strangers, particularly up North, how often does he yield to the impulse to suppress the identifying idiom, to avoid the awkward subject, and to blend inconspicuously into the national pattern — to act the role of the standard American? Has the Southern heritage become an old hunting jacket that one slips on comfortably while at home but discards when he ventures abroad in favor of some more conventional or modish garb? Or is it perhaps an attic full of ancestral wardrobes useful only in connection with costume balls and play acting — staged primarily in Washington, D.C.?

Asking himself some similar questions about the New England heritage, Professor George W. Pierson of Yale has come forth with some disturbing concessions about the integrity of his own region. Instead of an old hunting jacket, he suggests that we call New England "an old kitchen floor, now spatter-painted with many colors." He points out that roughly six out of every ten Connecticut "Yankees" are either foreign-born or born of foreign or mixed parentage, while only three have native forebears going as far back as two generations, and they are not necessarily New England forebears at that. "Like it or not," writes Pierson, "and no matter how you measure it — geographically, economically, racially or religiously, there is no New England Region today." It has become instead, he says, "an optical illusion and a land of violent contrast and change." And yet in spite of the wholesale and damaging concessions of his essay, which he calls "A Study in Denudation," he concludes that, "as a region of the heart and mind, New England is still very much alive."

One wonders if the Southerner, for his part, can make as many damaging admissions of social change and cultural erosion as our New England friend has made and come out with as firm a conclusion about the vitality of his own regional heritage. More doubt than assurance probably comes to mind at first. The South is still in the midst of an economic and social revolution that has by no means run its course, and it will not be possible to measure its results for a long time to come. This revolution has already leveled many of the old monuments of regional distinctiveness and may end eventually by erasing the very consciousness of a distinctive tradition along with the will to sustain it. The sustaining will and consciousness are also under the additional strain of a moral indictment against a discredited part of the tradition, an indictment more uncompromising than any since abolitionist times.

The Southerner may not have been very happy about many of those old monuments of regional distinctiveness that are now disappearing. He may, in fact, have deplored the existence of some — the one-horse farmer, one-crop agriculture, one-party politics, the sharecropper, the poll tax, the white primary, the Jim Crow car, the lynching bee. It would take a blind sentimentalist to mourn their passing. But until the day before yesterday there they stood, indisputable proof that the South was different. Now that they are vanished or on their way toward vanishing, we are suddenly aware of the vacant place they have left in the landscape and of our habit of depending upon them in final resort as landmarks of regional identification. To establish identity by reference to our faults was always simplest, for whatever their reservations about our virtues, our critics were never reluctant to concede us our vices and shortcomings.

It is not that the present South has any conspicuous lack of faults, but that its faults are growing less conspicuous and therefore less useful for purposes of regional identification. They are increasingly the faults of other parts of the country, standard American faults, shall we say. Many of them have only recently been acquired — could, in fact, only recently be afforded. For the great changes that are altering the cultural landscape of the South almost beyond recognition are not simply negative changes, the disappearance of the familiar. There are also positive changes, the appearance of the strikingly new.

The symbol of innovation is inescapable. The roar and groan and dust of it greet one on the outskirts of every Southern city. That symbol is the bulldozer, and for lack of a better name this might be called the Bulldozer Revolution. The great machine with the lowered blade symbolizes the revolution in several respects: in its favorite area of operation, the area where city meets country; in its relentless speed; in its supreme disregard for obstacles, its heedless methods; in what it demolishes and in what it builds. It is the advance agent of the metropolis. It encroaches upon rural life to expand urban life. It demolishes the old to make way for the new.

It is not the amount of change that is impressive about the Bulldozer Revolution so much as the speed and concentration with which it has come and with which it continues. In the decade of the forties, when urbanization was growing at a swift pace in the country as a whole, the cities of the South's fifty-three metropolitan areas grew more than three times as fast as comparable cities in the rest of the country, at a rate of 33.1 per cent as compared with 10.3 per cent elsewhere. For every three city dwellers in the South at the beginning of that decade there were four at the end, and for every five farm residents there were only four. An overwhelmingly rural South in 1930 had 5.5 millions employed in agriculture; by 1950, only 3.2 millions. A considerable proportion of these Southerners were moving directly from country to suburb, following the path of the bulldozer to "rurbanization" and skipping the phase of urbanization entirely. Rural Negroes, the most mobile of all Southerners, were more likely to move into the heart of the urban areas abandoned by the suburban dwellers. In the single decade of the forties the South lost a third of its rural-farm Negro population. If the same trend were continued through the present decade, it would reduce that part of the colored population to about one-fifth of the Negroes living in the region.

According to nearly all of the indices, so the economists find, economic growth of the South in recent years greatly exceeds the rate maintained in the North and East. The fact is the South is going through economic expansion and reorganization that the North and East completed a generation or more ago. But the process is taking place far more rapidly than it did in the North. Among all the many periods of change in the history of the South it is impossible to find one of such concentration and such substantive impact. The period of Reconstruction might appear a likely rival for this distinction, but that revolution was largely limited to changes in legal status and the ownership of property. The people remained pretty much where they were and continued to make their living in much the same way. All indications are that the bulldozer will leave a deeper mark upon the land than did the carpetbagger.

It is the conclusion of two Southern sociologists, John M. Maclachlan and Joe S. Floyd, Jr., that the present drive toward uniformity "with national demographic, economic, and cultural norms might well hasten the day when the South, once perhaps the most distinctively 'different' American region, will have become in most such matters virtually indistinguishable from the other urban-industrial areas of the nation."

The threat of becoming "indistinguishable," of being submerged under a national steamroller, has haunted the mind of the South for a long time. Some have seen it as a menace to regional identity and the survival of a Southern heritage. Premonitions of the present revolution appeared during the industrial boom that followed the First World War. Toward the end of the twenties two distinctive attempts were made by Southerners to dig in and define a perimeter of defense against further encroachment.

One of these entrenchments was that of the twelve Southerners who wrote *I'll*

Take My Stand. They sought to define what they called "a Southern way of life against what may be called the American or prevailing way," and they agreed "that the best terms in which to represent the distinction are contained in the phrase, Agrarian *versus* Industrial." Agrarianism and its values were the essence of the Southern tradition and the test of Southern loyalty. Their credo held that "the whole way in which we live, act, think, and feel," the humanist culture, "was rooted in the agrarian way of life of the older South." They called for "anti-industrial measures" which "might promise to stop the advances of industrialism, or even undo some of them."

Even in 1930 the agrarians were prepared to admit "the melancholy fact that the South itself has wavered a little and shown signs of wanting to join up behind the common or American industrial ideal." They admonished waverers among the younger generation that the brave new South they contemplated would "be only an undistinguished replica of the usual industrial community."

Three decades later the slight "wavering" in the Southern ranks that disturbed the agrarians in 1930 would seem to have become a pell-mell rout. Defections came by the battalion. Whole regiments and armies deserted "to join up behind the common or American industrial ideal." In its pursuit of the American Way and the American Standard of Living the South was apparently doing all in its power to become what the agrarians had deplored as "only an undistinguished replica of the usual industrial community." The voice of the South in the 1950's had become the voice of the chamber of commerce, and Southerners appeared to be about as much absorbed in the acquirement of creature comforts and adult playthings as any other Americans. The twelve Southerners who took their stand in 1930 on the proposition that the Southern way stands or falls with the agrarian way would seem to have been championing a second lost cause. If they were right, then our questions would have already been answered, for the Southerner as a distinctive species of American would have been doomed, his tradition bereft of root and soil. The agrarian way contains no promise of continuity and endurance for the Southern tradition.

Two years before the agrarian pronouncement appeared, another attempt was made to define the essence of the Southern tradition and prescribe the test of Southern loyalty. The author of this effort was the distinguished historian, Professor Ulrich B. Phillips. His definition had no reference to economic institutions but was confined to a preoccupation with race consciousness. The essential theme of continuity and unity in the Southern heritage, wrote Professor Phillips, was "a common resolve indomitably maintained" that the South "shall be and remain a white man's country." This indomitable conviction could be "expressed with the frenzy of a demagogue or maintained with a patrician's quietude," but it was and had been from the beginning "the cardinal test of a Southerner and the central theme of southern history."

Professor Phillips' criterion of Southernism has proved somewhat more durable and widespread in appeal than that of the agrarians. It is not tied so firmly to an ephemeral economic order as was theirs. Nor does it demand — of the dominant whites, at least — any Spartan rejection of the flesh pots of the American living standard. Its adherents are able to enjoy the blessings of economic change and remain traditionalists at the same time. There are still other advantages in the Phillipsian doctrine. The traditionalist who has watched the Bulldozer Revolution plow under cherished old values of individualism, localism, family, clan, and rural folk culture has felt helpless and frustrated against the mighty and imponderable agents of change. Industrialism, urbanism, unionism, and big government conferred or promised too many coveted benefits. They divided the people and won support in the South, so that it was impossible to rally unified opposition to them.

The race issue was different. Advocates and agents of change could be denounced as outsiders, intruders, meddlers. Historic memories of resistance and cherished constitutional principles could be invoked. Racial prejudices, aggressions, and jealousies could be stirred to rally massive popular support. And with this dearly bought unity, which he could not rally on other issues, the frustrated traditionalist might at last take his stand for the defense of all the defiled, traduced, and neglected values of the traditional order. What then is the prospect of the Phillipsian "cardinal test" as a bulwark against change? Will it hold fast where other defenses have failed?

Recent history furnishes some of the answers. Since the last World War old racial attitudes that appeared more venerable and immovable than any other have exhibited a flexibility that no one would have predicted. One by one, in astonishingly rapid succession, many landmarks of racial discrimination and segregation have disappeared, and old barriers have been breached. Many remain, of course — perhaps more than have been breached — and distinctively Southern racial attitudes will linger for a long time. Increasingly the South is aware of its isolation in these attitudes, however, and is in defense of the institutions that embody them. They have fallen rapidly into discredit and under condemnation from the rest of the country and the rest of the world.

Once more the South finds itself with a morally discredited Peculiar Institution on its hands. The last time this happened, about a century ago, the South's defensive reaction was to identify its whole cause with the one institution that was most vulnerable and to make loyalty to an ephemeral aspect which it had once led in condemning the cardinal test of loyalty to the whole tradition. Southerners who rejected the test were therefore forced to reject the whole heritage. In many cases, if they were vocal in their rejection, they were compelled to leave the South entirely and return only at their peril. Unity was thus temporarily achieved, but with the collapse of the Peculiar Institution the whole tradition was jeopardized and discredited for having been so completely identified with the part abandoned.

Historical experience with the first Peculiar Institution ought strongly to discourage comparable experiments with the second. If Southernism is allowed to become identified with a last ditch defense of segregation, it will increasingly lose its appeal among the younger generation. Many will be tempted to reject their entire regional identification, even the name "Southern," in order to dissociate themselves from the one discredited aspect. If agrarianism has proved to be a second lost cause, segregation is a likely prospect for a third.

With the crumbling of so many defenses in the present, the South has tended to substitute myths about the past. Every self-conscious group of any size fabricates myths about its past: about its origins, its mission, its righteousness, its benevolence, its general superiority. But few groups in the New World have had their myths subjected to such destructive analysis as those of the South have undergone in recent years. While some Southern historians have contributed to the mythmaking, others have been among the leading iconoclasts, and their attacks have spared few of the South's cherished myths.

The Cavalier Legend as the myth of origin was one of the earlier victims. The Plantation Legend of ante bellum grace and elegance has not been left wholly intact. The pleasant image of a benevolent and paternalistic slavery system as a school for civilizing savages has suffered damage that is probably beyond repair. Even the consoling security of Reconstruction as the common historic grievance, the infallible mystique of unity, has been rendered somewhat less secure by detached investigation. And finally, rude hands have been laid upon the hallowed memory of the Redeemers who did in the Carpetbaggers, and doubt has been cast upon the antiquity of segregation folkways. These faded historical myths have become weak material for buttressing Southern defenses, for time has dealt as roughly with them as with agrarianism and racism.

Would a hard-won immunity from the myths and illusions of Southern sectionalism provide some immunity to the illusions and myths of American nationalism? Or would the hasty divestment merely make the myth-denuded Southerner hasten to wrap himself in the garments of nationalism? The danger in the wholesale rejection of the South by the modern Southerner bent on reaffirming his Americanism is the danger of affirming more than he bargains for.

While the myths of Southern distinctiveness have been waning, national myths have been waxing in power and appeal. National myths, American myths have proved far more sacrosanct and inviolate than Southern myths. Millions of European immigrants of diverse cultural backgrounds have sought and found identity in them. The powerful urge among minority groups to abandon or disguise their distinguishing cultural traits and conform as quickly as possible to some national norm is one of the most familiar features in the sociology of American nationalism. European ethnic and national groups with traditions far more ancient and distinctive than those of the South have eagerly divested themselves of their cultural heritage in order to conform.

The conformist is not required nor expected to abandon his distinctive religion. But whether he remains a Protestant, a Catholic, or a Jew, his religion typically becomes subordinate or secondary to a national faith. Foreign observers have remarked that the different religions in America resemble each other more than they do their European counterparts. "By every realistic criterion," writes Will Herberg in his study of American religious sociology, "the American Way of Life is the operative faith of the American people." And where the mandates of the American Way of Life conflict with others, they take undisputed sway over the masses of all religions. Herberg describes it as "a faith that has its symbols and its rituals, its holidays and its liturgy, its saints and its sancta," and it is common to all Americans. "Sociologically, anthropologically, if one pleases," he writes, the American Way of Life "is the characteristic American religion, undergirding American life and overarching American society despite all indubitable differences of region, section, culture, and class." Differences such as those of region and section, "indubitable" though he admits them to be, he characterizes as "peripheral and obsolescent."

If the American Way of Life has become a religion, any deviation from it has become a sort of heresy. Regionalism in the typical American view is rather like the Turnerian frontier, a section on the move — or at least one that should keep moving, following a course that converges at not too remote a point with the American Way. It is a season's halt of the American caravan, a temporary encampment of an advancing society, eternally on the move toward some undefined goal of progress. If the encampment of regionalism threatens to entrench or dig in for a permanent stand, it comes to be regarded as "peripheral and obsolescent," an institutionalized social lag.

The same urge to conformity that operates upon ethnic or national minorities to persuade them to reject identification with their native heritage or that of their forebears operates to a degree upon the Southerner as well. Since the cultural landscape of his native region is being altered almost beyond recognition by a cyclone of social change, the Southerner may come to feel as uprooted as the immigrant. Bereft of his myths, his peculiar institutions, even his familiar regional vices, he may well reject or forget his regional identification as completely as the immigrant.

Is there nothing about the South that is immune from the disintegrating effect of nationalism and the pressure for conformity? Is there not something that has not changed? There is only one thing that I can think of, and that is its history. By that I do not mean a Southern brand of Shintoism, the worship of ancestors. Nor do I mean written history and its interpretation, popular and mythical, or professional and scholarly, which have changed often and will change again. I mean rather the collective experience of the Southern people. It is in just this respect that the South remains the most distinctive region of the country. In their unique historic experience as Americans the Southerners should not only be able to find the basis for continuity of their heritage but also make contributions that balance and complement the experience of the rest of the nation.

At this point the risks of our enterprise multiply. They are the risks of spawning new myths in place of the old. Awareness of them demands that we redouble precautions and look more cautiously than ever at generalizations.

To start with a safe one, it can be assumed that one of the most conspicuous traits of American life has been its economic abundance. From early colonial days the fabulous riches of America have been compared with the scarcity and want of less favored lands. Immense differentials in economic welfare and living standards between the United States and other countries still prevail. In an illuminating book called *People of Plenty,* David Potter persuasively advances the thesis that the most distinguishing traits of national character have been fundamentally shaped by the abundance of the American living standard. He marshals evidence of the effect that plenty has had upon such decisive phases of life as the nursing and training of babies, opportunities for education and jobs, ages of marriage and childbearing. He shows how abundance has determined characteristic national attitudes between parents and children, husband and wife, superior and subordinate, between one class and another, and how it has molded our mass culture and our consumer oriented society. American national character would indeed appear inconceivable without this unique experience of abundance.

The South at times has shared this national experience and, in very recent years, has enjoyed more than a taste of it. But the history of the South includes a long and quite un-American experience with poverty. So recently as 1938, in fact, the South was characterized by the President as "The Nation's Economic Problem No. 1." And the problem was poverty, not plenty. It was a poverty emphasized by wide regional discrepancies in living standard, per capita wealth, per capita income, and the good things that money buys, such as education, health, protection,and the many luxuries that go to make up the celebrated American Standard of Living. This striking differential was no temporary misfortune of the great depression but a continuous and conspicuous feature of Southern experience since the early years of the Civil War. During the last half of the nineteenth and the first half of the twentieth centuries, when technology was multiplying American abundance with unprecedented rapidity, the South lagged far behind. In 1880 the per capita wealth of the South, based on estimated true valuation of property, was $376 as compared with $1,186 per capita in the states outside the South. In the same year the per capita wealth of the South was 27 per cent of that of the Northeastern states. That was just about the same ratio contemporaneously existing between the per capita wealth of Russia and that of Germany.

Generations of scarcity and want constitute one of the distinctive historical experiences of the Southern people, an experience too deeply embedded in their memory to be wiped out by a business boom and too deep not to admit of some uneasiness at being characterized historically as a "People of Plenty." That they should have been for so long a time a "People of Poverty" in a land of plenty is one mark of enduring cultural distinctiveness. In a nation known around the world for the hedonistic ethic of the American Standard of Living, the Southern heritage of scarcity remains distinctive.

A closely related corollary of the uniquely American experience of abundance is the equally unique American experience of success. During the Second World War Professor Arthur M. Schlesinger made an interesting attempt to define the national character, which he brought to a close with the conclusion that the American character "is bottomed upon the profound conviction that nothing in the world is beyond its power to accomplish." In this he gave expression to one of the great American legends, the legend of success and invincibility. It is a legend with a foundation in fact, for much can be adduced from the American record to support it and explain why it has flourished. If the history of the United States is lacking in some of the elements of variety and contrast demanded of any good story, it is in part because of the very monotonous repetition of successes. Almost every major collective effort, even those thwarted temporarily, succeeded in the end. American history *is* a success story. Why should such a nation not have a "profound conviction that nothing in the world is beyond its power to accomplish"? Even the hazards of war — including the prospect of war against an unknown enemy with untried weapons — proves no exception to the rule. The advanced science and weaponry of the Russian challenger are too recent to have registered their impact on the legend. The American people have never known the chastening experience of being on the losing side of a war. They have, until very recently, solved every major problem they have confronted — or had it solved for them by a smiling fortune. Success and victory are still national habits of mind.

This is but one among several American legends in which the South can participate only vicariously or in part. Again the Southern heritage is distinctive. For Southern history, unlike American, includes large components of frustration, failure, and defeat. It includes not only an overwhelming military defeat but long decades of defeat in the provinces of economic, social, and political life. Such a heritage affords the Southern people no basis for the delusion that there is nothing whatever that is beyond their power to accomplish. They have had it forcibly and repeatedly borne in upon them that this is not the case. Since their experience in this respect is more common among the general run of mankind than that of their fellow Americans, it would seem to be a part of their heritage worth cherishing.

American opulence and American success have combined to foster and encourage another legend of early origin, the legend of American innocence. According to this legend Americans achieved a sort of regeneration of sinful man by coming out of the wicked Old World and removing to an untarnished new one. By doing so they shook off the wretched evils of feudalism and broke free from tyranny, monarchism, aristocracy, and privilege — all those institutions which, in the hopeful philosophy of the Enlightenment, accounted for all, or nearly all, the evil in the world. The absence of these Old World ills in America, as well as the freedom from much of the injustice and oppression associated with them, encouraged a singular moral complacency in the American mind. The self-image implanted in Americans was one of innocence as compared with less fortunate people of the Old World. They were a chosen people and their land a Utopia on the make. Alexis de Tocqueville's patience was tried by this complacency of the American. "If I applaud the freedom which its inhabitants enjoy, he answers, 'Freedom is a fine thing, but few nations are worthy to enjoy it.' If I remark on the purity of morals which distinguishes the United States," complained Tocqueville, " 'I can imagine,' says he, 'that a stranger, who has been struck by corruption of all other nations, is astonished at the difference.' "

How much room was there in the tortured conscience of the South for this national self-image of innocence and moral complacency? Southerners have repeated the American rhetoric of self-admiration and sung the perfection of American institutions ever since the Declaration of Independence. But for half that time they lived intimately with a great social evil and the other half with its aftermath. It was an evil that was even condemned and abandoned by the Old World, to which America's moral superiority was supposedly an article of faith. Much of the South's intellectual energy went into a desperate effort to convince the world that its peculiar evil was actually a "positive good," but it failed even to convince itself. It writhed in the torments of its own conscience until it plunged into catastrophe to escape. The South's preoccupation was with guilt, not with innocence, with the reality of evil, not with the dream of perfection. Its experience in this respect, as in several others, was on the whole a thoroughly un-American one.

An age-long experience with human bondage and its evils and later with emancipation and its shortcomings did not dispose the South very favorably toward such popular American ideas as the doctrine of human perfectibility, the belief that every evil has a cure, and the notion that every human problem has a solution. For these reasons the utopian schemes and the gospel of progress that flourished above the Mason and Dixon Line never found very wide acceptance below the Potomac during the nineteenth century. In that most optimistic of centuries in the most optimistic part of the world, the South remained basically pessimistic in its social outlook and its moral philosophy. The experience of evil and the experience of tragedy are parts of the Southern heritage that are as difficult to reconcile with the American legend of innocence and social felicity as the experience of poverty and defeat are to reconcile with the legends of abundance and success.

One of the simplest but most consequential generalizations ever made about national character was Tocqueville's that America was "born free." In many ways that is the basic distinction between the history of the United States and the history of other great nations. We skipped the feudal stage, just as Russia skipped the liberal stage. Louis Hartz has pointed up the complex consequences for the history of American political thought. To be a conservative and a traditionalist in America was a contradiction in terms, for the American Burke was forever conserving John

Locke's liberalism, his only real native tradition. Even the South, in its great period of reaction against Jefferson, was never able fully to shake off the grip of Locke and its earlier self-image of liberalism. That is why its most original period of theoretical inspiration, the "Reactionary Enlightenment," left almost no influence upon American thought.

There is still a contribution to be derived from the South's un-American adventure in feudal fantasy. While the South was not born Lockean, it went through a Lockean phase in its youth. But as Hartz admits, it was "an alien child in a liberal family, tortured and confused, driven to a fantasy life." There *are* Americans, after all, who were not "born free." They are also Southerners. They have yet to achieve articulate expression of their uniquely un-American experience. This is not surprising, since white Southerners have only recently found expression of the tragic potentials of their past in literature. The Negro has yet to do that. His first step will be an acknowledgment that he is also a Southerner as well as an American.

One final example of a definition of national character to which the South proves an exception is an interesting one by Thornton Wilder. "Americans," says Mr. Wilder, "are abstract. They are disconnected. They have a relation, but it is to everywhere, to everybody, and to always." This quality of abstraction he finds expressed in numerous ways — in the physical mobility of Americans, in their indifference or, as he might suggest, their superiority to place, to locality, to environment. "For us," he writes, "it is not *where* genius lived that is important. If Mount Vernon and Monticello were not so beautiful in themselves and relatively accessible, would so many of us visit them?" he asks. It is not the concrete but the abstract that captures the imagination of the American and gives him identity, not the here-and-now but the future. " 'I am I,' he says, 'because my plans characterize me.' Abstract! Abstract!" Mr. Wilder's stress upon abstraction as an American characteristic recalls what Robert Penn Warren in a different connection once described as "the fear of abstraction" in the South, "the instinctive fear, on the part of black or white, that the massiveness of experience, the concreteness of life, will be violated; the fear of abstraction."

According to Mr. Wilder, "Americans can find in environment no confirmation of their identity, try as they may." And again, "Americans are disconnected. They are exposed to all place and all time. No place nor group nor movement can say to them: we are waiting for you; it is right for you to be here." The insignificance of place, locality, and community for Thornton Wilder contrasts strikingly with the experience of Eudora Welty of Mississippi. "Like a good many other [regional] writers," she says, "I am myself touched off by place. The place where I am and the place I know, and other places that familiarity with and love for my own make strange and lovely and enlightening to look into, are what set me to writing my stories." To her, "place opens a door in the mind," and she speaks of "the blessing of being located — contained."

To do Mr. Wilder justice, he is aware that the Southern states constitute an exception to his national character of abstraction, "enclaves or residual areas of European feeling," he calls them. "They were cut off, or resolutely cut themselves off, from the advancing tide of the country's modes of consciousness. Place, environment, relations, repetitions are the breath of their being."

The most reassuring prospect for the survival of the South's distinctive heritage is the magnificent body of literature produced by its writers in the last three decades — the very years when the outward traits of regional distinctiveness were crumbling. The Southern literary renaissance has placed its writers in the vanguard of national letters and assured that their works will be read as long as American literature is remembered. The distinguishing feature of the Southern school, according to Allen Tate, is "the peculiar historical consciousness of the Southern writer." He defines the literary renaissance as "a literature conscious of the past in the present." The themes that have inspired the major writers have not been the flattering myths nor the romantic dreams of the South's past. Disdaining the polemics of defense and justification, they have turned instead to the somber realities of hardship and defeat and evil and "the problems of the human heart in conflict with itself." In so doing they have brought to realization for the first time the powerful literary potentials of the South's tragic experience and heritage. Such comfort as they offer lies, in the words of William Faulkner, in reminding us of "the courage and honor and hope and pride and compassion and pity and sacrifice" with which man has endured.

After Faulkner, Wolfe, Warren, and Welty no literate Southerner could remain unaware of his heritage or doubt its enduring value. After this outpouring it would seem more difficult than ever to deny a Southern identity, to be "merely American." To deny it would be to deny our history. And it would also be to deny to America participation in a heritage and a dimension of historical experience that America very much needs, a heritage that is far more closely in line with the common lot of mankind than the national legends of opulence and success and innocence. The South once thought of itself as a "peculiar people," set apart by its eccentricities, but in many ways modern America better deserves that description.

The South was American a long time before it was Southern in any self-conscious or distinctive way. It remains more American by far than anything else, and has all along. After all, it fell the lot of one Southerner from Virginia to define America. The definition he wrote in 1776 voiced aspirations that were rooted in his native region before the nation was born. The modern Southerner should be secure enough in his national identity to escape the compulsion of less secure minorities to embrace uncritically all the myths of nationalism. He should be secure enough also not to deny a regional heritage because it is at variance with national myth. It is a heritage that should prove of enduring worth to him as well as to his country.

• REMINISCENCES •

. JAMES . AGEE

from

A Death in the Family

Knoxville: Summer, 1915

WE ARE TALKING NOW of summer evenings in Knoxville, Tennessee, in the time that I lived there so successfully disguised to myself as a child. It was a little bit mixed sort of block, fairly solidly lower middle class, with one or two juts apiece on either side of that. The houses corresponded; middle-sized gracefully fretted wood houses built in the late nineties and early nineteen hundreds, with small front and side and more spacious back yards, and trees in the yards, and porches. These were softwooded trees, poplars, tulip trees, cottonwoods. There were fences around one or two of the houses, but mainly the yards ran into each other with only now and then a low hedge that wasn't doing very well. There were few good friends among the grown people, and they were not poor enough for the other sort of intimate acquaintance, but everyone nodded and spoke, and even might talk short times, trivially, and at the two extremes of the general or the particular, and ordinarily nextdoor neighbors talked quite a bit when they happened to run into each other, and never paid calls. The men were mostly small businessmen, one or two very modestly executives, one or two worked with their hands, most of them clerical, and most of them between thirty and forty-five.

But it is of these evenings, I speak.

Supper was at six and was over by half past. There was still daylight, shining softly and with a tarnish, like the lining of a shell; and the carbon lamps lifted at the corners were on in the light, and the locusts were started, and the fire flies were out, and a few frogs were flopping in the dewy grass, by the time the fathers and the children came out. The children ran out first hell bent and yelling those names by which they were known; then the fathers sank out leisurely in crossed suspenders, their collars removed and their necks looking tall and shy. The mothers stayed back in the kitchen washing and drying, putting things away, recrossing their traceless footsteps like the lifetime journeys of bees, measuring out the dry cocoa for breakfast. When they came out they had taken off their aprons and their skirts were dampened and they set in rockers on their porches quietly.

It is not of the games children play in the evening that I want to speak now, it is of a contemporaneous atmosphere that has little to do with them: that of the fathers of families, each in his space of lawn, his shirt fishlike pale in the unnatural light and his face nearly anonymous, hosing their lawns. The hoses were attached at spigots that stood out of the brick foundations of the houses. The nozzles were variously set but usually so there was a long sweet stream of spray, the nozzle wet in the hand, the water trickling the right forearm and the peeled-back cuff, and the water whishing out a long loose and low-curved cone, and so gentle a sound. First an insane noise of violence in the nozzle, then the still irregular sound of adjustment, then the smoothing into steadiness and a pitch as accurately tuned to the size and style of stream as any violin. So many qualities of sound out of one hose: so many choral differences out of those several hoses that were in earshot. Out of any one hose, the almost dead silence of the release, and the short still arch of the separate big drops, silent as a held breath, and the only noise the flattering noise on leaves and the slapped grass at the fall of each big drop. That, and the intense hiss with the intense stream; that, and that same intensity not growing less but growing more quiet and delicate with the turn of the nozzle, up to that extreme tender whisper when the water was just a wide bell of film. Chiefly, though, the hoses were set much alike, in a compromise between distance and tenderness of spray (and quite surely a sense of art behind this compromise, and a quiet deep joy, too real to recognize itself), and the sounds therefore were pitched much alike; pointed by the snorting start of a new hose; decorated by some man playful with the nozzle; left empty, like God by the sparrow's fall, when any single one of them desists: and all, though near alike, of various pitch; and in this unison. These sweet pale streamings in the light lift out their pallors and their voices all together, mothers hushing their children, the hushing unnaturally prolonged, the men gentle and silent and each snail-like withdrawn into the quietude of what he singly is doing, the urination of huge children stood loosely military against an invisible wall, and gentle happy and peaceful, tasting the mean goodness of their living like the last of their suppers in their mouths; while the locusts carry on this noise of hoses on their much higher and sharper key. The noise of the locust is dry, and it seems not to be rasped or vibrated but urged from him as if through a small orifice by a breath that can never give out. Also there is never one locust but an illusion of at least a thousand. The noise of each locust is pitched in some classic locust range out of which none of them varies more than two full tones: and yet you seem to hear each locust discrete from all the rest, and there is a long, slow, pulse in their noise, like the scarcely defined arch of a long and high set bridge. They are all around in every tree, so that the noise seems to come from nowhere and everywhere at once, from the whole shell heaven, shivering in your flesh and teasing your eardrums, the boldest of all the sounds of night. And yet it is habitual to summer nights, and is of the great order of noises, like the noises of the sea and the blood her precocious grandchild, which you realize you are hearing only when you catch yourself listening. Meantime from low in the dark, just outside the swaying horizons of the hoses, conveying always grass in the damp of dew and its strong green-black smear of smell, the regular yet spaced noises of the crickets, each a sweet cold silver noise three-noted, like the slipping each time of three matched links of a small chain.

But the men by now, one by one, have silenced their hoses and drained and coiled them. Now only two, and now only one, is left, and you see only ghostlike shirt with the sleeve garters, and sober mystery of his mild face like the lifted face of large cattle enquiring of your presence in a pitchdark pool of meadow; and now he too is gone; and it has become that time of evening when people sit on their porches, rocking gently and talking gently and watching the street and the standing up into their sphere of possession of the trees, of birds hung havens, hangars. People go by; things go by. A horse, drawing a buggy, breaking his hollow iron music on the asphalt; a loud auto; a quiet auto; people in pairs, not in a hurry, scuffling, switching their weight of aestival body, talking casually, the taste hovering over them of vanilla, strawberry, pasteboard and starched milk, the image upon them of lovers and horsemen, squared with clowns in hueless amber. A street car raising its iron moan; stopping, belling and starting; stertorous; rousing and raising again its iron increasing moan and swimming its gold windows and straw seats on past and past and past, the bleak spark crackling and cursing above it like a small malignant spirit set to dog its tracks; the iron whine rises on rising speed; still risen, faints; halts; the faint stinging bell; rises again, still fainter, fainting, lifting, lifts, faints forgone: forgotten. Now is the night one blue dew.

> Now is the night one blue dew, my father has
>   drained, he has coiled the hose.
> Low on the length of lawns, a frailing of fire who
>   breathes.
> Content, silver, like peeps of light, each cricket makes

his comment over and over in the drowned grass.
A cold toad thumpily flounders.
Within the edges of damp shadows of side yards are
    hovering children nearly sick with joy of fear,
    who watch the unguarding of a telephone pole.
Around white carbon corner lamps bugs of all sizes
    are lifted elliptic, solar systems. Big hardshells
    bruise themselves, assailant: he is fallen on his
    back, legs squiggling.
Parents on porches: rock and rock: From damp strings
    morning glories: hang their ancient faces.
The dry and exalted noise of the locusts from all the
    air at once enchants my eardrums.

On the rough wet grass of the back yard my father and mother have spread quilts. We all lie there, my mother, my father, my uncle, my aunt, and I too am lying there. First we were sitting up, then one of us lay down, and then we all lay down, on our stomachs, or on our sides, or on our backs, and they have kept on talking. They are not talking much, and the talk is quiet, of nothing in particular, of nothing at all in particular, of nothing at all. The stars are wide and alive, they seem each like a smile of great sweetness, and they seem very near. All my people are larger bodies than mine, quiet, with voices gentle and meaningless like the voices of sleeping birds. One is an artist, he is living at home. One is a musician, she is living at home. One is my mother who is good to me. One is my father who is good to me. By some chance, here they are, all on this earth; and who shall ever tell the sorrow of being on this earth, lying, on quilts, on the grass, in a summer evening, among the sounds of night. May God bless my people, my uncle, my aunt, my mother, my good father, oh, remember them kindly in their time of trouble; and in the hour of their taking away.

After a little I am taken in and put to bed. Sleep, soft smiling, draws me unto her: and those receive me, who quietly treat me, as one familiar and well-beloved in that home: but will not, oh, will not, not now, not ever; but will not ever tell me who I am.

ERSKINE CALDWELL

from

You Have Seen Their Faces

IF OUTSIDERS WOULD STOP sticking their noses into other people's business, we'd get along all right down here. We know how to run this part of the country, and we're going to see that it's run like we want it. Every time a nigger kills a white man or rapes a white woman, they say we're railroading him because he is a nigger. We know how to take care of the niggers, because we know them better than anybody else. We live with them all the time, that's why we've come to know them so well. Outsiders think we're hard on niggers just because they're black. Sometimes we are hard on them, but that's because they have to be taught a lesson. The rest of the time we leave them alone. I've been dealing with niggers on my farm for thirty-two years, and I know them a lot better than some jack-leg who comes down here and says I don't treat them right. They get what they deserve, and that's enough for anybody. If I started out tomorrow asking one of my field hands if he would like for me to build him a bungalow with electric lights and a bathroom, by breakfast time the next morning he'd be coming up to the house expecting me to let him sit down at my own table, and by night he'd be wanting to marry one of my daughters. Give a nigger an inch and he'll take a mile. I know them. That's why you have to keep them in their place, and the less you give them, the less they'll try to take from you. Those outsiders who come down here don't know no more about running niggers than I know how to get to the moon. But don't think those know-it-alls don't think they know how. They'll argue your ear off saying the niggers have a right to have this, that, and the other thing, but I just laugh at what they're saying because I know they're making damn fools of themselves. The white people down here are hard on the bad niggers sometimes, but we love the good ones.

MAGEE, MISSISSIPPI

The Mississippi Valley Delta is the garden spot of the South, but it is a relatively small spot on the map. For every thousand-acre Delta plantation there are a great many tenant farms on the scrawny uplands and eroded hillsides. From the Atlantic to the Ozarks and from the Gulf of Mexico to the Tennessee River, in eleven Southern States, there are thousands and thousands of tenant farmers vainly struggling to squeeze a meager existence from an almost totally impoverished soil. The day will come when there will not be left enough fertility in the earth to grow and mature an ear of corn or a boll of cotton.

But the Delta country can and does produce one and two bales of cotton an acre; every rain and flood in the Ohio and Missouri River valleys brings downstream more silt and loam to add to its fertility. The eroded and depleted tenant farms in the hills do well to produce from one-eighth to one-half bale of cotton an acre; every bale that is gathered from these hardscrabble acres hastens the land's depletion.

The Negro tenant in the Delta receives as much as two hundred dollars a year for his labor; most of the hill-country white tenant farmers consider themselves fortunate when they receive a hundred dollars for their year's work.

There is nothing extraordinary in seeing poverty walking hand in hand with luxury, sterility with lushness. It is an everyday sight in the South, as common as weeds and flowers, and every region in America furnishes comparable contrasts. Likewise, there is no goal or interest to be gained by attempting to make out a case either for or against the South.

What has happened is that the plantation system has been wringing the blood and marrow from the South for two hundred years and, as fast as that is accomplished, the institution of sharecropping is being set up as a means of extracting the last juice of life from its prostrate body. It so happens that there are now more than ten million persons in one and three-quarters million tenant families in the grip of this system. It may or it may not be a coincidence that many of them are lacking in food, clothing, and houses; wanting in education, health, and hope.

Farm tenancy, and particulary sharecropping, is not self-perpetuating. It can survive only by feeding upon itself, like an animal in a trap eating its own flesh and bone. The only persons interested in its continuation are the landlords who accumulate wealth by extracting tribute not from the products of the earth but from the labor of the men, women, and children who till the earth.

The white tenant farmer has not always been the lazy, slipshod, good-for-nothing person that he is frequently described as being. His shiftlessness, when apparent, is an occupational disease of which he is generally well aware. There are times when he will readily admit that he is improvident and in the habit of putting off to a later day a task that could just as well be done at the moment; and he will add casually that most postponed tasks are never begun, much less completed. There are times when he is even proud and boastful of his slothfulness.

This same white tenant farmer grew from child to boy to man with many of the same ambitions and incentives that motivate the lives of all human beings. He had normal instincts. He had hope.

Somewhere in his span of life he became frustrated. He felt defeated. He felt the despair and dejection that comes with defeat. He was made aware of the limitations of life imposed upon those unfortunate enough to be made slaves of sharecropping. Out of his predicament grew desperation, out of desperation grew resentment. His bitterness was a taste his tongue would always know.

In a land that has long gloried in the supremacy of the white race, he directed his resentment against the black man. His normal instincts became perverted. He became wasteful and careless. He became bestial. He released his pent-up emotions by lynching the black man in order to witness the mental and physical suffering of another human being. He became cruel and inhuman in everyday life as his resentment and bitterness increased. He released his energy from day to day by beating mules and dogs, by whipping and kicking an animal into insensibility or to death. When his own suffering was more than he could stand, he could live only by witnessing the suffering of others.

The institution of sharecropping does things to men as well as to land. Conservation of the soil, when attained, will be only half a victory. A man here has his vision of life impaired by a lack of education, a man there has his vision of life restricted by ill health and poverty. But no man, providing he is normal mentally and physically, is a member of an inferior race specifically bred to demonstrate such characteristics as indolence and thriftlessness, cruelty and bestiality. Plantation- and tenant-farm-owners alike are to be held responsible, and in the end to be called upon to answer for the degeneration of man as well as for the rape of the soil in the South.

The white tenant farmer lives in a flimsy house and eats too little of the right kind of food, not because he wishes to, but because he has no other choice. If he has six or eight children — and he probably has or will have before he dies — and if the house has only three rooms — and it is more likely to have that number than four or five — there is also the probability that there are only two beds in the dwelling and that half the family must sleep on the floor.

If there are only enough warm clothes to dress three or four of the children in winter, the others must stay at home instead of going to school. If in the spring and fall half the children in the family are needed to help produce and gather the crops, the demands of the farm come before the advantages of the school, the landlord's cotton comes before education.

The white tenant farmer might have acted differently under other circumstances but, when the time came, he was moved by necessity and not by choice. That time comes when bread and meat and shelter are at stake. That time comes also when he must go out to find a husband for his twelve-year-old daughter because by placing her in another man's charge there will be one less mouth for him to feed, and more for those others who look to him for food. He is once and for all a victim of circumstances, the hard and fast rules governing the lives and thoughts of those men and women who are the slaves of sharecropping.

In Emanuel County, Georgia, there is a sharecropper whose name is John Sanford. He is forty-seven years old, and he has worked on tenant farms since he was a boy of eleven. He was born in Emanuel County and has never left it except for infrequent trips to near-by towns.

Sanford has been married twice, his first wife dying after the birth of her first child. He has already had four children by his second wife, who also had one child by her first husband. Inevitably they expect others to come, since both are resigned to the conclusion that there is no way to stop having them. There are ten persons now living in the Sanford home. Sanford's son by his first wife married his wife's daughter by her first husband. This union has produced two children. These four live in the house with Sanford and his wife and their four children. The building has four rooms.

Sanford is a sharecropping cotton farmer. He has been sharecropping since the age of twenty, first on one tenant farm and then on another, for twenty-seven years. Once he made enough to buy two beds, half a dozen chairs, a dresser, a washstand, and the kitchen stove. Another time he made enough to buy cheaply a second-hand automobile. The furniture has lasted, except for three of the chairs; the automobile did not last. He does not own anything else, except a change of clothes and a few odds and ends. His wife cuts his hair; he pulls the children's teeth when they begin to bother. He has a form for making concrete grindstones; and when he can get the cement, he makes several every year to sell to his neighbors.

Three times a day the family eats cornbread and molasses. With one of the meals they generally have meat with the cornbread and molasses. The meat comes from one of the hogs running at range, since some of the hogs belong to him, although he does not know how many do; or the meat comes from a rabbit caught in a rabbit-gum. They have twelve or fourteen hens and a rooster; every year his wife saves enough eggs to make two or three sittings, and the rest of the eggs laid are used to make cornbread batter.

The twenty-acre farm is worked on shares. The landlord furnishes a mule and half the fertilizer used; he furnishes also half the seed for corn and cotton. One of the acres is a canefield, planted every year to supply molasses; the landlord does not take a half-share of that. There is also a garden, about a quarter-acre in size, planted every year in cabbage, turnips, and sweet potatoes. There are several acres of wasteland on the farm. Some of it has grown up in brush; some is gully-washed. Sanford has no cow, nor has he had one for six years.

The land that Sanford farms borders a brook that runs most of the year. In midsummer it usually runs dry for a month or six weeks. The land slopes upward from it, away from the brush and undergrowth that hide it from view. The soil is sandy. When Sanford first began farming it, the soil was fairly productive, making almost, in good seasons, a bale of cotton to the acre. After seven years, the length of time he has farmed it, the rains have washed much of the loam and top-soil away, and what remains is sandy white earth that becomes whiter after every rain. The sand acts as though it were a filter. The fertilizer that is mixed with it each year in the spring produces what cotton there is to gather in the fall.

Sanford has never made any money, as making money goes in the United States, except during the two years when he had enough left over after food and clothing to buy the furniture and the automobile. He has sharecropped for twenty-seven years, on seven or eight tenant farms, but there has hardly ever been enough to buy food and clothes for the family. He raises four acres of corn each year, half of it going to the landlord, and half being ground into meal to make the cornbread with.

He raises watermelons and keeps them all. There have never been enough to sell, and sometimes the crop is stricken with a blight that spoils all but two or three dozen.

Twelve of the twenty acres are planted in cotton every year. With the help of his son by his first wife, his son's wife, and his own wife, and, when needed, of their children, he grows cotton. He grows cotton as though cotton were food and drink and wine and music. When he can make a pound of cotton, he has made a little sugar for the table, a little tobacco for his pipe. Cotton will keep them and, next to corn and cane, nothing else can. He plants cotton, cultivates it, and picks it; he works every dry day during the season from dawn to dusk. The last crop was an average one. He made three bales of cotton on twelve acres.

After dividing the cotton in halves with the landlord, Sanford's part amounted to six hundred and forty pounds of lint. The ginned cotton was sold for ten and a quarter cents per pound. The seed did not amount to anything; his share had to be kept to plant the next year's crop. He received, in cash, sixty-five dollars and sixty cents for his crop of cotton. He received also, as his share of the government's crop benefit payment, four dollars and eighty-eight cents. The two sums made a total of seventy dollars and forty-eight cents. He did not receive any other money during the year.

Seventy dollars and forty-eight cents for his year's labor bought Sanford and his family some salt and pepper, snuff for his wife; some sugar and coffee-and-chicory; it bought smoking tobacco for the boy and himself, some candy for the children; it bought several yards of gingham, thread, and buttons for his married daughter; two dresses for his wife, and a pair of shoes; material to clothe three of the children so they could attend school; it bought several bottles of 666 medicine, a cane knife, kerosene, and stamps for letters to his wife's relations.

There were several articles which his wife expressed either a wish or a need for. One of them was soap. Soap could be made from hog fat, but all the hogs ran at range, and the ones that were caught and butchered supplied lean meat but not enough fat for soap-making. Clothing was another. Most of the time during the cold months the children took turns going to school, since there were not enough coats for all.

Sanford works hard. Not as hard as some men; harder than many. He was the son of a tenant farmer, and he learned from childhood from his father that tenant farming required all the energy a man could bring to it. He works a little harder each year, because the soil grows thinner after every rain, because the children grow larger and ask for more food, because he is not satisfied with what he makes.

John Sanford is not the kind of sharecropper a landlord takes pride in. He has grown surly. He accuses the landlord of weighing the cotton short. He tells the landlord he wants more than half the cotton because making a crop requires more labor on farmed-out land. The landlord does not visit him any more as he once did; now he comes only two or three times a year to see what condition the dwelling is in, to see if Sanford has cut any of the timber in the pine grove on the hill. He thinks Sanford might be a dangerous person to have around some day.

Sanford is not a good farmer now. There is no incentive for him to take care of the land. The erosion could have been checked by terracing. The last time he terraced a cottonfield he was living on a tenant farm three miles away. He also put new posts in a fence, and cleared ground for a new garden. When the terracing and fencing and clearing were finished, the landlord told him he was acting as though he owned the place, and that it would be a good thing for him to move off the farm before he got that idea too firmly fixed in his head. He left that farm and moved to his present place.

After twenty-seven years of sharecropping, Sanford might have become lazy and shiftless, as many men do. He might have become broken in health, unable to stand two hours' work in the sun. As it is, he is a little lazy, but still energetic enough to work in the cotton when the cotton needs it. He cannot stand the sun so well as some men now, but by putting green leaves in the crown of his hat he can work through the hottest part of the day without stopping.

He might have become much lazier than he is. Instead, he became resentful. He became critical. He wanted to know why a bank would not lend him enough money to start buying a farm of his own. He wanted to know why landlords were afraid to let sharecroppers terrace and take care of the land. He wanted to know why he could not get credit at a store. He wanted to know why it was that a landlord would give a Negro sharecropper the best land, taking it away from a white sharecropper if necessary. He wanted to know, finally, why all the white sharecroppers in the country did not get together and run all the Negroes out.

He is of little or no value to his landlord. He has talked about renting some cotton land in another part of the county, but has not made any efforts to find land to rent. He has tried to find a new landlord who will give him a farm to work on shares, but most of the men he has seen are afraid he will not be able either to make enough cotton to pay the rent on shares, or to support his family, or both.

They are afraid they would have to supply food for the family once Sanford moved on their land.

As long as the land was fertile enough to produce a living, Sanford was able to make a living. Now the land is eroded and washed thin, Sanford himself is almost broken in health and spirit, and he has become resentfully outspoken in a country where talking out loud against the agricultural system of farm tenancy signals a man's own doom. It is the last cry of a man defeated by sharecropping.

One of these days the tractor and the mechanical picker are going to catch up with cotton, but by that time it's going to be too late to help the tenant farmer. He'll have ruined the soil for raising any other crop, and broken his back, to boot. Don't ask me whose fault it is. I don't know. I don't even know anybody who thinks he knows. All I know is that one man out of ten makes a living, and more, out of cotton, and that the other nine poor devils get the short end of the stick. It's my business to sit here in the bank and make it a rule to be in when that one farmer shows up to borrow money, and to be out when those other nine show up. I don't even know how to make money raising cotton myself. If I knew, I'd be out there doing it, instead of sitting here trying to lend money to one farmer while trying to keep nine others from knowing I don't want to lend them money. Some nights I can't sleep at all for lying awake wondering what's going to happen to all those losing tenant farmers. A lot of them are hungry, ragged, and sick. Everybody knows about it, but nobody does anything about it. The tractor and the mechanical picker, if it comes or if it doesn't come, won't make any difference in the end. The world can get along without cotton as soon as something comes along that's a cheaper substitute, and as soon as it does, cotton will pass out just like spinning-wheels and one-horse buggies. What it all adds up to is that cotton has ruined ten million people living in the cotton States, and it's going to ruin a lot more before it's through. The rest of the country doesn't care what happens to all these people. They might make a show of caring, but they've got troubles of their own, and a man's own troubles are more important to him than somebody else's. If the government doesn't do something about the losing cotton farmers, we'd be doing them a favor to go out and shoot them out of their misery.

AUGUSTA, GEORGIA

. HARRY .
CREWS

from

A Childhood: The Biography of a Place

AS WINTER GREW DEEPER and we waited for hog-killing time, at home the center was not holding. Whether it was because the crops were in and not much work was to be done or whether it was because of my having just spent so long a time crippled in the bed, daddy had grown progressively crazier, more violent. He was gone from home for longer and longer periods of time, and during those brief intervals when he was home, the crashing noise of breaking things was everywhere about us. Daddy had also taken to picking up the shotgun and screaming threats while he waved it about, but at that time he had not as yet fired it.

While that was going on, it occurred to me for the first time that being alive was like being awake in a nightmare.

I remember saying aloud to myself: "Scary as a nightmare. Jest like being awake in a nightmare."

Never once did I ever think that my life was not just like everybody else's, that my fears and uncertainties were not universal. For which I can only thank God. Thinking so could only have made it more bearable.

My sleepwalking had become worse now that I could get out of bed on my unsure legs. I woke up sometimes in the middle of the night in the dirt lane by the house or sometimes sitting in my room in a corner chewing on something. It didn't matter much what: the sleeve of my gown or the side of my hand or even one time the laces of a shoe. And when I would wake up, it was always in terror, habitually remembering now what Auntie had said about the birds spitting in my mouth. No, more than *remembering* what she had said. Rather, seeing what she had said, the image of a bird burned clearly on the backs of my eyelids, its beak hooked like the nose of a Byzantine Christ, shooting spit thick as phlegm on a solid line into my open and willing mouth. With such dreams turning in my head it came time for us to all help kill and butcher hogs. Daddy was laid up somewhere drunk; we had not seen him in four days. So he did not go with us to Uncle Alton's to help with the slaughter. Farm families swapped labor at hog-killing time just as they swapped labor to put in tobacco or pick cotton. Early one morning our tenant farmers, mama, my brother, and I walked the half mile to Uncle Alton's place to help put a year's worth of meat in the smokehouse. Later his family would come and help us do the same thing.

Before it was over, everything on the hog would have been used. The lights (lungs) and liver — together called haslet — would be made into a fresh stew by first pouring and pouring again fresh water through the slit throat — the exposed throat called a goozle — to clean the lights out good. Then the fat would be trimmed off and put with the fat trimmed from the guts to cook crisp into cracklins to mix with cornbread or else put in a wash pot to make soap.

The guts would be washed and then turned and washed again. Many times. After the guts had been covered with salt overnight, they were used as casings for sausage made from shoulder meat, tenderloin, and — if times were hard — any kind of scrap that was not entirely fat.

The eyes would be removed from the head, then the end of the snout cut off, and the whole thing boiled until the teeth could be picked out. Whatever meat was left, cheeks, ears, and so on, would be picked off, crushed with herbs and spices and packed tightly into muslin cloth for hog's headcheese.

The fat from the liver, lungs, guts, or wherever was cooked until it was as crisp as it would get and then packed into tin syrup buckets to be ground up later for cracklin cornbread. Even the feet were removed, and after the outer layer of split hooves was taken off, the whole thing was boiled and pickled in vinegar and peppers. If later in the year the cracklins started to get rank, they would be thrown into a cast-iron wash pot with fried meat's grease, any meat for that matter that might have gone bad in the smokehouse, and some potash and lye and cooked into soap, always made on the full of the moon so it wouldn't shrink. I remember one time mama out in the backyard making soap when a chicken for some reason tried to fly over the wash pot but didn't make it. The chicken dropped flapping and squawking into the boiling fat and lye. Mama, who was stirring the mixture with an old ax handle, never missed a beat. She just stirred the chicken right on down to the bottom. Any kind of meat was good for making soap.

By the time we got to Uncle Alton's the dirt floor of the smokehouse had been covered with green pine tops. After the pork stayed overnight in tubs of salt, it would be laid on the green pine straw all night, sometimes for two nights, to get all the water out of it. Then it was taken up and packed again in salt for three or four days. When it was taken out of the salt for the last time, it was dipped into plain hot water or else in a solution of crushed hot peppers and syrup or wild honey. Then it was hung over a deep pile of smoldering hickory spread across the entire floor of the smokehouse. The hickory was watched very carefully to keep any sort of blaze from flaring up. Day and night until it was over, light gray smoke boiled continuously from under the eaves and around the door where the meat was being cured. It was the sweetest smoke a man was ever to smell.

It was a bright cold day in February 1941, so cold the ground was still frozen at ten o'clock in the morning. The air was full of the steaming smell of excrement and the oily, flatulent odor of intestines and the heavy sweetness of blood — in every way a perfect day to slaughter animals. I watched the hogs called to the feeding trough just as they were every morning except this morning it was to receive the ax instead of slop.

A little slop *was* poured into their long communal trough, enough to make them stand still while Uncle Alton or his boy Theron went quietly among them with the ax, using the flat end like a sledgehammer (shells were expensive enough to make a gun out of the question). He would approach the hog from the rear while it slopped at the trough, and then he would straddle it, one leg on each side, patiently waiting for the hog to raise its snout from the slop to take a breath, showing as it did the wide bristled bone between its ears to the ax.

It never took but one blow, delivered expertly and with consummate skill, and the hog was dead. He then moved with his hammer to the next hog and straddled it. None of the hogs ever seemed to mind that their companions were dropping dead all around them but continued in a single-minded passion to eat. They didn't even mind when another of my cousins (this could be a boy of only eight or nine because it took neither strength nor skill) came right behind the hammer and drew a long razor-boned butcher knife across the throat of the fallen hog. Blood spurted with the still-beating heart, and a live hog would sometimes turn to one that was lying beside it at the trough and stick its snout into the spurting blood and drink a bit just seconds before it had its own head crushed.

It was a time of great joy and celebration for the children. We played games and ran (I gimping along pretty well by then) and screamed and brought wood to the boiler and thought of that night, when we would have fresh fried pork and stew made from lungs and liver and heart in an enormous pot that covered half the stove.

The air was charged with the smell of fat being rendered in tubs in the backyard and the sharp squeals of pigs at the troughs, squeals from pure piggishness at the slop, never from pain. Animals were killed but seldom hurt. Farmers took tremendous precautions about pain at slaughter. It is, whether or not they ever admit it when they talk, a ritual. As brutal as they sometimes are with farm animals and with themselves, no farmer would ever eat an animal he had willingly made suffer.

The heel strings were cut on each of the hog's hind legs, and a stick, called a gambreling stick, or a gallus, was inserted into the cut behind the tendon and the hog dragged to the huge cast-iron boiler, which sat in a depression dug into the ground so the hog could be slipped in and pulled out easily. The fire snapped and roared in the depression under the boiler. The fire had to be tended carefully because the water could never quite come to a boil. If the hog was dipped in boiling water, the hair would set and become impossible to take off. The ideal temperature was water you could rapidly draw your finger through three times in succession without being blistered.

Unlike cows, which are skinned, a hog is scraped. After the hog is pulled from the water, a blunt knife is drawn over the animal, and if the water has not been too hot, the hair slips off smooth as butter, leaving a white, naked, utterly beautiful pig.

To the great glee of the watching children, when the hog is slipped into the water, it defecates. The children squeal and clap their hands and make their delightfully obscene children's jokes as they watch it all.

On that morning, mama was around in the back by the smokehouse where some hogs, already scalded and scraped, were hanging in the air from their heel strings being disemboweled. Along with the other ladies she was washing out the guts, turning them inside out, cleaning them good so they could later be stuffed with ground and seasoned sausage meat.

Out in front of the house where the boiler was, I was playing pop-the-whip as best I could with my brother and several of my cousins. Pop-the-whip is a game in which everyone holds hands and runs fast and then the leader of the line turns sharply. Because he is turning through a tighter arc than the other children, the line acts as a whip with each child farther down the line having to travel through a greater space and consequently having to go faster in order to keep up. The last child in the line literally gets *popped* loose and sent flying from his playmates.

I was popped loose and sent flying into the steaming boiler of water beside a scalded, floating hog.

I remember everything about it as clearly as I remember anything that ever happened to me, except the screaming. Curiously, I cannot remember the screaming. They say I screamed all the way to town, but I cannot remember it.

What I remember is John C. Pace, a black man whose daddy was also named John C. Pace, reached right into the scalding water and pulled me out and set me on my feet and stood back to look at me. I did not fall but stood looking at John and seeing in his face that I was dead.

The children's faces, including my brother's, showed I was dead, too. And I knew it must be so because I knew where I had fallen and I felt no pain — not in that moment — and I knew with the bone-chilling certainty most people are spared that, yes, death does come and mine had just touched me.

John C. Pace ran screaming and the other children ran screaming and left me standing there by the boiler, my hair and skin and clothes steaming in the bright cold February air.

In memory I stand there alone with the knowledge of death upon me, watching steam rising from my hands and clothes while everybody runs and, after everybody has gone, standing there for minutes while nobody comes.

That is only memory. It may have been but seconds before my mama and Uncle Alton came to me. Mama tells me she heard me scream and started running toward the boiler, knowing already what had happened. She has also told me that she could not bring herself to try to do anything with that smoking ghostlike thing standing by the boiler. But she did. They all did. They did what they could.

But in that interminable time between John pulling me out and my mother arriving in front of me, I remember first the pain. It didn't begin as bad pain, but rather like maybe sandspurs under my clothes.

I reached over and touched my right hand with my left, and the whole thing came off like a wet glove. I mean, the skin on the top of the wrist and the back of my hand, along with the fingernails, all just turned loose and slid on down to the ground. I could see my fingernails lying in the little puddle my flesh made on the ground in front of me.

Then hands were on me, taking off my clothes, and the pain turned into something words cannot touch, or at least my words cannot touch. There is no way for me to talk about it because when my shirt was taken off, my back came off with it. When my overalls were pulled down, my cooked and glowing skin came down.

I still had not fallen, and I stood there participating in my own butchering. When they got the clothes off me, they did the worse thing they could have done; they wrapped me in a sheet. They did it out of panic and terror and ignorance and love.

That day there happened to be a car at the farm. I can't remember who it belonged to, but I was taken into the backseat into my mama's lap — God love the lady, out of her head, pressing her boiled son to her breast — and we started for Alma, a distance of about sixteen miles. The only thing that I can remember about the trip was that I started telling mama that I did not want to die. I started saying it and never stopped.

The car we piled into was incredibly slow. An old car and very, very slow, and every once in a while Uncle Alton, who was like a daddy to me, would jump out of the car and run alongside it and helplessly scream for it to go faster and then he would jump on the running board until he couldn't stand it any longer and then he would jump off again.

But like bad beginnings everywhere, they sometimes end well. When I got to Dr. Sharp's office in Alma and he finally managed to get me out of the sticking sheet, he found that I was scalded over two-thirds of my body but that my head had not gone under the water (he said that would have killed me), and for some strange reason I have never understood, the burns were not deep. He said I would probably even outgrow the scars, which I have. Until I was about fifteen years old, the scars were puckered and discolored on my back and right arm and legs. But now their outlines are barely visible.

The only hospital at the time was thirty miles away, and Dr. Sharp said I'd do just as well at home if they built a frame over the bed to keep the covers off me and also kept a light burning over me twenty-four hours a day. (He knew as well as we did that I couldn't go to the hospital anyway, since the only thing Dr. Sharp ever got for taking care of me was satisfaction for a job well done, if he got that. Over the years, I was his most demanding and persistent charity, which he never mentioned to me or mama. Perhaps that is why in an age when it is fashionable to distrust and hate doctors, I love them.)

So they took me back home and put a buggy frame over my bed to make it resemble, when the sheet was on it, a covered wagon, and ran a line in from the Rural Electrification Administration so I could have the drying light hanging just over me. The pain was not nearly so bad now that I had for the first time in my life the miracle of electricity close enough to touch. The pain was bad enough, though, but relieved to some extent by some medicine Dr. Sharp gave us to spray out of a bottle onto the burns by pumping a black rubber ball. When it dried, it raised to form a protective, cooling scab. But it was bad to crack. The bed was always full of black crumbs, which Auntie worked continually at. When they brought me home, Auntie, without anybody saying a word to her, came back up the road to take care of me.

The same day Hollis Toomey came, too. He walked into the house without knocking or speaking to anyone. Nobody had sent for him. But whenever anybody in the county was burned, he showed up as if by magic, because he could talk the fire out of you. He did not call himself a faith healer, never spoke of God, didn't even go to church, although his family did. His was a gift that was real, and everybody in the county knew it was real. For reasons which he never gave, because he was the most reticent of men and never took money or anything else for what he did, he was drawn to a bad burn the way iron filings are drawn to a magnet, never even saying, "You're welcome," to those who thanked him. He was as sure of his powers and as implacable as God.

When he arrived, the light had not yet been brought into the house, and the buggy frame was not yet over my bed and I was lying in unsayable pain. His farm was not far from ours, and it was unlike any other in the county. Birds' nests made from gourds, shaped like crooked-necked squash with a hole cut in one side with the seeds taken out, hung everywhere from the forest of old and arching oak trees about his house. Undulating flocks of white pigeons flew in and out of his hayloft. He had a blacksmith shed, black as smut and always hot from the open hearth where he made among other things iron rims for wagon wheels. He could handcraft a true-shooting gun, including the barrel which was not smooth-bore but had calibrated riflings. He owned two oxen, heavier than mules, whose harness, including the double yoke, he had made himself. His boys were never allowed to take care of them. He watered them and fed them and pulled them now and again to stumps or trees. But he also had the only Belgian draft horse in the county. The horse was so monstrously heavy that you could hitch him to two spans of good mules — four of them — and he would walk off with them as though they were goats. So the oxen were really useless. It just pleased him to keep them.

He favored very clean women and very dirty men. He thought it was the natural order of things. One of the few things I ever heard him say, and he said it looking off toward the far horizon, speaking to nobody: "A man's got the *right* to stink."

His wife always wore her hair tightly bunned at the back of her head under a stiffly starched white bonnet. Her dresses were nearly to her ankles, and they always looked and smelled as if they had just come off the clothesline after a long day in the sun.

Hollis always smelled like his pockets were full of ripe chicken guts, and his overalls were as stiff as metal. He didn't wear a beard; he wore a stubble. The stubble was coal black despite the fact he was over sixty, and it always seemed to be the same length, the length where you've got to shave or start telling everybody you're growing a beard. Hollis Toomey did neither.

When I saw him in the door, it was as though a soothing balm had touched me. This was Hollis Toomey, who was from my county, whose boys I knew, who didn't talk to God about your hurt. He didn't even talk to *you*; he talked to the *fire*. A mosquito couldn't fly through a door he was standing in he was so wide and high, and more, he was obviously indestructible. He ran on his own time, went where he needed to go. Nobody ever thought of doing anything for him, helping him. If he wanted something, he made it. If he couldn't make it, he took it. Hollis Toomey was not a kind man.

My daddy had finally come home, red-eyed and full of puke. He was at the foot of the bed, but he didn't say a word while Hollis sat beside me.

Hollis Toomey's voice was low like the quiet rasping of a file on metal. I couldn't hear most of what he had to say, but that was all right because I stopped burning before he ever started talking. He talked to the fire like an old and respected adversary, but one he had beaten consistently and had come to beat again. I don't remember him once looking at my face while he explained: "Fire, this boy is mine. This bed is mine. This room is mine. It ain't nothing here that's yours. It's a lot that is, but it ain't nothing here that is."

At some point while he talked he put his hands on me, one of them spread out big as a frying pan, and I was already as cool as spring water. But I had known I would be from the moment I had seen him standing in the door. Before it was over, he cursed the fire, calling it all kinds of sonofabitch, but the words neither surprised nor shocked me. The tone of his voice made me know that he was locked in a real and terrible conflict with the fire. His hands flexed and hurt my stomach, but it was nothing compared to the pain that had been on me before he came.

I had almost dozed off when he suddenly got up and walked out of the room. My daddy called, "Thank you," in a weak, alcohol-spattered voice. Hollis Toomey did not answer.

When they finally got the buggy frame up, it was not as terrible as I at first thought it was going to be. I was, of course, by then used to the bed and that was no problem and the buggy frame gave a new dimension, a new feeling to the sickbed. With the frame arching over me it was a time for fantasy and magic because I lived in a sort of a playhouse, a kingdom that was all mine.

At least I pretended it was a kingdom, pretended it in self-defense. I did not want to be there, but there was no help for it, so I might as well pretend it was a kingdom as anything else. And like every child who owns anything, I ruled it like a tyrant. There was something very special and beautiful about being the youngest member of a family and being badly hurt.

Since it pleased me to do so, I spent a lot of time with the Sears, Roebuck catalogue, started writing and nearly finished a detective novel, although at that time I had never seen a novel, detective or otherwise. I printed it out with a soft-lead pencil on lined paper, and it was about a boy who, for his protection, carried not a pistol but firecrackers. He solved crimes and gave things to poor people and doctors. The boy was also absolutely fearless.

I was given a great deal of ginger ale to drink because the doctor or mama or somebody thought that where burns were concerned, it had miraculous therapeutic value. This ginger ale was the store-bought kind, too, not some homemade concoction but wonderfully fizzy and capped in real bottles. Since Hoyet and I almost never saw anything from the store, I drank as much of it as they brought me, and they brought me a lot. I never learned to like it but could never get over my fascination with the bubbles that rose in the bottle under the yellow light hanging from the buggy frame.

But I was tired of being alone in bed, and since I was going into my second major hurt back to back. I decided I might as well assert myself.

Old Black Bill had sired several kids the previous spring, and one of them was himself black and a male, so I named him Old Black Bill, too, and he grew up with me under the buggy frame. No animal is allowed in a farmhouse in Bacon County, at least to my knowledge. Dogs stay in the yard. Cats usually live in the barn catching rats, and goats, well, goats only get in the house if they have first been butchered for the table.

But I had been scalded and I was special. And I knew even then that an advantage unused becomes no advantage at all. So I insisted Old Black Bill's kid be brought to my bed. I was only about three weeks into my recovery, and I thought that a goat would be good company.

They brought him in, and I fed him bits of hay and shelled corn under the buggy frame. We had long conversations. Or rather, I had long monologues and he, patiently chewing, listened.

The two tall windows at the foot of my bed opened onto a forty-acre field. Through the long winter days Old Black Bill and I watched it being prepared to grow another crop. First the cornstalks were cut by a machine with revolving blades, pulled by a single mule. Then two mules were hitched to a big rake, so big a man could ride on it. When all the stalks were piled and burned, the land had to be broken, completely turned under, the single hardest job on a farm for the farmer and his mules.

Every morning, when the light came up enough for me to see into the field, Willalee's daddy, Will, would already be out there behind a span of mules walking at remarkable speed, breaking the hard, clayish earth more than a foot deep. Sometimes daddy was out there plowing, too. Most of the time he was not.

Willalee's daddy would mark off an enormous square, fifteen acres or better, then follow that square around and around, always taking about a fourteen-inch bite with the turnplow so that when he went once around on each of the four sides of the square, the land still to be broken would have been reduced by fourteen inches on a side.

A man breaking land would easily walk thirty miles or more every day, day in and day out, until the entire farm was turned under. Even though the mules were given more corn and more hay than they were used to, they still lost weight. Every night when they were brought to the barn, they had high stiff ridges of salt outlining where their collars and backbands and trace chains and even their bridles had been.

With only my head out from under the buggy frame, continually dried and scabbed by the burning light, I watched the plows drag on through the long blowing days, Willalee's daddy moving dim as a ghost in the sickly half-light of the winter sun. Then after the longest, hardest time, the turnplow was taken out of the field, and the row marker brought in to lay off the lines in the soft earth where the corn would finally begin to show in the springtime. The row marker was made out of a trunk of a tree, sometimes a young oak, more often a pine, made by boring holes thirty-six inches apart and inserting a straight section of limb into each of the holes. Two holes were bored into the top of the log for handles and two holes in the front of the log for the shaves, between which the mule was hitched to drag the whole rig across the turned-under field, marking off four rows at a time.

Some farmers always had crops that grew in rows straight as a plumb line. Others didn't seem to care about it much, one way or the other. It was not unusual for a farmer bumping along in a wagon behind a steaming mule in the heat of the summer to comment on how the rows were marked off on each farm he passed.

"Sumbitch, he musta been drunk when he laid them off."

"I bet he has to git drunk again ever time he plows that mess."

"I guess he figgers as much'll grow in a crooked row as a straight one."

For reasons I never knew, perhaps it was nothing more complicated than pride of workmanship, farmers always associated crooked rows with sorry people. So much of farming was beyond a man's control, but at least he could have whatever nature allowed to grow laid off in straight rows. And the feeling was that a man who didn't care enough to keep his rows from being crooked couldn't be much of a man.

In all the years in Bacon County, I never saw any rows straighter than the ones Willalee's daddy put down. He would take some point of reference at the other end of the field, say a tree or a post, and then keep his eye on it as the mule dragged the row marker over the freshly broken ground, laying down those first critical rows. If the first four rows were straight, the rest of the field would be laid off straight, because the outside marker would always run in the last row laid down.

It didn't hurt to have a good mule. As was true of so many other things done on the farm, it was much easier if the abiding genius of a good mule was brought to bear on the job. There were mules in Bacon County that a blind man could have laid off straight rows behind. Such mules knew only one way to work: the right way. To whatever work they were asked to do, they brought a lovely exactitude, whether it was walking off rows, snaking logs, sledding tobacco without a driver, or any of the other unaccountable jobs that came their way during a crop year.

After the field was marked in a pattern of rows, Willalee's daddy came in with the middlebuster, a plow with a wing on both sides that opens up the row to receive first the fertilizer and then the seed. When all the rows had been plowed into shallow trenches, Will appeared in the field early one morning with a two-horse wagon full of guano, universally called *gyou-anner.* It was a commercial fertilizer sold in 200-pound bags, and Will had loaded the wagon before daylight by himself and brought it at sunup into the field where he unloaded one bag every three rows across the middle of the field.

Shortly after he left with the wagon, he came back with the guano strower and Willalee Bookatee. Willalee had a tin bucket with him. He plodded sleepily behind his daddy, the bucket banging at his knees. The guano strower was a kind of square wooden box that got smaller at the bottom, where there was a metal shaft shaped like a corkscrew and over which the guano had to fall as it poured into the trench opened by the middlebuster. The corkscrew shaft broke up any lumps in the fertilizer and made sure it kept flowing. Two little tongue-shaped metal plows at the back of the guano strower were set so that one ran on each side of the furrow. They covered up the thin stream of fertilizer the instant after it was laid down.

Willalee was out there to fill up the guano strower for his daddy, a bad, boring job and one reserved exclusively for small boys. Willalee would open one of the bags, fill the strower, and his daddy would head for the end of the row. As soon as he was gone, Willalee would go back to the sack, and since he could not pick up anything that heavy, he would have to dip the bucket full with his hands. Then he had nothing to do but shift from foot to foot, the fertilizer burning his arms and hands and before long his eyes, and wait for his daddy to come back down the row. When he did, Willalee would fill up the strower and the whole thing would be to do over again.

ZORA NEALE HURSTON

from

Mules and Men

I HEARD OF FATHER Watson the "Frizzly Rooster" from afar, from people for whom he had "worked" and their friends, and from people who attended his meetings held twice a week in Myrtle Wreath Hall in New Orleans. His name is "Father" Watson, which in itself attests his Catholic leanings, though he is formally a Protestant.

On a given night I had a front seat in his hall. There were the usual camp-followers sitting upon the platform and bustling around performing chores. Two or three songs and a prayer were the preliminaries.

At last Father Watson appeared in a satin garment of royal purple, belted by a gold cord. He had the figure for wearing that sort of thing and he probably knew it. Between prayers and songs he talked, setting forth his powers. He could curse anybody he wished — and make the curse stick. He could remove curses, no matter who had laid them on whom. Hence his title The Frizzly Rooster. Many persons keep a frizzled chicken in the yard to locate and scratch up any hoodoo that may be buried for them. These chickens have, no doubt, earned this reputation by their ugly appearance — with all of their feathers set in backwards. He could "read" anybody at sight. He could "read" anyone who remained out of his sight if they but stuck two fingers inside the door. He could "read" anyone, no matter how far away, if he were given their height and color. He begged to be challenged.

He predicted the hour and the minute nineteen years hence, when he should die — without even having been ill a moment in his whole life. God had told him.

He sold some small packets of love powders before whose powers all opposition must break down. He announced some new keys that were guaranteed to unlock every door and remove every obstacle in the way of success that the world knew. These keys had been sent to him by God through a small Jew boy. The old keys had been sent through a Jew man. They were powerful as long as they did not touch the floor — but if you ever dropped them, they lost their power. These new keys at five dollars each were not affected by being dropped, and were otherwise much more powerful.

I lingered after the meeting and made an appointment with him for the next day at his home.

Before my first interview with the Frizzly Rooster was fairly begun, I could understand his great following. He had the physique of Paul Robeson with the sex appeal and hypnotic what-ever-you-might-call-it of Rasputin. I could see that women would rise to flee from him but in mid-flight would whirl and end shivering at his feet. It was that way in fact.

His wife Mary knew how slight her hold was and continually planned to leave him.

"Only thing that's holding me here is this." She pointed to a large piece of brain-coral that was forever in a holy spot on the altar. "That's where his power is. If I could get me a piece, I could go start up a business all by myself. If I could only find a piece."

"It's very plentiful down in South Florida," I told her. "But if that piece if so precious, and you're his wife, I'd take it and let *him* get another piece."

"Oh my God! Naw! That would be my end. He's too powerful. I'm leaving him," she whispered this stealthily. "You get me a piece of that — you know."

The Frizzly Rooster entered and Mary was a different person at once. But every time that she was alone with me it was "That on the altar, you know. When you back in Florida, get me a piece. I'm leaving this man to his women." Then a quick hush and forced laughter at her husband's appoach.

So I became the pupil of Reverend Father Joe Watson, "The Frizzly Rooster" and his wife, Mary, who assisted him in all things. She was "round the altar"; that is while he talked with the clients, and usually decided on whatever "work" was to be done, she "set" the things on the altar and in the jars. There was one jar in the kitchen filled with honey and sugar. All the "sweet" works were set in this jar. That is, the names and the thing desired were written on paper and thrust into this jar to stay. Already four or five hundred slips of paper had accumulated in the jar. There was another jar called the "break up" jar. It held vinegar with some unsweetened coffee added. Papers were left in this one also.

When finally it was agreed that I should come to study with them, I was put to running errands such as "dusting" houses, throwing pecans, rolling apples, as the case might be; but I was not told why the thing was being done. After two weeks of this I was taken off this phase and initiated. This was the first step towards the door of the mysteries.

My initiation consisted of the Pea Vine Candle Drill. I was told to remain five days without sexual intercourse. I must remain indoors all day the day before the initiation and fast. I might wet my throat when necessary, but I was not to swallow water.

When I arrived at the house the next morning a little before nine, as per instructions, six other perons were there, so that there were nine of us — all in white except Father Watson who was in his purple robe. There was no talking. We went at once to the altar room. The altar was blazing. There were three candles around the vessel of holy water, three around the sacred sand pail, and one large cream candle burning in it. A picture of St. George and a large piece of brain coral were in the center. Father Watson dressed eight long blue candles and one black one, while the rest of us sat in the chairs around the wall. Then he lit the eight blue candles one by one from the altar and set them in the pattern of a moving serpent. Then I was called to the altar and both Father Watson and his wife laid hands on me. The black candle was placed in my hand; I was told to light it from all the other candles. I lit it at number one and pinched out the flame, and re-lit it at number two and so on till it had been lit by the eighth candle. Then I held the candle in my left hand, and by my right was conducted back to the altar by Father Watson. I was led through the maze of candles beginning at number eight. We circled numbers seven, five and three. When we reached the altar he lifted me upon the step. As I stood there, he called aloud, "Spirit! She's standing here without no home and no friends. She wants you to take her in." Then we began at number one and threaded back to number eight, circling three, five and seven. Then back to the altar again. Again he lifted me and placed me upon the step of the altar. Again the spirit was addressed as before. Then he lifted me down by placing his hands in my arm-pits. This time I did not walk at all. I was carried through the maze and I was to knock down each candle as I passed it with my foot. If I missed one, I was not to try again, but to knock it down on my way back to the altar. Arrived there the third time, I was lifted up and told to pinch out my black candle. "Now," Father told me, "you are made Boss of Candles. You have the power to light candles and put out candles, and to work with the spirits anywhere on earth."

Then all of the candles on the floor were collected and one of them handed to each of the persons present. Father took the black candle himself and we formed a ring. Everybody was given two matches each. The candles were held in our left hands, matches in the right; at a signal everybody stooped at the same moment, the matches scratched in perfect time and our candles lighted in concert. Then Father Watson walked rhythmically around the person at his right. Exchanged candles with her and went back to his place. Then that person did the same to the next so that the black candle went all around the circle and back to Father. I was then seated on a stool before the altar, sprinkled lightly with holy sand and water and confirmed as a Boss of Candles.

Then conversation broke out. We went into the next room and had a breakfast that was mostly fruit and smothered chicken. Afterwards the nine candles used in the ceremony were wrapped up and given to me to keep. They were to be used for lighting other candles only, not to be just burned in the ordinary sense.

In a few days I was allowed to hold consultations on my own. I felt insecure and said so to Father Watson.

"Of course you do now," he answered me, "but you have to learn and grow. I'm right here behind you. Talk to your people first, then come see me."

Within the hour a woman came to me. A man had shot and seriously wounded her husband and was in jail.

"But, honey," she all but wept, "they say ain't a thing going to be done with him. They say he got good white folks back of him and he's going to be let loose soon as the case is tried. I want him punished. Picking a fuss with my husband just to get chance to shoot him. We needs help. Somebody that can hit a straight lick with a crooked stick."

So I went in to the Frizzly Rooster to find out what I must do and he told me, "That a low fence." He meant a difficulty that was easily overcome.

"Go back and get five dollars from her and tell her to go home and rest easy. That man will be punished. When we get through with him, white folks or no white folks, he'll find a tough jury sitting on his case." The woman paid me and left in perfect confidence of Father Watson.

So he and I went into the workroom.

"Now," he said, "when you want a person punished who is already indicted, write his name on a slip of paper and put it in a sugar bowl or some other deep something like that. Now get your paper and pencil and write the name; alright now, you got it in the bowl. Now put in some red pepper, some black pepper — don't be skeered to put it in, it needs a lot. Put in one eightpenny nail, fifteen cents worth of ammonia and two door keys. You drop one key down in the bowl and you leave the other one against the side of the bowl. Now you got your bowl set. Go to your bowl every day at twelve o'clock and turn the key that is standing against the side of the bowl. That is to keep the man locked in jail. And every time you turn the key, add a little vinegar. Now I know this will do the job. All it needs is for you to do it in faith. I'm trusting this job to you entirely. Less see what you going to do. That can wait another minute. Come sit with me in the outside room and hear this woman out here that's waiting."

So we went outside and found a weakish woman in her early thirties that looked like somebody had dropped a sack of something soft on a chair.

The Frizzly Rooster put on his manner, looking like a brown, purple and gold throne-angel in a house.

"Good morning, sister er, er —"

"Murchison," she helped out.

"Tell us how you want to be helped, Sister Murchison."

She looked at me as if I was in the way and he read her eyes.

"She's alright, dear one. She's one of us. I brought her in with me to assist and help."

I thought still I was in her way but she told her business just the same.

"Too many women in my house. My husband's mother is there and she hates me and always puttin' my husband up to fight me. Look like I can't get her out of my house no ways I try. So I done come to you."

"We can fix that up in no time, dear one. Now go take a flat onion. If it was a man, I'd say a sharp pointed onion. Core the onion out, and write her name five times on paper and stuff it into the hole in the onion and close it back with the cut-out piece of onion. Now you watch when she leaves the house and then you roll the onion behind her before anybody else crosses the door-sill. And you make a wish at the same time for her to leave your house. She won't be there two weeks more." The woman paid and left.

That night we held a ceremony in the altar room on the case. We took a red candle and burnt it just enough to consume the tip. Then it was cut into three parts and the short lengths of candle were put into a glass of holy water. Then we took the glass and went at midnight to the door of the woman's house and the Frizzly Rooster held the glass in his hands and said, "In the name of the Father, in the name of the Son, in the name of the Holy Ghost." He shook the glass three times violently up and down, and the last time he threw the glass to the ground and broke it, and said, "Dismiss this woman from this place." We scarcely paused as this was said and done and we kept going and went home by another way because that was part of the ceremony.

Somebody came against a very popular preacher. "He's getting too rich and big. I want something done to keep him down. They tell me he's 'bout to get to be a bishop. I sho' would hate for that to happen. I got forty dollars in my pocket right now for the work."

So that night the altar blazed with the blue light. We wrote the preacher's name on a slip of paper with black ink. We took a small doll and ripped open its back and put in the paper with the name along with some bitter aloes and cayenne pepper and sewed the rip up again with the black thread. The hands of the doll were tied behind it and a black veil tied over the face and knotted behind it so that the man it represented would be blind and always do the things to keep himself from progressing. The doll was then placed in a kneeling position in a dark corner where it would not be disturbed. He would be frustrated as long as the doll was not disturbed.

When several of my jobs had turned out satisfactorily to Father Watson, he said to me, "You will do well, but you need the Black Cat Bone. Sometimes you have to be able to walk invisible. Some things must be done in deep secret, so you have to walk out of the sight of man."

First I had to get ready even to try this most terrible of experiences — getting the Black Cat Bone.

First we had to wait on the weather. When a big rain started, a new receptacle was set out in the yard. It could not be put out until the rain actually started for fear the sun might shine in it. The water must be brought inside before the weather faired off for the same reason. If lightning shone on it, it was ruined.

We finally got the water for the bath and I had to fast and "seek," shut in a room that had been purged by smoke. Twenty-four hours without food except a special wine that was fed to me every four hours. It did not make me drunk in the accepted sense of the word. I merely seemed to lose my body, my mind seemed very clear.

When dark came, we went out to catch a black cat. I must catch him with my own hands. Finding and catching black cats is hard work, unless one has been released for you to find. Then we repaired to a prepared place in the woods and a circle drawn and "protected" with nine horseshoes. Then the fire and the pot were made ready. A roomy iron pot with a lid. When the water boiled I was to toss in the terrified, trembling cat.

When he screamed, I was told to curse him. He screamed three times, the last time weak and resigned. The lid was clamped down, the fire kept vigorously alive. At midnight the lid was lifted. Here was the moment! The bones of the cat must be passed through my mouth until one tasted bitter.

Suddenly, the Rooster and Mary rushed in close to the pot and he cried, "Look out! This is liable to kill you. Hold your nerve!" They both looked fearfully around the circle. They communicated some unearthly terror to me. Maybe I went off in a trance. Great beast-like creatures thundered up to the circle from all sides. Indescribable noises, sights, feelings. Death was at hand! Seemed unavoidable! I don't know. Many things I have thought and felt, but I always have to say the same thing. I don't know. I don't know.

Before day I was home, with a small white bone for me to carry.

from DUST TRACKS ON A ROAD: AN AUTOBIOGRAPHY

My search for knowledge of things took me into many strange places and adventures. My life was in danger several times. If I had not learned how to take care of myself in these circumstances, I could have been maimed or killed on most any day of the several years of my research work. Primitive minds are quick to sunshine and quick to anger. Some little word, look or gesture can move them either to love or to sticking a knife between your ribs. You just have to sense the delicate balance and maintain it.

In some instances, there is nothing personal in the killing. The killer wishes to establish a reputation as a killer, and you'll do as a sample. Some of them go around, making their announcements in singing:

I'm going to make me a graveyard of my own,
I'm going to make me a graveyard of my own,
Oh, carried me down on de smoky road,
Brought me back on de coolin' board,
But I'm going to make me a graveyard of my own.

And since the law is lax on these big saw-mill, turpentine and railroad "jobs," there is a good chance that they never will be jailed for it. All of these places have plenty of men and women who are fugitives from justice. The management asks no questions. They need help and they can't be bothered looking for a bug under every chip. In some places, the "law" is forbidden to come on the premises to hunt for malefactors who did their malefacting elsewhere. The wheels of industry must move, and if these men don't do the work, who is there to do it?

So if a man, or a woman, has been on the gang for petty-thieving and mere mayhem, and is green with jealousy of the others who did the same amount of time for a killing and had something to brag about, why not look around for an easy victim and become a hero, too? I was nominated like that once in Polk County, Florida, and the only reason that I was not elected, was because a friend got in there and staved off old club-footed Death.

Polk County! Ah!
Where the water tastes like cherry wine.
Where they fell great trees with axe and muscle.

These poets of the swinging blade! The brief, but infinitely graceful, dance of body and axe-head as it lifts over the head in a fluid arc, dances in air and rushes down to bite into the tree, all in beauty. Where the logs march into the mill with its smokestacks disputing with the elements, its boiler room reddening the sky, and its great circular saw screaming arrogantly as it attacks the tree like a lion making its kill. The log on the carriage coming to the saw. A growling grumble. Then contact! Yeelld-u-u-ow! And a board is laid shining and new on a pile. All day, all night. Rumble, thunder and grumble. Yee-ee-ow! Sweating black bodies, muscled like gods, working to feed the hunger of the great tooth. Polk County!

Polk County. Black men laughing and singing. They go down in the phosphate mines and bring up the wet dust of the bones of pre-historic monsters, to make rich land in far places, so that people can eat. But, all of it is not dust. Huge ribs, twenty feet from belly to backbone. Some old-time sea monster caught in the shallows in that morning when God said, "Let's make some more dry land. Stay there, great Leviathan! Stay there as a memory and a monument to Time." Shark-teeth as wide as the hand of a working man. Joints of backbone three feet high, bearing witness to the mighty monster of the deep when the Painted Land rose up and did her first dance with the morning sun. Gazing on these relics, forty thousand years old and more, one visualizes the great surrender to chance and change when these creatures were rocked to sleep and slumber by the birth of land.

Polk County. Black men from tree to tree among the lordly pines, a swift, slanting stroke to bleed the trees for gum. Paint, explosives, marine stores, flavors, perfumes, tone for a violin bow, and many other things which the black men who bleed the trees never heard about.

Polk County. The clang of nine-pound hammers on railroad steel. The world must ride.

Hah! A rhythmic swing of the body, hammer falls, and another spike driven to the head in the tie.

> Oh, Mobile! Hank!
> Oh, Alabama! Hank!
> Oh, Fort Myers! Hank!
> Oh, in Florida! Hank!
> Oh, let's shake it! Hank!
> Oh, let's break it! Hank!
> Oh, let's shake it! Hank!
> Oh, just a hair! Hank!

The singing-liner cuts short his chant. The strawboss relaxes with a gesture of his hand. Another rail spiked down. Another offering to the soul of civilization whose other name is travel.

Polk County. Black men scrambling up ladders into orange trees, Singing, laughing, cursing, boasting of last night's love, and looking forward to the darkness again. They do not say embrace when they mean that they slept with a woman. A behind is a behind and not a form. Nobody says anything about incompatibility when they mean it does not suit. No bones are made about being fed up.

> I got up this morning, and I knowed I didn't want it,
> Yea! Polk County!
> You don't know Polk County like I do
> Anybody been there, tell you the same thing, too.
> Eh, rider, rider!
> Polk County, where the water tastes like cherry wine.

Polk County. After dark, the jooks. Songs are born out of feelings with an old beat-up piano, or a guitar for a mid-wife. Love made and unmade. Who put out dat lie, it was supposed to last forever? Love is when it is. No more here? Plenty more down the road. Take you where I'm going, woman? Hell no! Let every town furnish its own. Yeah, I'm going. Who care anything about no train fare? The railroad track is there, ain't it? I can count tires just like I been doing. I can ride de blind, can't I?

> Got on de train didn't have no fare
> But I rode some
> Yes I rode some
> Got on de train didn't have no fare
> Conductor ast me what I'm doing there
> But I rode some
> Yes I rode some
>
> Well, he grabbed me by de collar and he led me to de door
> But I rode some
> Yes I rode some
> Well, he grabbed me by de collar and he led me to de door
> He rapped me over de head with a forty-four
> But I rode some
> Yes I rode some.

Polk County in the jooks. Dancing the square dance. Dancing the scronch. Dancing the belly-rub. Knocking the right hat off the wrong head, and backing it up with a switch-blade.

"Fan-foot, what you doing with my man's hat cocked on *your* nappy head? I know you want to see your Jesus. Who's a whore? Yeah I sleeps with my mens, but they pays me. I wouldn't be a fan-foot like you — just on de road somewhere. Runs up and down de road from job to job making pay-days. Don't nobody hold her! Let her jump on me! She pay her way on me, and I'll pay it off. Make time in old Bartow jail for her."

Maybe somebody stops the fight before the two switch-blades go together. Maybe nobody can. A short, swift dash in. A lucky jab by one opponent and the other one is dead. Maybe one gets a chill in the feet and leaps out of the door. Maybe both get cut badly and back off. Anyhow, the fun of the place goes on. More dancing and singing and buying of drinks, parched peanuts, fried rabbit. Full drummy bass from the piano with weepy, intricate right-hand stuff. Singing the memories of Ella Wall, the Queen of love in the jooks of Polk County. Ella Wall, Planchita, Trottin' Liza.

It is a sad, parting song. Each verse ends up with:

> Quarters Boss! High Sheriff? Lemme git gone from here!
> Cold, rainy day, some old cold, rainy day
> I'll be back, some old cold, rainy day.

Oh de rocks may be my pillow, Lawd!
De sand may be my bed
I'll be back some old cold, rainy day.

"Who run? What you running from the man for, nigger? Me, I don't aim to run a step. I ain't going to run unless they run me. I'm going to live anyhow until I die. Play me some music so I can dance! Aw, spank dat box, man!! Them white folks don't care nothing bout no nigger getting cut and kilt, nohow. They ain't coming in here. I done kilt me four and they ain't hung me yet. Beat dat box!"

"Yeah, but you ain't kilt no women, yet. They's mighty particular 'bout you killing up women."

"And I ain't killing none neither. I ain't crazy in de head. Nigger woman can kill all us men she wants to and they don't care. Leave us kill a woman and they'll run you just as long as you can find something to step on. I got good sense. I know I ain't got no show. De white mens and de nigger women is running this thing. Sing about old Georgy Buck and let's dance off of it. Hit dat box!"

Old Georgy Buck is dead
Last word he said
I don't want no shortening in my bread
Rabbit on de log
Ain't got no dog
Shoot him wid my rifle, bam! bam!

And the night, the pay night rocks on with music and gambling and laughter and dancing and fights. The big pile of cross-ties burning out in front simmers down to low ashes before sun-up, so then it is time to throw up all the likker you can't keep down and go somewhere and sleep the rest off, whether your knife has blood on it or not. That is, unless some strange, low member of your own race has gone and pimped to the white folks about something getting hurt. Very few of those kind are to be found.

That is the primeval flavor of the place, and as I said before, out of this primitive approach to things, I all but lost my life.

It was in a saw-mill jook in Polk County that I almost got cut to death.

Lucy really wanted to kill me. I didn't mean any harm. All I was doing was collecting songs from Slim, who used to be her man back up in West Florida before he ran off from her. It is true that she found out where he was after nearly a year, and followed him to Polk County and he paid her some slight attention. He was knocking the pad with women, all around, and he seemed to want to sort of free-lance at it. But what he seemed to care most about was picking his guitar, and singing.

He was a valuable source of material to me, so I built him up a bit by buying him drinks and letting him ride in my car.

I figure that Lucy took a pick at me for three reasons. The first one was, her vanity was rubbed sore at not being able to hold her man. That was hard to own up to in a community where so much stress was laid on suiting. Nobody else had offered to shack up with her either. She was getting a very limited retail trade and Slim was ignoring the whole business. I had store-bought clothes, a lighter skin, and a shiny car, so she saw wherein she could use me for an alibi. So in spite of public knowledge of the situation for a year or more before I came, she was telling it around that I came and broke them up. She was going to cut everything off of me but "quit it."

Her second reason was, because of my research methods I had dug in with the male community. Most of the women liked me, too. Especially her sworn enemy, Big Sweet. She was scared of Big Sweet, but she probably reasoned that if she cut Big Sweet's protégée it would be a slam on Big Sweet and build up her own reputation. She was fighting Big Sweet through me.

Her third reason was, she had been in little scraps and been to jail off and on, but she could not swear that she had ever killed anybody. She was small potatoes and nobody was paying her any mind. I was easy. I had no gun, knife or any sort of weapon. I did not even know how to do that kind of fighting.

Lucky for me, I had friended with Big Sweet. She came to my notice within the first week that I arrived on location. I heard somebody, a woman's voice "specifying" up this line of houses from where I lived and asked who it was.

"Dat's Big Sweet" my landlady told me. "She got her foot on somebody. Ain't she specifying?"

She was really giving the particulars. She was giving a "reading," a word borrowed from the fortunetellers. She was giving her opponent lurid data and bringing him up to date on his ancestry, his looks, smell, gait, clothes, and his route through Hell in the hereafter. My landlady went outside where nearly everybody else of the four or five hundred people on the "job" were to listen to the reading. Big Sweet broke the news to him, in one of her mildest bulletins that his pa was a double-humpted camel and his ma was a grass-gut cow, but even so, he tore her wide open in the act of getting born, and so on and so forth. He was a bitch's baby out of a buzzard egg.

My landlady explained to me what was meant by "putting your foot up" on a person. If you are sufficiently armed — enough to stand off a panzer division — and know what to do with your weapons after you get 'em, it is all right to go to the house of your enemy, put one foot up on his steps, rest one elbow on your knee and play in the family. That is another way of saying play the dozens, which also is a way of saying low-rate your enemy's ancestors and him, down to the present moment for reference, and then go into his future as far as your imagination leads you. But if you have no faith in your personal courage and confidence in your arsenal, don't try it. It is a risky pleasure. So then I had a measure of this Big Sweet.

"Hurt who?" Mrs. Bertha snorted at my fears. "Big Sweet? Humph! Tain't a man, woman nor child on this job going to tackle Big Sweet. If God send her a pistol she'll send him a man. She can handle a knife with anybody. She'll join hands and cut a duel. Dat Cracker Quarters Boss wears two pistols round his waist and goes for bad, but he won't break a breath with Big Sweet lessen he got his pistol in his hand. Cause if he start anything with her, he won't never get a chance to draw it. She ain't mean. She don't bother nobody. She just don't stand for no foolishness, dat's all."

Right away, I decided that Big Sweet was going to be my friend. From what I had seen and heard in the short time I had been there, I felt as timid as an egg without a shell. So the next afternoon when she was pointed out to me, I waited until she was well up the sawdust road to the Commissary, then I got in my car and went that way as if by accident. When I pulled up beside her and offered her a ride, she frowned at me first, then looked puzzled, but finally broke into a smile and got in.

By the time we got to the Commissary post office we were getting along fine. She told everybody I was her friend. We did not go back to the Quarters at once. She carried me around to several places and showed me off. We made a date to go down to Lakeland come Saturday, which we did. By the time we sighted the Quarters on the way back from Lakeland, she had told me, "You sho is crazy!" Which is a way of saying I was witty. "I loves to friend with somebody like you. I aims to look out for you, too. Do your fighting for you. Nobody better not start nothing with you, do I'll get my switch-blade and go round de ham-bone looking for meat."

We shook hands and I gave her one of my bracelets. After that everything went well for me. Big Sweet helped me to collect material in a big way. She had no idea what I wanted with it, but if I wanted it, she meant to see to it that I got it. She pointed out people who knew songs and stories. She wouldn't stand for balkiness on their part. We held two lying contests, story-telling contests to you, and Big Sweet passed on who rated the prizes. In that way, there was no argument about it.

So when the word came to Big Sweet that Lucy was threatening me, she put her foot up on Lucy in a most particular manner and warned her against the try. I suggested buying a knife for defense, but she said I would certainly be killed that way.

"You don't know how to handle no knife. You ain't got dat kind of a sense. You wouldn't even know how to hold it to de best advantage. You would draw your arm way back to stop her, and whilst you was doing all dat, Lucy would run in under your arm and be done; cut you to death before you could touch her. And then again, when you sure 'nough fighting, it ain't enough to just stick 'em wid your knife. You got to ram it in to de hilt, then you pull *down*. They ain't no more trouble after dat. They's *dead*. But don't you bother 'bout no fighting. You ain't like me. You don't even sleep with no mens. I wanted to be a virgin one time, but I couldn't keep it up. I needed the money too bad. But I think it's nice for you to be like that. You just keep on writing down them lies. I'll take care of all de fighting. Dat'll make it more better, since we done made friends."

She warned me that Lucy might try to "steal" me. That is, ambush me, or otherwise attack me without warning. So I was careful. I went nowhere on foot without Big Sweet.

Several weeks went by, then I ventured to the jook alone. Big Sweet let it be known that she was not going. But later she came in and went over to the cooncan game in the corner. Thinking I was alone, Lucy waited until things were in full swing and then came in and went over to the coon-can game in the corner. Thinking I was alone, Lucy waited until things were in full swing and then came in with the very man to whom Big Sweet had given the "reading." There was only one door. I was far from it. I saw no escape for me when Lucy strode in, knife in hand. I saw sudden death very near that moment. I was paralyzed with fear. Big Sweet was in a crowd over in the corner, and did not see Lucy come in. But the sudden quiet of the place made her look around as Lucy charged. My friend was large and portly but extremely light on her feet. She sprang like a lioness and I think the very surprise of Big Sweet being there when Lucy thought she was over at another party at the Pine Mill unnerved Lucy. She stopped abruptly as Big Sweet charged. The next moment, it was too late for Lucy to start again. The man who came in with Lucy tried to help her out, but two other men joined Big Sweet in the battle. It took on amazingly. It seemed that anybody who had any fighting to do, decided to settle-up then and there. Switch-blades, ice-picks and old-fashioned razors were out. One or two razors had already been bent back and thrown across the room, but our fight was the main attraction. Big Sweet yelled to me to run. I really ran, too. I ran out of the place, ran to my room, threw my things in the car and left the place. When the sun came up I was a hundred miles up the road, headed for New Orleans.

One bit of research I did jointly for the Journal of Negro History and Columbia University, was in Mobile, Alabama. There I went to talk to Cudjo Lewis. That is the American version of his name. His African name was Kossola-O-Lo-Loo-Ay.

He arrived on the last load of slaves run into the United States and was the only Negro alive that came over on a slave ship. It happened in 1859 just when the fight between the South and the Abolitionists was moving toward the Civil War. He has died since I saw him.

I found him a cheerful, poetical old gentleman in his late nineties, who could tell a good story. His interpretation of the story of Jonah was marvelous.

He was a good Christian and so he pretended to have forgotten all of his African religion. He turned me off with the statement that his Nigerian religion was the same as Christianity. "We know it a God, you unner'stand, but we don't know He got a Son."

He told me in detail of the circumstances in Africa that brought about his slavery here. How the powerful Kingdom of Dahomey, finding the slave trade so profitable, had abandoned farming, hunting and all else to capture slaves to stock the barracoons on the beach at Dmydah to sell to the slavers who came from across the ocean. How quarrels were manufactured by the King of Dahomey with more peaceful agricultural nations in striking distance of Dahomey in Nigeria and Gold Coast; how they were assaulted, completely wiped off the map, their names never to appear again, except when they were named in boastful chant before the King at one of his "customs" when his glory was being sung. The able-bodied who were captured were marched to Abomey, the capital city of Dahomey and displayed to the King, then put into the barracoons to await a buyer. The too old, the too young, the injured in battle were instantly beheaded and their heads smoked and carried back to the King. He paid off on heads, dead or alive. The skulls of the slaughtered were not wasted either. The King had his famous Palace of Skulls. The Palace grounds had a massive gate of skull-heads. The wall surrounding the grounds were built of skulls. You see, the Kings of Dahomey were truly great and mighty and a lot of skulls were bound to come out of their ambitions. While it looked awesome and splendid to him and his warriors, the sight must have been most grewsome and crude to Western eyes.

One thing impressed me strongly from this three months of association with Cudjo Lewis. The white people had held my people in slavery here in America. They had bought us, it is true and exploited us. But the inescapable fact that stuck in my craw, was: my people had *sold* me and the white people had bought me. That did away with the folklore I had been brought up on — that the white people had gone to Africa, waved a red handkerchief at the Africans and lured them aboard ship and sailed away. I know that civilized money stirred up African greed. That wars between tribes were often stirred up by white traders to provide more slaves in the barracoons and all that. But, if the African princes had been as pure and as innocent as I would like to think, it could not have happened. No, my own people had butchered and killed, exterminated whole nations and torn families apart, for a profit before the strangers got their chance at a cut. It was a sobering thought. What is more, all that this Cudjo told me was verified from other historical sources. It impressed upon me the universal nature of greed and glory. Lack of power and opportunity passes off too often for virtue. If I were King, let us say, over the Western Hemisphere tomorrow, instead of who I am, what would I consider right and just? Would I put the cloak of Justice on my ambition and send her out a-whoring after conquests? It is something to ponder over with fear.

Cudjo's eyes were full of tears and memory of fear when he told me of the assault on his city and its capture. He said that his nation, the Takkoi, lived "three sleeps" from Dahomey. The attack came at dawn as the Takkoi were getting out of bed to go to their fields outside the city. A whooping horde of the famed Dahoman women warriors burst through the main gate, seized people as they fled from their houses and beheaded victims with one stroke of their big swords.

"Oh, oh! I runnee this way to that gate, but they there. I runnee to another one, but they there, too. All eight gates they there. Them women, they very strong. I nineteen years old, but they too strong for me. They take me and tie me. I don't know where my people at. I never see them no more."

He described the awful slaughter as the Amazons sacked the city. The clusters of human heads at their belts. The plight of those who fled through the gates to fall into the hands of the male warriors outside. How his King was finally captured and carried before the King of Dahomey, who had broken his rule and come on this expedition in person because of a grudge against the King of Takkoi, and how the vanquished monarch was led before him, bound.

"Now, that you have dared to send impudent words to me,", the King of Dahomey said, "your country is conquered and you are before me in chains. I shall take you to Abomey."

"No," the King of Takkoi answered. "I am King in Takkoi. I will not go to Dahomey." He knew that he would be killed for a spectacle in Dahomey. He chose to die at home.

So two Dahoman warriors held each of his hands and an Amazon struck off his head.

Later, two representatives of a European power attended the customs of the King at Abomey, and told of seeing the highly polished skull of the King of Takkoi mounted in a beautiful ship-model. His name and his nation were mentioned in the chant to the glory of Dahomey. The skull was treated with the utmost respect, as the King of Dahomey would expect his to be treated in case he fell in battle. That was custom in West Africa. For the same reason, no one of royal blood was sold into slavery. They were killed. There are no descendants of royal African blood among American Negroes for that reason. The Negroes who claim that they are descendants of royal African blood have taken a leaf out of the book of the white ancestor-hounds in America, whose folks went to England with William the Conqueror, got restless and caught the *Mayflower* for Boston, then feeling a romantic lack, rushed down the coast and descended from Pocahontas. From the number of her children, one is forced to the conclusion that Pocahontas wasn't so poky, after all.

Kossola told me of the March of Abomey after the fall of Takkoi. How they were yoked by forked sticks and tied in a chain. How the Dahomans halted the march the second day in order to smoke the heads of the victims because they were spoiling. The prisoners had to watch the heads of their friends and relatives turning on long poles in the smoke. Abomey and the palace of the King and then the march to the coast and the barracoons. They were there sometime before a ship came to trade. Many, many tribes were there, each in a separate barracoon, lest they war among themselves. The traders could choose which tribe they wanted. When the tribe was decided upon, he was carried into the barracoon where that tribe was confined, the women were lined up on one side and the men on the other. He walked down between the lines and selected the individuals he wanted. They usually took an equal number.

He described the embarcation and the trip across the ocean in the *Chlotilde*, a fast sailing vessel built by the Maher brothers of Maine, who had moved to Alabama. They were chased by a British man-of-war on the lookout for slavers, but the *Chlotilde* showed her heels. Finally the cargo arrived in Mobile. They were unloaded up the river, the boat sunk, and the hundred-odd Africans began a four-year life of slavery.

"We so surprised to see mule and plow. We so surprised to see man pushee and mule pullee."

After the war, these Africans made a settlement of their own at Plateau, Alabama, three miles up the river from Mobile. They farmed and worked in the lumber mills and bought property. The descendants of these people are still there.

Kossola's great sorrow in America was the death of his favorite son, David, killed by a train. He refused to believe it was his David when he saw the body. He refused to let the bell be tolled for him.

"If dat my boy, where his head? No, dat not my David. Dat not my boy. My boy gone to Mobile. No, No! Don't ringee de bell for David. Dat not him."

But, finally his wife persuaded him that the headless body on the window blind was their son. He cried hard for several minutes and then said, "Ringee de bell."

His other great sorrow was that he had lost track of his folks in Africa.

"They don't know what become of Kossola. When you go there, you tellee where I at." He begged me. He did not know that his tribe was no more upon this earth, except for those who reached the barracoon at Dmydah. None of his family was in the barracoon. He had missed seeing their heads in the smoke, no doubt. It is easy to see how few would have looked on that sight too closely.

"I lonely for my folks. They don't know. Maybe they ask everybody go there where Kossola. I know they hunt for me." There was a tragic catch in his voice like the whimper of a lost dog.

After seventy-five years, he still had that tragic sense of loss. That yearning for blood and cultural ties. That sense of mutilation. It gave me something to feel about.

WILLIE MORRIS

Always Stand in Against the Curve

THE WAR IN KOREA had just started, and the radio spoke of Yaks and Stormoviks and T-34s, and Trygve Lie and Warren Austin and Sigmond Rhee. I was 17 the year we won the state championship. American Legion Junior Baseball was flourishing in the South in those days, and our team in Yazoo was an all-star club from the whole county, an amalgam of town and country boys who played against each other during the high school season in the spring — bitter adversaries in April, reluctant allies in July. These country boys threw at your head in the springtime and came into second with their spikes high, and would not shake hands after the game. They were hard-nosed sons of the earth. Only baseball joined us, and then uneasily, and they viewed our town girls with lust and apprehension.

It was a good county for baseball, perhaps the finest in Mississippi. The Ole Miss baseball coach, one of the best in Dixie, was a Yazooan. One forlorn hamlet out in the hills would produce two pitchers for the Pittsburgh Pirates. The country boys from Satartia, Benton, Fugates, and Bentonia were tough, wily, and suspicious of the big city, Yazoo having almost nine thousand people. They read comic books, and they came to practice in the back of pick-up trucks, having worked on the farms since sun-up. They did not drink as much water as us city boys, and they were more durable in the heat. They did not like their Yazoo City teammates, thinking us soft and corrupted. They would have been in the ranks with Earl Van Dorn or N.B. Forrest in north Mississippi, or with Pemberton at Vicksburg, lean, barefoot, and hungry. They did not talk much. One of their number was a taciturn right-hander from Eden with mean eyes and the best fastball in the area. He later made Triple-A. The catcher from town would go on to star at Ole Miss, the shortstop at Mississippi State. The first-baseman's brother had just signed with the Yankees and was playing that summer with the Yankees' Class C team in Joplin, Missouri, with a fledgling shortstop he wrote his brother a postcard about which we all read, named Mantle.

Our coach was a country farmer who often complained that he was neglecting his crops. At first I thought him frivolous, with his pale eyes and his belligerent homilies, yet later I knew we would not have won without him. He quoted the Scriptures from the little concrete-block churches with impoverished graveyards far back in the woods. He had us running through the streets of Yazoo before each practice. At our field with its unpainted grandstand and precarious bleachers surrounded by row after row of young cotton, we lay down on our backs while he walked on our stomachs. Coca-Colas were infractions of the training rules. I can close my eyes now and smell the sharp, clean odor of the cotton poison deposited all around us by the cotton-duster mono-planes as I ran windsprints in the broiling sun.

The American Legionnaires who sponsored our team were mostly town people and had fought in World War I. They came to our practices and drove us to our out-of-town games. They were proud baseball men. One of them was my father, who had played semi-pro in western Tennessee and was nicknamed "Hooks" for the way he could hook-slide. He was thin and gaunt and was the bookkeeper for the wholesale grocery there in Yazoo City; he understood as much baseball as any man I ever knew. Another was Sammy Moses, who owned the tobacco and confectionery store and whose son Gerry, our batboy, would someday spend seven years in the major leagues as a catcher with the Red Sox, Angels, Indians, and Yankees. There was Joe Bush, who ran the laundry, and Jack Barrack, a farmer, and Red Hester, who sold insurance, and Herman Nolte, who owned a service station on Broadway. As World War I men they were a dwindling cadre, for the V.F.W. was more formidable with its numerous veterans of World War II: they lived, it seemed, for baseball. They are gone now from the earth, all of them.

It was a wickedly hot summer of 1950, and the swirling dust often got in my eyes from my post in centerfield and I had to carry a wet handkerchief in my pocket. We wore white uniforms with red lettering: "Roy Lammons Post 7, Yazoo City, Miss.", and the uniforms were cheap, heavy wool, which scratched and prickled the skin until the wool became soaked in sweat.

The teams we played were Rolling Fork, Greenville, Canton, Clarksdale, Belzoni, Vicksburg, Mendenhall, and Jackson. Once we journeyed to Neshoba County to play Philadelphia; I had no inkling then of the days and weeks I would someday spend there following Marcus Dupree. We always played in the afternoons, since our field and all the others were without lights. We would be a caravan of cars making our indolent odysseys out into the delta, listening to the ominous reports from Korea or to the Old Scotchman, Gordan McLendon, doing the major league games on the Liberty Broadcasting System. At one rural field, as Sammy Moses fungoed us flies before the game, I allowed a line drive to get past me. I went to retrieve the ball in deep centerfield, a formidable terrain with mounds of junk overgrown with Johnson grass. I sighted the ball near a pile of empty bottles. As I reached down to get it, two rattlesnakes — possibly man and wife — slithered toward me. I left the ball where it was.

On another day we were driving to a game in Greenville. The American Legionnaires had provided us with a most curious vehicle — an old Pontiac sedan welded to the backside of a station wagon, so that we had a makeshift omnibus with seven rows of seats. The welding on the outside resembled nothing if not scar-tissue, but this conveyance actually had a motor which worked, and was big enough to accommodate the entire team and our equipment. Our country pitcher, between his perusal of a Wonder Woman comic book, jibed me for ruining his no-hitter in a game that spring with an insipid, broken-bat single into shallow right field. Far up into the delta, our coach asked me to drive. I was negotiating the flat, straight highway at fifty miles an hour when I heard the sound of cracking metal. When I pulled over to the side of the road we discovered that our omnibus had broken in two at the point of the welding, so that the middle was hopelessly collapsed, while each end pointed upward at a slant. As our coach hitchhiked to a telephone, the team assembled in a nearby cow pasture and took batting practice. After a time the coach returned with a Negro farmer in a flatbed truck. We climbed in the back and headed for Greenville. Halfway to our destination, a delta thunderstorm descended, and by the time we reached the field the whole team was drenched, our uniforms as heavy as croker-sacks. Forgiveably, perhaps, we lost that game 8-0, one of our few losses of the summer.

We drew substantial crowds to our home games. The pretty girls with double-names came to watch, sitting cool and talcumed in the shade of the grandstand, sipping the forbidden Coca-Colas. They would sit apart from the country girls unless one of the latter's fathers owned a delta plantation. Town and country people also sat in the grandstand discussing the dubious cotton crop of that season. My father and the other Legionnaires chose the bleachers behind our bench, where they conferred on strategy and advised us in whispers between innings.

By the time of the regional playoffs, our record stood at seventeen and three, two of the losses being to Jackson. The regional finals were held in Newton, Mississippi. Two of the three other teams in the tournament were exceptionally strong. Newton, the home team, had a pitcher-shortstop named Pepper Thomas, the finest athlete in the state in that day, a white Marcus Dupree, who later would reach Triple-A with the Braves. There was the omniscient Jackson, a collection of metropolitan players accustomed to winning in every sport. The fourth team, Pelahatchie, was a feeble also-ran; we had beaten them 25-0 in an exhibition game earlier in June. We were half asleep in our dormitory the night before the first day's doubleheader when our coach entered, shouting: "We drew Pelahatchie!" In the first game, we eliminated the hapless Pelahatchians, 18-1, then got dressed in a barn that served as the fieldhouse and settled in to watch Newton and Jackson. Before the hundreds of home town followers, Jackson registered its usual victory.

Again that night, the coach came into our quarters, followed by the American

Legionnaires. "You just got a telegram," Sammy Moses said. "I'm gonna read this thing to you very slow." The telegram said: "We plan to whip you country hicks so bad tomorrow you won't ever play ball again. (signed) Jackson Legion Team." Sammy Moses read the telegram once more. "Now how does *that* make you feel?" he shouted. The country boys roused out of their beds, revenge in their eyes. Half-naked, they ran amuck. One of them kicked over a chair. Another threw his baseball glove against the wall. "We gonna *whup* their tails!" one of them yelled, but in the ensuing pandemonium, I alone noticed the Legionnaires exchanging sly winks.

The next afternoon there must have been two thousand Newtonians at the parched little field to cheer on their small-town compatriots. The whole Newton team sat behind our bench to support us in our quest. The ersatz telegram worked. In a burst of strength, we overwhelmed our opponents, 10-4, thus winning a place in the state finals the following week.

After that, the state finals seemed anti-climactic. On a warm and luminous Saturday afternoon, before an overflow crowd, we edged Greenwood, 4-3, for the championship of all of Mississippi. My father and the other Legionnaires hastened down from the stands, awash in joy, to shake hands all around, then joined us as we posed for the team photograph at home plate.

Our next stop would be the Southern finals, to be played at the LSU field in Baton Rouge, against the championship teams from Louisiana, Texas, and Arkansas. The winner would advance to the Atlantic Seaboard tournament, and the victor there to the Little World Series, and these possibilities were exhilarating. We were good, and anything could happen. There was a two-week respite before we went to Baton Rouge. The townspeople honored us with barbequed chicken suppers, where many speeches, some solicited, were made in our honor.

Yet as in most effervescent moments, there was a vexing problem, almost Biblical in nature. The games in Louisiana would be played at night. We had never played at night before. Would this make any difference? My father and Sammy Moses said it would indeed; the ball looked different under the lights, they warned. The closest lighted field was in Silver City, out in Humphreys County in the delta. This was a most distinctive ball park, where I had gone to see many semi-pro games as a boy. It had been built right on the plantation of the Reed Brothers, "Soup" and Jack; the latter of the two would later make it to the New York Yankees. The Reeds offered to let us practice on their field. We drove there late one afternoon. The stadium was enclosed on all sides by cotton. The lights were pale on this August night amidst the smells of growing things and the sonorous delta sounds. It was difficult to tell the balls from the bugs. I dropped three or four routine flies during the practice, and everyone else did too. The coach gathered us about him during a break and advised us to forget about the lights. He led us in prayer.

A crowd was there to see us off at Mr. Herman Nolte's service station. Our coach had a new suit and new shoes. Amid little clusters of barefoot children, white and black, and the pretty girls, Mayor Harry Applebaum delivered a final soliloquy about victory and adversity.

Most of us had never been out of Mississippi before, and the arcane culture of Louisiana — they even had liquor billboards along the highways — enhanced the adventure. The grand LSU campus was like a metropolis for me. We must have made an unlikely sight in those explorations around the campus, small-town and boondocks boys and wizened American Legionnaires and the coach in his squeaky new shoes, everyone a long way from home. The empty Tiger Stadium at twilight, scene of the mighty Ole Miss-LSU games we had heard on the radio, was a fulfillment of dreams, and the baseball field set next to it made my heart beat faster for the next night's drama.

That game is etched in my memory, as indelible as first love.

We had drawn the Louisiana champions, Shreveport, in the opening round. Waxahatchie, Texas, was playing Little Rock, Arkansas, in the first match of the twi-night doubleheader, and we waited the long moments in our dormitory before donning our abrasive wool uniforms and driving across the campus to Box Field. The stadium was packed with Louisiana partisans, several thousand, who cheered the Shreveport players in their trim and fancy uniforms. Shagging flies with the others in the outfield, I again had trouble tracking the ball, which approached one not like a daytime baseball, but as a half-orb.

Later, in the dugout, I gazed across the diamond where the Louisiana pitcher was warming up. He was a little southpaw, and I was absorbed by his easy, fluid motions. He had fine speed, but it was his curveball that drew my attention. Even from that distance I could tell it was fearsome. At that age a superlative curve is an entity of its own, for one does not see very many then, and confronting a great curve at sixteen is one of life's memorable junctures, almost sexual in its intensity, and there is no full expectation of it, and no one can prepare you for it, not even yourself.

"What's his name?" I asked Mr. Herman Nolte.

"Seth Morehead," he replied.

I peered across at him again. "They told me today he's the best your age in the South," he added. "But don't let that bother you. You can hit him. Always stand in against the curve."

I hoped that was to be. But when we came to the plate in the top of the first inning and our lead-off batter, Clarkie Martin, who had never once struck out in a game of baseball, went down on three pitches, I had a premonition of what we faced. Clarkie returned to the dug-out with woebegone features. "I couldn't even *see* it," he said.

This game exists for me now in a curious blur, every movement attenuated. Our all-state shortstop dropped two pop flies. Our left-fielder mishandled a casual line drive. Our catcher, the finest in Mississippi, allowed an easy pop foul behind homeplate to elude him under the unfamiliar lights. Louisiana took a swift 2-0 lead. In the second inning with no one on base, a towering fly came out in my direction. For one terrifying moment I lost it in the lights, then caught it with a desperate hand-over-heels lunge.

I batted eighth in the order and came to the plate in the third inning, carrying the Jackie Robinson Louisville Slugger my father had bought me in Jackson; it had accompanied me through the long season. I stood there in the box looking out at Seth Morehead as he gazed down at me, silent and poised. His first pitch was a slicing curve of a kind I had never seen before, so swift and deadly I could barely believe what I had just observed. "Good boy, Seth!," the big catcher shouted. "This guy's a joker." The second pitch was a hard fastball on the inside. I swung and tapped a harmless foul into the dirt. The third offering was another sharp curve which broke outside; perhaps it would be called a slider today. Whatever the name, I observed it in trepidation as the umpire called me out.

As the game progressed, we made more errors on routine plays, while our Louisiana contemporaries, who had played most of their games at night, were flawless in the field. Clarkie Martin struck out again. So did I. Yet somehow we held our own. Our heaviest country hitters, oblivious to the lights and to the drama, finally began to hit the dexterous little lefthander in the waning innings. Clarkie Martin and I both struck out a third time. Yet we trailed by only one run, 4-3, when I came up again in the top of the ninth, a runner on first and one out. This time I looked out fiercely at Seth Morehead, praying silently to the Mississippi Methodist Lord. "Please, God," I mumbled to myself, "let me hit this nighttime curve." But the first pitch was a fastball which went by me for a strike. The second was also a fastball, low and inside, kicking the dust. I dug in with determination. Seth Morehead looked down for the signal, stretched, then threw. I caught the twist of the curve several feet out, swinging mightily, hitting a sharp line drive that winged toward left field — foul by three or four feet. I had hit him! Momentarily, my adversary, unperturbed and assured as ever, was throwing again. The blistering curve came in. I swung, missing the breaker by more than a foot. "Go home and practice," the catcher snarled. Our last batter, the country pitcher, also went down ignominiously swinging. We had lost to Louisiana. The partisan crowd roared in support.

I do not know what made me do it — certainly not "sportsmanship," for I was much too crestfallen for that. Perhaps it was something deeper in the blood. But as the Louisiana players surrounded their victorious pitcher, and soon began to disperse, I found myself walking in their direction.

"Hey — Number Twelve — Seth. . . . Seth Morehead!" I shouted.

He looked up casually as he was putting on his jacket. "Yeah?"

"Well. . . ." I stumbled for the words. "You're great! You're a great pitcher."

"Hey!" he said. "Thanks. I appreciate it."

I noticed to my surprise that my teammate Clarkie Martin was right behind me.

"Hey, Morehead!" he shouted. "Number Twelve! Why don't you come live in Yazoo next summer? I don't want to hit against *you* no more."

He grinned up at us, his victims, then extended his hand to us both. "I might do that. Hey, I appreciate it. Say, good luck tomorrow."

Playing erratically again under the lights, anything but the team that had undergone the splendid Mississippi summer, we lost the next night to Waxahatchie, Texas, as if the effort against Morehead's curveball had desecrated forever our deepest aspirations. We were eliminated. In the dormitory the American Legionnaires were bleak and dejected. The coach led us again in prayer. We drove all the way home in the somber night, several sixteen-year-olds who had learned a little about loss.

Yet as the days drifted toward the autumn, it did not seem all that bad — not truly. What if we had faced that curve ball in broad daylight in the Sovereign State of Mississippi? The merchants of town took up a collection and sent us to St. Louis for three days to see the Cardinals play the Phillies, when the catcher and I would be interviewed by Harry Carey himself on the Griesedick Brothers Beer Network. Not long after that, we got our shiny blue jackets with "Miss. State Champs, 1950," emblazoned on the back. Football arrived, and basketball, and time came and went. The town boys and the country boys pitted inexorably against each other in the next high school baseball spring did not snarl as before. It was as if we were an elite comaraderie, and when our mean-eyed pitcher from the summer induced me into a tame pop fly with the bases loaded and two out in the ninth and Yazoo a run behind on their treacherous little field, he bounded off the mound and shook my hand, saying: "I'm sorry I had to do that." That August those of us still eligible were eliminated by the same Jackson team we had beaten the summer before.

I went away to college in Texas, still playing baseball in the summers on a semi-pro squad, until the day came when I was twenty-one and played my last game. I got a scholarship to England, married an American girl, and had a son there who cost 82 cents. I lost touch with the boys of our championship year, who scattered throughout the burgeoning cities of the New South. One by one the American Legionnaires died, including my father. Baseball was far away in Oxford, England. Yet even there, in that medieval town on the Thames, a grown-man and a father, too, I had a recurring dream of my grotesque adolescent efforts to hit a curve under the lights in Baton Rouge, Louisiana.

My wife and new son and I returned to our native land in the summer of 1960, on the *Isle de France* to New York. Then we drove southward, for I had a newspaper job in Texas. We stopped briefly in Mississippi, where I made a solitary nostalgic visit to our old baseball field.

One summer Saturday afternoon, only two weeks returned to America, I was lounging on the floor in my father-in-law's house in Houston, lazily watching the Major League Game of the Day on national television; Dizzy Dean and Pee Wee

Reese were calling the action. Only my six-month-old son was in the room with me, crawling about on the floor, knocking objects off tables, nibbling the cover of a *Life Magazine*. For a while I watched the game, which was between the Chicago Cubs and the Milwaukee Braves, absorbing again the satisfying old nuances of the sport I had forgotten all those years. Then I fell into a half-sleep, a mid-summer's reverie of displacement and homecoming. The words of Pee Wee Reese — something he was trying to tell me — suddenly stirred me from my lethargy.

"Now pitching for the Chicago Cubs, coming in from the bullpen . . . the fine little southpaw Seth Morehead."

I was fully awake, sitting on my haunches. There on the screen was the imperturbable figure from that long-ago night, tossing down his fast-breaking warmup curves, while Hank Aaron watched his moves from the on-deck circle.

I looked about the room for someone to talk to. The boy was crawling around the coffee table. "Hey!" I shouted at him, so emphatically that he paused for an instant. "See that lefthander? He once struck out Clarkie Martin and me four times under the lights in Baton Rouge, Louisiana!" The infant son pondered me as if I had uttered something momentous, or taken all leave of my wits. Then he resumed his peregrinations, just as Hank Aaron took a brisk curve on the inside corner for a strike.

WALKER PERCY

Introduction to
Lanterns on the Levee

I REMEMBER THE FIRST time I saw him. I was thirteen and he had come to visit my mother and me and my brothers in Athens, Georgia, where we were living with my grandmother after my father's death.

We had heard of him, of course. He was the fabled relative, the one you like to speculate about. His father was a United States senator and he had been a decorated infantry officer in World War I. Besides that, he was a poet. The fact that he was also a lawyer and a planter didn't cut much ice — after all, the South was full of lawyer-planters. But how many people did you know who were war heroes and wrote books of poetry? One had heard of Rupert Brooke and Joyce Kilmer, but they were dead.

The curious fact is that my recollection of him even now, after meeting him, after living in his house for twelve years, and now thirty years after his death, is no less fabled than my earliest imaginings. The image of him that takes form in my mind still owes more to Rupert Brooke and those photographs of young English officers killed in Flanders than to a flesh-and-blood cousin from Greenville, Mississippi.

I can only suppose that he must have been, for me at least, a personage, a presence, radiating that mysterious quality we call charm, for lack of a better word, in such high degree that what comes to mind is not that usual assemblage of features and habits which make up our memories of people but rather a quality, a temper, a set of mouth, a look through the eyes.

For his eyes were most memorable, a piercing gray-blue and strangely light in my memory, as changeable as shadows over water, capable of passing in an instant, we were soon to learn, from merriment — he told the funniest stories we'd ever heard — to a level gray gaze cold with reproof. They were beautiful and terrible eyes, eyes to be careful around. Yet now, when I try to remember them, I cannot see them otherwise than as shadowed by sadness.

What we saw at any rate that sunny morning in Georgia in 1930, and what I still vividly remember, was a strikingly handsome man, slight of build and quick as a youth. He was forty-five then, an advanced age, one would suppose, to a thirteen-year-old, and gray-haired besides, yet the abiding impression was of a youthfulness — and an exoticness. He had in fact just returned from the South Seas — this was before the jet age and I'd never heard of anybody going there but Gauguin and Captain Bligh — where he had lived on the beach at Bora Bora.

He had come to invite us to live with him in Mississippi. We did, and upon my mother's death not long after, he adopted me and my two brothers. At the time what he did did not seem remarkable. What with youth's way of taking life as it comes — how else can you take it when you have no other life to compare it with? — and what with youth's incapacity for astonishment or gratitude, it did not seem in the least extraordinary to find oneself orphaned at fifteen and adopted by a bachelor-poet-lawyer-planter and living in an all-male household visited regularly by other poets, politicans, psychiatrists, sociologists, black preachers, folk singers, itinerant harmonica players. One friend came to seek advice on a book he wanted to write and stayed a year to write it. It was, his house, a standard stopover for all manner of people who were trying to "understand the South," that perennial American avocation, and whether or not they succeeded, it was as valuable to me to try to understand them as to be understood. The observers in this case were at least as curious a phenomenon as the observed.

Now belatedly I can better assess what he did for us and I even have an inkling what he gave up to do it. For him, to whom the world was open and who felt more at home in Taormina than in Jackson — for though he loved his home country, he had to leave it often to keep loving it — and who in fact could have stayed on at Bora Bora and chucked it all like Gauguin (he told me once he was tempted), for him to have taken on three boys, age fourteen, thirteen, and nine, and raised them, amounted to giving up the freedom of bachelorhood and taking on the burden of parenthood without the consolations of marriage. Gauguin chucked it all, quit, cut out and went to the islands for the sake of art and became a great painter if not a great human being. Will Percy not only did not chuck anything; he shouldered somebody else's burden. Fortunately for us, he did not subscribe to Faulkner's precept that a good poem is worth any number of old ladies — for if grandmothers are dispensable, why not second cousins? I don't say we did him in (he would laugh at that), but he didn't write much poetry afterwards and he died young. At any rate, whatever he lost or gained in the transaction, I know what I gained: a vocation and in a real sense a second self, that is, the work and the self which, for better or worse, would not otherwise have been open to me.

For to have lived in Will Percy's house, with "Uncle Will" as we called him, as a raw youth from age fourteen to twenty-six, a youth whose only talent was a knack for looking and listening, for tuning in and soaking up, was nothing less than to be informed in the deepest sense of the word. What was to be listened to, dwelled on, pondered over for the next thirty years was of course the man himself, the unique human being, and when I say unique I mean it in its most literal sense: he was one of a kind: I never met anyone remotely like him. It was to encounter a complete, articulated view of the world as tragic as it was noble. It was to be introduced to Shakespeare, to Keats, to Brahms, to Beethoven — and unsuccessfully, it turned out, to Wagner whom I never liked, though I was dragged every year to hear Flagstadt sing Isolde — as one seldom if ever meets them in school.

"Now listen to this part," he would say as Gluck's *Orfeo* played — the old 78s not merely dropped from a stack by the monstrous Capehart, as big as a sideboard, but then picked up and turned over by an astounding hooplike arm — and you'd make the altogether unexpected discovery that music, of all things, can convey the deepest and most unnameable human feelings and give great pleasure in doing so.

Or: "Read this," and I'd read or, better still, he'd read aloud, say, Viola's speech to Olivia in *Twelfth Night:*

> Make me a willow cabin at your gate,
> And call upon my soul within the house;
> . . . .
> And make the babbling gossip of the air
> Cry out "Olivia!"

You see? he'd as good as say, and what I'd begin to see, catch on to, was the great happy reach and play of the poet at the top of his form.

For most of us, the communication of beauty takes two, the teacher and the hearer, the pointer and the looker. The rare soul, the Wolfe or Faulkner, can assault the entire body of literature single-handedly. I couldn't or wouldn't. I had a great teacher. The teacher points and says *Look;* the response is *Yes, I see.*

But he was more than a teacher. What he was to me was a fixed point in a confusing world. This is not to say I always took him for my true north and set my course accordingly. I did not. Indeed my final assessment of *Lanterns on the Levee* must register reservations as well as admiration. The views on race relations, for example, diverge from my own and have not been helpful, having, in my experience, played into the hands of those whose own interest in these matters is deeply suspect. But even when I did not follow him, it was usually in *relation* to him, whether with him or against him, that I defined myself and my own direction. Perhaps he would not have had it differently. Surely it is the highest tribute to the best people we know to use them as best we can, to become, not their disciples, but ourselves.

It is the good fortune of those who did not know him that his singular charm, the unique flavor of the man, transmits with high fidelity in *Lanterns on the*

Levee. His gift for communicating, communicating himself, an enthusiasm, a sense of beauty, moral outrage, carries over faithfully to the cold printed page, although for those who did not know him the words cannot evoke — or can they? — the mannerisms, the quirk of mouth, the shadowed look, the quick Gallic shrug, the inspired flight of eyebrows at an absurdity, the cold Anglo-Saxon gaze. (For he was this protean: one time I was reading *Ivanhoe*, the part about the fight between Richard and Saladin, and knowing Richard was one of Uncle Will's heroes, I identified one with the other. But wait: wasn't he actually more like Saladin, not the sir-knight defender of the Christian West but rather the subtle easterner, noble in his own right? I didn't ask him, but if I had, he'd have probably shrugged: both, neither . . .)

There is not much doubt about the literary quality of *Lanterns on the Levee*, which delivers to the reader not only a noble and tragic view of life but the man himself. But other, nonliterary questions might be raised here. How, for example, do the diagnostic and prophetic dimensions of the book hold up after thirty years? Here, I think, hindsight must be used with the utmost circumspection. On the one hand, it is surely justifiable to test the prophetic moments of a book against history itself; on the other hand, it is hardly proper to judge a man's views of the issues of his day by the ideological fashions of another age. Perhaps in this connection it would not be presumptuous to venture a modest hope. It is that *Lanterns on the Levee* will survive both its friends and its enemies, that is, certain more clamorous varieties of each.

One is all too familiar with both.

The first, the passionate advocate: the lady, not necessarily Southern, who comes bearing down at full charge, waving *Lanterns on the Levee* like a battle flag. "He is right! The Old South was right!" What she means all too often, it turns out, is not that she prefers agrarian values to technological but that she is enraged at having to pay her cook more than ten dollars a week; that she prefers, not merely segregation to integration, but slavery to either.

The second, the liberal enemy: the ideologue, white or black, who polishes off *Lanterns on the Levee* with the standard epithets: racists, white supremacist, reactionary, paternalist, Bourbon, etc., etc. (they always remind me of the old Stalinist imprecations: facist, cosmopolitan, imperialist running dog).

Lanterns on the Levee deserves better and of course has better readers. Its author can be defended against the more extreme reader, but I wonder if it is worth the effort. Abraham Lincoln was a segregationist. What of it? Will Percy was regarded in the Mississippi of his day as a flaming liberal and nigger-lover and reviled by the sheriff's office for his charges of police brutality. What of that? Nothing much is proved except that current categories and names, liberal and conservative, are weary past all thinking of it. Ideological words have a way of wearing thin and then, having lost their meanings, being used like switchblades against the enemy of the moment. Take the worlds *paternalism, noblesse oblige,* dirty words these days. But is it a bad thing for a man to believe that his position in society entails a certain responsibility toward others? Or is it a bad thing for a man to care like a father for his servants, spend himself on the poor, the sick, the miserable, the mad who comes his way? It is surely better than watching a neighbor get murdered and closing the blinds to keep from "getting involved." It might even beat welfare.

Rather than measure *Lanterns on the Levee* against one or another ideological yardstick, it might be more useful to test the major themes of the book against the spectacular events of the thirty years since its publication. Certainly the overall pessimism of *Lanterns on the Levee*, its gloomy assessment of the spiritual health of Western civilization, is hard to fault these days. It seems especially prescient when one considers that the book was mostly written in the between-wars age of optimism when Americans still believed that the right kind of war would set things right once and for all. If its author were alive today, would he consider his forebodings borne out? Or has the decline accelerated even past his imaginings? Would he see glimmerings of hope? Something of all three, no doubt, but mainly, I think, he'd look grim, unsurprised, and glad enough to have made his exit.

Certainly nothing would surprise him about the collapse of the old moralities, for example, the so-called sexual revolution which he would more likely define in less polite language as alley-cat morality. I can hear him now: "Fornicating like white trash is one thing, but leave it to this age to call it the new morality." Nor would he be shocked by the cynicism and corruption, the stealing, lying, rascality ascendant in business and politics — though even he might be dismayed by the complacency with which they are received: "There have always been crooks, but we've not generally made a practice of re-electing them, let alone inviting them to dinner." All this to say nothing of the collapse of civil order and the new jungle law which rules the American city.

Nothing new here then for him: if the horrors of the Nazi holocaust would have dismayed him and the moral bankruptcy of the postwar world saddened him, they would have done so only by sheer dimension. He had already adumbrated the Götterdämmerung of Western values.

But can the matter be disposed of simply: decline and fall predicted, decline and fall taking place? While granting the prescience of much of *Lantern on the Levee*'s pessimism, we must, I think, guard against a certain seductiveness which always attends the heralding of apocalypse, and we must not overlook some far less dramatic but perhaps equally significant counterforces. Yes, Will Percy's indictment of modern life has seemed to be confirmed by the holocaust of the 1940s and by American political and social morality in the 1970s. But what would he make of some very homely, yet surely unprecedented social gains which have come to pass during these same terrible times? To give the plainest examples: that for the first time in history a poor boy, black or white, has a chance to get an education, become what he wants to become, doctor, lawyer, even read *Lanterns on the Levee* and write poetry of his own, and that not a few young men, black and white, have done just that? Also: that for the first time in history a working man earns a living wage and can support his family in dignity. How do these solid social gains square with pronouncements of decline and fall? I ask the questions and, not knowing the answer, can only wonder how Will Percy would see it now. As collapse? Or as contest? For it appears that what is upon us is not a twilight of the gods but a very real race between the powers of light and darkness, that time is short and the issue very much in doubt. So I'd love to ask him, as I used to ask him after the seven o'clock news (Ed Murrow: *This* — is London): "Well? What do you think?"

The one change that would astonish him, I think, is the spectacular emergence of the South from its traditional role of loser and scapegoat. If anyone had told him in 1940 that in thirty years the "North" (i.e., New York, Detroit, California) would be in the deepest kind of trouble with race, violence, and social decay while the South had become, by contrast, relatively hopeful and even prosperous, he would not have believed it. This is not to say that he would find himself at home in the new Dallas or Atlanta. But much of *Lanterns on the Levee* — for example, the chapter on sharecropping — was written from the ancient posture of Southern apologetics. If his defense of sharecropping against the old enemy, the "Northern liberal," seems quaint now, it is not because there was not something to be said for sharecropping — there was a good deal to be said — and it is not because he wasn't naive about the tender regard of the plantation manager for the helpless sharecropper — he was naive, even about his own managers. It is rather because the entire issue and its disputants have simply been bypassed by history. The massive social and technological upheavals in the interval have left the old quarrel academic and changed the odds in the new one. It is hard, for example, to imagine a serious Southern writer nowadays firing off his heaviest ammunition at "Northern liberals." Not the least irony of recent history is that the "Northern liberal" has been beleaguered and the "Southern planter" rescued by the same forces. The latter has been dispensed by technology from the ancient problem, sharecroppers replaced by Farmall and Allis-Chalmers, while the former has fallen out with his old wards, the blacks. The displaced sharecroppers moved to the Northern cities and the liberals moved out. The South in a peculiar sense, a sense Will Percy would not necessarily have approved (though he could hardly have repressed a certain satisfaction), may have won after all.

So Will Percy's strong feelings about the shift of power from the virtuous few would hardly be diminished today, but he might recast his villains and redress the battle lines. Old-style demagogue, for example, might give way to new-style image manipulator and smooth amoral churchgoing huckster. When he spoke of the "bottom rail on top," he had in mind roughly the same folks as Faulkner's Snopeses, a lower-class, itchy-palmed breed who had dispossessed the gentry who had in turn been the true friends of the old-style "good" Negro. The upshot: an unholy hegemony of peckerwood politicans, a white hoi polloi keeping them in office, and a new breed of unmannerly Negroes misbehaving in the streets. But if he — or Faulkner for that matter — were alive today, he would find the battleground confused. He would find most members of his own "class" not exactly embattled in a heroic Götterdämmerung, not exactly fighting the good fight as he called it, but having simply left, taken off for the exurbs where, barricaded in patrolled subdivisions and country clubs and private academies, they worry about their kids and drugs. Who can blame them, but is this the "good life" Will Percy spoke of? And when some of these good folk keep *Lanterns on the Levee* on the bed table, its author, were he alive today, might be a little uneasy. For meanwhile, doing the dirty work of the Republic in the towns and cities of the South, in the schools, the school boards, the city councils, the factories, the restaurants, the stores, are to be found, of all people, the sons and daughters of the poor whites of the 1930s and some of those same uppity Negroes who went to school and ran for office, and who together are not doing so badly and in some cases very well indeed.

So it is not unreasonable to suppose that Will Percy might well revise his view of the South and the personae of his drama, particularly in favor of the lower-class whites for whom he had so little use. In this connection I cannot help but think of another book about the South, W.J. Cash's *The Mind of the South*, published oddly enough the same year by the same publisher as *Lanterns on the Levee*. Cash's book links Southern aristocrat and poor white much closer than the former ordinarily would have it. Both books are classics in their own right, yet they couldn't be more different; their separate validities surely testify to the diversity and complexity of this mysterious region. Yet in this case, I would suppose that Will Percy would today find himself closer to Cash in sorting out his heroes and villains, that far from setting aristocrat against poor white and both against the new Negro, he might well choose his present-day heroes — and villains — from the ranks of all three. He'd surely have as little use for black lawlessness as for white copping out. I may be wrong but I can't see him happy as the patron saint of Hilton Head or Paradise Estates-around-the-Country Club.

For it should be noted, finally, that despite conventional assessments of *Lanterns on the Levee* as an expression of the "aristocratic" point of view of the Old South, Will Percy had no more use than Cash for genealogical games, the old Southern itch for coats of arms and tracing back connections to the English squirearchy. Indeed if I know anything at all about Will Percy, I judge that in so far as there might be a connection between him and the Northumberland Percys, they, not he, would have to claim kin. He made fun of his ancestor Don Carlos, and if he claimed Harry Hotspur, it was a kinship of spirit. His own aristocracy was a meritocracy of character, talent, performance, courage, and quality of life.

It is just that, a person and a life, which comes across in *Lanterns on the Levee*.

And about him I will say no more than that he was the most extraordinary man I have ever known and that I owe him a debt which cannot be paid.

THEODORE ROSENGARTEN

from

All God's Dangers: The Life of Nate Shaw

ONE DAY I TOLD my wife, "Darlin, I'm goin to Apafalya to get me a load of cotton seed hulls for my cows and some meal."

She said, "Darlin, you goin to town, I want you to get Rachel and Calvin some shoes" — they was the two oldest.

Told her, "All right. I'll do that."

She didn't know what number they wore but here's what she done: she went and took the measure of their foots and told me to get em shoes just a little longer than the measure from the heel to the toe. Well, I was fully determined to do it — and that was some of my first trouble.

I drove in Apafalya, hitched my mules, and walked into Mr. Sadler's store to get some shoes for the children first thing; then I was goin to drive on down to the carbox at the depot and load me a load of hulls and meal. Had my cotton bodies on my wagon —

I went on into Mr. Sadler's store and there was a big crowd in there. The store was full of white people and two or three colored people to my knowin. And there was a crippled fellow in there by the name of Henry Chase — Mr. Sadler had him hired for a clerk, and several more, maybe three or four more clerks was in there and some was women clerks. I walked in the store and a white lady come up to me and asked me, "Can I wait on you?"

I told her, "Yes, ma'am, I wants a couple of pair of shoes for my children."

And she took the measures and went on to the west side of the store and I went on around there behind her. She got a ladder, set it up, and she clumb that ladder and me standin off below her. There was a openin between the counters — and I was standin down there, just out of the way of the little swing-door and she was searchin from the front of that store nearly down to where I was.

And this Chase fellow, he was kind of a rough fellow and it was known — a heap of his people there in town didn't like him. So she was busy huntin my shoes and she'd climb that ladder and take down shoes, measurin em, and she'd set em back up if they wouldn't do, didn't come up to that straw measure. And she was just rattlin around there, up the ladder and down it, and this here Chase fellow was standin off watchin. After a while he come around there, showin his hatred, showin what he was made of, that's all it was. And there was a old broke down — it had been cut in two at the bottom — a old, tough brogan shoe sittin there on the counter, a sample, you know. And he walked through there by me to get behind that counter where she was. I was standin on the outside waitin on her patiently, weren't saying nothin. And he didn't like that white lady waitin on me, that just set him afire — I knowed it was that; I'd never had no dealins with him, no trouble with him noway — and he remarked, "You been in here the longest —" right in my face.

I said, "No sir, I haven't been in here but just a little while."

The white lady spoke up too; said, "No, he hasn't been here very long. I'm trying to find him some shoes."

He said, "You been in here the longest, you too hard to suit."

I said, "No sir, all I'm tryin to do is buy me some shoes to match the measure for my children's foots."

She said, "No, he hasn't been here but a short while."

Good God, when she said that he grabbed that old shoe up — he didn't like her to speak up for me — grabbed that shoe up and hit at my head with it. I blocked his lick off. Well, when I blocked his lick off — he'd a hit me side the head with that old shoe, or on the face; no doubt he woulda cut me up — he throwed that shoe down. He seed he couldn't hit me with it, I was goin to block him off. He dropped that shoe back down on the counter and out from between there he come and run down to the low end of the store. And Mr. Sadler kept shovels, hoes, plow tools, and every kind of thing down there, on the low end, back end of the store. Chase runned down there and picked him up one of these long-handled shovels and he whirled around and come back — he just showed that he was goin to split me down with that shovel. He come back — he begin to get close to me and I sort of turned myself to him one-sided.

I said, "Don't you hit me with that shovel" — told him to his head, didn't bite my tongue — "don't you hit me with that shovel."

He wouldn't say nothin. Just stood there and looked at me, wouldn't move up on me. Kept that shovel drawed, lookin at me, lookin at me, lookin at me. I just dared him to hit me with that shovel — I never told him what I'd do and what I wouldn't. Well, he stood there and let into cussin. He disregarded that white lady, just stood there with that shovel on him, cussin me, lookin like all he wanted was a chance. I'd a turned my head and he'd a hit me, looked like from the way he acted.

All right. We got up a loud talk and all the people in the store noticed it. After a while, a fellow by the name of Howard Crabtree — old Dr. Crabtree was a horse doctor and this was his son — runned up there and started his big mouth. And this cripple man Chase tellin me all the time, "Get out of here, you black bastard. Get out of here." Trying to run me out the store and I hadn't done a thing to him.

And this Crabtree, he runned up, "Naw, he aint goin to him you, but goddamnit, get out of here like he tells you."

I said, "Both of you make me get out. Both of you make me get out."

Couldn't move me. The white lady had done disbanded and got away from there. I stood my ground when this here Howard Crabtree runned up and taken Chase's part. I said, "I aint gettin nowhere. Both of you make me get out."

Chase runned back and put the shovel where he got it from and down the aisle on the far side of the store he went. And there was a ring of guns there, breech-loaders. I kept my eyes on him, watchin him. I weren't goin nowhere. The white lady went on back to huntin my shoes after Chase left from there — he come out from the back of the store and went on down to where that ring of guns was, sittin right in the front as you go in the door. And he grabbed up one of them single barrel breech-loaders — that's when a white man befriended me and several more done so until I left town. There was a white gentleman clerkin in there, Mr. Tom Sherman — I seed this here Henry Chase grab that gun and break it down, run his hand in his pocket and take out a shell and put it in there. Totin shells in his pocket so if anything happened that he needed to shoot somebody — picked up a gun and broke it down and unbreeched it and run his hand in his pocket, pulled out a shell and stuck it in there, then breeched it back up and commenced a lookin for a clear openin to shoot at me. I just considered it for a bluff — he weren't goin to shoot me there in that man's store, surely. And I watched him close, he jumpin around lookin, first one way then the other, holdin that gun in his hands, lookin. And Mr. Tom Sherman just quit his business when he seed Chase drop a shell in that gun, walked right on up to him and snatched the gun away. Chase didn't resist Mr. Sherman — that was a heavy-built man. Mr. Sherman took that gun out of his hands, unbreeched it, took that shell out of it, set the gun back in the ring and stood there by that ring of guns. Out the store Chase went.

Well, by that time, the white lady done got my shoes. I turned around and paid her for em. She wrapped em nice and I took the shoes and went on out the back door — it was handy; I come in the back door and I went back out it. I didn't go down the front. Chase'd gone out of there and I didn't want no trouble with him.

So, out the back door I went and I turned to the left and walked on out in the middle of the street, goin to my wagon. And when I got out to where I could see clear, Aunt Betsey Culver, Uncle Jim Culver's second wife, was sittin in the street on a buggy. Uncle Jim was over there by Sadler's store, he seed all that happened there. I walked up to the buggy and howdyed with my auntie — didn't talk about that trouble neither. I just set my shoes in the foot of the buggy and was standin there talkin with her. And after a while I happened to look down the street and here come that cripple Chase fellow — he was a young fellow too, and he walked in kind of a hoppin way, one leg drawed back — and the police was with him, old man Bob Leech, settle-aged white man. They was lookin for me and they come up to me quick. Chase pointed at me and said, "That's him, standin right yonder; that's him, standin there at that buggy."

Old man Leech walked up to me, looked at me, looked me over. And by me standin kind of sideways at Chase in the store, he done went and told the police that I acted just like I had a pistol in my pocket. Well, he never did see my hand. I had on a big heavy overcoat that day, just what the weather called for. So, he pointed me out to the police; police walked on up to me but wouldn't come right up to me, not very close.

He said, "Consider yourself under arrest."

I looked at him, said, "Consider myself under arrest for what?"

"Uh, consider yourself under arrest."

I asked him again, "Consider myself under arrest for what?"

"That's all right; that's all right."

Come up to me and patted me, feelin for a gun. I said, "You want to search me" —. I just grabbed that big overcoat and throwed it back — "search me, search me, just as much as you please. Search me."

He got up close enough to run his hands around me, feelin my hip pockets. He didn't find no gun. I had no gun, I didn't tote no gun around thataway. He said — he talked kind of through his nose, funny. And I called him in question about every word he spoke to me. He said, "Well, c'mon go with me."

I said, "Go with you where?"

"Gowanup-t-th-maya-uvtawn."

I couldn't understand him.

"Gowanup-t-th-maya-uvtawn."

I said, "To the mayor of town?"

He talkin thataway and I couldn't hardly understand him, talkin through his nostrils, looked like. I understood him but I just kept him cross-talked. Well, I started not to go — my mind told me, 'Go ahead with him, don't buck him.'

He carried me on down the street and hit the left hand side of town goin in — left my shoes in my uncle's buggy. And I went on. Got down there and went up the stairs — the stairsteps come down to the walkway. The mayor of town was upstairs. And by golly, when I got up there, who was the mayor of town? Doctor Collins! Dr. Collins knowed me well, been knowin me a long time. Walked on into his office and old man Leech, the police, spoke to him. And before he could say anything, Dr. Collins seed who was with him. He said, "Why, hello. What you doin with Shaw up here?"

"Well, him and Henry Chase got into it down there in Sadler's store."

Dr. Collins said, "Um-hmm." Dr. Collins was a pretty heavybuilt man himself.

He said, "Well, Mr. Leech, where is Chase?"

"He down there in town somewhere, in the streets."

"Um-hmm."

"And they got into it in Sadler's store."

"Mr. Leech, go down there and get Chase and bring him up here."

The old police went down and got Chase, brought him up there. He come up hip-hoppin, hip-hoppin — that's the way he walked, doin just thataway every step he took. Chase said, when he got up there, "Hi, Doc."

Dr. Collins said, "Howdy, Henry."

I was standin there listenin. He said, "Henry, did you and this darky —" he wouldn't say nigger neither; that was a white man, and there was some more of em in this country wouldn't call you nigger. Dr. Collins said, "Henry, did you and this darky get into it down there in Sadler's store?"

He said, "Yeah." But wouldn't tell nary a thing he done, uncalled for. "He was down there in Sadler's store —" wouldn't tell what I was waitin on or nothin, just told what he wanted Dr. Collins to know — "was down there in Sadler's store and we got into it" — wouldn't tell him what we got into it about — "and I told him to get out of there and he gived me a whole lot of impudent jaw."

Dr. Collins said, "Um-hmm. Who seed that beside you, Henry?"

"Well, Howard Crabtree seed it."

And the whole store seed it but none of em weren't busyin theirselves with it. Mr. Tom Sherman seed it and he went and took that gun away from him. Dr. Collins said, "Um-hmm. Well, go down, Mr. Leech, and get Howard Crabtree and bring him up here."

Chase said, "And he kept his hand behind him like he had a gun in his hip pocket."

Crabtree walked up with his big-talkin self. Dr. Collins said, "Crabtree, did you see this darky and Henry Chase get into it down there in Sadler's store?"

"I did. I did. I seed it every bit."

"Well, Crabtree, would you —"

"He had his hand behind him —" told the same lie Chase told — "had his hand behind him and he kept a tellin Chase not to hit him, better not hit him, and givin up a lot of other impudent jaw."

Dr. Collins said, "Um-hmm. Crabtree, would you swear that he had his hand in his hip pocket?"

"No, no" — he jumped back then — "no, I wouldn't swear he had his hand in his hip pocket, but he looked like he had it in there. I don't know where his hand was, he had on that big overcoat."

"Um-hmm," Dr. Collins said, "Um-hmm."

Dr. Collins knowed me well. Never gived nobody no trouble, tended to my business, let other folks alone, I didn't meddle in things. And at that time I had a good name, right there in Apafalya, I'd been there since I was a little boy up till I was grown and after.

Dr. Collins said, "Well, the little old case don't amount to nothin. I'm just goin to throw it out."

After Crabtree told him he wouldn't swear I had my hand in my hip pocket, Dr. Collins asked me, "Shaw, did you have a pistol?"

I said, "No, Doctor, I aint seed a pistol in I don't know when. I had no pistol."

Chase allowed to him, "He went out the back way; he coulda carried it out there and stashed it."

Well, good devil, just as sure as my Savior's at his restin place today, I didn't have no pistol, never thought about no pistol.

All right. They whirled and left from up there when Dr. Collins said he was just goin to throw the little case out. And when they started out, I started out right behind em. Dr. Collins throwed his finger at me — "Shaw, this way; Shaw, Shaw."

I was lookin back at him and I stopped. He said, "Just be yourself and stay up here a few minutes; that'll give em time to get away from down there, clear em out, then you can go."

I just made myself at home, stood there. After a while, Dr. Collins said, "Well, you can go ahead now. Mess don't amount to nothin nohow, that's the reason I throwed it out."

When I got down the stairsteps onto the walkway, there was Mr. Harry Black, man I had done my guano dealin with, and there was a fellow went around there in Apafalya, heap of folks called him Tersh Hog — that was Mr. Bob Soule, went for a cousin to Cliff Soule. He lived out about a mile from Apafalya and he didn't take no backwater off nobody. If a thing weren't right, he were goin to fix it right. Some of em didn't like him because they had to pass around him, white folks. And I seed him walk the streets right there in Apafalya with his pistol in his — just like a law, only he'd carry his pistol in his coat pocket, and that handle was hangin out over the pocket. Didn't nobody give Mr. Bob Soule no trouble in Apafalya and nowheres else he went. So, Mr. Bob Soule was standin there at them steps when I come down, and Mr. Harry Black and Mr. Ed Hardy — I knowed them definitely and there was a couple more of em, bout five altogether standin there when I come down. They said, "Hello, Nate. Hello, Nate."

I stopped and spoke to em polite and they was polite to me. Well, Uncle Jim Culver had done stood there too at the bottom of the steps while this trial business was goin on and he heard them white men speak this: "If that nigger comes down from up there with any charges against him, we goin to paint this damn place red."

I didn't know — I didn't hear em say it. Uncle Jim told me, "They was standin there for a purpose. I done stood here and listened at em. Said, 'If that nigger comes down from up there with any charges against him, we goin to paint this damn place red.'"

All of em knowed me well: I'd traded with Mr. Harry Black and Mr. Ed Hardy and they had passed confidence with me. And Mr. Bob Soule, he loved justice. When I walked down amongst em, all of em, I knowed em, looked in their faces, standin huddled there where the stairway hit the walkway. They was satisfied. They left there when I left.

Uncle Jim added his advice: "Things are hot here, son. Now you go on up the street and get your mules and wagon and turn around and go on back home."

I said to myself, 'The devil will happen before I do that.'

And he said, "Don't come back, don't come back through town. Go on home. Take your mules and go on home now."

I went on up there and pulled my mules back and hitched the traces and untied em from the post they was hitched to — both of em hitched to the same post and them inside traces dropped — set up on my wagon and went just as straight, just as dead straight right back down through Apafalya as I could go. Uncle Jim was standin there and he told some fellow. "There that boy goin right back through town and I told him to get his mules and wagon and go on back home."

But I was game as a peacock. I just went straight to his buggy and got my shoes out and carried em to my wagon, hitched my mules back, crawled up in the wagon over them high bodies, right down dead through town I went. And when I got down close to where the railroad runned under that bridge there in Apafalya I turned to my left and went on down to the depot. Loaded my hulls and meal — and when I left, I had a straight way right out from there up the back streets of town toward home.

One day after that, Uncle Jim got at me bout goin back down through town. I told him, "I aint no rabbit, Uncle Jim. When a man's mistreated thataway and he got friends and they proves it, he don't need to be scared. Of course, it's a dangerous situation and if I'd a been guilty of anything, why, I'd a took low."

There was a old colored fellow down at the door at Sadler's store the whole time this ruckus was goin on inside. Mighta been inside himself at the start but he runned out if he was; he acted like he runned out. And he stood where he could see me. And do you know he just stood there and beckoned to me that whole time, he beckoned to me to run out. That just roused the whole store up. The old man tickled me. He was a pretty heavy-built old man and he weren't as high — his head, he could have walked under a tall horse and never touched it. Heavy-built old colored man. And he had on one of these old frock-tail coats and it hit him just below the knee and it was cut back like a bug's wings. And he just stood there and bowed and beckoned for me to run out there. And every time he'd bow, that old coat would fly up behind him and when he straightened up it would hit him right back there below the bend in his legs. Tickled me, it tickled me. I thought it was the funniest thing I ever saw. He was scared for me and wanted me to run out of there. I didn't run nowhere. I stood just like I'm standin today — when I know I'm right and I aint harmin nobody and nothing else. I'll give you trouble if you try to move me.

LOUIS D. RUBIN, JR.

The Boll Weevil, The Iron Horse, and the End of the Line: Thoughts on the South

I. *The Boll Weevil*

On hot afternoons in the summertime — this was in the middle-to-late 1930s — I sat in the bleachers at College Park in Charleston and when the baseball game was not too interesting I watched for the Boll Weevil at the Seaboard Air Line railway station. It was called the Boll Weevil because when the little gas-electric locomotive-coach was placed in service in the early 1920s the black folk of the South Carolina sea islands through which the little train passed fancied its resemblance to the bug that had moved northward and then eastward from Mexico to devastate the cotton crops.

The little Seaboard gas-electric coach, of course, devastated no cotton crops. As a railroad train the Boll Weevil wasn't much. There were two of them in actuality, a northbound and a southbound train, operating each day between Savannah, Georgia, and Hamlet, North Carolina, the latter being a railroad junction point a few miles beyond the border between the two Carolinas. The trackage they traversed was not the Seaboard's main line, which was the New York-Florida route that crossed through South Carolina well to the interior. Rather, the railroad's low-country branch constituted a large bow in the line, a two-hundred-mile-long loop that dropped southward from the main line junction at Hamlet down toward the seacoast, then southwestward to Charleston and to Savannah not quite a hundred miles farther, where it rejoined the main line. It served the truck farming and — until the coming of the little black bug — the cotton industry along the coast, and transported passengers, mostly black, who wished to travel between the little way stations, towns, and flag stops and Charleston or Savannah, the only two communities of any size along the route.

The northbound Boll Weevil came through Charleston from Savannah shortly before midday. Its southbound counterpart from Hamlet customarily arrived about three o'clock in the afternoon. It was the latter that I watched for. At some point during the weekend doubleheader Municipal League baseball games it would make its appearance, clattering across Rutledge Avenue and rolling to a halt at the little stucco railroad station at Grove Street just beyond the left-field limits. No ceremony attended its advent. Perhaps there would be a taxicab or two, but usually only a railroad baggageman and a handful of outward-bound passengers were there to greet it.

The Boll Weevil's route lay closer to the coast than the Coast Line's. Until the 1900s the only way to travel between Charleston and the numerous coastal islands had been by slow boat; shallow-draft launches with steam and later make-and-break gasoline engines had traversed the creeks, estuaries, bays, and rivers with passengers and cargoes from the islands, made their way to the city, and tied up at Adger's Wharf. But now most of the sea islands were linked to the mainland by bridges, and the remoteness of the low country, which had lasted from colonial times, was coming to an end.

The Boll Weevil, however unprepossessing in appearance, thus represented a phase in the process whereby the several centuries of comparative isolation that had characterized the life of the Carolina seacoast were giving way to the mobility of modern industrial America. No longer were goods dependent upon water transport, or upon horse and mule drayage along rutted, sandy roads, to get into the hinterlands. And if there was no job for a black farmhand in the low country — no need, for example, to pick cotton any more, thanks to the little black bug from Mexico — the train was there to take him to the city.

So the sleepy little Boll Weevil gas-electric train that waited around for such an interminably long time at the stucco station up at College Park, just beyond left field, and which I would watch on summer afternoons during the 1930s, was in its own way emblematic of something perhaps every bit as disruptive, as devastating, as the insect that had moved up from Mexico in the 1910s to eradicate the cotton crop. What it represented and embodied was *change*.

Throughout the South there were many trains like the little Boll Weevil. In Eudora Welty's beautiful novel *Delta Wedding,* a little train named the Yellow Dog — in actuality the Yazoo and Delta — brings cousin Laura McRaven from the city of Jackson to the cotton lands of the Mississippi Delta — a mixed train, "four cars, freight, white, colored, and caboose, its smoke like a poodle tail curled overhead." Into the flat plantation country of the Delta it transported travelers from Jackson and from the world beyond, and though it seemed so diminutive and harmless, with its friendly engineer Mr. Dolittle who occasionally halted the train en route so that the conductor could gather goldenrod, it was not harmless but instead powerful and inexorable, as Miss Welty suggested, and what it brought and signified was ultimately irresistible; time and change, the world outside the confines of the plantation.

Nowadays there is no more Yellow Dog, and no more Boll Weevil. Even when I sat in the bleachers at the baseball games in the 1930s and watched the little train arrive at the Seaboard station, it was already outmoded, for the trains had been an earlier phase of the change. By the 1930s automobiles, buses, and trucks were the principal means of conveyance between the city and the islands. The dirt roads were being widened and paved. There were highway bridges connecting most of the sea islands with the mainland. Few places in the low country were really remote any more. All over the South this was taking place — had, indeed, already taken place by the middle 1930s.

The old isolation was ended, and the towns and cities were expanding into the open countryside. When I had first begun attending the games at College Park I had walked home through fields, leaving the built-up area along Grove Street to cut through a mile of open land, crossed a marsh creek over a little wooden bridge, then walked through a grove of trees to our house on a bluff overlooking the Ashley River. But by the late 1930s the entire area was rapidly being built up, and where for two hundred years there had been planted fields and marshland were now frame houses and multiple-occupancy dwellings. For there was a growing need for new housing in Charleston, occasioned by the influx of new people into the city to work at the Navy Yard, the steel mill, and other industrial installations to the north of the city limits. True, those city limits were still where they had been located at the time of the Civil War, along Mount Pleasant Street, a block north of our house. But now there was a sprawling and largely unlovely industrial community stretching out for ten miles and more to the northward.

One day I was waiting for a bus — the trolley cars were gone by then — at the corner of King and Wentworth streets downtown. When it pulled up to the curb there were already so many riders aboard that there was no room for anyone else. It was the going-home hour and another bus would be along shortly, I knew, so I prepared to wait. A woman who was standing near me was not willing to wait, however. She went up to the closed doors of the bus and began rapping on the glass panels in a vain attempt to gain admittance. "I want in!" she called. "I want in!"

She could not be a native Charlestonian, I knew, because she would never have said it that way if she were. She would have called, "I want to come in!" or "I want to get in!" No doubt she and her family had come from Ohio or somewhere else in the Midwest to work at the Navy Yard. Many people were moving to Charleston, from the Upstate, the other southern states, and the Midwest and North as well, for there were imminent signs of another war, and a tremendous defense industry was getting into high gear. There were many more buses in service, but also more waiting, because the area north of the city was becoming so thickly populated that the South Carolina Power Company simply could not purchase new buses rapidly enough to accommodate the demand.

Meanwhile the Boll Weevil kept to its rounds. I would catch sight of it from time to time while riding downtown or coming home on the bus. Sometimes I wished I might go for a trip aboard the little train. I wanted to board it at the station on Grove Street and make the journey with it up the coast and then inland, all the way to its northern terminus at Hamlet, North Carolina. I could then transfer to a main line Seaboard train such as the streamliner, the Silver Meteor, and continue on to Richmond, where my aunts, uncles, and cousins lived. But of course that was not the way to travel from Charleston to Richmond. To go there one drove up to North Charleston and boarded one of the Atlantic Coast Line trains.

By then the Second World War had come. My family moved from Charleston to Richmond, where my mother had come from, and soon after that I was in the Army. I was stationed first in Alabama and then in Connecticut, and most of my fellow soldiers were from the North and Midwest. Some were quick to point out to me, when I attempted to describe what I so liked about life back home, that many of the more pleasant qualities of that life were possible because of the availability of a disadvantaged labor force to do the unpleasant work and thus permit the famous "gracious living" enjoyed by the white folks. But if that were true — and I began to see that in certain crucial respects it was all too true — I could not feel that it was a sufficient explanation for what I felt about life in my part of the country.

Later I was sent to Fort Benning, and for almost two years I lived near the city of Columbus, Georgia. Here was a community of less than 50,000 which almost overnight was the civilian adjunct of an army camp of 120,000 troops! Housing, transportation, business, entertainment, recreation facilities were inconceivably overcrowded and inadequate. From my occasional visits to Columbus I could understand why it was that when sometimes I encountered a fellow soldier who had been stationed at or near Charleston, his attitude toward my own home city as a place to visit was usually so very hostile. Of course the city he had found so unpleasant and inhospitable was not the real Charleston, as I always hastened to explain, but a place that within a matter of several years had suddenly been forced to accommodate itself to the presence of three times its own population, ringed as it was with military installations. The chances were that on his visits to the city he had encountered very few actual Charlestonians; most of those storekeepers, taxi drivers, USO workers, shop girls and other civilians he had met were recent arrivals.

I doubt that the question ever occurred to me whether, when the war was done, my native city could or would go back to being what it had been just a few years ago. Yet had it not been changing even when I was living there? "I want in!" the woman at the bus stop had declared in her midwestern accent and idiom. Was the city I remembered, with the fishing boats and the White Stack tugboats tied up at Adger's Wharf, the little train waiting at the station just past the ball park, the barber shop which like my father I always patronized (with its familiar clientele and its barbers who conducted themselves so professionally and yet so accommodatingly), Broad Street with its lawyers, bankers, realtors, insurance men, the local "establishment" as it were, where my aunt was a secretary and where there were so many persons I knew and who knew me and my family — was this place, which I knew so well and liked so much, both for its virtues and its vices (and both were numerous), not the real, unchanging Charleston? And after the war was won would I not go back there to live, as I was sure I wanted to do?

Several times when I visited my relatives in Charleston during the war while on leave from Fort Benning, I had seen the little Boll Weevil in its familiar setting up by the station at College Park. But there was one occasion when I caught sight of the little train in a very different context. It was when I was on furlough to Richmond, where my parents were living. The train to Richmond, which I boarded at Atlanta, stopped at Hamlet, North Carolina, sometime after midnight to change crews and engines, and I made my way out of the crowded coach, which was filled with sleeping travelers, and stepped down onto the platform to look around. It was cold. The station was a large, old-fashioned wooden affair, with tracks on both sides. I walked back along the platform, past the station and toward the rear of the train, and gazed out into the winter night at the town's main thoroughfare. Except for the lights in the lobby of a railroad hotel, all was dark. After a minute I strolled back toward the station, and on the way I happened to glance down a section of track along a side street that crossed the main line, whereupon I spied a familiar silhouette. It was the Boll Weevil, waiting overnight for the next day's run down to Charleston and through the low country to Savannah.

Unlit and unnoticed, on a siding, not far from a station which even though the hour was well past midnight was crowded with servicemen, civilians, railroad crewmen, porters, passengers on the main line passenger train from Atlanta paused there en route northward, the little Boll Weevil seemed out of place, far from its proper element. To come upon it here, waiting mutely and, as it seemed, forlornly on a side track, was a shock. It belonged to sunny afternoons and the stucco station at College Park.

I went back to my coach, made my way to my seat, and waited for my journey to resume.

When the war was done and the troops came home, the South did not go back to being what it had been. Cities such as Charleston did not shrink back to prewar size; with only minor interruptions they proceeded to develop peacetime industries and enterprises to replace the war installations, and not only retained their prosperity and population but kept right on expanding in size and importance. The small cities of the South became large cities, the towns became smaller cities, the countryside, joined to the cities by networks of highways, lost what still remained of its remoteness and isolation. The traditional patterns of southern agriculture were being diversified. Cotton was king no more. Sharecropping and tenant farming no longer characterized much of the land-use arrangements. The rural population, in particular the blacks, moved to the cities as never before, and there was also a steady outmigration of blacks and whites to the big industrial cities of the North. The tractor, the mechanical cotton picker, the mechanized tobacco harvester displaced the mule and the field hand. There was money available in the South now. The postwar boom was on, but on a much more solid foundation than in the years just after the First World War.

As for myself, I did not go back to Charleston to live after all. There was no job for me there, for I was now a newspaperman and the Charleston newspapers had no place for me, nor, after I had left journalism for graduate study and teaching, was there a teaching position at home until long after I was at the stage in the profession that would make it impossible for me to go back. I realized a little later that even if I had been able to return home to live, the chances are that I should not have remained there for long. Charleston had changed in many ways, and my loyalty and attachment were really not so much to a place as to a time — to the years when I had been a child and an adolescent growing up in a small southern city. And Charleston was not that any more: this was borne in on me whenever I went back to visit. The familiar, medium-sized southern community that I had known was now only the center of a vast, sprawling metropolitan area of suburbs, subdivisions, manufacturing plants, shopping centers. Once I went outside the downtown area I hardly knew my way around. What had been fields, woods, marshland, open country now were urban areas. Many of the people I knew best, in particular most of those with whom I had attended high school and college and in whose company I had passed most of my time, were gone; like myself they had not come back home after the war.

As for the little Boll Weevil train, it had long since gone. I found this out rather vividly in the early 1950s. Returning to Charleston for a visit I decided that just for the fun of it I would not ride the Coast Line train but instead take the Seaboard down to Hamlet, spend the night in the railroad hotel near the station, and the next day get on board the Boll Weevil and ride down through the low country to Charleston. I checked the timetables; the little train was still listed as operating. So I rode down to Hamlet, stopped overnight in the railroad hotel, and the next morning went over to the passenger station to purchase my ticket. Instead of the familiar little gas-electric combine, I found a train made up of a diesel locomotive, a baggage car, and several air-conditioned coaches.

As the train rolled along down the single track line into South Carolina the conductor told me that the Boll Weevils had been removed from service several months ago. Nor was he regretful of their passing; the gas-electric combination coaches had always given much trouble, he said, and were constantly breaking down and falling behind schedule, so that he and his fellow trainmen had been happy to see them go. So I rode from Hamlet to Charleston in an air-conditioned coach. When the train arrived at the stucco station at College Park I got off and walked over to Rutledge Avenue to take the bus downtown. I thought to myself that even if the Boll Weevil was gone, at least I had finally made the trip.

It was none too soon, for within a few years all passenger service on the Hamlet-Charleston-Savannah branch was discontinued. And in the 1960s when the Seaboard and Atlantic Coast Line railroads were merged, even freight traffic along the tracks that led by the ball park and over the trestle at the foot of Grove Street was ended. The old wooden bridge across the Ashley River was torn down. No longer would young Charlestonians lie in bed at night as I had once done and hear the night freight train from the south whistling far off in the darkness, and then gradually draw near the bridge, until as the wheels rolled onto the timbered structure the iron flanges set up a deep, singing reverberation on the rails, which grew hoarser as the train crossed over the river and entered the city.

No, the train was gone for good, as indeed were steam locomotives, the Boll Weevil, Adger's Wharf down on the waterfront with the shrimp boats and tugboats and little cargo launches with their make-and-break engines, and many another artifact of youth and young manhood. And each separate visit, over the years, seemed to broaden the loss. The barber shop down on King Street, where once there had been eight barbers, all of whom I knew by name and who knew me, was now down to one elderly man, tending shop by himself. The comfortable old Fort Sumter Hotel on the Battery was converted into condominium apartments. The hulk of the ferryboat *Sappho*, moored throughout my youth in the tidal flats just beyond Gadsden Street, had long since disappeared under a landfill. The old Southern Railway roundhouse on Columbus Street, where on Sunday mornings my father used to take us to see the trains, was gone, and a supermarket occupied its former place. East Bay Street, where the wholesale houses had been located in antebellum buildings, had lost its hegemony to more accessible places in the built-up northern area; there was little but empty store fronts and a few conversions into apartments. Missing in particular was a red wagon wheel which had always hung suspended from a bracket above the entrance to one hardware dealer. My father had installed it in 1913, when he had been a youth working there.

Gone, too, along with the places and the emblems were those Charlestonians of my father's generation who had once lived among these things and made them substantial and significant. For almost all of those men and women, my elders, the adult citizens of the city when I was a child, and whose lives and positions and concerns and opinions had seemed so important and so formidable, were dead now, while the few who still survived and whom I sometimes encountered here and there were frail and old, human relics as it seemed, more like tourists such as myself than inhabitants, now that their onetime peers and companions, the social context in which they had fitted, were gone. They appeared oddly diminished and shrunken in stature, caricatures of their former selves. So that on each successive visit to what had once been my home, I found that what had constituted its substance and accidence both had dwindled. To the extent that the places, objects, people, and associations of my childhood — a southern childhood, in and of a southern city — had constituted whatever there was of reality and permanence to my younger experience, then that reality was becoming more and more a matter of absence, loss, and alienation. I was, that is, steadily being dispossessed.

2. *Will Barrett's Iron Horse*

The experience recounted thus far, however intensely felt by myself, is in no sense unique. It differs from similar experience for others only in the particular details in which it has been presented. Insofar as it is appropriate to most persons who, like myself, have grown away from a community that has been very much caught up in social transition and widespread change, it is valid for numerous modern southerners. Moreover, though its meaning lies, I think, at the center of the southern literary experience of our time, in the form that I have reported it so far it is inert, useless: merely a species of nostalgia. As presented, it presupposes a kind of absolute cultural, social, and historical order, designed and believed to exist permanently, and then interprets all subsequent changes within that order, all alteration in the complex substance of its embodiment, as a diminution of reality, an erosion of what should by rights have been immutable: in short, as disorder, loss, chaos.

But while such a way of viewing one's experience is perhaps unavoidable as a starting point, it is also partial, superficial, and really a distortion of reality rather than an evocation of it. And if that were all there was to the southern literary imagination as it views the past, there would be little point in paying much heed to it. For the truth is that, as I have suggested earlier on, just as there was at no time an absolute, unchanging, permanent form to the life of the Carolina low country, but instead at all times change and alteration, so my own memories of places, people, institutions, and artifacts of my own childhood and young manhood are composed not of fixity and diuturnity but of elements that were very much caught up in change, however they may have once seemed immutable to me.

I had thought of the little Boll Weevil train as fixed and determined in its arrivals and departures at the Seaboard station. But the railroad crew that operated it reported that it had constantly broken down and been behind schedule, and what it meant for the agricultural life of the low country had been mobility, change, the coming of the city to the sea islands and the movement of the black folk to the city. When during the war I had caught sight of the Boll Weevil late one winter night in North Carolina, and had felt so powerfully that it belonged not there on the unfamiliar siding but to summer afternoons at the stucco station in Charleston, I had been facile. It was not the little train, but myself, who was in what seemed to be the wrong place and wrong season. And what made the present time and place seem unsatisfactory was that I was attributing a greater emotional importance, a more self-sufficient identity and a freedom from contingency, to the earlier experience. Whereas the truth was that only *because* of the later experience — because I *saw* the little train in Hamlet that night — was the earlier experience made to seem so important, so intense, to seem, in short, so very *real*. In actuality the authenticity of the experience, and its importance for me, lay neither in the isolated memory of the little train at College Park as such, which was an act of mere nostalgia, nor in my reencounter with the train at Hamlet, which because of its seeming inappropriateness was so pathetic. Rather, the authenticity and importance resided in the relation of the one to the other — in the profound vividness of the experience of time and change, a vividness that I myself, through my participation, was able to bring to it. And it has been just such vividness, but magnified and enriched many times through artistic genius, that has constituted the achievement of the best of the modern southern writers.

There comes immediately to mind a scene from a brilliant novel by Walker Percy, *The Last Gentleman,* in which precisely this kind of perception is delineated, and which I now propose to discuss at some length. The novel, which like much of Percy's fiction contains strong autobiographical elements, involves the hegira of one Williston Bibb Barrett from Mississippi to New York City and then back southward and later westward in search of a way to unite action and conviction, and much of the motivation for Barrett's journey is ascribable to the collapse and futility, as he sees it, of the old southern stoic attitude of aristocratic fortitude he had been taught to believe in, a collapse exemplified by his own father's suicide.

Like more than one young man in southern literature, Will Barrett has the expectation of a proper and assured role for himself, but cannot identify the possibility of any such role existing in his own changed circumstance, even while he remains unwilling and unable to accept the kind of moral and social wasteland in which no such assurance is available. Like the speaker in Allen Tate's beautiful "Ode to the Confederate Dead," he stands at the cemetery gate, as it were, grieves at the inescapability of the fact that he cannot believe in the validity of the communal pieties, yet also cannot settle for an existence in which no such pieties are possible. "What shall we say who have knowledge / Carried to the heart?" Tate's protagonist asks. "Shall we take the act / To the grave?" In Will Barrett's instance he manages to stop, en route westward, outside his old home in Mississippi one night and look on from the darkness of the oak trees while his aunts sit out on the porch in traditional southern style — watching a give-away quiz show on television!

He remembers the night when his father, a lawyer (and much resembling Percy's cousin, William Alexander Percy), had walked up and down the street beneath the oak trees as usual, awaiting the outcome of a public battle he has led against a lower-class faction that seems to resemble the Ku Klux Klan of the 1920s. His son sat on the steps, tending the old-fashioned 78-rpm drop-record phonograph, on which a Brahms symphony was being played in the darkness. By and by the police come to tell the father that his fight has been won, the riffraff have broken up their meeting and left town. Instead of rejoicing in his victory, however, the father tells his son that its price has been the destruction of any pretense to superior moral and ethical standards on the part of his own class of onetime ladies and gentlemen. The illusion of aristocratic virtue and rectitude having been shattered, the father has only his private isolated sensibility to fall back upon. "In the last analysis, you are alone," he tells his son, and walks off again. *"Don't leave,"* his son begs. But the father goes into the house, climbs the stairs up to the attic, places the muzzle end of a shotgun against his breast, and pulls the trigger.

Now an older Will Barrett stands among the oaks remembering the sound of the shot, and meanwhile hearing the television commercial that his aunts are watching. He reaches out in the darkness and his hand encounters an iron hitching post, molded in the form of a horse's head, about the base of which an oak tree has grown until now it entirely surrounds it. He touches the tree bark:

> *Wait*. While his fingers explored the juncture of iron and bark, his eyes narrowed as if he caught a glimmer of light on the cold iron skull. *Wait*. I think he was wrong and that he was looking in the wrong place. No, not he but the times. The times were wrong and one looked in the wrong place. It wasn't even his fault because that was the way he was and the way the times were, and there was no other place a man could look. It was the worst of times, a time of fake beauty and fake victory. *Wait*. He had missed it! It was not in the Brahms that one looked and not in solitariness and not in the old sad poetry but — he wrung out his ear — but here, under your nose, here in the very curiousness and drollness and extraness of the iron and the bark that — he shook his head — that —

This is a marvelous passage. What Will Barrett wishes he could tell his dead father is that those public values and truths upon which his life and conduct had been predicated, and which had finally seemed to have so eroded that he had killed himself, were false, or at best only partial and ancillary. *Wait,* he keeps telling his father in his imaginary expostulation, in repetition of that traumatic moment in the past when he had vainly begged his father not to leave. The triumph over the riffraff, the great horn theme of Brahms, he insists, were false victory and false loveliness because the ideals they were being made to embody were illusory, a species of ideality removed from the world, as it were. His father had felt that his struggle with the red-necks (corresponding, one should note, to Walker Percy's grandfather's victory over the Klan in the 1920s, as described by

Will Percy in *Lanterns On the Levee*) was the assertion of absolute integrity in a graceless modern world. In being achieved it had revealed to his father his own isolation, since it had forced him to see that those who were on his side in the dispute, and who supposedly represented the lofty morality that he believed in, were in no way absolutely superior in ethics and morality to those they had defeated. He tells his son that the lower orders had once been "the fornicators and the bribers and the takers of bribes and we were not and that was why they hated us. Now we are like them."

But what Will Barrett knows, out of his own subsequent experience and observation, is that there never was any such generation of earlier heroes who were exempt from human stain and contingency, so that his father's ideal of aristocratic virtue, however nobly motivated, was actually a romantic escape from the compromised actuality of human life in time. Such a view necessarily presupposed a former time in which men were better and wiser, more disinterested and virtuous than humans could ever be, as well as a society that had been more nearly free from all temptations to covetousness, avarice, lust, and cruelty than had ever existed on earth.

Thus any change in circumstances and conduct would have to constitute a falling away from perfection, and to the extent that the change continued in time, the arrival of crass days, a moral and social wasteland, the death of the gods. So his father's belief that a mere political victory would reaffirm the antique virtues and insure their permanence was doomed to disappointment once his father realized that the golden age had not thereby been re-created. What his father had done was to attempt to insulate himself from time, change, and mortality by retreating into a private code of aristocratic virtue and honor, truth and beauty that gave him the illusion of human perfectibility, and when this was shattered by being tested in the actual world, there seemed nothing left for him but to be destroyed with it.

In the same way, the notion that the great horn theme of Brahms, to which the father had been listening on the night of his suicide, enunciated an ideal of absolute and timeless beauty was also ultimately self-contradictory. For as Will Barrett sensed, "The mellowness of Brahms had gone overripe, the victorious serenity of the Great Horn Theme was false, oh fake fake." Percy is alluding, I think, to a characteristic of Brahms' symphonic music that I have also noticed. Brahms builds up to huge, slow-moving thematic statements that seem to assert a kind of hard-won triumph of spirit, and which in their massive harmonics pronounce an ultimate resolution superior to merely human difficulties and leaving no further occasion for striving or disruption. Thus when the last notes of the symphony die out, one has a sense not of triumph but of sadness, for since so supernal a resolution cannot be continued indefinitely but must come to an end, one feels, as it were, alone and abandoned in a jaded world. The quality that Will Barrett identifies and deplores in Brahms seems to be a sort of victorious exhaustion, an elimination of all further possibility of growth or extension, that corresponds mightily to the *fin de siècle* romanticism of Swinburne, Dowson, the *Rubaiyat,* "The City of Dreadful Night," and, be it noted, of the poetry of William Alexander Percy himself. Thus, in having Will Barrett declare that his father had looked for beauty in the wrong place, what Walker Percy means, I think, is that music that asserts as an ideal a quality of perfection that seems to rule out all further human involvement can only become hollow and intolerable.

The place to look for beauty and for truth, rather, is "here, right under your nose, here in the very curiousness and drollness and extraness of the iron and the bark." For the iron horse's head of the hitching post, though ornamental, was cast for use by men, while the oak that has grown around it has drawn it into time and change rather than abstracted it from all future contingency, and in the union of the two is the miracle of growth and fusion, producing a quality of excess and uniqueness that goes beyond the merely usable or fortuitously natural, even while deriving its strength and beauty from time and change.

Such an achievement cannot ever involve a static perfection. The iron hitching post was given its form by men, to serve a purpose and yet to be ornamental as well, and though that purpose is outmoded, the very element that has outmoded it — change — has given it its marvelous new possibility: of being as one with the oak tree.

All this, it seems to me, is implicit in that remarkable passage from *The Last Gentleman. Wait!* Will Barrett begs his father. *Don't leave!* For the boy needed his father, but the father's way of seeing himself and his duty did not, finally, encompass any obligation to or need for a future so fallen from perfection as to seem meaningless. The father could not see that the presence of the boy there with him in the dark, tending the phonograph as he walked back and forth beneath the trees, was itself a refutation of his premise that *"in the last analysis,* you are alone" (italics mine) — for human virtue and meaning were not to be found solely within oneself, as measured against an autonomous, static ideal of timeless perfection, but instead were human qualities growing out of continuing existence in time, never perfect, never complete and self-sufficient in themselves, but always in vital relationship with ongoing experience.

The great horn theme seemed to separate itself from all regeneration, assert an ideal of pure, abstract beauty that mocked mere human striving. Similarly, the worship of the past as an age of super-human heroes made the present into a time of certain decline and fall, and the future into something meaningless. Instead of the past being allowed to illuminate and strengthen the authenticity of the present, it is made to destroy it. For the presence of the boy there on the steps, overseeing the drop-record phonograph and watching his father, is what the past has created; and the boy's need of his father — *don't leave!* — validates the genuineness of the past, because it provides a means for the best qualities of that past to continue to have meaning in time. And it is *that* kind of continuity, and not the blind preservation of what had once been human existence in time as static, changeless icon, untouched by the hurly-burly of continued experience, that keeps the past meaningful and makes its exemplars truly heroic. Otherwise that past, which Will Barrett's father saw as the sole repository of virtue, is rendered empty and abstract — as futile as the world-weary, life-denying "victory" of the great horn theme, a beauty so removed and isolated from human need and desire as to produce emptiness and despair.

Looking out from under the shadow of the oaks, Will Barrett does not blame his father for having left him. On the contrary, he is filled with love and pity for his father, for he knows that his father, like himself, was caught in a situation not of his own making, and was unable to extricate himself from it. Indeed, it might even be said that it was *because* his father had taken his life, in despair over what he considered the impossibility of being able to stay with him, that he was now able to recognize the murderous falseness and inadequacy of the ideal of the solitary man. The sound of that shotgun blast in the night, the hopelessness that had caused his father to pull the trigger of the twelve-gauge Greener, was what had sent him on his own search, which however prolonged and agonizing represented the only way that he might ever learn to break through the walls of solitude that might otherwise have imprisoned him as well.

What he learns, finally, is that solitary integrity is not enough for a man, that one cannot live merely in private measurement against a personal ideal. There can be no *I* without a *Thou*. The plea, "Wait. Don't leave!" is the recognition of human need, and the heeding of the plea is the acknowledgment not only that one is needed by another, but that acceptance of another's need is *in itself an assertion of need*. It is there, in ongoing involvement with what is outside of one's own otherwise solitary self, that one's identity in time can be affirmed: not through a strong-willed transcending of life but *in* and *through* life, immanently: the iron horse encircled by the living cortex of the great oak, the two elements become extraordinary in their marvelous need-in-separateness: unique and mysterious in their configuration — the handiwork of God.

The difference, as I see it, between my experience with the Boll Weevil and that given by Walker Percy to Williston Bibb Barrett in *The Last Gentleman* is that in effect the novel commences where I was willing to leave off. What I had done was to see the past — the little Seaboard gas-electric coach in its place at the station in Charleston — as something absolute and completely self-contained, in and of itself. And God said, Let there be Light, one might say; and He created the Boll Weevil. Because the train was there for me to see, it became part of my experience, and it belonged there at the ball park. But since, being human, I existed in time, I grew away from the experience it symbolized, and because its vivid, emblematic quality was important to me, I could only interpret any change in my relationship to it, any distancing of its image in time, as a falling away from perfection. Each subsequent stage in my relationship to it — seeing it at night on the siding, far from its familiar context; finding the diesel locomotive in its place when I went to board it at Hamlet; and finally, seeing the tracks along which it ran and the trestle over which it crossed the river torn up and removed — constituted a diminution of its reality to me. For I had associated the little train, to repeat, with a time and place that had seemed very real and permanent to me. The memory of the train was nostalgic, in that it revived the memory of the time and place, as a kind of golden age before the Fall; but since it was no more than that, I had to confront the fact that it was gone forever, with nothing in my present experience seemingly able to replace it in its vividness and solidity.

In the same way, Will Barrett's father in *The Last Gentleman*, confronting the fact that the old times, the old standards of aristocratic probity, were gone, and not even the temporary victory over the rabble can restore them, saw no further hope, no standard of moral conduct that could adequately replace what had been lost.

But not so his son, who out of his grief and loss at his father's death is made to see the limitations of such a way of viewing oneself and one's place in time in the inevitable hopelessness of his father's plight. Through an act of the resolute will his father had managed for a period of time to convince himself that the old times were not gone; but the evidence of his eyes and senses finally shattered the illusion. Will Barrett will make no such attempt, because he cannot; his father's suicide made it impossible for him to be satisfied with any repetition of his father's way. What he comes to see, therefore, after a long and painful search, is that no man may impose his heart's-desire view of reality upon the world without isolating himself from that world. Human reality in time, and his relationship to it, must be found in one's continuing engagement with the world, an engagement that because it takes place in human time must accept and incorporate change as well as continuity. Acceptance of that relationship involves an acceptance of one's need for what is outside oneself, and the obligation to seek to be oneself *in* that exterior world. A difficult task, truly, requiring as it does neither abject surrender nor prideful disdain, but ongoing engagement.

3. *End of the Line*

And what has that to do with the present and future South, whether Walker Percy's or mine or anyone else's? Simply (yet with what complication!) that we live in a region upon which history has enforced so pervasive a heritage of order and form and community, so powerful a set of loyalties and expectations, that we cannot sidestep the extraordinary strength of our identification with it. So decisive is that sense of identification, even today, that to an important degree it determines our personality. When I say, "I am a southerner," or "I am from Charleston," I am, no matter how I may disguise it, uttering an expression of pride in identity. It matters not that Walker Percy's experience of the South and his role within it may be in certain respects very different from mine or someone else's (his grandfather owned plantations in the Delta and served in the Senate of the United States, while mine owned a little grocery store down by the railroad tracks in Florence, South Carolina, and spoke in a German Jewish accent); the similarities are far more important than the differences, and that fact of itself might help to explain *why* the region could and still can exert so strong an influence upon its inhabitants and command so much of their loyalties. For genuine human communities, as contrasted with mere economic and social combinations, are hard to come by in this world, and that is what the South has been.

But the temptations and dangers involved in such an identification are perilous, too. It is too easy, and too tempting, to surrender one's own individual personality to it, to construct an absolute moral and ethical entity out of a relationship which, because it is human and in time, cannot ever afford absolute certainty to one. That way lies idolatry. This is what Allen Tate meant when he wrote to his friend Donald Davidson in 1942 that "you have always seemed to me to hold to a kind of mystical secularism, which has made you impatient and angry at the lack of results. We live in a bad age in which we cannot give our best; but no age is good." Donald Davidson, like Will Barrett's father, sought valiantly to fuse his own identity with the community he loved in its time and place, and when, as was inevitable, that community, being made up of humans, changed, he saw the change as a fall from perfection, and thus as a betrayal, and he spent his energies in a vain attempt to arrest the change and deny its manifestations. Increasingly the South that he loved became a heart's-desire land which bore less and less relationship to the actual Tennessee community he lived in, until his life became almost totally a rear guard action against any accommodation with change, and in which each engagement was fought as if it were Armageddon, or perhaps Gettysburg. Entered into with the noblest of motives, waged with unremitting courage and high personal honor, Donald Davidson's battle ultimately deprived him of all contact with the real world that poetry must inhabit if it is to take its images and meanings from life.

It is temptingly easy to forget what Stark Young warned his fellow Nashville Agrarians about when he declared in his contribution to the Agrarian symposium *I'll Take My Stand* that "we must remember that we are concerned first with a quality itself, not as our own but as found anywhere; and that we defend certain qualities not because they belong to the South, but because the South belongs to them." But it is also rather too easy to pursue the opposite course: to give in utterly and uncritically to change, to attempt to abdicate any responsibility for determining one's own moral and ethical relationship to it. For one's identity lies not in the change as such, but in what is undergoing change, and though we cannot arrest change, neither can we yield ourselves over to it entirely and still hope to retain any worthwhile integrity or identity in time. We are, in human terms at least, the product of our past, and our task is always therefore to adapt what we are to the inevitability of change, so as to secure and strengthen what we are and can be: to seek to control and shape change so as to help it become part of *us*. In that transaction lies human identity in time, and it would be foolish indeed for us not to attempt to preserve such hard-won virtues and accomplishments as we possess. For we have no way of knowing that adequate and acceptable replacements will be available if we give them up uncritically in exchange for the unknown.

The South has been with us for some time now, and there seems to be little reason not to assume that it will continue to be the South for many years to come. It has changed a great deal — it is always changing, and in recent decades the change has been especially dramatic. But there is little conclusive evidence that it is changing into something that is less markedly southern than in the past. After all, why should it? Does anyone, for example, seriously believe that the liberation of an entire segment of its population, its black folk, into full participation in the region's political and economic life will make the region *less* distinctively southern in its ways? Is not the reverse more likely? Does it seem plausible that, merely because they now live and work in towns and cities rather than in rural areas, the bulk of the southern population both white and black will abruptly cease to hold and to share most of the values, attitudes, concerns, and opinions that have hitherto characterized their lives?

Is the South becoming the "no-South"? Does the southern community cease to exist once it becomes urban and industrial? Not if we are to place any stock in what the sociological and political indices report, or what Walker Percy and other novelists and poets tell us. To think of change simply as destruction of the South's distinctiveness is misleading. Instead of concentrating our attention solely upon what industrialization, urbanization, racial integration, and so forth are going to do to the South, we might consider what so powerful and complex a community as our South is going to do to and with them. For the South has long had a habit of incorporating seemingly disruptive change within itself, and continuing to be the South. The historian George Tindall wryly records the long chronology of supposed demises of the "Old South." Each juncture in the region's history — the Civil War, the end of slavery, Reconstruction, the New South movement of the 1880s and 1890s, the Populist revolt, the impact of the First World War, the boosterism and business expansion of the 1920s, the Great Depression, the New Deal, the downfall of King Cotton and the rise of a more diversified agriculture, the break-up of the one-party system and the Solid South, *Brown v. Board of Education* and the end of legal segregation, the sweeping industrialization and urbanization of the 1960s and 1970s, the newfound prosperity of the so-called Sun Belt, the election of Jimmy Carter as President with strong backing from black southerners — has been proclaimed as signalizing the end of the line, so far as the preservation of regional identity and distinctiveness are concerned. Yet an identifiable and visible South remains, and its inhabitants continue to face the same underlying human problems as before, however much the particular issues may change.

At the conclusion of *The Last Gentleman,* Will Barrett, having lived in New York and journeyed to Santa Fe, will presumably go back to Birmingham, Alabama. He will not return to Things As They Were; but then, things are never as they once were. Those who proclaim Walker Percy's fiction as existential, thereby symbolizing the passing of the South and the conclusion of the twentieth-century southern literary mode as such, miss the point, it seems to me. The details of the southern heritage are deeply embodied in Percy's imagination, and in taking on the continuing human problems of self-definition, belief, good and evil, man's place in society from the perspective of a changed set of social and historical circumstances, Percy is doing what every major southern author before him has done. For at no time was there ever a static, changeless society known as the South, inhabited by fully realized, timeless human exemplars known as southerners, for whom there was no problem of self-definition in changing times. The evidence of southern literature, it seems to me — of which Percy is the latest practitioner — is that in every time and place men have faced the task of reconciling individual and private virtue with an inescapable need for fulfillment within a community of men and women, and there is always the requirement to redefine the ethical and moral assumptions of one's rearing and one's present social circumstance amid change. In *The Last Gentleman* Will Barrett has no doubt, really, that he wants to live a "normal" life; his consuming problem is the discovery of a way whereby he can believe in the virtue and value of such a life, rather than merely viewing his role in it as a kind of game plan, a calculated, abstract exercise of the will in which he imposes a private meaning upon what is outside and around him entirely in terms of its usefulness for himself. What he realizes, finally, is his absolute need for what goes on and is involved in that life — for what is ultimately outside of and unknown to him. Only with this acknowledgment of absolute dependence can he go back to his girl and his job and his life in Birmingham.

Now it seems to me that far from representing an end to the so-called traditional southern literary mode, *The Last Gentleman* is a redefinition of it, one that is necessary if it is to continue to have any significance. It represents, on its author's part, a reassessment of certain fundamental human truths, involving community, order, mutability, and belief, in a changed social circumstance. Without such a reassessment, whereby ethical and moral assumptions are translated into a usable idiom, the assumptions would soon become empty and meaningless. And as Will Barrett well recognizes, any such redefinition can be only partial and inexact, for the human beings who hold to the assumptions and seek to act upon them are finite men and women.

Once more, and for the last time, the Boll Weevil: for its demise, the merger of the Seaboard and Coast Line railroads, the discontinuance of all railroading along the trackage that led by the baseball field in Charleston, the removal of the old wooden trestle across the Ashley River, were not after all the end of my imaginative involvement with the little gas-electric coach that plays so inordinately emblematic a role in my memory of the past. There was a summer day, only several years ago, when I was driving from Charleston back to my home in North Carolina. The route led through the town of Hamlet, and since it was getting on toward midday when I neared there, I decided that I would leave the marked route, drive over to where the railway passenger station had been located, have a look around, and then find a place to eat lunch.

It has been twenty-five years since the day I had ridden down from Richmond, spent the night at the railroad hotel, and then gone to board the Boll Weevil, only to find it replaced by a diesel locomotive and air-conditioned coaches. Now I found the station itself, looking much as it had in the past, except that save for one small area reserved for Amtrak passengers, it was all boarded up. I went over to look at the train announcement board. There were only two passenger trains a day each way listed upon it. Not only had the branch line service to Charleston been long since discontinued, along with other such branches, but with the takeover of all passenger service by Amtrak, the onetime Seaboard service to Atlanta and Birmingham had been eliminated. Now the only passenger trains were New York-to-Florida runs.

The station platform was empty. I remembered it as it had been during the war, when the station had been filled with travelers, the lunch room crowded, porters busy with baggage carts along the ramps, railroad workers checking the condition of the wheels and braking equipment on the strings of coaches, switch engines shunting coaches, pullmans, baggage and mail cars back and forth to make up consists for the northbound, southbound, westbound, and eastbound runs. The life of the town of Hamlet, I thought, had once centered upon the activities at this station. Now it was deserted, boarded up.

I found the place where one night during the war I had spied the little Boll Weevil waiting alone in the darkness, far away from where in my mind's eye I felt it ought to be. Now there was only an empty stretch of siding next to an old brick warehouse, with the weeds grown high about the crossties and the rails rusty from long disuse.

I wondered whether the old wooden railroad hotel was still functioning. I walked a block southward. It was still there and, surprisingly, still doing business. No doubt its clientele of trainmen still found it useful for overnight stays between freight runs.

The restaurant was open, so I went in and sat down at a booth to order lunch. The room was crowded, and as I waited for my meal to be served, I looked around at my fellow customers. To judge from their age and appearance, most were not railroad workers but employees in the stores and offices along the main street nearby. What caught my eye, however, were four young women installed in a booth diagonally across from where I sat, eating lunch together while several youths stood nearby bantering with them. Three of the girls were white. One was black.

Twenty-five years ago, if I had been here at lunch time, such a sight would have been inconceivable. As they talked away, eating, chattering, making jokes, laughing, giggling, I thought of how much political rhetoric, how much scheming and planning and denouncing and defying and editorializing and drawing up of legal briefs and passing laws and the like had been expended in my part of the country in the vain effort to prevent those four girls from eating lunch together in that restaurant. How many dire predictions of social catastrophe, how many lamentations over the imminent destruction of the Southern Way of Life, the violation of all that was sacred and noble, had come thundering forth on all sides!

Yet here they were now, eating lunch together, and here was this restaurant in a southeastern North Carolina town on a summer day, with the clientele laughing and talking and eating, and the waitresses serving up the hamburgers and salads and cokes and coffee and iced tea and pie, and the floor fans droning away, and except for the presence of the black girl there and several other black customers at other tables, whom I now saw, nothing seemed importantly different from what I might have seen there had I stopped in for lunch on that day when I rode the successor to the Boll Weevil down to Charleston, or for that matter, from what I would have seen if a decade before that I had been able to board the train at the station near the ball park as I had dreamed of doing, and made the trip all the way up to Hamlet.

How remarkable it was, to have been part of all that had happened since then! For indeed I had been part of it; nor was it yet concluded. Here was I, at the place where a third of a century earlier I had known that the train was bound for, and had wanted to go there with it. Only now there was no more train. Those same years that had contained the stress and struggle and strife which had ultimately made it possible for those four girls, three white and one black, to go out for lunch together after three centuries of law and tradition to the contrary, had also witnessed the decline and the demise of the little passenger train that I had once so admired and loved. Yet could I honestly say, if in effect the end of a place for the Boll Weevil in the scheme of things had been, symbolically, the price that had to be paid in order for me to see those four girls eating lunch together in this restaurant, that the cost had been too high?

So that I could not and must not think of the memory of the little train as something unique and unqualified, frozen in time and inviolate, and of which all subsequent encounters and experiences were a species of decline and fall. For both I and the train had been part of a complex fabric of social experience, having moral and ethical validity, whose form had been the shape of time. It had been *real*, it had *existed,* and for me the little train was process: identity *in* time, not outside it. Its diminution did not represent merely loss, but change, of which I was a part, and which, because it had happened to me in my time, was mine to cherish. And it was not ghostly and subjective, with no further existence except as I could remember it, but substantial and in the world, authentic *because* it was part of time and change, emblematic of my own involvement in that world, and proof that I had been and still was alive. It was *in* time that it was able to be what it was for me, *in* its contingency: droll in its extraordinary extraness — the oak tree growing around the iron horse's head. And if I wanted to understand who I was, what my country was and why, it was there that I must learn to look.

JEAN TOOMER

Blood-Burning Moon

1

UP FROM THE SKELETON stone walls, up from the rotting floor boards and the solid hand-hewn beams of oak of the pre-war cotton factory, dusk came. Up from the dusk the full moon came. Glowing like a fired pine-knot, it illumined the great door and soft showered the Negro shanties aligned along the single street of factory town. The full moon in the great door was an omen. Negro women improvised songs against its spell.

Louisa sang as she came over the crest of the hill from the white folks' kitchen. Her skin was the color of oak leaves on young trees in fall. Her breasts, firm and up-pointed like ripe acorns. And her singing had the low murmur of winds in fig trees. Bob Stone, younger son of the people she worked for, loved her. By the way the world reckons things, he had won her. By measure of that warm glow which came into her mind at thought of him, he had won her. Tom Burwell, whom the whole town called Big Boy, also loved her. But working in the fields all day, and far away from her, gave him no chance to show it. Though often enough of evenings he had tried to. Somehow, he never got along. Strong as he was with hands upon the ax or plow, he found it difficult to hold her. Or so he thought. But the fact was that he held her to factory town more firmly than he thought for. His black balanced, and pulled against, the white of Stone, when she thought of them. And her mind was vaguely upon them as she came over the crest of the hill, coming from the white folks' kitchen. As she sang softly at the evil face of the full moon.

A strange stir was in her. Indolently, she tried to fix upon Bob or Tom as the cause of it. To meet Bob in the canebrake, as she was going to do an hour or so later, was nothing new. And Tom's proposal which she felt on its way to her could be indefinitely put off. Separately, there was no unusual significance to either one.

But for some reason, they jumbled when her eyes gazed vacantly at the rising moon. And from the jumble came the stir that was strangely within her. Her lips trembled. The slow rhythm of her song grew agitant and restless. Rusty black and tan spotted hounds, lying in the dark corners of porches or prowling around back yards, put their noses in the air and caught its tremor. They began plaintively to yelp and howl. Chickens woke up and cackled. Intermittently, all over the countryside dogs barked and roosters crowed as if heralding a weird dawn or some ungodly awakening. The women sang lustily. Their songs were cotton-wads to stop their ears. Louisa came down into factory town and sank wearily upon the step before her home. The moon was rising towards a thick cloud-bank which soon would hide it.

> Red nigger moon. Sinner!
> Blood-burning moon. Sinner!
> Come out that fact'ry door.

2

Up from the deep dusk of a cleared spot on the edge of the forest a mellow glow arose and spread fan-wise into the low-hanging heavens. And all around the air was heavy with the scent of boiling cane. A large pile of cane-stalks lay like ribboned shadows upon the ground. A mule, harnessed to a pole, trudged lazily round and round the pivot of the grinder. Beneath a swaying oil lamp, a Negro alternately whipped out at the mule, and fed cane-stalks to the grinder. A fat boy waddled pails of fresh ground juice between the grinder and the boiling stove. Steam came from the copper boiling pan. The scent of cane came from the copper pan and drenched the forest and the hill that sloped to factory town, beneath its fragrance. It drenched the men in circle seated around the stove. Some of them chewed at the white pulp of stalks, but there was no need for them to, if all they wanted was to taste the cane. One tasted it in factory town. And from factory town one could see the soft haze thrown by the glowing stove upon the low-hanging heavens.

Old David Georgia stirred the thickening syrup with a long ladle, and ever so often drew it off. Old David Georgia tended his stove and told tales about the white folks, about moonshining and cotton picking, and about sweet nigger gals, to the men who sat there about his stove to listen to him. Tom Burwell chewed cane-stalk and laughed with the others till some one mentioned Louisa. Till some one said something about Louisa and Bob Stone, about the silk stockings she must have gotten from him. Blood ran up Tom's neck hotter than the glow that flooded from the stove. He sprang up. Glared at the men and said, "She's my gal." Will Manning laughed. Tom stode over to him. Yanked him up and knocked him to the ground. Several of Manning's friends got up to fight for him. Tom whipped out a long knife and would have cut them to shreds if they hadnt ducked into the woods. Tom had had enough. He nodded to Old David Georgia and swung down the path to factory town. Just then, the dogs started barking and the roosters began to crow. Tom felt funny. Away from the fight, away from to stove, chill got to him. He shivered. He shuddered when he saw the full moon rising towards the cloud-bank. He who didnt give a godam for the fears of old women. He forced his mind to fasten on Louisa. Bob Stone. Better not be. He turned into the street and saw Louisa sitting before her home. He went towards her, ambling, touched the brim of a marvelously shaped, spotted, felt hat, said he wanted to say something to her, and then found that he didnt know what he had to say, or if he did, that he couldnt say it. He shoved his big fists in his overalls, grinned, and started to move off.

"Youall want me, Tom?"

"Thats what us wants, sho, Louisa."

"Well, here I am —"

"An here I is, but that aint ahelpin none, all th same."

"You wanted to say something? . ."

"I did that, sho. But words is like th spots on dice: no matter how y fumbles em, there's times when they jes wont come. I dunno why. Seems like th love I feels fo yo done stole m tongue. I got it now. Whee! Louisa, honey, I oughtnt tell y, I feel I oughtnt cause yo is young an goes t church an I has had other gals, but Louisa I sho do love y. Lil gal, Ise watched y from them first days when youall sat right here befo yo door befo th well an sang sometimes in a way that like t broke m heart. Ise carried y with me into th fields, day after day, an after that, an I sho can plow when yo is there, an I can pick cotton. Yassur! Come near beatin Barlo yesterday. I sho did. Yassur! An next year if ole Stone'll trust me, I'll have a farm. My own. My bales will buy yo what y gets from white folks now. Silk stockings an purple dresses — course I dont believe what some folks been whisperin as t how y gets them things now. White folks always did do for niggers what they likes. An they jes cant help alikin yo, Louisa. Bob Stone likes y. Course he does. But not th way folks is awhisperin. Does he, hon?"

"I dont know what you mean, Tom."

"Course y dont. Ise already cut two niggers. Had t hon, t tell em so. Niggers always tryin t make somethin out a nothin. An then besides, white folks aint up t them tricks so much nowadays. Godam better not be. Leastawise not with yo. Cause I wouldnt stand f it. Nassur."

"What would you do, Tom?"

"Cut him jes like I cut a nigger."

"No, Tom —"

"I said I would an there aint no mo to it. But that aint th talk f now. Sing, honey Louisa, an while I'm listenin t y I'll be makin love."

Tom took her hand in his. Against the tough thickness of his own, hers felt soft and small. His huge body slipped down to the step beside her. The full moon sank upward into the deep purple of the cloud-bank. An old woman brought a lighted lamp and hung it on the common well whose bulky shadow squatted in the middle of the road, opposite Tom and Louisa. The old woman lifted the well-lid, took hold the chain, and began drawing up the heavy bucket. As she did so, she sang. Figures shifted, restlesslike, between lamp and window in the front rooms of the shanties. Shadows of the figures fought each other on the gray dust of the road. Figures raised the windows and joined the old woman in song. Louisa and Tom, the whole street, singing:

> Red nigger moon. Sinner!
> Blood-burning moon. Sinner!
> Come out that fact'ry door.

3

Bob Stone sauntered from his veranda out into the gloom of fir trees and magnolias. The clear white of his skin paled, and the flush of his cheeks turned purple. As if to balance this outer change, his mind became consciously a white man's. He passed the house with its huge open hearth which, in the days of slavery, was the plantation cookery. He saw Louisa bent over that hearth. He went in as a master should and took her. Direct, honest, bold. None of this sneaking that he had to go through now. The contrast was repulsive to him. His family had lost ground. Hell no, his family still owned the niggers, practically. Damned if they did, or he wouldnt have to duck around so. What would they think if they knew? His mother? His sister? He shouldnt mention them, shouldnt think of them in this connection. There in the dusk he blushed at doing so. Fellows about town were all right, but how about his friends up North? He could see them incredible, repulsed. They didnt know. The thought first made him laugh. Then, with their eyes still upon him, he began to feel embarrassed. He felt the need of explaining things to them. Explain hell. They wouldnt understand, and moreover, who ever heard of a Southerner getting on his knees to any Yankee, or anyone. No sir. He was going to see Louisa to-night, and love her. She was lovely — in her way. Nigger way. What way was that? Damned if he knew. Must know. He'd known her long enough to know. Was there something about niggers that you couldnt know? Listening to them at church didnt tell you anything. Looking at them didnt tell you anything. Talking to them didnt tell you anything — unless it was gossip, unless they wanted to talk. Of course, about farming, and licker, and craps — but those werent nigger. Nigger was something more. How much more? Something to be afraid of, more? Hell no. Who ever heard of being afraid of a nigger? Tom Burwell. Cartwell had told him that Tom went with Louisa after she reached home. No sir. No nigger had ever been with his girl. He'd like to see one try. Some position for him to be in. Him, Bob Stone, of the old Stone family, in a scrap with a nigger over a nigger girl. In the good old days . . . Ha! Those were the days. His family had lost ground. Not so much, though. Enough for him to have to cut through old Lemon's canefield by way of the woods, that he might meet her. She was worth it. Beautiful nigger gal. Why nigger? Why not, just gal? No, it was because she was nigger that he went to her. Sweet . . . The scent of boiling cane came to him. Then he saw the rich glow of the stove. He heard the voices of the men circled around it. He was about to skirt the clearing when he heard his own name mentioned. He stopped. Quivering. Leaning against a tree, he listened.

"Bad nigger. Yassur, he sho is one bad nigger when he gets started."

"Tom Burwell's been on th gang three times fo cuttin men."

"What y think he's agwine t do t Bob Stone?"

"Dunno yet. He aint found out. When he does — Baby!"

"Aint no tellin."

"Young Stone aint no quitter an I ken tell y that. Blood of th old uns in his veins."

"Thats right. He'll scrap, sho."

"Be gettin too hot f niggers round this away."

"Shut up, nigger. Y dont know what y talkin bout."

Bob Stone's ears burned as though he had been holding them over the stove. Sizzling heat welled up within him. His feet felt as if they rested on red-hot coals. They stung him to quick movement. He circled the fringe of the glowing. Not a twig cracked beneath his feet. He reached the path that led to factory town. Plunged furiously down it. Halfway along, a blindness within him veered him aside. He crashed into the bordering canebrake. Cane leaves cut his face and lips. He tasted blood. He threw himself down and dug his fingers in the ground. The earth was cool. Cane-roots took the fever from his hands. After a long while, or so it seemed to him, the thought came to him that it must be time to see Louisa. He got to his feet and walked calmly to their meeting place. No Louisa. Tom Burwell had her. Veins in his forehead bulged and distended. Saliva moistened the dried blood on his lips. He bit down on his lips. He tasted blood. Not his own blood; Tom Burwell's blood. Bob drove through the cane and out again upon the road. A hound swung down the path before him towards factory town. Bob couldnt see it. The dog loped aside to let him pass. Bob's blind rushing made him stumble over it. He fell with a thud that dazed him. The hound yelped. Answering yelps came from all over the countryside. Chickens cackled. Roosters crowed, heralding the bloodshot eyes of southern awakening. Singers in the town were silenced. They shut their windows down. Palpitant between the rooster crows, a chill hush settled upon the huddled forms of Tom and Louisa. A figure rushed from the shadow and stood before them. Tom popped to his feet.

"Whats y want?"

"I'm Bob Stone."

"Yassur — an I'm Tom Burwell. Whats y want?"

Bob lunged at him. Tom side-stepped, caught him by the shoulder, and flung him to the ground. Straddled him.

"Let me up."

"Yassur — but watch yo doins, Bob Stone."

A few dark figures, drawn by the sound of scuffle, stood about them. Bob sprang to his feet.

"Fight like a man, Tom Burwell, an I'll lick y."

Again he lunged. Tom side-stepped and flung him to the ground. Straddled him.

"Get off me, you godam nigger you."

"Yo sho has started somethin now. Get up."

Tom yanked him up and began hammering at him. Each blow sounded as if it smashed into a precious, irreplaceable soft something. Beneath them, Bob staggered back. He reached in his pocket and whipped out a knife.

"Thats my game, sho."

Blue flash, a steel blade slashed across Bob Stone's throat. He had a sweetish sick feeling. Blood began to flow. Then he felt a sharp twitch of pain. He let his knife drop. He slapped one hand against his neck. He pressed the other on top of his head as if to hold it down. He groaned. He turned, and staggered towards the crest of the hill in the direction of white town. Negroes who had seen the fight slunk into their homes and blew the lamps out. Louisa, dazed, hysterical, refused to go indoors. She slipped, crumbled, her body loosely propped against the woodwork of the well. Tom Burwell leaned against it. He seemed rooted there.

Bob reached Broad Street. White men rushed up to him. He collapsed in their arms.

"Tom Burwell. . . ."

White men like ants upon a forage rushed about. Except for the taut hum of their moving, all was silent. Shotguns, revolvers, rope, kerosene, torches. Two high-powered cars with glaring searchlights. They came together. The taut hum rose to a low roar. Then nothing could be heard but the flop of their feet in the thick dust of the road. The moving body of their silence preceded them over the crest of the hill into factory town. It flattened the Negroes beneath it. It rolled to the wall of the factory, where it stopped. Tom knew that they were coming. He couldnt move. And then he saw the search-lights of the two cars glaring down on him. A quick shock went through him. He stiffened. He started to run. A yell went up from the mob. Tom wheeled about and faced them. They poured down on him. They swarmed. A large man with dead-white face and flabby cheeks came to him and almost jabbed a gun-barrel through his guts.

"Hands behind y, nigger."

Tom's wrists were bound. The big man shoved him to the well. Burn him over it, and when the woodwork caved in, his body would drop to the bottom. Two deaths for a godam nigger. Louisa was driven back. The mob pushed in. Its pressure, its momentum was too great. Drag him to the factory. Wood and stakes already there. Tom moved in the direction indicated. But they had to drag him. They reached the great door. Too many to get in there. The mob divided and flowed around the walls to either side. The big man shoved him through the door. The mob pressed in from the sides. Taut humming. No words. A stake was sunk into the ground. Rotting floor boards piled around it. Kerosene poured on the rotting floor boards. Tom bound to the stake. His breast was bare. Nails' scratches let little lines of blood trickle down and mat into the hair. His face, his eyes were set and stony. Except for irregular breathing, one would have thought him already dead. Torches were flung onto the pile. A great flare muffled in black smoke shot upward. The mob yelled. The mob was silent. Now Tom could be seen within the flames. Only his head, erect, lean, like a blackened stone. Stench of burning flesh soaked the air. Tom's eyes popped. His head settled downward. The mob yelled. Its yell echoed against the skeleton stone walls and sounded like a hundred yells. Like a hundred mobs yelling. Its yell thudded against the thick front wall and fell back. Ghost of a yell slipped through the flames and out the great door of the factory. It fluttered like a dying thing down the single street of factory town. Louisa, upon the step before her home, did not hear it, but her eyes opened slowly. They saw the full moon glowing in the great door. The full moon, an evil thing, an omen, soft showering the homes of folks she knew. Where were they, these people? She'd sing, and perhaps they'd come out and join her. Perhaps Tom Burwell would come. At any rate, the full moon in the great door was an omen which she must sing to:

> Red nigger moon. Sinner!
> Blood-burning moon. Sinner!
> Come out that fact'ry door.

EUDORA WELTY

Ida M'Toy

FOR ONE HUMAN BEING to point out another as "unforgettable" seems a trifle condescending, and in the ideal world we would all keep well aware of each other, but there are nevertheless a few persons one meets who are as inescapable of notice as skyrockets, it may be because like skyrockets they are radiant with their own substance and shower it about regardlessly. Ida M'Toy, an old negro woman, for a long time a midwife in my little Mississippi town and for another long time a dealer in second-hand clothes in the same place, has been a skyrocket as far back as most people remember. Or, rather, she is a kind of meteor (for she is not ephemeral, only sudden and startling). Her ways seem on a path of their own without regard to any course of ours and of a somewhat wider circuit; she will probably leave a glow behind and return in the far future on some other lap of her careening through all our duller and steadier bodies. She herself deals with the rest of us in this mighty and spacious way, calling in allegories and the elements, so it is owing to her nature that I may speak a little grandly.

The slave traders of England and New England, when they went capturing, took away the most royal of Africans along with their own slaves, and I have not much doubt that Ida has come down from a race of tall black queens. I wish I might have seen her when she was young. She has sharp clever features, light-filled black eyes, arched nostrils, and fine thin mobile lips, and her hair, gray now, springs like a wild kind of diadem from the widow's peak over her forehead. Her voice is indescribable but it is a constant part of her presence and is filled with invocation. She never speaks lightly of any person or thing, but she flings out her arm and points at something and begins, "O, precious, I'm telling you to look at that — *look* at it!" and then she invokes about it, and tolerates no interruptions. I have heard long chants and utterances on the origin and history and destination of the smallest thing, any article or object her eye lights on; a bit of candle stuck on the mantlepiece will set her off, as if its little fire had ignited her whole mind. She invokes what she wishes to invoke and she has in all ways something of the seer about her. She wields a control over great numbers of her race by this power, which has an integrity that I believe nothing could break, and which sets her up, aloof and triumphant, above the rest. She is inspired and they are not. Maybe off by themselves they could be inspired, but nobody else could be inspired in the same room with Ida, it would be too crowded.

Ida is not a poor old woman, she is a rich old woman. She accepts it that she is held in envy as well as respect, but it is only another kind of tribute as far as she is concerned, and she is not at all prouder of being rich or of having been married in the home of a white lady, "in her bay window," than she is of being very wise. She expects to be gaped at, but she is not vain.

Ida's life has been divided in two (it is, in many ways, eloquent of duality); but there is a thread that runs from one part into the other, and to trace this connection between delivering the child and clothing the man is an interesting speculation. Moreover, it has some excuse, for Ida herself helps it along by a wild and curious kind of talk that sashays from one part to the other and sounds to some of her customers like "ranting and raving." It is my belief that if Ida had not been a midwife she would not be the same kind of second-hand clothes dealer she is. Midwifery set her off, it gave her a hand in the mysteries, and she will never let go that flying hold merely because she is engaged in something else. An ex-alchemist would run a second-hand clothes business with extra touches — a reminiscence of glitter would cling to the garments he sold, and it is the same with Ida. So it is well when you meet her to think what she was once.

Ida's memory goes back to her beginnings, when she was, she says, the first practical nurse in Jackson at the age of twenty-one, and she makes the past sound very dark and far back. She thanks God, she says, that today Capitol Street is not just three planks to walk on and is the prettiest place on earth, but that "people white and black is too high and don't they know Ida seen them when they carried a little tin coal-oil lamp that wasn't any bigger than their little fingers?" Ida speaks of herself in the third person and in indirect discourse often and especially when she says something good of herself or something of herself long ago. She will intone, "Ida say that she was good to the poor white people as she was to the rich, as she made a bargain to nurse a poor white lady in obstetrical case for a peck of peas. Ida said no, she couldn't see her suffer, and therefore a peck of blackeyed peas would be sufficient." She wants all she says to be listened to with the whole attention, and declares she does wish it were all written down. "Let her keep it straight, darling, if she remember Ida's true words, the angels will know it and be waiting around the throne for her." But Ida's true words are many and strange. When she talks about the old days it is almost like a story of combat against evil. "Ida fitted a duel from twenty-one to fifty-six, and then they operated on her right side and she was never able to stoop down to the floor again. She was never like those young devils that pace around in those white shoes and those white clothes and up and down the streets of an evening while their patient is calling for a drink of water down poor parched throat — though I wore those white shoes and those white clothes. Only, my heart was in another direction."

Ida said, "I was nursing ever since there was a big road in Jackson. There was only nine doctors, and they were the best in all the world, all nine, right here in Jackson, but they were weak in finance. There wasn't nary hospital nowhere — there wasn't nary brick in Jackson, not one brick, no brick walk, no brick store, no brick nothing-else. There wasn't no Old Ladies' Home at the end of the street, there wasn't no stopping place but the country. Town was as black as tar come night, and praise God they finally put some gas in bottles on the corners. There wasn't no such thing in the world as a nice buggy. Never heard tell of a cotton mattress, but tore up shucks and see the bed, so high, and the hay pillow stand up so beautiful! Now they got all this electric light and other electricity. Can't do nothing without the clickety-click. And bless God they fly just like buzzards up in the air, but Ida don't intend to ride till she ride to Glory."

In those early days when Jackson seems to have been a Slough of Despond with pestilence sticking out its head in the nights as black as tar, Ida was not only a midwife, she nursed all diseases. "It was the yellow fever first, and the next after that was the worst pox that there ever was in the world — it would kill you then, in my girl-days, six or seven a day. They had to stretch a rope across the road to keep the poor sick ones apart and many's the day I've et at the rope and carried the food back to the ones suffering." Ida remembers epidemics as major combats in which she was a kind of giant-killer. She nursed through influenza "six at a blow, until the doctor told me if I didn't quit nursing by sixes I would drop dead in the room." She says the doctors wrote her a recommendation as long as where she will show you up her arm, saying that when they called, it never was too cold and it never was too hot for Ida to go, and that the whole town would bow and say Amen, from the Jews on. "Bless my patients," she says, "nary one ever did die under my nursing, though plenty were sick enough to die. But laugh here," she directs. "My husband stayed sick on me twenty-one years and cost me one thousand whole dollars, but you can't nurse the heart to do no good, and in the night he fallen asleep and left me a widow, and I am a widow still."

When Ida found she could no longer stoop to the floor she stopped being a midwife and began selling clothes. She was successful at once in that too, for there is natural flowering-ground for the second-hand clothes business in the small American community where the richest people are only a little richer than the poor people and the poorest have ways to save pride and not starve or go naked. In Jackson the most respectable matron, if she would like a little extra cash to buy a new camellia bush or take the excursion to New Orleans, can run over to Ida's with her husband's other suit and Ida will sell it to a customer as a bargain at $5 and collect 25% for herself, and everybody except the husband ("Right off my back! Perfectly good suit!") will be satisfied.

It could be a grubby enough little business in actual fact, but Ida is not a grubby person, and in her handling it has become an affair of imagination, and to my notion, an expression of a whole attitude of life as integrated as an art or a philosophy.

Ida's store is her house, a white-painted little house with a porch across the front, a picket-fence around, and the dooryard planted to capacity in big flowers. Inside, it is a phantasmagoria of garments. Every room except the kitchen is hung with dresses or suits (the sexes are segregated) three and four times around the walls, for the turnover is large and unpredictable, though not always rapid — people have to save up or wait for cotton-money. She has assumed all the ceremonies of Business and employs its practices and its terms to a point within sight of madness. She puts on a show of logic and executive order before which the customer is supposed to quail; sometimes I think her customers take on worth with her merely as witnesses of the miracles of her workings, though that is unfair. Her house turns year by year into a better labyrinth, more inescapable, and she delights in its complication of aisles and curtains and its mystery of closed doors with little signs on ruled paper, "Nobody can come in here." Some day some little colored girl is going to get lost in Ida's house. The richer she gets, the more "departments" she builds and adds on to the house, and each one is named for the color of its walls, the pink department, or the blue. Even now her side yard is filled with miscellaneous doors, glass panes, planks, and little stacks of bricks that she is accumulating for a new green department she says she will build in 1943.

Her cupboards and drawers are a progressive series of hiding places, which is her interpretation of the filing system. She hides trinkets of mysterious importance or bits of paper filled with abbreviated information; she does not hide money, however, and she tells how much she has on hand ($660.60 is the latest figure), and her life insurance policy is nailed up on the wall over the mantel. Everybody knows her to be an old woman living with only a small grandchild to guard her in a house full of cash money, and yet she has not been murdered. She never will be. I have wondered what Ida would do if she saw a burglar coming after her money. I am convinced that she has no axe or gun ready for him, but a flow of words will be unstoppered that will put the fear of God in him for life; and I think the would-be burglars have the same suspicion, and will continue to keep away, not wanting so much fear of God as that.

She keeps as strict and full a ledger of transaction as the Book of Judgment, and in as enthusiastic and exalted a spirit of accuracy as an angel bookkeeper should have. The only trouble is, it is almost impossible to find in it what she is looking for — but perhaps there will be confusion on Doomsday too. The book, a great black one, which she now has little William, her grandson, to hold for her while she consults it (and he will kneel under it like a little mural figure), covers a period of twenty-six years, concerns hundreds of people, "white and black," and innumerable transactions, all noted down in a strange code full of flourishes, for Ida properly considers all she does confidential. "You could find anything in the world in this book," she says reverently, then slamming it shut in your face, "if you turn enough pages and go in the right direction. Nothing in here is wrong," she says. Loose slips are always flying out of the ledger like notes in the Sybil's book, and she sets William flying to chase them and get them inside again.

She writes her own descriptions of the garments brought to her to sell, and a lady giving over her finest white dress of last summer must not be surprised, if she looks over Ida's shoulder, to see her pen the words, "Rally Day, $2.00" or note down her best spring straw hat as "Tom Boy, 75¢." The customer might be right, but Ida does not ever ask the customer. After a moment of concentration Ida goes and hangs the object for sale on the wall in the room of her choice, and a tag is pinned to the sleeve, saying simply, "Mrs. So-and-So." Accuracy is a passion with Ida, and so is her belief in her own conscience, and I do not know what it must have cost her to pin a tag on one poor sagging dress that has hung there year in, year out, saying "Don't know who this is."

She bears respect to clothes in the same degree as she bears it to the people from whose backs they come; she treats them like these people, until indeed it seems that dignity is in them, shapeless and even ridiculous as they have seemed at first; she gives them the space on the wall and the room in the house that correspond to the honor in which she holds the human beings, and she even speaks in the proper tone of voice when she is in the room with them. They hang at human height from the hangers on the walls, the brighter and more important ones in front and on top. With the most serene impartiality she makes up her mind about client and clothes, and she has been known to say, "For God's sake take it back. Wouldn't a man white or black wear that suit out of here."

There is a magnificence in Ida's business, an extent and an influence at which she hints without ceasing, that undoubtedly inspire the poorest or idlest customer with almost an anxiety to buy. It is almost like an appeasement, and the one that goes off with nothing must feel mean, foolish, and naked indeed, naked to scorn. "I clothe them," she says, "from Jackson to Vicksburg, Meridian to Jackson, Big Black to 'Azoo, Memphis to New Orleans — Clinton! Bolton! Edwards! Bovina! Pocahontas! Flora! Bentonia! 'Azoo City! Everywhere. There ain't nobody hasn't come to Ida, or sooner or later will come."

If no one else had thought of the second-hand clothes business, Ida would have originated it, for she did originate it as far as she is concerned; and likewise I am forced to believe that if there had never been any midwives in the world Ida would have invented midwifery, so ingenious and delicate-handed and wise she is, and sure of her natural right to take charge. She loves transformation and bringing things about, she simply cannot resist it. The negro midwives of this state have a kind of organization these days and lesser powers, they do certain things in certain book-specified ways, and all memorize and sing at meetings a song about "First we put — Drops in their eyes," but in Ida's day a midwife was a lone person, invested with the whole charge of life; she had to draw upon her own resources and imagination. Ida's constant gestures today still involve a dramatic outthrust of the right hand, and let any prominent names be mentioned (and she mentions them) and she will fling out her palm and cry into the conversation, "Born in this hand!" "Four hundred little white babies — or more," she says. "My God, I was bringing them all the time. I got 'em everywhere — doctors, lawyers, school teachers, and preachers, married ladies." She has been in the clothes business for twenty-six years, but she was a midwife for thirty-five.

She herself has been married, twice, and by her first husband she had one son, "the only one I ever did have and I want his name written down: Julius Knight." Her mother (before she died) and her brothers live out in the country, and only one little grandson has lived with her for a long time. Her husband, Braddie M'Toy, whom she called Toy, is remembered collecting and delivering clothes in a wagon when he was young, and was to be seen always on some street if not another, moving very slowly on account of his heart.

Now without Toy, Ida uses a telephone down the road and a kind of de luxe grapevine service to rouse up her clients and customers. Anybody who is asked to by Ida feels a duty to phone any stranger for her and "tell them for God's sake to come get their money and bring the change." Strange negroes call people at dawn, giving news of a sale, white ladies call unknown white ladies, notes on small rolls or scraps of paper folded like doctors' "powders" are conscientiously delivered, and the whole town contrives in her own spirit of emergency to keep Ida's messages on their way. Ida takes 25% of the sales price and if she sells your dress for a dollar you have to take her a quarter when you go, or come back another time, for she will not make change for anybody. She will not violate her system of book-keeping any more than she would violate her code of ethics or her belief in God — down to the smallest thing all is absolute in Ida's sight.

Whether it is due to a savage ancestry or a philosophical turn of mind, Ida finds all Ornament a wonderful and appropriate thing, the proper materializing of the rejoicing or sorrowing soul. I believe she holds Ornament next to birth and somehow kin to it. She despises a drab color and welcomes bright clothes with a queenly and triumphant smile, as if she acknowledges the bold brave heart that chose that. Inferior color means inferior spirit, and an inferior person should not hope to get or spend more than four-bits for an outfit. She dearly loves a dress that is at once identifiable as either rich mourning or "rally-day" — the symbolic and celebrating kind appeal to her inevitably over the warm, or the serviceable, and she will ask and (by oratory) get the finest prices for rather useless but splendid garments. "Girl, you buy this spangle-dress," she says to a customer, and the girl buys it and puts it on and shines. Ida's scale of prices would make a graph showing precisely the rise from her condemnation of the subdued and nondescript to her acclaim of the bright and glorious. Her customers, poverty-bound little cooks and maids and cotton-choppers, go away feeling that they have turned into queens. Ida has put second-hand clothes on their backs and, with all the abrupt bullying of a busy fairy, wrapped them in some glowing raiment of illusion, set them in a whirl of bedazzlement; and they skitter out with shining eyes and empty hands, with every hoarded penny spent. Ida has put them in inner spangles and she has taken an actual warm moist fifty-cent piece out of their palms, and in that world both items exchanged are precious above price, fifty cents being as miraculous as glory. With something second-hand, worn, yet finer than could ever be bought new, she brings to them a perfection in her own eyes and in theirs. She dresses them up and turns them with a little ceremonial jerk towards the mirror, and a magic must hang over the green cracked glass, for (I have seen it happen a hundred times) the glances that go into its surface begin to shine with a pride that could only be a kind of enchantment. It is nice on Saturdays to pass in front of Ida's house on the edge of town and see the customers emerge. With some little flash of scarf, some extra glitter of trimming for which they have paid dearly, dressed like some visions in Ida's speculations on the world, glorious or menial as befits their birth, merit, and willingness, but all rampant and somehow fulfilled by this last touch of costume as though they float dizzily down the steps and through the flowers out the gate; and you could not help thinking of the phrase "going out into the world," as if Ida had just birthed them anew.

I used to think she must be, a little, the cross between a transcendentalist and a witch, with the happiness and kind of self-wonder that this combination must enjoy. They say that all things we write could be; and sometimes in amazement I wonder if a tiny spark of the wonderful Philosopher of Clothes, Diogenes Teufelsdröchk, could be flashing for an instant, and somewhat barbarically, in the wild and enthusiastic spirit of this old black woman. Her life like his is proudly emblematic — she herself being the first to see her place in the world. It is she literally who clothes her entire world, as far and wide as she knows — a hard-worked midwife grown old, with a memory like a mill turning through it all the lives that were born in her hand or have passed through the door.

When she stalks about, alternately clapping her hand over her forehead and flinging out her palm and muttering "Born in this hand!" as she is likely to do when some lady of the old days comes bringing a dress to sell, you can not help believing that she sees them all, her children and her customers, in the double way, naked and clothed, young and then old, with love and with contempt, with open arms or with a push to bar the door. She is moody now, if she has not always been, and sees her customers as a procession of sweet supplicant spirits that she has birthed, who have returned to her side, and again sometimes as a bunch of scarecrows or even changelings, that she wishes were well gone out of sight. "They would steal from their own mother," she says, and while she is pinning up some purchase in a newspaper and the customer is still counting out the pennies, she will shout in a deep voice to the grandchild that flutters around like a little blackbird, "Hold the door, William."

I have never caught Ida doing anything except selling clothes or holding forth on her meditations, but she has a fine garden. "If you want to carry me something I really like," she will say, bringing up the subject first, "carry me dallion potatoes (dahlia bulbs) *first*, and old newspapers second." Ida has the green finger from her mother, and she says, "You're never going to see any flowers prettier than these right here." She adores giving flowers away; under your protest she will cut every one in the garden, every red and white rose on the trellis, which is a wooden sunset with painted rays, the blossoms with little two-inch stems the way a child cuts them, and distribute them among all present and those passing in the road. She is full of all the wild humors and extravagances of the godlike toward this entire town and its environs. Sometimes, owing to her superior wisdom, she is a little malign, but much oftener she will become excruciatingly tender, holding, as if in some responsibility toward all the little ones of the world, the entire population to her great black cameoed breast. Then she will begin to call people "It." "It's all hot and tired, it is, coming so far to see Ida. Ah, take these beautiful flowers Ida grew with her own hand, *that's* what it would like. Put 'em in its bedroom," and she presses forward all the flowers she has cut and then, not content, a bouquet dripping from a vase, one of a kind of everything, all into your arms.

She loves music too, and in her house she has one room, also hung with clothes, called the music room. "I got all the music in the world in here," she used to say, jabbing a finger at a silent radio and an old gramophone shut up tight, "but what's the use of letting those contrivances run when you can make your own music?" And ignoring the humble customers waiting she would fling herself down at the old pump-organ in the corner and tear into a frenzy of chords. "I make my own!" she would shout into the turmoil. She would send for little William, with a voice like a little bird's, and he knew how to sing with her, though he would give out. "Bass, William!" she would shout, and in his tiny treble he sang bass, bravely.

When Ida speaks of her mother it is in a strange kind of pity, a tender amazement. She says she knew when her mother was going to die, and with her deep feeling for events and commemorations, she gave her a fine big party. Ida would no more shrink from doing anything the grand way than she would shrink from other demands upon her greatness. "Hush now," she told me, "don't say a word while I tell you this. All that day long I was cooking dinner between niggers. I had: four turkeys, four hens, four geese, four hams, red cake, white cake, chocolate cake, caramel cake, every color cake known. The table reached from the front door to the ice box. I had all the lights burning up electricity, and all the flowers cut. I had the plates changed seven times, and three waiters from the hotel. I'd got Mama a partner. Mama was eighty years old and I got her another lady eighty years old to march with. I had everybody come. All her children — one son, the big shot, came all the way from Detroit, riding in a train, to be at Mama's grand dinner. We had somebody play "Silent Night" and march music to follow later. And there was Mama: look at Mama! Mama loved powder. Mama had on a little old-fashioned hat, but she wouldn't take it off — had nice hair, too. Mama did all right for the march, she marched all right, and sat down on time at the right place at the head of the table, but she wouldn't take off her hat. So the waiters, they served the chicken soup first, and Mama says, 'Where my coffee! Bring on turnip and cornbread. Didn't you make a blackberry pie?' I said, 'Mama, you don't eat coffee first.' But she said, 'Where my coffee? Bring on turnip and cornbread. Didn't you make a blackberry pie? What's the matter with you?' Everything was so fine, you know. It took her two big sons, one on each side, to quiet her, that's the way Mama acted!" And Ida ended the story laughing and crying. It was plain that there was one person who had no recognition of Ida's grandeur and high place in the world, and who had never yielded at all to the glamour as others did. It was a cruelty for Ida, but perhaps all vision has lived in the house with cruelty.

Nowadays, she is carried to such heights of business and power, and its paraphernalia crowds her so, that she is overcome with herself, and suddenly gives way to the magnitude of it all. A kind of chaos comes over her. Now and then she falls down in a trance and stays "dead as that chair for three days." White doctors love her and by a little struggle take care of her. Ida bears with them. "They took my appendix," she will say. "Well, they took my teeth." She says she has a paralyzed heel, though it is hard to see how she can tell — perhaps like Achilles she feels that her end is coming by entering that way. "The doctor told me I got to rest until 1945," she declares, with a lifted hand warding you off. "Rest! Rest! Rest! I must rest." If a step is heard on the front porch she instantly cries warning from within the house, "Don't set your heels down! When you speak to me, whisper!" When a lady that was a stranger came to see her, Ida appeared, but said in haste, "Don't tell me your name, for I'm resting my mind. The doctors don't want me to have any more people in my head than I got already." Now on Saturdays if a dusty battered car full of customers from across the cottonfields draws up, one by one all the shades in the house are yanked down. Ida wishes to see no one, she wishes to sell nothing.

Perhaps the truth is that she has expended herself to excess and now suffers with a corresponding emptiness that she does not want anyone to see. She can show you the track of the pain it gives her: her finger crosses her two breasts. She is as hard to see as a queen.

And I think she lives today the way she would rather be living, directly in symbols. People are their vestures now. Memories, the great memories of births and marriages and deaths, are nearly the same as the pieces of jewelry ("$147.65 worth") she has bought on anniversary days and wears on her person. "That's Mama's death," she says — a silver watch on a silver chain. She holds out for your admiration the yellow hands that she asserts most of this country was born in, on which now seven signet rings flash. "Don't go to church any longer," she says — "or need to go. I just sit at home and enjoy my fingers."

> 1119 Pinehurst St.
> Jackson, Mississippi
> March 28, 1942

Dear Mr. Shattuck,

Thanks for your letter and I am glad you like the little piece on Ida and are going to use it. I told Mr. Russell when I wrote him just now, so that's all right about letting him know.

As to the points you mention, I am in complete agreement that the title is a bad one, and if you can think of anything, use it — I can never write a title to anything. In my own mind I had changed this to the simple name, "Ida M'Toy," but seem capable of no more. (1) I don't think the first sentence would be affected to amount to anything by a change in the title, and can be left as is. (2) The dates could be made to connect by changing, on page 3, 53 to 56. I am outdone that I left something wrong about the date for I had had a terrible time with the ones Ida gave me, and had to write the whole first page over taking them every one out, because they threw the entire thing into hopeless confusion and would have made her begin midwifery at the age of 3 — I am poor at figures but I did catch that. (3) I think leaving the "however" to modify "hiding information" is all right as it is. (4) That sentence does go on, and if it would be clarified by enclosing "and he will kneel . . . mural figure" in a parenthesis, enclose it; Mark Twain of course said that anybody who will wilfully use a parenthesis would steal. (5) Yes, change the "very slowly moving" to "moving very slowly," much better. (6) It's all right to cut the two last sentences in the second paragraph.

Since you seem to like Ida as much as I could hope a reader would, I feel cheered and you will be interested to learn that she is waiting as impatiently as possible for this to appear in print. I told her that it is no reflection on her, but only on me, that it is not printed yet — I wrote it Christmas, and I think it will do to take her for an Easter present, a little late. She hasn't read it, but will of course think it only the faithful writing down of her own words and will scarcely bother to read it. I hope you will send me two copies so that I can take her one, for she will frame it and hang it on the wall during her lifetime and it will, I am afraid, be buried with her if and when she dies. She is really a remarkable person and I wish I might have done her better justice, but it is easy to see how the task can stop you almost before you begin.

I'm glad you like "Powerhouse" and thanks for the kind words about my book.

> Sincerely yours,
> Eudora Welty

Jackson, Miss.
Aug. 25, 1942

Dear Mr. Shattuck —

Thanks for the extra copy of the magazine, which I took out to Ida right away. She shut off all the musical things going and regally took hold of the magazine and kissed it. She set it on her bed up against her pillow where her head goes, took me by the hand and put a kiss on it, and said, "Here's where I get out my glasses." She said "That's my Christmas present." She didn't say she was going to nail it to the wall but she did announce that it was going to the very bottom of her trunk and the trunk would be locked. "Then I'll get it out when I'm ninety, darling." She said only an angel would have got all that written down. And she was glad the task finally got done. Then she led me to the front room where she had set up a big glass china closet full of jelly and told me to pick out a glass for Christmas. Just thought you'd like to hear how it went. She said she would read that book on her till she died, she supposed a thousand times, because it *couldn't* be read enough. — I'm enjoying the magazine too.

Yours sincerely,
Eudora Welty

Jackson, Miss.
September 1, 1942

Dear Mr. Shattuck:

Do not be surprised at what follows. The other morning at crack of dawn Ida M'Toy telephoned me to for God's sake come straight out there, as she had read the book on her life. When I got there she greeted me with three fingers stuck up in the air — I had three things wrong. First, I had said her watch was silver, when it was gold — how could I have done a thing like that to her? and she took it out of its hiding place and put it under my eyes. Second, I had left out Sudie, who had helped her in the store for six years and Sudie felt so bad about it — "Sudie, Sudie! Come stand here and let Miss Wealthy see how bad you feel — that's right — that's all, Sudie, get on back." Third, why did I think that one copy of her life was going to be enough for her and all her friends? Two hundred would be more like it. I then apologized for 1 and 2, and said it was unlikely that I could get 200 copies and besides the price of each was 30¢. "Thirty cents! My God, there are people would be glad to pay thirty dollars cash on the barrel head to have a copy right at their hand of Ida's life." In the end I said I would write and see if there were about ten copies you could send me. I'd of course pay you, and let Ida do the grand distribution, I think she wants to take orders and force it on her customers.

She says she wants a copy in Camp Shelby for sure, to teach those soldiers to live right. She had pride in the article, but was dismayed that I had come without a pencil, for she assumed that immediately on finishing and printing that much up, I would go on and write up all that was left out. "It wrote what it could remember," she said compassionately, "there's just so *much.*" She calls this copy of *Accent* "The Book of Ida" so you can see I would hate to deprive her of spreading it to her world. When you have time, do let me know if you can spare me ten or twelve copies, and thanks a lot. Ida is really beside herself and has guaranteed that you and I both will go to heaven and see the angels.

Yours sincerely,
Eudora Welty

1119 Pinehurst St.
Jackson, Miss.
September 14, 1942

Dear Mr. Shattuck,

Thanks ever so much for the letter and for the magazines, which arrived safely. I'm touched that Ida and her story have been received so wholeheartedly by everybody at *Accent*. Ida would be gratified and I guess I'd better tell her, that the Book of Ida will be at at least *some* soldiers' camps where it will be of such value. I enclose check for the magazines and the other dollar is for subscription — it's good that *Accent* is to go forward and I wish you luck. Ida received the 10 copies and hid them right away, and now to pick out the ten people who most deserve to buy first. If you have some flawed copies it would be wonderful to let her have them, and it's generous of you but I fear a lot of trouble. I doubt if any magazine ever pleased anybody so by printing an article than *Accent* has done by printing this — Ida refers to you all as "those precious people up near Chicago that has my life." Thanks again, and my best wishes.

Sincerely,
Eudora Welty

P.S. It was perfectly OK about any omissions etc. This was *enough.*

1119 Pinehurst
Jackson, Miss.
September 23

Dear Mr. Shattuck,

Your nice letter came and so did the stack of books, so I went straight out to Ida with the present — and it was her only thought to write you a letter on the spot. Here it is, and I only hope you can put your imagination to bear on it, because (of course I had to sit there all the time, never to take part but just to be a witness) for every sentence she got written, ten were being simultaneously said, and acted out. I doubt if Ida has written many letters and it wouldn't occur to her that you would only receive the written down words, not the augmentation or the physical accompaniments of shouts and groans — when she was writing about Mama's Dinner and wrote "in sulted" she jumped up out of the chair and yelled MAD! then sank down and added "mad" but you would have to imagine such things. She would have gone on forever with the letter, because she wanted to set you straight on some things I got wrong or left out, taking your desire to hear from her perfectly seriously in that way, but her tablet gave out. She is so overcome by your printing this much of the life that her mind really wanders and staggers under the load more than is good for her! She will never rest, maybe, until the account is perfect & complete. The copies I first took her she went and sold as if they were dresses and as you see from the enclosed envelope has given me the money — I declined to take out her commission — this in spite of the fact that the books were a present to her. She is also going to sell the ones you sent, in spite of all, and turn the money over to me for the army or navy. I'll get it to the U.S.O., I guess, to make things right and just so. I'm sending two pictures I took of her, and asked her to write on them for you. She declared writing would spoil their perfect beauty but consented to write on the "darling one" — she doesn't like the other one because it shows old freckles. They don't do her total justice but here they are. She has changed the spelling of her name to Torry, for unknown reasons, but it's on her husband's tombstone M'Toy, she used to have a photo of her on the wall that showed her kneeling at the grave with a sheaf of lilies, which she pointed out as "Me Mournin'."

I'm doubly pleased to have *Accent* for two years, and thanks for fixing it that way. With many good wishes to it and good luck to you.

Sincerely,
Eudora Welty

• INTERVIEWS •

• WILLIAM • FAULKNER

(with Jean Stein, 1956)

Q: Mr. Faulkner, you were saying a while ago that you don't like interviews.

FAULKNER: The reasons I don't like interviews is that I seem to react violently to personal questions. If the questions are about the work, I try to answer them. When they are about me, I may answer or I may not, but even if I do, if the same question is asked tomorrow, the answer may be different.

Q: How about yourself as a writer?

FAULKNER: If I had not existed, someone else would have written me, Hemingway, Dostoevsky, all of us. Proof of that is there are about three candidates for the authorship of Shakespeare's plays. But what is important is *Hamlet* and *Midsummer Night's Dream*, not who wrote them, but that somebody did. The artist is of no importance. Only what he creates is important, since there is nothing new to be said. Shakespeare, Balzac, Homer have all written about the same things and if they had lived 1,000 or 2,000 years longer, the publishers wouldn't have needed anyone since.

Q: But even if there seems nothing more to be said, isn't perhaps the individuality of the writer important?

FAULKNER: Very important to himself. Everybody else should be too busy with the work to care about the individuality.

Q: And your contemporaries?

FAULKNER: All of us failed to match our dream of perfection. So I rate us on the basis of our splendid failure to do the impossible. In my opinion, if I could write all my work again, I am convinced that I would do it better, which is the healthiest condition for an artist. That's why he keeps on working, trying again; he believes each time and this time he will do it, bring it off. Of course he won't, which is why this condition is healthy. Once he did it, once he matched the work to the image, the dream, nothing would remain but to cut his throat, jump off the other side of that pinnacle of cut perfection into suicide. I'm a failed poet. Maybe every novelist wants to write poetry first, finds he can't and then tries the short story which is the most demanding form after poetry. And failing at that, only then does he take up novel writing.

Q: Is there any possible formula to follow in order to be a good novelist?

FAULKNER: 99% talent . . . 99% discipline . . . 99% work. He must never be satisfied with what he does. It never is as good as it can be done. Always dream and shoot higher than you know you can do. Don't bother just to be better than your contemporaries or predecessors. Try to be better than yourself. An artist is a creature driven by demons. He don't know why they choose him and he's usually too busy to wonder why. He is completely amoral in that he will rob, borrow, beg, or steal from anybody and everybody to get the work done.

Q: Do you mean the writer should be completely ruthless?

FAULKNER: The writer's only responsibility is to his art. He will be completely ruthless if he is a good one. He has a dream. It anguishes him so much he must get rid of it. He has no peace until then. Everything goes by the board: honor, pride, decency, security, happiness, all, to get the book written. If a writer has to rob his mother, he will not hesitate; the *Ode on a Grecian Urn* is worth any number of old ladies.

Q: Then could the *lack* of security, happiness, honor, be an important factor in the artist's creativity?

FAULKNER: No. They are important only to his peace and contentment, and art has no concern with peace and contentment.

Q: Then what would be the best environment for a writer?

FAULKNER: Art is not concerned with environment either; it doesn't care where it is. If you mean me, the best job that was ever offered to me was to become a landlord in a brothel.[1] In my opinion it's the perfect milieu for an artist to work in. It gives him perfect economic freedom; he's free of fear and hunger; he has a roof over his head and nothing whatever to do except keep a few simple accounts and to go once every month and pay off the local police. The place is quiet during the morning hours which is the best time of the day to work. There's enough social life in the evening, if he wishes to participate, to keep him from being bored; it gives him a certain standing in his society; he has nothing to do because the madam keeps the books; all the inmates of the house are females and would defer to him and call him "Sir." All the bootleggers in the neighborhood would call him "Sir." And he could call the police by their first names.

So the only environment the artist needs is whatever peace, whatever solitude, and whatever pleasure he can get at not too high a cost. All the wrong environment will do is run his blood-pressure up; he will spend more time being frustrated or outraged. My own experience has been that the tools I need for my trade are paper, tobacco, food and a little whisky.

Q: Bourbon, you mean?

FAULKNER: No, I ain't that particular. Between scotch and nothing, I'll take scotch.

Q: You mentioned economic freedom. Does the writer need it?

FAULKNER: No. The writer doesn't need economic freedom. All he needs is a pencil, and some paper. I've never known anything good in writing to come from having accepted any free gift of money The good writer never applies to a foundation. He's too busy writing something. If he isn't first rate he fools himself by saying he hasn't got time or economic freedom. Good art can come out of thieves, bootleggers or horse swipes. People really are afraid to find out just how much hardship and poverty they can stand. They are afraid to find out how tough they are. Nothing can destroy the good writer. The only thing that can alter the good writer is death. Good ones don't have time to bother with success or getting rich. Success is feminine and like a woman, if you cringe before her, she will override you. So the way to treat her is to show her the back of your hand. Then maybe she will do the crawling.

Q: Can working for the movies hurt your own writing?

FAULKNER: Nothing can injure a man's writing if he's a first rate writer. If a man is not a first rate writer, there's not anything can help it much. The problem does not apply if he is not first rate, because he has already sold his soul for a swimming pool.

Q: Does a writer compromise in writing for the movies?

FAULKNER: Always, because a moving picture is by its nature a collaboration and any collaboration is compromise because that is what the word means - to give and to take.

Q: Which actors do you like to work with most?

FAULKNER: Humphrey Bogart is the one I've worked with best. He and I worked together in *To Have and to Have Not* and *The Big Sleep*.

Q: Would you like to make another movie?

FAULKNER: Yes, I would like to make one of George Orwell's *1984*. I have an idea for an ending which would prove the thesis which I'm always hammering at: that man is indestructible because of his simple will to freedom.

Q: How do you get the best results in working for the movies?

FAULKNER: The moving picture work of my own which seemed best to me was done by the actors and the writer throwing the script away and inventing the scene in actual rehearsal just before the camera turned. If I didn't take, or felt I was capable of taking, motion picture work seriously, out of simple honesty to motion pictures and myself too, I would not have tried. But I know now that I will never be a good motion picture writer; so that work will never have the urgency for me which my own medium has.

Q: Would you comment on that legendary Hollywood experience you were involved in?

FAULKNER: I had just completed a contract at M.G.M. and was about to return home. The director I had worked with said, "If you would like another job here, just let me know and I will speak to the studio about a new contract." I thanked him and came home. About six months later I wired my director friend that I would like another job. Shortly after that I received a letter from my Hollywood agent enclosing my first week's paycheck. I was surprised because I had expected first to get an official notice or recall and a contract from the studio. I thought to myself the contract is delayed and will arrive in the next mail. Instead, a week later I got another letter from the agent enclosing my second week's paycheck. That began in November 1932 and continued until May 1933. Then I received a telegram from the studio. It said: *William Faulkner, Oxford, Miss. Where are you? M.G.M. Studio.*

I wrote out a telegram *M.G.M. Studio, Culver City, California. William Faulkner.*

The young lady operator said: "Where is the message, Mr. Faulkner?" I said, "That's it." She said: "The rule book says that I can't send it without a message, you have to say something." So we went through her samples and selected I forget which one — one of the canned anniversary greeting messages. I sent that. Next was a long distance telephone call from the studio directing me to get on the first airplane, go to New Orleans and report to Director Browning. I could have got on a train in Oxford and been in New Orleans eight hours later. But I obeyed the studio and went to Memphis where an airplane did occasionally go to New Orleans. Three days later one did.

I arrived at Mr. Browning's hotel about six P.M. and reported to him. A party was going on. He told me to get a good night's sleep and be ready for an early start in the morning. I asked him about the story. He said, "Oh, yes. Go to room so and so. That's the continuity writer. He'll tell you what the story is."

I went to the room as directed. The continuity writer was sitting there alone. I told him who I was and asked him about the story. He said: "When you have written the dialogue I'll let you see the story." I went back to Browning's room and told him what had happened. "Go back," he said, "and tell that so and so — never mind, you get a good night's sleep so we can get an early start in the morning."

So the next morning in a very smart rented launch, all of us except the continuity writer sailed down to Grand Isle, about a hundred miles away where the picture was to be shot, reaching there just in time to eat lunch and have time to run the hundred miles back to New Orleans before dark.

That went on for three weeks. Now and then I would worry a little about the story but Browning always said, "Stop worrying. Get a good night's sleep so we can get an early start tomorrow morning."

One evening on our return I had barely entered my room when the telephone range. It was Browning. He told me to come to his room at once. I did so. He had a telegram. It said: *Faulkner is fired. MGM Studio.* "Don't worry," Browning said. "I'll call that so and so up this minute and not only make him put you back on the payroll but send you a written apology." There was a knock on the door. It was a page with another telegram. This one said: *Browning is fired. MGM Studio.* So I came back home. I presume Browning went somewhere too. I imagine that continuity writer is still sitting in a room somewhere with his weekly salary check clutched tightly in his hand. They never did finish the film. But they did build a shrimp village — a long platform on piles in the water with sheds built on it something like a wharf. The studio could have bought dozens of them for forty or fifty dollars a piece. Instead, they built one of their own, a false one. That is, a platform with a single wall on it so that when you opened the door and stepped through it, you stepped right on off to the ocean itself. As they built it, on the first day, the Cajun fisherman paddled up in his narrow tricky pirogue made out of hollow log. He would sit in it all day long in the broiling sun watching the strange white folks building this strange imitation platform. The next day he was back in the pirogue with his whole family, his wife nursing the baby, the other children, and the mother-in-law, all to sit all that day in the broiling sun to watch this foolish and incomprehensible activity. I was in New Orleans two or three years later and heard that the Cajun people were still coming in for miles to look at that imitation shrimp platform which a lot of white people had rushed in and built and then abandoned.

Q: You say that the writer must compromise in working for the motion pictures. How about his writing? Is he under any obligation to his reader?

FAULKNER: His obligation is to get the work done the best he can do it; whatever obligation he has left over after that he can spend any way he likes. I myself am too busy to care about the public. I have no time to wonder who is reading me. I don't care about John Doe's opinion on mine or anyone else's work. Mine is the standard which has to be met, which is when the work makes me feel the way I do when I read *La Tentation de Saint Antoine*, or the Old Testament. They make me feel good. So does watching a bird make me feel good . . . you know that if I were reincarnated, I'd want to come back a buzzard. Nothing hates him or envies him or wants him or needs him. He is never bothered or in danger, and he can eat anything.

Q: What technique do you use to arrive at your standard?

FAULKNER: Let the writer take up surgery or bricklaying if he is interested in technique. There is no mechanical way to get the writing done, no short cut. The young writer would be a fool to follow a theory. Teach yourself by your own mistakes; people learn only by error. The good artist believes that nobody is good enough to give him advice. He has supreme vanity. No matter how much he admires the old writer he wants to beat him.

Q: Then would you deny the validity of technique?

FAULKNER: By no means. Sometimes technique charges in and takes command of the dream before the writer himself can get his hands on it. That is *tour de force* and the finished work is simply a matter of fitting bricks neatly together, since the writer knows probably every single word right to the end before he puts the first one down. This happened with *As I Lay Dying*. It was not easy. No honest work is. It was simple in that all the material was already at hand. It took me just about six weeks in the spare time from a 12 hour a day job at manual labor. I simply imagined a group of people and subjected them to the simple universal natural catastrophes which are flood and fire with a simple natural motive to give direction to their progress. But then, when technique does not intervene, in another sense writing is easier too. Because with me there is always a point in the book where the characters themselves rise up and take charge and finish the job — say somewhere about page 275. Of course, I don't know what would happen if I finished the book on page 274. The quality an artist must have is objectivity in judging his work, plus the honesty and courage not to kid himself about it. Since none of my work has met my own standards, I must judge it on the basis of that one which caused me the most grief and anguish, as the mother loves the child who became the thief or murderer more than the one who became the priest.

Q: What work is that?

FAULKNER: *The Sound and the Fury*. I wrote it five separate times trying to tell the story, to rid myself of the dream which would continue to anguish me until I did. It's a tragedy of two lost women: Caddy and her daughter. Dilsey is one of my own favorite characters because she is brave, courageous, generous, gentle and honest. She's much more brave and honest and generous than me.

Q: How did *The Sound and the Fury* begin?

FAULKNER: It began with a mental picture. I didn't realize at the time it was symbolical. The picture was of the muddy seat of a little girl's drawers in a pear tree where she could see through a window where her grandmother's funeral was taking place and report what was happening to her brothers on the ground below. By the time I explained who they were and what they were doing and how her pants got muddy, I realized it would be impossible to get all of it into a short story and that it would have to be a book. And then I realized the symbolism of the soiled pants, and that image was replaced by the one of the fatherless and motherless girl climbing down the rainpipe to escape from the only home she had, where she had never been offered love or affection or understanding. I had already begun to tell it through the eyes of the idiot child since I felt that it would be more effective as told by someone capable only of knowing what happened, but not why. I saw that I had not told the story that time. I tried to tell it again, the same story through the eyes of another brother. That was still not it. I told it for the third time through the eyes of the third brother. That was still not it. I tried to gather the pieces together and fill in the gaps by making myself the spokesman. It was still not complete, not until 15 years after the book was published when I wrote as an appendix to another book the final effort to get the story told and off my mind, so that I myself could have some peace from it. It's the book I feel tenderest towards. I couldn't leave it alone, and I never could tell it right, though I tried hard and would like to try again, though I'd probably fail again.

Q: What emotion does Benjy arouse in you?

FAULKNER: The only emotion I can have for Benjy is grief and pity for all mankind. You can't feel anything for Benjy because he doesn't feel anything. The only thing I can feel about him personally is concern as to whether he is believable as I created him. He was a prologue like the gravedigger in the Elizabethan dramas. He serves his purpose and is gone. Benjy is incapable of good and evil because he had no knowledge of good and evil.

Q: Could Benjy feel love?

FAULKNER: Benjy wasn't rational enough even to be selfish. He was an animal. He recognized tenderness and love though he could not have named them, and it was the threat to tenderness and love that caused him to bellow when he felt the change in Caddy. He no longer had Caddy; being an idiot he was not even aware that Caddy was missing. He knew only that something was wrong, which left a vacuum in which he grieved. He tried to fill that vacuum. The only thing was he had one of Caddy's discarded slippers. The slipper was his tenderness and love which he could not have named, but he knew only that it was missing. He was dirty because he couldn't coordinate and because dirt meant nothing to him. He could no more distinguish between dirt and cleanliness than between good and evil. The slipper gave him comfort even though he no longer remembered the person to whom it had once belonged, any more than he could remember why he grieved. If Caddy had reappeared he probably would not have known her.

Q: Does the narcissus given to Benjy have some significance?

FAULKNER: The narcissus was given to Benjy to distract his attention. It was simply a flower which happened to be handy that 5th of April.[2] It was not deliberate.

Q: Are there any artistic advantages in casting the novel in the form of an allegory, as the Christian allegory you used in *A Fable*.

FAULKNER: Same advantage the carpenter finds in building square corners in order to build a square house. In *A Fable* the Christian allegory was the right allegory to use in that particular story, like an oblong square corner is the right corner with which to build an oblong rectangular house.

Q: Does that mean an artist can use Christianity simply as just another tool, like a carpenter would borrow a hammer?

FAULKNER: The carpenter we are speaking of never lacks that hammer. No one is without Christianity, if we agree on what we mean by the word. It is every individual's individual code of behavior by means of which he makes himself a better human being than his nature wants to be, if he followed his nature only. Whatever its symbol — cross or crescent or whatever — that symbol is man's reminder of his duty inside the human race. Its various allegories are the charts against which he measures himself and learns to know what he is. It cannot teach man to be good as the text book teaches him mathematics. It shows him how to discover himself, evolve for himself a moral code and a standard within his capacities and aspirations, by giving him a matchless example of suffering and sacrifice and the promise of hope. Writers have always drawn, and always will, on the allegories of moral consciousness, for the reason that the allegories are matchless — the three men in *Moby Dick*, who represent the trinity of conscience: knowing nothing, knowing but not caring, knowing and caring. The same trinity is represented in *A Fable* by the young Jewish pilot officer who said 'This is terrible. I refuse to accept it, even if I must refuse life to do so,' the old French Quartermaster General who said, 'This is terrible, but we can weep and bear it,' and the English battalion runner who said, 'This is terrible, I'm going to do something about it.'

Q: Are the two unrelated themes in *The Wild Palms* brought together in one book for any symbolic purpose? Is it as certain critics intimate a kind of esthetic counterpoint, or is it merely haphazard?

FAULKNER: No, no. That was one story — the story of Charlotte Rittenmeyer and Harry Wilbourne, who sacrified everything for love, and then lost that. I did not know it would be two separate stories until after I had started the book. When I reached the end of what is now the first section of *The Wild Palms*, I realized suddenly that something was missing, it needed emphasis, something to lift it like counterpoint in music. So I wrote on the "Old Man" story until "The Wild Palms" story rose back to pitch. Then I stopped the "Old Man" story at what is now its first section, and took up "The Wild Palms" story until it began again to sag. Then I raised it to pitch again with another section of its antithesis, which is the story of a man who got his love and spent the rest of the book fleeing from it, even to the extent of voluntarily going back to jail where he would be safe. They are only two stories by chance, perhaps necessity. The story is that of Charlotte and Wilbourne.

Q: How much of your writing is based on personal experience?

FAULKNER: I can't say. I never counted up. Because 'how much' is not important. A writer needs 3 things: *experience, observation, imagination,* any two of which, at times any one of which, can supply the lack of the others. With me, the story usually begins with a single idea or memory or mental picture. The writing of the story is simply a matter of working up to that moment, to explain why it happened or what it caused to follow. A writer is trying to create believable people in credible moving situations in the most moving way he can. Obviously he must use as one of his tools the environment which he knows. I would say that music is the easiest means in which to express, since it came first in man's experience and history. But since words are my talent, I must try to express clumsily in words what the pure music would have done better. That is, music would express better and simpler, but I prefer silence to sound, and the image produced by words occurs in silence. That is, the thunder and the music of the prose take place in silence.

Q: You mentioned experience, observation, and imagination as being important for the writer. Would you include inspiration?

FAULKNER: I don't know anything about inspiration because I don't know what inspiration is — I've heard about it, but I never saw it.

Q: As a writer you are said to be obsessed with violence.

FAULKNER: That's like saying the carpenter is obsessed with his hammer. Violence is simply one of the carpenter's tools. The writer can no more build with one tool than the carpenter can.

Q: Can you say how you started as a writer?

FAULKNER: I was living in New Orleans, doing whatever kind of work was necessary to earn a little money now and then. I met Sherwood Anderson. We would walk about the city in the afternoon and talk to people. In the evenings we would meet again and sit over a bottle or two while he talked and I listened. In the forenoon I would never see him. He was secluded, working. The next day we would repeat. I decided that if that was the life of a writer, then becoming a writer was the thing for me. So I began to write my first book. At once I found that writing was fun. I even forgot that I hadn't seen Mr. Anderson for three weeks until he walked in my door, the first time he ever came to see me, and said "What's wrong? Are you mad at me?" I told him I was writing a book. He said "My God" and walked out. When I finished the book — it was *Soldiers' Pay* — I met Mrs. Anderson on the street. She asked how the book was going and I said I finished it. She said, "Sherwood says that he will make a trade with you. If he doesn't have to read your manuscript he will tell his publisher to accept it." I said "Done" and that's how I became a writer.

Q: What were the kinds of work you were doing to earn that "little money now and then"?

FAULKNER: Whatever came up. I could do a little of almost anything — run boats, paint houses, fly aeroplanes. I never needed much money because living was cheap in New Orleans then, and all I wanted was a place to sleep, a little food, tobacco, and whisky. There were many things I could do for two or three days and earn enough money to live on for the rest of the month. By temperament I'm a vagabond and a tramp. I don't want money badly enough to work for it. In my opinion it's a shame that there is so much work in the world. One of the saddest things is that the only thing a man can do for eight hours a day, day after day, is work. You can't eat eight hours a day nor drink for eight hours a day nor make love for eight hours — all you can do for eight hours is work. Which is the reason why man makes himself and everybody else so miserable and unhappy.

Q: You must feel indebted to Sherwood Anderson, but how do you regard him as a writer?

FAULKNER: He was the father of my generation of American writers and the tradition of American writing which our successors will carry on. He has never received his proper evaluation. Dreiser is his older brother and Mark Twain the father of them both.

Q: What about the European writers of that period?

FAULKNER: The two great men in my time were Mann and Joyce. You should approach Joyce's *Ulysses* as the illiterate Baptist preacher approaches the Old Testament: with faith.

Q: How did you get your background in the Bible?[3]

FAULKNER: My Great-Grandfather Murry was a kind and gentle man, to us children anyway. That is, although he was a Scot, he was (to us) neither especially pious nor stern either: he was simply a man of inflexible principles. One of them was, everybody, children on up through all adults present, had to have a verse from the Bible ready and glib at tongue-tip when we gathered at the table for breakfast each morning; if you didn't have your scripture verse ready, you didn't have any breakfast; you would be excused long enough to leave the room and swot one up (there was a maiden aunt, a kind of sergeant-major for this duty, who retired with the culprit and gave him a brisk breezing which carried him over the jump next time).

It had to be an authentic, correct verse. While we were little, it could be the same one, once you had it down good, morning after morning, until you got a little older and bigger, when one morning (by this time you would be pretty glib at it, galloping through without even listening to yourself since you were already five or ten minutes ahead, already among the ham and steak and fried chicken and grits and sweet potatoes and two or three kinds of hot bread) you would suddenly find his eyes on you — very blue, very kind and gentle, and even now not stern so much as inflexible; and next morning you had a new verse. In a way, that was when you discovered that your childhood was over; you had outgrown it and entered the world.

Q: Some people say they can't understand your writing, even after they read it two or three times. What approach would you suggest for them?

FAULKNER: Read it four times.

Q: Do you read your contemporaries?

FAULKNER: No, the books I read are the ones I knew and loved when I was a young man and to which I return as you do to old friends: the Old Testament, Dickens, Conrad, Cervantes — *Don Quixote*. I read that every year, as some do the Bible. Flaubert, Balzac — he created an intact world of his own, a blood-stream running through twenty books — Dostoevsky, Tolstoi, Shakespeare. I read Melville occasionally, and of the poets: Marlowe, Campion, Jonson, Herrick, Donne, Keats and Shelley. I still read Housman. I've read these books so often that I don't always begin at page 1 and read on to the end. I just read one scene, or about one character, just as you'd meet and talk to a friend for a few minutes.

Q: And Freud?

FAULKNER: Eveybody talked about Freud when I lived in New Orleans, but I have never read him. Neither did Shakespeare. I doubt if Melville did either, and I'm sure Moby Dick didn't.

Q: Do you ever read mystery stories?

FAULKNER: I read Simenon because he reminds me something of Chekhov.

Q: What about your favorite characters?

FAULKNER: My favorite characters are Sarah Gamp — a cruel, ruthless woman, a drunkard, opportunist, unreliable, most of her character was bad, but at least it was character; Mrs. Harris, Falstaff, Prince Hal, Don Quixote and Sancho, of course. Lady Macbeth I always admire. And Bottom, Ophelia, and Mercutio — both he and Mrs. Gamp coped with life, didn't ask any favors, never whined. Huck Finn, of course, and Jim. Tom Sawyer I never liked much — an awful prig. And then I like Sut Lovingood from a book written by George Harris about 1840 or '50 in the Tennessee mountains. He had no illusions about himself, did the best he could; at certain times he was a coward and knew it and wasn't ashamed; he never blamed his misfortunes on anyone and never cursed God for them.

Q: Would you comment on the future of the novel?

FAULKNER: I imagine as long as people will continue to read novels, people will continue to write them, or vice versa; unless of course the pictorial magazines and comic strips finally atrophy man's capacity to read, and literature really is on its way back to the picture writing in the Neanderthal cave.

Q: And how about the function of the critics?

FAULKNER: The artist doesn't have time to listen to the critics. The ones who want to be writers read the reviews, the ones who want to write don't have the time to read the reviews. The critic too is trying to say "Kilroy was here." His function is not directed towards the artist himself. The artist is a cut above the critic, for the artist is writing something which will move the critic. The critic is writing something which will move everybody but the artist.

Q: So you never feel the need to discuss your work with anyone?

FAULKNER: No, I am too busy writing it. It has got to please me and if it does, I don't need to talk about it. If it doesn't please me, talking about it won't improve it, since the only thing to improve it is to work on it some more. I am not a literary man but only a writer. I don't get any pleasure from talking shop.

Q: Critics claim that blood relationships are central in your novels.

FAULKNER: That is an opinion and as I have said I don't read critics. I doubt that if a man trying to write about people is any more interested in blood relationships than in the shape of their noses, unless they are necessary to help the story move. If the writer concentrates on what he does need to be interested in, which is the truth and the human heart, he won't have much time left for anything else, such as ideas and facts like the shape of noses or blood relationships, since in my opinion ideas and facts have very little connection with truth.

Q: Critics also suggest that your characters never consciously choose between good and evil.

FAULKNER: Life is not interested in good and evil. Don Quixote was constantly choosing between good and evil, but then he was choosing in his dream state. He was mad. He entered reality only when he was so busy trying to cope with people, that he had no time to distinguish between good and evil. Since people exist only in life, they must devote their time simply to being alive. Life is motion and motion is concerned with what makes man move — which are ambition, power, pleasure. What time man can devote to morality, he must take by force from the motion of which he is a part. He is compelled to make choices between good and evil sooner or later. Because that moral conscience demands that from him in order that he can live with himself tomorrow. His moral conscience is the curse he had to accept from the Gods in order to gain from them the right to dream.

Q: Could you explain more what you mean by motion in relation to the artist?

FAULKNER: The aim of every artist is to arrest motion, which is life, by artificial means and hold it fixed so that 100 years later when a stranger looks at it, it moves again since it is life. Since man is mortal, the only immortality possible for him is to leave something behind him that is immortal since it will always move. This is the artist's way of scribbling "Kilroy was here" on the wall of the final and irrevocable oblivion through which he must someday pass.

Q: It has been said by Malcolm Cowley that your characters carry a sense of submission to their fate?

FAULKNER: That is his opinion. I would say that some of them do and some of them don't, like everybody else's characters. I would say that Lena Grove in *Light in August* coped pretty well with hers. It didn't really matter to her in her destiny whether her man was Lucas Burch or not. It was her destiny to have a husband and children and she knew it, and so she went out and attended to it without asking help from anyone. She was the captain of her soul. One of the calmest, sanest speeches I ever heard was when she said to Byron Bunch at the very instant of repulsing his final desperate and despairing attempt at rape, "Ain't you ashamed? You might have woke the baby." She was never for one moment confused, frightened, alarmed. She did not even know that she didn't need pity. Her last speech for example: "Here I ain't been traveling but a month, and I'm already in Tennessee. My, my, a body does get around."

The Bundren family in *As I Lay Dying* pretty well coped with theirs. The Father having lost his wife would naturally need another one, so he got one. At one blow he not only replaced the family cook, he acquired a gramophone to give them all pleasure while they were resting. The pregnant daughter failed this time to undo her condition, but she was not discouraged. She intended to try again and even if they all failed right up to the last, it wasn't anything but just another baby.

Q: And Mr. Cowley says you find it hard to create characters between the ages of 20 and 40 who are sympathetic.

FAULKNER: People between 20 and 40 are not sympathetic. The child has the capacity to do but it can't know. It only knows when it is no longer able to do — after 40. Between 20 and 40 the will of the child to do gets stronger, more dangerous, but it has not begun to learn to know yet. Since his capacity to do is forced into channels of evil through environment and pressures, man is strong before he is moral. The world's anguish is caused by people between 20 and 40. The people around my home who have caused all the interracial tension — the Milams and the Bryants (in the Emmett Till murder) and the gangs of Negros who grab a white woman and rape her in revenge, the Hitlers, Napoleons, Lenins — all these people are symbols of human suffering and anguish, all of them between 20 and 40.

Q: You gave a statement to the papers at the time of the Emmett Till killing. Have you anything to add to it here?

FAULKNER: No, only to repeat what I said before: that if we Americans are to survive it will have to be because we choose and elect and defend to be first of all Americans; to present to the world one homogeneous and unbroken front whether of white Americans or blacks ones or purple or blue or green. Maybe the purpose of this sorry and tragic error committed in my native Mississippi by two white adults on an afflicted Negro child is to prove to us whether or not we deserve to survive. Because if we in America have reached that point in our desperate culture when we must murder children, no matter for what reason or what color, we don't deserve to survive, and probably won't.

Q: What happened to you between *Soldiers' Pay* and *Sartoris* — that is what caused you to begin the Yoknapatawpha saga?

FAULKNER: With *Soldiers' Pay* I found out writing was fun. But I found out after that not only each book had to have a design but the whole output or sum of an artist's work had to have a design. With *Soldiers' Pay* and *Mosquitoes* I wrote for the sake of writing because it was fun. Beginning with *Sartoris* I discovered that my own little postage stamp of native soil was worth writing about and that I would never live long enough to exhaust it, and by sublimating the actual into apocryphal I would have complete liberty to use whatever talent I might have to its absolute top. It opened up a gold mind of other peoples, so I created a cosmos of my own. I can move these people around like God, not only in space but in time too. The fact that I have moved my characters around in time successfully, at least in my own estimation, proves to me my own theory that time is a fluid condition which has no existence except in the momentary avatars of individual people. There is no such thing as *was* — only *is*. If *was* existed there would be no grief or sorrow. I like to think of the world I created as being a kind of keystone in the Universe; that, as small as that keystone is, if it were ever taken away, the universe itself would collapse. My last book will be the Doomsday Book, the Golden Book, of Yoknapatawpha County. Then I shall break the pencil and I'll have to stop.

Notes

1. According to *Time* (May 28, 1956) Faulkner respoded to a question as to whether he meant this literally by saying: "I am a fiction writer and I am not responsible for any construction made on any interview I have ever given."
2. The fourth section of *The Sound and the Fury* is actually dated April 8.
3. This question and its answer first appeared in the *Writers at Work* text and was apparently not part of the original interview. Malcolm Cowley, in a letter to one of the editors, recalled that he expressed to the interviewer a wish that Faulkner had said more about his familiarity with the Bible, and that she asked the additional question of Faulkner on a subsequent occasion.

SHELBY FOOTE

(with John Griffin Jones, 1979)

Jones: I suppose it's best if we start at the beginning, if you could tell me some of your early background, when and where you were born.

Foote: Well, I was born in Greenville, Mississippi, at the Greenville Sanatorium on the seventeenth of November, 1916, in room 31 although it was room 13. The don't have room 13s in hospitals, I guess. The doctor was Dr. A. G. Payne. My daddy was working for a gin down in Rolling Fork and came up on a freight train when he heard my mother had gone into labor.

Jones: What did your daddy do?

Foote: He didn't do anything until after he got married. He was sort of a rich man's son that never thought he would do anything in this world. About the time he got married, his father lost all his money. My mother's father, Morris Rosenstock, got him a job as a shipping clerk with Armour and Company there in Greenville. That was about 1915 or so. He just suddenly caught fire and he lived another seven or eight years. By the time seven years were up he was manager of all the Armour and Companies in the South. But he died in Mobile, Alabama, in September of 1922.

Jones: So your mother raised you?

Foote: Yes. I was not quite six years old when he died and my mother never remarried. She did indeed raise me. We lived back in Greenville until I was — well, to get it straight, while my father was alive we lived in various places because he was rising up the business ladder. We lived in Vicksburg, Jackson, Pensacola, and he had just been transferred to Mobile at the time he died. He got a promotion each time. He'd had a good life. He was born in 1890, a planter's son. He was more interested in hunting and gambling and drinking whiskey and fooling around than he was in anything else, until he and mother got married.

Jones: Born at Mount Holly?

Foote: No. He was born at Mounds Plantation near Rolling Fork. He's buried there now. He lived at Mount Holly through his boyhood. My grandfather had three or four plantations down there. There was Mount Holly, Mounds, Egremont, and one called Hardscrabble. My Daddy grew up with that kind of life. His father had come from Macon, Mississippi — this is Huger Lee Foote I'm talking about, my father's father. His father was Hezekiah William Foote from Macon, Mississippi, a wealthy man there. He had been a Colonel in the Confederate army, was at Shiloh — in fact, got the tail shot off his horse at Shiloh. My father never had any intentions of doing anything with his life, so far as I know, until he and my mother got married. He did not go to a university. He went to Brannam and Hughes to school, and when college time came around he wasn't interested in that; he didn't go, he stayed around home. By the time he would have been a junior or senior in college he was getting married.

Jones: So your grandfather was the first Foote in the Greenville area?

Foote: Yes, he was the first one. He was the youngest son of old Hezekiah William, and his father sent him to Chillicothe Business College up in Ohio. I still can't imagine some Southern boy going to Chilliocothe Business College. But his father sent him there — to learn bookkeeping, I suppose, and that kind of thing — and then sent him over to the Delta to manage four plantations. Mounds Plantation was one, where my father was born, and another was Mount Holly where they lived soon after that. Mount Holly was his favorite of all the places he was running for his father, so as soon as he began to run those places he began paying his father for Mount Holly. He wanted to buy it from him. He made the last payment the year the old man died, and then it was left him in his will.

Jones: I've heard that story.

Foote: That's hard.

Jones: And who gambled it away?

Foote: He did. He finally sold Mount Holly and moved to town and spent all his time gambling, some at the Elks Club there in Greenville, but he also went many places. I've talked with old men who knew him in poker games all over that region. He died of apparent cancer. I'm sure it was cancer; I'm not sure whether it was stomach or intestines or what it was. I remember them telling me he was sitting on a pillow during the last of his poker playing days. He also had one of the first operations that was known as the Murphy Button; something to do with an intestinal bypass. It was a daring technique in those days. My mother has told me about seeing him. He died a year before I was born. She told me about seeing him, but when she knew him best he was already in the hospital, lying up in bed there. My first novel *Tournament* is written out of sort of a conception of him, but it's only a conception. It's not even founded much on fact. I'd never seen him, I'd never talked about him a great deal with his widow or my mother, except for small things.

Jones: Was the Foote family always centered in Mississippi? When did they come down to this area?

Foote: They were originally in Virginia, went from there to Chester County, South Carolina, and from there across Alabama to the black prairie region of Mississippi, where my great-grandfather settled. He was, I've heard, the first man in Mississippi to bring in blooded cattle, to raise pedigree cattle. There's no trace of him left around Macon, no kinfolks even. I go there every now and then; I like to see the old man buried in the cemetery there — he's got an obelisk over his grave, and his four wives are buried around him, one to each of the four main points of the compass.

Jones: Is your mother still in Greenville?

Foote: She died ten years ago but she lived there nearly all her life.

Jones: Are there any of your close relatives in Greenville,

Foote: I have an aunt, Elizabeth Foote. I have another aunt, Katherine, her older sister, who's paralytic and in a nursing home in Greenville, and that's all.

Jones: What about the governor in the 1850s, Henry Stuart Foote, is he related?

Foote: He's a distant cousin, not close kin.

Jones: Where was he from?

Foote: Well, it's rather confusing. He's really a Tennessean. There is a connection though, he and my great-grandfather were among two of the founders of Vanderbilt, so they were connected that way. I don't know the exact kinship of old Hezekiah William to Henry Stuart Foote. Henry Stuart Foote's an interesting man. He was sort of a renegade. He left the Confederacy and went abroad.

Jones: Did he?

Foote: Yes. He was a fiery man, something of a blowhard, I think, and a mortal enemy of Jefferson Davis's, before the war and during it.

Jones: Had a fist fight with him, didn't he?

Foote: Yes, it was at a boarding house in Washington. He made a remark that Davis took exception to, about a young lady or something. Those fist fights never amounted to much; like any two fifty-year old men swinging away at each other.

Jones: Well, he was quite a duelist in his time too, wasn't he?

Foote: Yes. You never know how serious those things are. There's a scene of him in the Confederate Senate, or House, I've forgotten which. He was attacked by a fellow member, a man named Dargan, I believe, from Alabama, with a Bowie knife. Foote managed to scramble out of the way, and some of the other Senators grabbed Dargan and pinned him to the floor, and Foote came back within range and said, "I defy the steel of the assassin!"

Jones: When you were growing up in Greenville, was your family literary?

Foote: No, my family was not literary on either side. I've done some speculating about that and there are several answers to where the devil the literary thing came from. So far as blood goes, and kinship, if it comes from anywhere it comes from my mother's father who was born in Vienna, Austria, and left there when he was seventeen years old and came to this country, probably to escape conscription; we don't really know why because he wouldn't talk about it. He was a Viennese Jew. His name was Rosenstock. He came over here when he was seventeen, and how he got to Mississippi from probably landing in New York I do not know. But anyway he came down the river and settled here and was keeping books on a plantation at Avon for a man named Peters, who was a planter there at Avon. This man Peters had a redheaded daughter who was a true belle, a beautiful woman. I've got some of her trinkets, and my grandfather married her. How a Jew bookkeeper managed to marry the daughter of a planter I don't know, but he swung it somehow. He had three daughters by her and she died bearing the third one. My mother was the middle daughter of the three. The oldest one had a great influence on me because I loved her very much and she was very fond of me and we were close. Her name was Maude. The youngest daughter was named Minnie, and I suppose strident is one of the kindest words you can use to describe her. She's still living in Nashville, I think; a dreadful woman. My mother — I couldn't say too many nice things about her. She supported me in every sense all my life. A lot of bad things happened to me and she stood by me through all of them. She got discouraged I'm sure from time to time, but she never reproached me for any of my mistakes. I could see her disappointment. But she never said what I would have said in her place: "There you go again. You're always acting like this." She never did that. The best way to describe her attitude toward me, and it's by no means a complete description, is that she never once hurt my feelings. It is a very strange thing to be that close to someone and never hurt their feelings. I hurt her feelings many times, in anger, in scorn. But she never hurt mine, though she had plenty of reason to.

Jones: What did she think about your work?

Foote: She liked it, and she was happy that I had found what I wanted to do. She would have been happy no matter what I'd done, if I enjoyed doing it.

Jones: At what age do you think that the notion of becoming a novelist and writer came to you?

Foote: It came to me, thank God, not too soon. I was editor of the high school paper there in Greenville, *The Pica*, it's called, so that I suppose I had some literary pretensions. But it didn't interfere with my life before then or even at that time. It took over my life later on. I lived a very normal Delta boyhood in spite of an interest in books. Incidentally, my first interest in books ran from *Bunny Brown and his Sister Sue* through *Tom Swift* up through *Tarzan*. So I've always been glad that I enjoyed dances and helling around the Delta. It's where I got much of the material I use now, so that I'm glad that I didn't become a recluse. When I got to be about sixteen or seventeen I discovered good reading and found out there was another whole world I had scarcely suspected up to then. The real thing that happened to me, I can almost pinpoint it, was when I was about twelve years old. For some reason or other, not having anything to do with school, I read *David Copperfield*. I had done a lot of reading of what I suppose can only be called trash. But reading *David Copperfield* I suddenly got aware that there was a world, if anything, more real than the real world. There was something about that book that made me realize what art is, I suppose, translating now. It made a tremendous impression on me. I didn't then and there rush in to read the rest of Dickens nor fan out into reading other things, but it was the first real clue I had as to the existence of this other world. I had a delayed reaction to it because I was about sixteen or seventeen before I came around to really reading. When I did finally come around to it, for the next five or six years I read quite literally almost everything I could get my hands on, especially modern things. I heard somewhere, probably from Will Percy, that the most important three novels of the twentieth century were Thomas Mann's *Magic Mountain*, Joyce's *Ulysses* and Proust's *Remembrance of Things Past*. So, the first few months after my seventeenth birthday when my mother gave me the Proust, I read those novels because I considered that I should read them. It was a great time; I was like a colt in clover with that stuff. It was marvelous. That's what, if anything, made me a writer. The other strong influence was the Percy family. I remember I was about fourteen, something like that, out at the country club, swimming, and Will Percy came over. He'd been playing golf — he was a dreadful golfer, but he liked to play occasionally in those days — he came over and said, "Some kinsmen of mine are coming here to spend the summer with me. There are three boys in the group and the two older boys are about your age. I hope you'll come over to the house often and help them enjoy themselves while they're here." I said, "Mr. Will, I'll be glad to." That was the first I heard of Walker, LeRoy, and Phinizy. Soon afterwards they arrived and I began to go over to their house and they began to come over to my house, and we became good and close friends, which we have been ever since.

Jones: I have read that a lot of people think that the fact that there wasn't ever a lynching in Washington County, and the fact that the Klan never gained a foot in the local politics . . .

Foote: Yes.

Jones: And even the fact that Hodding Carter could come there and write freely his type of journalism, was due to the atmosphere that the Percy family created.

Foote: There's a lot of truth in that, but there are other factors. The Percy influence was the main current sociological bar to the Klan. They set a style and an adherence to truth and justice that the Klan could have no part in, and people subscribed to that, so they had a high example in the community to go by, to guide them. They had other things to, though. Jews had always been prominent in Greenville. I was amazed to find anti-Semitism outside of Greenville in the Delta itself and, of course, elsewhere in the country. I was amazed to hear that Jews couldn't belong to the country club in Greenwood. I didn't know what to make of that because there were more Jews than any one religion in the founders of the country club in Greenville. It surprised me greatly. That, too, was a factor. Jews were among the most prominent people in town. If anybody knew Jake Stein and they heard somebody talking anti-Semitic they knew how absurd it was because they knew what a fine man Jake Stein was, and others too. It never caught on. But the Percys must not be underrated in their influence in that fight. Senator Percy was strongly anti-Klan and expressed himself so at every opportunity. Mr. Will as a young man did what he could in that direction, too. In *Lanterns on the Levee*, he tells about the election that was held and how the Klan candidates were defeated. There are still some prominent men in Greenville who were members of the Klan, and old citizens know who they are and don't feel too kindly toward them to this day. It was not really as horrendous a thing as it sounds now. The Klan was political, almost social. I don't think that they intended to lynch anybody or put anybody in ovens or anything like that. Most of the members of it were politicians who were looking for bloc votes.

Jones: What type of effect do you think that Will Percy and his writing has had on Walker?

Foote: That's an interesting question, because Mr. Will's values are not Walker's values. Walker would find the old Grecian, Roman stoicism perhaps admirable as broadsword virtues, but he doesn't think that's the path to heaven. He would have no satisfaction in it as a solution to what makes a man or what makes his soul. He would find some admiration for those qualities in a man as to character, but as to what made him really a man, Walker would find those unsatisfactory. That's partly because of the difference in their ages. Certain things were satisfactory fifty years ago that no longer are. The attitude toward the Negro, for instance, takes some understanding. Mr. Will, and Senator Percy before him, believed that the best thing any man could do was do his best in his circumstances and be a shining example, I suppose you'd call it, to the people around him. Therefore, the Negro's solution to his oppression and its various problems was to excel in spite of them so that when he made a claim for decent treatment and fair treatment, it had to be respected because of his excellence. That's basically the Booker T. Washington view: "Let your buckets down where you are." By the time Mr. Will came along, people were beginning to see that that might be a pretty good rule for the world at large, but it's not a good rule in a country where all men are supposed to be equal from the outset. A man is not supposed to have to prove he's equal in this country. That was one of the flaws in it. The other was that some of us poor souls are not equipped to do what superior men like Booker T. Washington can do. And it's a dreadful thing to see the government itself passing laws discriminating against you. So this solution of individual excellence was not a satisfactory solution, and Walker would never have found it so. Senator Percy now, before Will Percy, Will Percy's father, he came at the end of his life, as a result of political failures — he lost any popular election he ever ran for — to believe that, as he said, "Shooting at the stars had always seemed to (him) to be pretty poor marksmanship." A man should succeed in his own area. Take his own little postage stamp piece of the country and be a good man inside that, and he would have done what he was put on this earth for. How much of that is sour grapes I don't know. I do know that he enjoyed his term as a Senator back in the days when he was elected by the Legislature, and I'm sure he would have liked to have gone on with that. And I think that this late view about "shooting for the stars" is an expression of his disappointment more than anything else, although it was his outlook at the end of his life. I remember Senator Percy, but only vaguely. I remember him as a dignified gentleman with a white mustache playing golf mainly out at the club. I remember his wife, Miss Camille, a marvelous woman, had a deep voice, very likeable. But they were dead a couple of years before the boys came.

Jones: Knowing Walker like you do, what do you think of the characters he's created: Binx Bolling, Will Barrett, Dr. Tom More. . .

Foote: Well, my judgment of Walker's work is really interfered with. When I read Walker I can hear him talking, and I know some of the stories he's told and some of the experiences we've had together that went into the books. He's not an autobiographical writer in the ordinary sense of Tom Wolfe, of somebody like that, but he does use things out of his life. I read him; I'm a great admirer of his work. I think he's a substantial artist of our time.

Jones: I've read in an article or some place where he said, "You can be sure that I didn't learn to write by sitting at the feet of old men on the front porch listening to them tell stories."

Foote: Right.

Jones: How would you rate that influence on you?

Foote: I would rate it highly. I learned a great deal from listening to old men on the front porch, and so did Walker. He just meant that writing is not something that is picked up out of the air — which, of course, it's not. But he didn't mean by that to slight his material. The material was there for him and he absorbed a great deal of it listening to people talk.

Jones: When did you write for the *Delta Democrat-Times?*

Foote: I never really worked for the *Delta Democrat-Times*. I worked for the *Delta Star*.

Jones: Before they merged.

Foote: Hodding Carter came to Greenville and started the *Delta Star*, and I was a reporter on the *Star*. It was Hodding himself who worked harder than anybody, unless maybe it was his wife Betty who worked harder than he did, and then Donald Weatherbee was the managing editor who worked very hard, then I was the reporter who did not work very hard.

Jones: This was after you got back from college?

Foote: Yes, right after. One of the reasons I didn't go back to school — the main one was I didn't want to, but there was another one — was that the war was heading up in Europe. We all saw it coming. When it started in September of 1939 I joined the Mississippi National Guard, knowing that we'd be put into federal service pretty soon. We didn't go into federal service until November of '40. But during that year I was in the National Guard at home there. We met once a week and went to summer camp, and I knew I was biding my time until we went into service. I was very much in favor of our getting into the war because of Hitler. It was during that year that I worked mostly at the *Delta Star* and I also wrote the first draft of my first novel *Tournament* at that time.

Jones: It seems like your experience as a reporter has affected you, it comes out in your writing — *Follow Me Down*.

Foote: Sure, it would. *Follow Me Down*, for example, is an attempt to show the reaction of a town to a crime of passion, including the court trial. There were such crimes and I attended many such trials, as a reporter and just as a spectator. So, yeah, all that goes into it.

Jones: Was there any factual base behind *Follow Me Down*?

Foote: Yes. There was a man named Floyd Myers who drowned a girl name Emma Jean somebody, I've forgotten her name, and was tried for it and did get life imprisonment at Parchman. That was merely the basis for it. They didn't live on the island or anything like that, but he did drown her in Lake Ferguson there at home. There was that much to it. And I did attend his trial, which I learned a lot from.

Jones: What about the Parker Nowell character?

Foote: He's based in part on a lawyer named Ben Wilkes who was Myer's lawyer in that case, only in part though. Ben Wilkes didn't have a wife who ran off with somebody else. He certainly didn't listen to any thousand dollar phonograph and all that kind of thing. But Nowell was in part based on him. Nobody uses a real character entirely on his own in a book. You use parts of four or five people to make a character. And so I did with Parker Nowell. Nowell's phonograph, for instance, belonged to Mr. Will, which, incidentally, Mr. Will could never operate. He had less mechanical ability than anyone I've ever known in my life. He couldn't operate an automatic pencil. Walker and LeRoy and Phin got together one Christmas. He liked to listen to the radio, but he never could operate one. So, push button radios came out about 1936 or so. It had push buttons on it for getting the different stations. Below, where the push button was, there were celluloid tabs that a light shown through, and you could take a pencil and write WQXR or whatever on the little tabs. The boys showed him how to operate it, said, "All you have to do is push this button and that shows you the station." They came in the next day and he had used a pencil and pushed the pencil through the little celluloid things. He could never operate anything. He couldn't drive a car. He could never operate anything mechanical. He was funny, faced with a mechanical problem.

Jones: He was a small man physically, wasn't he?

Foote: Yes. You didn't think of him as small, but he certainly was, just as you didn't think of Faulkner being small and Faulkner was smaller than Mr. Will. Mr. Will would make personal judgments against artists. He didn't think they were exempt from the rules that required you to be well-mannered. Faulkner came over there once in the late twenties, I guess it was. Mr. Will had a tennis court in the back there, and he took tennis pretty seriously. It was the one sport he really did take seriously. Faulkner had been drinking and got out on the tennis court and made a fool of himself. Faulkner never had Mr. Will's admiration as a writer or a man or anything else after that display on the tennis court; he'd shake his head about it every time he would remember it. He didn't think anything good could come from anybody who would to a thing like that.

Jones: Your earliest influences were Proust, Mr. Will, and who else?

Foote: Certainly William Faulkner. *Light in August* was one of the first current novels I read. It came out around 1932 when I started reading earnestly. I read *Light in August* and I was tremendously impressed by it, and also puzzled by it. I've never written a letter to an author saying how much I liked his work or didn't like his work, but I had a very strong inclination to sit down and write Mr. Faulkner a letter saying, "You had such a good story to tell, why didn't you tell it instead of confusing me the way you did?" I've always been glad I didn't write that letter.

Jones: Did you come to know him?

Foote: Yes. I was with Faulkner maybe five, six times; spent the night in his house once, took a trip with him up to Shiloh once, had dinner with him and Miss Estelle a couple of times. I liked him very much. He was a friendly, even outgoing man with certain reticences. His reticences never bothered me; I figured a man with that big a genius strapped to his back would be bound to have some pretty hard times.

Jones: But you didn't see any great incongruities in him?

Foote: No, I didn't. I've read where other people did; I didn't. He seemed like William Faulkner to me, man and writer. I did not find any gap between the two. The man wasn't as great as the writer, but I'm sure that's nearly always true of great writers. I simply liked him. He was a good companion, a likeable man, a great deal of humor, a gracious host, and seemed like a fine husband — which I later found out he was not. But I liked him.

Jones: It seems to people, especially in my generation, the things that are taught to you about him are all rather dark concerning his personality.

Foote: Yep. Those things are rather hard to judge when you are young and a person's reputation is not overwhelming at that point. You'd just see him for what he was and you liked him or you didn't like him.

Jones: Was he interested in the Civil War, too?

Foote: Yes, he was interested in the Civil War, but only in an amateurish way. He didn't know much about it. Faulkner was never interested in the facts, the hard background, statistics, any of that. But he had a very fine if somewhat romantic view of the War, and he knew the general shape of it far better than most so-called buffs. He had a real good eye for terrain. I walked him over the field at Shiloh, surely one of the most confusing fields of the War, and he caught on to it fast. And I don't think he had ever been there before.

Jones: We talked earlier about how old people, sitting around talking and telling stories that even I still hear, influenced you a great deal. Were there stories passed around in your family about the War?

Foote: No; very few. I only saw about two or three Civil War veterans in my whole lifetime, and they had probably been drummer boys or something. Not much talk about the War. There were certain things left over from the War. There were old maiden aunts whose sweethearts had been killed in the War. There were widows of Confederate soldiers around; they'd married the old men when they were fairly young and the men were old. There were customs that were very much a part of it, although you didn't realize them too well. For example, we never celebrated the Fourth of July because that was the day Vicksburg fell. I remember there was one family — it was very unusual to have outsiders, even in Greenville in those days — but there was a family there from Ohio and on the Fourth of July they all got in their car and went up on the levee and had a picnic and they forgot to set the brakes and the car rolled down the levee and fell in the river. Everybody said it served them right for celebrating the Fourth of July.

Jones: Confederate history is something that has just always fascinated you?

Foote: Yes. I read background material on the Civil War at certain phases of my life the way other people read detective stories. It did fascinate me. The actual mechanics of the battles and everything interested me. I wanted to find out what happened. And certain people: Stonewall Jackson, Bedford Forrest, Robert E. Lee, interested me. I wanted to know about their lives. I would read biographies of them — Henderson's *Jackson* was one of the first that drew me to it, and Robert Self Henry's *Story of the Confederacy* was an important book for me as a young man, a child, really.

Jones: When you were in the Second World War, did you have combat experience?

Foote: No. I was in the Fifth Division, a regular Army division, and we were stationed in Northern Ireland during the training period for the year leading up to the invasion. I had a serious run-in with a colonel in my battalion, and out of that a serious run-in with the general of the whole damn brigade, and as a result of their watching and waiting they jumped on me for falsifying a trip ticket about a trip to Belfast and brought me before a general court-martial, and I was dismissed from the Army for falsifying a government document. It was a real con job. What happened was they had a rule that you could not use a government vehicle for pleasure beyond the range of fifty miles, and our battalion was fifty-two miles from Belfast. The other two battalions were inside the circumference. So, we commonly changed our trip ticket to forty-eight miles instead of fifty-two. Anyway, that was the thing I was charged with. It was just a simple con job. I came on home, worked for Associated Press for about three months in New York, and then joined the Marine Corps. I was in the Marine Corps a year, including combat intelligence school at Camp Lejeune, and then was in California waiting to go over when they dropped the bomb, and I got out on points. I had plenty of points because I had four years in the Army and a year in the Marine Corps. I was a captain in the Army and a private in the Marine Corps. The other Marines used to say, "You used to be a captain, didn't you? You ought to make a pretty good Marine private."

Jones: It would seem like you had some combat experience just because of the way you write so vividly about the Civil War battles.

Foote: Well, the Army experience itself was very useful to me. I learned a great many maneuvers of all kinds, and I did study hard the use of artillery and tactics.

Jones: Tell me the story of how you came to write the trilogy. Originally it didn't start off to be that, did it?

Foote: No, it started off to be a short history of the Civil War. Random House wanted me to do it and Bennett Cerf was happy about it and I signed a contract for a short history of the Civil War. It was going to be about 200,000 words, not a long book at all. But I hadn't any more than started before I saw I wasn't the one to write any short history of the Civil War; just a summary of what happened really didn't interest me. But I was enormously interested in the whole thing. So, about the time I got started — in fact, I hadn't done much more than block out what I call the plot — when I saw it was going to take a lot more space than that. My editor at Random House then was Robert Linscott, a very nice man, and I wrote him and told him I'd like to go spread-eagle, whole hog on the thing. It must have been a terrible shock to him, but he saw Cerf and whoever else he had to see and made his recommendations; they considered it, I suppose — I never heard any of that; he just wrote back and said, "Go ahead," So I did. What was really upsetting to them, this was supposed to be the first volume in an historical series they were going to do; one on the Civil War, one on the Revolution, and so forth. This first one turned into a gigantic trilogy, so they didn't try any more.

Jones: Immediately you saw how enormous your task was going to be?

Foote: Yes.

Jones: And at that time did you realize that you were going to put your fiction down for twenty years?

Foote: No, I had no idea. I knew how big it was going to be, but I thought I could write it fast. I thought it would take me two years instead of one to write a volume. Actually, as it turned out it took me five years each on the first two and ten years on the third.

Jones: And did you put down your fiction during that time?

Foote: Absolutely. I've never in my life been able to do but one thing at a time.

Jones: What were your sources, besides the *Official Records*?

Foote: Well, as you say, the *Official Records* were the main thing, but my sources were probably not over 250, 300 books. And I didn't use letters or things like that, manuscript stuff. I stuck to printed material.

Jones: Where did you get the insights that made it a narrative?

Foote: From learning how to write novels.

Jones: Is that right?

Foote: That's exactly what it is. Novelists know instinctively not to do things that historians do all the time. It's what makes historians such poor reading, and I'm not talking about being entertaining, I'm talking about what makes you dissatisfied with an historian, a dry, unskilled historian's history. There are great historians, I'm not talking about them. There has never been a greater novelist or writer of any kind than Tacitus, for instance, who was a great historian by any standards; Gibbon, Thucydides. It's just that a lot of modern historians are scared to death to suggest that life has a plot. They've got to take it apart and have a chapter on slavery, a chapter on "The Armies Meet," chapters on this, that, and the other. There's something almost low-life about trying to write about events from a human point of view. So they say. The result is they have no real understanding of the Civil War because they don't understand what Lincoln's problems were. They don't see them as problems impinging on a man; they see them as theoretical problems. I'm not saying what they do has no validity; I am saying it has no art. Of course, without their work I could have done nothing. They get along without me very well, but I couldn't get along without them.

Jones: Regimental histories, I've heard you say, played a large part.

Foote: Yes. They are not to be trusted for facts, but they are to be greatly admired for incidentals: how soldiers felt, what they did, sometimes humor, which is a necessary ingredient. I sometimes think that there's never been a single page of very great writing that did not have humor in it. It may be dark humor, it may be sardonic, it may be this and that and the other, but there's always humor in any good writing. There's scarcely a passage in Shakespeare that doesn't have humor in it, even if it's just a crazy juxtaposition of two words.

Jones: In your opinion, has history overrated or underrated any figures from the War?

Foote: Absolutely. The underrating of Jefferson Davis is almost like a giant conspiracy. Davis was a warm, friendly, outgoing man. When you read about him in history he sounds like a cold-blooded prig. It is almost unexplainable. It's just hard to believe how this gigantic conspiracy got formed, because some very fine historians think of Davis as a stiff, unbending man. He was not, not at all; he was the opposite of that. I just think, somehow, they don't pay any attention to things like his letters to his wife or those things, his fondness for his children. They would begin to question those things if they understood better the kind of man he really was.

Jones: Do you feel like he made the largest contribution to the Confederate war effort?

Foote: No, I wouldn't say that. Robert E. Lee is certainly a rival in that regard. He was the hardest working man in the Confederacy, I think — Jefferson Davis was. I agree with what Lee said; he said he didn't think anyone could have done a better job than Davis did, and so far as he personally was concerned he didn't know anyone who could have done as well. Davis had his shortcomings; he was too testy in his dealings with men like Joe Johnston and Beauregard. But I agree with Lee that, in sum, he did a better job than anybody else I know would have done.

Jones: What about on the Union side, who do you think was the most important individual?

Foote: Well, in this case there's no doubt at all because Lincoln was. But Lincoln was a genius. He was a true political genius, and those are rare. It's one of Mr. Davis's misfortunes to be compared to Lincoln. Almost nobody can be compared to Lincoln.

Jones: Do you think Davis had the foremost intellect of his time?

Foote: No, Davis was not even an intellectual, though most people think he was. He was not. His tastes were really quite simple. In poetry his favorite poet was Robert Burns, who is a good poet, but certainly not of heavy intellect. He had little humor, too little humor, far too little humor, although he had more than most people realize. No, Davis had determination, will, and enormous integrity. If he gave a man his word there was no way he could be persuaded to go back on it. Lincoln would break his word to his best friend on earth, in two minutes, if it would help the Union cause to do it. And he never kept his word beyond the point where the conditions under which he gave it pertained. His enormous flexibility, his pragmatism, were incredible.

Jones: Do you think Davis could have served the Confederacy better as commander of the Mississippi troops?

Foote: No, I think Davis was right where he belonged. I've never been satisfied that Davis would have been a first-rate soldier. He was too intelligent for that, if you see what I mean. A good general ought to be a little stupid, to keep from getting rattled. There was a genius on the Confederate side all right, but it wasn't Davis or Lee, it was Bedford Forrest. I once told General Forrest's granddaughter that I had thought long and hard about these matters and I had decided that there were two authentic geniuses in the Civil War; one was her grandfather, Beford Forrest, and the other was Abraham Lincoln. There was a pause at the other end of the telephone. Finally she said, "You know, we never thought much of Mr. Lincoln in my family." She didn't like that coupling, that comparison, at all, and didn't think much of me for making it.

Jones: What about individuals in the war who were overrated?

Foote: Well, there are a lot of those, but it's hard to know who is doing the overrating and does it matter and all that.

Jones: Yes.

Foote: There are generals I don't like personally; Joe Johnston's one of them. Phil Sheridan's another. But I don't say from that they were overrated, it is just that they had flaws that rubbed me the wrong way. I hope I didn't let that show in the book, though I'm sure it did to some degree. A historian has a great fondness for scoundrels. Edwin Stanton was a scoundrel, but he's very useful to me. He livens a page, picks it up. So too, just as there can't be any good without evil, he makes a good contrast for some other people who wouldn't show up as well if you didn't have Stanton to compare them to.

Jones: What about the notion that the North fought the War with one hand behind its back, do you think that's accurate?

Foote: Yes, I often say that, and I think it's quite true. In the course of the War, the North passed and acted on the Homestead Act. They developed the West while the War was going on. Incredible inventions were made during the Civil War — wars always bring on inventions — but things that you don't think of like the fountain pen, or the machine that sewed the uppers to the soles of shoes, were made where one person could do the work of forty people. There were many things like that. Some of our finest institutions of education were founded during the Civil War: Vassar, M.I.T., and a lot more. My point in this is that the North was doing all those things and fighting the War at the same time. If they had had to do more to win the War, they simply would have done a great deal more instead of these other things they were doing. The Confederacy put close to everything it had into that War, but the North, as I said, fought it with one hand tied behind its back, on purpose. And they got rich in the process — selling their wheat crop to England, for instance.

Jones: So to think that the War was lost at Vicksburg, or the War was lost at Gettysburg, is completely erroneous.

Foote: If I had to pick any one point at which I said the War was lost — and I never would — I would say Fort Donelson.

Jones: In '62.

Foote: Yes, way early; February of '62. It did about four different things: it caused the loss of Tennessee and Kentucky — in the sense that Kentucky was never going to be recovered. It led to the isolation of the Transmississippi. Above all, it marked the emergence of U.S. Grant, the man who was going to win the War. But Donelson was reversible at Shiloh, except they didn't reverse it, so that you slip back and say, "No, Shiloh was the decisive point," and then, "No, if we had done this at Gettysburg," and you keep on with these might-have-beens and you wind up nowhere. I think the truth of the matter is there was no way the South could have won that war. The one outside chance was British recognition, and help, and we were not going to get that, especially after Lincoln defined the War as a war against slavery. The English people would never have put up with their leaders taking them into a war that had been defined on those terms.

Jones: But isn't it true that there was a point where England and France, especially Napoleon III who had recommended it, were considering intervention?

Foote: Napoleon III wanted to intervene for his own reasons, primarily to get Confederate cotton, I think, also to weaken a growing opponent, and perhaps some political maneuvering to get England involved so that strength could be drawn off that way. But the high point that is often pointed to in recognition is a British cabinet meeting that went on about the time the Battle of Sharpsburg, or what the Union people called Antietam, was being fought. When the results of that reached England, Lee was in retreat and the time had passed when they could have recognized them. But I'm not at all convinced that if Lee had been successful in that invasion the British would have recognized and engaged in the War. That was a big step they weren't about to take. You have to remember certain consequences to England if they had come into that war. The War of 1812 had wiped the British merchant fleet off the seas, and the Northern navy would have done the same thing in the 1860s. England wasn't about to be crippled that greatly at a time when French power was growing and the Germans were a threat from another direction and all this was going on. There couldn't be any kind of winner in that kind of thing. And the English have never been famous for pulling anybody's chestnuts out of the fire. They had general admiration for the Confederates, but that admiration wasn't about to be translated into terms of anybody going over and fighting, or risking their fleet.

Jones: Even if things had worked out where Lee would have won at Gettysburg and had gone down and taken Washington, that, in your opinion, wouldn't have affected the ultimate outcome?

Foote: Well, it's problematical, of course, but not very profitable to speculate on.

Jones: Yes. Today, do you still visit the battlefields?

Foote: Very seldom. If I happen to be close to one I might drop by to see it. I get a particular satisfaction out of doing it because I feel that it sort of belongs to me now that I've written about it — all writers feel that. But not much anymore. I've been determined to wash the Civil War out of my head ever since I finished that third volume, and I've pretty well done it, too. I don't remember now where Stonewall Jackson was born.

Jones: Was it hard for you to get back into the field of fiction after twenty years on the War?

Foote: Writing is always hard work, but no, it wasn't any harder writing *September September* than it had been writing *The Civil War*.

Jones: Tell me where the idea for *September September* came from.

Foote: I really don't know; it's not based on anything. There was no case like that here or anything like it. I wanted to get my hand back in by writing a short, action novel; so I did. I researched it hard, the way I'd done in history. The whole book takes place in the month of September in 1957, which I could remember because I was in Memphis, and I went down and read the *Commercial Appeal* and the *Press-Scimitar* for the month of September 1957, as a way of starting. I took notes on what the temperatures were and how much rain fell on the various days, phases of the moon, changes that have been made in the city since then. So I wanted it to be accurate, but I always wanted that, in my earlier books too. The headlines and things that are quoted in *September* are right out of the two papers.

Jones: Seems like you have sort of mellowed from *Follow Me Down* to *September September*. Both of them are about a crime; yet in *September September* no one gets murdered.

Foote: Yes. What's more, I have a lot more tolerance of people's shortcomings than I had back in those days, I think, because I've discovered a good many of them in myself.

Jones: I personally enjoyed *September September* very much.

Foote: I'm glad. I expected it to be a runaway bestseller, which it certainly was not. Everybody always thinks something's going to be a runaway best-seller. I've been lately reading about Faulkner; he thought *Absalom, Absalom!* was going to take off like a rocket. It certainly did not. It came out about the same time as *Gone With the Wind*, in the same year, anyhow. I don't know whether Faulkner ever read *Gone With the Wind* or not. He said, "No story needs to be a thousand pages long!" I don't think he ever read *Gone With the Wind*.

Jones: I read once where a reporter had asked him who he had been reading presently, and he said, "I don't read my contemporaries," and walked across the room and proceeded to tell some writer that their work was directly related to this other writer's work.

Foote: Right. The only book I actually saw him read was a book called *Bugles in the Afternoon* by Ernest Haycox, a western. But he was an avid reader. I've talked with him about other books, but that's the only book I ever actually saw him read.

Jones: Let me ask you a pretty nebulous question that I think has a lot to do with what your fiction shows. What effect do you think the Southern defeat in the Civil War has had on us and our ideology and our character?

Foote: Profound effect. In the movie *Patton*, Patton stands up in front of an enormous American flag and says, "We Americans have never lost a war, and will never lose a war as long as we keep our qualities." Patton was from Virginia, and when he said, "We Americans have never lost a war," I couldn't believe he knew what he was saying. He had lost a war. Southerners are in close touch with some things that the rest of the country doesn't know much about, and one of them is military defeat. And it wasn't just defeat; it was grinding defeat. Without being annihilated, very few sides in a war have ever been trounced as thoroughly as the Confederacy was trounced. We were really beaten in war; we were beaten far worse than the Germans were in either of the world wars, for instance. We were ground down into the ground, and then ground down some more after it was over. Southerners who are at all aware of their history — and even if they aren't it's part of their heritage — are among the people on earth who know best what defeat is, and it has a great deal to do with the way we see the world. We are also thoroughly familiar with injustice, which can be recognized at a hundred yards from our treatment of the blacks over the century, so that a lot of American ideals are bound to sound pretty absurd to an observant Southerner who has been in touch with the underside of the American character. It's very important, the fact that we were defeated in a war.

Jones: Did you work on your trilogy when you were working at Hollins?

Foote: I've never done any work away from my home. I did do some research and take some notes and things like that, but I hadn't any more than started on that Hollins job, which I had agreed to, than my mother came down with cancer, and I had to commute between Hollins and here almost every weekend. She was in the hospital here in Memphis, and at home here too. She left Greenville and came up here to be with us during all this treatment. I had planned to do a good deal of work — I was up there by myself; my wife stayed here with our child — but because of my mother's critical illness during that time I didn't.

Jones: Was that the major reason you took ten years on your third volume?

Foote: Well, when I finished the second volume I thought I had another five years to go and I accepted this Ford Foundation grant with the Arena Stage in Washington as a sort of vacation, a way of resting up for starting the third volume. I enjoyed it. We got a townhouse in Georgetown with a swimming pool and all that. We spent Mr. Ford's money right and left. We were there about, I don't know, six or eight months, and it was very pleasant, and that six or eight months I deliberately used as a vacation. Following the Washington thing we had the brilliant idea of going down to the Alabama coast and building a house on the Gulf there. There were two things wrong with that: one, I got crossways with the Ku Klux Klan down there during the George Wallace days, and the other was we had an architect here in Memphis named Adalotte design a house for us. It was a three-story house with a nine-foot gallery all the way around the two top stories. It was a beautiful house; but we found that in a sixty-mile-an-hour wind it would fly. So we had a lot of delays on that, and finally decided not to build it.

Jones: What kind of pressure did you get in Alabama from the Klan?

Foote: It wasn't bad. It was the kind of pressure anybody would run into down there if he let it be known what his feelings were, different from theirs. They considered that their backs were to the wall and they even translated themselves into terms of being modern-day Confederates, which is what they were not, and I told them every time I had any kind of confrontation with one of them or saw them with a Confederate flag; I told them they were a disgrace to the flag, that everything they stood for was almost exactly the opposite of everything the Confederacy had stood for, that the Confederacy believed in law and order above all things. Its main hope was to get in front of the courts, while they were cussing the courts and wanting not to have anything to do with them and wanting to disobey the orders of the courts. I created a good deal of resentment against myself down there until they decided I was crazy and then they were more sympathetic.

Jones: You've said you've spent the last five years or so trying to wash the Civil War out of your head.

Foote: Yes.

Jones: Do you feel like your fiction is a more lasting literary contribution?

Foote: I don't know how I feel about that; I don't know that it is more lasting. It could be that I have more pride in and affection for my fiction than I have for my history because it all came out of my head rather than out of documents. But I'm satisfied with that job I did on the War; those three volumes suit me; I'm proud of them, and willing to stand by them. I'm also protective of the novels because most people think that the history is my serious work and the novels are not up to that standard. I disagree with that, violently.

Jones: Do you get more pleasure out of working with fiction?

Foote: No, they're not that different, writing history and writing fiction. All the same problems are there. Somewhere in one of the bibliographical notes I said it doesn't much matter if facts come out of documents or out of your head, they are still things you work with and respect. You are looking for the truth, and, as I said also, it's not a different truth, it's the same truth. You try and find out the truth, and it doesn't really make that much difference — to the person writing it, anyhow — whether you made up the facts, which you then must respect, or you found them in documents, which you must respect. I never felt cramped at all while writing the history. I felt just as free as I feel when I'm writing a novel. It's true, I couldn't make up the color of a man's eyes, but I could find out what color they were. It just meant a little harder work.

Jones: You didn't have any facts in the trilogy that weren't completely documented?

Foote: Absolutely not. If the work didn't have absolute historical integrity it would have been a total waste of time. There would be no point whatsoever in doing a novelistic treatment in the sense of inventing scenes that would explain Robert E. Lee or how Stonewall Jackson looked. All that has to come out of fact, and the whole thing would have been vitiated if I had invented anything or distorted anything. It wouldn't do. I've never known a modern historical instance where the truth wasn't superior to anybody's distortion. I would be willing for that book to be subjected to any kind of iron rule about accuracy. If I didn't do that, I would say that it was not worthwhile.

Jones: I was always fascinated by the incidentals in the narrative. You knew exactly at what point Stonewall Jackson was leaning up against a tree sucking on a lemon.

Foote: That's right. Those things are all in the documents. Nothing flatters me more than to have someone ask me if I made up some scene, because I hope it sounds as if a novelist wrote it, but I didn't make up anything in it. I may have done some conjectures of which I do very little in that book, and my interpretation of why somebody did something or the future effect of what had been done in the past is a contribution, I hope. But any facts in there are facts, whether it's the weather or the color of somebody's hair and eyes or his height and weight or his age or what his schooling was, what his voice sounded like; all those things are accurate. I'm not saying I didn't make some errors and mistakes, I'm sure I did. But they were as accurate as I knew how to make them.

Jones: What about when you were writing, did you read one sequence ahead in the *Official Records* or would you get a whole overall view and write from that?

Foote: I did a whole overall view, reread some of my favorite books, read other books that I had not read, biographies, general histories of the War, studies of individual campaigns, always the *Official Records of the War of the Rebellion*, that 128-volume monster. I read all that and that gave me the information with which to plot the whole three-volume work. Having done that and having straight in my mind how the plot was going, I then researched each individual incident as I came to it. I would generally research at night and write in the daytime.

Jones: But you could sit down and write the complete scene freehand?

Foote: Yes. I would have notes stuck up on the bulletin board for quotations or so I could remember what book something was in. I never had a typist or an assistant or a research person or anything like that. I did it all myself, and I couldn't have done it any other way. I couldn't have asked somebody to go find something in a book for me; I would have gone crazy waiting for them to find it, for one thing. And I certainly didn't want anybody turning out a whole bunch of notes for me, so I didn't want any kind of secretarial assistant. I didn't even want anybody typing it because that gave me another chance to improve it — each copy you make is that much better. But I would be sitting down writing a scene and I would remember something that happened and that somebody said something at that point; then I would scratch my head and remember what book it was in, and then when I went over and got the book I would remember that it was about two-thirds of the way down the page on the left-hand side, and I would find it. Sometimes I would be stopped dead cold in my tracks for two hours while I tried to remember what book and what part of that book it was in. But that was my way of doing it, and it suited me. Any short cut would have been an interference.

Jones: What about the criticism you got on the trilogy, was it mainly that you took too much of a Southern bias?

Foote: There was a little bit of that. There was some objection to winding up on the note of Jefferson Davis, for instance, as a continuation of this war against Jefferson Davis which was waged from 1861 to 1979, and will continue to be waged. There was a little bit of that, but to tell you the truth I saw very little criticism of anything about those books. It was all praise. There was no attack on it, almost none. I saw, I'd be guessing if I'd say, four or five hundred reviews, and practically none of them, some of them were lightweight and slight, but nobody really attacked it, said, "No, no, no." Some people were disappointed by the treatment I gave certain characters, favorites of theirs. I remember a very good historian named Vandiver had some objections to my depiction of Stonewall Jackson at the Seven Days, but that was just a difference of opinion; it was not a direct attack on any facts I had.

Jones: He said something about Stonewall Jackson delaying on the way to Mechanicsville or Gaines Mill?

Foote: He said that Jackson didn't delay, he did exactly what he was supposed to do.

Jones: Ordered.

Foote: Yes. Some truth in that, but it wasn't Jackson in his spread-eagle style, God knows. And Lee always wanted men to do more than they were told to do. In fact he said he learned from General Scott to bring the armies together, bring all his units together on the field; then the battle was up to them.

Jones: And you don't think you'll ever involve yourself in another novel or any type of history of the War?

Foote: I doubt it. Originally I thought I would do a short novel early in my writing life on a Civil War subject and that was to be *Shiloh*. I wrote that. Then in the middle of my writing life I hoped to do a big historical novel on the Siege of Vicksburg, and at the end of my writing life I wanted to write another short novel on the Battle of Brice's Crossroads, all of them basically Mississippi battles — Shiloh, of course, being just across the state line — but I won't write the Vicksburg novel and probably won't write the Brice's Crossroads novel; I've been there, you see. T. S. Eliot said an interesting thing that all writers know to be true. He said, it's in one of the *Four Quartets*, he said that writing — you're trying to do a thing that you don't know how to do, and, he said, it winds up a general mess of imprecision. Having done it you have learned how to do it, but having done it you're no longer interested in doing it again. That's the tragedy — if you know how to do it, it's because you've tried and bungled, but now that you've learned how, you are no longer interested because you wouldn't be learning. Many people think that writers are wise men who can impart to them the truth or some profound philosophy of life. It is not so. A writer is a skilled craftsman who discovers things along with the reader, and what you do with a good writer is you share the search; you are not being imparted wisdom, or if you are being imparted wisdom, it's a wisdom that came to him just as it came to you reading it.

Jones: That's a good point. Can you tell us something about other things you learned in writing the trilogy about the uniqueness of a Southern heritage?

Foote: I'll tell you a very simple thing that I got out of writing about the War that tremendous long time. It started at the very beginning and continued through the writing. I acquired a knowledge of and a love for Southern geography. It's great when you learn about the rivers and the mountains and the way the South physically is. That's a thing that is important to us. People do draw from their physical backgrounds. Whether you live in the mountains or on the seacoast makes a big difference in what kind of person you are. There are other things too. I'm from the Mississippi Delta which has a forty-foot top soil and is often said to be the richest farming land in the world — it's not, but it's often said to be — and I've known some people out in the hills too, and I've discovered that there's sort of an inverse ratio between the richness of the soil and the providence of the people who live on it. People who live down in the Delta don't worry too much about the future because the soil is so rich they don't have to, I guess. It's like Hawaiians;

when they get hungry they can reach up and pull a pineapple off the tree. An Eskimo, if he stops thinking about food for two hours in a row, would starve to death, and so he knows to think about it and to do something about it. Out in the hills of Mississippi you'll see people canning vegetables and doing all kinds of things looking forward to a hard winter. Down in the Delta they just go down to the supermarket and buy a can of beans. It's funny. George Washington Carver, one of the finest men I ever met, came to Greenville in the early or middle thirties to lecture to a big Negro gathering there celebrating one hundred years of progress or something, and he reproached them something awful. He said, "I've seen Buick automobiles in the yard of a house where you can study botany through the floor and astronomy through the roof." He wanted them to be frugal and look after themselves; be good, solid citizens. Dr. Carver was a fine man. I remember his speaking. I covered it as a reporter on the newspaper there as a high school boy when I was working for the paper in the summertime. I remember one thing that made a great impression on me. First, Dr. Carver did. I've seen about five or six great men in my life, and Dr. Carver was certainly one of them. Another one was a psychiatrist named Harry Stack Sullivan who came down and visited the Percy family back in the thirties. But what I remember about the Carver visit was there would be audiences of five or six hundred people — it was in the very hot summertime — and every person in that audience was dressed. They all had on ties and coats, and they were very proud. They were all black, no white people there, or scarcely any. I remember how proud they were and they showed their pride through dressing up, and it was hot. This was Mississippi in July or August, I think, when there was no air-conditioning ever heard of. They were great in that respect.

Jones: Did Mr. Will bring him to town?

Foote: He brought Harry Stack Sullivan, but not George Washington Carver. That was done by the blacks at home there; they brought him over from Georgia. I guess after the death of Booker T. Washington, Carver was probably the best known Negro in the country, because of his work with what he called, "the lowly peanut." He was a wonderful man.

Jones: Who else did Mr. Will bring to town that had an effect on you?

Foote: Oh, I'm trying to think of the many people I met at the Percy house. I remember Roark Bradford was there one time, a very funny man, really funny. Dave Cohn stayed there at the Percy house for about a year writing a book. He came on a visit and stayed a year. He was from Greenville and he'd been in New Orleans as manager of Sears Roebuck or something. By the time he was a little over forty years old he figured he'd worked enough and made enough money to live on and he didn't want to be a businessman any more, he wanted to be a writer. He came back home and went to see Mr. Will about it, and Mr. Will said, "It's all well enough to say you want to be a writer, but writers write. That's what you have to do, not talk about it." And Dave said he thought he would, and Mr.

Will said, "Well, fine. Why don't you stay here at this house? You can get it done." Dave Cohn stayed there and in less than a year wrote *God Shakes Creation*, probably his best book, and he wrote seven or eight more. I like Dave Cohn's work. He had a good ear. He was very good on blacks. He wasn't ashamed at all to see the absurd side of them, which Roark Bradford had pointed out so well by then. Dave was also interesting about certain provincial aspects of Memphis. It was Dave in *God Shakes Creation* who said, "The Delta begins in the lobby of the Peabody Hotel and ends on Catfish Row in Vicksburg." He was always welcome at the Peabody; they were glad to see him — he stayed there whenever he was in Memphis — but they never even gave him a cup of coffee, and he thought it was rather amusing that they had so little appreciation of this publicity. Any New York hotel would have put him up and fed him for years. The Pontchartrain in New Orleans would too. But not in Memphis.

Jones: Reading that type of thing and Hodding Carter's work, you get a different sense of the Delta than you do in your work. Your work is closer to Faulkner.

Foote: Yes; more influenced by Faulkner certainly. The Delta is generally misunderstood. For some reason we in the Delta think we are the aristocrats of Mississippi simply because we've had more money than most other sections of Mississippi. At the time I'm talking about there was damn little anybody had, but the Delta was better off than other sections. And we thought of ourselves as the aristocrats, with pure blood lines and all that foolishness. Actually the Delta is a great melting pot — God Almighty's a big dollar mark. It's not at all the way it's portrayed, say, in the work of Tennessee Williams. I've never understood Williams writing about the Delta when he had Columbus on the Tombigbee River, which is a much better place to write about than the Delta. What I mean is it is much better for Tennessee Williams to write about Columbus because he knew it, and he didn't know the Delta. I've always been interested — more than say Faulkner was — in the actual historical shaping of a society, the events which caused people to be the way they are, and their conflict with those events. I'll probably never write anything past the mid-sixties. I kind of stopped looking, about that time.

Jones: Are you going to return to Greenville in your work again?

Foote: Yes. I'm writing a big long family novel right now called *Two Gates to the City*. It's about a family in the Delta. It's not an historical novel. It's about a group of people, probably in the late forties. It's not a saga by any means. It's a family novel in the same sense as, say, *The Brothers Karamazov*.

Jones: What do you think is the truth behind the fact that so many writers come from Mississippi?

Foote: That's a question that's often asked, and there is no easy answer. There are good flippant answers, such as there's nothing else to do down there, so you write. There are only two movies in town so you haven't got much to do. You go to court and watch a trial. My day was before television, so that didn't take up an awful lot of people's time. I've seen recently that the average American boy watches something like six hours a day. It's unbelievable. And you have to subtract that from a lot of things, that six hours out of the waking eighteen. You've got six of that and six of school and six eating or something, you don't have much left for reading or doing many of the things I did when I was a boy.

Jones: So you think something basic is changing?

Foote: Oh, yes, a lot of things are changing. I always hesitate to say it's for the worse, no matter how worse it looks to me, because I've heard these dithyrambs before from people saying it's a miserable damn time. When our leading writers were Fitzgerald, Faulkner, Hemingway and Dos Passos, people were saying, "There are no good writers around anymore; Dreiser's dead," and so on.

Jones: But do you see something changing in the Southern character?

Foote: I'm sure it must change. For one thing, when I grew up we had a peasantry. That being gone has a profound effect on things. Imagine Russian novels without a peasantry. Imagine Faulknerian novels without blacks. Well, sure it's changed. That's not necessarily for the bad though; we'll just have to wait and see. You're always at the mercy of history, of events, as to whether you have good writers or not. You can't turn them out by any formula; you can't provide a society that will result in good writers. In fact there's a curious paradox there. Our best writers have come out of dreadful times, and out of dreadful systems. Mozart and Beethoven, Bach and Haydn composed under what was largely a patronage system — the worst of all systems, supposedly, but it produced some terrific work.

Jones: I read in a 1952 interview that somebody did with you where you said that you didn't have any other hobbies, that writing was your religion. Is that still the case with you?

Foote: Yes, yes, I don't play golf or even poker. I don't belong to any clubs or anything; don't do anything but write.

Jones: Do you write everyday now?

Foote: Try to, yes. I'm a slow writer, 500 words is a good day, but I always worked seven days a week. I don't do that anymore; I take off Sunday and I don't work eight hours a day like I used to, I work five or six hours. I've written and published over two million words, and so if I'm tired I feel I have a right to be.

Jones: Who do you think that today is writing the best fiction, besides Walker and you?

Foote: You mean for the whole country?

Jones: Yes.

Foote: There's some I like a lot. There is no one I think measures up to the big men before our time, certainly not Mailer or Styron or Capote, but there are writers I like. I think John Updike is a skillful writer. My favorite writer among people who have come along after me is Cormac McCarthy; I like his work a great deal. He had a new novel out about two months ago called *Suttree* that I like a lot. That's his fourth book. I like McCarthy's work very much. There's a South American writer that I put off reading and finally read about two months ago that I am really crazy about. His name is Garcia Marquez. He wrote a book called *One Hundred Years of Solitude*. It's one of the finest novels I've ever read in my life, unbelievably funny. It's got a huge, mythic sort of Faulknerian quality to it. I like it very much. That book came out in 1970 and I didn't read it until eight or nine years later. I called Walker right after I finished it. I was so pleased with it, I said, "Walker, Jesus Christ and God Almighty; I've discovered a very great novel!" He said, "Hey, what is it?" I said, "It's called *One Hundred Years of Solitude* by Garcia Marquez," and Walker said, "You son of a bitch, I did my best to get you to read that book five or six years ago and you wouldn't do it." I'd forgotten he ever said anything about it. It's a good book though.

There's a big gap in my reading of novels caused by my Civil War reading. I read very few novels during those years. I would go back and read *The Brothers Karamazov* or *The Magic Mountain*, but I wasn't reading modern novels, except writers that I was particularly interested in like John O'Hara or Styron and Mailer. Something has happened to writers in our time that's very serious. When they get early fame they get torn on the bias; they get pulled crossways. It's no easy thing to be twenty-six or seven years old and be on the cover of *Time* magazine and have people clamoring after you all the time. You get to believing the extravagant praise, you get to appearing on television talk shows, you get to attending conferences and all that kind of stuff. I don't know why they let themselves in for it, but it appears to be unavoidable. There're some who have managed to avoid it; Salinger steered away from it; but he appears to have gone down the chute even without it. I don't know. It's a hard time, though, because of instantaneous communications and the tremendous growth of television and that kind of thing. It really gets at you. I'm certainly comparatively obscure; and yet you wouldn't believe the amount of stuff that comes into this house — people wanting me to read and comment on their novels or do interviews or write for travel magazines, all this kind of stuff. And there's a lot of big money flying around. I'm not surprised that a lot of people are seduced by it. It's wrong. I have no idea about what to do about it. There are pressures out of nowhere, such as being writer-in-residence somewhere. A young writer learning his craft has got no business being a writer-in-residence. When I was coming up there was nobody that wanted me on any college campus whatsoever, but now they want all these young boys and a lot of them are on campuses and they're not doing a damn thing but laying the coeds. It's a bad scene, particularly for poets. Practically every poet you know is on a college campus somewhere if he's under sixty years old. It's had a bad effect, I think. He ought to be out in the world, writing about what he sees out there, not on a college campus. There are also all kinds of grants and things that are very bad. I ought to be in favor of anything that would help my fellow writers, and me too. I've had three Guggenheims and a Ford Foundation grant, but they were for purposes of researching the War when I had to travel and buy books, which I'd have a hard time doing without Mr. Guggenheim's money and Mr. Ford's money.

But I still think it's bad, particularly for young writers who are learning their craft. No matter how pitifully poor and small the living is that you earn with your pen, you get a tremendous strength by earning your living by your pen. If you're living off government money or grant money, you lose that, and it's a big loss. Now I'm talking particularly about a young writer. After you get a little soft in the belly and the head, I suppose such money doesn't do you much harm. But it diverts you from what should be your pride, it diverts you from what should be your concern. Wondering where your next meal is coming from is a splendid thing for a writer; it's not bad, it doesn't cripple him up, it doesn't keep him from working. Going out and having a job as a common laborer or a timekeeper or something like that is a hell of a lot better way to reinforce your income than teaching on a college campus. Writers used to know that. You can't imagine Hemingway or Fitzgerald or the early Faulkner or John O'Hara or any of those people doing any of those things. They simply did not do them. There was very little opportunity to do them, but they didn't do them. They knew it would interfere with their work, and they put their work first, not their wife and children.

Jones: What about the future of the Southern novel? It seems like a lot of things we always thought of as Northern qualities have come down on us.

Foote: Yes, there's a good deal of homogenization going on. When you're traveling and stop in a Holiday Inn, you can't tell by the looks of the room whether you're in Minnesota or Mississippi. When you go into a restaurant to eat you can't tell where you are. Regional food, regional lodgings, all that is pretty well over. And so I suppose, as a result of radio and the jet plane and those things, we'll all be evened out more and more as time goes on. When I was a boy, people didn't know how to pronounce Roosevelt's name, they called him R*oo*sevelt (vowel sound as in shoot). It was double O, and they had never heard anybody say it. So you had strong regional characteristics simply because of a lack of communication with the rest of the country. I think the attempt to preserve a heritage — not as a brake on progress, but as a matter of pride in that heritage — is a very valuable thing and should be hugged onto. I approve very much of these latest things such as you're doing here, trying to catch the time and fix it with the use of tape recorders and various other things, and the preservation of documents that would be destroyed. The Department of Archives and History there in Jackson has done some marvelous work on preserving things that would have been lost without it. But you can't have pride in your heritage if you don't know the heritage. I was driving through Mississippi, I think it was on a Monday, and I can't remember what year it was [1963], but I heard on the automobile radio that there'd been a bomb set off in a church in Birmingham the day before, and three little Negro girls had been killed. So I was going through a place called Prentiss, Mississippi, and I pulled into a roadside restaurant-cafe to get a newspaper to try to find out what had happened. I went in and the proprietor was standing behind the cash register talking to a Mississippi highway patrolman. There was a waitress down the counter there. I went up to the proprietor and said, "Do you have a morning paper?" and he said, "We're all sold out." I said, "I wanted to find out something if I could about this Birmingham explosion, a bombing or something in a church over there." He said, "Yeah, that was all in the paper this morning. I guess those niggers will learn sooner or later." I said, "Well, I must not have heard it right on the radio. It said three little girls were killed." He said, "That's right," and I said, "Thank you, anyhow," and went and sat down at the counter. The waitress came over and I said, "I just want a cup of coffee," and she went to get the coffee. I turned back around to the proprietor and said, "This town is called Prentiss," — I've left out one thing he said. "We've got to preserve our heritage," was one of the things he said in the extenuation of this bombing and everything else; his notion that we had to hold the blacks down if we were going to preserve our heritage, because it would be destroyed. Anyway, while she was getting me the coffee I turned back to him and the patrolman and I said, "This town is called Prentiss; is it named for Sergeant S. Prentiss?" He said, "I don't know," and I said, "It seems likely, but it might have been some other family name, Prentiss or something." He said to the waitress, "You know how Prentiss got its name?" She said, "No, I don't know," and the highway patrolman said he didn't have any idea. That showed you how much their heritage meant to them. It was a strange business though. There's a log of ugliness down here. Yet I know from my experiences in the North and in the South that that same man, if I had been broken down on the side of the road with car trouble or something, he would stop, get the jack out of his car and help me, get all greasy and dirty, and would not have expected anything more than a "thank you" for doing it. It's a curious mixup of traits. Most of the evil comes from ignorance. It seems that the good is inherent and the evil is acquired. I have a candidate to blame for all this. I think the planter is the "nigger in this woodpile." He's the son of a bitch who set the system up so he could rule the roost, and he managed to keep everybody under him quiet by promising them about this open society where they could be planters someday and live the way he lived. Sometimes I'm amazed at his genius, at how well the whole thing was designed. Even the giving of Christmas presents to plantation workers was designed to demean them. Almost everything about day-to-day life on the plantation — and I speak with some knowledge because I come from a long line of planters — was designed to hold these people down so that he could live the way he did. I don't know if people would even believe it nowadays, but it was quite common for a cook who worked seven days a week, all day, fixing breakfast, dinner and supper, to make three dollars, three-fifty and four dollars a week. What she got for that was money, which she used to pay her house rent, usually about five dollars a month for the cabin she lived in with no plumbing, and cast-off clothes, and food to take home to her husband and children at night. That can't be a good system. That's bound to be a bad system. And the people who were paying that to her, in many cases, were making a great deal of money. Something was very wrong at the core of it, not only in slavery days but in those days too, which practically amounted to peonage. My grandfather and two other men at home, including Senator Percy — it was my grandfather, Senator Percy and O. B. Crittenden — had a plantation across the river, where the bridge goes now, called Sunnyside. They brought in Italian and Sicilian workers; paid their passage over on the boat. The three men nearly got into serious trouble with the federal government because a Catholic priest who was ministering to those people saw what was being done to them. It amounted to peonage; they had to work off their passage and it never worked out so that they got clear. The three men were very nearly prosecuted for peonage, but they managed to get from under it by the fact that Theodore Roosevelt had met Senator Percy as a young man when he came down to my part of the country on a bear hunt with my other grandfather. This was my mother's father who was in on the plantation; his name was Rosenstock. My other grandfather Foote had had Roosevelt down here on a bear hunt, and they got to talking, "What are we going to do when we're not hunting with President Roosevelt? How are we going to talk with him? We'll bore him to death." So my grandfather said, "We'll ask Percy along; he can talk with him." So, as a result of that relationship they were able to get the indictment quashed, or anyhow not prosecuted on condition that they let the people go.

Jones: Mr. Foote, I've kept you long enough. Before I cut this off I want to say how much I appreciate your talking with me. It's been an honor to meet you.

• WALKER PERCY •

Questions They Never Asked Me
So He Asked Them Himself
(Self-Interview, 1977)

Question: Will you consent to an interview?

Answer: No.

Q: Why not?

A: Interviewers always ask the same questions, such as: What time of day do you write? Do you type or write longhand? What do you think of the South? What do you think of the New South? What do you think of southern writers? Who are your favorite writers? What do you think of Jimmy Carter?

Q: You're not interested in the South?

A: I'm sick and tired of talking about the South and hearing about the South.

Q: Do you regard yourself as a southern writer?

A: That is a strange question, even a little mad. Sometimes I think that the South brings out the latent madness in people. It even makes me feel nutty to hear such a question.

Q: What's mad about such a question?

A: Would you ask John Cheever if he regarded himself as a northeastern writer?

Q: What do you think of southern writers?

A: I'm fed up with the subject of southern writing. Northern writing, too, for that matter. I'm also fed up with questions about the state of the novel, alienation, the place of the artist in American society, race relations, the Old South.

Q: What about the New South?

A: Of all the things I'm fed up with,I think I'm fed up most with hearing about the New South.

Q: Why is that?

A: One of the first things I can remember in my life was hearing about the New South. I was three years old, in Alabama. Not a year has passed since that I haven't heard about a New South. I would dearly love never to hear the New South mentioned again. In fact my definition of a new South would be a South in which it never occurred to anybody to mention the New South. One glimmer of hope is that this may be happening.

Q: But people have a great curiosity about the South now that Jimmy Carter is President.

A: I doubt that. If there is anything more boring than the questions asked about the South, it is the answers southerners give. If I hear one more northerner ask about good ol' boys and one more southerner give an answer, I'm moving to Manaus, Brazil, to join the South Carolinians who emigrated after Appomattox and whose descendants now speak no English and have such names as Senhor Carlos Calhoun. There are no good ol' boys in Manaus.

Q: In the past you have expressed admiration for such living writers as Bellow, Updike, Didion, Mailer, Cheever, Foote, Barthelme, Gass, Heller. Do you still subscribe to such a list?

A: No.

Q: Why not?

A: I can't stand lists of writers. Compiling such a list means leaving somebody out. When serious writers make a list, they're afraid of leaving somebody out. When critics and poor writers do it, they usually mean to leave somebody out. It seems a poor practice in either case.

Q: Do you have any favorite dead writers?

A: None that I care to talk about. Please don't ask me about Dostoevski and Kierkegaard.

Q: How about yourself? Would you comment on your own writing?

A: No.

Q: Why not?

A: I can't stand to think about it.

Q: Could you say something about the vocation of writing in general?

A: No.

Q: Nothing?

A: All I can think to say about it is that it is a very obscure activity in which there is usually a considerable element of malice. Like frogging.

Q: Frogging?

A: Yes. Frogging is raising a charley horse on somebody's arm by a skillful blow with a knuckle in exactly the right spot.

Q: What are your hobbies?

A: I don't have any.

Q: What magazines do you read?

A: None.

Q: What are your plans for summer reading?

A: I don't have any.

Q: Do you keep a journal?

A: No.

Q: But don't writers often keep journals?

A: So I understand. But I could never think what to put in a journal. I used to read writers' journals and was both astonished and depressed by the copiousness of a single day's entry: thoughts, observations, reflections, descriptions, snatches of plots, bits of poetry, sketches, aphorisms. The one time I kept a journal I made two short entries in three weeks. One entry went so: *Four p.m. Thursday afternoon — The only thing notable is that nothing is notable. I wonder if any writer has ever recorded the observation that most time passes and most events occur without notable significance. I am sitting here looking out the window at a tree and wondering why it is that though it is a splendid tree, it is of not much account. It is no good to me. Is it the nature of the human condition or the nature of the age that things of value are devalued?* I venture to say that most people most of the time experience the same four-o'clock-in-the-afternoon devaluation. But I have noticed an interesting thing. If such a person, a person like me feeling lapsed at four o'clock in the afternoon, should begin reading a novel about a person feeling lapsed at four o'clock in the afternoon, a strange thing happens. Things increase in value. Possibilities open. This may be the main function of art in this peculiar age: to reverse the devaluation. What the artist or writer does is not depict a beautiful tree — this only depresses you more than ever — no, he depicts the commonplaceness of an everyday tree. Depicting the commonplace allows the reader to penetrate the commonplace. The only other ways the husk of the commonplace can be penetrated is through the occurrence of natural disasters or the imminence of one's own death. These measures are not readily available on ordinary afternoons.

Q: How would you describe the place of the writer and artist in American life?

A: Strange.

Q: How do you perceive your place in society?

A: I'm not sure what that means.

Q: Well, in this small Louisiana town, for example.

A: I'm still not sure what you mean. I go to the barbershop to get a haircut and the barber says: "How you doing, Doc?" I say: "Okay." I go to the post office to get the mail and the clerk says: "What's up, Doc?" Or I go to a restaurant on Lake Pontchartrain and the waitress says: "What you want, honey?" I say: "Some cold beer and crawfish." She brings me an ice-cold beer and a platter of boiled crawfish that are very good, especially if you suck the heads. Is that what you mean?

Q: What about living in the South, with its strong sense of place, of tradition, of rootedness, of tragedy — the only part of America that has ever tasted defeat?

A: I've read about that. Actually I like to stay in motels in places like Lincoln, Nebraska, or San Luis Obispo.

Q: But what about these unique characteristics of the South? Don't they tend to make the South a more hospitable place for writers?

A: Well, I've heard about that, the storytelling tradition, sense of identity, tragic dimension, community, history and so forth. But I was never quite sure what it meant. In fact, I'm not sure that the opposite is not the case. People don't read much in the South and don't take writers very seriously, which is probably as it should be. I've managed to live here for thirty years and am less well-known than the Budweiser distributor. The only famous person in this town is Isiah Robertson, linebacker for the Rams, and that is probably as it should be, too. There are advantages to living an obscure life and being thought an idler. If one lived in a place like France where writers are honored, one might well end up like Sartre, a kind of literary-political pope, a savant, an academician, the very sort of person Sartre made fun of in *Nausea*. On the other hand, if one is thought an idler and a bum, one is free to do what one pleases. One day a fellow townsman asked me: "What do you do, Doc?" "Well, I write books." "I know that, Doc, but what do you really do?" "Nothing." He nodded. He was pleased and I was pleased.

I have a theory of why Faulkner became a great writer. It was not the presence of a tradition and all that, as one generally hears, but the absence. Everybody in Oxford, Mississippi, knew who Faulkner was, not because he was a great writer but because he was a local character, a little bitty fellow who put on airs, wore a handkerchief up his sleeve, a ne'er-do-well, Count No-count they called him. He was tagged like a specimen under a bell jar; no matter what he wrote thereafter, however great or wild or strange it was, it was all taken as part of the act. It was part of "what Bill Faulkner did." So I can imagine it became a kind of game with him, with him going to extraordinary lengths in his writing to see if he could shake them out of their mild, pleasant inattention. I don't mean he wanted his fellow southerners to pay him homage, that his life and happiness depended on what they thought of him. No, it was a kind of game. One can imagine Robinson Crusoe on his island doing amazing acrobatics for his herd of goats, who might look up, dreamily cud chewing for a moment, then go on with their grazing. "That one didn't grab you?" Crusoe might say, then come out with something even more stupendous. But even if he performed the ultimate stunt, the Indian rope trick, where he climbs up a stiff rope and disappears, the goats would see it as no more or less than what this character does under the circumstances. Come to think of it, who would want it otherwise? There is a good deal of talk about community and the lack of it, but one of the nice things about living an obscure life in the South is that people don't come up to you, press your hand and give you soulful looks. I would have hated to belong to the Algonquin round table, where people made witty remarks and discussed Ezra Pound. Most men in the South don't read and the women who do usually prefer Taylor Caldwell and Phyllis Whitney to Faulkner and O'Connor.

No, it is the very absence of a tradition that makes for great originals like Faulkner and O'Connor and Poe. The South is Crusoe's island for a writer and there's the good and bad of it. There is a literary community of sorts in the North. The best northern writers are accordingly the best of a kind. As different as Bellow, Cheever, Updike and Pynchon are, their differences are within a genus, like different kinds of fruit: apples, oranges, plums, pears. A critic or reviewer can compare and contrast them with one another. But Faulkner, O'Connor, Barthelme? They're moon berries, kiwi fruit, niggertoes.

Q: Niggertoes?

A: That's what we used to call Brazil nuts.

Q: How did you happen to become a writer? Didn't you start out as a doctor?

A: Yes, but I had no special talent for it. Others in my class were smarter. Two women, three Irish Catholics, four Jews and ten WASPs were better at it than I. What happened was that I discovered I had a little knack for writing. Or perhaps it is desire, a kind of underhanded desire.

Q: What do you mean by knack?

A: It is hard to say.

Q: Try.

A: I suspect it is something all writers have in greater or lesser degree. Maybe it's inherited, maybe it's the result of a rotten childhood — I don't know. But unless you have it, you'll never be a writer.

Q: Can you describe the knack?

A: No, except in negative terms. It is not what people think it is. Most people think it is the perfecting of the ordinary human skills of writing down words and sentences. Everybody writes words and sentences — for example, in a letter. A book is thought to be an expanded and improved letter, the way a pro ballplayer is thought to do things with a ball most men can do, only better. Not so. Or if you have an unusual experience, all you have to do is "write it up," the more unusual and extraordinary the experience the better, like My Most Extraordinary Experience in *Reader's Digest*. Not so. Psychologists know even less about writing than laymen. Show me a psychologist with a theory of creativity and I'll show you a bad writer.

Q: Can't you say what the knack is?

A: No, except to say that it is a peculiar activity, as little understood as chicken fighting or entrail reading, and that the use of words, sentences, paragraphs, plots, characters and so forth are the accidents, not the substance, of it.

Q: What is it if not the putting together of words and sentences?

A: I can't answer that except to say two things. One is that it is a little trick one gets onto, a very minor trick. One does it and discovers to one's surprise that most people can't do it. I used to know a fellow in high school who, due to an anomaly of his eustachian tubes, could blow smoke out of both ears. He enjoyed doing it and it was diverting to watch. Writing is something like that. Another fellow I knew in college, a fraternity brother and a trumpet player, could swell out his neck like a puff adder — the way the old horn player Clyde McCoy used to do when he played *Sugar Blues*.

The other thing about the knack is that it has theological, demonic and sexual components. One is aware on the one hand of a heightened capacity for both malice and joy and, occasionally and with luck, for being able to see things afresh and even to make things the way the Old Testament said that God made things and took a look at them and saw that they were good.

The best novels, and the best part of a novel, is a creatio ex nihilo. Unlike God, the novelist does not start with nothing and make something of it. He starts with himself as nothing and makes something of the nothing with things at hand. If the novelist has a secret it is not that he has a special something but that he has a special nothing. Camus said that all philosophy comes from the possibility of suicide. This is probably not true, one of those intellectual oversimplifications to which the French regularly fall prey. Suicide, the real possibility of self-nihilation, has more to do with writing poems and novels. A novelist these days has to be an ex-suicide. A good novel — and, I imagine, a good poem — is possible only after one has given up and let go. Then, once one realizes that all is lost, the jig is up, that after all nothing is dumber than a grown man sitting down and making up a story to entertain somebody or working in a "tradition" or "school" to maintain his reputation as a practitioner of the *nouveau roman* or whatever — once one sees that this is a dumb way to live, that all is vanity sure enough, there are *two* possibilities: either commit suicide or not commit suicide. If one opts for the former, that is that; it is a *letzte Lösung* and there is nothing more to write or say about it. But if one opts for the latter, one is in a sense dispensed and living on borrowed time. One is not dead! Onc is alive! One is free! I won't say that one is like God on the first day, with the chaos before him and a free hand. Rather one feels, What the hell, here I am washed up, it is true, but also cast up, cast up on the beach, alive and in one piece. I can move my toe up and then down and do anything else I choose. The possibilities open to one are infinite. So why not do something Shakespeare and Dostoevski and Faulkner didn't do, for after all they are nothing more than dead writers, members of this and that tradition, much-admired busts on a shelf. A dead writer may be famous but he is also dead as a duck, finished. And I, cast up here on this beach? I am a survivor! Alive! A free man! They're finished. Possibilities are closed. As for God? That's his affair. True, he made the beach, which, now that I look at it, is not all that great. As for me, I might try a little something here in the wet sand, a word, a form . . .

Q: What's this about a sexual component?

A: I'd rather not say.

Q: Why not?

A: Because no end of dreary bullshit has been written on the subject, so much as to befoul the waters for good. Starting with Freud's rather stupid hydraulic model of art as the sublimation of libidinal energies: libido suppressed in the boiler room squirts up in the attic. There followed half a century of dull jokes about x orgasms equals y novels down the drain, and so forth and so forth. Freud's disciples have been even more stupid about "creative writing." At least Freud had the good sense to know when to shut up, as he did in Dostoevski's case. But stupider still is the more recent Hemingway machismo number. The formula is: Big pencil equals big penis. My own hunch is that those fellows have their troubles, otherwise why make love with a pencil? Renoir may have started it with a smart-ass statement: "I paint with my penis." If I were a woman, I wouldn't stand for such crap. No wonder women get enraged these days. Some of the most feminine women writers have this same knack, or better, and can use it to a fare-thee-well — southern women like K. A. Porter, Welty, O'Connor — look out for them!

The twentieth century, noted for its stupidity in human matters, is even stupider than usual in this case. And in this case Muhammad Ali is smarter than either Freud or Hemingway. Float like a butterfly, sting like a bee. Ali's exaltation and cunning and beauty and malice apply even more to writing than to fighting. Freud made a mistake only a twentieth-century professor would have been capable of: trying to explain the human psyche by a mechanical-energy model. Take away four hundred fifty psychic calories for love and that leaves you four hundred fifty short for art. Actually it's the other way around. The truth is paradoxical and can't be understood in terms of biological systems. Psychic energy is involved here, but it follows a different set of laws. Like Einstein's theory, it at times defies Newton's law of gravitation. Thus it is not the case that E minus one-half E equals one-half E (Newton, Freud) but rather E minus one-half E equals six E. Or simply, zero minus E equals E — which is more astounding than Einstein's E equals MC squared.

I will give you a simple example. Let us say a writer finds himself at 0, naught, zero, at four p.m. of a Thursday afternoon. No energy, depressed, strung out, impotent, constipated, a poet sitting on the kitchen floor with the oven door open and the gas on, an incarnated nothingness, an outer human husk encasing an inner cipher. The jig is up. The poem or novel is no good. But since the jig is up, why not have another look, or tear it up and start over? Then, if he is lucky — or is it grace, God having mercy on the poor bastard? — something opens. A miracle occurs. Somebody must have found the Grail. The fisher king is healed, the desert turns green — or better still: the old desert is still the old desert but the poet names it and makes it a new desert. As for the poet himself: in a strange union of polarities — wickedness/good, malice/benevolence, hatred/love, butterfly/bee — he, too, comes together, sticks his tongue in his cheek, sets pencil to paper: What if I should try this? Uh-huh, maybe . . . He works. He sweats. He stinks. He creates. He sweats and stinks and creates like a woman conceiving. Then what? It varies. Perhaps he takes a shower, changes clothes. Perhaps he takes a swim in the ocean. Perhaps he takes a nap. Perhaps he takes a drink, flatfoots half a glass of bourbon. Then, if he is near someone he loves or wants to love or should love or perhaps has loved all along but has not until this moment known it, he looks at her. And by exactly the same measure by which the novel has opened to him and he to it, he opens to her and she to him. Well now, why don't you come here a minute? That's it. Give me your hand. He looks at her hand. He is like the castaway on the beach who opens his eyes and sees a sunrise coquina three inches from his nose. Her hand is like the coquina. What an amazing sight! Well now, why don't we just sit down here on this cypress log? Imagine your being here at four-thirty in the afternoon. All this time I thought I was alone on this island and here you are. A miracle! Imagine Crusoe on his island performing the ultimate stunt for his goats, when he turns around and the *she* is. Who needs Friday? What he needs now is her, or she him, as the case may be.

Such is the law of conservation of energy through its expenditure: Zero minus E equals E.

Q: If writing is a knack, does the knack have anything to do with being southern?

A: Sure. The knack has certain magic components that once came in handy for southern writers. This is probably no longer the case.

Q: Why is that?

A: Well, as Einstein once said, ordinary life in an ordinary place on an ordinary day in the modern world is a dreary business. I mean *dreary*. People will do anything to escape this dreariness: booze up, hit the road, gaze at fatal car wrecks, shoot up heroin, spend money on gurus, watch pornographic movies, kill themselves, even watch TV. Einstein said that was the reason he went into mathematical physics. One of the few things that diverted me from the dreariness of growing up in a country-club subdivision in Birmingham was sending off for things. For example, sending off for free samples, such as Instant Postum. You'd fill in a coupon clipped from a magazine and send it off to a magic faraway place (Battle Creek?) and sure enough, one morning the mailman would hand you a *box*. Inside would be a small jar. You'd make a cup and in the peculiar fragrance of Postum you could imagine an equally fragrant and magical place where clever Yankee experts ground up stuff in great brass mortars.

That was called "sending off for something."

It was even better with Sears and Roebuck: looking at the picture in the catalog, savoring it, fondling it, sailing to Byzantium with it, then — even better than poetry — actually getting it, sending off to Chicago for it, saving up your allowance and mailing a postal money order for twenty-three dollars and forty-seven cents and getting back a gold-filled Elgin railroader's pocket watch with an elk engraved on the back. With a strap and a fob.

Writing is also going into the magic business. It is a double transaction in magic. You have this little workaday thing you do that most people can't do. But in the South there were also certain magic and exotic ingredients, that is, magic and exotic to northerners and Europeans, which made the knack even more mysterious. As exotic to a New Yorker as an Elgin pocket watch to an Alabama boy. I've often suspected that Faulkner was very much onto this trick and overdid it a bit.

You write something, send it off to a *publisher* in *New York* and back it comes as a — book! Print! Pages! Cover! Binding! Scribble-scratch is turned into measured paragraphs, squared-off blocks of pretty print. And even more astounding: in the same mail that brought the Elgin pocket watch come *reviews*, the printed thoughts of people who have *read* the book!

The less the two parties know about each other, the farther apart they are, the stronger the magic. It must be very enervating to be a writer in New York, where you know all about editing and publishing and reviewing, to discover that editors and publishers and reviewers are as bad off as anyone else, maybe worse. Being a writer in the South has its special miseries, which include isolation, madness, tics, amnesia, alcoholism, lust and loss of ordinary powers of speech. One may go for days without saying a word. Then, faced with an interviewer, one may find oneself talking the way one fancies the interviewer expects one to talk, talking southern — for example, using such words as "Amon": "Amon git up and git myself a drink." Yet there are certain advantages to the isolation. At best one is encouraged to be original; at worst, bizarre; sometimes both, like Poe.

It was this distance and magic that once made for the peculiarities of southern writing. Now the distance and magic are gone, or going, and southern writers are no better off than anyone else, perhaps worse, because now that the tricks don't work and you can't write strange like Faulkner, what do you do? Write like Bellow? But before — and even now, to a degree — the magic worked. You were on your own and making up little packages to send to faraway folk. As marooned as Crusoe, one was apt to be eccentric. That's why Poe, Faulkner, O'Connor and Barthelme are more different from one another than Bellow, Updike and Cheever are.

The southern writer at his best was a value because he was somewhat extraterrestrial. (At his worst he was overwhelmed by Faulkner: there is nothing more feckless than imitating an eccentric.) He was different enough from the main body of writers to give the reader a triangulation point for getting a fix on things. There are degrees of difference. If the writer is altogether different from the genus *Writer*, which is the only genus the reviewer knows, the reviewer is baffled — as New York reviewers like Clifton Fadiman were baffled by Faulkner; they were trying to compare him with such standard writers as Thornton Wilder, and it can't be done. But if the critic recognizes the value of difference, the possibility of an extraterrestrial point of view, he will be excited. That's why the French went nuts over Poe and Faulkner.

Meanwhile, Mississippians shrugged their shoulders.

Q: Would you care to say something about your own novels?

A: No.

Q: What about your last novel, *Lancelot*?

A: What about it?

Q: What do you have to say about it?

A: Nothing.

Q: How would you describe it?

A: As a small cautionary tale.

Q: That's all?

A: That's all.

Q: It has generally been well reviewed. What do you think of reviews?

A: Very little. Reading reviews of your own book is a peculiar experience. It is a dubious enterprise, a no-win game. If the review is flattering, one tends to feel vain and uneasy. If it is bad, one tends to feel exposed, found out. Neither feeling does you any good. Besides that, most reviews are of not much account. How could it be otherwise? I feel sorry for reviewers. I feel sorry for myself when I write a review. Book reviewing is a difficult and unrewarding literary form and right now no one is doing it. The reviewer's task is almost impossible. A writer may spend years doing his obscure thing, his little involuted sexual-theological number, and there's the poor reviewer with two or three days to figure out what he's up to. And even if the review is good, you're in no mood to learn anything from it. The timing is all bad. You're sick to death of the book and don't even want to think about it. Then, just when you think you're rid of this baby, have kicked him and his droppings out of the nest forever, along comes these folks who want to talk about him.

Q: Do you feel bad about a bad review?

A: Moderately bad. One likes to be liked. The curious thing is I always expect people to like me and my writing and am surprised when they don't. I suffer from the opposite of paranoia, a benign psychosis for which there is no word. I say "curious" because there is a good deal of malice in my writing — I have it in for this or that — but it is not personal malice and I'm taken aback when people take offense.

A rave review makes me feel even more uneasy. It's like being given an A plus by the teacher or a prize by the principal. All you want to do is grab your report card and run — before you're found out.

Q: Found out for what?

A: Found out for being what you are (and what in this day and age I think a serious writer has to be): an ex-suicide, a cipher, naught, zero — which is as it should be because being a naught is the very condition of making anything. This is a secret. People don't know this. Even distinguished critics are under the misapprehension that you are something, a substance, that you represent this or that tradition, a skill, a growing store of wisdom. Whereas in fact what you are doing is stripping yourself naked and putting yourself in the eye of the hurricane and leaving the rest to chance, luck or providence. Faulkner said it in fact: Writing a novel is like a one-armed man trying to nail together a chicken coop in a hurricane. I think of it as more like trying to pick up a four-hundred-pound fat lady: you need a lot of hands to hold up a lot of places at once.

There are four kinds of reviews, three of which are depressing and one of which is at best tolerable.

The first is the good good review. That is, a review that is not only laudatory but is also canny and on the mark. One is exhilarated for three seconds, then one becomes furtive and frightened. One puts it away quick, before it turns into a pumpkin.

The second is the bad good review. That is, it is the routine "favorable" review that doesn't understand the book. The only thing to say about it is that it is better to get a bad good review than a bad bad review.

The third is the bad bad review. It is a hateful review in which the reviewer hates the book for reasons he is unwilling to disclose. He is offended. But he must find other reasons for attacking the book than the cause of the offense. I don't blame this reviewer. In fact he or she is sharper than most. He or she is onto the secret that novel writing is a serious business in which the novelist is out both to give joy and to draw blood. The hateful review usually means that one has succeeded only in doing the latter. The name of this reviewer's game is: "Okay, you want to play rough? Very well, here comes yours." A hateful reviewer is like a street fighter: he doesn't let on where he's been hit and he hits you with everything he's got — a bad tactic. Or he lies low and waits for a chance to blindside you. A bad bad review doesn't really hurt. Getting hit by an offended reviewer reminds me of the old guy on *Laugh-In* who would make a pass at Ruth Buzzi on the park bench and get slammed across the chops by a soft purse. It's really a love tap. I can't speak for Ruth Buzzi but I can speak for the old guy: all he wants to say is, "Come on, honey, give us a kiss."

The fourth is the good bad review, a rare bird. It would be the most valuable if one were in any shape to learn, which one is not. It is the critical review that accurately assesses both what the novelist had in mind, was trying to do, and how and where he failed. It hurts because the failure is always great, but the hurt is salutary, like pouring iodine in an open wound. Here the transaction is between equals, a fair fight, no blind-sliding. It makes me think of old-movie fistfights between John Wayne and Ward Bond. Ward lets the Duke have one, racks him up real good. The Duke shakes his head to clear it, touches the corner of his mouth, looks at the blood, grins in appreciation. Nods. All right. That's a fair transaction, a frontal assault by an equal. But what the hateful reviewer wants to do is blind-side you, the way Chuck Bednarik blind-sided Frank Gifford and nearly killed him. Unlike Chuck Bednarik, the hateful reviewer can't hurt you. He gives away too much of himself. The only way he can hurt you is in the pocketbook — the way a playwright can be knocked off by a *Times* reviewer — but in the case of a book even that is doubtful.

Even so, one is still better off with hateful reviewers than with admiring reviewers. If I were a castaway on a desert island, I'd rather be marooned with six hateful reviewers than with six admiring reviewers. The hateful men would be better friends and the hateful women would be better lovers.

The truth is all reviewers and all your fellow novelists are your friends and lovers. All serious writers and readers constitute less than one percent of the population. The other ninety-nine percent don't give a damn. They watch *Wonder Woman*. We are a tiny shrinking minority and our worst assaults on each other are love taps compared with the massive indifference surrounding us. Gore Vidal and Bill Buckley are really two of a kind, though it will displease both to hear it. Both are serious moralists to whom I attach a high value.

Q: Do you see the Jimmy Carter phenomenon as a revival of Protestant Christianity or as a renascence of Jeffersonian populism or the southern political genius or all three, and if so, what is the impact on the southern literary imagination and race relations?

A: How's that again?

Q: Do you —

A: What was that about race relations?

Q: How do you assess the current state of race relations in the South?

A: Almost as bad as in the North.

Q: But hasn't there occurred a rather remarkable reconciliation of the races in the South as a consequence of its strong Christian tradition and its traditional talent for human relations?

A: I haven't noticed it. The truth is most blacks and whites don't like each other, North or South.

Q: But great changes have taken place, haven't they?

A: Yes, due mainly to court decisions and congressional acts and Lyndon Johnson. It was easier for the South to go along than to resist. After all, we tried that once. Anyhow, as Earl Long used to say, the feds have the bomb now.

Q: Can you say anything about the future of race relations?

A: No.

Q: Why not?

A: I'm white. It's up to the blacks. The government has done all it can do. The whites' course is predictable. Like anybody else, they will simply hold on to what they've got as long as they can. When did any other human beings behave differently? The blacks have a choice. They can either shoot up the place, pull the whole damn thing down around our ears — they can't win but they can ruin it for everybody — or they can join the great screwed-up American middle class. Of course what they're doing is both, mostly the latter. It is noteworthy that blacks, being smarter than whites about such things, have shown no interest in the Communist party. Blacks seem less prone than whites to fall prey to abstractions. Comradeship and brotherhood are all very well, but what I really want is out of this ghetto, and if I can make it and you can't, too bad about you, brother. But that's the American dream, isn't it? It will even make them happy like it did us — for a while. It will take them years to discover just how screwed up the American middle class is. I visualize a U.S. a few years from now in which blacks and whites have switched roles. The pissed-off white middle class will abandon suburbia just as they abandoned the cities, either for the countryside, where they will live in r.v.'s, mobile homes, converted farms, log cabins, antebellum outhouses, revolutionary stables, silos, sod huts, or to move back to the city, back to little ethnic cottages like Mayor Daley's, Victorian shotguns, stained-glass boardinghouses, converted slave quarters, abandoned streetcars — while the blacks move out to Levittown and the tracts, attend the churches of their choice, P.T.A.'s, Rotary, Great Books. In fact it's already happening. The only danger is that this happy little switch may not happen fast enough and the young blacks in the city who have little or nothing to lose may say the hell with it and shoot up everything in sight.

There is a slight chance, maybe one in a hundred, that blacks and whites may learn the best of each other rather than the worst.

Q: What is the worst?

A: Well, whites in the Western world don't know how to live and blacks don't know how to govern themselves. It would be nice if each could learn the gift of the other. But there are already signs in America that blacks are learning the white incapacity for life. For example, they've almost reached the white incidence of suicide and gastric ulcer and have surpassed them in hypertension. And some white politicians govern like Haitians and Ugandans. I've noticed that more and more blacks act like Robert Young as Dr. Marcus Welby, with that same tight-assed, suspect post-Protestant rectitude, while more and more white politicians act like Idi Amin.

Q: Can you describe the best thing that could happen?

A: No. All I can say is that it has something to do with southern good nature, good manners, kidding around, with music, with irony, with being able to be pissed off without killing other people or yourself, maybe with Jewish humor, with passing the time, with small unpretentious civic-minded meetings. Some whites and blacks are sitting around a table in Louisiana, eating crawfish and drinking beer at a P.T.A. fund raiser. The table is somewhat polarized, whites at one end, blacks at the other, segregated not ill-naturedly but from social unease, like men and women at a party. The talk is somewhat stiff and conversation making and highfaluting — about reincarnation in fact. Says a white to a white who has only had a beer or two: "I think I'd rather come back as an English gentleman in the eighteenth century rather than this miserable century of war, alienation and pollution." Says a black to a black who has had quite a few beers: "I'd rather come back as this damn crawfish than as a nigger in Louisiana." All four laugh and have another beer. I don't know why I'm telling you this. You wouldn't understand it. You wouldn't understand what is bad about it, what is good about it, what is unusual about it or what there is about it that might be the hundred-to-one shot that holds the solution.

Q: Why do you leave Christianity out as one of the ingredients of better race relations?

A: Because the Christians left it out. Maybe Jimmy Carter and Andrew Young and a few others mean what they say, I don't know, but look at the white churches. They generally practice the same brand of brotherhood as the local country club. If Jesus Christ showed up at the Baptist church in Plains, the deacons would call the cops. No, the law, government, business, sports, show business, have done more here than the churches. There seems to be an inverse relationship between God and brotherhood in the churches. In the Unitarian Church, it's all brotherhood and no God. Outside the churches the pocketbook has replaced the Holy Ghost as the source of brotherhood. Show me an A & P today that is losing money because it is not hiring blacks and I'll show you an A & P tomorrow that has hired blacks and, what is more, where blacks and whites get along fine.

Q: But aren't you a Catholic?

A: Yes.

Q: Do you regard yourself as a Catholic novelist?

A: Since I am a Catholic and a novelist, it would seem to follow that I am a Catholic novelist.

Q: What kind of Catholic are you?

A: Bad.

Q: No. I mean are you liberal or conservative?

A: I no longer know what those words mean.

Q: Are you a dogmatic Catholic or an open-minded Catholic?

A: I don't know what that means, either. Do you mean do I believe the dogma that the Catholic Church proposes for belief?

Q: Yes.

A: Yes.

Q: How is such a belief possible in this day and age?

A: What else is there?

Q: What do you mean, what else is there? There is humanism, atheism, agnosticism, Marxism, behaviorism, materialism, Buddhism, Muhammadanism, Sufism, astrology, occultism, theosophy.

A: That's what I mean.

Q: To say nothing of Judaism and Protestantism.

A: Well, I would include them along with the Catholic Church in the whole peculiar Jewish-Christian thing.

Q: I don't understand. Would you exclude, for example, scientific humanism as a rational and honorable alternative?

A: Yes.

Q: Why?

A: It's not good enough.

Q: Why not?

A: This life is much too much trouble, far too strange, to arrive at the end of it and then to be asked what you make of it and have to answer "Scientific humanism." That won't do. A poor show. Life is a mystery, love is a delight. Therefore I take it as axiomatic that one should settle for nothing less than the infinite mystery and the infinite delight, i.e., God. In fact I demand it. I refuse to settle for anything less. I don't see why anyone should settle for less than Jacob, who actually grabbed aholt of God and wouldn't let go until God identified himself and blessed him.

Q: Grabbed aholt?

A: A Louisiana expression.

Q: But isn't the Catholic Church in a mess these days, badly split, its liturgy barbarized, vocations declining?

A: Sure. That's a sign of its divine origins, that it survivies these periodic disasters.

Q: You don't act or talk like a Christian. Aren't they supposed to love one another and do good works?

A: Yes.

Q: You don't seem to have much use for your fellowman or do many good works.

A: That's true. I haven't done a good work in years.

Q: In fact, if I may be frank, you strike me as being rather negative in your attitude, cold-blooded, aloof, derisive, self-indulgent, more fond of the beautiful things of this world than of God.

A: That's true.

Q: You even seem to take a certain satisfaction in the disasters of the twentieth-century and to savor the imminence of world catastrophe rather than world peace, which all religions seek.

A: That's true.

Q: You don't seem to have much use for your fellow Christians, to say nothing of Ku Kluxers, A.C.L.U.'ers, northerners, southerners, fem-libbers, anti-fem-libbers, homosexuals, anti-homosexuals, Republicans, Democrats, hippies, anti-hippies, senior citizens.

A: That's true — though taken as individuals they turn out to be more or less like oneself, i.e., sinners, and we get along fine.

Q: Even Ku Kluxers?

A: Sure.

Q: How do you account for your belief?

A: I can only account for it as a gift from God.

Q: Why would God make you such a gift when there are others who seem more deserving, that is, serve their fellowman?

A: I don't know. God does strange things. For example, he picked as one of his saints a fellow in northern Syria, a local nut, who stood on top of a pole for thirty-seven years.

Q: We are not talking about saints.

A: That's true.

Q: We are talking about what you call a gift.

A: You want me to explain it? How would I know? The only answer I can give is that I asked for it, in fact demanded it. I took it as an intolerable state of affairs to have found myself in this life and in this age, which is a disaster by any calculation, without demanding a gift commensurate with the offense. So I demanded it. No doubt other people feel differently.

Q: But shouldn't faith bear some relation to the truth, facts?

A: Yes. That's what attracted me, Christianity's rather insolent claim to be true, with the implication that other religions are more or less false.

Q: You believe that?

A: Of course.

Q: I see. Moving right along now —

A: To what?

Q: To language. Haven't you done some writing about the nature of language?

A: Yes.

Q: Will you say something about your ideas about language?

A: No.

Q: Why not?

A: Because, for one thing, nobody is interested. The nature of language is such, I have discovered from experience, that even if anyone has the ultimate solution to the mystery of language, no one would pay the slightest attention. In fact most people don't even know there is a mystery. Here is an astounding fact, when you come to think of it. The use of symbols between creatures, the use of language in particular, appears to be the one unique phenomenon in the universe, is certainly the single behavior that most clearly sets man apart from the beasts, is also the one activity in which humans engage most of the time, even asleep and dreaming. Yet it is the least understood of all phenomena. We know less about it than about the back side of the moon or the most distant supernova — and are less interested.

Q: Why is that? Why aren't people interested?

A: Because there are two kinds of people, laymen and scientists. The layman doesn't see any mystery. Since he is a languaged creature and sees everything through the mirror of language, asking him to consider the nature of language is like asking a fish to consider the nature of water. He cannot imagine its absence, so he cannot consider its presence. To the layman, language is a transparent humdrum affair. Where is the mystery? People see things, are given the names of things when they are children, have thoughts, which they learn to express in words and sentences, talk and listen, read and write. So where is the mystery? That's the general lay attitude toward language. On the other hand there are the theorists of language, who are very much aware of the mystery and who practice such esoteric and abstruse disciplines as transformational generative grammar, formal semantics, semiotics, and who by and large have their heads up their asses and can't even be understood by fellow specialists. They remind me of nothing so much as the Scholastics of the fifteenth century, who would argue about the number of angels that could dance on the head of a pin.

Q: Haven't you written something about a theory of language?

A: Yes.

Q: Could you summarize your thoughts on the subject?

A: No.

Q: Why not?

A: It is not worth the trouble. What is involved in a theory of language is a theory of man, and people are not interested. Despite the catastrophes of this century and man's total failure to understand himself and deal with himself, people still labor under the illusion that a theory of man exists. It doesn't. As bad and confused as things are, they have to get even worse before people realize they don't have the faintest idea what sort of creature man is. Then they might want to know. Until then, one is wasting one's time. I'm not interested in butting my head against a stone wall. I've written something on the subject. Maybe ten years from now, fifty years from now, some people will be interested. That's their affair. People are not really interested in science nowadays. They are interested in pseudoscientific mysteries.

Q: Like what?

A: Laymen are more interested in such things as the Bermuda Triangle, U.F.O.'s, hypnotic regression, Atlantis, astrology — pseudomysteries. Scientists are more intereted in teaching apes to talk than in finding out why people talk. It is one of the peculiarities of the age that scientists are more interested in spending millions of dollars and man-hours trying to teach chimps to use language in order to prove that language is not a unique property of man than in studying the property itself. Scientists tend to be dogmatic about the nature of man. Again they remind me of the Scholastics battling with Galileo. Scholastics spent thousands of man-hours inside their heads trying to prove that Jupiter couldn't have moons and that the earth was at the center of the universe. To suggest otherwise offended their sense of the order of things. Galileo pointed to his telescope: Why don't you take a look?

Today we have plenty of scholastics of language. What we need is a Galileo who is willing to take a look at it.

Q: You still haven't said what you think of Jimmy Carter.

A: No.

Q: There is an extraordinary divergence of opinion. Some say he is the greatest of all southern con artists, that everything he says and does in the way of humility, sincerity, honesty, love, brotherhood and so forth is an act, a calculated living up to an image. Others say that these virtues are real. Which is it?

A: Is there a difference?

Q: Moving right along. . . . This is a pleasant room we're sitting in, over-looking a pleasant bayou.

A: Yes, it is. It is still a pretty country, despite the fact that the white man did his best to ruin it, ran the Indian off, cut down all the trees.

Q: Is that a portrait of you over the fireplace?

A: Yes. It was done by an artist friend of mine, Lyn Hill. I like it very much.

Q: I don't quite get it. What's going on there?

A: It shows me — well, not exactly me, a version of me — standing in front of what seems to be another framed painting. A picture within a picture, so to speak.

Q: What does it mean to you?

A: I can only say what I see. The artist may very well disagree, but after all the subject and viewer is entitled to his own ideas — like a book reviewer. I identify the subject of the portraits as a kind of composite of the protagonists of my novels, but most especially Lancelot. He is not too attractive a fellow and something of a nut besides. As we say in the South, he's mean as a yard dog. It is not a flattering portrait — he is not the sort of fellow you'd like to go fishing with. He is, as usual, somewhat out of it, out of the world that is framed off behind him. Where is he? It is an undisclosed place, a kind of limbo. It's a dark place — look at that background — if one believed in auras, his would be a foreboding one. It is a kind of desert, a bombed-out place, a place after the end of the world, a no-man's-land of blasted trees and barbed wire. As for him, he is neither admirable nor attractive. Rather, he is cold-eyed and sardonic. There is a gleam in his eyes, a muted and dubious satisfaction. He is looking straight at the viewer, soliciting him ironically: *You and I know something, don't we? Or do we?* Or rather: *The chances are ninety-nine in a hundred you don't know, but on the other hand you might be the one in a hundred who does — not that it makes much difference. True, this is a strange world I'm in, but what about the world you're in? Have you noticed it lately? Are we onto something, you and I? Probably not.*

But look at this apocalyptic world behind him. Something is going on. Is he aware of it? The dead blasted tree is undergoing a transformation. Into —? Into what? A bound figure? Figures? A woman? Lovers? The no-man's-land barbed wire is not really wire but a brier and it is blooming! A rose! Behind him there is a window of sorts, an opening out of his dark world onto a lovely sea-scape/skyscape. A new world! Yet he goes on looking straight at the viewer, challenging him: *Yes, I know about it, but do you? If you do, well and good. If you don't, there's no use in my telling you or turning around and pointing it out.* There's a limit to what writers can tell readers and artists can tell viewers. Perhaps he is Lancelot with the world and his life in ruins around him, but there is a prospect of a new world in the Shenandoah Valley. There was something wrong with the old world, the old things, the old flowers, the old skies, old clouds — or something wrong with his way of seeing them. They were used up. They have to be seen anew. Here is a new sky, a new sea, a new rose . . .

Q: Could you say something about your debt to Kierkegaard?

A: No.

Q: Could you at least explicate the painting in Kierkegaardian terms?

A: If I do, will you leave me alone?

Q: Yes.

A: Very well, I see the painting as depicting the very beginning of the Kierkegaardian stages of life — which can apply to an individual, a people, an age. It is the dawn of the aesthetic stage, the emergence of life from death, of light from darkness, the first utterance of words between people. The desert is just beginning to flower and there is the possibility that there may be survivors after the catastrophe. He, somewhat sardonic and smart-assed as usual, knows it but does not want to give away the secret too easily. So he keeps his own counsel, except for the faintest glimmer in his eye — of risibility, even hope? — which says to the viewer: *I doubt if you know what's going on, but then again you just might. Do you?*

Do you understand?

Q: No.

• Biographical Notes •

JAMES AGEE (1909-1955)
James Agee was born in Knoxville, Tennessee. After graduating from Harvard in 1932, he began a writing career in which he excelled in a number of different literary forms, including film criticism, novels (*The Morning Watch*, 1951, *A Death in the Family*, 1958), poetry, film scripts (*The African Queen, The Night of the Hunter*), journalism, and the exceptional literary documentary, *Let Us Now Praise Famous Men*, published in 1941 with the brilliant photographs of Walker Evans.

A. R. AMMONS (1926-   )
A. R. Ammons was born in Whiteville, North Carolina. He graduated from Wake Forest College in 1949, and worked at various jobs before taking a position at Cornell University where he is currently professor of English. His *Collected Poems: 1951-1971* was chosen for the National Book Award in 1972. He has also won the Bollingen Prize. Among his other volumes are *Sphere: The Form of a Motion* (1974), *Diversifications* (1975), *The Snow Poems* (1977), *A Coast of Trees* (1981), and *Wordly Hopes* (1982).

JAMES APPLEWHITE (1935-   )
James Applewhite was born in Stantonsburg, North Carolina. He grew up on a tobacco farm in Wilson County and studied at Duke University where he received his B.A., M.A., and Ph.D. degrees. He currently teaches creative writing at Duke. Among his volumes of poetry are *Statues of the Grass* (1975) and *Ode to the Chinaberry Tree and Other Poems* (1986).

WENDELL BERRY (1934-   )
Wendell Berry was born in Henry County, Kentucky, where he works a farm and writes. Since 1964, he has taught creative writing at the University of Kentucky. He has written novels, essays, and short stories. A good selection of his poetry can be found in *Collected Poems: 1957-1982*, published by North Point Press in 1985. His most recent book is a collection of short stories, *The Wild Birds: Six Stories of the Port William Membership* (1986).

DAVID BOTTOMS (1949-   )
David Bottoms was born in Canton, Georgia. He has a B.A. from Mercer University, a M.A. from West Georgia College, and a Ph.D. from Florida State. His collection of poetry, *Shooting Rats at the Bibb County Dump*, was winner in 1979 of the Walt Whitman Award sponsored by the Academy of American Poets, and in 1986 a group of poems from *Under the Vulture-Tree* was awarded the Levinson Prize from *Poetry* magazine.

ERSKINE CALDWELL (1902-   )
Erskine Caldwell was born in 1902 in Newnan, Coweta County, Georgia. He attended the Wrens Institute in Georgia, Erskine College in South Carolina, and the University of Virginia. Noted as a popular storyteller of the South, Caldwell published a number of famous novels, including *Tobacco Road* (1933), *God's Little Acre* (1933), and *Georgia Boy* (1943). From 1938 to 1941, he served as a foreign correspondent in Europe with Margaret Bourke-White, whom he married in 1939 (divorced in 1942). By 1946, *God's Little Acre* had sold 4.5 million copies, due in large measure to its availability in paperback to the armed forces.

TRUMAN CAPOTE (1923-1984)
Truman Capote was born in New Orleans. Though he lived much of his adult life outside the South, his early short stories owe much to his childhood in Louisiana and Alabama. His collections of stories include *A Tree of Night* (1949), *Breakfast at Tiffany's: A Short Novel and Three Stories* (1958), and *Music for Chameleons* (1981). Among his other books are *Other Voices, Other Rooms* (1948), *The Grass Harp* (1951), several plays, and the non-fiction "novel" *In Cold Blood* (1966).

W. J. CASH (1900-1941)
Wilbur Joseph Cash was born in Gaffney, South Carolina. He graduated from Wake Forest College, and began writing for newspapers. He joined the staff of the Charlotte *News* in 1926. In 1929, he began to contribute to H. L. Mencken's *American Mercury*. Cash's single book, *The Mind of the South*, was published in 1941. That same year he committed suicide in Mexico City.

FRED CHAPPELL (1936-   )
Fred Chappell was born in Canton, North Carolina. He studied at Duke University where he received his B.A. and M.A. degrees. He is currently professor of English at the University of North Carolina at Greensboro. He has published many volumes of poetry, five novels, including the recent *I Am One of You Forever* (1985), and a collection of short stories, *Moments of Light* (1980). In 1985 he was awarded the Bollingen Prize in Poetry.

HARRY CREWS (1935-   )
Harry Crews was born and grew up in Bacon County, Georgia. His auto-biographical memoir *A Childhood: The Biography of a Place* (1978), is a remarkable account of his boyhood years. He has published ten novels and many journalistic essays. Currently, he is a member of the English Department at the University of Florida. A recent collection of his writings about Florida, *Florida Frenzy*, was published in 1982.

DONALD DAVIDSON (1893-1968)
Donald Davidson was born in Campbellsville, Tennessee. He studied at Vanderbilt University where he remained as a teacher until his death. An early member of the Fugitive group, he wrote many poems and in 1930 was the leading spirit behind the Agrarian manifesto, *I'll Take My Stand*. He published several volumes of poetry, including the collection *Poems, 1922-1961* (1966), and many essays on the South, including the collections *The Attack on Leviathan* (1938) and *Still Rebels, Still Yankees* (1957).

JAMES DICKEY (1923-   )
James Dickey was born in Atlanta, Georgia. He attended Clemson College and Vanderbilt University where he received his B.A. and M.A. degrees. During World War II he served as a fighter pilot and was awarded a Silver Star and two Distinguished Flying Crosses. In 1966 he won the National Book Award for poetry with his collection *Buckdancer's Choice*. In addition to his volumes of poetry, he has published a novel, *Deliverance* (1970), and several collections of critical essays and autobiographical pieces. He is currently writer-in-residence at the University of South Carolina in Columbia.

WILLIAM FAULKNER (1897-1962)
Generally regarded as one of America's foremost modern novelists, William Faulkner was born in Albany, Mississippi. He lived for most of his life in nearby Oxford, where many of his Yoknapatawpha novels are set. Among his many works, the following stand out as vital classics of modern fiction: *The Sound and the Fury* (1929), *As I Lay Dying* (1930), *Light in August* (1932), *Absalom, Absalom!* (1936), *The Hamlet* (1940), *Go Down, Moses* (1942), and his *Collected Stories* (1950). In 1949 he was awarded the Nobel Prize for literature.

SHELBY FOOTE (1916-   )
Shelby Foote was born in Greenville, Mississippi. He attended the University of North Carolina and served in Europe during World War II. Though he has written several highly praised novels, including *Love in a Dry Season* (1951), *Jordon County* (1954), and *September, September* (1977), he is best known for his monumental history of the Civil War in three volumes, *The Civil War: A Narrative*, completed in 1974. He now lives in Memphis, Tennessee.

ERNEST J. GAINES (1933-   )
Ernest Gaines was born on a plantation in Pointe Coupée Parish near New Roads, Louisiana, which is the Bayonne of all his fiction. He is the author of five novels: *Catherine Carmier* (1964), *Of Love and Dust* (1967), *The Autobiography of Miss Jane Pittman* (1971), *In My Father's House* (1978), and *A Gathering of Old Men* (1983). His collection of short stories, *Bloodline*, was published in 1968. He divides his time between San Francisco and the University of Southwestern Louisiana, in Lafayette, where he teaches creative writing.

CAROLINE GORDON (1895-   )
Caroline Gordon was born in Trenton, Kentucky. She spent most of her life as a professor and writer-in-residence at various universities throughout the United States. She is the author of many stories, including the collections, *The Forest of the South* (1945) and *Old Red and Other Stories* (1963). Her *Collected Stories* appeared in 1981. Her novels include *Penhally* (1931), *Aleck Maury, Sportsman* (1934), *None Shall Look Back* (1937), *The Garden of Adonis* (1937), *The Women on the Porch* (1944), and *The Malefactors* (1956). She has also published an impressive body of literary criticism, including the influential anthology (with Allen Tate) *The House Of Fiction* (1950).

BARRY HANNAH (1942-   )
Barry Hannah was born in Meridian, Mississippi. He graduated from Mississippi College and received an M.F.A. from the University of Arkansas. He has been writer-in-residence at several universities and is currently at the University of Mississippi. He was awarded the William Faulkner Prize for his first novel *Geronimo Rex* (1972). Later novels include *Nightwatchman* (1973), *Ray* (1980), and *The Tennis Handsome* (1983). His collection of stories *Airships* (1978), won the Arnold Gingrich Short Fiction Award.

ZORA NEALE HURSTON (1903-1960)
Zora Neale Hurston was born in Eatonville, Florida. During her life, she worked at a variety of jobs, but her writing and research were always her central occupations. She wrote stories, essays, plays, novels, including *Jonah's Gourd Vine* (1934) and *Their Eyes Were Watching God* (1937), two books of Afro-American folklore, and an autobiography, *Dust Tracks in a Road* (1942). Never financially secure, she died in Fort Pierce, Florida, where she was befriended by several local sympathizers, including the Florida artist, A. L. Backus.

RANDALL JARRELL (1914-1965)
Randall Jarrell was born in Nashville, Tennessee. He studied under John Crowe
Ransom at Vanderbilt University where he received his M.A. in 1938. After World
War II, in which he served in the Army Air Force, he began a career as poet,
critic, teacher, and translator. His satirical novel, *Pictures From an Institution*, was
published in 1954. Among his essays of criticism are the collections *Poetry and
the Age* (1953) and *A Sad Heart at the Supermarket* (1962). In 1960 he was
awarded the National Book Award in poetry for *The Woman at the Washington
Zoo*. His *Complete Poems* was published in 1969.

MADISON JONES (1925-   )
Madison Jones was born in Nashville, Tennessee. He attended Vanderbilt University and the University of Florida and is currently writer-in-residence at Auburn
University. Among his many novels are *The Innocent* (1957), *Forest of the Night*
(1960), *A Buried Land* (1963), *An Exile* (1967), *A Cry of Absence* (1971), and
Passage to Gehenna (1978). A recent work, *Season of the Strangler* (1982), is a
linked collection of short stories in the tradition of *Winesburg, Ohio*.

DONALD JUSTICE (1925-   )
Donald Justice was born in Miami, Florida, where he attended public schools and
received his B.A. from the University of Miami. He then studied at the University
of North Carolina (M.A.) and the University of Iowa (Ph.D.). He has taught at
many universities and is currently professor of English at the University of Iowa.
Among his volumes of poetry are *The Summer Anniversaries* (1960), *Night Light*
(1967), and *Departures* (1973).

ETHERIDGE KNIGHT (1931-   )
Etheridge Knight was born in Corinth, Mississippi. He has been poet-in-residence
at the University of Pittsburgh, Hartford University, and Lincoln University.
Among his volumes of poetry are *Poems From Prison, A Poem for Brother Man*,
and *Belly Song and Other Poems*.

ANDREW LYTLE (1902-   )
Andrew Lytle was born in Murfreesboro, Tennessee. He studied at Vanderbilt
University where he was a friend of the Fugitives and one of the contributors to the
Agrarian manifesto *I'll Take My Stand* (1930). He attended the Yale School of
Drama where he studied under George Pierce Baker. For many years he taught at
the University of the South and edited *The Sewanee Review* (1961-1973). Among
his books are novels (*The Long Night*, 1936; *The Velvet Horn*, 1957), short stories,
a biography (*Bedford Forest and His Critter Company*, 1931), and critical essays
(*The Hero With the Private Parts*, 1966).

CARSON MCCULLERS (1917-1967)

Carson McCullers was born in Columbus, Georgia. At the age of nineteen, she published her first short story, "Wunderkind," in *Story*. In 1940, she published her best-known novel, *The Heart Is a Lonely Hunter*. Her other novels include *Reflections in a Golden Eye* (1941), *The Member of the Wedding* (1946), and *Clock Without Hands* (1961). In 1950, her play, a rewritten version of *The Member of the Wedding*, won the New York Critics Award. Her major short stories are collected in *The Ballad of the Sad Café* (1951).

WILLIAM MILLS (1935-   )

William Mills was born in Hattiesburg, Mississippi, and grew up in Louisiana. He holds a Ph.D. from Louisiana State University. He has taught at several universities in the South and is currently professor of English and creative writing at the University of Arkansas. His volumes of poetry are *Watch for the Fox* (1974), *Stained Glass* (1979), and *The Meaning of Coyotes* (1984). His latest book is a novel, *Those Who Blink* (1986).

WILLIE MORRIS (1934-   )

Willie Morris was born in Jackson, Mississippi, and grew up in Yazoo City, the center of many of his autobiographical essays. He studied at the University of Texas, was a Rhodes Scholar, and was editor of *The Texas Observer* (1960-1963). For four years (1967-1971) he was editor-in-chief of *Harper's Magazine*. He is currently journalist-in-residence at the University of Mississippi at Oxford. Among his books are *North Toward Home* (1967), *Good Old Boy* (1971), *Terrains of the Heart* (1981), *The Courting of Marcus Dupree* (1983), and *Always Stand in Against the Curve* (1983).

FLANNERY O'CONNOR (1925-1964)

Flannery O'Connor was born in Savannah, Georgia, but lived for most of her life in Milledgeville. She attended the Writers' Workshop at the University of Iowa, and published her first story, "Geranium," at the age of twenty-one. She is the author of two novels: *Wise Blood* (1952) and *The Violent Bear It Away* (1960). Her collections of stories are *A Good Man Is Hard To Find* (1955) and *Everything That Rises Must Converge* (1965). Her *Complete Stories* appeared in 1971 and won the National Book Award in 1972. A collection of essays, *Mystery and Manners*, edited by Sally and Robert Fitzgerald, was published in 1969. *The Habit of Being*, a collection of her remarkable letters, was edited by Sally Fitzgerald and was published in 1979.

WALKER PERCY (1916-   )

Walker Percy was born in Birmingham, Alabama, and grew up in Greenville, Mississippi, where after the death of his parents he lived with his father's cousin

William Alexander Percy, author of *Lanterns on the Levee* (1941). He attended the University of North Carolina and studied medicine at Columbia University where he received his M.D. in 1941. Forced to abandon practice because of tuberculosis, he eventually moved to Louisiana where he now lives in Covington. In 1961, his first novel, *The Moviegoer*, won the National Book Award. His other books are the novels *The Last Gentleman* (1966), *Love in the Ruins* (1971), *Lancelot* (1977), *The Second Coming* (1980), and two collections of essays: *The Message in the Bottle* (1975) and *Lost in the Cosmos* (1983).

KATHERINE ANNE PORTER (1890-1980)
Katherine Anne Porter was born in Indian Creek, Texas. Winner of the Pulitzer Prize and the National Book Award, she is chiefly known for her short stories. Her three major collections are *Flowering Judas and Other Stories* (1930), *Pale Horse, Pale Rider: Three Short Novels* (1938), and *The Leaning Tower and Other Stories* (1944). Her *Collected Stories* appeared in 1964. In 1962 she published a long novel, *Ship of Fools*. She also published essays, translations, and a memoir of the Sacco-Vanzetti case, *The Never-Ending Wrong* (1977).

REYNOLDS PRICE (1933-   )
Reynolds Price was born in Macon, North Carolina. He studied at Duke University and was a Rhodes Scholar. He has published two collections of short stories: *The Names and Faces of Heroes* (1963) and *Permanent Errors* (1970). His novels include *A Long and Happy Life* (1962), *A Generous Man* (1966), *Love and Work* (1968), *The Surface of Earth* (1975), *The Source of Light* (1981), and *Kate Vaiden* (1986). In 1978 he published a selection of translations from the Bible, *A Palpable God*. Since 1958 he has been on the English faculty at Duke University.

JOHN CROWE RANSOM (1888-1974)
John Crowe Ransom was born in Pulaski, Tennessee. He graduated from Vanderbilt in 1909 and was a Rhodes Scholar. In 1914 he joined the faculty at Vanderbilt where he taught until 1937 when he became professor of English at Kenyon College. He was one of the founding members of the Fugitives and a leading poet and literary critic during his lifetime. Among his volumes of poetry are *Poems About God* (1919), *Chills and Fever* (1924), *Two Gentlemen in Bonds* (1927), and *Selected Poems* (various editions). His critical writings are collected in *God Without Thunder* (1930), *The World's Body* (1938), and *The New Criticism* (1941).

THEODORE ROSENGARTEN (1944-   )
Theodore Rosengarten was born in Brooklyn, New York, and graduated from Amherst College in 1966. His doctoral dissertation from Harvard was *All God's Dangers: The Life of Nat Shaw*, which, after publication in 1974, won the National Book Award. His second book *Tombee: Portrait of a Cotton Planter* (1986)

contains a biography of Thomas Chaplin (1822-90), the master of Tombee Plantation, plus a journal Chaplin kept from 1845 to 1858.

LOUIS D. RUBIN, JR. (1923-   )

Louis D. Rubin, Jr., was born in Charleston, South Carolina, and was educated at the University of Richmond and The Johns Hopkins University where he received his Ph.D.. A leading critic of Southern culture and literature, he has written and edited a number of important books, including *The Faraway Country* (1963), *The Teller in the Tale* (1967), *George W. Cable* (1969), and *The American South* (1980). He is professor of English at the University of North Carolina at Chapel Hill and director of Algonquin Books, a publishing house.

JAMES SEAY (1939-   )

James Seay was born in Panola County, Mississippi. After graduating from the University of Mississippi, he took his M.A. at the University of Virginia. His two volumes of poetry are *Let Not Your Hart* (1970) and *Water Tables* (1974). He currently teaches creative writing at the University of North Carolina.

DAVE SMITH (1942-   )

Dave Smith was born in Portsmouth, Virginia, and educated at the University of Virginia (B.A.), Southern Illinois University (M.A.), and Ohio University (Ph.D.). Among his many volumes of poetry are *Homage to Edgar Allen Poe* (1981) and *In the House of the Judge* (1984). His own selection of his best work is contained in *The Roundhouse Voices: Selected and New Poems* (1985). Other publications include fiction, critical essays, and appreciations. He is currently professor of English at Virginia Commonwealth University.

ELIZABETH SPENCER (1921-   )

Elizabeth Spencer was born in Carollton, Mississippi. She was educated at Belhaven College and Vanderbilt University. Among her novels are *Fire in the Morning* (1948), *This Crooked Way* (1952), *The Voice at the Back Door* (1956), *The Light in the Piazza* (1960), *Knights and Dragons* (1965), *No Place for an Angel* (1967), *The Snare* (1972), and *The Salt Line* (1984). Her stories have been collected in *The Stories of Elizabeth Spencer* which was published in 1981.

DABNEY STUART (1937-   )

Dabney Stuart was born in Richmond, Virginia. He studied at Davidson College and at Harvard University where he received his M.A. He has taught at the College of William and Mary and at Washington and Lee University where he is professor of English and poetry editor of *Shenandoah*. Among his volumes of poetry are *The Diving Bell* (1966), *A Particular Place* (1969), *The Other Hand* (1974), and *Round and Round: A Triptych* (1977).

WILLIAM STYRON (1925-   )

William Styron was born in Newport News, Virginia. He attended Davidson College, but his education was interrupted by World War II and his service in the Marine Corps. He later graduated from Duke University. In Paris in the 1950's he helped found *The Paris Review* with George Plimpton. Among his fiction are the novels *Lie Down in Darkness* (1951), *Set This House on Fire* (1960), *The Confessions of Nat Turner* (1967), and *Sophie's Choice* (1979).

ALLEN TATE (1899-1979)

Allen Tate was born in Winchester, Clark County, in Kentucky. He entered Vanderbilt University in 1918 and quickly became a leading member of the Fugitive group, and later contributed to the Agrarian statement *I'll Take My Stand* (1930). He taught in many universities, edited (1944-1946) *The Sewanee Review*, and established himself as a major thinker on the South and on modern literary theory. He was awarded the Bollingen Prize in Poetry in 1956. His publications include biographies, essays, and a novel, *The Fathers* (1938). His *Collected Poems, 1919-1976* was published in 1978.

PETER TAYLOR (1919-   )

Peter Taylor was born in Trenton, Tennessee. He studied under John Crowe Ransom at Vanderbilt and at Kenyon College. After serving in the U.S. Army during World War II, he taught at many universities. He has recently retired from the University of Virginia. Best known for his short stories, he has published a novel and several plays. His major collections of stories include *A Long Fourth and Other Stories* (1948), *Happy Families Are All Alike* (1959), *Miss Leonora When Last Seen and Fifteen Other Stories* (1964), *In the Miro District* (1977), and *The Old Forest* (1985). His *Collected Stories* was published in 1969.

JEAN TOOMER (1894-1967)

Nathan Eugene Toomer was born in Washington, D.C., where he was raised in the household of his maternal grandfather, P.B.S. Pinchback, who had been the lieutenant governor of Louisiana during Reconstruction. In 1921, Toomer spent several months in Sparta, Georgia, and shortly after published *Cane* (1922), his best-known work. He published little afterwards, but a large number of unpublished manuscripts are held at Fisk University. Many of the imaginative sections in *Cane,* especially those involving women, can be considered prose poems in the form of a reminiscence.

ALICE WALKER (1944-   )

Alice Walker was born in Eatonton, Georgia. She has taught at Jackson State College and Tougaloo College in Mississippi, at Wellesley College, and the University of Massachusetts. She is the author of four collections of poems, including *Once* (1968) and *Revolutionary Petunias and Other Poems* (1973), two collections of stories, various essays and introductions, a biography of Langston Hughes, and three novels: *The Third Life of Granger Copeland* (1970), *Meridian* (1976) and *The Color Purple* (1983).

ROBERT PENN WARREN (1905-   )
Robert Penn Warren was born in Guthrie, Kentucky. He was educated at Vanderbilt University, the University of California, and at Oxford University as a Rhodes Scholar. One of America's most respected men of letters, he has excelled in most literary genres and has won virtually every major literary award, including the National Book Award, the Pulitzer, and the Bollingen Prize in Poetry. In 1986 he was chosen as the United States's first poet laureate. Of his many volumes of poetry, his most recent, *New and Selected Poems, 1923-1985*, was published in 1985. He is the author of an important body of literary criticism and ten novels, including *Night Rider* (1939), *All The King's Men* (1946), *World Enough and Time* (1950), *Band of Angels* (1955), and *A Place To Come To* (1977).

EUDORA WELTY (1909-   )
Eudora Welty was born in Jackson, Mississippi, and has lived there for most of her life. She was educated at Mississippi State College for Women and the University of Wisconsin. She is now generally considered as one of the most gifted short story writers of the century. Her major collections include *The Wide Net and Other Stories* (1943), *The Golden Apples* (1949), and *The Bride of the Innisfallen and Other Stories* (1955). Her *Collected Stories* was published in 1980. Among her novels are *The Robber Bridegroom* (1942), *Delta Wedding* (1946), *Losing Battles* (1970), and *The Optimist's Daughter* (1972). Her essays are collected in *The Eye of the Story* (1979). Recently, she has published an autobiography, *One Writer's Beginnings* (1983).

JAMES WHITEHEAD (1936-   )
James Whitehead was born in St. Louis, Missouri, and grew up in Mississippi. He earned his B.A. and M.A. degrees at Vanderbilt University and an M.F.A. at the University of Iowa. He has published a novel, *Joiner* (1971) and two collections of poetry, *Domains* (1966) and *Local Men* (1979). He is currently professor of English at the University of Arkansas where he teaches creative writing.

MILLER WILLIAMS (1930-   )
Miller Williams was born in Hoxie, Arkansas. He has a B.S. degree in biology from Arkansas State College and an M.S. in zoology from the University of Arkansas. He has taught biology and English at various Southern colleges and is now professor of English at the University of Arkansas. Among his collections of poetry are *Halfway From Hoxie: New and Selected Poems* (1977), *Why God Permits Evil* (1977), and *The Boys on Their Bony Mules* (1983).

TENNESSEE WILLIAMS (1911-1983)

Tennessee Williams was born in Columbus, Mississippi. One of America's most remarkable and celebrated dramatists, he is the author of *The Glass Menagerie* (1944), *A Streetcar Named Desire* (1947), *Cat on a Hot Tin Roof* (1955), and *Sweet Bird of Youth* (1959), among many others. He has also written numerous short stories, and an autobiography, *Memoirs* (1975).

THOMAS WOLFE (1900-1938)

Thomas Wolfe was born in Asheville, North Carolina. He studied at the University of North Carolina where he was a member of the Carolina Playmakers, and at Harvard where for three years he was a member of George Pierce Baker's drama workshop. Only two of his novels were published during his lifetime: *Look Homeward Angel* (1929) and *Of Time and the River* (1935). The rest of his work, including *The Web and the Rock* (1939), *You Can't Go Home Again* (1940), and *The Hills Beyond* (1941) were put together out of the mass of manuscript he left at his death.

C. VANN WOODWARD (1908-   )

C. Vann Woodward was born and grew up in rural Arkansas before moving to Georgia with his family in 1928. He studied at Emory University, the University of North Carolina, and Columbia University. For many years professor of history at Yale University, he is one of the foremost historians of the South. His most influential book, *The Burden of Southern History*, was first published in 1960. Among his other books are *The Strange Career of Jim Crow* (1955) and the monumental *Origins of the New South 1877-1913*, published in 1951. He has recently published an autobiographical memoir, *Thinking Back* (1986).

CHARLES WRIGHT (1935-   )

Charles Wright was born in Pickwick Dam, Tennessee. After graduating from Davidson College, he earned an M.A. at the University of Iowa. He currently teaches at the University of Virginia. In 1983 he won the American Book Award for poetry. His *Selected Poems* appeared in 1982.

RICHARD WRIGHT (1908-1960)

Richard Wright was born on a cotton plantation near Natchez, Mississippi. At fifteen, he left home to work in Memphis, and from there he went to Chicago, and later to New York. His first book, *Uncle Tom's Children*, appeared in 1938. In 1940, his best-known work, *Native Son*, was published. Among his other books are a fictionalized autobiography, *Black Boy* (1945), *The Outsider* (1953), *The Long Dream* (1958), and a posthumous collection of short stories, *Eight Men* (1961). He died in Paris where he had lived for a number of years.

• About the Editors •

BEN FORKNER, who received his Ph.D. in American Literature from the University of North Carolina, is Director of American Studies at the University of Angers, France. He is the editor of *Modern Irish Short Stories* and *Stories of the Modern South* (with Patrick Samway). He has been a Fulbright Lecturer and is a member of the National Humanities Faculty.

PATRICK SAMWAY, S.J., also an American Literature Ph.D. from the University of North Carolina, teaches at Fordham University and is Literary Editor of the weekly journal *America*. He has been a Fulbright Lecturer and is the author of a book on Faulkner's *Intruder in the Dust*, as well as co-editor of *Faulkner and Idealism: Perspectives from Paris* and *Stories of the Modern South*.

• CREDITS •

D# 231883

1/9/87 UR